African American Frontiers
Slave Narratives and Oral Histories

Alan Govenar

ABC-CLIO

Santa Barbara, California
Denver, Colorado
Oxford, England

Library of Congress Cataloging-in-Publication Data
Govenar, Alan B., 1952–
    African American frontiers : slave narratives and oral histories /
      Alan B. Govenar.
      p. cm.
    Includes bibliographical references and index.
    ISBN 0-87436-867-7 (alk. paper)
    1. Slaves—United States—Biography. 2. Afro-American pioneers—Biography. 3. Afro-Americans—Biography. 4. Afro-Americans —History. 5. Afro-Americans—Social conditions. 6. Slaves—United States—Social conditions. 7. Frontier and pioneer life—United States. 8. Oral history. 9. Slaves' writings, American.
I. Title.

E444 .G68 2000
973'.0496073'00922—dc21   00-011250

04 03 02 01 00   10 9 8 7 6 5 4 3 2 1

ABC-CLIO, Inc.
130 Cremona Drive
P.O. Box 1911
Santa Barbara, California 93116-1911

This book is printed on acid-free paper ∞ .
Manufactured in the United States of America

Contents

Section III: Oral Histories

Acknowledgments

In compiling this book, I have benefited from the input of many people. First and foremost, I am grateful to the many individuals who shared their time with me and whose life experiences propelled this work forward.

Lonn Taylor and Nianni Kilkenny of the Smithsonian Institution nurtured my research early on by inviting me to develop a public program on African American cowboys in Texas at the National Museum of American History. Subsequent presentations of that program at the Festival de Printemps in Lausanne, Switzerland, the National Black Arts Festival in Atlanta, and Colorado College in Colorado Springs refined my understanding of the questions often engendered by discussions of the migratory patterns of African Americans. Adrienne Seward challenged me to rethink existing literature on the frontier, and Paul Stewart and Ottawa Harris introduced me to the collections of the Black American West Museum and Heritage Center in Denver.

Nudie Williams coauthored the original prospectus for this book but had to withdraw due to unforeseen health problems. Still, his insights and enthusiasm were invaluable to me as I persisted to bring this work to completion.

My participation in the International Conference on African American Music and Europe at the Université de la Sorbonne Nouvelle, Paris, in 1996 was supported in part by Documentary Arts and the Florence Gould Foundation. This conference, organized by Michel Fabre and Henry Louis Gates, Jr., expanded the scope of my inquiry and provided me an opportunity to engage in a probing dialogue with Paul Oliver and Francis Hofstein about misconceptions of African American culture in southern and western regions of the United States.

As this book began to evolve through the arduous process of revision, Sterling Stuckey helped to clarify my study of published slave narratives. John Slate and Jay Brakefield assisted me in surveying the historical collections and archives in states west of the Mississippi River; both, at different points in the process, collaborated with me in conducting interviews and then helped with transcription and copyediting of the resulting oral histories.

My wife, Kaleta Doolin, suggested interview subjects and actively shared her thoughts as the final conceptualization of this book emerged. Tara Neal and my daughter, Breea Govenar, aided in the organization of references and primary source materials. My son, Alex Govenar, an avid researcher at age ten, inspired me to explore more deeply the unexpected stories of people I met for the first time.

Introduction

In recent years historians have attempted to expand the concept of the American frontier to reflect the diversity of the cultural groups that have settled across the United States. This book explores the frontier as both place and idea, specifically as it relates to African Americans. For African Americans, there were many frontiers that involved geographic movement and, perhaps more important, engendered new ways of thinking. These frontiers predicated unprecedented economic, political, social, and cultural changes that were a consequence of the migratory patterns of African Americans and the conditions of enslavement and racism to which they were subjected.

The first Africans to leave their continent were both explorers and captives. European explorers, including Columbus, Balboa, Ponce de Léon, Cortés, Pizarro, Menéndez, and Coronado, brought Africans on their expeditions to the New World. Generally, the role of these Africans is not well defined; clearly, some were indentured servants, while others were probably slaves, and a few were recognized as explorers in their own right.

The status of Africans in the New World prior to the sixteenth century varied from voyage to voyage. It is known that Africans sold slaves to Arab traders from northern Africa in ancient times. Yet the earliest Portuguese and Spanish explorers who took African captives did not necessarily consider them slaves. Some written accounts suggest that these captives were in fact servants and not "slaves" in a conventional sense.

However, by the year 1500, the fate of African captives changed significantly. As Spain and Portugal established colonies in Latin America and the West Indies, slavery became a means to facilitate rapid economic expansion. Historian Roger Hornsby points out that in 1496, shortly after the establishment of Santo Domingo (the first permanent European settlement in the New World), the Spanish exploited slave labor on their sugar plantations. "The first Africans were seen there as early as 1501. After the Spanish virtually exterminated the Carib Indians, natives of the Caribbean Islands, larger numbers of blacks were imported. Fearing that blacks would eventually outnumber Europeans in the region, Spanish authorities soon placed restrictions on their importation. In 1517, Bishop Bartholomew Las Casas and others persuaded King Charles I of Spain to rescind the restriction in order for Africans to augment the dwindling supply of Indian labor. Subsequently, in 1518, large numbers of blacks were imported directly from Africa. These newly arrived slaves were known as *bozal* Negroes, which distinguished them from the group of Africans who were initially transported to Europe and Christianized before being sent to the Caribbean."[1]

As the African population grew, fears among the European settlers intensified. Harsh slave codes were implemented to control the potential for violence and insurgency. Despite the relative success of the codes in punishing unruly Africans, some managed to escape and were not recaptured. They were known as Maroons, and they formed camps called *quilombos* (cabins). In time, these *quilombos* became autonomous colonies that resisted European attacks and established an economy based on agriculture, trade, and the raiding of local plantations.

Essentially, the *quilombos* represented the earliest movement of free Africans into the frontiers of Latin America. However, these frontiers for Africans of the sixteenth century were limited, because the patterns of African enslavement through the plantation system and Christianization became institutionalized.

Hernando Cortés and other conquistadors brought Spanish-speaking blacks to Mexico. In time, many of these Afro-Spaniards, as well as the slaves transported to colonial Mexico, intermarried with the Indian population, giving rise to a large Zambo (mixed Indian and African) population. Some of these, in turn, migrated to the frontiers of northern Mexico, regions that later became Texas, California, New Mexico, and Arizona.[2]

As early as 1526, the Spanish explorer Lucas Vasquez de Allyon brought approximately 100 African slaves and 500 colonists into what is now South Carolina to build a settlement near the mouth of the Pedee River. Within months, the colony was failing, due to widespread illness and the hostility of indigenous Indians. Many of the Africans rebelled and mounted the first recorded slave revolt in North America, escaping to the Indians they befriended and causing the remainder of the settlers to flee to Haiti.[3]

In 1528, the explorer Cabeza de Vaca and Esteban, a Moroccan slave, survived the Pánfilo de Navaréz expedition to Florida. They journeyed for eight years along the northern shores of the Gulf of Mexico, across Texas and Mexico to the Gulf of California, and finally reached Mexico City.

Esteban's prowess as an explorer was legendary. In 1538, he was retained as a guide by Fray Marcos de Niza in a search for the Seven Cities of Cibola, and was reportedly killed by Indians when the expedition was within two or three days of its destination.

In 1565, the Spanish established St. Augustine, Florida, and disparate accounts of African farmers and craftspeople among the settlers indicate that the status of these Africans was somewhat ambiguous. Most were enslaved, although within the social structure of the colony some were granted different degrees of personal freedom based on their skill level.

The earliest British colonies in North America seemed to afford more opportunities for Africans than those settlements established by the Spanish and French. In 1619, twenty Africans came to the British colony at Jamestown, Virginia. Although the origins of these Africans are unclear, historians generally concur that they were captured in Africa and sold to British settlers. Their status in the New World, however, is ambiguous; slavery had been moribund in England since the thirteenth century, but did exist in Virginia. Some historians have considered these Africans indentured servants; others insist that they were in fact slaves.

By definition, indentured servants worked for three to seven years to earn their freedom, and reportedly, most of the twenty Africans in Jamestown were granted this right. What happened to these Africans is not completely known, although records do exist for a few of them who apparently became property owners and politically active citizens. In Jamestown in 1619, no statutory procedure had been established to fix the legal standing of Africans. Anthony Johnson, who became one of the most prominent Africans in the colony during the seventeenth century, came to Virginia in 1621 aboard the *James* and was simply known as "Antonio the Negro." Over time, he acquired the surname Johnson and was able to acquire 250 acres of land on Pungoteague Creek, possibly by purchasing headright certificates from other planters.[4]

Clearly, for both the enslaved and the indentured, the possibility of freedom represented the first frontier. During the period from the seventeenth century onward to emancipation, the movement out of slavery, by escape or by any means necessary, offered the promise of new opportunities, although laws limiting the rights of freed Negroes posed definite obstacles. Nevertheless, these opportunities created new frontiers; in some instances, this involved westward migration, but in others, it entailed geographic movement elsewhere—to the frontiers of New York, Rhode Island or Massachusetts, or perhaps Canada or Mexico.

This book explores many of these frontiers through the personal accounts of a wide range of African Americans, focusing specifically on slave narratives and oral histories. It concentrates on the period from 1703, the date of the first published narrative of an African slave's attainment of freedom in the American colonies,[5] to 1948, the year in which President Harry S. Truman integrated the United States armed forces through Executive Order 9981. Truman's mandate for integration was an important catalyst in the struggle to systematically dismantle institutionalized racism, and it coincides with a major demographic shift in the African American population.

Propelled by the opportunities of higher-paying jobs in the shipyards, aircraft factories, and other wartime industries, thousands of African Americans migrated into the western United States. In the 1940s, the black population of the region grew 49 percent, from 1,343,930 to 1,996,036. In urban centers, this growth was the most dramatic. Between 1940 and 1944, the African American population in the San Franciso–Oakland area rose from 19,000 to 147,000; in Portland, from 1,300 to 22,000; in Los Angeles, from 75,000 to 218,000.

Organized as a reference book and providing an overview of more than 200 years of history, this work documents the process through which different frontiers emerged and developed. People, places, and events are chronicled through individual life experiences to reveal the complexities of the frontier experience over the course of day-to-day events. The broad subject areas covered include, but are not limited to, art and culture, business and commerce, politics and government, and social and demographic change. The emphasis is upon people themselves and the ways in which they participate in the process of history through what they say and do. Often, the slave narratives and oral histories express the extraordinary perspectives of ordinary people who have been overlooked in more general histories. In these everyday life experiences, the sense of time is usually more associative than chronological, but the accounts themselves are nonetheless valuable in enlarging our comprehension of the multifaceted human dynamics through which different frontiers were conceived, explored, and settled.

Slave Narratives

The *Transactions of the Colonial Society of Massachusetts in Boston, County of Suffolk,* on August 3 and November 2, 1703, under the heading *Adam Negro's Tryall,* details the plight of a slave, who had earned his emancipation but was denied his freedom.

> Adam was the slave of one John Saffin, a prosperous gentleman
> farmer of Suffolk County, whose troubles with his slave we first
> learn of in the tract that Saffin wrote and printed in Boston in

1701 in response to the recent publication by Samuel Sewell of the antislavery pamphlet *The Selling of Joseph*. It seems that Adam had not only capped a seven-year period of work-dodging with a flat refusal to accompany his master when Saffin was obliged to leave town, but he also had taken advantage of Saffin's absence to terminate his indentureship, going to Judge Sewell with a writ of promise Adam had obtained from Saffin years before to the effect that Saffin would give him his freedom after seven years of service.[6]

When the case finally came to trial on August 3, 1703, the jury decided that Adam was to remain Saffin's servant, but the judgment of the Court of the General Sessions was reversed on appeal. At Her Majesty's Superiour Court of Judicature, Suffolk County, Judge Sewell concluded: "It's therefore Considered by the Court That sd. Adam and his heirs be at peace and quite free with all their Chattles from the sd. John Saffin, Esqr and his heirs for Ever."[7]

Despite the limited details about Adam's life before and after the court proceedings, this short narrative is a remarkable account of one man's struggle for freedom—first, through acts of civil disobedience: "work-dodging and flat refusal" to comply with the directives of his master, and ultimately, by due process of law.

Historian Marion Wilson Starling suggests that Adam's narrative, like others of the eighteenth century, reveals "the slaves' awareness of a social prejudice against the slave as Negro, quite apart from his economic disadvantage of being a slave."[8] This awareness of racism is especially apparent in the narrative of Briton Hammon, published in 1760. A summary of its contents is contained on its title page:

> A Narrative of the Uncommon Sufferings, and Surprizing Deliverance of Briton Hammon, A Negro Man, Servant to General Winslow, of Marshfield, in New-England; Who Returned to Boston, after Having Been Absent Almost Thirteen Years. Containing An Account of the many Hardships he underwent from the Time he left his Master's House, in the Year 1747, to the Time of his Return to Boston.—How he was cast away in the Capes of Florida;—the horrid Cruelty and inhuman Barbarity of the Indians in murdering the whole Ship's Crew;—the Manner of his being carry'd by them into Captivity. Also, An Account of his being Confined Four Years and Seven Months in a close Dungeon;—And the remarkable Manner in which he met with his good old Master in London; who returned to New-England a Passenger, in the same Ship. (Boston; Printed and Sold by Green and Russell, in Queen-Street, 1760)

Like Adam, Briton Hammon mapped out his own destiny without the sanction of his master, but his escape was not successful and did not ultimately lead to freedom. In fact, while he initially seemed rebellious, his adventures over the next thirteen years, including confrontation with cannibalistic Indians off the coast of Florida, shipwrecks, and incarceration by pirates, made the reunion with his master an unexpectedly "joyful" occasion.

> I worked on board Captain Watt's ship almost three months, before she sail'd, and one Day being at work in the Hold, I overheard some Persons on board mention the name of Winslow, at the name of which I was very inquisitive, and having asked what Winslow they were talking about? They told me it was General Winslow; and that he was one of the Passengers. I ask'd them what General Winslow? For I never knew my good Master, by that Title before; but after enquiring more particularly I found it must be Master, and in a few Days Time the Truth was joyfully verify'd by a happy Sight of his Person, which so overcome me, that I could not speak to him for some Time—my good Master was exceeding glad to see me, telling me that I was like one arose from the Dead, for he thought I had been Dead a great many Years, having heard nothing of me for almost Thirteen Years.[9]

Overall, Hammon's narrative underscored his adventures and his quest for freedom, but failed to provide concrete information about the horrors of enslavement. The first narrative to express strong disdain for the social structure and conditions of slavery was written by Equiano, or Gustavus Vassa, and was first published in London in 1789.[10]

The Interesting Narrative of the Life of Olaudah Equiano, or Gustavus Vassa, the African, Written by Himself was subsequently reissued in thirty-six editions in English, Dutch, and German between that year and 1857. In the text Equiano recounts his experiences as a slave in Africa, the West Indies, Georgia, and Pennsylvania, and on board warships off the Spanish coast. Although the first twenty pages of Equiano's autobiography were apparently compiled by someone other than the author from handbooks on the history of Guinea, most of the text appears as firsthand recollections. Especially poignant are Equiano's first impressions of the slave ship on which he was placed against his will.

> The first object which saluted my eyes when I arrived on the coast was the sea, and a slave ship, which was then riding at anchor, and waiting for its cargo. These filled me with astonishment, which was soon converted into terror when I was carried on board. I was immediately handled, and tossed up to see if I

were sound, by some of the crew; and I was now persuaded that I had gotten into a world of bad spirits, and that they were going to kill me. Their complexions too differing so much from ours, their long hair, and the language they spoke … united to confirm me in this belief…. When I looked round the ship, too, and saw a large furnace or copper boiling, and a multitude of black people of every description chained together, every one of their countenances expressing dejection and sorrow, I no longer doubted of my fate; and, quite overpowered with horror and anguish, I fell motionless on the deck and fainted. When I recovered a little I found some black people about me, who I believed were some of those who had brought me on board, and had been receiving their pay; they talked to me in order to cheer me, but all in vain. I asked them if we were not to be eaten by those white men with horrible looks, red faces, and long hair. They told me I was not. [11]

Later in the narrative, Equiano describes in detail the detestable stench below deck, the wailing of the slaves, his brutal floggings for refusing to eat, and his attempted suicide by jumping overboard. During his enslavement, he traveled extensively with his master, Captain Pascal. After living in servitude in England, where he stayed in the homes of English families and received limited schooling, he was sold to his second master, the Quaker Robert King of Philadelphia. After several voyages between America and the West Indies, King was pressured to release his slaves by his fellow Quakers, and ultimately allowed Equiano to buy his freedom in 1766.

Like Equiano, Venture Smith recalls the conditions of his enslavement and the means through which he not only gained his freedom but became a relatively prosperous landowner. Smith's narrative is reproduced in its entirety in this book because of its relevance to an understanding of African American movement into a frontier region. Although Smith never actually uses the word *frontier,* its meaning is implicit in his plan of escape, his yearning for geographic exploration, and his fervent hope to settle in a different region of the country. In this context, *frontier* becomes synonymous with *opportunity* and the promise of the future that existed beyond the boundaries imposed by slavery.

The years between 1770 and 1810, historian Ira Berlin writes, were a formative period for African American culture. "The confluence of three events—freedom for large numbers of blacks with the abolition of slavery in the North and large-scale manumission in parts of the south; the maturation of a native-born Afro-American population after more than a century of captivity; and a new, if short-lived, flexibility in white racial attitudes—made these years the pivot point in the development of black life in the United States." [12]

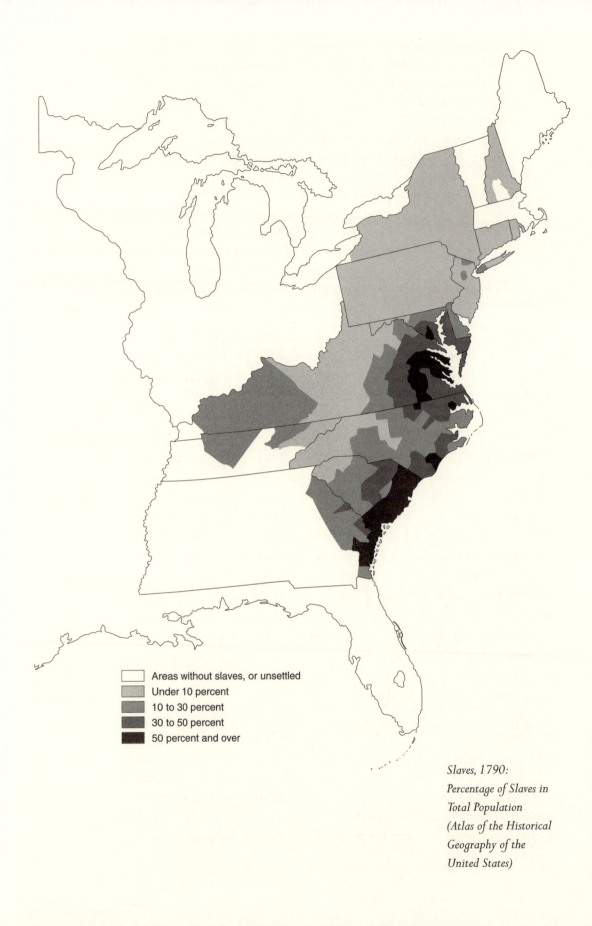

Areas without slaves, or unsettled
Under 10 percent
10 to 30 percent
30 to 50 percent
50 percent and over

Slaves, 1790:
Percentage of Slaves in
Total Population
(Atlas of the Historical
Geography of the
United States)

The number of free blacks in the nation increased from a few thousand in 1760 to more than 180,000 in 1810. Clearly, the onset of the American Revolution was the most significant catalyst for this change. In the 1770s, as the war dragged on, "military necessity forced the British, and then more reluctantly, Americans to muster black slaves into their armies by offering them freedom in exchange for their services."[13]

The acceptance of blacks into American colonial militias varied from region to region. The northern states, led by New England, were the first to solicit black recruits, and Rhode Island even created a black regiment. The southern states, however, were more stubborn because of their greater dependence upon slave labor and their fear that freeing only some of their slaves might lead to more widespread insurrections.

As Berlin notes, "Maryland authorized slave enlistments and eventually subjected free Negroes to the draft. Virginia allowed black freemen to serve in its army and navy, and Delaware and North Carolina, following Virginia, occasionally permitted slaves to stand as substitutes for their masters.... South Carolina and Georgia rejected the hesitant measures adopted in the Upper South...."[14]

After the Revolutionary War, the British carried thousands of blacks to freedom in Great Britain, the West Indies, Canada, and even Africa, while in the newly formed United States, opportunities for blacks widened. However, the divisions between the northern and southern states became more pronounced, and the obstacles for African Americans stiffened. Laws were passed to effectively limit the potential for social mobility, economic opportunity, and geographic movement. Racist attitudes proliferated, and the political rights of blacks narrowed.

Still, by the early years of the nineteenth century, some African Americans did prosper. In the West, African Americans were active in the fur trading business, both as trappers and traders, and were involved in the exploration of the Rocky Mountain region. Historian Quintard Taylor points out, "Trapper Peter Ranne in 1824 was a member of the first party of Americans to reach California overland. One year later, Moses Harris was the first non-Indian to explore the Great Salt Lake region. James Beckwourth and Edward Rose, among other 'mountain men,' traversed much of what become Montana, Idaho, Wyoming, and Colorado."[15]

In the North and along the eastern seaboard, many African Americans acquired land and pursued professions that had previously been forbidden: merchant, painter, poet, minister, and author. The almanacs of Benjamin Banneker, the poems of Phillis Wheatley and Jupiter Hammon, and the portraits of Joshua Johnson are testaments to the cultural growth among African Americans, while the public works of Prince Hall in Boston, Richard Allen in Philadelphia, Daniel Coker in Baltimore, Christopher

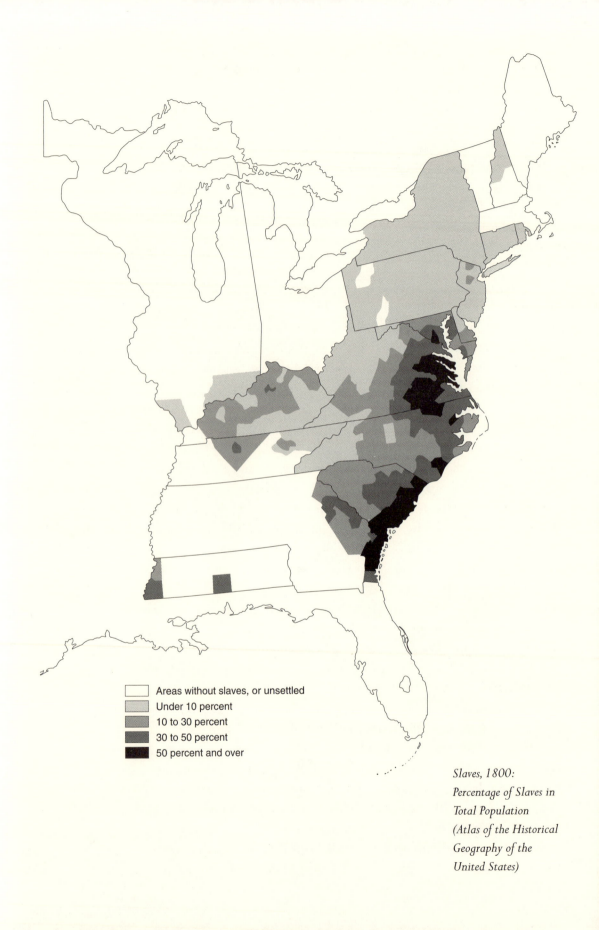

Areas without slaves, or unsettled
Under 10 percent
10 to 30 percent
30 to 50 percent
50 percent and over

Slaves, 1800:
Percentage of Slaves in
Total Population
(Atlas of the Historical
Geography of the
United States)

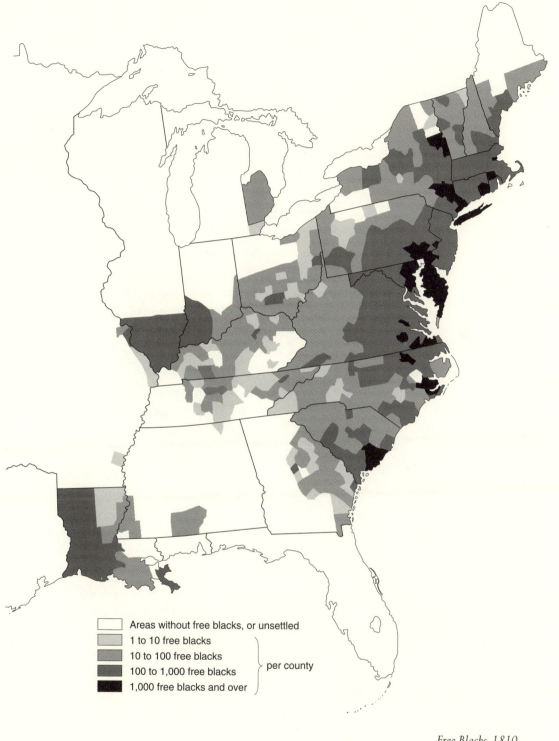

Legend:

- Areas without free blacks, or unsettled
- 1 to 10 free blacks
- 10 to 100 free blacks
- 100 to 1,000 free blacks
- 1,000 free blacks and over

} per county

Free Blacks, 1810
(Atlas of the Historical
Geography of the United
States)

McPherson in Richmond, and Andrew Bryan in Savannah combined with the financial success of merchant Robert Sheridan in Wilmington, North Carolina, sail manufacturer James Forten of Philadelphia, and sea captain Paul Cuffee of New Bedford, Massachusetts, were all indicative of the gradual transformation of American life. In this context, African Americans made important advances in the areas of education, medicine, and religion.

The African Methodist Episcopal (AME) Church was founded by Richard Allen, who had been born a slave in 1760 in Philadelphia. When he was young, he and his family were sold to a Mr. Stokely, a Delaware planter, who allowed Allen to purchase his freedom when he was seventeen. Stokely had been profoundly influenced by a Methodist minister, Freeborn Garrisson, who convinced him in a sermon he delivered that slaveholders fell short of the "weight needed for salvation." From then on Stokely made clear to Allen his intentions to permit him to work outside of his plantation to earn enough money to buy his freedom.

In his published narrative, Allen recalls: "I had it often impressed upon my mind that I should one day enjoy freedom; for slavery is a bitter pill, notwithstanding we had a good master. But when we would think that our day's work was never done, we often thought that after our master's death we were liable to be sold to the highest bidder, as he was much in debt; and thus my troubles were increased, and I was often brought to weep between the porch and the altar. But I have reason to bless my dear Lord that a door was opened unexpectedly for me to buy my time and enjoy my liberty." [16]

Allen's devoutness to his Christian faith led him to affiliate with the Methodists as an assisting preacher on the circuit south of Wilmington, Delaware, and then to become a preacher in his own right in Philadelphia. There, in 1793, he opened the "Bethel Church" in a dilapidated old blacksmith shop that he converted into a house of worship with the help of volunteers in the African American community. Rather than founding his own sect, Allen decided to make the church a division of the African Methodist Episcopal Church and committed himself to strengthening the quality of life for his fellow blacks:

"I was confident that there was no religious sect or denomination would suit the capacity of the colored people as well as the Methodist; for the plain and simple gospel suits best for my people; for the unlearned can understand, and the learned are sure to understand; and the reason that the Methodist is so successful in the awakening and conversion of the colored people ... is its having a good discipline.... We are beholden to the Methodists, under God, for the light of the Gospel we enjoy; for all other denominations preached so high-flown that we were not able to comprehend their doctrine." [17]

Paul Cuffe, born in 1759 on Cuttyhunk Island in the Massachusetts Bay Colony to a Wampanoag Indian and a former slave who had purchased his freedom, became a sea captain, ardent abolitionist, and black nationalist. In 1780, he and his brother, John, refused to pay taxes in Massachusetts to protest a clause in the state constitution that forbade suffrage for blacks. For this protest, Cuffe was briefly imprisoned but nonetheless continued his efforts to advance the cause of African Americans. Cuffe joined the Society of Friends in 1808 and was a devout Quaker for the remainder of his life. In 1811, he made the first of two trips to the British colony of Sierra Leone, where he hoped to establish a three-way trade route between the United States, England, and Africa. In 1815, he returned to Sierra Leone, bringing thirty-eight people from nine families as part of an emigration plan to improve the conditions of black Americans and to bring prosperity to Africa.

Of all the early white abolitionists, the Quakers were among the most effective. The Quakers actively sought to support the efforts of free blacks to purchase and seek the manumission of children and other relatives. With financial assistance provided by the Quakers combined with the independent means of free blacks themselves, Sterling Stuckey points out, "scores of Negroes were [successfully] purchased by relatives who wanted to see them set free."[18]

In 1827, a group of blacks in New York City, led by Samuel E. Cornish, a Presbyterian minister, and John Russwurm, a graduate of Bowdoin College, founded *Freedom's Journal,* the first African American weekly newspaper in the United States. *Freedom's Journal,* like other antebellum reform newspapers of the time, used current events, anecdotes, and editorials to champion social reform. Moreover, the editors focused public attention on racism, prejudice, and the threat of colonization by the American Colonization Society, started in 1816 by Presbyterian ministers in the District of Columbia to expatriate free blacks to Africa. Support for *Freedom's Journal* quickly spread beyond New York City. David Walker in Boston, an activist and pamphleteer originally from North Carolina, became an agent for the paper, collecting subscriptions and expanding its circulation. Walker also wrote for *Freedom's Journal* and advocated the unification of "the colored population, so far, through the United States of America, as may be practicable and expedient; forming societies, opening, extending and keeping up correspondences" (*Freedom's Journal,* December 19, 1828). In 1829, the same year *Freedom's Journal* ceased publication, Walker published his *Appeal to Colored Citizens of the World,* in which he urged his fellow African Americans to mobilize their efforts through self-help and mutual aid.

The relative success of Walker's *Appeal* inspired others to publish narratives and pamphlets advocating the abolition of slavery and the geographic

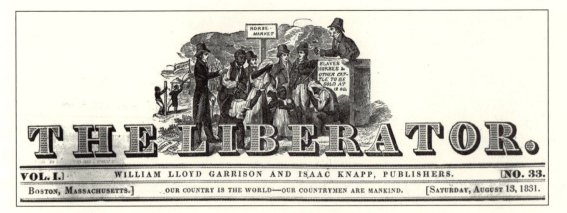

THE LIBERATOR.

VOL. I.]   WILLIAM LLOYD GARRISON AND ISAAC KNAPP, PUBLISHERS.   [NO. 33.

BOSTON, MASSACHUSETTS.]   OUR COUNTRY IS THE WORLD—OUR COUNTRYMEN ARE MANKIND.   [SATURDAY, AUGUST 13, 1831.

Masthead from The Liberator, *the abolitionist journal published by William Lloyd Garrison, 1831. (Library of Congress)*

movement of African Americans away from the all-too-prevalent conditions of racism and discrimination. Isolated free blacks were scattered throughout the American colonies, and after the American Revolution, the number of free blacks increased. Many of these had mixed-racial origins; some were freed at birth if their mother was white, because colonial law generally provided that a child's status followed that of its mother. The largest concentration of free blacks during the colonial period was in Maryland, though the restrictions placed upon this population severely limited movement to other states and unsettled areas of the country.

In the 1830s, slave narratives became an integral part of the abolitionist campaign. By 1836, there were twelve abolitionist journals published in the United States: *American Anti-Slavery Almanac, The Chronotype,* and *The Liberator,* in Boston; *American Anti-Slavery Record, Anti-Slavery Examiner, Anti-Slavery Record, The Emancipator, Human Rights, Quarterly Anti-Slavery Magazine,* and *Slave's Friend,* in New York; *National Enquirer* in Philadelphia; and *Observer* in St. Louis.[19]

Given the abolitionist underpinnings of the slave narratives during the antebellum period, their authenticity as autobiographical works has been challenged. In fact, the authorship of the first book-length slave narrative to directly address issues of social injustice, *Slavery in the United States: A Narrative of the Life and Adventures of Charles Ball, a Black,* has never been established. The controversy surrounding this work developed in 1836 during its first year of publication and has never been fully resolved.

No such doubt, however, attended the publication a year later of the narrative of Moses Roper, who was hailed as the first fugitive from slavery to escape to England from the southern United States. Roper was born in North Carolina, presumably around 1800, the child of a white slaveowner and his wife's young mistress (servant). As a mulatto, Roper suffered greatly:

> I was born in North Carolina, in Caswell County, I am not able
> to tell in what month or year. What I shall now relate, is what
> was told me by my mother and grandmother. A few months be-

fore I was born, my father married my mother's young mistress. As soon as my father's wife heard of my birth, she sent one of my mother's sisters to see whether I was white or black, and when my aunt had seen me she returned back as soon as she could, and told her mistress that I was white, and resembled Mr. Roper very much. Mr. Roper's wife not being pleased with this report, she got a large club-stick and knife, and hastened to the place in which my mother was confined. She went into my mother's room with a full intention to murder me with her knife and club, but as she was going to stick the knife into me, my grandmother happening to come in, caught the knife and saved my life. But as well as I can recollect from what my mother told me, my father sold her and myself, soon after her confinement.... I am not sure whether he exchanged me for another slave, or not, but think it very likely he did exchange me with one of his wife's brothers or sisters, because I remember when my mother's old master died, I was living with my father's wife's brother-in-law, whose name was Mr. Durham. My mother was drawn with the other slaves.... The way they divide their slaves is this: they write the names of different slaves on a small piece of paper, and put it into a box, and let them all draw. I think that Mr. Durham drew my mother, and Mr. Fowler drew me, we were separated a considerable distance, I cannot say how far. My resembling my father so much, and being whiter than the other slaves, caused me to be soon sold to what they call a Negro trader, who took me to the Southern States of America, several hundred miles from my mother. As well as I can recollect I was then about six years old. The trader, Mr. Mitchell, after travelling several hundred miles, and selling a good many of his slaves, found he could not sell me very well (as I was so much whiter than other slaves were) for he had been trying several months—left me with a Mr. Sneed, who kept a large boarding house, who took me to wait at table, and sell me if he could. I think I stayed with Mr. Sneed about a year, but he could not sell me. When Mr. Mitchell had sold his slaves, he went to the North, and brought up another drove, and returned to the South with them, and sent his son-in-law into Washington, Georgia, after me; so he came and took me from Mr. Sneed, and met his father-in-law with me, in a town called Lancaster, with his drove of slaves. We stayed in Lancaster a week, because it was court week, and there were a great many people there, and it was a good opportunity for selling the slaves; and there he was enabled to sell me to a gentleman, Dr. Jones, who was both a Doctor and a Cotton Planter. He took me into his shop to beat up and mix medicines, which was not a very hard employment, but I did not keep it long, as the Doctor soon sent me to his cotton plantation, that I might be burnt darker by the sun.[20]

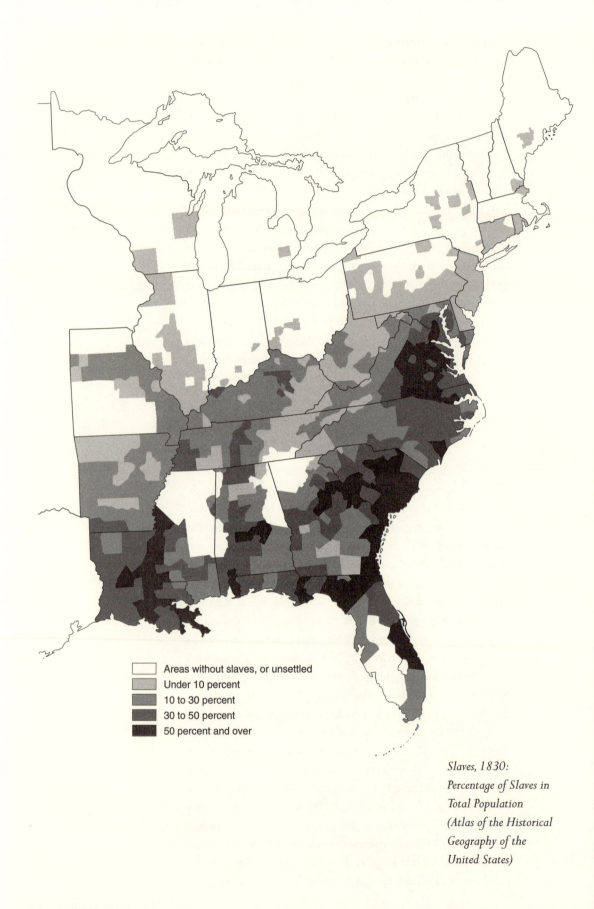

Areas without slaves, or unsettled
Under 10 percent
10 to 30 percent
30 to 50 percent
50 percent and over

Slaves, 1830:
Percentage of Slaves in
Total Population
(Atlas of the Historical
Geography of the
United States)

The pathos of Roper's narrative attracted considerable attention in abolitionist journals and newspapers, which actively pursued the stories of other slaves to bolster their campaign against slavery. Other influential narratives excerpted in this book include those of Lewis Clarke (1845), Frederick Douglass (1845), William Wells Brown (1847), Henry Bibb (1849), Henry Box Brown (1849), Jermain Loguen (1859), and William and Ellen Craft (1860). In assessing the value of slave narratives of the antebellum period, historian John W. Blassingame points out that "the fundamental problem confronting anyone interested in studying black views of bondage is that the slaves had few opportunities to tell what it meant to be chattel. Since antebellum narratives were frequently dictated or written by whites, any study of such sources must begin with an assessment of the editors. An editor's education, religious beliefs, literary skill, attitudes toward slavery, and occupation all affected how he recorded the account of the slave's life."[21]

Blassingame concludes that generally the editors of antebellum narratives were an impressive group of people noted for their integrity. "Most of those for whom biographical data were available were engaged in professions (lawyers, scientists, teachers, historians, journalists, ministers, and physicians) and businesses where they had gained a great deal of prior experience in separating truth from fiction, applying rules of evidence, and accurately portraying men and events."[22]

Blassingame maintains that many of the editors of published slave narratives were "either antagonistic to or had little connection with professional abolitionists."[23] This is not to say that they were not sympathetic to the escaped slaves whose life experiences they published. Clearly, the editors understood the importance of written history and its relevance to the ever-changing currents of public opinion.

Blassingame asserts that "many of the procedures the editors adopted are now standard in any biographical study or oral-history project. Generally, the ex-slave lived in the same locale as the editor and had given oral accounts of his bondage. If the fugitive believed that white men truly respected blacks, they discussed the advisability of publishing his account. Once the black was persuaded to record his experiences for posterity, the dictation might be completed in a few weeks or be spread over two or three years. Often, the editor read the story to the fugitive and asked for elaboration of certain points and clarification of confusing and contradictory details. When the dictation ended, the editor frequently compiled appendices to corroborate the ex-slave's narrative."[24]

The appendixes to slave narratives often included official reports by legislatures, courts, governors, churches, and agricultural societies and were supplemented by references to books or newspaper articles written

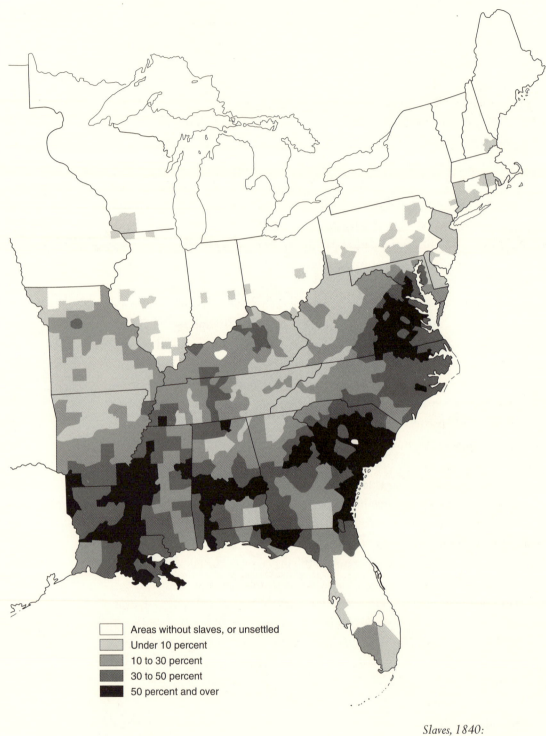

Slaves, 1840:
Percentage of Slaves in
Total Population
(Atlas of the Historical
Geography of the
United States)

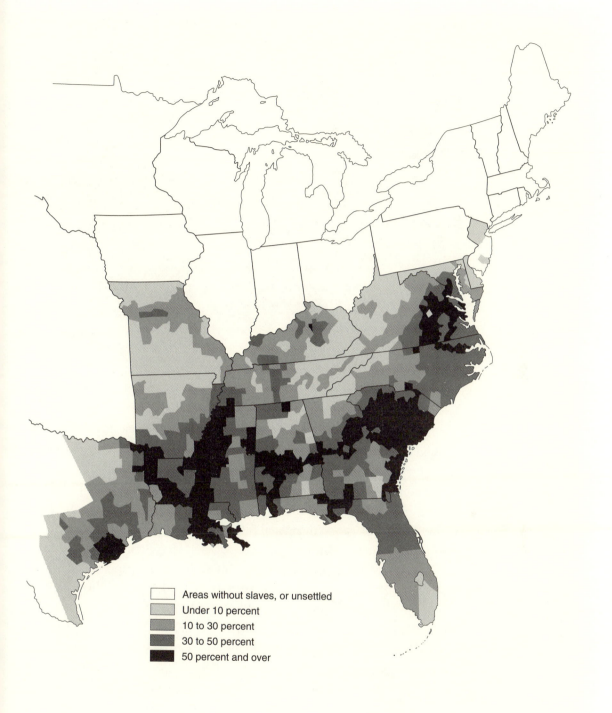

Areas without slaves, or unsettled
Under 10 percent
10 to 30 percent
30 to 50 percent
50 percent and over

Slaves, 1850:
Percentage of Slaves in
Total Population
(Atlas of the Historical
Geography of the
United States)

Unidentified men,
ambrotype, ca. 1860s
(Texas African
American
Photography Archive)

by southern whites. In some instances, however, there are literary devices and methods used in the narratives that were likely beyond the comprehension of unlettered slaves and were designed by the editors to evoke the strongest sympathies of their readers. Despite the abolitionist rhetoric that sometimes accompanied the narratives, they were usually reliable.

Scholars have substantiated the narratives of Olaudah Equiano, Lewis G. and Milton Clarke, William and Ellen Craft, and Henry Box Brown by investigating the judicial proceedings associated with them and by checking census records, diaries and letters of whites, newspapers, and city directories. In cases where blacks (such as Richard Allen, William Wells Brown, Frederick Douglass, Henry Bibb, and Jarmain Loguen) have purchased their freedom, been manumitted, or escaped from bondage and were able to acquire some formal education, the style of their narratives has been compared to their antebellum letters, speeches, and sermons and has thus essentially proved their similarity and authenticity.[25]

Nineteenth-century accounts of the escapes of slaves are energized by the incredible experiences of extraordinary individuals who risked their lives in pursuit of freedom. As primary sources they are, in and of themselves, remarkable, and they enlarge our understanding of how freedom from oppression was and is the ultimate frontier. Ellen and William Craft, who were slaves in Georgia, managed to escape by disguising themselves: Ellen, who was "fair enough to pass for white," pretended to be a gentleman, "a little lame" with his arm in a sling, accompanied by William, the

loyal servant. This ploy enabled them to escape north, first to Philadelphia and then to Boston.

Harriet Tubman, whose maiden name was Arminta Ross, was born a slave in Maryland in 1820 or 1821. About 1844, she married a "free colored man" named Henry Tubman but never had any children. Threatened by the prospects of her sale to a new owner, she escaped to Philadelphia, where she worked and saved her money. Two years later she returned to Maryland, disguised as a man, hoping to reunite with her husband, but much to her disappointment, he had taken another wife and declined to see her. Not deterred, she began the work that earned her the nickname "Moses," leading fugitive slaves through the "Underground Railroad" to the free states of the North and to Canada.

Henry Box Brown escaped to freedom in the 1840s by having himself packed in a box two feet wide and three feet long and then shipped to Philadelphia by the white Virginian Samuel A. Smith. The *Narrative of Henry Box Brown* was first published in 1851 and even became the subject of sheet music written to celebrate his exploits.

Overall, the more than 6,000 published antebellum slave narratives differ significantly in character from the 2,194 accounts of ex-slaves compiled in interviews by the Works Progress Administration (WPA) between 1936 and 1938. Although some scholars, including Benjamin A. Botkin, Norman R. Yetman, and Eugene D. Genovese, have argued that these accounts are more representative of the total slave population and less biased than the published narratives of former slaves, Blassingame has raised important questions about the methodology utilized by WPA interviewers.

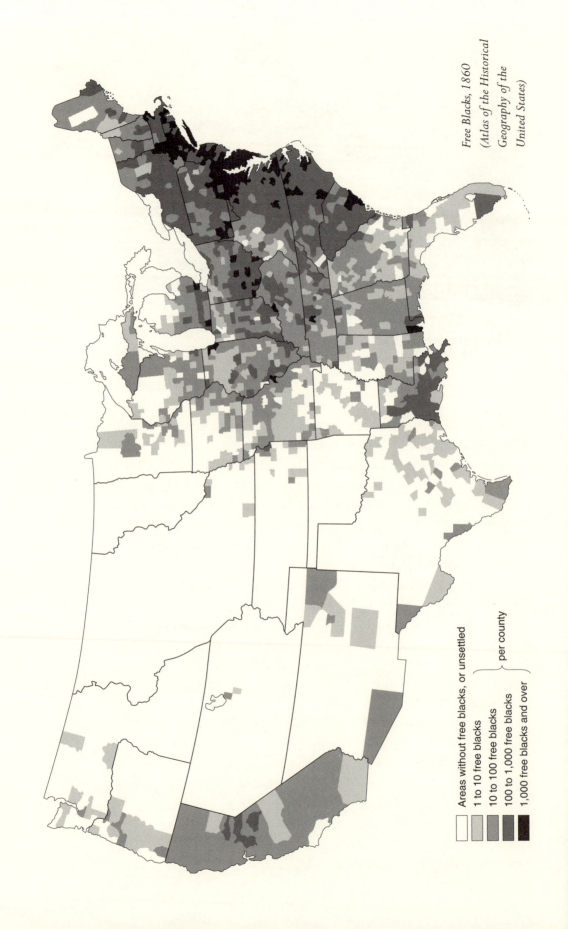

Free Blacks, 1860
(Atlas of the Historical
Geography of the
United States)

Areas without free blacks, or unsettled

1 to 10 free blacks

10 to 100 free blacks   per county

100 to 1,000 free blacks

1,000 free blacks and over

"The first and most important question one must raise about these sources," Blassingame writes, "is whether the interview situation was conducive to the accurate communication and recording of what the informants remembered of slavery. In this regard, it should be noted that black interviewers were virtually excluded from WPA staffs in all of the Southern states except Virginia, Louisiana, and Florida." [26]

Moreover, Blassingame cites references that indicate that "many of the WPA interviewers consistently referred to their informants as darkeys, niggers, auntys, mammies, and uncles. Reminiscent as these terms were of rigid plantation etiquette, they were not calculated to engender the trust of blacks.... Often the white interviewer-

Unidentified soldier, ca. 1870s (Texas African American Photography Archive)

author's actions and demeanor led to distortions and limitations of what the black informant told him.... A second weakness of the WPA interviews is that many of them are not verbatim accounts. The informant's stories were often edited or revised before they were typed and listed as official records.... Indications of deliberate distortion and interpolation of the views of WPA staffers pose a serious challenge to historians who rely on the interviews." [27]

Despite these limitations, WPA narratives do provide some valuable information about the lives of slaves. The seven WPA narratives included in this book reveal a distinct perspective on geographical movement. Phoebe Banks, who was interviewed in Muskogee, Oklahoma, discusses the relations between black slaves and the Creek Indians. Milton Starr, also from Oklahoma, talks about his family's associations with the Cherokee Indians. Felix Haywood from San Antonio explains that "sometimes someone would come long and try to get us to run up North and be free. There wasn't no reason to run up North. All we had to do was walk, but walk South, and we'd be free as soon as we crossed the Rio Grande. In Mexico you could be free." [28]

Oral Histories

Prior to the Civil War, approximately half a million free people of African descent lived in the United States. Known as free Negroes, free blacks, or free people of color, they comprised less than 2 percent of the nation's population and about 9 percent of all African Americans. Concentrated chiefly in the North, as a consequence of their participation in the

American Revolution, free blacks also occupied areas of the Upper South and West. Although economic autonomy was possible during this antebellum period, widespread discrimination stifled political activism and social mobility.

Emancipation engendered unparalleled geographical movement of the African American population. African American soldiers after the Civil War were reorganized into the Ninth and Tenth calvaries and Twenty-fourth and Twenty-fifth infantries and were stationed in different parts of the West. Their presence protected homesteaders, strengthened law enforcement, and helped facilitate the migration of African Americans. Between 1870 and 1900, 1,000 blacks settled in Colorado, 4,000 in Nebraska, 40,000 in Kansas, and over 100,000 in Oklahoma.[29] Smaller numbers moved to California, Washington, Oregon, the Dakotas, Utah, Nevada, and Arizona. Political initiatives led to the creation of all-black settlements, such as Boley and Langston in the Oklahoma territory, Allensworth in California, and Nicodemus in Kansas.[30]

Many African Americans achieved great success in the West during Reconstruction and helped to popularize its image as "the land of opportunity." Quintard Taylor's research demonstrates that African Americans worked in virtually every Western industry, including mining and the range cattle business. He estimates that African Americans composed 25 percent, or approximately 9,000, of the 35,000 cowboys in the West between 1860 and 1895.

> Barney L. Ford, a former slave who arrived in Denver in 1859, had by 1890 become one of the wealthiest men in Colorado. His property, which included a hotel, a dry-goods store, and real estate in Denver and Cheyenne, Wyoming, made him a millionaire. Sarah Gammon Bickford, who from 1888 to 1931 owned and operated the water system for Virginia City, Montana, became one of the city's most prominent citizens. William Gross arrived in Seattle in 1861 and opened the city's second hotel, as well as a restaurant and barbershop, and later bought a farm that would become the site of Seattle's black community. Biddy Mason, a former slave, acquired—and donated to African American institutions—a fortune in Los Angeles real estate before her death in 1891.
>
> (African Americans) participated in the gold rushes to Idaho, Montana, Colorado and the Black Hills in South Dakota. A few found gold on their claims. Californian Albert Callis amassed $90,000 in gold from his efforts in the 1850s, and John Frazier extracted $100,000 from his Colorado mine in 1866. Thaddeus Mundy, a soldier mustered out of service in Helena, Montana, in 1870, made a strike of $50,000 in nearby Dry Gulch the same year.[31]

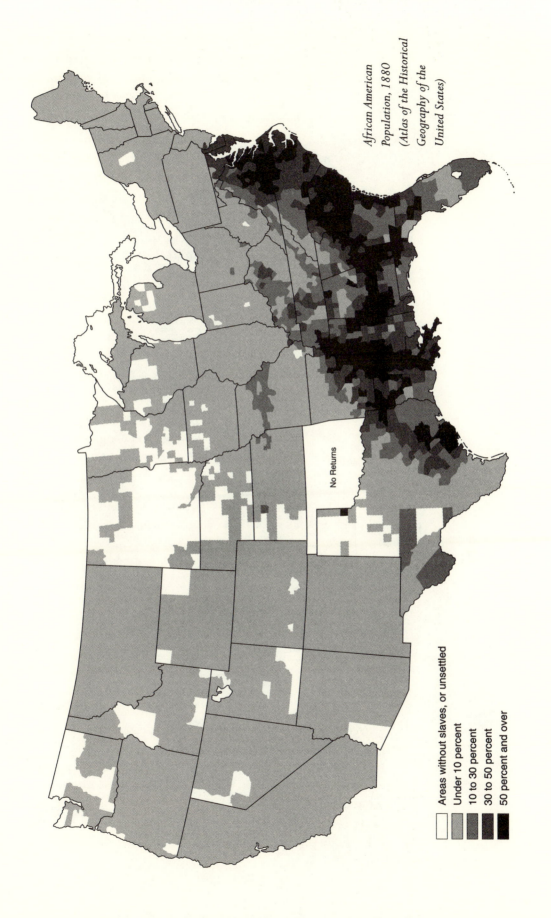

African American Population, 1880 (Atlas of the Historical Geography of the United States)

No Returns

Areas without slaves, or unsettled

Under 10 percent

10 to 30 percent

30 to 50 percent

50 percent and over

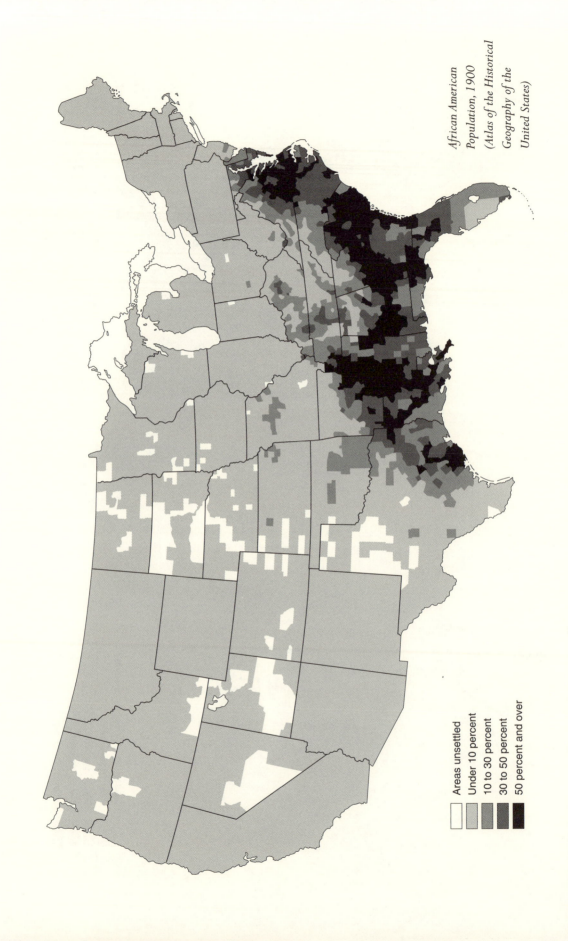

African American
Population, 1900
(Atlas of the Historical
Geography of the
United States)

Areas unsettled

Under 10 percent

10 to 30 percent

30 to 50 percent

50 percent and over

Cora Bell family, Sugar Land, Texas, ca. 1890s (Texas African American Photography Archive)

In addition to increased economic opportunities, the postbellum West attracted political leaders and civil rights activists, such as William J. Hardin of Denver and Charles Langston of Leavenworth, Kansas, who organized the campaigns for equal suffrage. Newspaper editors, including Philip Bell of the San Francisco *Elevator* and Horace Clayton of the Seattle *Republican,* were outspoken critics of segregation and discrimination.

After 1900, increasing numbers of African Americans migrated to urban areas: Denver, San Francisco, Los Angeles, and Seattle in the West; Chicago, Indianapolis, Cleveland, and Detroit in the Upper Midwest and North; and Boston, Philadelphia, and New York in the East. Despite the promise of a higher standard of living, occupational opportunities were limited. Many African Americans were able to find work only in factories and as hotel cooks and waiters, laborers, longshoremen, railway porters, maids, and clerks. A few became professionals—lawyers, doctors, teachers, and ministers. Most of these were educated at historically black colleges.

During the period from 1900 to 1948, many African American urban areas, especially in the South, suffered underemployment and segregated housing. Jim Crow laws propagated the "separate-but-equal" principle, affirmed by the U.S. Supreme Court in *Plessy v. Ferguson* (1896). Local and

state governments passed laws that restricted African American access to public facilities and to virtually every conceivable place where whites and blacks might have social contact. African Americans protested vigorously. In 1905, W. E. B. Du Bois and other black intellectuals founded the Niagara Movement. Opposed to the conciliatory ideology of Booker T. Washington and his followers, Du Bois focused national attention on the plight of African Americans and demanded the abolition of all distinctions based on racial identity. Though the Niagara Movement was relatively short-lived, it was a forerunner of the National Association for the Advancement of Colored People (NAACP), founded in 1909, and the National Urban League (1911). These organizations were strong advocates of civil rights and social reform through the process of "litigation, legislation and education." Together, they rallied the support of their community infrastructure and involved African American churches, colleges, businesses, clubs, sororities, and fraternal groups.

To document the growth of African American communities in the areas of politics, economics, medicine, art, culture, human rights, and social mobility, I engaged in extensive fieldwork, researching existing collections of oral histories and conducting interviews with as many individuals as possible. My principal focus was upon those regions of the country where the idea of the frontier seemed most relevant to geographic movement and the migratory patterns of African Americans. Initially, I explored the historical collections and archives in the states west of the Mississippi River, but as I began interviewing specific people, the scope of my work expanded.

For example, I was introduced to Bruce Lee by his son, whom I met at the Oklahoma Historical Society. Lee, who currently lives in the San

Francisco Bay area, grew up in Buffalo, New York, in an area that he calls the "Niagara Frontier" for the "community of coloreds," referring to his mixed Anglo-Saxon, Indian, and African descent. For Lee and his family, this region of upstate New York, prior to World War II, provided the greatest opportunity for economic and social advancement.

The Bruce Lee interview resulted in an account that was a kind of oral autobiography or life history, comparable in some ways to the nineteenth-century narratives included in the book, in which individuals related the stories of their lives from birth to the date of the interview. Although the nineteenth-century narratives were often dictated to the editor, I tape-recorded and transcribed the interviews. In editing my interviews, I deleted those elements of speech, including hesitations and interruptions, that might impede understanding. My intent was to make their speech fluent in written form and not to alter the grammar or vocabulary.

Unidentified woman, ca. 1920s (Texas African American Photography Archive)

The oral autobiography approach was appropriate for those individuals who were interested in taking the time to provide the most thorough overview of their life experiences as they related to the idea of the frontier. For Jacob Lawrence and Gwendolyn Knight, the frontier was New York City, a "mecca for black artists" during the Harlem Renaissance;[32] for John McLendon, playing, coaching, and struggling to integrate basketball; for Herb Jeffries, creating the role of the black cowboy in the Western movies of the 1930s and later exploring life outside the United States as an expatriate; for Katie Simms and her son, Charles, moving to California; for A. J. Walker, organizing his own ranch rodeo; for Tony Lott, working as a cowboy; for Charles Brown, moving from Texas City to Los Angeles and becoming a rhythm and blues musician; for Archie Reynolds, leaving New Orleans for San Francisco and establishing himself as a gospel singer and businessman; for Jay McShann, maturing as a jazz pianist and bandleader; for William Waddell, teaching at the Tuskegee Institute and building a career as a veterinarian; for Marvin Williams, playing Negro League baseball and trying out for the Boston Red Sox; for Herman Simmons, going on the road as a Pullman porter.

The oral histories with the above-mentioned people are supplemented by others I collected, as well as by those that were edited from existing oral histories in archives around the country. For organizational purposes,

Unidentified woman, ca. 1920s (Texas African American Photography Archive)

these are grouped together and arranged in alphabetical order by the subject's name.

At the Oklahoma Historical Society, I focused on a group of oral histories collected from residents of the Greenwood area of Tulsa. Despite their brevity, these oral histories, when considered together, provide a composite view of community life and the impact of the Tulsa Race Riot of 1921. Especially intense are the accounts of LaVerne Cooksey Davis and Eunice Jackson, who survived the riot. The oral histories collected from Charles Bate, Fannie Ezelle Hill, Hugh Hollins, and Wesley Young offer insight into the lives and work of African Americans in the Tulsa area.

The excerpt of the oral history with Clarence Ray on "Black Politics and Gaming in Las Vegas" was collected and edited by Helen M. Blue and Jamie Coughtry as part of the Oral History Program of the University of Nevada, Reno, in 1991. The oral history with Minnie Lee Haynes, granddaughter of Samuel D. Chambers (who accompanied Brigham Young on his spiritual journey to Utah), was done by William G. Hartley

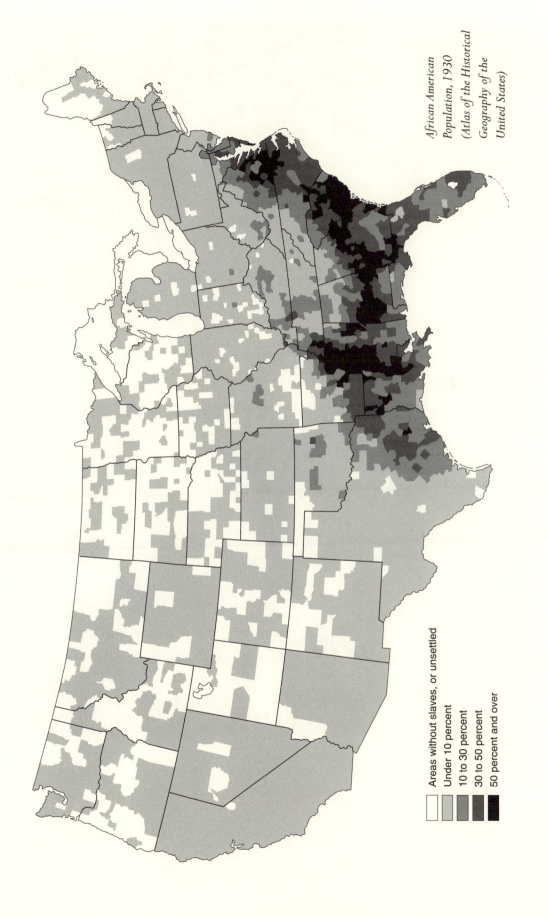

African American
Population, 1930
(Atlas of the Historical
Geography of the
United States)

Areas without slaves, or unsettled

Under 10 percent

10 to 30 percent

30 to 50 percent

50 percent and over

Unidentified men at a segregated drinking fountain, ca. 1930s (Corbis / Bettmann)

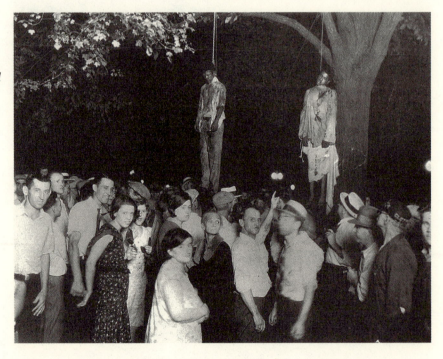

Lynching of Abram Smith and Thomas Shipp, two African American men accused of murder, Marion, Indiana, 1930 (UPI / Corbis / Bettmann)

as part of the Church of Jesus Christ of Latter-day Saints oral history project in 1972.

Unidentified group, ca. late 1940s (Texas African American Photography Archive)

The University of Washington provided interviews with Virginia Gayton (granddaughter of Lewis Clarke, who published a slave narrative in 1845) by Richard Berner in 1970 and Liola Woffort by Larry Gossett in 1968.

Additional oral histories were found at the Idaho State Historical Society, the Montana State Historical Society, and the library at Arizona State University. Folklorist Patrick Mullen shared excerpts from the oral history he is compiling on Jesse Truvillion. Wiley College historian Lloyd Thompson interviewed educator and college president Earl Rand. Jay Brakefield contributed interviews he did with bluesman Jesse Thomas and with Ollie Hunter Boyd and Barbara Wood, who were both part of a community of people from Abbeville, South Carolina, who migrated to Evanston, Illinois, after a lynching in 1916.

Underscoring all of the different primary sources in this book are the ways in which empowerment is achieved through the exploration of different frontiers. Within this context, however, not everyone was able to actualize his or her goals. Through the experiences of a wide range of individuals, the struggles of African American history are personalized. Minnie Lee Haynes brings to life the deep aspirations of her ancestors, but also relates the frustrations of her own life in Oregon. Charles Simms gives voice to the difficulties of growing up in Oakland, California, and weighs the potential merits of moving west against the reality of living in an inner-city, low-income neighborhood.

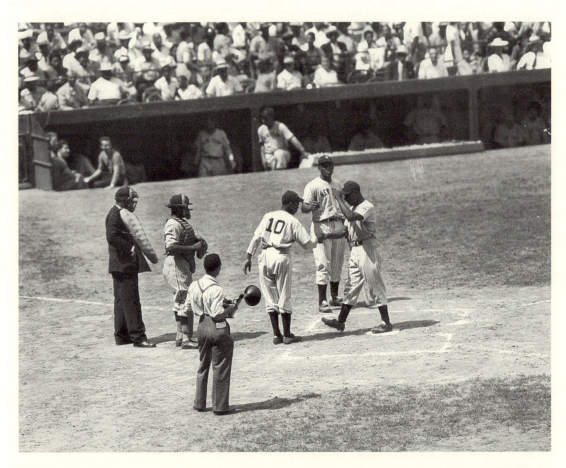

Black Yankees catcher Johnny Hayes crosses home plate after his home run. Greeting him is the pitcher Calhoun, New York, 1942 (UPI/Corbis/Bettmann)

From a geographical perspective, this book reveals the complexities of African American life in frontier regions, and the ways in which these frontiers were conceived, explored, and settled by different individuals during different historical periods. For each of these individuals, venturing out onto the frontier through geographical movement or, perhaps, professional development bestowed unforeseen responsibilities and predicated a new course of action.

In this book, the scope of different frontiers is delineated in human terms and shown to be as diverse as the people themselves and the places in which they lived and worked. Although this volume strives to broaden the definition of the frontier in terms of the vastness of the African American experience, it is ultimately an overview designed to stimulate dialogue about written history and the oral tradition by exploring the lives of people who defy generalization and who necessitate further study.

Notes

1. Roger Hornsby, Jr., *Chronology of African-American History: Significant Events and People from 1619 to the Present* (Detroit: Gale Research, Inc., 1991), p. xix.

2. In 1781, the first census of Los Angeles showed that 56 percent of the city's earliest settlers were part black. Similar statistics were also recorded that same year in San Jose, where 25 percent were identified as Zambo or mulatto, and in San Francisco, 14 percent. In 1790, 28 percent were listed in this manner in Albuquerque, and in 1794, 35 percent in San Antonio and 23 percent in California.

3. Herbert Aptheker, *American Negro Revolts* (New York: International Publishers, 1987), p. 163.

4. T. H. Breen and Stephen Innes, *Mine Owne Ground: Race and Freedom on Virginia's Eastern Shore, 1400–1676* (New York: Oxford University Press, 1980), pp. 8–9.

5. Marion Wilson Starling, *The Slave Narrative: Its Place in American History* (Boston: G. K. Hall, 1981), p. 50. Accounts of antislavery sentiments were published as early as 1646, when, by order of the Massachusetts General Court, a group of slaves were returned to Africa because they were unlawfully transported. For more information, see Starling, p. 2.

6. Starling, p. 50.

7. "Adam Negro's Tryall," in *Publications of the Colonial Society of Massachusetts Transactions, 1892–1894,* as Starling, p. 51.

8. Starling, p. 3.

9. Briton Hammon, *A Narrative of the Uncommon Sufferings and Suprising Deliverance of Briton Hammon, A Negro Man, Etc.* (Boston: Green and Russell, 1760).

10. After its publication in London in 1789, *The Interesting Narrative of the Life of Olaudah Equiano, or Gustavus Vassa, the African, Written by Himself* was subsequently reissued in thirty-six editions in English, Dutch, and German between that year and 1857.

11. Olaudah Equiano, *The Interesting Narrative of the Life of Olaudah Equiano, or Gustavus Vassa, The African, Written by Himself,* Vol. I (New York: W. Duell, 1791).

12. Ira Berlin, "The Revolution in Black Life," reprinted in Richard D. Brown, ed., *The Major Problems in the Era of the American Revolution, 1760–1791* (Lexington, Massachusetts: D.C. Heath, 1992), p. 330.

13. Ibid., p. 332.

14. Ibid., pp. 332–333.

15. Quintard Taylor, "Blacks in the West," in Jack Salzman, David Lionel Smith, and Cornell West, eds., *Encyclopedia of African-American Culture and History* (New York: Simon and Schuster, 1996), pp. 2804–2808. For more information, see Quintard Taylor, *In Search of the Racial Frontier: African Americans in the American West, 1528–1990* (New York: W. W. Norton, 1998).

16. Richard Allen, *The Life, Experience, and Gospel Labours of the Right Reverend Richard Allen. To Which Is Annexed the Rise and Progress of America, Etc.* (Philadelphia: 1841).

17. Starling, p. 50.

18. Sterling Stuckey, *Slave Culture: Nationalist Theory and the Foundations of Black America.* (New York: Oxford University Press, 1987), p.101.

19. *American Anti-Slavery Almanac,* published by the Boston Anti-Slavery Society from 1836 to 1840, then by the New York Anti-Slavery Society until about 1847; *The Chronotype,* published in Boston, ca. 1836 to 1847; *The Liberator,* edited by William Lloyd Garrison and published in Boston from 1831 to 1865; *The American Anti-Slavery Record,* published by the New York Anti-Slavery Society from 1835 to 1839, began as the *Anti-Slavery Reporter* in 1833. The name was changed in 1834 to the *American Anti-Slavery Reporter* and changed again in 1835; *Anti-Slavery Examiner,* published by the New York Anti-Slavery Society from 1836 to 1845; *Anti-Slavery Record,* published by the New York Anti-Slavery Society from 1835 to 1839; *The Emancipator,* published variously in New York and Boston from 1833 to 1850 by the American Anti-Slavery Society. (The title changed to *The Republican* in the 1840s, not to be confused with Elihu Embree's *The Emancipator,* published in 1820 in Jonesborough, Tennessee); *Human Rights,* published by the New York Anti-Slavery Society from 1835 to 1837; *Quarterly Anti-Slavery Magazine,* published by the New York Anti-Slavery Society from 1835 to 1837; *Slave's Friend,* a magazine for juveniles, published by the New York Anti-Slavery Society from 1836 to 1839; *National Enquirer,* Benjamin Lundy's paper, with which he merged the *Genius of Universal Emancipation,* published in Philadelphia from 1836 to 1837; *Observer,* edited by Elijah P. Lovejoy and published in St. Louis from 1833 to 1837 and in Alton, Illinois, in 1837.

20. Moses Roper, *Narrative of the Adventures and Escape of Moses Roper from American Slavery* (London: 1837).

21. John W. Blassingame, "Using the Testimony of Ex-Slaves: Approaches and Problems," in Charles T. Davis and Henry Louis Gates, Jr., *The Slave's Narrative* (New York: Oxford University Press, 1985), p. 79.

22. Ibid., p. 79.

23. Ibid., p. 80.

24. Ibid., p. 81.

25. Ibid., p. 83.

26. Ibid., p. 84.

27. Ibid., p. 86.

28. Felix Haywood, interviewed in San Antonio, Texas, n.d. *American Slave,* ser. 1, vol. 4 (Texas pt. 2), pp.130–134.

29. For more information, see Eugene Berwanger, *The West and Reconstruction* (Urbana: University of Illinois Press, 1981); Jimmie Lewis Franklin, *Journey Toward Hope* (Norman: University of Oklahoma Press, 1982); Nell Irvin Painter, *Exodusters: Black Migration to Kansas after Reconstruction* (Topeka: University Press of Kansas, 1986); and W. Sherman Savage, *Blacks in the West* (Westport, Connecticut: Greenwood Press, 1976).

30. The *Exodusters,* as they were called, consisted of about 20,000 African Americans, who, fearing they might be reenslaved when Reconstruction ended, migrated to Kansas from Mississippi, Louisiana, Texas, Kentucky, and Tennessee in the spring of 1879. Kansas was revered as a free state where blacks hoped to own land and control their own destiny. Ultimately, however, Kansas became segregated and was involved in one of the five U.S. Supreme Court cases that together are known as *Brown v. Board of Education,* which paved the way for school desegregation after 1954. For more information, see Robert G. Athearn, *In Search of Canaan: Black Migration to Kansas, 1879–80* (Lawrence, Kansas: University of Kansas Press, 1978).

31. Taylor, p. 2806.

32. For more information on the Harlem Renaissance, see Arna Bontemps, *The Harlem Renaissance Remembered: Essays with a Memoir* (New York: Dodd, Mead, 1972); Nathan I. Huggins, *Harlem Renaissance* (New York: Oxford University Press, 1971).

Section I

Slave Narratives

Emancipation,
an engraving by
Thomas Nast, 1865.
(Library of Congress)

Henry Bibb

Life dates: May 10, 1815–1854

Henry Bibb was the eldest of seven sons born to Mildred Jackson, a slave woman in Shelby, Kentucky. Like many slaves, he was uncertain about the identity of his father, who was reportedly James Bibb, a Kentucky state senator. After his marriage to a mulatto slave named Malinda in 1833, he made repeated attempts to escape slavery, but did not succeed until 1842, when he fled to Detroit, Michigan. In Detroit, Bibb became an ardent abolitionist, and in 1849 he published his autobiography, Narrative of the Life and Adventures of Henry Bibb, an American Slave. *In 1850 Congress passed the Fugitive Slave Act, which gave slave owners the right to reclaim escaped slaves and obligated Northerners to assist them. Bibb fled with his second wife, Mary Miles Bibb, to Ontario, Canada, where he founded the first black newspaper in that country, the* Voice of the Fugitive.

In the fall or winter of 1837 I formed a resolution that I would escape, if possible, to Canada, for my liberty. I commenced from that hour making preparations for the dangerous experiment, breaking the chains that bound me as a slave. My preparation for this voyage consisted in the accumulation of a little money, perhaps not exceeding two dollars and fifty cents, and a suit which I had never been seen or known to wear before; this last was to avoid detection.

On the twenty-fifth of December, 1837, my long anticipated time had arrived when I was to put into operation my former resolution which was to bolt for liberty or consent to die a slave. I acted upon the former, although I confess it to be one of the most self-denying acts of my whole life, to take leave of an affectionate wife who stood before me on my departure, with dear little Frances in her arms, and with tears of sorrow in her eyes as she bid me a long farewell. It required all the moral courage that I was master of to suppress my feelings while taking leave of my little family.

Had Malinda known my intention at that time, it would not have been possible for me to have got away, and I might have to this day been a slave. Notwithstanding every inducement which was held out to me to run away if I would be free, and the voice of liberty was thundering in my very soul, "Be free, oh, man! be free," I was struggling against a thousand obstacles which had cluttered around my mind to bind my wounded spirit still in the dark prison of mental degradation. My strong attachments to friends and relatives, with all the love of home and birth-place which is so natural among the human family, twined about my heart and were hard to

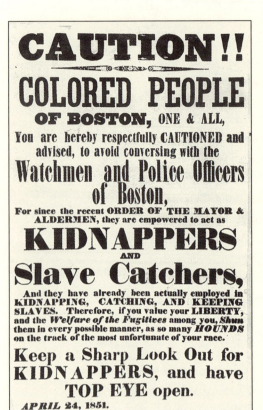

CAUTION!!

COLORED PEOPLE

OF BOSTON, ONE & ALL,

You are hereby respectfully **CAUTIONED** and advised, to avoid conversing with the

Watchmen and Police Officers of Boston,

For since the recent **ORDER OF THE MAYOR & ALDERMEN,** they are empowered to act as

KIDNAPPERS

AND

Slave Catchers,

And they have already been actually employed in **KIDNAPPING, CATCHING, AND KEEPING SLAVES.** Therefore, if you value your **LIBERTY,** and the *Welfare of the Fugitives* among you, *Shun* them in every possible manner, as so many *HOUNDS* on the track of the most unfortunate of your race.

Keep a Sharp Look Out for KIDNAPPERS, and have TOP EYE open.

APRIL 24, 1851.

This April 1851 placard, issued by the Vigilance Committee of Boston, warns slaves to be careful. (Bettmann / Corbis)

break away from. And withal, the fear of being pursued with guns and blood-hounds, and of being killed, or captured and taken to the extreme South, to linger out my days in hopeless bondage on some cotton or sugar plantation, all combined to deter me. But I had counted the cost, and was fully prepared to make the sacrifice. The time for fulfilling my pledge was then at hand. I must forsake friends and neighbors, wife and child, or consent to live and die a slave.

By the permission of my keeper, I started out to work for myself on Christmas. I went to the Ohio River, which was but a short distance from Bedford. My excuse for wanting to go there was to get work. High wages were offered for hands to work in a slaughter-house. But in place of my going to work there, according to promise, when I arrived at the river I managed to find a conveyance to cross over into a free state. I was landed in the village of Madison, Indiana, where steamboats were landing every day and night, passing up and down the river, which afforded me a good opportunity of getting a boat passage to Cincinnati. My anticipation being worked up to the highest pitch, no sooner was the curtain of night dropped over the village, than I secreted myself where no one could see me, and changed my suit ready for the passage. Soon I heard the welcome sound of a steamboat coming up the river Ohio, which was soon to waft me beyond the limits of the human slave markets of Kentucky. When the boat had landed at Madison, notwithstanding my strong desire to get off, my heart trembled within me in view of the great danger to which I was exposed in taking passage on board of a Southern steamboat; hence before I took passage, I kneeled down before the Great I Am, and prayed for his aid and protection, which He bountifully bestowed even beyond my expectation; for I felt myself to be unworthy. I then stept boldly on the deck of this splendid swift-running steamer, bound for the city of Cincinnati. This being the first voyage that I had ever taken on board of a steamboat, I was filled with fear and excitement, knowing that I was surrounded by the vilest enemies of God and man, liable to be seized and bound hand and foot, by any white man, and taken back into captivity. But I crowded myself back from the light among the deck passengers, where it would be difficult to distinguish me from a white man. Every time during the night that the mate came round with a light after the hands, I was afraid he would see I was a colored man, and take me up;

hence I kept from the light as much as possible. Some men love darkness rather than light, because their deeds are evil; but this was not the case with myself; it was to avoid detection in doing right. This was one of the instances of my adventures that my affinity with the Anglo-Saxon race, and even slaveholders, worked well for my escape. But no thanks to them for it. While in their midst they have not only robbed me of my labor and liberty, but they have almost entirely robbed me of my dark complexion. Being so near the color of a slaveholder, they could not, or did not find me out that night among the white passengers. There was one of the deck hands on board called out on his watch, whose hammock was swinging up near by me. I asked him if he would let me lie in it. He said if I would pay him twenty-five cents that I might lie in it until day. I readily paid him the price and got into the hammock. No one could see my face to know whether I was white or colored, while I was in the hammock; but I never closed my eyes for sleep that night. I had often heard of explosions on board of steamboats; and every time the boat landed, and blowed off steam, I was afraid the boilers had bursted and we should all be killed; but I lived through the night amid the many dangers to which I was exposed. I still maintained my position in the hammock, until the next morning about 8 o'clock, when I heard the passengers saying the boat was near Cincinnati; and by this time I supposed that the attention of the people would be turned to the city and I might pass off unnoticed.

There were no questions asked me on board the boat. The boat landed about 9 o'clock in the morning in Cincinnati, and I waited until after most of the passengers had gone off of the boat; I then walked as gracefully up the street as if I was not running away, until I had got pretty well up Broadway. My object was to go to Canada, but having no knowledge of the road, it was necessary for me to make some inquiry before I left the city. I was afraid to ask a white person, and I could see no colored person to ask. But fortunately for me I found a company of little boys at play in the street, and through these little boys, by asking them indirect questions, I found the residence of a colored man.

"Boys, can you tell me where that old colored man lives who
saws wood, and works at jobs around the streets?"
"What is his name?" said one of the boys.
"I forget."
"Is it old Job?"
"Is Dundy a colored man?"
"Yes, sir."
"That is the very man I am looking for; will you show me where
he lives?"
"Yes," said the little boy, and pointed me out the house.

Mr. D. invited me in, and I found him to be a true friend. He asked me if I was a slave from Kentucky, and if I ever intended to go back into slavery? Not knowing yet whether he was truly in favor of slaves running away, I told him I had just come over to spend my Christmas Holydays, and that I was going back. His reply was, "My son, I would never go back if I was in your place; you have a right to your liberty." I then asked him how I should get my freedom. He referred me to Canada, over which waved freedom's flag, defended by the British Government, upon whose soil there cannot be the foot print of a slave.

He then commenced telling me of the facilities for my escape to Canada; of the Abolitionists; of the Abolition Societies, and of their fidelity to the cause of suffering humanity. This was the first time in my life that ever I had heard of such people being in existence as the Abolitionists. I supposed that they were a different race of people. He conducted me to the house of one of these warmhearted friends of God and the slave. I found him willing to aid a poor fugitive on his way to Canada, even to the dividing of the last cent, or morsel of bread if necessary.

These kind friends gave me something to eat, and started me on my way to Canada, with a recommendation to a friend on my way. This was the commencement of what was called the underground railroad to Canada. I walked with bold courage, trusting in the arm of Omnipotence; guided by the unchangeable North Star by night, and inspired by an elevated thought that I was fleeing from a land of slavery and oppression, bidding farewell to handcuffs, whips, thumb-screws and chains.

I travelled on until I had arrived at the place where I was directed to call on an Abolitionist, but I made no stop: so great were my fears of being pursued by the pro-slavery hunting dogs of the South. I prosecuted my journey vigorously for nearly forty-eight hours without food or rest, struggling against external difficulties such as no one can imagine who has never experienced the same: not knowing what moment I might be captured while travelling among strangers, through cold and fear, breasting the north winds, being thinly clad, pelted by the snow storms through the dark hours of the night, and not a house in which I could enter to shelter me from the storm.

The second night from Cincinnati, about midnight, I thought that I should freeze; my shoes were worn through, and my feet were exposed to the bare ground. I approached a house on the roadside, knocked at the door, and asked admission to their fire, but was refused. I went to the next house, and was refused the privilege of their fire-side, to prevent my freezing. This I thought was hard treatment among the human family. But—

"Behind a frowning Providence there was a smiling face," which soon shed beams of light upon unworthy me.

The next morning I was still found struggling on my way, faint, hungry, lame, and rest-broken. I could see people taking breakfast from the roadside, but I did not dare to enter their houses to get my breakfast, for neither love nor money. In passing a low cottage, I saw the breakfast table spread with all its bounties, and I could see no male person about the house; the temptation for food was greater than I could resist.

I saw a lady about the table, and I thought that if she was ever so much disposed to take me up, that she would have to catch and hold me, and that would have been impossible. I stepped up to the door with my hat off, and asked her if she would be good enough to sell me a sixpence worth of bread and meat. She cut off a piece and brought it to me; I thanked her for it, and handed her the pay, but instead of receiving it, she burst into tears, and said "never mind the money," but gently turned away bidding me go on my journey. This was altogether unexpected to me: I had found a friend in the time of need among strangers, and nothing could be more cheering in the day of trouble than this. When I left that place I started with bolder courage. The next night I put up at a tavern, and continued stopping at public houses until my means were about gone. When I got to the Black Swamp in the county of Wood, Ohio, I stopped one night at a hotel, after travelling all day through mud and snow; but I soon found that I should not be able to pay my bill. This was about the time that the "wild-cat banks" were in a flourishing state, and "shin plasters" (paper money) in abundance; they would charge a dollar for one night's lodging.

After I had found out this, I slipped out of the bar room into the kitchen where the landlady was getting supper; as she had quite a number of travellers to cook for that night, I told her if she would accept my services, I would assist her in getting supper; that I was a cook. She very readily accepted the offer, and I went to work.

She was very much pleased with my work, and the next morning I helped her to get breakfast. She then wanted to hire me for all winter, but I refused for fear I might be pursued. My excuse to her was that I had a brother living in Detroit, whom I was going to see on some important business, and after I got that business attended I would come back and work for them all winter.

When I started the second morning they paid me fifty cents beside my board, with the understanding that I was to return; but I've not gone back yet.

I arrived the next morning in the village of Perrysburgh, where I found quite a settlement of colored people, many of whom were fugitive slaves. I made my case known to them and they sympathized with me. I was a stranger, and they took me in and persuaded me to spend the winter in Perrysburgh, where I could get employment and go to Canada the next spring, in a steamboat which ran from Perrysburgh, if I thought it proper so to do.

I got a job of chopping wood during that winter which enabled me to purchase myself a suit, and after paying my board the next spring, I had saved fifteen dollars in cash. My intention was to go back to Kentucky after my wife.

When I got ready to start, which was about the first of May, my friends all persuaded me not to go, but to get some other person to go, for fear I might be caught and sold off from my family into slavery forever. But I could not refrain from going back myself, believing that I could accomplish it better than a stranger.

The money that I had would not pass in the South, and for the purpose of getting it off to a good advantage, I took a steamboat passage to Detroit, Michigan, and there I spent all my money for dry goods, to peddle out on my way back through the state of Ohio. I also purchased myself a pair of false whiskers to put on when I got back to Kentucky, to prevent any one from knowing me after night, should they see me. I then started back after my little family.

Jacob Blockson

Life dates: unknown

The narrative of Jacob Blockson was published in William Still's The Underground Railroad *(1878). Blockson escaped from slavery and traveled the Underground Railroad to St. Catherines, Canada. The narrative is supplemented by a letter written by Blockson to his wife, whom he was unable to take with him.*

Jacob was a stout and healthy-looking man, about twenty-seven years of age, with a countenance indicative of having no sympathy with Slavery. Being invited to tell his own story, describe his master, etc., he unhesitatingly relieved himself somewhat after this manner; "I escaped from a man by the name of Jesse W. Paten [Layton]; he was a man of no business, except drinking whiskey, and farming. He was a light-complected man, tall, large, and full-faced, with a large nose. He was a widower. He belonged to no society of any kind. He lived near Seaford, in Sussex County, Delaware.

I left because I didn't want to stay with him any longer. My master was about to be sold out this fall, and I made up my mind that I did not want to be sold like a horse, the way they generally sold darkies then; so when I started I resolved to die sooner than I would be taken back; this was my intention all the while.

I left my wife, and one child; the wife's name was Lear [Lea], and the child was called Alexander. I wanted to get them on soon too. I made some arrangements for their coming if I got off safe to Canada.

Jacob Blockson, after reaching Canada, true to the pledge that he made, wrote back as follows:

> Saint Catharines. Canada West, Dec. 26th, 1858
>
> Dear Wife: I now inform you I am in Canada and am well and hope you are the same, and would wish you to be here next August. You come to suspension bridge and from there to St. Catherines, write and let me know. I am doing well working for a Butcher this winter, and will get good wages in the spring. I now get $2.50 a week.
>
> I, Jacob Blockson, George Lewis, George Alligood and James Alligood are all in St. Catherines, and met George Ross from Lewis Wright's. Jim Blockson is in Canada West, and Jim Delany, Plunnoth Cannon. I expect you my wife Lea Ann Blockson, my son Alexander & Lewis and Ames will all be here and Isabella also. If you can't bring all bring Alexander surely. Write when you will come and I will meet you in Albany. Love to you all, from your loving Husband,
>
> Jacob Blockson

Henry Box Brown
Life dates: c. 1815–?

Henry Brown was born a slave in 1816 on a plantation near Richmond, Virginia. As a young man, he worked at a tobacco factory. In 1848, after his wife and three children were sold to a North Carolina clergyman, Brown vowed to escape from slavery, and a year later, had himself shipped in a wooden crate to Philadelphia by Adams Express. Brown added "Box" as a middle name as a permanent reminder of his method of escape. He settled in Boston and became active in the abolitionist movement. Samuel A. Smith, the white Virginian who crated Brown, was convicted and imprisoned for eight years after he was caught in two similar attempts to help slaves escape by shipping them in wooden crates to the North. In 1849, the first edition of the Narrative of Henry Box Brown *was published with the assistance of Charles Stearns. A second edition of the* Narrative *appeared in Manchester, England, in 1861. William Still in* The Underground Railroad *(1878) included a description of Brown's escape.*

Portrait of Henry Box Brown that appeared in the edition of Narrative of Henry Box Brown *published in 1849.* (*Library of Congress*)

I call upon you, Sons of the North, if your blood has not lost its bright color of liberty, and is not turned the blackened gore which surrounds the slaveholder's polluted hearts, to arise in your might, and demand the liberation of slaves. If you do not, at the day of final account, I shall bear witness against you, as well as against the slaveholders themselves, as the cause of my brethren's bereavement. Think you, at that dread hour, you escape the scrutinizing look of the Judge of all the earth, as he "maketh inquisition for the blood of the innocents"? Oh, no: but equally with the Southern slaveholders, will your character be condemned by the Ruler of the universe.

The next day, I stationed myself by the side of the road, along which the slaves, amounting to three hundred and fifty, were to pass. The purchaser of my wife was a Methodist minister, who was about to starting for North Carolina. Pretty soon five wagonloads of little children passed, and looking at the foremost one, what should I see but a little child, pointing its tiny hand towards me, "There's my father; I knew he would come and bid me good-bye." It was my eldest child! Soon the gang approached in which my wife was chained. I looked, and beheld her familiar face; but O, reader, that glance of agony! May God spare me ever again enduring the excruciating horror of that moment! She passed, and came near to where I stood. I seized hold of her hand, intending to bid her farewell; but words failed me; the gift of utterance had fled, and I remained speechless. I followed her for some distance, with her hand grasped in mine, as if to save her from her fate, but I could not speak, and I was obliged to turn away in silence.

This is not an imaginary scene, reader; it is not a fiction, but an every-day reality at the South; and all I can say more to you, in reference to it is, that if you will not, after being made acquainted with these facts, consecrate your all to the slaves' release from bondage, you are utterly unworthy the name of a man, and should go and hide yourself, in some impenetrable cave, where no eye can behold your demon form.

One more scene occurs in the tragical history of my life, before the curtain drops, and I retire from the stage of observation, as far as past events are concerned; and not, however, to shrink from public gaze, as if ashamed of my perilous adventures, or to retire into private life, lest the bloodhounds of the South should scent my steps, and start in pursuit of their missing property. No, reader, for as long as three million of my countrymen pine in cruel bondage, on Virginia's exhausted soil, and in Carolina's pestilential rice swamps; in the cane breaks of Georgia, and on the cotton fields of Louisiana and Mississippi, and in the insalubrious climate of Texas; as well as suffer under slave-driver's cruel lash, all over the God-forsaken South; I shall never refuse to advocate their claims to your sympathy, whenever a fitting occasion occurs to speak in their behalf.

But you are eager to learn the particulars of my journey from freedom to liberty. The first thing that occurred to me, after the cruel separation of my wife and children from me, and I had recovered my senses, so as to know how to act, was, thoughts of freeing myself from slavery's iron yoke. I had suffered enough under its heavy weight, and I determined I would endure it no longer; and those reasons which often deter the slave from attempting to escape, no longer existed in reference to me, for my family were gone, and slavery now had no mitigating circumstances, to lessen the bitterness of its cup of woe. It is true, as my master had told me, that I could "get another wife"; but no man, excepting a brute below the human species, would have proposed such a step to a person in my circumstances; and as I was not such a degrade human being, I did not dream of so conducting. Marriage was not a thing of personal convenience with me, to be cast aside as a worthless garment, whenever the slaveholder's will require it: but was a sacred institution binding upon me, as long as the God who had "joined us together," refrained from untying the nuptial knot. What! Leave the wife of my bosom for another! And while my heart was leaping from its abode, to pour its strong affections upon the kindred soul of my devoted partner, could I receive a stranger, another person to my embrace, as if the ties of love existed only in the presence of the object loved! Then, indeed, should I have been a traitor to that God, who had linked our hearts together in fond affection, and cemented our union, by so many additional cords, twining around our hearts; as a tree and an arbor are held together by the clinging tendrils of the adhering vine, which winds itself about them so closely. Slavery, and slave abettors, seize hold of these tender scions, and cut and prune them away from both tree and arbor, as remorselessly as a gardener cuts down the briars and thorns which disturb the growth of his fair plants; but all humane, and every virtuous man, must instinctively recoil from such transactions, as they would from soul murder, or from the commission of some enormous deed of villainy.

Reader, in the light of these scenes you may behold, as in a glass, your true character. Refined and delicate you may pretend to be, and may pass yourself off as a pure and virtuous person; but if you refuse to exert yourself for the overthrow of a system, which thus tramples human affection under its bloody feet, and demands of its crushed victims, the sacrifice of all that is noble, virtuous and pure, upon its smoking altars; you may rest assured, that if the balances of purity were extended before you,

He who "searches the hearts, and trieth the reins," would say to you, as your character underwent his searching scrutiny, "Thou art weighed in the balance and found wanting."

I went to Mr. Allen, and requested of him permission to refrain from labor a short time, in consequence of a disabled finger; but he refused to grant me this permission, on the ground that my hand was not lame enough to justify him in so doing. Nothing daunted by this rebuff, I took some oil of vitriol, intending to pour a few drops upon my finger, to make it sufficiently sore, to disable me from work, which I succeeded in, beyond my wishes; for in my hurry, a larger quantity than it was my purpose to apply to my finger, found its way there, and my finger was soon eaten through to the bone. The overseer then was obliged to allow me to absent myself from business, for it was impossible for me to work in that situation. But I did not waste my precious furlough in idle mourning over my fate. I armed myself with determined energy, for action, and in the words of one of old, in the name of God, "I leaped over a wall and run through a troop" of difficulties. After searching for assistance for some time, I at length was so fortunate as to find a friend, who promised to assist me, and for one half the money I had about me, which was one hundred and sixty dollars. I gave him eighty-six, and he was to do his best in forwarding my scheme. Long did we remain together, attempting to devise ways and means to carry me away from the land of separation of families, of whips and thumb-screws, and auction blocks; but as often as a plan was suggested by my friend, there would appear some difficulty in the way of its accomplishment. Perhaps it may not be best to mention what these plans were, as some unfortunate slaves may thereby be prevented from availing themselves of these methods of escape.

At length, after praying earnestly to Him, who seeth afar off, for assistance, in my difficulty, suddenly, words, "Go and get a box, and put yourself in it." I pondered the words over in my mind. "Get a box?" thought I; "what can this mean?" But I was "not disobedient unto the heavenly vision," and I determined to put into practice this direction, as I considered it, from my heavenly Father. I went to the depot, and there noticed the size of the largest boxes, which commonly were sent by the cars, and returned with their dimensions. I then repaired to a carpenter and induced him to make me a box of such a description as I wished, informing him of the use I intended to make of it. He assured me I could not live in it; but as it was dear liberty I was in pursuit of, I thought it best to make the trial.

When the box was finished, I carried it, and placed it before my friend, who had promised to assist me, who asked if that was to "put my clothes in?" I replied that it was not, but to "put Henry Brown in!" He was astonished at my temerity; but I insisted upon his placing me in it, and nailing me up, and he finally consented.

After corresponding with a friend in Philadelphia, arrangements were made for my departure, and I took my place in this narrow prison, with a mind full of uncertainty as to the result. It was a critical period of my life, I can assure you, reader; but if you have never been deprived of your liberty, as I was, you cannot realize the power of that hope of freedom, which was to me, indeed, "an anchor to the soul, both sure and steadfast."

I laid me down in my darkened home of three feet by two, and like one about to be guillotined, resigned myself to my fate. My friend was to accompany me, but he failed to do so; and contented himself with sending a telegraph message to his correspondent in Philadelphia, that such a box was on its way to his care.

I took with me a bladder filled with water to bathe my neck with, in case of too great heat; and with no access to fresh air, excepting three small gimlet holes, I started on my perilous cruise. I was first carried to the express office, the box being placed on its end, so that I started with my head downwards, although the box was directed, and "this side up with care." From the express office, I was carried to the depot and from thence tumbled roughly into the baggage car, where I happened to fall "right side up," but no thanks to my transporters. But after a while the cars stopped, and I was put aboard a steamboat, and placed on my head. In this dreadful position, I remained the space of an hour and a half, it seemed to me, when I began to feel of my eyes and head, and found to my dismay, that my eyes were almost swollen out of their sockets, and the veins on my temple seemed ready to burst. I made no noise however, determining to obtain "victory or death," but endured the terrible pain, as well as I could, sustained under the whole by the thoughts of sweet liberty. About half an hour afterwards, I attempted again to lift my hands to my face, but found I was not able to move them. A cold sweat now covered me from head to foot. Death seemed my inevitable fate, and every moment I expected to feel the blood flowing over me, which had burst from my veins. One half hour longer and my sufferings would have ended in that fate, which preferred to slavery; but I lifted up my heart to God in prayer, believing that he would yet deliver me, when to my joy, I overheard two men say, "We have been here two hours and have traveled twenty miles, now let us sit down, and rest ourselves." They suited the action to the word, and turned the box over, containing my soul and body, thus delivering me from the power of the grim messenger of death, who a few moments previously, had aimed his fatal shaft at my head, and had placed his icy hands on my throbbing heart. One of these men inquired of the other, what he supposed the box contained, to which his comrade replied, that he guessed it

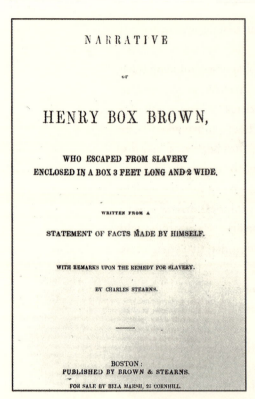

Title page of the published account of Henry Box Brown's adventures. (Library of Congress)

was the mail. "Yes," thought I, "it is a male, indeed, although not the mail of the United States."

Soon after this fortunate event, we arrived at Washington, where I was thrown from the wagon, and again as my luck would have it, fell on my head. I was then rolled down a declivity, until I reached the platform from which the cars were to start. During this short but rapid journey, my neck came very near being dislocated, as I felt it crack, as if it had snapped asunder. Pretty soon, I heard some one say, "there is no room for this box, it will have to remain behind." I then again applied to the Lord, my help in all my difficulties, and in a few minutes I heard a gentleman direct the hands to place it aboard, as it came with into the car, my head downwards again, as I seemed to be destined to escape on my head; a sign probably, of the opinion of American people respecting such bold adventurers as myself; that our heads should be held downwards, whenever we attempt to benefit ourselves. Not the only instance of this prosperity, on the part of the American people, towards the colored race. We had not proceeded far, however, before more baggage was placed in the car, at a stopping place, and I was again turned to my proper position. No farther difficulty occurred until my arrival at Philadelphia. I reached this place at three o'clock in the morning, and remained in the depot until six o'clock A.M, at which time, a wagon drove up, and a person inquired for a box directed to such a place, "right side up." I was soon placed on this wagon, and carried to the house of my friend's correspondent, where quite a number of persons were waiting to receive me. They appeared to be some afraid to open the box at first, but at length one of them rapped upon it, and with a trembling voice, asked, "Is all right within?" to which I replied, "All right." The joy of these friends was excessive, and like the ancient Jews, who repaired to the rebuilding of Jerusalem, each one seized hold of some, and commenced opening my grave. At length the cover was removed, and I arose, and shook myself from the lethargy into which I had fallen; but exhausted nature proved too much for my frame, and I swooned away.

After my recovery from this fainting fit, the first impulse of my soul, as I looked around, and beheld my friends, and was told that I was safe, was to break out in a song of deliverance, and praise to the most high God, whose arm had been signally manifest in my escape. Great God, was I a freeman! Had I indeed succeeded in effecting my escape from the human wolves of Slavery? O what ecstatic joy thrilled through every nerve and fiber of my system! My labor was accomplished, my warfare was ended, and I stood erect before my equal fellow men; no longer a crouching slave, forever at the look and nod of a whimsical and tyrannical slave-owner. Long had seemed my journey, and terribly hazardous had my attempt to gain my birth-right; but it all seemed a comparatively light price to pay for the precious boon of Liberty. O ye, who know not the value of "pearl of great price," by having been all your life shut out from its life-giving presence; learn of how much importance its possession is regarded, by the panting fugitive, as he traces his way through the labyrinths of snares, placed between him and the object of his fond desires! Sympathize with the three millions of crushed and mangled ones who this day pine in cruel bondage, and arouse yourself to action in their behalf! This you will do, if you are not traitors to your God and to humanity. Aid not in placing in high offices, baby-stealers and women-whippers; and if these wicked men, all covered with the clotted gore of their mangled victims, come among you, scorn the idea of bowing in homage to them, whatever may be the character of their claims to your regard. No matter, if they are called presidents of your nation, still utterly refuse to honor them; which you will most certainly do, if you are true to the Slave!

After remaining a short time in Philadelphia, it was thought expedient that I should proceed to Massachusetts, and accordingly funds sufficient to carry me there, were raised by some anti-slavery friends, and I proceeded to Boston. After remaining a short time in that city, I concluded to go to New Bedford, in which place I remained a few weeks, under the care of Mr. Joseph Rickerston of that place, who treated me very kindly. At length hearing of a large anti-slavery meeting to be held in Boston, I left New Bedford, and found myself again in that city, so famous for its devotion to the days of the American revolution; and here, in the presence of several thousand people, did I first relate in public, the story of my sufferings, since which time I have repeated my simple tale in different parts of Massachusetts, and in the State of Maine.

I now stand before you as a freeman, but since my arrival among you, I have been informed that your laws require that I should still be held as a slave; and that if my master should espy me in any nook or corner of the free states, according to the constitution of the United States, he could secure me and carry me back into Slavery; so that I am confident I am not safe, even here, if what I have heard concerning your laws is true. I cannot imagine why you should uphold such strange laws. I have been told that every time a man goes to the polls and votes, he virtually swears to sustain them, frightful as they are. It seems to me to be hard case, for a man to endure what I have endured in effecting my escape, and then to continually exposed to be seized by my master, and carried back into that horrid pit from which I have escaped. I have been told, however, that the people here would not allow me to be thus returned, that they would break their own laws in my behalf, which seems quite curious to me; for why should you make laws, and swear to uphold them, and then break them? I do not understand much about laws, to be sure, as the law of my master is the one I have been subject to all my life, but somehow, it looks a little singular to me, that wise people should be obliged to break their own laws, or else do a very wicked act. I have been told that there are twice as many voters at the North, as there are at the South, and much more wealth, as well as other things of importance, which makes me study much, why the Northern people live under such laws. If I was one of them, and had any influence among them, it appears to me, I should advocate the overthrow of such laws, and the establishment of better ones in their room. Many people tell me besides, that if the slaves should rise up, and do as they did in Nat Turner's time, endeavor to fight their way to freedom, that the Northern people are pledged to shoot them down, and keep them in subjection to their masters. Now I cannot understand this, for almost all the people tell me, that they "are opposed to Slavery," and yet they swear to prevent the slaves from obtaining their liberty! If these things could be made clear to my mind, I should be glad; but a fog hangs over my eyes at present in reference to this matter.

William Wells Brown
Life dates: 1814–1864

William Wells Brown was born a slave in Lexington, Kentucky, in 1814, the son of a slave woman and a white relative of her owner. He remained enslaved in Missouri until his escape in January 1834. Narrative of William Wells Brown, A Fugitive Slave, Written by Himself *was published by the Anti-Slavery Office of Boston in 1847. Two years later, Brown traveled to France to attend the Paris Peace Congress and to generate support for the American abolitionist movement. In addition to delivering over a thousand speeches, he wrote the first African American travelog, entitled* Three Years in Europe; or, Places I Have Seen and People I Have Met *(1852; reprinted in the United States in 1855 as* The American Fugitive in Europe; Sketches of Places and People Abroad, with a Memoir of the Author). *In London in 1853 he published a book that many historians consider the first African American novel:* Clotel; or, The President's Daughter: A Narrative of Slave Life in the

United States, with a Sketch of the Author's Life. *When Brown left Europe in 1854, his supporters purchased his freedom from Enoch Price, his last master. In America Brown wrote a satirical dramatic work,* Experience; or How to Give a Northern Man a Backbone *(1856), and in 1858 he completed* The Escape; or A Leap for Freedom, *the earliest play published by an African American. His other books include* The Black Man: His Antecedents, His Genius, and His Achievements *(1863),* The Negro in the American Rebellion: His Heroism and His Fidelity *(1867),* The Rising Son; or The Antecedents and Advancement of the Colored Race *(1874), and* My Southern Home; or, The South and Its People *(1880).*

The following selection from Brown's 1847 slave narrative chronicles his escape, detailing the customs of slave marriages, the derivation of his name from an Ohio Quaker, and his involvement in the abolitionist movement as a free man.

XI

The love of liberty that had been burning in my bosom, had well nigh gone out. I felt as though I was ready to die. The boat moved gently from the wharf, and while she glided down the river, I realized that my mother was indeed

Gone,——Gone,——sold and gone,
To the rice swamp dank and lone!

After the boat was out of sight, I returned home; but my thoughts were so absorbed in what I had witnessed, that I knew not what I was about half of the time. Night came, but it brought no sleep to my eyes.

In a few days, the boat upon which I was to work being ready, I went on board to commence. This employment suited me better than living in the city, and I remained until the close of navigation; though it proved anything but pleasant. The captain was a drunken, profligate, hard-hearted creature, not knowing how to treat himself, or any other person.

The boat, on its second trip, brought down Mr. Walker, the man of whom I have spoken in a previous chapter, as hiring my time. He had between one and two hundred slaves, chained and manacled. Among them was a man that formerly belonged to my old master's brother, Aaron Young. His name was Solomon. He was a preacher, and belonged to the same church with his master. I was glad to see the old man. He wept like a child when he told me how he had been sold from his wife and children.

The boat carried down, while I remained on board, four or five gangs of slaves. Missouri, though a comparatively new state, is very much engaged in raising slaves to supply the southern market. In a former chapter, I have mentioned that I was once in the employ of a slave-trader, or driver, as he is called at the South. For fear that some may think that I have misrepresented a slave-driver, I will here give an extract from a paper published

*William Wells Brown
(Boston Public
Library)*

in a slaveholding state, Tennessee, called the "Millennial Trumpeter." "Droves of negroes, chained together in dozens and scores, and hand-cuffed, have been driven through our country in numbers far surpassing any previous year, and these vile slave-drivers and dealers are swarming like buzzards around a carrion. Through this country, you cannot pass a few miles in the great roads without having every feeling of humanity insulted and lacerated by this spectacle, nor can you go into any county or any neighborhood, scarcely, without seeing or hearing of some of these despicable creatures, called negro-drivers.

"Who is a negro-driver? One whose eyes dwell with delight on lacerated bodies of helpless men, women and children; whose soul feels diabolical raptures at the chains, and hand-cuffs, and cart-whips, for inflicting tortures on weeping mothers torn from helpless babes, and on husbands and wives torn asunder forever!"

Dark and revolting as is the picture here drawn, it is from the pen of one living in the midst of slavery. But though these men may cant about negro-drivers, and tell what despicable creatures they are, who is it, I ask, that supplies them with the human beings that they are tearing asunder? I answer, as far as I have any knowledge of the state where I came from, that those who raise slaves for the market are to be found among all classes, from Thomas H. Benton down to the lowest political demagogue, who may be able to purchase a woman for the purpose of raising stock, and from the Doctor of Divinity down to the most humble lay member in the church.

It was not uncommon in St. Louis to pass by an auction-stand, and behold a woman upon the auction-block, and hear the seller crying out, *"How much is offered for this woman? She is a good cook, good washer, a good obedient servant. She has got religion!"* Why should this man tell the purchasers that she has religion? I answer, because in Missouri, and as far as I have any knowledge of slavery in the other states, the religious teaching consists in teaching the slave that he must never strike a white man; that God made him for a slave; and that, when whipped, he must not find fault,—for the Bible says, "He that knoweth his master's will, and doeth it not, shall be beaten with many stripes!" And slaveholders find such religion very profitable to them.

After leaving the steamer Ohio, I resided at home, in Mr. Willi's family, and again began to lay my plans for making my escape from slavery. The anxiety to be a freeman would not let me rest day or night. I would think of the northern cities that I had heard so much about;—of Canada, where so many of my acquaintances had found refuge. I would dream at night that I was in Canada, a freeman, and on waking in the morning, weep to find myself so sadly mistaken.

> I would think of Victoria's domain,
> And in a moment I seemed to be there!
> But the fear of being taken again,
> Soon hurried me back to despair.

Mr. Willi treated me better than Dr. Young ever had; but instead of making me contented and happy, it only rendered me the more miserable, for it enabled me to better appreciate liberty. Mr. Willi was a man who loved money as most men do, and without looking for an opportunity to sell me, he found one in the offer of Captain Enoch Price, a steamboat owner and commission merchant, living in the city of St. Louis. Captain Price tendered seven hundred dollars, which was two hundred more than Mr. Willi had paid. He therefore thought best to accept the offer. I was wanted for a carriage driver, and Mrs. Price was very much pleased with the captain's bargain. His family consisted besides of one child. He had three servants beside myself—one man and two women.

Mrs. Price was very proud of her servants, always keeping them well dressed, and as soon as I had been purchased, she resolved to have a new carriage. And soon one was procured, and all preparations were made for a turn-out in grand style, I being the driver.

One of the female servants was a girl some eighteen or twenty years of age, named Maria. Mrs. Price was very soon determined to have us united, if she could so arrange matters. She would often urge upon me the necessity of having a wife, saying that it would be so pleasant for me to take one in the same family! But getting married, while in slavery, was the last of my thoughts; and had I been ever so inclined, I should not have married Maria, as my love had already gone in another quarter. Mrs. Price soon found out that her efforts at this match-making between Maria and myself would not prove successful. She also discovered (or thought she had) that I was rather partial to a girl named Eliza, who was owned by Dr. Mills. This induced her at once to endeavor the purchase of Eliza, so great was her desire to get me a wife!

Before making the attempt, however, she deemed it best to talk to me a little upon the subject of love, courtship, and marriage. Accordingly one afternoon she called me into her room—telling me to take a chair and sit down. I did so, thinking it rather strange, for servants are not very often asked thus to sit down in the same room with the master or mistress. She said that she had found out that I did not care enough about Maria to marry her. I told her that was true. She then asked me if there was not a girl in the city that I loved. Well, now, this was coming into too close quarters with me! People, generally, don't like to tell their love stories to everybody that think fit to ask about them, and it was so with me. But, after blushing awhile and recovering myself, I told her that I did not want a wife. She then asked me, if I did not think something of Eliza. I told her that I did. She then said that if I wished to marry Eliza, she would purchase her if she could.

I gave but little encouragement to this proposition as I was determined to make another trial to get my liberty, and I knew that if I should have a wife, I should not be willing to leave her behind; and if I should attempt to bring her with me, the chances would be difficult for success. However, Eliza was purchased, and brought into the family.

XII

But the more I thought of the trap laid by Mrs. Price to make me satisfied with my new home, by getting me a wife, the more I determined never to marry any woman on earth until I should get my liberty. But this secret I was compelled to keep to myself, which placed me in a very critical position. I must keep upon good terms with Mrs. Price and Eliza. I therefore promised Mrs. Price that I would marry Eliza; but said that I was not then ready. And I had to keep upon good terms with Eliza, for fear that Mrs. Price would find out that I did not intend to get married.

I have here spoken of marriage, and it is very common among slaves themselves to talk of it. And it is common for slaves to be married; or at least have the marriage ceremony performed. But there is no such thing as slaves being lawfully married. There has never yet a case occurred where a slave has been tried for bigamy. The man may have as many women as he wishes, and the women as many men; and the law takes no cognizance of such acts among slaves. And in fact some masters, when they have sold the husband from the wife, compel her to take another.

There lived opposite Captain Price's, Doctor Farrar, well known in St. Louis. He sold a man named Ben to one of the traders. He also owned Ben's wife, and in a few days he compelled Sally (that was her name) to marry Peter, another man belonging to him. I asked Sally "why she married Peter so soon after Ben was sold." She said, "because master made her do it."

Mr. John Calvert, who resided near our place, had a woman named Lavinia. She was quite young, and a man to whom she was about to be married was sold, and carried into the country near St. Charles, about twenty miles from St. Louis. Mr. Calvert wanted her to get a husband; but she had resolved not to marry any other man, and she refused. Mr. Calvert whipped her in such a manner that it was thought she would die. Some of the citizens had him arrested, but it was soon hushed up. And that was the last of it. The woman did not die, but it would have been the same if she had.

Captain Price purchased me in the month of October, and I remained with him until December, when the family made a voyage to New Orleans, in a boat owned by himself, and named the "Chester." I served on board, as one of the stewards. On arriving at New Orleans, about the middle of the month, the boat took in freight for Cincinnati; and it was decided that the family should go up the river in her, and what was of more interest to me, I was to accompany them.

The long-looked-for opportunity to make my escape from slavery was near at hand.

Captain Price had some fears as to the propriety of taking me near a free State, or a place where it was likely I could run away, with a prospect of liberty. He asked me if I had ever been in a free State. "Oh yes," said I, "I have been in Ohio; my master carried me into that State once, but I never like a free State."

It was soon decided that it would be safe to take me with them, and what made it more safe, Eliza was on the boat with us, and Mrs. Price, to try me, asked if I thought as much as ever of Eliza. I told her that Eliza was very dear to me indeed, and that nothing but death should part us. It was the same as if we were married. This had the desired effect. The boat left New Orleans, and proceeded up the river.

I should have stated, that before leaving St. Louis, I went to an old man named Frank, a slave, owned by a Mr. Sarpee. This old man was very distinguished (not only among the slave population, but also the whites) as a fortune-teller. He was about seventy years of age, something over six feet high, and very slender. Indeed, he was so small around his body that it looked as though it was not strong enough to hold up his head.

Uncle Frank was a very great favorite with the young ladies, who would go to him in great numbers to get their fortunes told. And it was generally believed that he could really penetrate into the mysteries of futurity. Whether true or not, he had the name, and that is about half of what one needs in this gullible age. I found Uncle Frank seated in the chimney corner, about ten o'clock at night. As soon as I entered, the old man left his seat. I watched his movement as well as I could by the dim light of the fire. He soon lit a lamp, and coming up, looked me full in the face, saying, "Well, my son, you have come to get uncle to tell your fortune, have you?" "Yes," said I. But how the old man should know what I had come for, I could not tell. However, I paid the fee of twenty-five cents, and he commenced by looking into a gourd, filled with water. Whether the old man was a prophet, or the son of a prophet, I cannot say; but there is one thing certain, many of his predictions were verified.

I am no believer in soothsaying; yet I am sometimes at a loss to know how Uncle Frank could tell so accurately what would occur in the future. Among the many things he told was one which was enough to pay me for all the trouble of hunting him up. It was that *I should be free!* He further said, that in trying to get my liberty, I would meet with many severe trials. I thought to myself, any fool could tell me that!

The first place in which we landed in a free State was Cairo, a small village at the mouth of the Ohio River. We remained here but I had at different times obtained little sums of money, which I had reserved for a "rainy day." I procured some cotton cloth, and made me a bag to carry provisions in. The trials of the past were all lost in hopes for the future. The love of liberty, that had been burning in my bosom for years, and had been well nigh extinguished, was now resuscitated. At night, when all around was peaceful, I would walk the decks, meditating upon my happy prospects.

During the last night that I served in slavery, I did not close my eyes a single moment. When not thinking of the future, my mind dwelt on the past. The love of a dear mother, a dear sister, and three dear brothers, yet living, caused me to shed many tears. If I could only have been assured of their being dead, I should have felt satisfied; but I imagined I saw my dear mother in the cotton-field, followed by a merciless task-master, and no one to speak a consoling word to her! I beheld my dear sister in the hands of a slave-driver, and compelled to submit to his cruelty! None but one placed in such a situation can for a moment imagine the intense agony to which these reflections subjected me.

XIII

At last the time for action arrived. The boat landed at a point which appeared to me the place of all others to start from. I found that it would be impossible to carry anything with me, but what was upon my person. I had some provisions, and a single suit of clothes, about half worn. When the boat was discharging her cargo, and the passengers engaged carrying their baggage on and off shore, I improved the opportunity to convey myself with my little effects on land. Taking up a trunk, I went up the wharf, and was soon out of the crowd. I made directly for the woods, where I remained until night, knowing well that I could not travel, even in the State of Ohio, during the day, without danger of being arrested.

I had long since made up my mind that I would not trust myself in the hands of any man, white or colored. The slave is brought up to look upon every white man as an enemy to him and his race; and twenty-one years in slavery had taught me that there were traitors, even among colored people. After dark, I emerged from the woods into a narrow path, which led me into the main travelled road. But I knew not which way to go. I did not know North from South, East from West. I looked in vain for the North Star; a heavy cloud hid it from my view. I walked up and down the road until near midnight, when the clouds disappeared, and I welcomed the sight of my friend,—truly the slave's friend,—the North Star!

As soon as I saw it, I knew my course, and before daylight I travelled twenty or twenty-five miles. It being in the winter, I suffered intensely from the cold; being without an overcoat, and my other clothes rather thin for the season. I was provided with a tinder-box, so that I could make up a fire when necessary. And but for this, I should certainly have frozen to death; for I was determined not to go to any house for shelter. I knew of a man belonging to Gen. Ashly, of St. Louis, who had run away near Cincinnati, on the way to Washington, but had been caught and carried back into slavery; and I felt that a similar fate awaited me, should I be seen by any one. I travelled at night, and lay by during the day.

On the fourth day, my provisions gave out, and then what to do I could not tell. Have something to eat, I must; but how to get it was the question! On the first night after my food was gone, I went to a barn on the road-side, and there found some ears of corn. I took ten or twelve of them, and kept on my journey. During the next day, while in the woods, I roasted my corn and feasted upon it, thanking God that I was so well provided for.

My escape to a land of freedom now appeared certain, and the prospects of the future occupied a great part of my thoughts. What should be my occupation, was a subject of much anxiety to me; and the next think what should be my name? I have before stated that my old master, Dr. Young, had no children of his own, but had with him a nephew, the son of his brother, Benjamin Young. When this boy was brought to Doctor Young, his name being William, the same as mine, my mother was ordered to change mine to something else. This, at the time, I thought to be one of the most cruel acts that could be committed upon my rights; and I received several very severe whippings for telling people that my name was William, after orders were given to change it. Though young, I was old enough to place a high appreciation upon my name. It was decided, however, to call me "Sandford," and this name I was known by, not only upon my master's plantation, but up to the time that I made my escape. I was sold under the name of Sandford.

But as soon as the subject came to my mind, I resolved on adopting my old name of William, and let Sandford go by the board, for I always hated it. Not because there was anything peculiar in the name; but because it had been forced upon me. It is sometimes common at the south, for slaves to take the name of their masters. Some have a legitimate right to do so. But I always detested the idea of being called by the name of either of my masters. And as for my father, I would rather have adopted the name of "Friday," and been known as the servant of some Robinson Crusoe, than to have taken his name. So I was not only hunting for my liberty, but also hunting for a name; though I regarded the latter as of little consequence, if I could but gain the former. Travelling along the road, I would sometimes speak to myself, sounding my name over, by way of getting used to it, before I should arrive among civilized human beings. On the fifth or sixth day, it rained very fast, and it froze about as fast as it fell, so that my clothes were one glare of ice. I travelled on at night until I became so chilled and benumbed—the wind blowing into my face—that I found it impossible to go any further, and accordingly took shelter in a barn, where I was obliged to walk about to keep from freezing.

I have ever looked upon that night as the most eventful part of my escape from slavery. Nothing but the providence of God, and that old barn, saved me from freezing to death. I received a very severe cold, which settled upon my lungs, and from time to time my feet had been frostbitten, so that it was with difficulty I could walk. In this situation I travelled two days, when I found that I must seek shelter somewhere, or die.

The thought of death was nothing frightful to me, compared with that of being caught, and again carried back into slavery. Nothing but the prospect of enjoying liberty could have induced me to undergo such trials, for

> Behind I left the whips and chains,
> Before me were sweet freedom's plains!

This, and this alone, cheered me onward. But I at last resolved to seek protection from the inclemency of the weather, and therefore I secured myself behind some logs and brush, intending to wait there until some one should pass by; for I thought it probable that I might see some colored person, or, if not, some one who was not a slaveholder; for I had an idea that I should know a slaveholder as far as I could see him.

XIV

The first person that passed was a man in a buggy-wagon. He looked too genteel for me to hail him. Very soon, another passed by on horseback. I attempted speaking to him, but fear made my voice fail me. As he passed, I left my hiding-place, and was approaching the road, when I observed an old man walking towards me, leading a white horse. He had on a broad-brimmed hat and a very long coat, and was evidently walking for exercise. As soon as I saw him, and observed his dress, I thought to myself, "You are the man that I have been looking for!" Nor was I mistaken. He was the very man!

On approaching me, he asked me, "if I was not a slave." I looked at him some time, and then asked him "if he knew of any one who would help me, as I was sick." He answered that he would; but again asked, if I was not a slave. I told him I was. He then said that I was in a very pro-slavery neighborhood, and if I would wait until he went home, he would get a covered-wagon for me. I promised to remain. He mounted his horse, and was soon out of sight.

After he was gone, I meditated whether to wait or not; being apprehensive that he had gone for some one to arrest me. But I finally concluded to remain until he should return; removing some few rods to watch his movements. After a suspense of an hour and a half or more, he returned with a two horse covered-wagon, such as are usually seen under the shed of a Quaker meeting-house on Sundays and Thursdays; for the old man proved to be a Quaker of the George Fox stamp.

He took me to his house, but it was some time before I could be induced to enter it; not until the old lady came out, did I venture into the house. I thought I saw something in the old lady's cap that told me I was not only safe, but welcome, in her house. I was not, however, prepared to receive their hospitalities. The only fault I found with them was their being too kind. I had never had a white man to treat me as an equal, and the idea of a white lady waiting on me at the table was still worse! Though the table was loaded with the good things of this life, I could not eat. I thought if I could only be allowed the privilege of eating in the kitchen, I should be more than satisfied!

Finding that I could not eat, the old lady, who was a "Thomsonian," made me a cup of "composition," or "number six"; but it was so strong and hot, that I called it "number seven!" However, I soon found myself at home in this family. On different occasions, when telling these facts, I have been asked how I felt upon finding myself regarded as a man by a white family; especially just having run away from one. I cannot say that I have ever answered the question yet.

The fact that I was in all probability a free man, sounded in my ears like a charm. I am satisfied that none but a slave could place such an appreciation upon liberty as I did at that time. I wanted to see mother and sister, that I might tell them "I was free!" I wanted to free my fellow slaves in St. Louis, and let them know that the chains were no longer upon my limbs. I wanted to see Captain Price, and let him learn from my own lips that I was no more a chattel, but a man! I was anxious, too, thus to inform Mrs. Price that she must get another coachman. And I wanted to see Eliza more than I did either Mr. or Mrs. Price!

The fact that I was a free man—could walk, talk, eat and sleep as a man, and no one to stand over me with the blood-clotted cowhide—all this made me feel that I was not myself.

The kind friend that had taken me in was named Wells Brown. He was a devoted friend of the Slave; but was very old, and not in the enjoyment of good health. After being by the fire awhile, I found that my feet had been very much frozen. I was seized with a fever which threatened to confine me to my bed. But my Thomsonian friends soon raised me, treating me as kindly as if I had been one of their own children. I remained with them twelve or fifteen days, during which time they made me some clothing, and the old gentleman purchased me a pair of boots.

I found that I was about fifty or sixty miles from Dayton, in the State of Ohio, and between one and two hundred miles from Cleveland, on Lake Erie, a place I was desirous of reaching on my way to Canada. This I know will sound strangely to the ears of people in foreign lands, but it is nevertheless true. An American citizen was fleeing from a Democratic, Republican, Christian government, to receive protection under the monarchy of Great Britain. While the people of the United States boast of their freedom, they at the same time keep three millions of their own citizens in chains; and while I am seated here in sight of Bunker Hill Monument, writing this narrative, I am a slave, and no law, not even in Massachusetts, can protect me from the hands of the slaveholder!

Before leaving this good Quaker friend, he inquired what my name was besides William. I told him that I had no other name. "Well," said he, "thee must have another name. Since thee has got out of slavery, thee has become a man, and men always have two names."

I told him that he was the first man to extend the hand of friendship to me, and I would give him the privilege of naming me.

"If I name thee," said he, "I shall call thee Wells Brown, after myself."

"But," said I, "I am not willing to lose my name of William. As it was taken from me once against my will, I am not willing to part with it again upon any terms."

"Then," said he, "I will call thee William Wells Brown."

"So be it," said I; and I have been known by that name ever since I left the house of my first white friend, Wells Brown.

After giving me some little change, I again started for Canada. In four days I reached a public house, and went in to warm myself. I there learned that some fugitive slaves had just passed through the place. The men in the bar-room were talking about it, and I thought that it must have been myself they referred to, and I was therefore afraid to start, fearing they would seize me; but I finally mustered courage enough, and took my leave. As soon as I was out of sight, I went into the woods, and remained there until night, when I again regained the road, and travelled on until the next day.

Not having had any food for nearly two days, I was faint with hunger, and was in a dilemma what to do, as the little cash supplied me by my adopted father, and which had contributed to my comfort, was now all gone. I however concluded to go to a farmhouse, and ask for something to eat. On approaching the door of the first one presenting itself, I knocked, and was soon met by a man who asked me what I wanted. I told him that I would like something to eat. He asked where I was from, and where I was going. I replied that I had come some way, and was going to Cleveland.

After hesitating a moment or two, he told me that he could give me nothing to eat, adding, "that if I would work, I could get something to eat."

I felt bad, being thus refused something to sustain nature, but did not dare tell him that I was a slave.

Just as I was leaving the door, with a heavy heart, a woman, who proved to be the wife of this gentleman, came to the door, and asked her husband what I wanted. He did not seem inclined to inform her. She therefore asked me herself. I told her that I had asked for something to eat. After a few other questions, she told me to come in, and that she would give me something to eat.

I walked up to the door, but the husband remained in the passage, as if unwilling to let me enter.

She asked him two or three times to get out of the way, and let me in. But as he did not move, she pushed him on one side, bidding me walk in! I was never before so glad to see a woman push a man aside! Ever since that act, I have been in favor of "woman's rights"!

After giving me as much food as I could eat, she presented me with ten cents, all the money then at her disposal, accompanied with a note to a friend, a few miles further on the road. Thanking this angel of mercy from an overflowing heart, I pushed on my way, and in three days arrived at Cleveland, Ohio.

Being an entire stranger in this place, it was difficult for me to find where to stop. I had no money, and the lake being frozen, I saw that I must remain until the opening of navigation, or go to Canada by way of Buffalo. But believing myself to be somewhat out of danger, I secured an engagement at the Mansion House, as a table waiter, in payment for my board. The proprietor, however, whose name was E. M. Segur, in a short time, hired me for twelve dollars per month; on which terms I remained until spring, when I found good employment on board a lake steamboat.

I purchased some books, and at leisure moments perused them with considerable advantage to myself. While at Cleveland, I saw, for the first time, an anti-slavery newspaper. It was the *Genius of Universal Emancipation,* published by Benjamin Lundy, and though I had no home, I subscribed for the paper. It was my great desire, being out of slavery myself, to do what I could for the emancipation of my brethren yet in chains, and while on Lake Erie, I found many opportunities of "helping their cause along."

It is well known, that a great number of fugitives make their escape to Canada, by way of Cleveland; and while on the lake, I always made arrangement to carry them on the boat to Buffalo or Detroit, and thus effect their escape to the "promised land." The friends of the slave, knowing that I would transport them without charge, never failed to have a delegation when the boat arrived at Cleveland. I have sometimes had four or five on board, at one time.

In the year 1842, I conveyed, from the first of May to the first of December, sixty-nine fugitives over Lake Erie to Canada. In 1843, I visited Malden, in Upper Canada, and counted seventeen, in that small village, who owed their escape to my humble efforts.

Soon after coming North, I subscribed for the *Liberator,* edited by that champion of freedom, William Lloyd Garrison. I labored a season to promote the temperance cause among the colored people, but for the last three years, have been pleading for the victims of American slavery.

WILLIAM WELLS BROWN
Boston, Mass., June 1847

Lewis Clarke
Life dates: 1815–1897

Lewis Clarke was born a slave in Madison County, Kentucky, the son of a mulatto plantation slave, Letitia, and her white, Scottish-born husband, Daniel Clarke. His escape from slavery is chronicled in Narratives of the Sufferings of Lewis and Milton Clarke, Sons of a Soldier of the Revolution; during a Captivity of More than Twenty Years among the Slaveholders of Kentucky, One of the So-Called Christian States of North America *(1848). In the1850s Clarke toured the country as an ardent abolitionist delivering public lectures. He met Harriet Beecher Stowe, who purportedly based the character of George Harris, the husband of Eliza, on him in her novel* Uncle Tom's Cabin.

At length, the report was started that I was to be sold for Louisiana. Then I thought it was time to act. My mind was made up. This was about two weeks before I started. The first plan was formed between a slave named Isaac and myself. Isaac proposed to take one of the horses of his mistress, and I was to take my pony, and we were to ride off together; I as master and he as slave. We started together, and went on five miles. My want of confidence in the plan induced me to turn back. Poor Isaac plead like a good fellow to go forward. I am satisfied from experience and observation that both of us must have been captured and carried back. Everything would have been done in such an awkward manner that a keen eye would have seen through our plot at once. I did not know the roads, and could not have read the guideboards; and ignorant as many people are in Kentucky, they would have thought it strange to see a man with a waiter, who could not read a guide-board. I was sorry to leave Isaac, but I am satisfied I could have done him no good, in the way proposed.

After this failure, I staid about two weeks; and after having arranged every thing to the best of my knowledge, I saddled my pony, went into the cellar where I kept my grass-seed apparatus, put my clothes into a pair of saddle-bags, and them into my seed bag, and, thus equipped, set sail for the North Star. O what a day that was to me! This was on Saturday, in August, 1841. I wore my common clothes, and was very careful to avoid special suspicion, as I already imagined the administrator was very watchful of me. The place from which I started was about fifty miles from Lexington. The reason why I do not give the name of the place, and a more accurate location, must be obvious to anyone who remembers that, in the eye of the law, I am yet accounted a slave, and no spot in the United States affords an asylum for the wanderer. True, I feel protected in the hearts of many warm friends of the slave by whom I am surrounded; but this protection does not come from the laws of any one of the United States.

But to return. After riding about fifteen miles, a Baptist minister overtook me on the road, saying, "How do you do, boy? Are you free? I always thought you were free, till I saw them try to sell you the other day." Then I wished him a thousand miles off, preaching, if he would, to the whole plantation, "Servants, obey your masters"; but I wanted neither sermons, questions, nor advice from him. At length I mustered resolution to make some kind of a reply. "What made you think I was free?" He replied, that he had noticed I had great privileges, that I did much as I liked, and that I was almost white. "O yes," I said, "but there are a great many slaves as white as I am." "Yes," he said, and then went on to name several; among others, one who had lately, as he said, run away. This was touching altogether too near upon what I was thinking of. Now, said I, he must know, or at least reckons, what I am at—running away.

However, I blushed as little as possible, and made strange of the fellow who had lately run away, as though I knew nothing of it. The old fellow looked at me, as it seemed to me, as though he would read my thoughts. I wondered what in the world slaves could run away for, especially if they had

Lewis Clarke (Boston Public Library)

such a chance as I had had for the last few years. He said, "I suppose you would not run away on any account, you are so well treated." "O," said I, "I do very well, sir. If you should ever hear that I had run away, be certain it must be because there is some great change in my treatment."

He then began to talk with me about the seed in my bag, and said that he should want to buy some. Then, I thought, he means to get at the truth by looking in my seed bag, where, sure enough, he would not find grass seed, but the seeds of liberty. However, he dodged off soon, and left me alone. And although I have heard say, poor company is better than none, I felt much better without him than with him.

When I had gone on about twenty-five miles, I went down into a deep valley by the side of the road, and changed my clothes. I reached Lexington before and stopped with him, it excited no attention from the slaveholding gentry. Moreover, I had a pass from the administrator, of whom I had hired my time. I remained over the Sabbath with Cyrus, and we talked over a great many plans for future operations, if my efforts to escape should be successful. Indeed, we talked over all sorts of ways for me to proceed. But both of us were very ignorant of the roads, and of the best way to escape suspicion. And I sometimes wonder that a slave, so ignorant, so timid, as he is, ever makes the attempt to get his freedom. "Without are foes, within are fears."

Monday morning, bright and early, I set my face in good earnest toward the Ohio River, determined to see and tread the north bank of it, or die in the attempt. I said to myself, One of two things,—FREEDOM OR DEATH! The first night I reached Mayslick, fifty odd miles from Lexington. Just before reaching this village, I stopped to think over my situation, and determine how I would pass that night. On that night hung all my hopes. I was within twenty miles of Ohio. My horse was unable to reach the river that night. And besides, to travel and attempt to cross the river in the night, would excite suspicion. I must spend the night there. But how? At one time, I thought, I will take my pony out into the field and give him some corn, and sleep myself on the grass. But then the dogs will be out in the evening, and, if caught under such circumstances, they will take me for a thief if not for a runaway. That will not do. So, after weighing the matter all over, I made a plunge right into the heart of the village, and put up at the tavern.

After seeing my pony disposed of, I looked into the bar-room, and saw some persons that I thought were from my part of the country, and would know me. I shrunk back with horror. What to do I did not know. I looked across the street, and saw the shop of a silversmith. A thought of a pair of spectacles, to hide my face, struck me. I went across the way, and began to barter for a pair of double-eyed green spectacles. When I got them on, they blind-folded me, if they did not others. Every thing seemed right up in my eyes. Some people buy spectacles to see out of; I bought mine to keep from being seen. I hobbled back to the tavern, and called for supper. This I did to avoid notice, for I felt like any thing but eating.

At tea, I had not learned to measure distances with my new eyes, and first pass I made with my knife and fork at my plate went right into my lap. This confused me still more, and, after drinking one cup of tea, I left the table, and got off to bed as soon as possible. But not a wink of sleep that night. All was confusion, dreams, anxiety, and trembling.

As soon as day dawned, I called for my horse, paid my reckoning, and was on my way, rejoicing that that night was gone, any how. I made all diligence on my way, and was across the Ohio, and in Aberdeen by noon, that day!

What my feelings were, when I reached the free shore, can be better imagined than described. I trembled all over with deep emotion, and I could feel my hair rise up on my head. I was on what was called a free soil, among a people who had no slaves. I saw white men at work, and no slave smarting beneath the lash. Everything was indeed new and wonderful. Not knowing where to find a friend, and being ignorant of the country— unwilling to inquire, lest I should betray my ignorance, it was a whole week before I reached Cincinnati. At one place, where I put up, I had a great many more questions put to me than I wished to answer. At another place, I was very much annoyed by the officiousness of the landlord, who made a point to supply every guest with newspapers. I took the copy handed me, and turned it over, in a somewhat awkward manner, I suppose. He came to point out a veto, or some other very important news. I thought it best to decline his assistance, and gave up the paper, saying my eyes were not in a fit condition to read much.

At another place, the neighbors, on learning that a Kentuckian was at the tavern, came, in great earnestness, to find out what my business was. Kentuckians sometimes came there to kidnap their citizens. They were in the habit of watching them close. I at length satisfied them, by assuring them that I was not, nor my father before me, any slaveholder at all; but lest their suspicions should be excited in another direction, I added, my grandfather was a slaveholder.

At Cincinnati, I found some old acquaintances, and spent several days. In passing through some of the streets, I several times saw a great slave-dealer from Kentucky, who knew me, and, when I approached him,

I was very careful to give him a wide berth. The only advice that I here received was from a man who had once been a slave. He urged me to sell my pony, go up the river, to Portsmouth, then take the canal for Cleveland, and cross over to Canada. I acted upon this suggestion, sold my horse for a small sum, as he was pretty well used up, took passage for Portsmouth, and soon found myself on the canal-boat, headed for Cleveland. On the boat, I became acquainted with a Mr. Conoly, from New York. He was very sick with fever and ague, and, as he was a stranger, and alone, I took the best possible care of him, for a time. One day, in conversation with him, he spoke of the slaves, in the most harsh and bitter language, and was especially severe on those who attempted to run away. Thinks, I, you are not the man for me to have much to do with. I found the spirit of slaveholding was not all south of the Ohio River.

No sooner had I reached Cleveland, than a trouble came upon me from a very unexpected quarter. A rough, swearing, reckless creature, in the shape of a man, came up to me, and declared I had passed a bad five dollar bill upon his wife, in the boat, and he demanded the silver for it. I had never seen him, nor his wife, before. He pursued me into the tavern, swearing and threatening all the way. The travellers, that had just arrived at the tavern, were asked to give their names to the clerk, that he might enter them upon the book. He called on me for my name, just as this ruffian was in the midst of his assault upon me. On leaving Kentucky, I thought it best, for my own security, to take a new name, and I had been entered on the boat as Archibald Campbell. I knew, with such a charge as this man was making against me, it would not do to change my name from the boat to the hotel. At the moment, I could not recollect what I had called myself, and for a few minutes, I was in a complete puzzle. The clerk kept calling, and I made believe deaf, till, at length, the name popped back again, and I was duly enrolled a guest at the tavern, in Cleveland. I was heard, before, of persons being frightened out of their Christian names, but I was fairly scared out of both of mine for a while. The landlord soon protected me from the violence of the bad-meaning man, and drove him away from the house.

I was detained at Cleveland several days, not knowing how to get across the lake, into Canada. I went out to the shore of the lake again and again, to try and see the other side, but I could see no hill, mountain, nor city of the asylum I sought. I was afraid to inquire where it was, lest it would betray such a degree of ignorance as to excite suspicion at once. One day, I heard a man ask another, employed on board a vessel, "and where does this vessel trade?" At last, the answer came, "over here in Kettle Creek, near Port Stanley." "And where is that?" said I. "O, right over here in Canada." That was the sound for me; "over here in Canada." The captain asked me if I wanted a passage to Canada. I thought it would not do to be too earnest about it, lest it would betray me. I told him I some thought of going, if I could get a passage cheap. We soon came to terms on this point, and that evening we set sail. After proceeding only nine miles, the wind changed, and the captain returned to port again. This, I thought, was a very bad omen. However, I stuck by, and the next evening, at nine o'clock, we set sail once more, and at daylight we were in Canada.

When I stepped ashore here, I said sure enough, I AM FREE. Good heaven! what a sensation, when it first visits the bosom of a full-grown man; one born to bondage—one who had been taught, from early infancy, that this was his inevitable lot for life. Not till then did I dare to cherish, for a moment, the feeling that one of the limbs of my body was my own. The slaves often say, when cut in the hand or foot, "Plague on the old foot" or "the old hand; it is master's—let him take care of it. Nigger don't care, if he never get well." My hands, my feet, were now my own. But what to do with them, was the next question. A strange sky was over me, a new earth under me, strange voices all around; even the animals were such as I had never seen. A flock of prairie-hens and some black geese were altogether new to me. I was entirely alone; no human being, that I had ever seen before, where I could speak to him or he to me.

And could I make that country ever seem like home? Some people are very much afraid all the slaves will run up north, if they are ever free. But I can assure them that they will run back again, if they do. If I could have been assured of my freedom in Kentucky, then, I would have anything in the world for the prospect of spending my life among old acquaintances where I first saw the sky, and the sun rise and go down. It was a long time before I could make the sun work right at all. It would rise in the wrong place, and go down wrong; and, finally, it behaved so bad, I thought it could not be the same sun.

There was a little something added to this feeling of strangeness. I could not forget all the horrid stories slaveholders tell about Canada. They assure the slave that, when they get hold of slaves in Canada, they make various uses of them. Sometimes they skin the head, and wear the wool on their coat collars—put them into the lead-mines, with both eyes out— the young slaves they eat; and as for the red coats, they are sure death to the slave. However ridiculous to a well-informed person such stories may appear, they work powerfully upon the excited imagination of an ignorant slave. With these stories all fresh in mind, when I arrived at St. Thomas, I kept a bright look-out for the red coats. As I was turning the corner of one of the streets, sure enough, there stood before me a red coat, in full uniform, with his tall bear-skin cap, a foot and a half high, his gun shouldered, and he standing as erect as a guide-post. Sure enough, that is the fellow that they tell about catching a slave. I turned on my heel, and sought another street. On turning another corner, the same soldier, as I thought, faced me, with his black cap and stern look. Sure enough, my time has come now. I was near scared to death, then, as a man can be and breathe. I could not have felt any worse if he had shot me right through the heart. I made off again, as soon as I dared to move. I inquired for a tavern. When I came up to it, there was a great brazen lion sleeping over the door, and, although I knew it was not alive, I had been so well frightened that I was almost afraid to go in. Hunger drove me to it at last, and I asked for something to eat.

On my way to St. Thomas I was so badly frightened. A man asked me who I was. I was afraid to tell him a runaway slave, lest he should have me to the mines. I was afraid to say, "I am an American," lest he shoot me, for I know there had been trouble between the British and Americans. I inquired, at length, for the place where the greatest number of colored soldiers were. I was told there were a great many at New London; so for New London I started. I got a ride, with some country people, to the latter place. They asked me who I was, and I told them from Kentucky; and they, in a familiar way, called me "Old Kentuck." I saw some soldiers, on the way, and asked the men what they had soldiers for. They said they were kept "to get drunk and be whipped"; that was the chief use they made of them. At last, I reached New London, and here I found soldiers in great numbers. I attended at their parade, and saw the guard driving the people back; but it required no guard to keep me off. I thought, "If you will let me alone, I will not trouble you." I was much afraid of a red coat as I would have been a bear. Here I asked again for the colored soldiers. The answer was, "Out at Chatham." The first night, I stopped at a place called the Indian Settlement. The door was barred, at the house where I was, which I did not like so well, as I was yet somewhat afraid of their Canadian tricks. Just before I got to Chatham, I met two colored soldiers, with a white man, bound and driving along before them. This was something quite new. I thought, then, sure enough, this the land for me. I had seen a great many colored people bound, and in the hands of whites, but this was changing things right about. This removed all my suspicions, and ever after, I felt quite easy in Canada.

Ellen Craft

Life dates: 1826–1891

William Craft

Life dates: 1824–February 1900

Ellen and William Craft were fugitive slaves who fled Macon, Georgia, in 1848. Together they devised a detailed plan in advance of their departure. First, they procured passes to visit friends for several days during the Christmas season. Ellen, who had a fair complexion, posed as an invalid white male slave owner traveling north to consult doctors. William pretended he was her black slave. Together they traveled by train, steamer, and ferry through Georgia, South Carolina, North Carolina, Virginia, and Maryland, and finally arrived in free territory in Philadelphia on Christmas Day, 1848. In Philadelphia, they became friends with William Wells Brown and William Lloyd Garrison and soon became abolitionist lecturers. In 1860 William Craft published their narrative, Running a Thousand Miles for Freedom: or, The Escape of Willliam and Ellen Craft from Slavery, *in London. The following narrative of the Crafts' escape was originally published in the* Portland Transcript *(July 7, 1849). Note that the surname in the text is Crafts, while in later publications the spelling is changed to Craft.*

In a city about nine hundred miles south of Mason and Dixon's line, Ellen Crafts was held as a slave. Because we find her in this degrading condition, let it not be understood that she is a negro. Ellen Crafts, though a slave, is white; or, rather to be strictly correct, a brunette. She is now about nineteen or twenty years of age, and will readily pass in any circle as a dark-colored white girl. Girls as dark as Ellen, are as often met with, as those of fairer skins. We are not describing the chief attraction of a ballroom, but something more, when we say that firmness, intelligence and perseverance are distinctly and impressively marked upon her countenance. Her hair is long, straight and dark-colored; nose prominent, eyes dark, large and expressive. We are thus particular, to show her connection with the Anglo-Saxon, and to show how little there is, of any feature by which the enslaved race is so readily recognized.

In the city from which Ellen fled, she acted as a body servant or slave to another young woman, possibly her sister—for our knowledge of the "patriarchal institution," leads us readily and naturally to that inference.

While in this situation, she married. It is for the profit of the master that early marriages should be a law of custom. The union contracted by

Ellen Craft's disguise as an "invalid young man" included "a double story hat," glasses to make her appear older, and a sling for her right arm that disguised the fact she could not write. (The Granger Collection)

Ellen proved to be a happy one. The husband, William—slaves have no right to other names—has proved himself to be in every way, worthy of her. By his industry, and by turning night into day, he contrived to procure enough money to purchase a portion of his time from the man who claimed to own him. It cost William all he had, but it procured him privileges which enabled him, by assiduous application, to lay by another store—a larger portion of which, the lion's share, went to swell the master's ill-gotten gains—for new and dear-bought privileges.

By dint of saving and starving, William contrived to accumulate for himself and wife, enough to purchase for each, many little comforts and privileges. They were thus enabled to ameliorate their condition, and were for a time happy. Though not permitted to see her oftener than once a week, they had many secret meetings.

These stolen interviews were sweet and precious. Were they not, ye, who love the wife of your affections? Thoughts of their condition, their hard lot, mingled with unavailing regrets, without doubt, were the principal ones exchanged between them. But this condition they were constrained to endure, almost joyfully, in view of their greater deprivation and sufferings of their fellow slaves.

Privileges like these, however, were destined to bear a rich harvest. Thoughts of liberty are never long absent from a slave or a prisoner. Hope beckons forever, even through sorest ills. This was the great subject, between Ellen and William. In the long, lone hours of the night, that were but ushering in, to them, another day of bondage, the spirit of liberty, visited them. Not inappropriate to their condition is the exclamation of David: "As the hart panteth after the water-brooks, so panteth my soul after thee, O God."

It is quite certain that they could have escaped from the city in which they were. But whither could they flee? Without a place, without means of support, hunted by every slave catcher, "like the partridge upon the mountains," surrounded by enemies, their capture was certain; and stripes, separation, acclimated woes, would be their lot.

These considerations filled their hearts with sadness. But liberty, ever bright and fair, bid them to hope on. For many weeks they thought over every plan of escape, which promised success, but could fine none.

They had heard vaguely, of the abolitionists of the North; but they had been represented to them as monsters more to be dreaded, than the slave-driver himself, and their hopes led them not that way. Still they would inquire concerning them, and one day sufficient was learned to determine their course. They would flee to the abolitionists.

Their star in the east, had indeed arisen, but how could they follow their glorious path? The nearest city to them was Philadelphia, a distance of 1,000 miles, a weary way for fugitives from slavery. But the determination once formed, every obstacle was to be overcome. Accordingly their sleeping and waking thoughts were given to find out the way to the spot where liberty dwelt.

The first obstacle to be overcome was to secure the necessary funds for the proposed flight. By double toil, by a more than miserly saving, a sufficient sum was acquired. They were, for slaves, really rich, and now freedom or death, rather than slavery, was their joint language.

The plan adopted, displays a degree of ingenuity which could not have been acquired under the ordinary circumstances of life; solitary confinement or a life of perpetual bondage are the only incentives which bring out all the latent ingenuity of the man. The thoughts of the captives are upon one point. The whole energy and strength of his mind are directed to one aim. Let such and one see but the slightest probability of success, though it be but the faintest glimmer, and that faith, which overcomes mountains, lifts the man into the paradise he would gain. That faith secures the boon.

It was decided that Ellen should personate an invalid young man, and that William should represent the servant. The plan proposed involved a large expenditure, since young men who travel with their servants are supposed to be rich. But it secured this great, this abounding advantage. By this disguise they could take the public highway, and the most rapid conveyances. Besides, the very boldness, the originality of the plan was designed to be their greatest safeguard for, who would look for a fugitive from slavery under the hat of a palefaced, sickly youth, pursuing his way north, in quest of health, attended by a serving man?

So much for the plan. Its execution was now the great point. Could a disguise, impenetrable to the slave catchers, whose scent is like the blood-hound's and with the blood-hound, be procured? Over this vital question, Ellen and William pondered day and night, with palpitating hearts. But that genius which gave the bold scheme birth, was yet fertile in resources. The first idea was a prestige of its full accomplishment.

William Craft posed as the traveling servant to Ellen Craft's "palefaced, sickly youth" as part of the couple's daring scheme to flee slavery in Macon, Georgia, in 1848. (The Granger Collection)

There was no point, however, minute, in the habiliments of a young man, that was not studied with as much care as ever Newton or Herschell studied the heavens. This was necessary, for a young woman who first attempts the apparel of a boy, is sure to be discovered at the first glance, by an accurate observer. Hence Ellen practised nightly in her new garb until she had been thoroughly trained.

But to the dress itself. A slave cannot purchase a suit unquestioned, as another person may. Therefore extreme caution became necessary, else the cherished scheme of months would have been discovered and overthrown. Then they must die, for "if hope be dead, why seek to live."

William was the purchaser. At various places and different times, under numerous pretexts he bought the required articles. The hat was a very high bell crowned, as he stated it, "a double story hat." Next he bought a sack which, on being on, proved "a world too wide," but Ellen thought that was no objection, as "sacks never fit!" The vest proved a very long one, reaching below the hips, but fashionably cut; and as it was "all the go," was adopted without demur, especially as the sack could be buttoned over and hide the disproportion of its size. Then the pantaloons were of the most liberal dimensions, and boots, more easily obtained, completed this part of the wardrobe. A pair of green glasses were procured for the purpose of making Ellen look older, when fitted out in her new rig. She looked exceedingly young, besides her features might be recognized by any person whom they might meet, that knew them, while upon their journey.

These preparations having been made, a day was appointed for their flight. That day, so fraught with their wildest hopes arrived. Nothing had been omitted. Two trunks were obtained, sufficiently ponderous for the baggage of a young man on his travels. Nothing had been forgotten. As it became necessary to register names at hotels and sign a certificate for the slave, "the servant who accompanied young master," a bandage, a sling for Ellen's right arm was thought of; why? She could not read or write. As impertinent travelers might scan the young man's face too closely, a convenient swelling, which required poulticing, enveloped her cheeks. As voluble and inquisitive persons might be too particular in their inquiries, sickness, fatigue of travelling and then swelling would be a sufficient excuse against rudeness for not answering.

Thus equipped, William, having nerved his courage up, went boldly to the ticket office, and purchased a "through ticket" for "young master" and myself to "filadelfy [Philadelphia]." No questions were asked and the tickets were obtained.

Next morning, the fearful and dangerous passage was commenced. At the depot, Ellen was not recognized. So complete was her disguise, a porter there, one of her early suitors, addressed her as "young master." She kindly bestowed upon him a small trifle to encourage him in politeness.

Along the road, at the various stopping places, the "sickly youth" received the blessing of many for his liberality in rewarding any slight service. Their custom was to put up at the first hotels, for they were determined to travel as "big-bugs."

They passed through many perils and hair-breadth escapes, but not once did Ellen's courage fail, or her inimitable and unapproachable endurance and perseverance give way, during all their journey through the slave states. After the cars left Baltimore, for Philadelphia, William, wearied with anxiety and watching, laid himself down to sleep in the "Jim Crow car," where he invariably rode; for a slave could not presume to ride with his master. It was his invariable practice to run nervously back at every stopping place to see that "young master was safe." For this affectionate attention, he received the approbation of many passengers, and was rewarded with several presents. And from Washington to Baltimore, his devotedness to his master's health was pointed out to several northern gentlemen as an evidence of the close bonds of affection subsisting between master and slave.

We left William sleeping in the "Jim Crow car." At Havre de Grace, where the Ferry is crossed, William remained sleeping. Ellen was called upon with other passengers to change cars. But, where was her husband? Her courage began to fail, and despair to seize upon her. She dreaded the worst, a woeful disappointment, so near the goal of their desires. She could not be comforted until the baggagemaster relieved her, by rudely waking the "black rascal" who so neglected his master. We will not attempt to describe Ellen's feelings when she was relieved from her fears.

They arrived in Philadelphia on Sabbath morning, God's day of rest to them, for all their toils and sufferings. What an appropriate ending for such a journey. It was commenced on Wednesday, and they consequently traveled one thousand miles in four days and a half, thro' the enemy's country. An escape as difficult—and to them far more glorious—than Bonaparte's journey from Egypt through a coast and sea studded with the British fleet.

Frederick Douglass

Life dates: February 1818–February 20, 1895

Frederick Douglass was an abolitionist, journalist, orator, and social reformer. Born a slave in Maryland, he escaped to the North with the aid of Anna Murray, a free African American woman in Baltimore. Douglass married Murray and together they moved to New Bedford, Massachusetts (1838), Lynn, Massachusetts (1841), Rochester, New York (1847), and Washington, D.C. (1872). In 1841 the abolitionist William Lloyd Garrison asked Douglass to join him as a lecturer. In 1845 Narrative of the Life of Frederick Douglass, an American Slave, Written by Himself *was published to great acclaim and heightened Douglass's popularity in the United States and Great Britain. This success prompted Douglass to publish* My Bondage and My Freedom *(1855) and* Life and Times of Frederick Douglass *(1881; revised 1892). After the Civil War, Douglass persisted in his work as an advocate for fair and equal rights for all African Americans and was appointed to numerous public positions, including U.S. marshal for the District of Columbia (1877–1881), recorder of deeds for the District of Columbia (1881–1886), and charge d'affaires for Santo Domingo and minister to Haiti (1889–1891). In 1884, a year and a half after the death of his first wife, Douglass married Helen Pitts, his white secretary, and endured criticism from both blacks and whites. Undeterred, Douglass, the consummate humanist, continued to articulate his commitment to a unified American nationality that transcended race and embodied the principles of a democratic country.*

The following text is excerpted from Douglass's 1855 biography.

On Monday, the third day of September, 1838, in accordance with my resolution, I bade farewell to the city of Baltimore, and to that slavery which had been my abhorrence from childhood....

Before, however, proceeding with this narration, it is, perhaps, proper that I should frankly state, in advance, my intention to withhold a part of the facts connected with my escape from slavery. There are reasons for this suppression, which I trust the readers will deem altogether valid. It may be easily conceived, that a full and complete statement of all the facts pertaining to the flight of a bondman, might implicate and embarrass some who may have, wittingly or unwittingly, assisted him; and no one can wish me to involve any man or woman who has befriended me, even in the liability of embarrassment or trouble....

I have never approved of the very public manner, in which some of our western friends have conducted what they call the "Underground Rail-

road," but which, I think, by their open declarations, has been made, most emphatically, the "Upperground Railroad." Its stations are far better known to the slaveholders than to the slaves. I honor those good men and women for their noble daring, in willingly subjecting themselves to persecution, by openly avowing their participation in the escape of slaves; nevertheless, the good resulting from such avowals, is of a very questionable character. It may kindle an enthusiasm, very pleasant to inhale; but that is of no practical benefit to themselves, nor to the slaves escaping. Nothing is more evident, than that such disclosures are a positive evil to the slaves remaining, and seeking to escape. In publishing such accounts, the anti-slavery man addresses the slaveholder, not the slave; he stimulates the former to greater watchfulness, and adds to his facilities for capturing his slave. We owe something to the slaves, south of Mason and Dixon's line, as well as to those north of it; and, in discharging the duty of aiding the latter, on their way to freedom, we

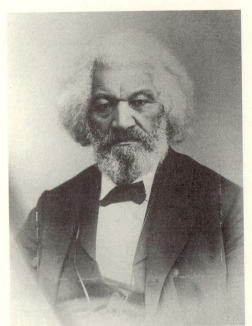

Frederick Douglass in a 1903 photograph (Texas African Photography Archive)

should be careful to do nothing which would be likely to hinder the former, in making their escape from slavery....

My condition in the year (1838) of my escape, was, comparatively, a free and easy one, so far, at least, as the wants of the physical man were concerned; but the reader will bear in mind, that my troubles from the beginning, have been less physical than mental, and he will thus be prepared to find, after what is narrated in the previous chapters, that slave life was adding nothing to its charms for me, as I grew older, and became better acquainted with it. The practice, from week to week, of openly robbing me of all my earnings, kept the nature and character of slavery constantly before me. I could be robbed by indirection, but this was too open and barefaced to be endured. I could see no reason why I should, at the end of each week, pour the reward of my honest toil into the purse of any man. The thought itself vexed me, and the manner in which Master Hugh received my wages, vexed me more than the original wrong. Carefully counting the money and rolling it out, dollar by dollar, he would look me in the face, as if he would search my heart as well as my pocket, and reproachfully ask me, "Is that all?"—implying that I had, perhaps, kept back part of my wages; or, if not so, the demand was made, possibly, to make me feel, that, after all, I was an "unprofitable servant." Draining me of the last cent of my hard earnings, he would, however, occasionally—when I brought home an extra large sum—dole out to me a sixpence or a shilling, with a view, perhaps, of kindling up my gratitude; but this practice had the opposite effect—it was an admission of my right to the whole sum. The fact, that he gave me any part of my wages, was proof that he suspected that I had a right to the whole of them. I always felt uncomfortable, after having received anything in this way, for I feared that the giving me a few cents, might, possibly, ease his conscience, and make him feel himself a pretty honorable robber, after all!

Held to a strict account, and kept under a close watch—the old suspicion of my running away not having been entirely removed—escape from slavery, even in Baltimore, was very difficult. The railroad from Baltimore to Philadelphia was under regulations so stringent, that even free colored travelers were almost excluded. They must have free papers; they must be measured and carefully examined, before they were allowed to enter the cars; they only went in the day time, even when so examined. The steamboats were under regulations equally stringent. All the great turnpikes, leading northward, were beset with kidnappers, a class of men who watched the newspapers for advertisements for runaway slaves, making their living by the accursed reward of slave hunting.

My discontent grew upon me, and I was on the lookout for means of escape. With money, I could easily have managed the matter, and, therefore, I hit upon the plan of soliciting the privilege of hiring my time. It is quite common, in Baltimore, to allow slaves this privilege, and it is the practice, also, in New Orleans. A slave who is considered trustworthy, can, by paying his master a definite sum regularly, at the end of each week, dispose of his time as he likes. It so happened that I was not in very good odor, and I was far from being a trustworthy slave....

My object, therefore, in working steadily, was to remove suspicion, and in this I succeeded admirably. He probably thought I was never better satisfied with my condition, than at the very time I was planning my escape. The second week passed, and again I carried him my full week's wages—nine dollars; and so well pleased was he, that he gave me twenty-five cents! and "bade me make good use of it!" I told him I would, for one of the uses to which I meant to put it, was to pay my fare on the underground railroad.

The laws of Maryland required every free negro to carry papers describing him accurately and to pay liberally for this protection. Slaves often escaped by borrowing papers from a friend, to whom the precious documents would be returned by mail. Whenever a colored man came with free papers to the railroad station to buy a ticket, he was always examined carefully enough to insure the detection of a runaway, unless the resemblance was very close. Our hero was not acquainted with any free negro who looked much like him; but he found out that passengers who paid on the cars were not scrutinized so minutely as those who bought tickets, and also that sailors were treated with peculiar indulgence by the conductors. The dominant party was doing all it could to encourage the shipping interest, and rapidly reducing the tariff. The cry of "Free Trade and Sailors' Rights" meant in this instance "Free Labor and the Rights of the Slave."

Among his friends was a sailor who was of much darker hue than he was himself, but who owned a protection, setting forth his occupation, and bearing the sacred figure of the American eagle. This was borrowed; sailor's clothes were purchased and, on Monday morning, the fugitive jumped on the train just as it started. His baggage had been put aboard by a friendly hackman. He was greatly troubled, for, as he wrote to his master, ten years later, I was making a leap in the dark. The probabilities, so far as I could by reason determine them, were stoutly against the undertaking. The preliminaries and precautions I had adopted previously, all worked badly. I was like one going to war without weapons—ten chances of defeat to one of victory. One in whom I had confided, and one who had promised me assistance, appalled by fear at the trial hour, deserted me. However, gloomy as was the prospect, thanks be to the Most High, who is ever the God of the oppressed, at the moment which was to determine my whole earthly career, His grace was sufficient; my mind was made up.

His anxiety increased in consequence of the harshness with which the conductor questioned other passengers in the negro car. The sailor, however, was addressed kindly and told, after a mere glance at the protection, that it was all right. Thus far he was safe; but there were several people on the train who would have known him at once in any other clothes. A German blacksmith looked at him intently, and apparently recognized him, but said nothing. On the ferry boat, by which they crossed the Susquehanna, he found an old acquaintance employed, and was asked some dangerous questions. On they went, however, until they stopped to let the train from Philadelphia pass. At a window sat a man under whom the runaway had been at work but a few days before. He might easily have recognized him, and would certainly have him arrested; but fortunately he was looking another way. The passengers went on from Wilmington by steamer to Philadelphia, where one of them took the train for New York and arrived early on Tuesday. In less than twenty-four hours the slave had made himself a free man. It was but a few months since he had become twenty-one.

The flight was a bold and perilous one; but here I am, in the great city of New York, safe and sound, without loss of blood or bone. In less than a week after leaving Baltimore, I was walking amid the hurrying throng, and gazing upon the dazzling wonders of Broadway. The dreams of my childhood and the purposes of my manhood were now fulfilled. A free state around me, and a free earth under my feet! What a moment was this to me! A whole year was pressed into a single day. A new world burst upon my agitated vision. I have often been asked, by kind friends to whom I have told my story, how I felt when first I found myself beyond the limits of slavery; and I must say here, as I have often said to them, there is scarcely anything about which I could not give a more satisfactory answer. It was a moment of joyous excitement, which no words can describe. In a letter to a friend, written soon after reaching New York, I said I felt as one might be supposed to feel, on escaping from a den of hungry lions. But, in a moment like that, sensations are too intense and too rapid for words. Anguish and grief, like darkness and rain, may be described, but joy and gladness, like the rainbow of promise, defy alike the pen and pencil....

Free and joyous, however, as I was, joy was not the only sensation I experienced. It was like the quick blaze, beautiful at the first, but which subsiding, leaves the building charred and desolate. I was soon taught that I was still in an enemy's land. A sense of loneliness and insecurity oppressed me sadly. I had been but a few hours in New York, before I was met in the streets by a fugitive slave, well known to me, and the information I got from him respecting New York, did nothing to lessen apprehension of danger. The fugitive in question was "Allender's Jake," in Baltimore; but, said he, I am "William Dixon," in New York! I knew Jake well, and knew when Tolly Allender and Mr. Price (for the latter employed Master Hugh as his foreman, in his shipyard on Fell's Point) made an attempt to recapture Jake, and failed. Jake told me all about his circumstances, and how narrowly he escaped being taken back to slavery; that the city was now full of southerners, returning from the springs, that the black people in New York were not to be trusted; that there were hired men on the lookout for fugitives from slavery, and who, for a few dollars, would betray me into the hands of the slave-catchers; that I must trust no man with my secret; that I must not think of going either on the wharves to work, or to a boarding-house to board; and, worse still, this same Jake told me it was not in his power to help me. He seemed, even while cautioning me, to be fearing lest, after all, I might be a party to a second attempt to recapture him. Under the inspiration of this thought, I must suppose it was, he gave signs of a wish to get rid of me, and soon left me—his whitewash brush in hand—as he said, for his work. He was soon lost to sight among the throng, and I was alone again, an easy prey to the kidnappers, if any should happen to be on my track.

New York, seventeen years ago, was less a place of safety for a runaway slave than now, and all know how unsafe it now is, under the new fugitive slave bill. I was much troubled. I had very little money—enough to buy me a few loaves of bread, but not enough to pay board, outside a lumber yard. I saw the wisdom of keeping away from the shipyards, for if Master Hugh pursued me, he would naturally expect to find me looking for work among the calkers. For a time, every door seemed closed against me. A sense of my loneliness and helplessness crept over me, and covered me with something bordering on despair. In the midst of thousands of my fellowmen, and yet a perfect stranger! In the midst of human brothers, and yet more fearful of them than of hungry wolves! I was without home, without friends, without work, without money, and without any definite knowledge of which way to go, or where to look for succor....

I found my man in the person of one who said his name was Stewart. He was a sailor, warm-hearted and generous, and he listened to my story with a brother's interest. I told him I was running for my freedom—knew not where to go—money almost gone—was hungry—thought it unsafe to go to the shipyards for work, and needed a friend. Stewart promptly put me in the way of getting out of trouble. He took me to his house, and went in search of the late David Ruggles, who was then the secretary of the New York Vigilance Committee, and a very active man in all anti-slavery works. Once in the hands of Mr. Ruggles, I was comparatively safe. I was hidden with Mr. Ruggles several days. In the meantime, my intended wife, Anna, came on from Baltimore—to whom I had written, informing her of my safe arrival at NewYork—and, in the presence of Mrs. Mitchell and Mr. Ruggles, we were married, by Rev. James W. C. Pennington.

Mr. Ruggles was the first officer on the underground railroad with whom I met after reaching the North, and, indeed, the first of whom I ever heard anything. Learning that I was a calker by trade, he promptly decided that New Bedford was the proper place to send me. "Many ships," said he, "are there fitted out for the whaling business, and you may there find work at your trade, and make a good living." Thus, in one fortnight after my flight from Maryland, I was safe in New Bedford, regularly entered upon the exercise of the rights, responsibilities, and duties of a freeman.

Olaudah Equiano

Life dates: 1745–1797

The excerpts from the narrative The Interesting Narrative of the Life of Olaudah Equiano, or Gustavus Vassa, the African, Written by Himself *exemplify the quest for and consequences of a freedom that was at once hard-won and retained despite adversity and the temptation to betray other slaves. This narrative was first published in London in 1789 and was subsequently reissued in 36 editions in English, Dutch, and German by 1857. In the text Equiano, who was born in Nigeria, recounts his experiences as a slave in Africa, the West Indies, Georgia, Pennsylvania, and on board warships off the Spanish coast.While the first twenty pages of Equiano's autobiography were apparently compiled by someone other than the author from handbooks on the history of Guinea, most of the text appears as first-hand recollections. Especially poignant are Equiano's descriptions of his first encounter with a slave ship and the horrors of the middle passage. Equiano describes in detail the detestable stench below deck on the slave ship, the wailing of the slaves, his brutal floggings for refusing to eat, and his attempted suicide by jumping overboard. During his enslavement, he traveled extensively with his master, Captain Pascal. After living in servitude in England, where he stayed in the homes of English families and received limited schooling, he was sold to his second master, the Quaker Robert King of Philadelphia. After several voyages between America and the West Indies, King was pressured to release his slaves by his fellow Quakers, and ultimately allowed Equiano to buy his freedom in 1766. Equiano died the next year in England.*

Chapter 7

Every day now brought me nearer my freedom, and I was impatient till we proceeded again to sea, that I might have an opportunity of getting a sum large enough to purchase it. I was not long ungratified; for in the beginning of the year 1766, my master bought another sloop, named the *Nancy,* the largest I had ever seen. She was partly laden, and was to proceed to Philadelphia. Our captain had his choice of three, and I was well pleased he chose this, which was the largest; for, from his having a large vessel, I had more room, and could carry a larger quantity of goods with me. Accordingly, when we had delivered our old vessel the *Prudence,* and completed the lading of the *Nancy,* having made near three hundred per cent by four barrels of pork I brought from Charlestown, I laid in as large a cargo as I could, trusting to God's Providence to prosper my undertaking. With these views I sailed for Philadelphia. On our passage, when we drew near the land, I was for the first time surprised at the sight of some whales, having never seen any such large sea-monsters before; and, as we sailed by the land, one morning I saw a puppy whale close by the vessel; it was about the length of a wherry-boat, and it followed us all the day until we got within the Capes. We arrived safe and in good time at Philadelphia, and I sold my goods there chiefly to the Quakers. They always appeared to be a very honest and discreet sort of people, and never attempted to impose on me; I therefore liked them, and ever after chose to deal with them in preference to any others.

One Sunday morning while I was here, as I was going to church, I chanced to pass a meeting-house. The doors being open, and the house full of people, it excited my curiosity to go in. When I entered the house, to my great surprise, I saw a very tall woman standing in the midst of them, speaking in an audible voice something which I could not understand. Having never seen any thing of this kind before, I stood and stared about me for some time, wondering at this odd scene. As soon as it was over, I took an opportunity to make enquiry about the place and people, when I was informed they were called Quakers. I particularly asked what that woman I saw in the midst of them had said, but none of them were pleased to satisfy me; so I quitted them, and soon after, as I was returning, I came to a church crowded with people; the church-yard was full likewise, and a number of people were even mounted on ladders, looking in at the windows. I thought this a strange sight, as I had never seen churches, either in England or the West-Indies, crowded in this manner before. I therefore made bold to ask some people the meaning of all this, and they told me the Rev. George Whitfield was preaching. I had often heard of this gentleman, and had wished to see and hear him; but I had never before had an opportunity. I now therefore resolved to gratify myself with the sight, and pressed in amidst the multitude. When I got into the church I saw this pious man exhorting the people with the greatest fervour and earnestness, and sweating as much as ever I did while in slavery on Montserrat-beach. I was very much struck and impressed with this; I thought it strange I had never seen divines exert themselves in this manner before; and was no longer at a loss to account for the thin congregations they preached to. When we had discharged our cargo here, and were loaded again, we left this fruitful land once more, and set sail for Montserrat. My traffic had hitherto succeeded so well with me, that I thought, by selling my goods when we arrived at Montserrat, I should have enough to purchase my freedom. But as soon as our vessel arrived there, my master came on board, and gave orders for us to go to St. Eustatia, and discharge our cargo there, and from thence to proceed for Georgia. I was much disappointed at this; but thinking, as usual, it was of no use to murmur at the decrees of fate, I submitted without repining, and we went to St. Eustatia.

After we had discharged our cargo there, we took in a live cargo, as we call a cargo of slaves. Here I sold my goods tolerably well; but not being able to lay out all my money in this small island to as much advantage as in many other places, I laid out only part, and the remainder I brought away with me neat. We sailed from hence to Georgia, and I was glad when we got there, though I had not much reason to like the place from my last adventure in Savannah; but I longed to get back to Montserrat and procure my freedom, which I expected to be able to purchase when I returned. As soon as we had arrived here I waited on my careful doctor, Mr. Brady, to whom I made the most grateful acknowledgments in my power, for his former kindness and attention during my illness.

While we remained here, an odd circumstance happened to the captain and me, which disappointed us both a great deal. A silversmith, whom we had brought to this place some voyages before, agreed with the captain to return to the West-Indies, and promised at the same time to give the captain a great deal of money, having pretended to take a liking to him, and being, as we thought, very rich. But while we stayed to load our vessel this man was taken ill, in a house where he worked, and in a week's time became very bad. The worse he grew the more he used to speak of giving the captain what he had promised him, so that he expected something considerable from the death of this man, who had no wife or child, and he attended him day and night.

I used also to go with the captain, at his own desire, to attend him; especially when we saw there was no appearance of his recovery: and in order to recompence me for my trouble, the captain promised me ten pounds, when he should get the man's property. I thought this would be

GUSTAVUS VASSA,

OR

Olaudah Equiano

A NATIVE AFRICAN FROM THE COAST OF GUINEA

*who, after being freed from American Slavery, made voyages
to Europe, the West Indies, &c. and accompanied an Expedition
to explore a North West passage. He was a worthy, pious, and
enlightened Negro, and published his own Narrative dedicated
to the British Parliament.*

of great service to me, although I had nearly money enough to purchase my freedom, if I should get safe this voyage to Montserrat. In this expectation I laid out above eight pounds of my money for a suit of superfine clothes to dance in at my freedom, which I hoped was then at hand. We still continued to attend this man, and were with him even on the last day he lived, till very late at night when we went on board. After we were got to bed, about one or two o'clock in the morning, the captain was sent for, and was informed the man was dead. On this he came to my bed, and, waking me, informed me of it, and desired me to get up, procure a light, and to go immediately with him. I told him I was very sleepy, and wished he would take somebody else with him; or else, as the man was dead, and could want no further attendance, to let all things remain as they were till the next morning. "No, no," said he, "we will have the money tonight. I cannot wait till tomorrow; so let us go." Accordingly I got up and struck a light, and away we both went, and saw the man as dead as we could wish. The captain said he would give him a grand burial, in gratitude for the promised treasure; and desired that all the things belonging to the deceased might be brought forth. Amongst others there was a nest of trunks, of which he had kept the keys whilst the man was ill; and when they were produced, we opened them with no small eagerness and expectation; as there were a great number within one another, with much impatience we took them out of each other. At last, when we came to the smallest, and had opened it, we saw it was full of papers, which we supposed to be notes; at the sight of which our hearts leapt for joy; and that instant the captain, clapping his hands, cried out "Thank God! Here it is!"

But when we began to examine the supposed treasure and long-looked-for bounty, alas! alas! how uncertain and deceitful are all human affairs! What had we found? While we thought we were embracing a substance, we grasped an empty nothing. The whole amount in the nest of trunks was only a dollar and a half; and all that the man possessed would not pay for his coffin! Our sudden and exquisite joy was now succeeded by as sudden and exquisite pain; and my captain and I exhibited, for some time, most ridiculous figures pictures of chagrin and disappointment! We went away greatly mortified, and left the deceased to do as well as he could for himself, as we had taken so good care of him when alive for nothing.

We set sail once more for Montserrat, and arrived there safe; but much out of humour with our friend, the silversmith. When we had unladen the vessel, and I had sold my venture, finding myself master of about forty-seven pounds, I consulted my true friend, the captain, how I should proceed in offering my master the money for my freedom. He told me to come on a certain morning, when he and my master would be at breakfast together. Accordingly, on that morning I went, and met the captain there, as he had appointed. When I went in I made my obeisance to my master, and with my money in my hand, and many fears in my heart, I prayed him to be as good as his offer to me, when he was pleased to promise me my freedom as soon as I could purchase it. This speech seemed to confound him; he began to recoil; and my heart that instant sunk within me. "What," said he, "give you your freedom? Why, where did you get the money? Have you got forty pounds sterling?" "Yes, sir," I answered. "How did you get it?" replied he. I told him, "very honestly." The captain then said he knew I got the money very honestly and with much industry, and that I was particularly careful. On which my master replied, I got money much faster than he did; and said he would not have made me the promise which he did, had he thought I should have got the money so soon. "Come, come," said my worthy captain, clapping my master on the back, "come, Robert, (which was his name) I think you must let him have his freedom. You have laid your money out very well; you have received good interest for it all this time, and here is now the principal at last. I know Gustavus has earned you more than a hundred a year, and he will still save you money, as he will not leave you. Come, Robert, take the money." My master then said, he would not be worse than his promise; and, taking the money, told me to go to the Secretary at the Register Office, and get my manumission drawn up.

These words of my master were like a voice from heaven to me: in an instant all my trepidation was turned into unutterable bliss, and I most reverently bowed myself with gratitude, unable to express my feelings, but by the overflowing of my eyes, and a heart replete with thanks to God; while my true and worthy friend, the Captain, congratulated us both with a peculiar degree of heartfelt pleasure. As soon as the first transports of my joy were over, and that I had expressed my thanks to these my worthy friends in the best manner I was able, I rose with a heart full of affection and reverence, and left the room, in order to obey my master's joyful mandate of going to the Register Office. As I was leaving the house I called to mind the words of the Psalmist, in the 126th Psalm, and like him, "I glorified God in my heart, in whom I trusted." These words had been impressed on my mind from the very day I was forced from Deptford to the present hour, and I now saw them, as I thought, fulfilled and verified.

My imagination was all rapture as I flew to the Register Office; and in this respect, like the apostle Peter (whose deliverance from prison was so sudden and extraordinary, that he thought he was in a vision) I could scarcely believe I was awake. Heavens! Who could do justice to my feelings at this moment? Not conquering heroes themselves, in the midst of a triumph—Not the tender mother who has just regained her long-lost infant, and presses it to her heart—Not the weary, hungry mariner, at the sight of the desired friendly port—Not the lover, when he once more embraces his beloved mistress, after she has been ravished from his arms!— All within my breast was tumult, wildness, and delirium! My feet scarcely touched the ground; for they were winged with joy, and, like Elijah, as he rose to Heaven, they "were with lightning sped" as I went on. Every one I met I told of my happiness, and blazed about the virtue of my amiable master and captain.

When I got to the office and acquainted the Register with my errand, he congratulated me on the occasion, and told me he would draw up my manumission for half-price, which was a guinea. I thanked him for his kindness; and, having received it and paid him, I hastened to my master to get him to sign it, that I might be fully released. Accordingly he signed the manumission that day; so that, before night, I, who had been a slave in the morning, trembling at the will of another, was become my own master, and completely free. I thought this was the happiest day I had ever experienced; and my joy was still heightened by the blessings and prayers of many of the sable race, particularly the aged, to whom my heart had ever been attached with reverence.

In short, the fair as well as black people immediately styled me by a new appellation, to me the most desirable in the world, which was "Freeman," and, at the dances I gave, my Georgia superfine blue clothes made no indifferent appearance, as I thought. Some of the sable females, who formerly stood aloof, now began to relax and appear less coy; but my heart was still fixed on London, where I hoped to be ere long. So that my worthy captain, and his owner, my late master, finding that the bent of my mind was towards London, said to me, "We hope you won't leave us, but that you will still be with the vessels." Here gratitude bowed me down; and none but the generous mind can judge of my feelings, struggling between inclination and duty. However, notwithstanding my wish to be in London, I obediently answered my benefactors that I would go in the vessel, and not leave them; and from that day I was entered on board as an able-bodied seaman, at thirty-six shillings per month, besides what perquisites I could make. My intention was to make a voyage or two, entirely to please these my honoured patrons; but I determined that the year following, if it pleased God, I would see Old England once more, and surprise my old master, Captain Pascal, who was hourly in my mind; for I still loved him, notwithstanding his usage to me, and I pleased myself with thinking of what he would say when he saw what the Lord had done for me in so short a time, instead of being, as he might perhaps suppose, under the cruel yoke of some planter.

With such reveries I used often to entertain myself, and shorten the time till my return; and now, being as in my original free African state, I embarked on board the *Nancy,* after having got all things ready for our voyage. In this state of serenity we sailed for St. Eustatia; and having smooth seas and calm weather, we soon arrived there; after taking our cargo on board, we proceeded to Savannah in Georgia, in August, 1766. While we were there, as usual, I used to go for the cargo up the rivers in boats; and, when on this business, I have been frequently beset by alligators, which were very numerous on that coast and river. I have shot many of them when they have been near getting into our boats; which we have with great difficulty sometimes prevented, and have been very much frightened at them. I have seen a young one sold in Georgia alive for sixpence.

During our stay at this place, one evening a slave belonging to Mr. Read, a merchant of Savannah, came near our vessel, and began to use me very ill. I entreated him, with all the patience of which I was master, to desist, as I knew there was little or no law for a free negro here. But the fellow, instead of taking my advice, persevered in his insults, and even struck me. At this I lost all temper, and fell on him, and beat him soundly. The next morning his master came to our vessel, as we lay alongside the wharf, and desired me to come ashore that he might have me flogged all round the town, for beating his negro slave! I told him he had insulted me, and had given the provocation by first striking me. I had also told my captain the whole affair that morning, and desired him to go along with me to Mr. Read, to prevent bad consequences; but he said that it did not signify, and if Mr. Read said any thing he would make matters up, and desired me to go to work, which I accordingly did.

The captain being on board when Mr. Read came and applied to him to deliver me up, he said he knew nothing of the matter, I was a free-man. I was astonished and frightened at this, and thought I had better keep where I was, than go ashore and be flogged round the town, without judge or jury. I therefore refused to stir; and Mr. Read went away, swearing he would bring all the constables in the town, for he would have me out of the vessel. When he was gone, I thought his threat might prove too true to my sorrow; and I was confirmed in this belief, as well by the many instances I had seen of the treatment of free negroes, as from a fact that had happened within my own knowledge here a short time before.

There was a free black man, a carpenter, that I knew, who for asking a gentleman that he had worked for, for the money he had earned, was put into gaol [jail]; and afterwards this oppressed man was sent from Georgia, with false accusations, of an intention to set the gentleman's house on fire, and run away with his slaves. I was therefore much embarrassed, and very apprehensive of a flogging at least. I dreaded, of all things, the thoughts of being stripped, as I never in my life had the marks of any violence of that kind. At that instant a rage seized my soul, and for a little I determined to resist the first man that should attempt to lay violent hands on me, or basely use me without a trial; for I would sooner die like a freeman, than suffer myself to be scourged, by the hands of ruffians, and my blood drawn like a slave.

The captain and others, more cautious, advised me to make haste and conceal myself; for they said Mr. Read was a very spiteful man, and he would soon come on board with constables and take me. At first I refused this counsel, being determined to stand my ground; but at length, by the prevailing entreaties of the captain and Mr. Dixon, with whom we lodged, I went to Mr. Dixon's house, which was a little out of the town, at a place called Yea-ma-chra. I was but just gone when Mr. Read, and the constables, came for me, and searched the vessel; but, not finding me there, he swore he would have me dead or alive. I was secreted about five days; however the good character which my captain always gave me, as well as some other gentlemen, who also knew me, procured me some friends. At last some of them told my captain that he did not use me well, in suffering me thus to be imposed upon, and said they would see me redressed, and get me on board some other vessel. My captain, on this, immediately went to Mr. Read, and told him, that ever since I eloped from the vessel his work had been neglected, and he could not go on with her loading, himself and mate not being well; and as I had managed things on board for them, my absence must have retarded his voyage, and consequently hurt the owner. He therefore begged of him to forgive me, as he said he never heard any complaint of me before, during the several years I had been with him. After repeated entreaties, Mr. Read said I might go to hell; and that he would not meddle with me; on which my captain came immediately to me at his lodging, and telling me how pleasantly matters had gone on, desired me to go on board.

Some of my other friends then asked him if he had got the constable's warrant from them; the captain said, "No." On this I was desired by them to stay in the house; and they said they would get me on board of some other vessel before the evening. When the captain heard this he became almost distracted. He went immediately for the warrant, and, after using every exertion in his power, he at last got it from my hunters; but I had all the expences to pay.

After I had thanked all my friends for their kindness, I went on board again to my work, of which I had always plenty. We were in haste to complete our lading, and were to carry twenty head of cattle with us to the West-Indies, where they are a very profitable article. In order to encourage me in working, and to make up for the time I had lost, my captain promised me the privilege of carrying two bullocks of my own with me; this made me work with redoubled ardour. As soon as I had got the vessel loaded, in doing which I was obliged to perform the duty of the mate as well as my own work, and when the bullocks were near coming on board, I asked the captain leave to bring my two, according to his promise; but, to my great surprise, he told me there was no room for them. I then asked him to permit me to take one; but he said he could not. I was a good deal mortified at this usage, and told him I had no notion that he intended thus to impose on me; nor could I think well of any man that was so much worse than his word. On this we had some disagreement, and I gave him to understand that I intended to leave the vessel. At this he appeared to be very much dejected; and our mate, who had been very sickly, and whose duty had long devolved upon me, advised him to persuade me to stay. In consequence of which he spoke very kindly to me, making many fair promises, telling me that, as the mate was so sickly, he could not do without me; and that, as the safety of the vessel and cargo depended greatly upon me, he therefore hoped that I would not be offended at what had passed between us, and swore he would make up all matters when we arrived in the West Indies; so I consented to slave on as before.

Soon after this, as the bullocks were coming on board, one of them ran at the captain, and butted him so furiously in the breast, that he never recovered of the blow. In order to make me some amends for his treatment about the bullocks, the captain now pressed me very much to take some turkeys, and other fowls, with me, and gave me liberty to take as many as I could find room for; but I told him he knew very well I had never carried any turkeys before, as I always thought they were such tender birds as were not fit to cross the seas. However, he continued to press me to buy them for once; and, what seemed very surprising to me, the more I was against it, the more he urged my taking them, insomuch that he insured me from all losses that might happen by them, and I was prevailed on to take them. But I thought this very strange, as he had never acted so with me before. This, and not being able to dispose of my paper-money in any other way, induced me at length to take four dozen. The turkeys, however, I was so dissatisfied about that I determined to make no more voyages to this quarter, nor with this captain; and was very apprehensive that my free voyage would be the worst I had ever made.

We set sail for Montserrat. The captain and mate had been both complaining of sickness when we sailed, and as we proceeded on our voyage they grew worse. This was about November, and we had not been long at sea before we began to meet with strong northerly gales and rough seas; and in about seven or eight days all the bullocks were near being drowned, and four or five of them died. Our vessel, which had not been tight at first, was much less so now: and, though we were but nine in the whole, including five sailors and myself, yet we were obliged to attend to the pumps, every half or three quarters of an hour. The captain and mate came on deck as often as they were able, which was now but seldom; for they declined so fast, that they were not well enough to make observations above four or five times the whole passage. The whole care of the vessel rested therefore upon me, and I was obliged to direct her by mere dint of reason, not being able to work a traverse.

The captain was now very sorry he had not taught me navigation, and protested, if ever he should get well again, he would not fail to do so. But in about seventeen days his illness increased so much, that he was obliged to keep his bed, continuing sensible, however, until the last, constantly having the owner's interest at heart; for this just and benevolent man ever appeared much concerned about the welfare of what he was intrusted with. When this dear friend found the symptoms of death approaching, he called me by my name; and, when I came to him, he asked (with almost his last breath) if he had ever done me any harm. "God forbid I should think so!" I replied, "I should then be the most ungrateful of wretches to the best of benefactors." While I was thus expressing my affection and sorrow by his bedside, he expired without saying another word, and the day following we committed his body to the deep. Every man on board loved him, and regretted his death; but I was exceedingly affected at it, and found that I did not know, till he was gone, the strength of my regard for him. Indeed I had every reason in the world attached to him; for, besides that he was in general mild, affable, generous, faithful, benevolent, and just, he was to me a friend and father; and had it pleased Providence that he had died but five months before, I verily believe I should not have obtained my freedom when I did; and it is not improbable that I might not have been able to get it at any rate afterwards.

The captain being dead, the mate came on the deck, and made such observations as he was able, but to no purpose. In the course of a few days more, the few bullocks that remained were found dead; but the turkeys I had, though on the deck, and exposed to so much wet and bad weather, did well, and I afterwards gained near three hundred per cent on the sale of them. So that in the event it proved a happy circumstance for me that I had not bought the bullocks I intended, for they must have perished with the rest. I could not help looking upon this, otherwise trifling, circumstance, as a particular providence of God; and was accordingly thankful. The care of the vessel took up all my time, and engaged my attention entirely. As we were now out of the variable winds, I thought I should not be much puzzled to hit the islands. I was persuaded I steered right for Antigua, which I wished to reach, as the nearest to us; and in the course of nine or ten days we made that island to our great joy, and the day after we came safe to Montserrat.

Many were surprised when they heard of my conducting the sloop into the port; and I now obtained a new appellation, and was called "Captain." This elated me not a little and it was quite flattering to my vanity to be thus styled by as high a title as any sable freeman in this place possessed. When the death of the captain became known, he was much regretted by all who knew him; for he was a man universally respected. At the same time the sable captain lost no fame; for the success I had met with increased the affection of my friends in no small measure; and I was offered, by a gentleman of the place, the command of his sloop, to go amongst the islands, but I refused.

Daniel Fisher

Life dates: 1808–?

The narrative of Daniel Fisher appeared in the New Era Press *of Deep River,
Connecticut, on November 23, 1900. Fisher recounts his escape from slavery in
South Carolina and his travel to Washington, Baltimore, Philadelphia, New York,
New Haven, and Deep River, where he was given the name William Winters to
protect his identity.*

I was born in Westmoreland County, Virginia, about the year of 1808. I
had five brothers and two sisters and was known as Daniel Fisher. Our
master's name was Henry Cox. When I was about twenty years of age my
master was obliged, on account of heavy losses, to sell me, and I was sent
to Richmond to be sold on the block to the highest bidder. The sale took
place and the price paid for me was five hundred and fifty dollars. I was
taken by my new master to South Carolina. This was in the month of
March. I remained there until October when, in company with another
slave, we stole a horse and started to make our escape. In order not to tire
the animal, we traveled from ten o'clock at night until daybreak the next
morning when we ran the horse into the woods and left him, for we knew
what would happen to us if two slaves were seen having a horse in their
possession. We kept on our way on foot, hiding by day and walking by
night. We were without knowledge of the country, and with nothing to
guide us other than the North Star, which was oftentimes obscured by
clouds, we would unwittingly retrace our steps and find ourselves back at
the starting point. Finally, after days of tedious walking and privations,
fearing to ask for food and getting but little from the slaves we met, we
reached Petersburg. From Petersburg we easily found our way to Richmond and then, after wandering in the woods for three days and nights,
we came to my old home at Westmoreland Court House.

One of the greatest obstacles we had to contend with was the crossing of rivers, as slaves were not allowed to cross bridges without a pass
from their masters. For that reason, when we came to the Rappahannock
we had to wait our chance and steal a fisherman's boat in order to cross.
Upon my arrival at my old plantation, I called upon my young master and
begged him to buy me back. He said he would gladly do it, but he was
poorer than when he sold me. He advised me to stow myself away on
some vessel going north, and as the North meant freedom I decided to act
upon his advice. While awaiting the opportunity to do so, we (the same slave
who had accompanied me from South Carolina being with me) secured
shovels and dug us three dens in different localities in the neighboring

woods. In these dens we lived during the day, and foraged for food in the night time, staying there about three months. At the end of that time we managed to stow ourselves away on a vessel loaded with wood bound for Washington. We were four days without food and suffered much. When we reached Washington the captain of the vessel put on a coat of a certain color, and started out for the public market, telling us to follow and keep him in sight.

At the market he fed us and told us in what direction to go, starting us on our journey, giving us two loaves of bread each for food. We took the railroad track and started for Baltimore. We had gone scarcely a mile before we met an Irishman, who decided that we were runaways, and was determined to give us to the authorities. However, by telling him a smooth story that we were sent for by our masters to come to a certain house just ahead, he let us by. Thinking our bundles of bread were endangering our safety by raising suspicion, we threw them away. After we went several days without food, traveling day and night, we reached the Delaware [Susquehanna?] River. We walked along the bank of the river for some five miles in search of a bridge. We finally came to one, but on attempting to cross were stopped, as we had no passes. It was a toll bridge, and there was a woman in charge of it, who upon our payment of a penny for each and the promise to come back immediately, allowed us to go by. By this time we were hungry, but had no food. At the other end of the bridge we were stopped again, as the gates were opened only for teams. However, by exercising our ingenuity and pretending to look around, we finally managed to slip by in the shadow of a team, and then—glorious thought!— we were at last on the free soil of Pennsylvania.

We again took to the woods, knowing that we were liable to be apprehended at any time. We made a fire, which attracted attention, and we were soon run out of our hiding place. We sought another place and built another fire, and again we were chased away. We made no more fires. In the course of our further wanderings we were chased by men and hounds, but managed to escape capture, and finally arrived in Philadelphia, being three days on the road. In Philadelphia we found friends who gave us the choice of liquor or food. I took the food; my companion, the liquor.

As kidnappers were plenty, it was thought best for our safety that we separate, and we parted. The only weapon for defense which I had was a razor, one which I had carried all through my wanderings. In company with some Philadelphia colored people, I was taken to New York, and it was there I first met members of the Abolition party. At New York I was put on board a steamboat for New Haven. Arrived in that city, a colored man took me to the Tontine Hotel, where a woman gave me a part of a suit of clothes. I was fed and made comfortable, and then directed to Deep River, with instructions that upon arriving there I was to inquire for George Read or Judge Warner. I walked all the way from New Haven to Deep River, begging food by the way from the women of the farm houses, as I was afraid to apply to the men, not knowing but what they would detail me and give me up. I traveled the Old Stage Road from New Haven to Deep River and in going through Killingworth I stopped at the tavern kept by Landlord Redfield but was driven away. Upon reaching the "Plains" this side of Winthrop, I could not read the signs on the post at the forks of the road, and asked the way of Mrs. Griffing. She drove me away, but called out, "Take that road," and pointed to it. Further on I met Harrison Smith, who had a load of wood which he said was for Deacon Read, the man I was looking for.

I reached Deep River at last, weary and frightened. I called at Deacon Read's, told him my circumstances and gave him my name as Daniel Fisher. All this was in secret. The good deacon immediately told me that I must nevermore be known as Daniel Fisher, but must take the name of "William Winters," the name which I have borne to this day. He furthermore told me that I must thereafter wear a wig at all times and in all places. After that I worked at different times for Ambrose Webb and Judge Warner in Chester, and for Deacon Stevens in Deep River, getting along very nicely, though always afraid of being taken by day or night and carried again to the South.

Francis Henderson
Life dates: 1822–?

Francis Henderson described the brutal conditions of slavery and the circumstances that led to his escape. He focused specifically on the "patrols" of poor white men that watched the slaves and made their living by "plundering and stealing." Henderson was a member of the Methodist Church in Washington, D.C.

I escaped from slavery in Washington City, D.C., in 1841, aged nineteen. I was not sent to school when a boy, and had no educational advantages at all. My master's family were Church of England people themselves and wished me to attend there. I do not know my age, but suppose thirty-three.

I worked on a plantation from about ten years old till my escape. They raised wheat, corn, tobacco, and vegetables—about forty slaves on the place. My father was a mulatto, my mother dark; they had thirteen children, of whom I was the only son. On that plantation the mulattoes were more despised than the whole-blood blacks. I often wished from the fact of my condition that I had been darker. My sisters suffered from the same cause. I could frequently hear the mistress say to them, "you yellow hussy! you yellow wench!" etc. The language to me generally was, "go do so and so." But if a hoe-handle were broken or any thing went wrong, it would be every sort of a wicked expression—so bad I do not like to say what—very profane and coarse.

Our houses were but log huts—the tops partly open—ground floor—rain would come through. My aunt was quite an old woman, and had been sick several years; in rains I have seen her moving from one part of the house to the other, and rolling her bedclothes about to try to keep dry—every thing would be dirty and muddy. I lived in the house with my aunt. My bed and bedstead consisted of a board wide enough to sleep on—one end on a stool, the other placed near the fire. My pillow consisted of my jacket—my covering was whatever I could get. My bedtick [mattress] was the board itself. And this was the way the single men slept—but we were comfortable in this way of sleeping, being used to it. I only remember having but one blanket from my owners up to the age of nineteen, when I ran away.

Our allowance was given weekly—a peck of sifted corn meal, a dozen and a half herrings, two and a half pounds of pork. Some of the boys would eat this up in three days—then they had to steal, or they could not perform their daily tasks. They would visit the hog-pen, sheep-pen, and granaries. I do not remember one slave but who stole some things—they were driven to it as a matter of necessity. I myself did this—many a time have I, with others, run among the stumps in chase of a sheep, that we might have something to eat. If colored men steal, it is because they are brought up to it. In regard to cooking, sometimes many have to cook at one fire, and before all could get to the fire to bake hoe cakes, the overseer's horn would sound: then they must go at any rate. Many a time I have gone along eating a piece of bread and meat, or herring broiled on the coals—I never sat down at a table to eat except in harvest time, all the time I was a slave. In harvest time, the cooking is done at the great house, as the hands they have are wanted in the field. This was more like people, and we liked it, for we sat down then at meals. In the summer we had one pair of linen trousers given us—nothing else; every fall, one pair of woollen pantaloons, one woollen jacket, and two cotton shirts.

My master had four sons in his family. They all left except one, who remained to be a driver. He would often come to the field and accuse the slaves of having taken so and so. If we denied it, he would whip the grown-up ones to make them own it. Many a time, when we didn't know he was anywhere round, he would be in the woods watching us—first thing we would know, he would be sitting on the fence looking down upon us, and if any had been idle, the young master would visit him with blows. I have known him to kick my aunt, an old woman who had raised and nursed him, and I have seen him punish my sisters awfully with hickories from the woods.

The slaves are watched by the patrols, who ride about to try to catch them off the quarters, especially at the house of a free person of color. I have known the slaves to stretch clothes lines across the street, high enough to let the horse pass, but not the rider; then the boys would run, and the patrols in full chase would be thrown off by running against the lines. The patrols are poor white men, who live by plundering and stealing, getting rewards for runaways, and setting up little shops on the public roads. They will take whatever the slaves steal, paying in money, whiskey, or whatever the slaves want. They take pigs, sheep, wheat, corn—any thing that's raised they encourage the slaves to steal: these they take to market next day. It's all speculation—all a matter of self-interest, and when the slaves run away, these same traders catch them if they can, to get the reward. If the slave threatens to expose his traffic, he does not care—for the slave's word is good for nothing—it would not be taken. There are frequent quarrels between the slaves and the poor white men. About the city on Sundays, the slaves, many of them, being fond of dress, would appear nicely clad; which seemed to provoke the poor white men. I have had them curse and damn me on this account. They would say to me, "Where are you going? Who do you belong to?" I would tell them—then, "Where did you get them clothes ? I wish you belonged to me—I'd dress you up!" Then I have had them throw water on me. One time I had bought a new fur hat, and one of them threw a watermelon rind, and spoiled the hat. Sometimes I have seen them throw a slave's hat on the ground, and trample on it. He would pick it up, fix it as well as he could, put it on his head, and walk on. The slave had no redress, but would sometimes take a petty revenge on the man's horse or saddle, or something of that sort.

I knew a free man of color, who had a wife on a plantation. The patrols went to his house in the night time—he would not let them in; they broke in and beat him: nearly killed him. The next morning he went before the magistrates, bloody and dirty just as he was. All the redress he got was, that he had no right to resist a white man.

An old slaveholder married into the family, who introduced a new way of whipping—he used to brag that he could pick a "nigger's" back as he would a chicken's. I went to live with him. There was one man that he used to whip every day, because he was a foolish, peevish man. He would cry when the master undertook to punish him. If a man had any spirit, and would say, "I am working—I am doing all I can do," he would let them alone—but there was a good deal of flogging nonetheless.

Just before I came away, there were two holidays. When I came home to take my turn at the work, master wanted to tie me up for a whipping. Said he, "You yellow rascal, I hate you in my sight." I resisted him, and told him he should not whip me. He called his son—they both tried, and we had a good deal of pulling and hauling. They could not get me into the stable. The old man gave up first—then the young man had hold of me. I threw him against the barn, and ran to the woods. The young man followed on horseback with a gun. I borrowed a jacket, my clothes having been torn off in the scuffle, and made for Washington City, with the intention of putting myself in jail, that I might be sold. I did not hurry, as it was holiday. In about an hour or so, my father came for me and said I had done nothing. I told him I would return in the course of the day, and went in time for work next morning. I had recently joined the Methodist Church, and from the sermons I heard, I felt that God had made all men free and equal, and that I ought not to be a slave—but even then, that I ought not to be abused. From this time I was not punished. I think my master became afraid of me; when he punished the children, I would go and stand by, and look at him—he was afraid, and would stop.

I belonged to the Methodist Church in Washington. My master said, "You shan't go to that church—they'll put the devil in you." He meant that they would put me up to running off. Then many were leaving; it was two from here, three from there, etc.—perhaps forty or fifty a week.... I heard something of this: master would say, "Why don't you work faster? I know why you don't; you're thinking of running off!" And so I was thinking, sure enough. Men would disappear all at once: a man who was working by me yesterday would be gone today—how, I knew not. I really believed that they had some great flying machine to take them through the air. Every man was on the lookout for runaways. I began to feel uneasy, and wanted to run away too. I sought for information—all the boys had then gone from the place but just me. I happened to ask in the right quarter. But my owners found that I had left the plantation while they had gone to church. They took steps to sell me. On the next night I left the plantation. At length I turned my back on Washington, and had no difficulty in getting off. Sixteen persons came at the same time—all men—I was the youngest of the lot.

There is much prejudice here against us. I have always minded my own business and tried to deserve well. At one time, I stopped at a hotel and was going to register my name, but was informed that the hotel was "full." At another time, I visited a town on business, and entered my name on the register, as did the other passengers who stopped there. After-wards I saw that my name had been scratched off. I went to another hotel and was politely received by the landlady; but in the public room—the bar—were two or three persons, who as I sat there, talked a great deal about "niggers"—aiming at me. But I paid no attention to it, knowing that when "whiskey is in, wit is out."

John Jackson

Life dates: unknown

The narrative was first printed in the Rochester, New York, Union and Advertiser *on August 9, 1893. Jackson was born and raised as a slave in Charleston, South Carolina. Although he was allowed to play with his master's children when he was a child, his "overseer was a mean fellow," who whipped him on numerous occasions. Jackson became determined to escape after his wife was taken from him and he was whipped until he "fainted." He escaped by hiding in the hold of a ship leaving Charleston for Boston.*

I was born and bred on the plantation of old Marse [Master] Robert English, one hundred miles from Charleston. My younger days were happy ones. I played with the massa's children until I became seven or eight years old, then I had to go into the field with the other black folks and work hard all day from earliest dawn till late at night. We ate twice a day, that is, when we got up in the morning we were driven out into the fields and were called into breakfast at noon by the blast of an old tin horn.

All we got to eat then was three corn cake dumplins and one plate of soup. No meat unless there happened to be a rotten piece in the smoke house. This would be given to us to make our soup. Why the dogs got better eating than we poor colored folks. We would go out into the fields again and work very hard until dark, when we were driven in by the crack of the overseer's lash and frequently that crack meant blood from some unfortunate creature's back, who, becoming weary had shown signs of faltering.

In the evening those of us who felt inclined would play on something we had made from corn stalks and skin, but not very often. Our overseer was a mean fellow, that he was, sir. I was whipped before my father's face many and many a time. My poor father couldn't help himself, though. After [the overseer] had whipped me to his heart's content—it didn't seem as if he had a heart—he would send me back bleeding and sore to work on until noon, when he blowed the horn.

I would have to tell him about half past seven o'clock every morning, to go and get his breakfast while we worked on in the boiling sun, without food since the night before. I growed up and married when I was very young and I loved my little girl wife. Life was not a burden then. I never minded the whippings I got.

I was happy and it made old Marse Robert angry. He frequently would come out and whip me himself and say "you will have to give up that wife of yours or I will thrash you till you can't stand." I always declared I wouldn't and then he would whip me, oh! how he would whip me. My flesh even now has a quivering feeling when I think of those horrible times. Old Marse Robert went crazy soon afterward and then he could not whip me any more.

One day the overseer said to me, "I'm going to marry that girl of yours to Enoch." He was another slave. I said to him that no one should take her while I was around and then he whipped me till I fainted. That night I determined to run away to the free North and see if I could not get some one to help me steal my girl wife out of slavery. It was a dark, rainy night. Everybody had gone to sleep and even the bloodhounds had crept into their master's house for shelter.

I kissed my wife and babe goodbye. I can see her now, my poor wife, with the tears glistening in her eyes. The dying fire cast its fitful glow upon the wall and I was going from my dear ones never to see them more, for they married my dear wife to another slave and she and my baby boy died soon after and got out of slavery, thank the good Lord.

I made way to Charleston and got into the hold of a northern bound sailing vessel. I remained for seven days and nights in my hiding place. Hunger and thirst at last compelled me to bore a hole through the planking of the ship with the gimlet I had. I stuck out a straw and attracted the attention of the captain, who ordered the sailors to release me. After a long while I was taken out of my close confinement and was taken to the captain, who asked me if I knew him or his vessel. I said I did not. He said all right and took me down to the cabin and gave me something to eat.

The vessel was bound for Boston. I asked the captain if he could help me get my wife and child. He told me to get some minister to write, as I could not write myself. I did and then learned she had been married to another slave and a short time afterward died.

I made my way to Toronto from Boston and from there to England. While in England I belonged to the Rev. Mr. Spurgeon's church and was the only black man in the congregation.

I came back to this country after the war. I'm getting old and feeble and I only want to live till I get the money for the home, and then I will go down to Old Carliny [South Carolina] and there is where I want to die, down in my old cabin home.

Jarmain Wesley Loguen
Life dates: unknown

Jarmain W. Loguen escaped from slavery via the Tennessee Underground Railroad, traveling north to Canada. Loguen later settled in Syracuse, New York, where he became a minister and station keeper on the Underground Railroad, working with Gerrit Smith and Samuel Ward. The following letters between Loguen and his former owner were published in Loguen's book, The Reverend Jermain W. Loguen, as a Slave and as a Freeman: A Narrative of a Real Life.

Maury Co., State of Tennessee
February 20th, 1860

To Jarm:

...I write you these lines to let you know the situation we are in—partly in consequence of your running away and stealing Old Rock, our fine mare.... I am cripple, but I am still able to get about. The rest of the family are all well.... Though we got the mare back, she was never worth much after you took her, and, as I now stand in need of some funds, I have determined to sell you. If you will send me one thousand dollars and pay for the old mare I will give up all claim I have to you....

In consequence of your running away, we had to sell Abe and Ann and twelve acres of land; and I want you to send me the money that I may be able to redeem the land that you was the cause of our selling, and on receipt of the above named sum of money, I will send you your bill of sale. If you do not comply with my request, I will sell you to some one else....

I understand that you are a preacher.... I would like to know if you read your Bible? If so, can you tell what will become of the thief if he does not repent? And, if the blind lead the blind, what will the consequence be?...You know that we reared you as we reared our own children; that you was never abused, and that shortly before you ran away, when your master asked you if you would like to be sold, you said you would not leave him to go with any body.

—Sarah Logue
Syracuse, N.Y., March 28th, 1860

Mrs. Sarah Logue:

…You sold my brother and sister, Abe and Ann, and twelve acres of land, you say, because I run away. Now you have the unutterable meanness to ask me to return and be your miserable chattel, or in lieu thereof send you one thousand dollars to enable you to redeem the land, but not to redeem my poor brother and sister! If I were to send you money it would be to get my brother and sister, and not that you should get land. You say you are cripple, and doubtless you say it to stir my pity, for you know I was susceptible in that direction. I do pity you.…Wretched woman! Be it known to you that I value my freedom, to say nothing of my mother, brothers, and sisters, more than your whole body; more indeed, than my own life; more than all the lives of all the slaveholders and tyrants under heaven.…

You say, "You know we raised you as we did our own children?" Woman, did you raise your own children for the market? Did you raise them for the whipping post? Did you raise them to be drove off in a coffle in chains? Where are my poor bleeding brothers and sisters? Can you tell? Who was it that sent them off into sugar and cotton fields, to be kicked, and cuffed, and whipped, and to groan and die; and where no kin can hear their groans, or attend and sympathize at their dying bed, or follow in their funeral?

…You say I am a thief, because I took the old mare along with me. Have you got to learn that I had a better right to the old mare, as you call her, than Master Logue had to me? Is it a greater sin for me to steal his horse, than it was for him to rob my mother's cradle and steal me? If he and you infer that I forfeit all my rights to you, shall not I infer that you forfeit all your rights to me? Have you got to learn that human rights are mutual and reciprocal, and if you take my liberty and life, you forfeit me your own liberty and life? Before God and High Heaven, is there a law for one man which is not law for every other man?

If you or any other speculator on my body and rights, wish to know how I regard my rights, they need but come here and lay their hands on me to enslave me. Do you think to terrify me by presenting the alternative to give my money to you, or give my body to Slavery?… I stand among a free people, who, I thank God, sympathize with my rights, and the rights of mankind; and if your emissaries and venders come here, to re-enslave me, and escape the unshrinking vigor of my own right arm, I trust my strong and brave friends, in this city and state, will be my rescuers and avengers.

Yours,

—J. W. Loguen

James Mars

Life dates: unknown

James Mars was born and raised as a slave in Canaan, Viriginia. When he was a child, his father secretly planned his family's escape from Canaan to Norfolk, Virginia, but James and his brother, Joseph, were eventually captured and sold back into slavery. In time, James's parents and sister were set free. Joseph remained a slave until age twenty-five, and James became a freeman at twenty-one.

The Life of James Mars, a Slave Born and Sold in Connecticut, Written by Himself, contains the following account of slavery and the *circumstances that led to his escape, capture, and emancipation.*

The treatment of slaves was different at the North from the South; at the North they were admitted to be a species of the human family. I was told when a slave boy, that some of the people said that slaves had no souls, and that they would never go to heaven, let them do ever so well.

My father was born in the state of New York, I think in Columbia County. He had, I think, three different masters in that state, one by the name of Vanepps, and he was Gen. Van Rensallaer's slave in the time of the Revolution, and was a solider in that war; he was then owned by a man whose name was Rutser, and then was owned in Connecticut, in Salisbury, and then by the minister in North Canaan.

My mother was born in old Virginia, in Loudon County; I do not remember the name of the town. The minister of North Canaan, whose name was Thompson, went to Virginia for a wife, or she came to him; in some way they got together, so that they became man and wife. He removed her to Canaan, and she brought her slaves with her, and my mother was one of them. I think there were two of my mother's brothers also. The Rev. Mr. Thompson, as he was then called, bought my father, and he was married to my mother by him. Mr. Thompson ministered to the people of Canaan in holy things; his slaves worked his farm. For a short time things went on very well; but soon the North and the South, as now, fell out; the South must rule, and after a time the North would not be ruled. The minister's wife told my father if she only had him South, where she could have at her call a half dozen men, she would have him stripped and flogged until he was cut in strings, and see if he would do as she bid him. She told him, "You mind, boy, I will have you there yet, and you will get your pay for all that you have done." My father was a man of considerable muscular strength, and was not easily frightened into obedience. I have heard my mother say she has often seen her mother tied up and whipped until the blood ran across the floor in the room where she was tied and whipped.

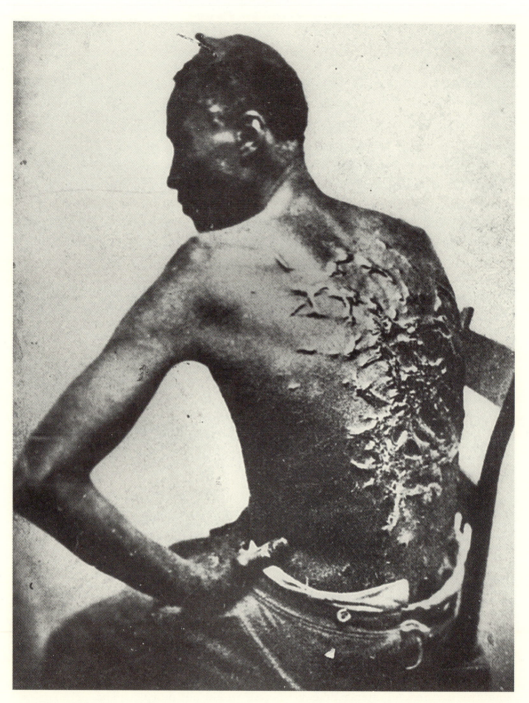

*Slave named Peter,
whipped by plantation
overseer named Artayou
Carrier, Baton Rouge,
Louisiana, 1863 (Corbis)*

Abolitionist engraving, ca. 1835 (Library of Congress)

Well, as I said, the South and the North could not agree; the South seceded and left the North; the minister's wife would not live North, and she and her husband picked up and went South, and left my father and mother in Canaan to work the farm, and they lived on the farm until I was eight years old. My mother had one child when she came from the South; I was the first she had after she was married. They had five children born in Canaan—three died in infancy. I was born March 3d, 1790. Mr. Thompson used to come up from Virginia and talk about our going South.

He would pat me on the head and tell me what a fine boy I was. Once when he was in Canaan, he asked me if I would like to go with him and drive the carriage for my mistress.

Venture Smith

Life Dates: c. 1729–September 19, 1805

Venture Smith recalls the conditions of his enslavement and the means through which he not only gained his freedom but became a relatively prosperous landowner. Smith's narrative is reproduced in its entirety because of its relevance to an understanding of African American movement onto the frontier. While Smith never actually used the word "frontier," its meaning is implicit in the thoughts and actions of the individuals represented. In this context, the frontier is synonymous with opportunity and the promise of the future that existed beyond the boundaries imposed by slavery.

NARRATIVE OF LIFE OF VENTURE.

CHAPTER I

CONTAINING AN ACCOUNT OF HIS LIFE, FROM HIS BIRTH TO
THE TIME OF HIS LEAVING HIS NATIVE COUNTRY

I was born at Dukandarra, in Guinea, about the year 1729. My father's name was Saungm Furro, Prince of the tribe of Dukandarra. My father had three wives. Polygamy was not uncommon in that country, especially among the rich, as every man was allowed to keep as many wives as he could maintain. By his first wife he had three children. The eldest of them was myself, named by my father, Broteer. The other two were named Cundazo and Soozaduka. My father had two children by his second wife, and one by his third. I descended from a very large, tall and stout race of beings, much larger than the generality of people in other parts of the globe, being commonly considerable above six feet in height, and every way well-proportioned.

The first thing worthy of notice which I remember, was a contention between my father and mother, on account of my father marrying his third wife without the consent of his first and eldest, which was contrary to the custom generally observed among my countrymen. In consequence of this rupture, my mother left her husband and country, and travelled away with her three children to the eastward. I was then five years old. She took not the least sustenance along with her, to support either herself or children. I was able to travel along by her side; the other two of her off-spring she carried, one on her back, the other, being a sucking child, in her arms. When we became hungry, our mother used to set us down on the ground and gather some of the fruits that grew spontaneously in that climate. These served us for food on the way. At night we all lay down together in the most secure place we could find and reposed ourselves until morning. Though there were many noxious animals there, yet so kind was our Almighty protector that none of them were ever permitted to hurt or molest us.

Thus we went on our journey until the second day after our departure from Dukandarra, when we came to the entrance of a great desert. During our travel in that, we were often affrighted with the doleful howlings and yellings of wolves, lions and other animals. After five days' travel we came to the end of this desert, and immediately entered into a beautiful and extensive interval country. Here my mother was pleased to stop and seek a refuge for me. She left me at the house of a very rich farmer. I was then, as I should judge, not less than one hundred and forty miles from my native place, separated from all my relatives and acquaintances. At this place, my mother took her farewell of me and set out for her own country. My new guardian, as I shall call the man with whom I was left, put me into the business of tending sheep immediately after I was left with him. The flock, which I kept with the assistance of a boy, consisted of about forty. We drove them every morning between two and three miles to pasture, into the wide and delightful plains. When night drew on, we drove them home and secured them in the cote. In this round I continued during my stay here. One incident which befell me when I was driving my flock from pasture, was so dreadful to me at that age, and is to this time so fresh in my memory, that I cannot help noticing it in this place. Two large dogs sallied out of a certain house and set upon me. One of them took me by the arm and the other by the thigh, and before their master could come and relieve me, they lacerated my flesh to such a degree that the scars are very visible to the present day. My master was immediately sent for. He came and carried me home, as I was unable to go myself on account of my wounds. Nothing remarkable happened afterwards until my father sent for me to return home.

Before I dismiss this country, I must first inform my reader what I remember concerning this place. A large river runs through this country in a westerly course. The land for a great way on each side is flat and level, hedged in by a considerable rise in the country at a great distance from it. It scarce ever rains there, yet the land is fertile; great dews fall in the night which refresh the soil. About the latter end of June or first of July, the river begins to rise, and gradually increases until it has inundated the country for a great distance, to the height of seven or eight feet. This brings on a slime which enriches the land surprisingly. When the river has subsided, the natives begin to sow and plant, and the vegetation is exceedingly rapid. Near this rich river my guardian's land lay. He possessed, I cannot exactly tell how much, yet this I am certain of respecting it, that he owned an immense tract. He possessed likewise a great many cattle and goats. During my stay with him I was kindly used, and with as much tenderness, for what I saw, as his only son, although I was an entire stranger to him, remote from friends and relatives. The principal occupations of the inhabitants there were the cultivation of the soil and the care of their flocks. They were a people pretty similar in every respect to that of mine, except in their persons, which were not so tall and stout. They appeared to be very kind and friendly. I will now return to my departure from that place.

My father sent a man and horse after me. After settling with my guardian for keeping me, he took me away and went for home. It was then about one year since my mother brought me here. Nothing remarkable occurred to us on our journey until we arrived safe home. I found then that the difference between my parents had been made up previous to their sending for me. On my return, I was received both by my father and mother with great joy and affection, and was once more restored to my paternal dwelling in peace and happiness. I was then about six years old.

Not more than six weeks had passed after my return, before a message was brought by an inhabitant of the place where I lived the preceding year to my father, that that place had been invaded by a numerous army, from a nation not far distant, furnished with musical instruments, and all kinds of arms then in use; that they were instigated by some white nation who equipped and sent them to subdue and possess the country; that his nation had made no preparation for war, having been for a long time in profound peace; that they could not defend themselves against such a formidable train of invaders, and must, therefore, necessarily evacuate their lands to the fierce enemy, and fly to the protection of some chief; and that if he would permit them they would come under his rule and protection when they had to retreat from their own possessions. He was a kind and merciful prince, and therefore consented to these proposals.

He had scarcely returned to his nation with the message before the whole of his people were obligated to retreat from their country and come to my father's dominions. He gave them every privilege and all the protection his government could afford. But they had not been there longer than four days before news came to them that the invaders had laid waste their country, and were coming speedily to destroy them in my father's territories. This affrighted them, and therefore they immediately pushed off to the southward, into the unknown countries there, and were never more heard of.

Two days after their retreat, the report turned out to be but too true. A detachment from the enemy came to my father and informed him that the whole army was encamped not far from his dominions, and would invade the territory and deprive his people of their liberties and rights, if he did not comply with the following terms. These were, to pay them a large sum of money, three hundred fat cattle, and a great number of goats, sheep, asses, etc.

My father told the messenger he would comply rather than that his subjects should be deprived of their rights and privileges, which he was not then in circumstances to defend from so sudden an invasion. Upon turning out those articles, the enemy pledged their faith and honor that they would not attack him. On these he relied, and therefore thought it unnecessary to be on his guard against the enemy. But their pledges of faith and honor proved no better than those of other unprincipled hostile nations, for a few days after, a certain relation of the king came and informed him that the enemy who sent terms of accommodation to him, and received tribute to their satisfaction, yet meditated an attack upon his subjects by surprise, and that probably they would commence their attack in less than one day, and concluded with advising him, as he was not prepared for war, to order a speedy retreat of his family and subjects. He complied with this advice.

The same night which was fixed upon to retreat, my father and his family set off about the break of day. The king and his two younger wives went in one company, and my mother and her children in another. We left our dwellings in succession, and my father's company went on first. We directed our course for a large shrub plain, some distance off, where we intended to conceal ourselves from the approaching enemy, until we could refresh ourselves a little. But we presently found that our retreat was not secure. For having struck up a little fire for the purpose of cooking victuals, the enemy, who happened to be encamped a little distance off, had sent out a scouting party who discovered us by the smoke of the fire, just as we were extinguishing it and about to eat. As soon as we had finished eating, my father discovered the party and immediately began to discharge arrows at them. This was what I first saw, and it alarmed both me and the women, who, being unable to make any resistance immediately betook ourselves to the tall, thick reeds not far off, and left the old king to fight alone. For some time I beheld him from the reeds defending himself with great courage and firmness till at last he was obliged to surrender himself into their hands.

They then came to us in the reeds, and the very first salute I had from them was a violent blow on the head with the fore part of a gun, and at the same time a grasp around the neck. I then had a rope put about my neck, as all the women in the thicket with me, and were immediately led to my father, who was likewise pinioned and haltered for leading. In this condition we were all led to the camp. The women and myself, being submissive, had tolerable treatment from the enemy, while my father was closely interrogated respecting his money, which they knew he must have. But as he gave them no account of it, he was instantly cut and pounded on his body with great inhumanity, that he might be induced by the torture he suffered to make the discovery. All this availed not in the least to make him give up his money, but he despised all the tortures which they inflicted, until the continued exercise and increase of torment obliged him to sink and expire. He thus died without informing his enemies where his money lay. I saw him while he was thus tortured to death. The shocking scene is to this day fresh in my memory, and I have often been overcome while thinking on it. He was a man of remarkable stature. I should judge as much as six feet and six or seven inches high, two feet across the shoulders, and every way well proportioned. He was a man of remarkable strength and resolution, affable, kind and gentle, ruling with equity and moderation.

The army of the enemy was large, I should suppose consisting of about six thousand men. Their leader was called Baukurre. After destroying the old prince, they decamped and immediately marched towards the sea, lying to the west, taking with them myself and the women prisoners. In the march, a scouting party was detached from the main army. To the leader of this party I was made waiter, having to carry his gun, etc. As we were a-scouting, we came across a herd of fat cattle consisting of about thirty in number. These we set upon and immediately wrested from their keepers, and afterwards converted them into food for the army. The enemy had remarkable success in destroying the country wherever they went. For as far as they had penetrated they laid the habitations waste and captured the people. The distance they had now brought me was about four hundred miles. All the march I had very hard tasks imposed on me, which I must perform on pain of punishment. I was obliged to carry on my head a large flat stone used for grinding our corn, weighing, as I should suppose, as much as twenty-five pounds; besides victuals, mat and cooking utensils. Though I was pretty large and stout of my age, yet these burdens were very grievous to me, being only six years and a half years old.

We were then come to a place called Malagasco. When we entered the place, we could not see the least appearance of either house or inhabitants, but on stricter search found that instead of houses above ground they had dens in the sides of hillocks, contiguous to ponds and streams of water. In these we perceived they had all hid themselves, as I suppose they usually did on such occasions. In order to compel them to surrender, the enemy contrived to smoke them out with faggots. These they put to the entrance of the caves and set them on fire. While they were engaged in this business, to their great surprise some of them were desperately wounded with arrows which fell from above on them. This mystery they soon found out. They perceived that the enemy discharged these arrows through holes on the top of the dens directly into the air. Their weight brought them back, point downwards, on their enemies heads, whilst they were smoking the inhabitants out. The points of their arrows were poisoned, but their enemy had an antidote for it which they instantly applied to the wounded part. The smoke at last obliged the people to give themselves up. They came out of their caves, first spatting the palms of their hands together, and immediately after extended their arms, crossed at their wrists, ready to be bound and pinioned. I should judge that the dens above mentioned were extended about eight feet horizontally into the earth, six feet in height, and as many wide. They were arched overhead and lined with earth, which was of the clay kind and made the surface of their walls firm and smooth.

The invaders then pinioned the prisoners of all ages and sexes indiscriminately, took their flocks and all their effects, and moved on their way towards the sea. On the march, the prisoners were treated with clemency, on account of their being submissive and humble. Having come to the next tribe, the enemy laid siege and immediately took men, women, children, flocks, and all their valuable effects. They then went on to the next district, which was contiguous to the sea, called in Africa, Anamaboo. The enemies' provisions were then almost spent, as well as their strength. The inhabitants, knowing what conduct they had pursued, and what were their present intentions, improved the favorable opportunity, attacked them, and took enemy, prisoners, flocks and all their effects. I was then taken a second time. All of us were then put into the castle and kept for market. On a certain time, I and other prisoners were put on board a canoe, under our master, and rowed away to a vessel belonging to Rhode Island, commanded by Captain Collingwood, and the mate, Thomas

Mumford. While we were going to the vessel, our master told us to appear to the best possible advantage for sale. I was bought on board by one Robertson Mumford, a steward of said vessel, for four gallons of rum and a piece of calico, and called Venture on account of his having purchased me with his own private venture. Thus I came by my name. All the slaves that were bought for that vessel's cargo were two hundred and sixty.

CHAPTER II

CONTAINING AN ACCOUNT OF HIS LIFE FROM THE TIME OF HIS
LEAVING AFRICA TO THAT OF HIS BECOMING FREE

After all the business was ended on the coast of Africa, the ship sailed from thence to Barbados. After an ordinary passage, except great mortality by the small pox, which broke out on board, we arrived at the island of Barbadoes; but when we reached it, there were found, out of the two hundred and sixty that sailed from Africa, not more than two hundred alive. These were all sold, except myself and three more, to the planters there.

The vessel then sailed for Rhode Island, and arrived there after a comfortable passage. Here my master sent me to live with one of his sisters until he could carry me to Fisher's Island, the place of his residence. I had then completed my eighth year. After staying with his sister some time, I was taken to my master's place to live.

When we arrived at Narragansett, my master went ashore in order to return a part of the way by land, and gave me the charge of the keys of his trunks on board of the vessel, and charged me not to deliver them up to anybody, not even to his father, without his orders. To his directions I promised faithfully to conform. When I arrived with my master's articles at his house, my master's father asked me for his son's keys, as he wanted to see what his trunks contained. I told him that my master intrusted me with the care of them until he should return, and that I had given him my word to be faithful to the trust, and could not, therefore, give him, or any other man, the keys without my master's directions. He insisted that I should deliver to him the keys on pain of punishment. But I let him know that he should not have them, let him say what he would. He then laid aside trying to get them. But notwithstanding he appeared to give up trying to obtain them from me, yet I mistrusted that he would take some time when I was off my guard, either in the daytime or at night, to get them, therefore, I slung them round my neck, and in the daytime concealed them in my bosom, and at night I always slept with them under me, that no person might take them from me without my being apprized of it. Thus I kept the keys from everybody until my master came home. When he returned he asked where Venture was. As I was within hearing, I came and said, "Here, sir, at your service." He asked for his keys, and I immediately took them off my neck and reached them out to him. He took them, stroked my hair, and commended me, saying in presence of his father that his young Venture was so faithful that he never would have been able to have taken the keys from him but by violence; that he should not fear to trust him with his whole fortune, for that he had been in his native place so habituated to keeping his word, that he would sacrifice even his life to maintain it.

The first of the time of living at my master's own place, I was pretty much employed in the house, carding wool and other household business. In this situation I continued for some years, after which my master put me to work out of doors. After many proofs of my faithfulness and honesty, my master began to put great confidence in me. My behavior had as yet been submissive and obedient. I then began to have hard tasks imposed on me. Some of these were to pound four bushels of ears of corn every night in a barrel for the poultry, or be rigorously punished. At other seasons of the year, I had to card wool until a very late hour. These tasks I had to perform when only about nine years old. Some time after, I had another difficulty and oppression which was greater than any I had ever experienced since I came into this country. This was to serve two masters. James Mumford, my master's son, when his father had gone from home in the morning and given me a stint to perform that day, would order me to do this and that business different from what my master had directed me. One day in particular, the authority which my master's son had set up had like to have produced melancholy effects. For my master having set me off my business to perform that day and then left me to perform it, his son came up to me in the course of the day, big with authority, and commanded me very arrogantly to quit my present business and go directly about what he should order me. I replied to him that my master had given me so much to perform that day, and that I must faithfully complete it in that time. He then broke out into a great rage, snatched a pitchfork and went to lay me over the head therewith, but I as soon got another and defended myself with it, or otherwise he might have murdered me in his outrage. He immediately called some people who were within hearing at work for him, and ordered them to take his hair rope and come and bind me with it. They all tried to bind me, but in vain, though there were three assistants in number. My upstart master then desisted, put his pocket handkerchief before his eyes and went home with a design to tell his mother of the struggle with young Venture. He told that their young Venture had become so stubborn that he could not control him, and asked her what he should do with him. In the meantime I recovered my temper, voluntarily caused myself to be bound by the same men who tried in vain before, and carried before my young master, that he might do what he pleased with me. He took me to a gallows made for the purpose of hanging cattle on, and suspended me on it. Afterwards he ordered one of his hands to go to the peach orchard and cut him three dozen of whips to punish me with. These were brought to him, and that was all that was done with them, as I was released and went to work after hanging on the gallows about an hour.

After I had lived with my master thirteen years, being then about twenty-two years old, I married Meg, a slave of his who was about my own age. My master owned a certain Irishman, named Heddy, who about that time formed a plan of secretly leaving his master. After he had long had this plan in meditation, he suggested it to me. At first I cast a deaf ear to it, and rebuked Heddy for harboring in his mind such a rash undertaking. But after he had persuaded and much enchanted me with the prospect of gaining my freedom by such a method, I at length agreed to accompany him. Heddy next inveigled two of his fellow-servants to accompany us. The place to which we designed to go was the Mississippi. Our next business was to lay in a sufficient store of provisions for our voyage. We privately collected out of our master's store, six great old cheeses, two firkins of butter, and one batch of new bread. When we had gathered all our own clothes and some more, we took them all about midnight and went to the water side. We stole our master's boat, embarked, and then directed our course for the Mississippi River.

We mutually confederated not to betray or desert one another on pain of death. We first steered our course for Montauk Point, the east end of Long Island. After our arrival there, we landed, and Heddy and I made an incursion into the island after fresh water, while our two comrades were left a little distance from the boat, employed in cooking. When Heddy and I had sought some time for water, he returned to our companions and I continued on looking for my object. When Heddy had performed his business with our companions who were engaged in cooking, he went directly to the boat, stole all the clothes in it, and then travelled away for East Hampton, as I was informed. I returned to my fellows not long after. They informed me that our clothes were stolen, but could not determine who was the thief, yet they suspected Heddy, as he was missing. After reproving my comrades for not taking care of our things which were in the boat, I advertised Heddy and sent two men in search of him. They pursued and overtook him at Southampton and returned him to the boat. I then thought it might afford some chance for my freedom, or at least be a palliation for my running away, to return Heddy immediately to his master, and inform him that I was induced to go away by Heddy's address.

Accordingly, I set off with him and the rest of my companions for my master's, and arrived there without any difficulty. I informed my master that Heddy was the ringleader of our revolt, and that he had used us ill. He immediately put Heddy into custody, and myself and companions were well received and went to work as usual.

Not a long time passed after that before Heddy was sent by my master to New London gaol [jail]. At the close of that year I was sold to a Thomas Stanton, and had to be separated from my wife and one daughter, who was about one month old. He resided at Stonington Point. To this place I brought with me from my late master's, two Johannes, three old Spanish dollars, and two thousand of coppers, besides five pounds of my wife's money. This money I got by cleaning gentlemen's shoes and drawingboots, by catching muskrats and minks, raising potatoes and carrots, etc., and by fishing in the night, and at odd spells.

All this money, amounting to near twenty-one pounds York currency, my master's brother, Robert Stanton, hired of me, for which he gave me his note. About a year and a half after that time, my master purchased my wife and her child for seven hundred pounds old tenor. One time my master sent me two miles after a barrel of molasses, and ordered me to carry it on my shoulders. I made out to carry it all the way to my master's house. When I lived with Capt. George Mumford, only to try my strength I took upon my knees a tierce of salt containing seven bushels, and carried it two or three rods. Of this fact there are several eye witnesses now living.

Towards the close of the time I resided with this master, I had a falling out with my mistress. This happened one time when my master was gone to Long Island a-gunning. At first the quarrel began between my wife and her mistress. I was then at work in the barn, and hearing a racket in the house, induced me to run there and see what had broken out. When I entered the house, I found my mistress in a violent passion with my wife, for what she informed me was a mere trifle—such a small affair that I forbear to put my mistress to the shame of having it known. I earnestly requested my wife to beg pardon of her mistress for the sake of peace, even if she had given no just occasion for offence. But whilst I was thus saying, my mistress turned the blows which she was repeating on my wife to me. She took down her horse whip, and while she was glutting her fury with it, I reached out my great black hand, raised it up and received the blows of the whip on it which were designed for my head. Then I immediately committed the whip to the devouring fire.

When my master returned from the island, his wife told him of the affair, but for the present he seemed to take no notice of it, and mentioned not a word of it to me. Some days after his return, in the morning as I was

TO BE SOLD, on WEDNESDAY 3d AUGUST next,

By Cowper & Telfairs,
A CARGO

Of 170 prime young likely healthy
GUINEA SLAVES,

laft imported, in the Bark Friends, William Rofs Mafter, directly from
Angola.   Savannah, July 25, 1774.

To be Sold at Private Sale, any Time before the 18th of
next Month,

THE PLANTATION, containing one hundred acres, on which the
subfcriber lives, very pleafantly fituated on Savannah River in fight
of town. The terms of fale may be known by applying to
July 21, 1774   RICHARD WYLLY.

WANTED,

AN OVERSEER thoroughly qualified to undertake the fettlement of
a River Swamp Plantation on the Alatamaha River. Any fuch
perfon, who can bring proper recommendations, may hear of great encouragement by applying to   NATHANIEL HALL.

THE fubfcriber being under an abfolute neceffity of clofing his concerns without delay, gives this laft publick notice, that all perfons indebted to him by bond,
note or otherwife, who do not difcharge the fame by the firft day of October next,
will find their refpective obligations, &c in the hands of an Attorney to be fued for
without diftinction. It is hoped thofe concerned will avail themfelves of this notice.
                                  PHILIP BOX.

RUN AWAY the 20th of May laft from John Forbes, Efq.'s plantation in St.
John's parifh, TWO NEGROES, named BILLY and QUAMINA, of the
Guinea Country, and fpeak good Englifh. Billy is lufty and well made, about 5 feet
10 or 11 inches high, of a black complection, has loft fome of his upper teeth, and
had on when he went away a white negroe cloth jacket and trowfers of the fame.
Quamina is ftout and well made, about 5 feet 10 or 11 inches high, very black,
has his country marks on his face, had on when he went away a jacket, trowfers
and robbin, of white negroe cloth. Whoever takes up faid Negroes, and deliver
them to me at the above plantation, or to the Warden of the Work-Houfe in Savan
nah, fhall receive a reward of 20s. befides what the law allows.
                               DAVIS AUSTIN.

*Engraving from
Savannah, Georgia,
1774 (Library of
Congress)*

putting on a log in the fireplace, not suspecting harm from any one, I received a most violent stroke on the crown of my head with a club two feet long and as large around as a chair post. This blow very badly wounded my head, and the scar of it remains to this day. The first blow made me have my wits about me as you may suppose, for as soon as he went to renew it I snatched the club out of his hands and dragged him out of the door. He then sent for his brother to come and assist him, but I presently left my master, took the club he wounded me with, carried it to a neighboring justice of the peace, and complained of my master. He finally advised me to return to my master and live contented with him till he abused me again, and then complain. I consented to do accordingly. But before I set out for my master's, up he came and his brother Robert after me. The justice improved this convenient opportunity to caution my master. He asked him for what he treated his slave thus hastily and unjustly, and told him what would be the consequence if he continued the same treatment towards me. After the justice had ended his discourse with my master, he and his brother set out with me for home, one before and the other behind me. When they had come to a by-place, they both dismounted their respective horses and fell to beating me with great violence. I became enraged at this and immediately turned them both under me, laid one of them across the other, and stamped them both with my feet what I would.

This occasioned my master's brother to advise him to put me off. A short time after this, I was taken by a constable and two men. They carried me to a blacksmith's shop and had me handcuffed. When I returned home my mistress enquired much of her waiters whether Venture was handcuffed. When she was informed that I was, she appeared to be very contented and was much transported with the news. In the midst of this content and joy, I presented myself before my mistress, showed her my handcuffs, and gave her thanks for my gold rings. For this my master commanded a negro of his to fetch him a large ox chain. This my master locked on my legs with two padlocks. I continued to wear the chain peaceably for two or three days, when my master asked me with contemptuous hard names whether I had not better be freed from my chains and go to work. I answered him, "No." "Well, then," said he, "I will send you to the West Indies, or banish you, for I am resolved not to keep you." I answered him, "I crossed the waters to come here and I am willing to cross them to return."

For a day or two after this not anyone said much to me, until one Hempstead Miner of Stonington asked me if I would live with him. I answered that I would. He then requested me to make myself discontented and to appear as unreconciled to my master as I could before that he bargained with him for me, and that in return he would give me a good chance to gain my freedom when I came to live with him. I did as he requested me. Not long after, Hempstead Miner purchased me of my master for fifty-six pounds lawful. He took the chain and padlocks off me immediately after.

It may here be remembered that I related a few pages back that I hired out a sum of money to Mr. Robert Stanton, and took his note for it. In the fray between my master Stanton and myself, he broke open my chest containing his brother's note to me and destroyed it. Immediately after my present master bought me, he determined to sell me at Hartford. As soon as I became apprized of it, I bethought myself that I would secure a certain sum of money which lay by me safer than to hire it out to Stanton. Accordingly I buried it in the earth, a little distance from Thomas Stanton's, in the road over which he passed daily. A short time after, my master carried me to Hartford, and first proposed to sell me to one William Hooker of that place. Hooker asked whether I would go to the German Flats with him. I answered, "No." He said I should; if not by fair means, I should by foul. "If you will go by no other measures, I will tie you down in my sleigh." I replied to him, that if he carried me in that manner no person would purchase me, for it would be thought he had a murderer for sale. After this he tried no more, and said he would not have me as a gift.

My master next offered me to Daniel Edwards, Esq., of Hartford, for sale. But he not purchasing me, my master pawned me to him for ten pounds, and returned to Stonington. After some trial of my honesty, Mr. Edwards placed considerable trust and confidence in me. He put me to serve as his cup-bearer and waiter. When there was company at his house, he would send me into his cellar and other parts of his house to fetch wine and other articles occasionally for them. When I had been with him some time, he asked me why my master wished to part with such an honest negro, and why he did not keep me himself. I replied that I could not give him the reason, unless it was to convert me into cash and speculate with me as with other commodities. I hope that he can never justly say it was on account of my ill conduct that he did not keep me himself. Mr. Edwards told me that he should be very willing to keep me himself, and that he would never let me go from him to live, if it was not unreasonable and inconvenient for me to be parted from my wife and children; therefore, he would furnish me with a horse to return to Stonington, if I had a mind for it. As Miner did not appear to redeem me, I went, and called at my old master Stanton's first to see my wife, who was then owned by him. As my old master appeared much ruffled at my being there, I left my wife before I had spent any considerable time with her, and went to Col. O. Smith's. Miner had not as yet wholly settled with Stanton for me, and had before my return from Hartford given Colonel Smith a bill of sale of me. These men once met to determine which of them should hold me, and upon my expressing a desire to be owned by Colonel Smith, and upon my master's settling the remainder of the money which was due to Stanton for me, it was agreed that I should live with Colonel Smith. This was the third time of my being sold, and I was then thirty-one years old.

As I never had an opportunity of redeeming myself whilst I was owned by Miner, though he promised to give me a chance, I was then very ambitious of obtaining it. I asked my master one time if he would consent to have me purchase my freedom. He replied that he would. I was then very happy, knowing that I was at that time able to pay part of the purchase money by means of the money which I some time buried. This I took out of the earth and tendered to my master, having previously engaged a free negro man to take his security for it, as I was the property of my master, and therefore could not safely take his obligation myself. What was wanting in redeeming myself, my master agreed to wait on me for, until I could procure it for him. I still continued to work for Colonel Smith. There was continually some interest accruing on my master's note to my friend, the free negro man above named, which I received, and with some besides, which I got by fishing, I laid out in land adjoining my old master Stanton's. By cultivating this land with the greatest diligence and economy, at times when my master did not require my labor, in two years I laid up ten pounds. This my friend tendered my master for myself, and received his note for it.

Being encouraged by the success which I had met in redeeming myself, I again solicited my master for a further chance of completing it. The chance for which I solicited him was that of going out to work the ensuing winter. He agreed to this on condition that I would give him one-quarter of my earnings. On these terms I worked the following winter, and earned four pounds and sixteen shillings, one quarter of which went to my master for the privilege, and the rest was paid him on my account. I was then about thirty-five years old.

The next summer I again desired he would give me a chance of going to work. But he refused and answered that he must have my labor this summer, as he did not have it the past winter. I replied that I considered it as hard that I could not have a chance to work out when the season became advantageous, and that I must only be permitted to hire myself out in the poorest season of the year. He asked me after this what I would give him for the privilege per month. I replied that I would leave it wholly to his own generosity to determine what I should return him a month. Well then, said he, if so, two pounds a month. I answered him that if that was the least he would take I would be contented.

Accordingly I hired myself out at Fisher's Island, earning twenty pounds; thirteen pounds six shillings of which my master drew for the privilege and the remainder I paid for my freedom. This made fifty-one pounds two shillings which I paid him. In October following I went and wrought six months at Long Island. In that six months' time I cut and corded four hundred cords of wood, besides threshing out seventy-five bushels of grain, and received of my wages down only twenty pounds, which left remaining a larger sum. Whilst I was out that time, I took up on my wages only one pair of shoes. At night I lay on the hearth, with one coverlet over and another under me. I returned to my master and gave him what I received of my six months' labor. This left only thirteen pounds eighteen shillings to make up the full sum of my redemption. My master liberated me, saying that I might pay what was behind if I could ever make it convenient, otherwise it would be well. The amount of the money which I had paid my master towards redeeming my time, was seventy-one pounds two shillings. The reason of my master for asking such an unreasonable price, was, he said, to secure himself in case I should ever come to want. Being thirty-six years old, I left Colonel Smith once and for all. I had already been sold three different times, made considerable money with seemingly nothing to derive it from, had been cheated out of a large sum of money, lost much by misfortunes, and paid an enormous sum for my freedom.

CHAPTER III

CONTAINING AN ACCOUNT OF HIS LIFE FROM THE TIME OF
PURCHASING HIS FREEDOM TO THE PRESENT DAY

My wife and children were yet in bondage to Mr. Thomas Stanton. About this time I lost a chest, containing, besides clothing, about thirty-eight pounds in paper money. It was burnt by accident. A short time after I sold all my possessions at Stonington, consisting of a pretty piece of land and one dwelling house thereon, and went to reside at Long Island. For the first four years of my residence there, I spent my time in working for various people on that and at the neighboring islands. In the space of six months I cut and corded upwards of four hundred cords of wood. Many other singular and wonderful labors I performed in cutting wood there, which would not be inferior to the one just recited, but for brevity's sake I must omit them. In the aforementioned four years, what wood I cut at Long Island amounted to several thousand cords, and the money which I earned thereby amounted to two hundred and seven pounds ten shillings. This money I laid up carefully by me. Perhaps some may inquire what maintained me all the time I was laying up my money. I would inform them that I bought nothing which I did not absolutely want. All fine clothes I despised in comparison with my interest, and never kept but just what clothes were comfortable for common days, and perhaps I would have a garment or two which I did not have on at all times, but as for superfluous finery, I never thought it to be compared with a decent homespun dress, a good supply of money and prudence. Expensive gatherings of my mates I commonly shunned, and all kinds of luxuries I was perfectly a stranger to; and during the time I was employed in cutting the aforementioned quantity of wood, I never was at the expense of six pence worth of spirits. Being after this labor forty years of age, I worked at various places, and in particular on Ram Island, where I purchased Solomon and Cuff, two sons of mine, for two hundred dollars each.

It will here be remembered how much money I earned by cutting wood in four years. Besides this, I had considerable money, amounting to all to near three hundred pounds. After this I purchased a negro man, for no other reason than to oblige him, and gave for him sixty pounds. But in a short time after he ran away from me, and I thereby lost all that I gave for him, except twenty pounds which he paid me previous to his absconding. The rest of my money I laid out in land, in addition to a farm which I owned before, and a dwelling house thereon. Forty-four years had then completed their revolution since my entrance into this existence of servitude and misfortune.

Solomon, my eldest son, being then in his seventeenth year, and all my hope and dependence for help, I hired him out to one Charles Church, of Rhode Island, for one year, on consideration of his giving him twelve pounds and an opportunity of acquiring some learning. In the course of the year, Church fitted out a vessel for a whaling voyage, and being in want of hands to man her, he induced my son to go, with the promise of giving him on his return, a pair of silver buckles, besides his wages. As soon as I heard of his going to sea, I immediately set out to go and prevent it if possible. But on my arrival at Church's, to my great grief, I could only see the vessel my son was in, almost out of sight, going to sea. My son died of the scurvy in this voyage, and Church has never yet paid me the least of his wages. In my son, besides the loss of his life, I lost equal to seventy-five pounds.

My other son being but a youth, still lived with me. About this time I chartered a sloop of about thirty tons burthen, and hired men to assist me in navigating her. I employed her mostly in the wood trade to Rhode Island, and made clear of all expenses above one hundred dollars with her in better than one year. I had then become something forehanded, and being in my forty-fourth year, I purchased my wife Meg, and thereby prevented having another child to buy, as she was then pregnant. I gave forty pounds for her.

During my residence at Long Island, I raised one year with another, ten cart loads of watermelons, and lost a great many besides by the thievishness of the sailors. What I made by the watermelons I sold there, amounted to nearly five hundred dollars. Various other methods I pursued in order to enable me to redeem my family. In the night time I fished with set nets and pots for eels and lobsters, and shortly after went a whaling voyage in the service of Col. Smith. After being out seven months, the vessel returned laden with four hundred barrels of oil. About this time I became possessed of another dwelling house, and my temporal affairs were in a pretty prosperous condition. This and my industry was what alone saved me from being expelled from that part of the island in which I resided, as an act was passed by the selectmen of the place, that all negroes residing there should be expelled.

Next after my wife, I purchased a negro man for four hundred dollars. But he having an inclination to return to his old master, I therefore let him go. Shortly after, I purchased another negro man for twenty-five pounds, whom I parted with shortly after.

Being about forty-six years old, I bought my oldest child, Hannah, of Ray Mumford, for forty-four pounds, and she still resided with him. I had already redeemed from slavery, myself, my wife and three children, besides three negro men.

About the forty-seventh year of my life I disposed of all my property at Long Island, and came from thence into East Haddam, Conn. I hired myself out first to Timothy Chapman for five weeks, the earnings of which time I put up carefully by me. After this I wrought for Abel Bingham for about six weeks. I then put my money together and purchased of said Bingham ten acres of land lying at Haddam Neck, where I now reside. On this land I labored with great diligence two years, and shortly after purchased six acres more of land contiguous to my other. One year from that time I purchased seventy acres more of the same man, and paid for it mostly with the produce of my other land. Soon after I bought this last lot of land, I set up a comfortable dwelling house on my farm, and built it from the produce thereof. Shortly after I had much trouble and expense with my daughter Hannah, whose name has been before mentioned to this account. She was soon married after I redeemed her, to one Isaac, and shortly after her marriage fell sick of a mortal disease. Her husband, a dissolute and abandoned wretch, paid but little attention to her illness. I therefore thought it best to bring her to my house and nurse her there. I procured her all the aid mortals could afford, but notwithstanding this she fell a prey to her disease, after a lingering and painful endurance of it. The physician's bill for attending her illness amounted to forty pounds.

Having reached my fifty-fourth year, I hired two negro men, one named William Jacklin, and the other, Mingo. Mingo lived with me one year, and having received his wages, run in debt to me eight dollars, for which he gave me his note. Presently after he tried to run away from me without troubling himself to pay up his note. I procured a warrant, took him, and requested him to go to Justice Throop's of his own accord but he refusing, I took him on my shoulders and carried him there, distant about two miles. The justice asking me if I had my prisoner's note with me. I applied to several gentlemen for counsel in this affair, and they advised me, as my adversary was rich, and threatened to carry the matter from court to court till it would cost me more than the first damages would be, to pay the sum and submit to the injury, which I accordingly did, and he has often since insultingly taunted me with my unmerited misfortune. Such a proceeding as this committed on a defenseless stranger, almost worn out in the hard service of the world, without any foundation in reason or justice, whatever it may be called in a Christian land, would in my native country have been branded as a crime equal to highway robbery. But Captain Hart was a white gentleman, and I a poor African, therefore it was all right, and good enough for the black dog.

I am now sixty-nine years old. Though once straight and tall, measuring without shoes six feet, one inch and an half, and every way well proportioned, I am now bowed down with age and hardship. My strength, which was once equal if not superior to any man whom I have ever seen, is now enfeebled so that life is a burden, and it is with fatigue that I can walk a couple of miles, stooping over my staff. Other griefs are still behind, on account of which some aged people, at least, will pity me. My eye-sight has gradually failed, till I am almost blind, and whenever I go abroad one of my grandchildren must direct my way; besides for many years I have been much pained and troubled with an ulcer on one of my legs. But amidst all my griefs and pains, I have many consolations; Meg, the wife of my youth, whom I married for love and bought with my money, is still alive. My freedom is a privilege which nothing else can equal. Notwithstanding all the losses I have suffered by fire, by the injustice of knaves, by the cruelty and oppression of false-hearted friends, and the perfidy of my own countrymen whom I have assisted and redeemed from bondage, I am now possessed of more than one hundred acres of land, and three habitable dwelling houses. It gives me joy to think that I have and that I deserve so good a character, especially for truth and integrity. While I am now looking to the grave as my home, my joy for this world would be full—IF my children, Cuff for whom I paid two hundred dollars when a boy, and Solomon who was born soon after I purchased his mother—IF Cuff and Solomon—Oh! that they had walked in the way of their father. But a father's lips are closed in silence and in grief! Vanity of vanities, all is vanity.

Stonington, Conn., November 3, 1798.

These may certify, that VENTURE is a free negro man, aged about 69 years, and was, as we have ever understood, a native of Africa, and formerly a slave to Mr. James Mumford, of Fisher's Island, in the State of New York, who sold him to Mr. Thomas Stanton, 2d, of Stonington, in the State of Connecticut, and said Stanton sold said Venture to Col. Oliver Smith, of the aforesaid place. That said Venture hath sustained the character of a faithful servant, and that of a temperate, honest and industrious man, and being ever intent of obtaining his freedom, he was indulged by his master after the ordinary labor on the days of his servitude, to improve the nights in fishing and other employments to his own emolument, in which time he procured so much money as to purchase his freedom from his late master, Colonel Smith; after which he took upon himself the name of Venture Smith, and has since his freedom purchased a negro woman, called Meg, to whom he was previously married, and also his children who were slaves and said Venture has since removed himself and family to the town of East Haddam, in this State, where he hath purchased lands on which he hath built a house, and there taken up his abode.

NATHANIEL MINOR, ESQ.

CAPT. AMOS PALMER. ACORS SHEFFIELD.

EDWARD SMITH

Harriet Tubman

Life dates: c.1820–March 10, 1913

Harriet Tubman, whose maiden name was Araminta Ross, was born a slave in Maryland. About 1844 she married a "free colored man" named Henry Tubman but never had any children. Threatened by the prospects of her sale to a new owner, she escaped to Philadelphia, where she worked and saved her money. Two years later she returned to Maryland, disguised as a man, hoping to reunite with her husband, but much to her disappointment, he had taken another wife and declined to see her. Not deterred, she began the work that earned her the nickname "Moses," leading fugitive slaves through the Underground Railroad to the free states of the North and to Canada. The material here is from interviews appearing in the Commonwealth *of July 17, 1863, and in the first volume of the* Freeman's Record *of March 1865.*

One of the teachers lately commissioned by the New-England Freedmen's Aid Society is probably the most remarkable woman of this age. That is to say, she has performed more wonderful deeds by the native power of her own spirit against adverse circumstances than any other. She is well known to many by the various names which her eventful life has given her; Harriet Garrison, Gen. Tubman, &c.; but among the slaves she is universally known by her well earned title of Moses—Moses the deliverer. She is a rare instance, in the midst of high civilization and intellectual culture, of a being of great native powers, working powerfully, and to beneficent ends, entirely untaught by schools or books.

Her maiden name was Araminta Ross. She is the granddaughter of a native African, and has not a drop of white blood in her veins. She was born in 1820 or 1821, on the Eastern Shore of Maryland. Her parents were slaves, but married and were faithful to each other, and the family affection is very strong. She claims that she was legally freed by a will of her first master, but his wishes were not carried into effect.

She seldom lived with her owner, but was usually "hired out" to different persons. She once "hired her time," and employed it in rudest farming labors, ploughing, carting, driving the oxen, &c., to so good advantage that she was able in one year to buy a pair of steers worth forty dollars.

When quite young she lived with a very pious mistress; but the slaveholder's religion did not prevent her from whipping the young girl for every slight or fancied fault. Araminta found that this was usually a morning exercise; so she prepared for it by putting on all the thick clothes she could procure to protect her skin. She made sufficient outcry, however, to convince her mistress that her blows had full effect; and in the afternoon she would take off her wrappings, and dress as well as she could. When invited into family prayers, she preferred to stay on the landing, and pray for herself; "and I prayed to God," she says "to make me strong and able to fight and that's what I've allers prayed for ever since." It is in vain to try to persuade her that her prayer was a wrong one. She always maintains it to be sincere and right, and it has certainly been fully answered.

In her youth she received a severe blow on her head from a heavy weight thrown by her master at another slave, but which accidentally hit her. The blow produced a disease of the brain which was severe for a long time, and still makes her very lethargic. She cannot remain quiet fifteen minutes without appearing to fall asleep. It is not refreshing slumber; but a heavy, weary condition which exhausts her. She therefore loves great physical activity, and direct heat of the sun, which keeps her blood actively circulating. She was married about 1844 to a free colored man named

John Tubman, but never had any children. Owing to changes in her owner's family, it was determined to sell her and some other slaves; but her health was so much injured, that a purchaser was not easily found. At length she became convinced that she would soon be carried away, and she decided to escape. Her brothers did not agree with her plans; and she walked off alone, following the guidance of the brooks, which she had observed to run North. The evening before she left, she wished very much to bid her companions farewell, but was afraid of being betrayed, if any one knew of her intentions; so she passed through the street singing, "Good bye, I'm going to leave you, Good bye, I'll meet you in the kingdom," and similar snatches of Methodist songs. As she passed on singing, she saw her master, Dr. Thompson, standing at his gate, and her native humor breaking out, she sung yet louder, bowing down to him, "Good bye, I'm going for to leave you." He stopped and looked after her as she passed on; and he afterwards said, that, as her voice came floating back in the evening air it seemed as if "A wave of trouble never rolled across her peaceful breast."

Wise judges are we of each other!—She was only quitting home, husband, father, mother, friends, to go out alone, friendless and penniless into the world.

She remained two years in Philadelphia working hard and carefully hoarding her money. Then she hired a room, furnished it as well as she could, bought a nice suit of men's clothes, and went back to Maryland for her husband. But the faithless man had taken to himself another wife. Harriet did not dare venture into her presence, but sent word to her husband where she was. He declined joining her. At first her grief and anger were excessive. She said, "she did not care what massa did to her, she thought she would go right in and make all the trouble she could, she was determined to see her old man once more"; but finally she thought "how foolish it was just for temper to make mischief"; and that, "if he could do without her, she could without him," and so "he dropped out of her heart," and she determined to give her life to brave deeds. Thus all personal aims died out of her heart; and with her simple brave motto, "I can't die but once," she began the work which has made her Moses,—the deliverer of her people. Seven or eight times she has returned to the neighborhood of her former home, always at the risk of death in the most terrible forms, and each time has brought away a company of fugitive slaves, and led them safely to the free States, or to Canada. Every time she went, the dangers increased. In 1857 she brought away her old parents, and, as they were too feeble to walk, she was obliged to hire a wagon, which added greatly to the perils of the journey. In 1860 she went for the last time, and among her troop was an infant whom they were obliged to keep stupefied with laudanum to prevent its outcries. This was at the period of great excite-

Harriet Tubman
(Culver Pictures, Inc.)

ment, and Moses was not safe even in New York State; but her anxious friends insisted upon her taking refuge in Canada. So various and interesting are the incidents of the journeys, that we know not how to select from them. She has shown in them all the characteristics of a great leader: courage, foresight, prudence, self-control, ingenuity, subtle perception, command over others' minds. Her nature is at once profoundly practical and highly imaginative. She is economical as Dr. Franklin, and as firm in the conviction of supernatural help as Mahomet. A clergyman once said, that her stories convinced you of their truth by their simplicity as do the gospel narratives. She never went to the South to bring away fugitives without being provided with money; money for the most part earned by drudgery in the kitchen, until within the last few years, when friends have aided her. She had to leave her sister's two orphan children in slavery the last time, for the want of thirty dollars. Thirty pieces of silver; an embroidered handkerchief or a silk dress to one, or the price of freedom to two orphan children to another! She would never allow more to join her than she could properly care for, though she often gave others directions by which they succeeded in escaping. She always came in the winter when the nights are long and dark, and people who have homes stay in them. She was never seen on the plantation herself; but appointed a rendezvous for her company eight or ten miles distant, so that if they were discovered at the first start she was not compromised. She started on Saturday night; the slaves at that time being allowed to go away from home to visit their friends—so that they would not be missed until Monday morning. Even then they were supposed to have loitered on the way, and it would often be late on Monday afternoon before the flight would be certainly known. If by any further delay the advertisement was not sent out before Tuesday morning, she felt secure of keeping ahead of it; but if it were, it required all her ingenuity to escape. She resorted to various devices, she had confidential friends all along the road. She would hire a man to follow the one who put up the notices, and take them down as soon as his back was turned. She crossed creeks on railroad bridges by night, she hid her company in the woods while she herself not being advertised went into the towns in search of information. If met on the road, her face was always to the south, and she was always a very respectable looking darkey, not at all a poor fugitive. She would get into the cars near her pursuers and manage to hear their plans.

The expedition was governed by the strictest rules. If any man gave out, he must be shot. "Would you really do that?" she was asked. "Yes," she replied, "if he was weak enough to give out, he'd be weak enough to betray us all, and all who had helped us; and do you think I'd let so many die just for one coward man." "Did you ever have to shoot any one?" she was asked. "One time," she said, "a man gave out the second night; his feet were sore and swollen, he couldn't go any further; he'd rather go back and die, if he must." They tried all arguments in vain, bathed his feet, tried to strengthen him, but it was of no use, he would go back. Then she said, "I told the boys to get their guns ready, and shoot him. They'd have done it in a minute; but when he heard that, he jumped right up and went on as well as any body." She can tell the time by the stars, and find her way by natural signs as well as any hunter; and yet she scarcely knows of the existence of England or any other foreign country.

When going on these journeys she often lay alone in the forests all night. Her whole soul was filled with awe of the mysterious Unseen Presence, which thrilled her with such depths of emotion, that all other care and fear vanished. Then she seemed to speak with her Maker "as a man talketh with his friend"; her child-like petitions had direct answers, and beautiful visions lifted her up above all doubt and anxiety into serene trust and faith. No man can be a hero without this faith in some form; the sense that he walks not in his own strength, but leaning on an almighty arm. Call it fate, destiny, what you will, Moses of old, Moses of today, believed it to be Almighty God.

She loves to describe her visions, which are very real to her; but she must tell them word for word as they lie in her untutored mind, with endless repetitions and details; she cannot shorten or condense them, whatever be your haste. She has great dramatic power; the scene rises before you as she saw it, and her voice and language change with her different actors. Often these visions came to her in the midst of her work. She once said, "We'd been carting manure all day, and t'other girl and I were gwine home on the sides of the cart, and another boy was driving, when suddenly I heard such music as filled all the air"; and, she saw a vision which she described in language which sounded like the old prophets in its grand flow; interrupted now and then by what t'other girl said, by Massa's coming and calling her to wake up, and her protests that she wasn't asleep.

One of her most characteristic prayers was when on board a steamboat with a party of fugitives. The clerk of the boat declined to give her tickets, and told her to wait. She thought he suspected her, and was at a loss how to save herself and her charge, if he did; so she went alone into the bow of the boat, and she says, "I drew in my breath and I sent it out to the Lord, but that was all I could say; and then again the third time, and just then I felt a touch on my shoulder, and looked round, and the clerk said, 'Here's your tickets.'"

Her efforts were not confined to the escape of slaves. She conducted them to Canada, watched over their welfare, collected clothing, organized them into societies, and was always occupied with plans for their benefit. She first came to Boston in the spring of 1859, to ask aid of the friends of her race to build a house for her aged father and mother. She brought recommendations from Gerrit Smith, and at once won many friends who aided her to accomplish her purpose. Her parents are now settled in Auburn, and all that Harriet seems to desire in reward for her labors is the privilege of making their old age comfortable. She has a very affectionate nature, and forms the strongest personal attachments. She has great simplicity of character; she states her wants very freely, and believes you are ready to help her; but if you have nothing to give, or have given to another, she is content. She is not sensitive to indignities to her color in her own person; but knows and claims her rights. She will eat at your table if she sees you really desire it; but she goes as willingly to the kitchen. She is very abstemious in her diet, fruit being the only luxury she cares for. Her personal appearance is very peculiar. She is thoroughly negro, and very plain. She has needed disguise so often, that she seems to have command over her face, and can banish all expression from her features, and look so stupid that nobody would suspect her of knowing enough to be dangerous; but her eye flashes with intelligence and power when she is roused.

Section II

WPA Slave Narratives

The following narratives are edited from the texts prepared by the FederalWriters' Project of theWorks Progress Administration (WPA) during the period 1936 to 1938 and deposited in the Library of Congress, where they are assembled under the title Slave Narratives: A Folk History of Slavery in the United States from Interviews with Former Slaves.

Phoebe Banks

Born:Wagoner County, Oklahoma, 1860

Age when interviewed: 78

Place interviewed: Muskogee, Oklahoma

Master: Mose Perryman

Location: Vol. 7A, pp. 8–11

Phoebe Banks was seventy-eight years old when her account of slavery was recorded by theWPA in the winter of 1937–1938. Born to a Creek Indian master, Mose Perryman, in 1860, Banks remained in Oklahoma after the Civil War. Her narrative tells of a failed escape attempt led by her father and uncle and offers insight into the relations between African Americans and American Indians on the Oklahoma frontier.

In 1860, there was a little Creek Indian town of Sodom on the north bank of the Arkansas river in a section the Indians called Choska Bottoms where Mose Perryman had a big farm or ranch for a long time before the CivilWar. That same year, October 17, I was born on the Perryman place, which was northwest of where I live now in Muskogee; only in them days Fort Gibson and Olomulgee was the biggest towns around and Muskogee hadn't shaped up yet.

My mother belonged to Mose Perryman when I was born; he was one of the best known Creeks in the whole nation, and one of his younger brothers, Legus Perryman, was made the big chief of the Creeks (1887) a long time after the slaves was freed. Her name was Eldee; my father's name was William McIntosh, belonging to a Creek Indian family named McIntosh. Everybody say the McIntoshs was leaders in the Creek doings away back there in Alabama long before they come out here.

With me, there was twelve children in our family: Daniel, Stroy, Scott, Segal, Neil, Joe, Phillip, Mollie, Harriett, Sally and Queenie.

African Americans
drive wagons in the
first '89er parade,
Guthrie, Oklahoma.
(Western History
Collections,
University of
Oklahoma Libraries)

The Perryman slave cabins were all alike—just two room log cabins, with a fireplace where mammy do the cooking for us children at night after she get through working in the master's house.

Mother was the house girl—cooking, waiting on the table, cleaning the house, spinning the yarn, knitting some of the winter clothes, taking care of the mistress girl, washing the clothes—yes, she was always busy and worked mighty hard all the time while them Indians wouldn't hardly do nothing for themselves.

On the McIntosh plantation my daddy said there was a big number of slaves and lots of slave children. The slave men work in the fields chopping cotton, raising corn, cutting rails for the fences, building log cabins and fireplaces. One time when father was cutting down a tree it fell on him and after that he was only strong enough to rub down the horses and do light work around the yard. He got to be a good horse trainer, and long time after slavery he helped to train horses for the free fairs around the country, and I suppose the first money he ever earned was made that way.

Lots of the supplies was freighted up the Arkansas river by the steamboats; sometimes daddy take me down to the river when he go to help unload the freight, but I don't remember the names on them boats.

Some of the slave owners didn't want their slaves to learn reading and writing, but the Perrymans didn't care, they even help the younger slaves with that stuff. Mother said her master didn't care much what the slaves do, he was so lazy he didn't care for nothing.

They tell me about the war times, that's all I remember of it. Before the war is over some of the Perryman slaves and some from the McIntosh place fix up to run away from their masters.

My father and my uncle, Jacob Perryman, were some of the fixers. Some of the Creek Indians already lost a few slaves who slip off to the North, and they take what was left down into Texas so's they could get away. Some of the other Creeks were friendly to the North and away up there; that's the ones my daddy and uncle were fixing to join, for they were afraid their masters would take up and move to Texas before they could get away.

They call the old Creek, who was leaving for the North, "Old Gouge" (Opoethleyoholo). All our family join up with him, and there was lots of Creek Indians and slaves in the outfit when they made a break for the North. The runaways were riding ponies stolen from their masters.

When they get into the hilly country farther north in the country that belong to the Cherokee Indians they make camp on a big creek and there the rebel Indian soldiers catch up but they was fought back.

Then long before morning lighten the sky, the men hurry and sling the camp kettles across the pack horses, tie the littlest children to the horses' backs and get on the move farther into the mountains. They kept moving fast as they could, but the wagons made it mighty slow in the brush and the lowland swamps, so just about the time they ready to ford another creek the Indian soldiers catch up and the fighting begin all over again.

The Creek Indians and the slaves with them try to fight off them soldiers like they did before, but they get scattered around and separated so's they lose the battle. Lost their horses and wagons, and the soldiers killed lots of the Creeks and negroes, and some of the slaves were captured and take back to their masters.

Dead all over the hills when we got away; some of the Negroes shot and wounded so bad the blood run down the saddle skirts, and some fall off their horse miles from the battle ground and lay still on the ground. Daddy and Uncle Jacob keep our family together somehow and head across the line to Kansas. We all get to Fort Scott where there was a big army camp; daddy work in the blacksmith shop and Uncle Jacob join with the northern soldiers to fight against the South. He come through the war and live to tell about the fighting he been in.

He went with the soldiers down around Fort Gibson where they fight the Indians who stayed with the South. Uncle Jacob say he killed many a man during the war, and showed me the musket and sword he used to fight with; said he didn't shoot the women and children—just whack their heads off with the sword, and almost could I see the blood dripping from the point!—it make me so scared at his stories.

The captain of his company want his men to be brave and not get scared, so before the fighting start he put out a tub of white liquor (corn whiskey) and steam them up so's they'd be mean enough to whip their grannie. The soldiers do lots of riding and the saddle sores get so bad they grease their body every night with snake oil so's they could keep going on.

Uncle Jacob said the biggest battle was at Honey Springs (1863). That was down near Elk Creek, close by Checotah, below Rentersville. He said it was the most terrible fighting he seen, but the Union soldiers whipped and went back into Fort Gibson. The Rebels were chased all over the country and couldn't find each other for a long time, the way he tell it.

After the war our family come back here and settle at Fort Gibson, but it ain't like the place my mother told me about. There were big houses and buildings of brick setting on the high land above the river when I first see it, not like she know it when the Perrymans come here years ago.

She heard the Indians talk about the old fort (1824), the one that rot down long before the Civil War. And she seen it herself when she go with the master for trading with the stores. She said it was made by Mathew Arbuckle and his soldiers, and she talk about Company's B, C, D, K and the 7th Infantry who was there and made the Osage Indians stop fighting the Creeks and the Cherokees. She talk of it, but that old place all gone when I first see the fort.

Then I hear about how after the Arbuckle soldiers leave the old log fort, the Cherokee Indians take over the land and start up the town of Keetoowha. The folks who move in there make the place so wild and rascally the Cherokees give up trying to make a good town and it kind of blow away.

My husband was Tom Banks, but the boy I got ain't my own son, but I found him on my doorstep when he's about three weeks old and raise him like he is my own blood. He went to school at the manual training school at Tullahassee and the education he got get him a teacher job at Taft, Oklahoma, where he is now.

David A. Hall

Born: Wayne County, North Carolina, 1847
Age when interviewed: 90
Place interviewed: Tiffin, Ohio
Master: Lifich Famer
Location: Vol. 160 (OH), pp. 39–44

David A. Hall grew up in Goldsboro, North Carolina, and moved to Canton,
Ohio, in 1866. In this WPA narrative collected on August 16, 1937, Hall
discusses his life as a slave and the invasion of Yankee soldiers during the Civil
War. Hall talks briefly about the "night riders" who attacked blacks after
emancipation. He recalls how a Yankee soldier brought him to the North and
helped him find a job in a flour mill in Tiffin, Ohio, that he kept for seventy
years.

I never knew who owned my father, but my mother's name was Lifich Famer. My mother did not live on the plantation but had a little cabin in town. You see, she worked as a cook in the hotel and her master wanted her to live close to her work. I was born in the cabin in town.

I never went to school but I was taught a little by my master's daughter, and can read and write a little. As a slave boy I had to work in the military school in Goldsboro. I waited table and washed dishes, but my wages went to my master the same as my mother's.

I was about fourteen when the war broke out and remember when the Yankees came through our town. There was a Yankee soldier by the name of Kuhns who took charge of the government store. He would sell tobacco and such to the soldiers. He was the man who told me I was free and then gave me a job working in the store.

I had some brothers and sisters but I do not remember them—can't tell you anything about them.

Our beds were homemade out of poplar lumber and we slept on straw ticks. We had good things to eat and a lot of corn cakes and sweet potatoes. I had pretty good clothes, shoes, pants and a shirt, the same winter and summer.

I don't know anything about the plantation as I had to work in town and did not go out there very much. I don't know how big it was or how many slaves there was. I never heard of any uprisings either.

Our overseer was "poor white trash," hired by the master. I remember the master lived in a big white house and he was always kind to his slaves. So was his wife and children, but we didn't like the overseer. I heard of some slaves being whipped, but I never was and I did not see any of the others get punished. Yes, there was a jail on the plantation where slaves had to go if they wouldn't behave. I never saw a slave in chains but I have seen colored men in the chain gang since the war.

We had a Negro church in town and slaves that could be trusted could go to church. It was a Methodist church and we sang Negro spirituals.

We could go to the funeral of a relative and quit work until it was over and then went back to work. There was a graveyard on the plantation.

A lot of slaves ran away, and if they were caught they were brought back and put in the stocks until they were sold. The master would never keep a runaway slave. We used to have fights with the "white trash" sometimes and once I was hit by a rock throwed by a white boy and that's what this lump on my head is.

We had to work every day but Sunday. The slaves did not have any holidays. I did not have time to play games but used to watch the slaves sing and dance after dark. I don't remember any stories.

When the slaves heard that they had been sent free, I remember a lot of them were sorry and did not want to leave the plantation. I never heard of any in our section getting any mules or land.

I do remember the "night riders" that come through our country after the war. They put the horse shoes on the horses backwards and wrapped the horses feet in burlap so we couldn't hear them coming. The colored folks were deathly afraid of these men and would all run and hide when they heard they were coming. These "night riders" used to steal everything the colored people had—even their beds and straw ticks.

Right after the war I was brought north by Mr. Kuhns I spoke of, and for a short while I worked at the milling trade in Tiffin and came to Canton in 1866. Mr. Kuhns owned a part in the old flour mill here (now the Ohio Builders and Milling Co.) and he gave me a job as a miller. I worked there until the end of last year, 70 years, and I am sure this is a record in Canton. I never worked any other place.

I was married July 4, 1871, to Jennie Scott in Massillon. We had four children but they were all dead except one boy. Our first baby—a girl named Mary Jane, born February 21, 1872, was the first colored child born in Canton. My wife died in 1926. I did not know when she was born, but I do know she was not a slave.

I started to vote after I came north but I did not ever vote in the South. I do not like the way the young people of today live; they are too fast and drink too much. I think this is true of the white children the same as the colored.

I saved my money when I worked and when I quit I had three properties. I sold one of these, gave one to my son, and am living on the other.

I never did ask for charity. I get a pension check from the mill where I worked so long.

I joined church simply because I thought it would make me a better man and I think every one should belong. I have seen a member of St. Paul's A.M.E. church here in Canton for 54 years. Yesterday (Sunday, August 15, 1937) our church celebrated by burning the mortgage. As I was the oldest member, I was one of the three who lit it, the other two are the only other living charter members. My church friends made me a present yesterday of $100.00 which was a birthday gift. I was 90 years old on the 25th of last month.

Felix Haywood

Born: Bexar County, Texas, 1845
Age when interviewed: 92
Place interviewed: San Antonio, Texas
Master: William Gudlow
Location: Vol. 4B, pp. 130–133

Felix Haywood was born a slave in Bexar County (San Antonio), Texas, in 1845. He was ninety-two when his account of slavery was recorded by the WPA in 1938. Haywood discusses his reluctance to harm his master, William Gudlow, as a means to obtain his freedom. He also explains that if he had been able to escape, he would have gone to Mexico instead of traveling into the North. After emancipation, Haywood continued to live in close proximity to his former master.

It's a funny thing how folks always want to know about the war. The war wasn't so great as folks suppose. Sometimes you didn't knowed it was goin' on. It was the ending of it that made the difference. That's when we all wakes up that somethin' had happened. Oh, we knew what was going on in it all the time, 'cause old man Gudlow went to the post office every day and we knew. We had papers in them days, just like now.

But the war didn't change nothing. We saw guns and we saw soldiers, and one member of master's family, Colmin Gudlow, was gone fighting—somewhere. But he didn't get shot no place but one—that was in the big toe. Then there was neighbors went off to fight. Some of them didn't want to go. They was took away (conscription). I'm thinking lots of them pretended to want to go as soon as they had to go.

Cowboys in South
Texas, ca. 1920.
(Institute of Texan
Cultures)

The ranch went on just like it always had before the war. Church
went on. Old Mew Johnson, the preacher, seen to it church went on. The
kids didn't know war was happening. They played marbles, see-saw and
rode. I had old Buster, an ox, and he took me about plenty good as a horse.
Nothing was different. We got layed-onto (whipped) time on time, but
generally life was good—just as good as a sweet potato. The only misery I
had was when a black spider bit me on the ear. It swelled up my head and
stuff came out. I was plenty sick and Dr. Brennen, he took good care of
me. The whites always took good care of people when they were sick.
Hospitals couldn't do no better for you today. Maybe it was a black widow
spider, but we called it the "devil biter."

Sometimes someone would come along and try to get us to run up
North and be free. We used to laugh at that. There wasn't no reason to run
up North. All we had to do was to walk, but walk South, and we'd be free
as soon as we crossed the Rio Grande. In Mexico you could be free. They
didn't care what color you was, black, white, yellow or blue. Hundreds of
slaves did go to Mexico and got on all right. We would hear about them
and they was goin' to be Mexicans. They brought up their children to
speak only Mexican.

But what I want to say is, we didn't have no idea of running and
escaping. We was happy. We got our lickings, but just the same we get our
fill of biscuits every time the white folks had them. Nobody knew how it
was to lack food. I tell my chillen we didn't know no more about pants

than a hog knows about heaven; but I tells them that to make them laugh. We had all the clothes we wanted and if you wanted shoes bad enough you got them shoes with a brass square toe. And shirts! Mister, them was shirts that was shirts! If someone gets caught by his shirt on a limb of a tree, he had to die there if he weren't cut down. Them shirts wouldn't rip no more than buckskin.

> The end of the war, it come jus' like that—like you snap your fingers
> Hallelujah broke out—
> Abe Lincoln freed the nigger
> With the gun and the trigger;
> And I ain't goin' to get whipped any more.
> I got my ticket, leavin' the thicket,
> And I'm a-headin' for the Golden Shore!

Soldiers, all of a sudden, was everywhere—coming in bunches, crossing and walking and riding. Everyone was a-singing. We were all walking on golden clouds. Hallelujah!

> Union forever
> Hurrah, boys, hurrah!
> Although I may be poor,
> I'll never be a slave—
> Shoutin' the battle cry of freedom.

Everybody went wild. We all felt like horses and nobody had made us that way but ourselves. We were free. Just like that, we were free. I didn't seem to make the whites mad, either. They went right on giving us food just the same. Nobody took our homes away, but right off colored folks started on the move. They seemed to want to get closer to freedom, so they'd know what it was—like it was a place or a city. Me and my father stuck, stuck close as a lean tick to a sick kitten. Gudlows started us out on a ranch. My father, he'd round up cattle, unbranded cattle, for the whites. They was cattle that they belonged to, all right; they had gone to find water along the San Antonio River and the Guadalupe. Then the whites gave me and my father some cattle for our own. My father had his own brand, (7 B), and we had a herd to start out with of seventy.

We knowed freedom was on us, but we didn't know what was to come with it. We thought we was going to get rich like the white folks. We thought we was going to be richer than the white folks, 'cause we were stronger and knowed how to work, and the whites didn't and they didn't have us to work for them anymore. But it didn't turn out that way. We soon found out that freedom could make folks proud but it didn't make them rich.

Did you ever stop to think that thinking don't do any good when you do it too late? Well, that how it was with us. If every mother's son of a black had thrown away his hoe and took up a gun to fight for his own freedom along with the Yankees, the war'd been over before it began. But we didn't do it. We couldn't help stick to our master. We couldn't more shoot them than we could fly. My father and me used to talk it out. We decided we was too soft and freedom wasn't going to be much to our good even if we had a education.

Silas Jackson

Born: Ashbie's Gap, Virginia, 1846 or 1847
Age when interviewed: 90
Place interviewed: Baltimore, Maryland
Master: Tom Ashbie
Location: Vol. 16M, pp. 29–37

Silas Jackson grew up as a slave near Ashbie's Gap, Virginia. His grandfather had escaped from slavery with the assistance of Harriet Tubman and went to Philadelphia, where he saved enough money to purchase the freedom of his grandmother. In his WPA narrative, Jackson describes the work and living conditions on the plantation where he was enslaved. He recounts beatings and persecution of his fellow slaves, who had little recourse against their masters, although he does mention one incident in which two white men were murdered by "colored people" and "it was never known whether by free people or slaves."

I was born at or near Ashbie's Gap in Virginia, either in the year of 1846 or '47. I do not know which, but I will say that I am 90 years of age. My father's name was Sling and mother's Sarah Louis. They were purchased by my master from a slave trader in Richmond, Virginia. My father was a man of large stature and my mother was tall and stately. They originally came from the eastern shore of Maryland, I think from the Legg estate, beyond that I do not know. I had three brothers and two sisters. My brothers older than I, and my sisters younger. Their names were Silas, Cater, Rap or Raymond, I do not remember; my sisters were Jane and Susie, both of whom are living in Virginia now. Only one I have ever seen and he came north with General Sherman, he died in 1925. He was a Baptist minister like myself.

The only things I know about my grandparents were: My grandfather ran away through the aid of Harriet Tubman and went to Philadelphia

and saved $350, and purchased my grandmother through the aid of a Quaker or an Episcopal minister, I do not know. I have on several occasions tried to trace this part of my family's past history, but without success.

I was a large boy for my age, when I was nine years of age my task began and continued until 1864. You see, I was a slave.

In Virginia where I was, they raised tobacco, wheat, corn and farm products. I have had a taste of all the work on the farm, besides digging and clearing up new ground to increase the acreage to the farm. We all had task work to do—men, women and boys. We began work on Monday and worked until Saturday. That day we were allowed to work for ourselves and to garden and do extra work. When we could get work, or work on someone else's place, we got a pass from the overseer to go off the plantation, but to be back by nine o'clock on Saturday night or when cabin inspection was made. Some time we could earn as much as 50 cents a day, which we used to buy cakes, candies, or clothes.

On Saturday each slave was given 10 pounds of corn meal, a quart of black strap, 6 pounds of fat back, 3 pounds of flour and vegetables, all of which were raised on the farm. All of the slaves hunted or those who wanted, hunted rabbits, opossums or fished. These were our choice food as we did not get anything special from the overseer.

Our food was cooked by our mothers or sisters and for those who were not married by the old women and men assigned for that work.

Harriet Tubman (far left) with slaves she helped escape to freedom, ca. 1850 (Corbis/Bettmann)

Each family was given three acres to raise their chickens or vegetables and if a man raised his own food he was given $10.00 extra at Christmas time, besides his presents.

In the summer or when warm weather came each slave was given something, the women, linsey goods or gingham clothes, the men overalls, muslin shirts, top and underclothes, two pair of shoes, and a straw hat to work in. In the cold weather, we wore woolen clothes, all made at the sewing cabin.

My master was named Tom Ashbie, a meaner man was never born in Virginia—brutal, wicked and hard. He always carried a cowhide with him. If he saw anyone doing something that did not suit his taste, he would have the slave tied to a tree, man or woman, and then would cowhide the victim until he got tired, or sometimes, the slave would faint.

The Ashbies home was a large stone mansion, with a porch on three sides. Wide halls in the center up and down stairs, numerous rooms and a stone kitchen built on the back connected with the dining room.

Mrs. Ashbie was kind and lovely to her slaves when Mr. Ashbie was out. The Ashbies did not have any children of their own, but they had boys and girls of his own sister and they were much like him, they had maids or private waiters for the young men if they wanted them.

I have heard it said by people in authority, Tom Ashbie owned 9,000 acres of farm land besides of wood land. He was a large slave owner having more than 100 slaves on his farm. They were awakened by blowing of the horn before sunrise by the overseer, started work at sunrise and worked all day to sundown, with no time to go to the cabin for dinner. You carried your dinner with you. The slaves were driven at top speed and whipped at the snap of the finger by the overseer. We had four overseers on the farm, all hired white men. I have seen men beaten until they dropped in their tracks or knocked over by clubs, women stripped down to their waist and cowhide.

I have heard it said that Tom Ashbie's father went to one of the cabins late at night, the slaves were having a secret prayer meeting. He heard one slave ask God to change the heart of his master and deliver him from slavery so that he may enjoy freedom. Before the next day the man disappeared, no one ever seeing him again; but after that down in the swamp at certain times of the moon, you could hear the man who prayed in the cabin praying. When old man Ashbie died, just before he died he told the white Baptist minister, that he killed Zeek for praying and that he was going to hell.

There was a stone building on the farm, it is there today. I saw it this summer while visiting in Virginia. The old jail, it is now used as a garage. Downstairs there were two rooms, one where some of the whipping was done, and the other used by the overseer. Upstairs was used for women and girls. The iron bars have corroded, but you can see where they were. I have never seen slaves sold on the farm, but I have seen them taken away, and brought there. Several times I have seen slaves chained, taken away and chained when they came.

No one on the place was taught to read or write. On Sunday the slaves who wanted to worship would gather at one of the large cabins with one of the overseers present and have their church. After which, the overseer would talk. When communion was given, the overseer was paid for staying there with half of the collection taken up, some time he would get 25 cents. No one could read the Bible. Sandy Jasper, Mr. Ashbie's coachman was the preacher, he would go to the white Baptist church on Sunday with family and would be better informed because he heard the white preacher.

Twice each year, after harvest and after New Year's the slaves would have their protracted meeting or revival and after each closing they would baptize the creek. Sometimes in the winter they would break the ice singing "Going to the Water" or some other hymn of that nature. And at each funeral, the Ashbies would attend the service conducted in the cabin where the deceased was, from there to the slave graveyard. A lot dedicated for that purpose, situated about a quarter of a mile from the cabins near a hill.

There were a number of slaves on our plantation who ran away, some were captured and sold to a Georgia trader, others who were never captured. To intimidate the slaves, the overseers were connected with the patrollers, not only to watch our slaves, but sometimes for the rewards for other slaves who had run away from other plantations. This feature caused a great deal of trouble between the whites and the blacks. In 1858 two white men were murdered near Warrenton on the road by colored people, it was never known whether by free people or slaves.

When work was done the slaves retired to their cabins, some played games, others cooked or rested or did what they wanted. We did not work on Saturdays unless harvest time, then Saturdays were days of work. At other times, on Saturdays you were at leisure to do what you wanted. On Christmas day Mr. Ashbie would call all the slaves together, give them presents, money, after which they spent as they liked. On New Year's day we all were scared, that was the time for selling, buying and trading slaves. We did not know who was to go or come.

I do not remember of playing any particular game, my sport was fishing. You see, I do not believe in ghost stories nor voodooism, I have nothing to say. We boys used to take the horns of a dead cow or bull, cut the end off of it, we could blow it, some having different notes. We could tell who was blowing and from what plantation.

When a slave took sick, she or he would have to depend on herbs, salves or other remedies prepared by someone who knew the medicinal value. When a valuable hand took sick, one of the overseers would go for a doctor.

James Calhart James

Born: Ft. Sumter, South Carolina, 1846
Age when interviewed: unknown
Place interviewed: Baltimore, Maryland
Master: Franklin Randolph
Location: Vol. 16M, pp. 34–37

James Calhart James grew up in South Carolina, the son of a white landowner, Franklin Pearce Randolph, and Lottie Virginia James, daughter of an Indian and a slave woman. As a young man, James's father told his mother that he was going to free James and send him to the North to be educated, but instead he was freed by emancipation. In 1865, when he was twenty-one years old, he left South Carolina and enrolled at Howard University, where he graduated in 1873. He taught in schools in Virginia, North Carolina, and Maryland and retired in 1910. In this WPA narrative, James recounts his early life as a slave and the ways in which he received an education.

My father's name was Franklin Pearce Randolph of Virginia, a descendant of the Randolphs of Virginia who migrated to South Carolina and located near Fort Sumter, the fort that was surrendered to the Confederates in 1861 or the beginning of the Civil War. My mother's name was Lottie Virginia James, daughter of an Indian and a slave woman, born on the Rapidan River in Virginia about 1823 or 24, I do not know which; she was a woman of fine features and very light in complexion with beautiful, long black hair. She was purchased by her master and taken to South Carolina when about 15 years old. She was the private maid of Mrs. Randolph until she died and then continued as housekeeper for her master. While there and in that capacity I was born on the Randolph's plantation August 23, 1846. I was half brother to the children of the Randolphs, four in number. After I was born mother and I lived on the servants quarters of the big house enjoying many pleasures that the other slaves did not: eating and sleeping in the big house, playing and associating with my half-brothers and sisters.

As for my ancestors I have no recollection of them, the history of the Randolphs in Virginia is my background.

My father told mother when I became of age, he was going to free me, send me north to be educated, but instead I was emancipated. During my slave days my father gave me money and good clothes to wear. I bought toys and games. My clothes were good both winter and summer according to the weather.

My master was my father, he was kind to me but hard on the field hands who worked in the rice fields. My mistress died before I was born. There were three girls and one boy, they treated me fairly good—at first or when I was small or until they realized their father was my father, then they hated me. We lived in a large white farm house containing about 15 rooms with every luxury of that day, my father being very rich.

I have heard the Randolph plantation contained about 4,000 acres and about 300 slaves. We had white overseers on the plantation, they worked hard producing rice on a very large scale, and late and early. I know they were severely punished, especially for not producing the amount of work assigned them or for things that the overseers thought they should be punished for.

We had a jail over the rice barn where the slaves were confined, especially on Sundays, as punishment for things done during the week.

I could read and write when I was 12 years old. I was taught by the teacher who was the governess for the Randolph children. Mother could also read and write. There was no church on the plantation, the slaves attended church on the next plantation, where the owner had a large slave church, he was a Baptist preacher. I attended the white church with the Randolph children. I was generally known and called Jim Randolph. I was baptized by the white Baptist minister and christened by a Methodist minister.

There was little trouble between the white and the blacks. You see I was one of the children of the house, I never came in contact much with the other slaves. I was told that the slaves had a drink that was made of corn and rice which they drank. The overseers sometimes themselves drank it very freely. On holidays and Sundays the slaves had their times, and I never knew any difference as I was treated well by my father and did not associate with the other slaves.

In the year of 1865, I left South Carolina, went to Washington, entered Howard University 1868, graduated 1873, taught schools in Virginia, North Carolina and Maryland, retired 1910. Since then I have been connected with A.M.E. educational board. Now I am home with my granddaughter, a life well spent.

One of the songs sung by the slaves on the plantation I can remember a part of it. They sang it with great feeling and happiness—

Oh, where shall we go when the great day comes
An the blowing of the trumpets and the bangins of the drums
When General Sherman comes.
No more rice and cotton fields
We will hear no more crying
Old master will be sighing.

I can't remember the tune, people sang it according to their own tune.

Bill Simms

Born: St. Clair County, Missouri, 1839
Age when interviewed: unknown
Place interviewed: Ottawa, Kansas
Master: Simms
Location: Vol. 16A, pp. 8–13

The WPA narrative of Bill Simms was recorded in Topeka, Kansas, in 1936. In the narrative, Simms recounts growing up on a plantation in Osceola, Missouri, and provides information about the sale of slaves, the splitting up of his family, the living conditions of slaves, the Confederate army, and the Civil War. Simms moved to Lawrence, Kansas, in June 1874, and moved to Ottawa, Kansas, five months later. Simms worked as a field hand and did whatever odd jobs he could find. Although the details of his life are fragmentary, the narrative does provide a glimpse of the Kansas frontier.

I lived on a farm with my mother, and my master, whose name was Simms. I had an older sister, about two years older than I was. My master needed some money so he sold her, and I have never seen her since except just a time or two.

On the plantation we raised cows and sheep and cotton, tobacco and corn, which were our principal crops. There were plenty of wild hogs, turkey, and deer and other game. The deer used to come up and feed with the cattle in the feed yards, and we could still get all the wild hogs we wanted by simply shooting them in the timber.

A man who owned ten slaves was considered wealthy, and if he got hard up for money, he would advertise and sell some slaves, like my oldest sister was sold on the block with her children. She sold for eleven hundred dollars, a baby in her arms sold for three hundred dollars. Another sold for six hundred dollars and the other for a lot less than that. My master was offered fifteen hundred dollars for us several times, but he refused to sell me, because I was considered a good, husky slave. My family is all dead, and I am the only one living.

The slaves usually lived in a two-room house made of native lumber. The houses were all small. A four- or five-room house was considered a mansion. We made our own clothes, had spinning wheels and raised and combed our own cotton, clipped the wool from our sheep's backs, combed and spun it into cotton and wool clothes. I learned how to make shoes when I was just a boy and I made shoes for the whole family. I used to chop wood and make rails and do all kinds of farm work.

I had a good master. Most of the masters were good to their slaves. When a slave got too old to work they would give him a small cabin on the plantation and have the other slaves to wait on him. They would furnish him with victuals and clothes until he died.

Slaves were never allowed to talk to white people or someone their master knew, as they were afraid the white man might have the slave run away. The master aimed to keep their slave in ignorance and the ignorant slaves were all in favor of the Rebel army, only the more intelligent were in favor of the Union army.

When the war started, my master sent me to work for the Confederate army. I worked most of the time for three years on and off, hauling canons, driving mules, hauling ammunition, and provisions. The Union army pressed in on us and the Rebel army moved back. I was sent home. When the Union army came close enough I ran home and joined the Union army. There I drove six-mule team and worked at wagon work, driving ammunition and all kinds of provisions until the war was ended. Then I returned home to my old master, who had stayed there with my mother. My master owned about four hundred acres of good land, and had about ten slaves. Most of the slaves stayed at home. My master hired me to work for him. He gave my mother forty acres of land with a cabin on it, and sold me forty acres, for twenty dollars, when I could pay him. This was timbered land and had lots of good trees for lumber, especially walnut. One tree on this ground was worth one hundred dollars. If I could only get it out and marketed, I could pay for my land. My master's wife had been dead for several years and they had no children. The nearest relative was a nephew. They wanted my master's land and was afraid that he would give it all away to us slaves, so they killed him, and would have killed us if we had stayed at home. I took my mother and ran into the adjoining, St. Clair County. We settled there and stayed for sometime, but I wanted to see Kansas, the state I had heard so much about.

I couldn't get nobody to go with me, so I started out afoot across the prairies for Kansas. After I got some distance from home it was all prairie. I had to walk all day long following the buffalo trail. At night I would go

A PULPITEER and GOSPEL SINGER

Go ye into all the world and preach the gospel, teaching men to observe the things that I have commanded you and lo I am with you even unto the end of the world.

Rev. John R. KELLUM, B. D.
Minister and Pastor of the
PILGRIM BAPTIST CHURCH

Mrs. LELLA KELLUM
Member Pilgrim Baptist Church
Rep. Women's Mission in the Kaw Valley
District Association

~~316 W. Laurent St.~~   **TOPEKA KANSAS**   **Phone 2-1060**
910 n. Topeka ave

off a little ways from the trail and lay down and sleep. In the morning I'd wake up and see nothing but the sun and prairie. Not a house, not a tree, no living thing, not even could I hear a bird. I had little to eat, I had a little bread in my pocket. I didn't even have a pocket knife, no weapon of any kind. I was not afraid, but I wouldn't start my way out again. The only shade I could find was the rosin weed on the prairie. I would lay down so it would throw the shade in my face and rest, then get up and go again. It was in the spring of the year in June. I came to Lawrence, Kansas, and stayed two years working on the farm. In 1874 I went to work for a man by the month at $38 a month and I made more money than the owner did, because the grasshoppers ate up the crops. I was hired to cut up the corn for him, but the grasshoppers ate it up first. He could not pay me for sometime. Grasshoppers were so thick that you couldn't step on the ground without stepping on a dozen at each step. I got my money and came to Ottawa in December 1874, about Christmas time.

My master's name was Simms and I was known as Simm's Bill, just like horses. When I came out here I just changed my name from Simm's Bill, to Bill Simms.

Ottawa was very small at the time I came here, and there were several Indians close by that used to come to town. The Indians held their war dance on what is now courthouse grounds. I planted trees that are now standing on courthouse grounds. I still planted trees until three or four years ago. There were few farms fenced and what were, were on the streams. The prairie land was all open. This is what North Ottawa was, nothing but prairie north of Logan Street and the river. Ottawa didn't have many business houses. There was also an oil mill where they bought castor beans, and made castor oil on the north side of the Marais des Cygnes River one block west of Main Street. There was one hotel, which was called Leafton House and it stood on what is now the southwest corner of Main and Second Streets.

I knew Peter Fraiser, when I came here, and A.P. Elder was just a boy then.

The people lived pretty primitive. We didn't have kerosene. Our only lights were tallow candles, mostly grease lamps, they were just a pan with grease in it, and one end of the rag dragging out over the side which we could light. There were no sewers at the time.

I had no chance to go to school when I was a boy, but after I came to Kansas I was too old to go to school, and I had to work, but I attended night school, and learned how to read and write and figure.

The farm land was nearly all broke up by ox teams, using about six oxen on a plow. In Missouri we lived near the Santa Fe trail, and the settlers traveling on the trail used oxen, and some of them used cows. The cows seem to stand the road better than the oxen and also gave some milk. The travelers usually aimed to reach the prairie states in the spring, so they could have grass for their oxen and horses during the summer.

I have lived here since I came here. I was married when I was about thirty years old. I married a slave girl from Georgia. Back in Missouri, if a slave wanted to marry a woman from another plantation, he had to ask the master, and if both masters agreed they were married. The man stayed at his owners, and the wife, at her owners. He could go and see her on Saturday night and on Sunday. Sometimes only every two weeks. If a man was a big strong man, neighboring plantation owners would come over to see his gals, hoping that he might want to marry one of them, but if a Negro was a small man, he was not cared for as a husband, as they valued their slaves for what they could do, just like they would horses. When they married and if they had children they belonged to the man who owned the woman. Osceola is where the saying originated, "I'm from Missouri, show me." After the war the smart guys came through and talked the people into voting bonds, but there was no railroad built and most counties paid their bonds, but the county in which Osceola stands refused to pay for their bonds because there was no railroad built, and they told the collectors to "show me the railroad and we will pay," and that is where "show me" originated.

My wife died when we had three children. She had to work hard all her life and she said she didn't want her children to have to work as hard as she had, and I promised her on her death bed, that I would educate our girls. So I worked and sent the girls to school. My two girls both graduated from Ottawa University, the oldest one being the first colored girl ever to graduate from that school. After graduation she went to teach school in Oklahoma, but only got twenty-five dollars a month, and I had to work to send her money to pay her expenses. The younger girl also graduated and went to teach school, but she did not teach school long, until she married a well-to-do farmer in Oklahoma. The older girl got her wages raised until she got one hundred and twenty-five dollars a month. I have worked at farm work and tree husbandry all my life. My oldest daughter bought me my first suit of clothes I ever had.

I have been living alone about twenty-five years. I don't know how old I was, but my oldest daughter had written my mother before she died, and got our family record, which my mother kept in her old Bible. Each year she writes me and tells me on my birthday how old I am.

Milton Starr

Born: Cherokee Nation, Oklahoma, 1858
Age when interviewed: 80
Place interviewed: Gibson Station, Oklahoma
Master: Jerry Starr
Location: Vol. 12S, pp. 293–298

Milton Starr was seven at the time the Emancipation Proclamation was signed to end slavery. His memories of slavery are minimal, although he does remember that he was born the son of a slave woman and his master. His mother and father never married. Starr's narrative was collected by the WPA in 1938.

I was born a slave, but was not treated like other slaves and my folks never told me anything about slavery. So there is very little I can tell of those days. My birthplace was in the old Flint district of the Cherokee Nation; the nearest town was Russellville, Arkansas, and the farm was owned by Jerry Starr, half-breed Cherokee, who was my master and father. They told me I was born February 24, 1858, right in my master's house, and when I was a baby had the care of the average white child.

My mother was Jane Coursey of Tennessee, a slave girl picked up by the Starrs when they left that country with the rest of the Cherokee Indians. My mother wasn't bought, just stolen by them Indians, and when she

was freed she went back to Tennessee; I stayed with Starr family being raised by Millie and Jerry Starr.

Jerry Starr said when the Cherokees come to this country they crossed Baron Fork Creek east of Proctor (Okla.) They were riding in a government wagon and they crossed Baron Fork on ice 80 inches thick the mules and wagons didn't break through.

My master had a brother named Tom Starr, and he come to this country with some earlier Cherokees than did Jerry. Tom settled at Walking-Stick Spring east of Tahlequah, where he had 20 slaves working on a 40-acre patch of rocks and sand, that's the way Jerry Starr always talked about Tom's place. He said all them slaves done was fish and hunt.

Them Starrs got mixed up with some pretty bad folks too, after the War. I hear about it when I was a young man; about how Tom Starr had a son named Sam who married a white woman the folks called Belle Star. She was the baddest woman in the whole country before she got killed down on her farm near Briartown, about 1888, I think it was. Shot from her horse but they never found out who killed her.

Old Tom was a kind of outlaw too, but not like his son's wife. He never went around robbing trains and banks, his troubles were all account of Indian doings long before the War, so they say. Seem like they said he killed a man name Buffington and run away to Texas for a long time, but he come back when the Cherokee government send word for Tom to come back home and behave himself.

Jerry Starr was close kin to another mixed-blood Cherokee who was a bad man that most of the folks nowadays remember pretty well. He was Henry Starr and it ain't been long ago that he robbed a bank over in Arkansas and got himself shot in the back before he could get away with the money. Them Starr boys always seem to be in a peck of trouble most of the time.

Jerry Starr was known best around the place of Tahlequah where we all move to after the War. I saw a hanging there; Lizzie Redbird was hanged for selling dope of some kind. The hanging tree was an old oak that stood near the little creek that runs on the edge of town. Don't know if it's still there or not.

There's one Indian law I remember Jerry Starr told me about, and it was the death law. If an Indian found any silver, or gold, or any kind of mineral that was rich, he was to hide it and never tell anybody about it or where it was. If anybody went against that law he was bound to die.

My mistress and stepmother had three girls: Mamie, Ella and Tiger. They had some slave girls and one of them, Jessie, I married long after the War, in 1883. We went to Tyler, Texas, for awhile, but she died and years later I married Jenona Alberty. We had two girls, Irena and Esther, but they both dead.

But, like I said, my folks never told me about slavery; they never whipped me, always treated me like I was one of the family, because I was, so, I can't tell nothing about them days.

Section III

Oral Histories

Charles James Bate, M.D.

Physician

Born: January 1, 1914, Castalian, Tennessee

Charles James Bate provides an overview of his career as a physician and his work in Tulsa, Oklahoma. This oral history was found in the collections of the Oklahoma Historical Society. While the text is informative, it does not include important information concerning the details of Bate's early life and his education. The narrative is nonetheless important in that it offers a glimpse of the difficulties encountered by African American physicians and their patients during the years of segregation.

We must never forget the past. We must especially tell the story of what black doctors went through in the past to pave the way for the present generation of doctors and caregivers. Oh my, we had a rough time! Young doctors today have everything handed to them on a silver platter—scholarships, free books, fancy internships—and when they start to practice, they get subsidized and they get big, fancy cars. It was different in the old days. The boys in my class worked in all kinds of places and at all kinds of jobs trying to scrape up tuition, which was $40 to $50 a year. That doesn't sound like much now, but then it was awful hard to come by. We worked on farms, in wheat fields, cotton fields, tobacco fields, on boats, railroad tracks, and Pullman cars—just anyplace that would hire strong, young men. We scrimped and saved our money. Sometimes we wouldn't get a haircut for three or four months.

When we got ready to intern, there were very few places for young black doctors. Washington, D.C., Nashville, Tennessee, New Orleans, Louisiana, and St. Louis, Missouri, took a few. Intern pay ranged from $5 a month in some places to a maximum of $15 a month in "good places."

When we did start our own practice in the black community, it was heartbreaking to see the conditions then. I sometimes pray to forget some of the things I saw. For instance, due to segregation laws, blacks could not be admitted to white hospitals then. Before there was a black hospital in Tulsa, most black women delivered their babies at home with midwives in attendance. Or some of them sent for a white doctor who didn't mind treating "colored" folks in their own homes. Black people who needed operations were especially susceptible; they were operated on in their own homes in unsterile, inadequate surroundings. Then they were left to recuperate in the midst of noisy families. It is no wonder that so many of them hemorrhaged and died!

Graduating class, Howard University School of Medicine, ca. 1930s (Texas African American Photography Archive)

It is interesting how Tulsa's white hospitals first "opened up" to blacks long before civil rights acts mandated it. Rich white oil men and other businessmen were often very fond of their black servants, and when the servants became ill, they would often just show up at Hillcrest Hospital (then known as Morningside Hospital) at 11th and Utica streets, or at St. John's Catholic Hospital up on 21st and Utica with their ailing black servants. These hospitals had been built with Masonic money and contributions from wealthy oil men and wealthy businessmen. So, even though the state of Oklahoma was entrenched in segregation, white doctors couldn't ignore the demands of these wealthy white benefactors. In the 1920s, Hillcrest set up an area on the first floor, in the north wing, where black servants could be treated, but after a short period of recuperation in "colored rooms" in the basement, they were sent home to recover.

One incident that occurred in Hillcrest Hospital caused me to hold a grudge against a white doctor for many years. It involved a childbirth case and a black woman. A very obese black woman showed up at Hillcrest in great distress. The attending physician examined her and determined that she needed an operation immediately for a large ovarian tumor; the "tumor" turned out to be a healthy black baby! The perplexed white doctor didn't know what to do with the baby; the mother was put in the "colored ward" in the basement, but he couldn't put a screaming baby in there with recuperating adults. So the good doctor put the baby in a broom closet! That really bothered me, and I did hold a grudge against that doctor. But one day when he and I were talking, he told me that the incident, as I had heard, was true. He said he was ashamed to be a part of a system that would treat another human being that way, but he said that he had no choice. At that time, he simply could not have put that little black baby in the nursery with white babies in Oklahoma. I thought about it, and I knew that he was telling the truth. So my grudge against him just dissolved, and we became close friends.

Oh, we had some rough times then. Black people didn't have the opportunities then that they have now, and they didn't get proper credit for their inventions and creativity. Why, they discovered things, in the medical profession, and in all other segments of society, for which white people got the credit! I could write a book about it. In fact, I did write a book about the medical profession. Don't let people forget what we, black Americans, have been through. All Americans need to know this history—black, white, young, old, rich, poor—everybody. Young blacks today are ignorant of their rich cultural heritage, and white youth are arrogant because they don't know the heritage of black people. They think that everything was invented by white people. Yes, there is a great need for setting the record straight in the United States. Don't let people ever forget what we, as black people, went through. It was especially difficult in the medical profession, and we must never forget the rocky road that others went over in the past to make the path smoother for all of us today.

INTERVIEW BY EDDIE FAYE GATES, MAY–AUGUST, 1994
COURTESY OKLAHOMA HISTORICAL SOCIETY
ARCHIVES AND MANUSCRIPTS DIVISION, ORAL HISTORY DEPARTMENT

Ollie Hunter Boyd

Dry cleaner
Born: April 21, 1919, Abbeville, South Carolina

Ollie Hunter Boyd always wanted to get out of Abbeville, South Carolina. She grew up near the tall tree where a prosperous black farmer, Anthony Crawford, was lynched in 1916, three years before she was born. The lynching began an African American exodus from Abbeville and the surrounding area. Boyd's parents were sharecroppers with sixteen children. After the lynching, they were frightened for the children and began sending them north to Evanston, Illinois, a relatively

progressive Chicago suburb where work was available. Ollie Boyd moved to Evanston in the mid-1930s. Within a few years, both parents had moved there as well, and their home became a way station for new immigrants from the South. The close-knit community of former Abbeville residents cushioned the shock of adjusting to a new, urban culture.

My father was a farmer. He grew everything but peanuts and pop-corn. His name was Will Hunter. My mother's name was Mamie Rice Hunter. I didn't know my grandfather and grandmother on either side, but I knew my uncles, my mother's brothers. My mother came from a large family, too; it was like eighteen in her family. And my daddy—it's all in the history there. They lynched a man named Mr. Anthony Crawford. He was a kinda rich colored man. He had his own everything, an old T-Model Ford. He didn't work for nobody. He lived kinda out in what we call Sandburg. And he would bring his cotton to town and sell it. The boss man didn't have to bring it. And for one thing, he had a T-Model Ford of his own. And he was supposed to have accidentally insulted a man's daughter. Maxwell, old man Maxwell. That's what they told us. T. J. Maxwell, I think that was his name. He owned the fish market. And he had a great big daughter, 'bout this big, sit out in the front with a great big tub and sold fish to people. And he was supposed to have insulted her, asked her for a date or something like that, this colored man. So they caught him and whipped him all around Abbeville County. Abbeville was just a square block. You could stand on one corner and holler all the way to the other end. It was much smaller than Davis Street. And they caught him and beat him in the square there, then they hooked him to a car and drug him. First out from town was our house. We lived not right in town; we lived like out of town because all behind us was farmland. And they drug him there, and there was a big old pine tree. Wasn't in our backyard, but it was in a little field. It was thirteen men, they drug him and put him up in that tree and shot, but he was dead when they did it. And then they ran everybody in town that had a business out of town. And the only reason they didn't lynch us, we had a great big old barnlike house. We lived on a man's farm called Saul Rosenberg. He was a rich Jew. That was the only reason they didn't take any of us out. They ran Gus Richards, Butler, it was quite a few of them. They had to get out of town, or they was going to kill them because they were the people that had something. They had a store, a little business. Mr. Beltry, he had a little restaurant. Gus Richards, he was the undertaker man. Holmes was an undertaker man. And they all got out of town. But they were gone about two or three days; they came back. But after then, nobody could rest. Mama was just so scared for us. They just packed them up and started sending them north. My oldest brother came first. Roosevelt. "Pick." Well, I had an uncle already up here that had moved up here. He moved up here because they had moved from down there because things was getting bad. And Uncle Henry and Uncle Pete, and they had moved up here. And he came up to stay with them. I don't know why they picked Evanston. They worked at the steel mill, most of them, in Gary, Indiana. Before they went to the steel mill, they worked right across on the other side of the high school, Clayton and Marx, manufacturing steel things. I came to Evanston in 1934. We moved up here. But the rest of them, sisters older than me, soon as they would finish high school, then my mother would send them here. We had uncles and things up here. Just the thoughts of them hanging a man, might as well say in our backyard, just killed the spirit of everybody, and that's why the majority of the people moved away from Abbeville was because of that lynching. After we left, everybody left. Wasn't any work left. In the Greenwood area, McCormick, right around in there. The lynching of this man was all the colored people in Abbeville was going to take. And they just left. I don't know what happened to Crawford's land. Wasn't no community, just a house on the side of the road. Rosenberg was all right. In fact, his son, the baby boy, after we moved from there, he moved in the house and built a house where we were living. I think he died last year. They had a store there, Rosenberg's store. And they sold goods, clothes, and shoes. One of Mr. Rosenberg's sons was a doctor there. And David—I think it's in the book. I finished high school. Well, I never did have any trouble with them. I didn't go out and work in nobody's house or nothing, you know. So we kinda lived from the street. But they were nice. "Mamie was a good nigger." Mama raised vegetables, and they would come over and get vegetables out of our garden. Mama never did charge 'em nothing. We had a peach orchard, about thirtysome peach trees. A pecan tree. It wasn't ours. It was Mr. Rosenberg's, and we took care of them. We all moved up here. I come with my mother. I left my daddy and two younger than me home. They gave the stuff away that we had in our house, and then they moved up here the next year, '36. Daddy worked at Clayton and Marx for a while. My sisters and brothers didn't want my daddy to work. And my mother, didn't want her working, either. But my mother, I guess my mother wish she could have gotten out and worked because she cooked for about eighteen every day. And with all of us having friends, we brought people home. But we loved our mama. She died in '65. There's four of us still living. One sister has the beauty parlor right here on Emerson Street, Blanche Hunter. And I have a sister living at 1043 Darrow, Christine Samuels; that's the baby girl. And Helen, she lives downtown in Chicago. Helen Robinson. I traveled everywhere. (We were) known as the Hunter Sisters. I went along and sang solos. They used to broadcast every Sunday morning over Jack L. Cooper's program in Chicago. It was fun. Everybody, practically, in Abbeville, moved up here. They'd move and come to our house.

INTERVIEW BY JAY BRAKEFIELD

Charles Brown

Rhythm and blues pianist
Life dates: September 24, 1920–January 21, 1999

Charles Brown began studying classical piano in Texas City, Texas, when he was ten years old, encouraged by his grandmother, who raised him after his mother died. His father followed the crop harvests, traveling from town to town, picking cotton and doing whatever other work he could find. Brown excelled at school in academics and music, influenced early on by the recordings of jazz great Art Tatum. Brown earned a B.S. degree in chemistry from Prairie View A&M in Texas, but had difficulty finding good jobs because of the limited opportunities available to blacks during the years of segregation. In 1944, Brown moved to Los Angeles and joined The Three Blazers, a musical group that epitomized the West Coast sound by blending classical techniques and dynamics with elements of rhythm and blues and jazz. With The Three Blazers, Brown recorded some of his biggest hits, "Driftin' Blues," "Merry Christmas Baby," and "Sunny Road." In the 1950s, Brown toured with Fats Domino, Bill Doggett, Roy Brown, Amos Milburn, and others. By the late 1960s, the black audience for rhythm and blues had started to decline, but Brown continued performing, bringing his distinctive "California Fusion" sound to festivals abroad. In 1997, Brown was awarded a National Heritage Fellowship by the National Endowment for the Arts.

My mother died when I was six months old. My dad got killed by a train when I was going on eight years old, 1928. And he planned to come back and steal me. In 1927, he had come down to Texas City, and he took me around in his old T-Model Ford and went to Galveston, Texas. He was crazy about prostitutes and whatnot, but I can't tell you all about that. But anyway he told me, "If I come and get you, will you go back with me?"

And I told him, "Yes."

He said, "Well, don't you let your grandmother know it."

But then when he got ready to come and steal me, February the 28th, that morning, he got killed. The train ran into him. Foggy. They didn't have a signal up there. And he got killed. But he was able to tell them that he had a son down in Texas City.

And so when these two fellows came to my aunt's house, around about twelve o'clock, he says, "Well, boy, is your mama here?"

I said, "No, sir. My Aunt Dee is here."

Said, "Well, tell her to come to the door." So Aunt Dee was in the kitchen, washing dishes, and she came in there. He said, "Do you know a Mose Brown?"

So Aunt Dee said, "Yes, that's this boy's daddy."

"Well, he's just been hit by a train. We don't know how serious it is."

And I started screaming and hollering because I figured if you get hit by a train, you won't be living. But that's all right, because my grandmother said later on, she said, "You better be glad that he didn't steal you. You would have been a cotton picker and picking up potatoes 'cause we believe in education." So that's why I didn't even go to his funeral. I went to hollering.

Charles Brown, Fort Worth, Texas, ca. 1955. (African American Museum of Dallas)

But she said, "If you go to that funeral, it'll stunt your growth. I'm not going to let you go."

My grandfather was named Conquest Simpson, and my grandmother's name was Sewanee Simpson. They used the old name Conquest. And my grandmother was named after the Sewanee River. My mother's name was Mattie Evelyn Simpson, and my father's name was Mose Brown. They would always get the biblical names like Amos, Mose, you know, like that. And so, they named me Charles Mose Brown.

My grandmother was from North Carolina—Rocky Mount, North Carolina. And I don't know how my grandparents really met, but my grandfather was from Louisiana, and he has people there, Creole people.

I used to go with my grandmother to the post office. They had a postmaster named Mr. Ambrin. He says, "Swan, Sewanee. You need a pension."

She said, "Why, Mr. Ambrin?"

"You're an Indian. You can get a pension."

She said, "Oh, Mr. Ambrin, I'm not no Indian."

So she just went on like that. She looked beautiful, black, pretty hair, that beautiful Indian skin. She was slightly bowlegged with a little waistline and big hips. And she directed that choir. She could really direct it. And I watched her. But I think it wiped off on me in a different way. And so, that's why I'm still here.

My grandmother talked about her mother. They used to go down on Saturday morning to this mercantile store. And when they went to the mercantile store, you know, they would have comments about being black or whatnot.

So this white fellow said to my great-grandmother, "Auntie, move this wagon."

She said, "I'm not your Auntie and I'm not your mother's sister. I'm Mrs. Harrison." And she said, "You call me by my name if you want to know me, but since you don't know me (don't call me at all), because I'll shoot the hell out of you." So that's the only thing my grandmother told me about (with regard to her mother).

And my grandfather told me about one other situation. Why we went to Texas City with my mother, they were living sixty miles way down in Wharton, Texas. And they were living behind plantation houses. And they would raise the farms, and they had credit at the mercantile store until the crops came out. And they would pay. And he said that these two little boys were very good-looking, and one of the people that they worked for had a daughter, and she was in love, wanted this black boy to be with her. And he was scared of her. And she tried to make him, and he wouldn't bat an eye with her. And she said, "If you don't do this with me, I'm going to tell my daddy that you tried to rape me." And so she told her daddy that. So it went, on a Saturday when these guys went downtown on the wagon with their father, her daddy started looking for them. Then he found them, and he dragged these two sons off the wagon, dragged them through the neighborhood where these houses were sitting behind the plantation house. And my grandfather said they were ready to move. Nobody could do nothing about it. He said he had a little money saved and they caught the train, SP train coming out of Wharton, Texas, going to Texas City. He said he got off four miles from Texas City with my mother. I wasn't born yet. And they walked four miles and didn't know where they were going. They didn't have a job. So there was a man named Mr. John Hunter, saw them walking and he picked them up. And he said that he was asking Mr. John Hunter, do they have any places that they could live?

He says, "Well, I own a lot of houses here." He says, "I'm a longshoreman. I can get you a job." And Papa (that's what I called my grandfather) explained everything to him. And Papa stayed in his house, one of these big houses. And that's when I was born.

That happened about 1902, 1903, because my mother was born maybe 1905. But the latter part, because my grandfather was born in 1875. He married my grandmother when she was twenty-five.

When I was growing up, my grandmother was a choir director at the Barber's Chapel Baptist Church. And she could sing bass up to soprano. Then when my mother died, my grandmother wanted—that was her daughter—she wanted to give me the best education that was possible. But at the time, nobody had too much money, though my grandfather made a little bit more money than the average person made. And my lessons were $5 dollars a lesson. But now when I was six years old, she took me to a teacher named Miss Jones to help get me into the music business. And so she'd sit there and watch, because she always would see to it that if I had some notes she missed, she could help me. Well, Miss Jones gave me the lesson. She hit my knuckles and hurt them, trying to play my fingers in the right keys. So when we left there, my grandmother said, "How did you like Miss Jones?"

I said, "Mama, I didn't like Miss Jones. Because she hurt my knuckles."

She said, "I'll tell you what. I'm not going to take you back there anymore." She says, "You know, I play, and I read notes, but I'll tell you what. You have to get a better teacher, but I'm not able to do it right now.

But I want to teach you all I know. But those long notes with those flags on them, I don't know what they are. You have to get a teacher."

So we went along with that. She taught up to when I was about eleven years old. And then, she was fascinated with a girl named Janice Felder, from Galveston, Texas. She went to Bishop College. She had won every contest between the colleges for the best classical pianist. So my grandmother said, "I know Janice Felder's playing out about twenty miles from here with the Reverend Cole at a Baptist church out on this highway." And so, she took me out there. And man, I'm telling you the truth, this Reverend Cole was a big, black preacher, and he had the sisters rollin', carrying them out on stretchers. And Janice was playing that, jazzing up those spirituals, just like the blues. And I was just listening.

And I said, "Mama, can a piano sound like that?"

She said, "Yes, it can, but you have to take lessons." And so, she said, "I'm going to ask Janice Felder can she teach you."

So we went up there, when it was over. And Janice Felder was very tall, a light-skinned native of Galveston. Her daddy was the janitor at this Central High School where everybody went. So she took me up there and she asked Janice, "My little boy's crazy about the way you play that piano. Do you have any time to teach any music?"

She says, "Well, I don't have much time because I'm getting ready to go back and get my master's degree at Bishop College." She said, "But this is the summer session. I'm home usually two months, you know, before we go back to school." Then she said, "Well, bring him over here to Galveston and let me see what I can do."

And so my grandmother took me over there and she had me play little things, "The Old Rugged Cross," "Amazing Grace," with those half notes and whole notes. And so Janice says, "I'll take him." And she looked at my hands. And I had these great big fingers, and she said, "Oh, yes, I'll teach him."

So my lesson began at $5, and two times a week. That was Tuesdays and Thursdays that I had to study after that. So then my grandmother wanted, you know, she loved Fats Waller. Her daughter had a little place called Hollywood, and she had the jukeboxes in there. And every time a new record would come out by the Ink Spots or Fats Waller, she would put it on the jukebox and they would dance by it. So my grandmother was fascinated with the piano playing of Fats Waller. She was talking about the stride piano playing. She says, "Now, I really would love for you to play like that." And so, my grandmother, after we went to the teacher, she went downtown, I think, to one of those music stores, and bought some of Fats Waller's music. There was "Honeysuckle Rose," "When My Dreamboat Comes Home," and "Lulu's Back in Town."

Then she asked the teacher, "Janice, can you teach my little boy how to play and solo these songs?"

She said, "Well, I can show him how to play a few things. But I don't want the people at the church to know that I'm interested in this sheet music of Fats Waller and stuff." She said, "Just keep that quiet if anybody asks you."

Grandmother said, "Janice, I'm not concerned about that. I'm concerned with teaching."

So that's when I started to play, before I went to high school.

My first exposure to blues was through my grandmother's one son named James Simpson. We called him Uncle Jet. Uncle Jet had his own little old record player back in the room. He would listen to Big Boy Crudup, Tampa Red, Bessie Smith, Leroy Carr, and many of the other people who at that time were very popular. And he said, "Plunt," he called me "Plunt." "Come on back here and let's listen to some of this good old music. Man, it's so good. This is what I really like, and maybe you'll like this."

So I'd go back there and listen. And I was fascinated with Bessie Smith singing, you know, because she was very popular then. "You better get it and bring it right here, if you don't get it," something like that, I'll swear. Oh, I loved Bessie Smith.

Then I told my grandmother, "Uncle Jet had me listen to some this good music, you know. The blues and everything."

She said, "If you listen to those blues, I'm going to get on him. I'm going to knock the *h-e-double ll* out of him. Listening to this music, and I'm trying to get you to another class of music. A classical class of music."

And so I was scared to go back there.

So when I went to college, we had a chance to listen to good music. And that was inspiring to me, because every time we'd go Friday evening, we had a seminar and a movie picture would show. Then they would play all these things by Tommy Dorsey. And I was crazy about Helen O'Connell with Jimmy Dorsey. And so I think a little of that wiped off on me because she sang this style. You know (sings), "Take me. I'm yours. You take. Please darling, awake me." You know, and so that kinda wiped off on me.

I said, "You know what? My grandmother said I can listen to this kind of music, but if I wanted to sing, I'd rather sing those type of songs." I was interested more in "Embraceable You."

In 1942, I finished Prairie View College. Now it's the Prairie View University. I majored in chemistry at Prairie View, mathematics minor. My training in the piano field was always good, and I could read flies on paper. But I didn't really know my talent was the piano. So I taught school because my grandmother thought that a white-collar job would be wonderful, to be a principal in the town where she was and could praise the son, the grandson that she reared. So later on, I began to reflect back and saw that I could really play this piano. And studying these books, and shoot, I said, "Well, I mean, I should have taken four years of piano." But I took advanced piano one semester. And I was way ahead of a lot of them, the musicians.

But my first job (after I finished Prairie View) was in Baytown, Texas, as head of the science department. Well, Mr. Archer, the principal, said, "I want you to compete in my school. Carver High School." Said, "I want you to be there because I just think the world of you. The kids will love you." And I was only nineteen, going on twenty. And I got the job the first year, in September of that year. And I stayed there till 1943.

In 1943, I found out that the government had put out bulletins about how they wanted junior chemists. But now when I was working as a schoolteacher, I wasn't getting but $90 a month. That means $45 every two weeks. And I thought a schoolteacher was making plenty of money and I could really help my grandfather through these things, to show him my appreciation. But I got to be a teacher. But when I worked down in Baytown, I hardly had $5 left over. I had to pay my room rent and board and then that was leaving me not anything but barely $5.

So I said, "Well, this is not going to work." I said, "I don't like this." So when the government sent out the bulletins for junior chemists, I answered one of them and passed the examination, and they said that I could go to the Pine Bluff Arsenal or the Maryland Arsenal. And when they told me that, I chose the Pine Bluff Arsenal, where they made mustard gas. All right, I got the job there, but I had to pass on through the majors and the second lieutenants and the first lieutenants. I don't know what they called it; audition, before you get the job. So I went to this place early in the morning, Pine Bluff, Arkansas, waiting for my time, for them to call me. It was so cold, and they had only two big potbellied steel stoves, one side was colored, one side was white. But on the colored side, there was no fire. And I sat there on the white side. So I sat there at seven o'clock in the morning till around eleven o'clock, and they never called me. And I walked back up to the gate.

I said, "I'm Charles Brown. I was supposed to have an interview with the lieutenants and the major for this job."

She said, "I'll tell you what. You'll be called if you get away from that white stove."

I said, "But I'm so cold." But then I sat over in the colored area. I obeyed her, and she called me, and then they had this little Jeep to come pick me up and take me over to this interviewing section.

And the major seemed to really like me, and he talked to me, asked me questions about, "What do you think about race relations?"

I said, "Well, I learned to appreciate a person not on the basis of race, but on what they have to contribute to civilization."

He said, "Well, where are you from?"

I said, "I'm from Texas."

He said, "Well, you're very different from the average Texas person."

And then he said, "Now, we have a lot of fellows working around those vat machines where the mustard gas come in, sulfur, and they may not have as much education as you have. What do you think about that, if you have to obey them?"

I said, "Well, I was taught military science in Prairie View, and I learned to obey my superior officer."

He said, "That's it. We're going to try you in Plant Number Two. But you're quite different from anyone else." And he said, "I'll tell you what. You have to be very careful not to get any mustard gas on you because we have inspection." He said that if you waste anything, those samples on the table, use carbon tetrachloride to really absolve it. And so he said, "Now when we do inspection, we don't want anything against you." He said, "against your technique." And so I did that.

But then I had a run-in with this second lieutenant; he wanted to give me some raggedy clothes, and I wanted the clothes that were nice up on the top shelf. So he would go under the counter to give me these clothes.

And I said, "Oh, I don't want that outfit. That's torn. I want the other one up on top."

He said, "I can't give you this, you better take what I give you." So this was an argument, so they called the major down. And the major came down and he bowed his head to the major and whatnot. And major asked what was going on between Charles Brown and him.

He said, "He wanted one of those uniforms up on this other shelf, and I have the uniforms for these colored folks down on this other shelf."

He said, "I'll tell you what. You give Charles Brown any one of those uniforms he wants on the top shelf."

And that's when he tried to fight me and that's when I really got disgusted, because I called Washington, D.C., and wrote a letter, too, that I wanted to be moved. And I said I wanted to come out to California, to the Western Research Laboratory in Berkeley, California. So they got an opening for me to come out here. But when I got out here, it was closed. They had put someone in my place. And then they classified me 1A. Then I got to thinking about the 1A. A friend of mine was going to UC (University of California) in Berkeley. I was staying up there with him until I registered for the fall session.

Dr. Lawrence Harrison, he's dead now, he said, "Well, you can stay with me."

But then I said, "Well, I can't go on being a 1A, because sometime they're going to call me."

I said, "I'd rather volunteer." So I called Mr. Rhodes, who was head of the inductions. I told him, "Mr. Rhodes, I'm Charles Brown."

He said, "I know you. You're the only one from Texas City that went to school up in Prairie View. I know you. Know all your people."

I said, "Well, I don't think I'll be good on the front lines. I think I'd be good behind the lines doing service work and in the chemistry department."

He said, "Well, you just go on and see what you can do, and when the time comes, we'll call you."

That didn't satisfy me. I really wanted to volunteer. I said, "I'm gonna volunteer."

So they sent me to the induction center down in Houston, Texas. I had to take off all my clothes and pass through all these doctors and what-not. Well, a lot of guys were there ahead of me.

One guy said, "Can you read this?"

He said, "No, I can't read that. I can't read." Said, "Mr. Brown, can you read this?" I read it. Those guys followed the line into the service. So when we got to the heart specialist, he felt my heart and put the things up to his ear and he said, "Have you ever had heart troubles?"

I said, "I've had asthma in my younger days."

He said, "Well, I tell you what. Uncle Sam wants assets, not liabilities." He said, "I'm gonna put this on your chart. DISQ."

And I said, "What does that mean?"

And one guy back there answered, "Man, you're disqualified. You don't have to go in the service no more."

So he told me to follow this line out the door. And one sergeant was out there. He said, "Do you want the government to pay for your return to your household, Texas City?"

I said, "No, I got the money for myself." And that's when I went to Texas City by the Texas bus line. But my aunts and all the people, before I left there, they were crying. "That boy, he ain't never coming back." But then they didn't know that if I didn't pass, I would be back. So they watched every bus that stopped there. And so when I got off this bus, they were looking out of the doors, my aunts and all of them, hollering and scream-ing: "There's that boy. Lord have mercy." Oh, you know. And then they had this big affair for me, that dinner, that night.

Then I said, "Papa, I'm going back to California." I said, "Because I'm going to go back, and I'm going to make some records." Now, I had never thought about making any records. I just said that. And when I went back, I was looking for a job as a pianist in some hotel, just playing the piano. I had had my formal training, I had studied Art Tatum books, I had studied Count Basie books, that style, Eddie Duchin, Claude Thornhill, all them great piano players, and their style kind of wiped off on me. But I didn't play like them, but it gave me some poise about playing the piano. And I went back to California, looking for a good job.

One guy said, "Well, you can play, because you got the experience."

I had played with the Prairie View Collegians the three years that I was there, at Prairie View. And when I went to Central High School, Mr. James had me play on the beach because I could read well. So, all of this gave me a foundation into the music world, playing any kind of music: I could play Count Basie and the plinking little solos that he did. Plink, plink, with the bass, plink, plink. So all of that wiped off on me. Then another fellow named B. H. Grimes, who was about to graduate from Prairie View, showed me how to solo. And when he showed me how to solo, I was very alert about taking in the things that I was interested in. And so that helped me. And when I went out to California, it's a long story, but I got a job at the Broadway Department Store as elevator operator. Then I won the amateur contest at the Lincoln Theater in 1943. And then Ivy Anderson's husband, who used to sing with Duke Ellington, asked me to play in his Chickenshack band. Chickenshack, with wines and beers and steaks served. So, then I met some of the great artists that came there. Bobby Short was one. He was a young Bobby Short. Then Billy Taylor came. Ethel Waters came. Hattie McDaniel came. The young Dorothy Donegan and her mother came. Lionel Hampton and Gladys Hampton came to eat there. Man Tan Moreland, the comedian with Ben Carter.

Ben Carter was one of the fellows who was the in-between between the Negro talent and going to Hollywood. And they would contact him for whatever they wanted. And so I was in between there. I had been living in Watts. The government passed a law that they pay taxes, and they said you have to pay taxes on your money. They have to take it out of your money. And I said, "Well, Mr. Neely, if you take out the money, can I make the same amount of money and raise my salary?"

He said, "No, I'll have to talk to my wife, Ivy, she works out in Hollywood at the Circle Bar." And she'd bring in a lot of the white people to eat steaks from where she were. A lot of the white people come down on the Avenue after hours, you know. And so when I talked to her, she said, "Oh, when I come back from Mexico, maybe you'll get a raise."

I said, "Miss Anderson, when you come back from Mexico, I won't be here." So I gave my little job to a girl named Richidell Archie. She's living today. Her daddy was the principal at the school that I taught in, and so she wanted a job. She was going to USC, studying piano, master's degree. So when I decided I could move out to Sugar Hill, where all these black movie stars were, I said, "I want to get into the know of this business, and maybe somebody might see me."

Reginald Bean was playing for Ethel Waters, and he was her pianist. So I contacted him and he says, "Well, if I see an opening, I'll get it for you." So Ethel Waters, I was just crazy about her. And I went to Sugar Hill. Then that's when Johnny Moore came looking for me, The Three Blazers, he was head of The Three Blazers. Oscar Moore, with King Cole, was his brother. The King Cole Trio was really popular because they were on Excelsior Records, Otis Rene's record company. Leon Rene was the brother. He had Exclusive Records. But Nat Cole showed them when the big band era was going out, a trio could do just as much as a big band. And so everybody resorted to trios. But when we made our first audition at the Talk of the Town, for $600, The Three Blazers won. Nat Cole was playing over on Eighth Street at a club called 333 or Three Thirty Something. But we were making more than him. We made $600. Nat and them was working for only $300. And so we were into the circle of movie stars. Sontag Drugstore, all these people from Mexico would come. Lena Romay, Xavier Cugat, we had Martha Raye come in. And she wanted me to play for her parties out in Coldwater Canyon. And I did that for $300. She had just married one of the Condos brothers. So I tried to be in the upgraded sections of Hollywood. I didn't work on Central Avenue. John didn't want to work down there either because he said that most of the promoters run away with your money and you can't find them.

So Carlos Gastell, after he got the King Cole Trio and signed them up, he took them to Johnny Mercer. But the one that set the pace for Capitol Records was Nellie Lutcher. Nellie Lutcher and Julia Lee were the only black people that were on Capitol Records. So when Carlos Gastell talked to us, he said, "You are two top trios." He said, "But now, I can't do justice to both of you." Say, "I want Nat Cole to do this with me and get paid."

And Johnny Moore said, "Okay," said, "Well, that's it."

So we all were good friends, and then Johnny Moore wanted to go down south and do one-nighters. But King Cole didn't do one-nighters. So then we were made with the black public. We put out "Driftin' Blues." And that was one of the greatest records of its time. And because "St. Louis Blues" had been warranted as one of the great records, blues records. But we took Louis Jordan out of first place at the *Billboard*.

But getting around to all of this is just to tell you from the horse's mouth, and if you really want to know more about me, there are going to be books about me that you can read.

I knew T-Bone Walker. We played together at some places, Dayton, Ohio, right there. Then I used to go see him quite often when he played the Harlem Club in Watts, California. And so, we all got tougher because most of the good people, I think, from Texas and Louisiana, went to California. Then the Mississippi people, Georgia and Alabama, they went to Chicago. So they set up their own way of doing their music. They were running, they weren't the twelve-bar blues, they'd run sixteen bars. So they didn't care. But we had to be meticulous about Hollywood because people were not used to blues. So we had to take those standard numbers and do a little to make it presentable for the people to listen. So we all came up in that era, so when I talk about anything from Texas, at the time, 1943, or 1944, I know about it.

When I was with Johnny Moore, we recorded "Driftin' Blues" and that was the first big hit. I'll tell you when I wrote "Driftin' Blues," my Uncle Johnny, who was my grandmother's brother, he weighed about 375 pounds. We used to call him "One cock-eye." For he would come to Texas City and play for the little rent parties and out on the highway at this club, and he and my grandmother on a Friday night sometimes, they'd go to choir rehearsal and they'd think we were in the bed. And we'd slip and go to hear Uncle Johnny play. And we were peeping through these cracks and we would hear this lilting melody (sings, no words), you know. Then I started putting words to it. Then my cousin, she's dead now, started putting the real words to it. And that's when I fixed "Driftin' Blues." We recorded that for Philo Records. Then they changed the name (of the label) after "Driftin' Blues."

Whenever I learned to play, I said, "Well, I want to select what I want to do." And so there was not anything about blues. We studied a higher class then. Well, blues is okay, but I wasn't into that. I didn't really know what to do or whether I was going to be a blues pianist, blues singer, whatnot. It's just a period of time, came to be in there. And I was there to do it.

T-Bone Walker was kind of like that, too. He was a little more so-phisticated, too, then. He didn't play the lowdown blues because he couldn't play it out in California. He played a good blues. Johnny Moore taught him how to make the more complex chords on the guitar. That's the trio I was with.

Well, I've been around a long time. I've heard a lot and I've seen a lot, too. The things about it that make me want to go on: What else can I do? I was a schoolteacher; it didn't work. I found out that music works. But we've had ups and downs in it. I was blackballed from the union because I wanted to go home to my grandfather, who was sick, and these agencies had deposits up there. And they didn't want me to go home and lose the deposit. So they sued me for $40,000, and I became a scab musician.

But anyway, music's the only thing I know now that I could do for so long. Duke Ellington, Count Basie, he played in a wheelchair till he died. So when you're on the battlefield, that's what you know. I couldn't sit home in a rocking chair and say, "Oh, I'm just going to sit here." I mean, I'm retired, I couldn't do that. But now there are things that come up like operations on my legs. And you know, it discourages you sometimes that you can't get around, look like it's a mile apart. But you can play. I say, "I don't play with my feet. I play with my hands and my mind. It's still active."

Well, I'll tell you what motivates me. Now, my grandfather used to travel with me everywhere I went. He brought a little counter, clock, where the promoters would say, "Well, we had 500 people." They would have 700, and they would cheat me out of my money. But he used to sit on the side of the stage with his cigar and I'd play these different songs. And he would say to me, my nickname, he'd say, "Plunt, what is that song you playing?" He'd say, "That sure sounds good." And I can see him right now, the image, to be sitting there, playing to him. I wouldn't be looking at all the audience. I'd be thinking about Papa. Then everything would come down for me.

Oh, I still travel, seventy-four years old, seventy-five now, and I got more work than I can really do. But I have my guitarist, he takes care of all the business. He finds out all the places we're going to play. And I'm just, I don't feel that I want to know too much about it. He just tells me about it and I'm ready to go if it's right. And actually, I don't feel nothing, I'm inspired to do what people like me to do. And this young generation right now seems to be, some of them, seem to say, "Well, Charles, we can feel the love in your music." And when you hear that, that's some of your flowers while you're living. Yeah, that's the biggest flower. That somebody's gathering what you are about.

INTERVIEW BY ALAN GOVENAR, OCTOBER 6, 1998

Anna Mae Conley

Nanny and domestic worker
Born: March 16, 1919, Dallas, Texas

Anna Mae Conley has lived her entire life in Dallas, Texas. In this oral history, Conley traces the migratory patterns of her family, beginning with her grandmother, Jeano Evelina Fisher Beverly, who was a slave in Bunkie, Louisiana, and moved to Dallas after emancipation. She talks candidly about her life with her parents in Dallas, the conditions of racism and segregation, her schooling and interactions with African American folklorist J. Mason Brewer, her brief meetings with George Washington Carver and President Franklin Delano Roosevelt at the Texas Centennial celebration in 1936, her work as a domestic and nanny, and her decision to stay in Dallas and not move to California like some members of her family. Conley's narrative introduces the oral histories collected from her first cousin, Katie Simms, who did relocate to California, and her nephew Charles Simms (Katie's son), who discusses the difficulties of growing up in Oakland during the civil rights era. Separate narratives for Charles Simms and for Katie Simms appear on pages 407 and 415, respectively.

My mother came from Bunkie, Louisiana. Her name was Ophelia Beverly. "Beverly" means beautiful or pretty. That was her family name. She was Ophelia Beverly Conley when she married. My father was from Fort Worth. His name was Will Conley. Actually, William, but even his business papers identified him as Will.

Well, Bunkie was a very small place, and my mother was reared there. Her mother had fourteen children and all of them were leaving. Some went to California, and some went to Oklahoma. No one stayed there. When she left, my grandmother was there with two of her sons, so she moved to Dallas along with one of her sisters, who was living here in Dallas. And she found a job and she met my father. And after a pretty long courtship, they married. Now, she married in 1911 or 1912, somewhere along in there.

My grandmother's maiden name was Jeano Evelina Fisher Beverly. Well, she really didn't know how to spell it. See, it was French. And the girl's name was Jeanette. This happened during slavery. My grandmother was born a slave. And the little white girl was named Jeanette. And they wanted my grandmother's name to be close to hers, so they called her Jeano. But Jeano is a masculine name. So they didn't put the "t" on it.

My grandmother remembered a whole lot about slavery. Fisher was the slave owner's name. She said that they were owned by some masters who were very kind and generous. But she saw people beaten to death

Anna Mae Conley,
ca. 1940s (courtesy
Anna Mae Conley)

when she was in the field. And her master would say, well, even if he hated the person, if the person had done something very bad, that he was throwing away money when he killed his slave, and that he should have sold him.

But the master educated my grandmother, and her brother. They were educated right along with the white children of the house. They had a tutor that would come in, and all of them were tutored.

My grandmother said that one day, this old man came up, and he was talking to one of his daughters. And he said he didn't even have time to have children. He just died. Such a waste of a life. Something like that. And she says, "Well, yes, he has two children." And that was my grandmother and her brother. Now, I get tangled up on the names. All of them had names that were kind of intertwined. One was Alger Fisher, and one was Willie Fisher. They weren't brothers, but they were all kin, and I didn't know those people. They were dead. She just said "my brother" when she referred to him.

But she did know her mother. Her mother was named Julia Mantee, and Julia Mantee's mother was a white woman. Her father went around; he had a great big buggy, a wagon or whatever, and he sold things. And he was traveling. It was in the wintertime. And this lady was pregnant. And she had the baby, but she died. And the man had the baby there with him, but he could not take care of the baby. So he stopped at one of the plantations and went to the door and explained the situation, that he was a long way from home. It was cold. He did not know how to take care of the baby. And he wasn't asking for the baby to be brought into the house, but would they please let one of the slaves raise the little baby? And so they did. They took the baby. And the baby was raised up back in the slave quarters. And when she was of age where she could marry, well, they let her marry a slave. And from that came Julia Mantee. This was highly unusual. Most of the slaves who had white parents, the fathers were white and the mothers were black. But in Julia Mantee's situation, her mother was white and her father was black.

The slave owners were French. Now, I don't know how French they were. But I know that their background was French. Most of Louisiana was like that way back then. I know that the slave owner was a pretty well-to-do person because he owned this plantation and he had a lot of people working for him. And he seems to have had a good many slaves.

My grandmother told me stories about what happened at other plantations, but she did know about people being beaten to death in the fields, about teenage girls having babies they didn't want and trying to kill themselves and trying to kill the babies. Now, I don't know how often that happened. But she told me a lot about things that happened right after slavery. Things were hard for them because the people who owned the slaves had suffered a lot. They'd lost a lot. And they didn't really have the money to hire the slaves and pay them wages. They'd been getting all that for free. And even if they wanted to keep the slaves and let them stay there, the slaves would not be paid, and that was against the law. It was all tangled up like that. So people had to leave and go other places, and a lot of them went to places like Arizona and Oklahoma. That was just the situation that they found themselves in after slavery was over because they really didn't know how to conduct business and things like that. But they did come across people being very cruel to them, working them and not paying them and accusing them of things that they didn't do.

Now, my grandmother and her people didn't suffer because they were given land and they lived on this land, and I assume that some of that land still belongs to the ones who stayed, on my grandmother's brother's side. I think that maybe some of those people still live on that land. But it was just a typical situation with things that were bad that you heard about

Anna Mae Conley, ca. 1940s (courtesy Anna Mae Conley)

slavery. But the worst one was separation of families. If they were angry with you, they usually sold you and separated the family. They'd take part of the family and keep it, and you would be sent far away where you wouldn't know about how your family was doing and they wouldn't know where you were. And I think that was almost the worst thing that could happen to a person because after slavery, they still didn't know where the rest of their family was.

My mother mostly stayed home and took care of her children. I know where she applied for jobs. Well, she did say that she and another lady went to apply for a job, and she got it but she wasn't applying. That was at Weyland's Funeral Home. Now, that would have been before she married.

When my father was real young, he was living in Fort Worth and he lived near downtown. He worked at a bar that sold food, and he cooked. He would also deliver the food. And in that day and time, my father was delivering some food, and a policeman jerked him and made him drop the tray.

The policeman said, "You're the one we're looking for. You're the one we're looking for." It had to do with a white woman, but I don't think that he did anything but say something to the woman. Which was a death penalty in itself. But another policeman ran up and said, "No, he didn't. We have the man. The man has confessed. And the lady says it's the man."

But the policeman with my father said, "No, he's the one who did it." And he started beating my father. And my father started fighting back, and the other man (whom they had detained) pulled out his gun and shot the policeman. And all the people around there in the downtown section took up money and gave it to my father and put him on a train, said, "Don't you come back here because we know what happened. But we would be hurting ourselves if we got up in court and said it because we can't testify for you. So don't ever come back."

So my father went to Chicago and he was living with his grandmother, and his grandmother was blind. Her name was Anna Mae Conley, too. And he would send money back, but he couldn't send money to her. So he sent the money next door. And he did not know whether or not the people were giving my great-grandmother the money or how she was doing because they didn't write and say. It worried him, so he came back home. And they had just buried her the day before. They had told him, "Don't stay in Fort Worth."

So, he came to Dallas, and he married another lady, a very nice lady. And they had two children, but finally they divorced and he met my mother and married her. Before they married they lived in the same neighborhood. And all the people in those days in black neighborhoods, everyone knew each other and they called each other "Aunt" or "Uncle." And my grandmother lived with a lady named Aunt Mattie. And that's where her sister was living. And I think my father was living with Aunt Mattie's sister, Aunt Mitt. And they met, and they married.

I think it was on Paris Street, right off of Pearl Street, between Pearl and Preston. That was in South Dallas. I guess the market would be part of that now. I haven't been there in years.

I went to J. P. Starks School right here in Dallas. And one of the first things that I noticed was, we didn't ever have new books. They were always written in. And there was no place where it said "property of." All of that page was filled out. And the books came from the City Park School, which I had to pretty much pass going to my school, only I didn't go that way because the children would tease you. And sometimes they would chase you and you were afraid you'd have to fight. And they would have to have policemen or truant officers come and help those kids to cross Park Avenue and those streets so that there wouldn't be any friction, because both of the schools turned out at the same time. A little later, they fixed it so that the children wouldn't get out at the same time.

Most of what I remember about segregation is we only went to the seventh grade, the high seventh. And then we went to high school, and that was the ninth grade. We skipped a grade, going to school. Now, we have no idea what it was we missed in the eighth grade. We had four years of high school. But teachers, all of the teachers, knew what the situation was, and I imagine that most of them came up in a situation even worse.

Now, I have a friend who stopped in the sixth grade. In these little one-room schoolhouses, like they had in West Dallas, which wasn't very well populated, the teacher taught all the grades. She only went to the sixth grade. When they finished the sixth grade, they came over to our school and went to school. And they didn't have streetcars and buses out in West Dallas in those days, so they would have people who had cars, big cars, and they would take them to school and back for a nickel. But you had to meet them down at the train station. All the kids would walk from my school to the train station to get this car. It wasn't a bus, it was a car (called a jitney), and he'd take them over to West Dallas.

My friend, when she finished in the sixth grade in West Dallas, they thought that she could do well enough to go on to high school, and

Dallas, Texas
ca. late 1930s
(Library of Congress)

she did. And she ended up being an English major in college, and she taught for many years until she retired. But she only went to the sixth grade in elementary school.

When I was in school, I wanted to be a writer, and I wanted to be a nurse. And I took Latin from grades one through eight in high school because they said Latin would help. They also said that Latin would help you with your words and sentence construction and things like that. And I liked Latin, but it was hard. You had to remember the words and things, how to not just translate, but be able use the right verb with the right noun and the things that modified the noun and the verb.

Well, when I was growing up, we heard about the Klan. We heard that people would disappear. If a black man stood up for his rights, he might think he had won, but they'd come and get him at night.

And my father worked downtown. He knew all of the policemen, and all of them seemed to like him. My father had a very nice personality. He joked and he just had a good sense of humor. So almost everybody liked him, including the policemen.

I know once when I was working out at the Texas Centennial in '36, the streetcars would line up downtown at twelve o'clock and everybody would have a chance to go and catch their last streetcar coming home. And I didn't want to be sitting on the streetcar waiting that long. I was afraid. So I would come, I'd get off on Elm, Commerce, or Main, depending on which streetcar I rode from the Fair Park, and I would just run on down St. Paul until I got home. And it was much quicker. It would be a long time after I got home before you'd hear the Ervay streetcar coming down Ervay Street. So one night the police, they said they were police, I don't know whether they were or not, they said, "Hey, girl, where you going? Come over here." And I looked at that car, and all I was doing was coming down the street real fast. And I knew they didn't have any business stopping me. So the Dallas Power and Light Company had a parking lot where they parked their cars during the night. And I ran through that parking lot and hid in there. It was just right across the street from me, in the same block. I knew how to get out of it. But I ran home and I hit that door and Daddy opened it: "What's wrong, Mae?" So I told him.

He said, "Well, Mae, I told you to get on the streetcar and stay on there, that nothing would happen to you. Do you want me to come and walk you home?"

And I got to thinking, well, if they stopped me, they'd stop him.

I said, "No, Daddy, I don't want you to do that."

And so he said, "Well, I'll take care of it tomorrow." And he told me when he got home, he said, "Well, no one's going to stop you; you can come down Ervay or St. Paul." So he took care of it. All the policemen knew us. And they knew that we had a very good reputation—matter of fact, almost everyone in our neighborhood was a pretty nice person.

I had heard about cross burnings. I just heard about them. But I do know that there was a man who was hung from the Cotton Exchange. And the reason it happened was now this happened between black people. A woman asked a man who worked at the Cotton Exchange to loan her either a quarter or fifty cents. And he said he didn't have it. And she argued with him about it. And he still said he didn't have it. So she went and told some white people that he had said something out of the way to a white woman. And they took that man and they hung him there from on the top of the Cotton Exchange. And then later in the day, they were telling the woman that they had taken care of what had happened, and she didn't know a thing about it. I don't know when this happened, it was evidently before I was born, or a little bit after I was born. I was born in 1919.

At the Texas Centennial, I was an usher. I worked at the Hall of Negro Life. It was a very nice building, and they sent for a man from Pennsylvania to come and be over it. Now I applied for a job, I went downtown and applied for a job where I thought I could get one. But I didn't realize that they were going to give me such a nice job. At the Centennial, in the Hall of Negro Life, I explained the Tuskegee exhibit. There was a man who was a sculptor, and he sculpted a bust of himself. He just looked in the mirror and did it, and it looked just like him. And when we were out at one of the churches where my husband pastored, we met that man, and he remembered me. That was in 1948 when we went there. And it had been '36 when I was working at the Centennial when Texas was 100 years old. And we had all kinds of exhibits. We had these exhibits that George Washington Carver had made; from the sweet potato he made a lot of products and the peanut. And one day while I was there, explaining the exhibit, this man just kept asking me questions and things, and so he said, "Well, you did very well."

I said, "Well, thank you."

"I'm George Washington Carver." And I was just very happy to meet him. I also met President Roosevelt and John Connally, all of the people who were in politics here in Texas. And I met senators and representatives from all the states because they all came and they all came to our building. And right after the Centennial was over with, they tore down our building.

When I went to Booker T. Washington, I went in the evening first, from twelve twenty to five o'clock in the afternoon. We had a half day; we had two half-day sessions because we only had the one high school and there were too many students to put them in there all at one time. J. Mason Brewer was at Booker T. Washington then. He wasn't my teacher. He taught Spanish, so he never would have been my teacher because I took Latin. He was over the Quill Club. That was a writing club that I belonged to.

Mr. Brewer was very friendly. He was kind of comical at times. And he had been injured in the war, and at times he would have to pull at his collar. Seemed like he was trying to let air through so that he could speak. He had a lot of Hispanic friends, and once a year, to raise money for our Quill Club, he would have a Spanish band come to the school for the assembly, and we'd pay to get in. It was five cents, but that helped us to publish our books.

I read his books. They had them in the library. I know he had written some books on poetry. Most of them were in dialect.

I was in that Quill Club from the time I started in school until I finished. But I also worked on the school newspaper. I took journalism. Everything that I thought would help me. I was interested in writing poems because my grandmother would just set you on fire with all kinds of things. She was a schoolteacher. And she would just tell you all kinds of things—they weren't really bad things. I would not have written anything different from what I write right now. But Mr. Brewer and others told me that I could not publish those poems because they would incite people and that they would probably ride us out of town on a rail and they would tar and feather us first. And I told that to my father, and my father was just very, very tickled about it because he had almost been put out of town on a rail.

And I said, "Well, what must I do?"

He says, "You do what you want to do."

But I just wrote other things that were not as interesting to me. And some of them disappeared. My sister took some of them to California. When I married, I had to leave a lot of things at home. And when we got a house that was big enough, they had disposed of everything that I had. But I think my friend Lucille finally found one of the books. They were just little booklets, poem booklets. Much like what they publish now with poems in them.

In our family, we weren't allowed to call anybody black. But they could call me yellow. I'm talking about in my family. I had a sister who was very contentious. Oh, I was lighter than the rest of them in my family, my brother and I were. And they'd call me "yellow dog" and "yellow cow." See, my father was black. So there were degrees, from black to as light as I am or my brother was. So you didn't talk about people's color in our family.

But my grandmother looked like a white woman. And my grandmother was forever calling somebody black. In Louisiana, people were very conscious of color. And people who were very black didn't make it that well. I don't care how sweet and kind and gentle they were, how industrious, how educated. They didn't stand much of a chance if there were people who were lighter. And they could be telling a lie, and the people who were dark were telling the truth. You'd still believe that— they were just more preferred, lighter people. So that was a problem then, and I guess it's a problem even now.

I wanted to go to Denver and live. I thought that would be a real nice place, a scenic place. And I had thought of going to California because most of our people that went anyplace either went there or to Oklahoma. But I had an opportunity to go to Denver and I was in the train station. It was during the war, just about two days before the war was over. And I had to make a reservation. You couldn't just go and get a ticket and get on the train. And I saw a chair and I sat in it. There were two white people on either side of this chair. And I sat in it, and they got up. And see, that hadn't ever happened to me in Dallas. I knew right away because I knew some of the things that happened during segregation. So, when it was time for me to stand in line, I could tell that some of the people didn't want to be next to me. Now, that was Denver, the place where I thought there was no segregation.

I finally made it to Denver, but I didn't stay but about a week. I went to help my sister. My sister's husband passed. She had been married one month. She married on the Fourth of July, and her husband died on the fourth of August, and I think it was the sixth when the war ended [when they bombed Hiroshima].

In the forties I remember Joe Louis. And he was fighting Schmeling, and we were out at Fair Park. And from place to place, where we would go, we could hear the radio because everyone had that radio on, and they wanted a white savior. And he was beating Joe Louis. And you could tell that all the white people were just elated. And the black people were walking around with their heads down. Joe Louis lost. But we just thought Joe Louis was the strongest man on earth. But we knew that he didn't have a good education, and he didn't know how to handle his money.

Well, my brother-in-law fought in the Japanese arena and he got jungle rot there in the jungles. But he didn't have enough of it, because he reenlisted twice after the war was over with. He went to Alaska. And he liked Alaska, and he was trying to settle there, and he wanted to open up a place of business there.

A lot of my family went out to California. They wanted to make more money, and they did pay more in California. And then you could sit where you wanted to on the bus, and you didn't have to drink "colored water." And if you were downtown here in Dallas, they had a rest room, but if you were not near it, you could be caught in a terrible push. We lived near the downtown; we practically lived in downtown. And people we didn't even know knew that we lived there, and they would use the rest room. But now the rest room was outside so they would just ask if they could use it, and they could. But we had problems like that in Dallas, and then they knew that the housing situation was better in California. And the children would get better educations in California. So they went.

Katie Simms's mother passed when she was about five years old. And her father, well, her father and her mother had been married about a year when she was born. Aunt Minnie was Katie's mother. Her mother was a schoolteacher. But she was sick; she had heart trouble. Aunt Minnie's first husband passed. He had this flu that took so many lives. So when Katie was born, right after, her mother took down sick again. Well, she had married Katie's father. And he had a farm, and they had a lot of work to do. Katie's mother had two daughters and five boys. And when Katie was real young like that, her mother passed, too. And my aunt here went and got Katie and the family and brought them to Texas. And they divided the children up, and for a while, three of the boys stayed with us, and Katie and one of the boys went with my grandmother and my aunt. The older daughter went to live in Beaumont with one of my aunts because there were too many for this man that my Aunt Minnie married.

Katie's father was very, very poor. And sometimes he didn't even have two cents to send a postcard. And when Katie started to school, they wrote and asked him to send fifty cents so they could buy some cloth to make her a dress. And he didn't have that. And he told them he had to borrow the money to send the postcard. My grandmother and my aunt were very angry about that because they lived up here in Dallas. It was easier to make money in Dallas than it was in Boyington, Oklahoma.

They said, "Well now, she's going to start to school and we're not even going to let her wear his name. She'll be Lawson just like the rest of them."

My grandmother finally moved two doors from us, and I stayed over at my grandmother's most of the time during the day. My mother was real glad to get rid of me because I talked all the time.

Katie and I lived close to each other, and it just bothered me that they were pulling up and going to California because I didn't know whether they could make it there. But everyone else did, and things like that just went through my mind. Ultimately though, I think they were better off for moving. The children had better opportunities for an education. But then the schools were somewhat segregated out there, too, because your schools were in your neighborhood. They lived in a black neighborhood. Well, I was married before Katie left, and Katie was married. She had three children when they left. And I promised my mother before she passed that I would stay with the children until they were big enough to look after themselves. She did not want them separated. She wanted them all raised together so they would love one another, and, if they needed help, one could help the other. And she said my father would tell me when I could get married. And I married when I was twenty-four; I was fourteen when our mother passed. And it was almost ten years to the day because I married December the fourth, 1943, and she had passed December the first, 1933.

Anyway, I stayed married twenty-one years and seven months, and I've forgotten how many days. It worked out fine for a while, but we had to split up. I liked the work of being married to a minister; I enjoyed the minister's work. It was just fine. I liked reading the Bible. I had already taught Sunday school. I enjoyed working with young people. And I worked with the young people's missionary department when I was a young person. So when I was grown, they put me over that at the church where I was. And I was the first person who was over it. And I felt so proud. The little children would come to my home sometimes and I would teach them. And sometimes we'd meet at church. And they seemed so interested in mission work and people in the Bible who did mission work. And I joined the regular Missionary Society, and I enjoyed working with the Missionary Society, and I do to this day. That's the Smith Chapel AME Church. I've been there thirty-one years, and I've been on that missionary board ever since I've been there.

Well, the church has always been a place of refuge. We always felt that God was our only hope and our only help and if we got help, we'd get help from our church or from white people who were Christians. And that pretty much was the way that it was. In these later years, like during the war, and during the freedom rallies, they would meet at the churches. The NAACP would have meetings there, and other freedom groups. And so often, after a meeting, maybe three or four weeks later, that church would be burned down. Just like they're burning down churches now. So it wasn't a new thing. When it started again, the church where I was raised, Bethel AME Church on Leonard and Cochran, was burned down. Good Street Baptist Church on Good-Latimer was burned down. And even white churches were burned if the pastor got up and said something that indicated that they were for people being treated as they should be, that you treat all people alike. Black people knew that our churches were being burned down because some of the freedom people came and spoke at our church.

I worked at Parkland Hospital for close to four years. And then I switched over to Baylor, but I didn't stay there hardly a year. I gathered up the laundry; I was a housekeeper. And I had to answer the phone and take messages, and then I would help them fix the dinner at night.

I had one job that wasn't really like a home. There were six girls. Only two of them were related. But they had this large apartment and they needed someone who could pay bills and who could do the shopping.

And they told me when I started working for them, they said, "You don't have to make beds, and you don't have to do washing. All you have to do is help us with the cooking in the evening, take our messages, and see that everything looks neat because of our boy-friends"—all of them were single.

This was during the war. And sometimes their parents would come up. And they would also come and ask me what the girls were doing and thank me for looking after them. Now we were all about the same age. But I remember at Thanksgiving time, they were going to invite some people who were officers. And they wanted to know what a jigger was. Well, I didn't know what a jigger was either. So I asked my father.

And so he says, "Well, these are young ladies around your age?"

I said, "Yes, they are."

He said, "You tell them if those men want to drink, let them bring it with them. Don't let those girls sit up there and get those men drunk. They wouldn't be able to handle that."

So, I went back and I told them. And every one of them, when their parents came up, they thanked me for telling them. Because they were like eighteen and nineteen and twenty. You know they wouldn't have been able to handle that. But I wouldn't have known it because I'd never served any liquor to anybody either. But they always felt that I knew more about things than they did. And I guess I did, in a way. All of them were from small towns like Mineola, Groesbeck, and Cooper, small places in Texas.

Well, black women worked as nannies and domestics because that was the only job they could get. I guess the "American Dream" means about the same thing to blacks as it means to others, opportunities to get a home and to have a little nest egg in the bank. To be able to take vaca-tions and go places. If something good comes up, you want an opportu-nity at it, to be able to improve yourself educationally, or have a nice place of worship. Be able to go and see nice shows, or maybe the opera, or the symphony if you want to, or to even buy a burial plot where you want it. I think that the American Dream is just having the same opportunities for happiness that everyone else has. And to be able to have friends and not feel that you are imposing on people when you meet people. To be able to stop and talk with people.

When I was growing up I lived in a nice neighborhood, and school was about five blocks from my house. And some of those kids would come down and play baseball with us. But then there were others who didn't, you know, who would fight. But the city park was there. And there was segregation in that park. It wasn't even segregation. They didn't allow us in it. The park, the one park we had, was in North Dallas, and there was no way my mother could take us to North Dallas, to the park.

I believe in God. I know that he is the one who takes care of me. And I feel that he's with me, so I trust him. And he has done many, many things for me that I just hoped would happen. And I'd even be afraid to ask because it would look like I was asking for too much. But he would give them to me just the same.

I think the world is a better place today, but it's also a worse place. They have so many means of doing things that are not good, they have so many means of doing things that are very good. And so it kind of balances out. And there are so many people who are so nice, and kind, and thoughtful, and compassionate. But there are equally as many people that you don't even know are not good and kind, people that you don't really expect anything from. But if they can do something to hurt you, they will. And so it's just that way. You never know when you're meeting somebody like that.

INTERVIEW BY KALETA DOOLIN, AUGUST 30, 1997

Madge E. Copeland

Beauty shop operator
Born: March 31, 1895, Minden, Louisiana

Madge Copeland grew up in Minden, Louisiana. She attended segregated schools and aspired to be a piano accompanist, but had limited opportunities to perform outside of her church because of the social prejudice leveled against African Americans. She married shortly after her graduation from high school and had two children. In 1919, she separated from her husband and moved to Phoenix, Arizona. Although the living conditions for African Americans were restricted, she was enthusiastic about the promise of migration into the West. At first, she had difficulty finding work, but was able to establish herself as a hairdresser and became active as a missionary in the African Methodist Episcopal Church and as a volunteer for the Democratic Party. Copeland was eighty-six years old when she was interviewed by Maria Hernandez for the Department of Archives and Manuscripts at Arizona State University.

My family life was very good. My grandmother raised me mostly because my mother taught school in the rural district. That was my father's mother. Her name was Sara Johnson. She taught me how to cook and how to clean and she taught me many things about life, about being honest and always walk straight with my head up, my shoulders back, and be proud. So, we had a lot of fun together and I loved her very much.

My father's name was David Johnson. He was a compress man and a musician. A compress man is one that works at a compress mill where the bales of cotton were pressed. They are very large when they are sent to the mill, when they come in from the gin, but when they send them over to the plant where they compress them, they are made smaller for shipment. He (my father) was the compress man that made these bales of cotton smaller for shipment. And as a musician he played for dances on certain nights, especially weekends. And he was also a cook, camp cook. He worked two years with the Geodetic Society going from Florida all the way up the coast to New York. They surveyed that coast for some reason. He was the cook all the way.

When I was growing up, Minden was very small. Not over 6,000. They had a big, good school system. Very good teachers, and we learned so much from those teachers that were very interested in the children. And we were taught how to sing, how to act in numerous plays at the school, and I was given music lessons. And I would play for a lot of programs they had after I was advanced in music.

Well, in those days they did not have one class to a teacher. They had children—well, in grammar school, my mother would just teach the school. Different classes would be taught at different times during the day. She taught five days a week and she went into the rural district by horse and buggy. So, she wasn't there a lot. My grandmother reared me.

I'm eleven years older than my brother, and I would have to take care of him. But he was really in my way because I was playing play house where we cooked pies. And I didn't want to take care of him but I had to.

I would have to take care of him and it was time for me to cook mud pies. And then we made play houses because Louisiana was just full of all kinds of trees, especially pine trees, and they had the straw that fell from the pine trees. We fashioned all of the furniture in our play houses with this straw: Living room, kitchen, dining room, bathroom, bedroom, and all, and we were so busy with that until I didn't want to nurse the baby. But I had that to do, so I had to stop once in a while and take care of him and my father was very strict when it came to cooking and I had to have everything just right for him, but especially coffee. The coffee beans were bought—you had no coffee prepared as you do now in cans. We bought the beans out of the store, they were green, and he wanted them posh— what I mean by that—roasted in a pan in the oven and he wanted each grain the same color. So it was really a hard task and my mind was on the play house. I had to really work while the house was being run by the other playmates. We had quite a neighborhood. They had preaching. They had one girl who could really preach and we had an old cowbell on one of the wire fences. Anything that would happen, well, somebody would ring that bell and all the rest of us would know that there was something doing, church or to bury a chicken, which it took us all day to bury a chicken. So we had to dress for the funeral and we took the chicken in a shoe box and tied a string on there and someone would pull this chicken ahead of the family—the grieving family—and we had to bury him in that 'cause it took us all day to find the old clothes that our parents had to wear and we had a lot of fun.

Then we would go out into the woods in the spring and gather fruit. They had a lot of different kinds of fruit growing out in the forest, and in the fall we would gather hickory nuts and walnuts right from the trees. So we were busy out in the forest.

I was always busy. I had to cook for my father quite a bit because my mother was away and my father wanted to teach me. Of course, he would leave instructions at the house before he went to work and I would have to cook for him. So I had quite a schedule with that cooking.

And I had to keep up the yard, and in those days we just had a plain yard with no grass growing at all. We had to sweep the yard because large trees would shed their leaves and we would have to keep that clean. The house and the yard were mostly my responsibility as my brother was so much younger and my grandmother was too old to do that. I had to do all of that kind of work. But it was all enjoyable, at home, at school, and at church.

I was Methodist, and I had to go to church all day. We had Sunday school, eleven o'clock service and a number of times we had a program at three o'clock, our preaching service, and then at six o'clock the youth would have their meeting. I took care of the youth, and my classmates in the literary department. So, we would always have a program every Sunday afternoon. I was taught early in life about programming and playing and religious play and also the secular plays at school.

When graduation time came (at school), there were only two of us that graduated. We had a class of twenty some odd. But most of them had moved away or married or stopped school. So, there were only two to graduate from high school that year. Of course, they combined schools. They didn't have any separate high schools. They had the grammar school and the high school in the same building and different graduation exercises.

Even though there were only two of us graduating, we had our regular service as though we had a large class. Of course, we included others from the school. I had to play seven selections (on the piano) from various composers—Brahms, Bach, and Beethoven.

My music teacher had quite a large class of music students. She had to divide them into parts, and then she would have a program or a large recital and she would have the two divisions compete, and I was so glad to compete. Just had to compete; a Beethoven bust was offered as a prize, and she would give it to the division that won. And I worked hard to win that bust of Beethoven and did. I won that. I was so glad. I nearly cut meals to practice for the selections from Beethoven, and I was so glad to win. That was the thing. I was taught how to play piano. She was a very competent teacher, and knew how to arrange it for her students. And in those days there just wasn't any question about getting it, you had to know it, and there wasn't any arguing with the teacher that I can't or don't want to, you just were required to know that. So we didn't miss a note.

I would rather be an accompanist than anything else. I liked it. I enjoyed it and I can hear every voice as they get out of tune just a tiny bit. I would know who it was or what group it was, but I would prefer that than anything else to accompany a group or a soloist.

It was very hard (after I graduated). You hardly know what to do or which way you would like to turn, but I taught school for a short while, not too long. But it is very hard to make a decision. Now, think about the children, how when they are trying to decide, because I remember how hard it was for me. I didn't know what direction to go, but I knew I wanted to be an accompanist, but in those days, of course, Negroes were very limited. They and myself. I had opportunities to accompany the visiting artists, but that was restricted to church programs or recitals, and those coming into town, of course, I was selected to accompany them.

I was limited to church because of prejudice. Performance anyplace else wasn't even thought about. I am glad that things have opened up, and a lot of the prejudice disappeared where artists can appear anyplace because there are so many talented black people. There are so many of them, but they did not get the opportunity to express themselves.

Prejudice was very much evident in Minden. It really was. Lynching was very prevalent. It was fading after I grew up. My father, he told me about some of the lynchings around there, but I don't recall any. But the prejudice was very strong. On election day, it was best for Negroes to stay home because the white people thought you might come to vote and then they would start beating you up, you know, cause a lot of trouble. So most Negroes stayed home on election day. They weren't even allowed to register in those days. It was so evident you didn't have to talk about it. No, it wasn't discussed very much in the home. You just knew it was there and everywhere and everyplace. There wasn't much discussion there about the race prejudice.

I married shortly after that (graduation from school). My husband went to the same church. I knew him quite a while, but we didn't grow up together. He worked at the lumber mills. So it was family life then. It was quite a different life. You have to learn as you go along because I didn't particularly have any expectations.

I cleaned the house, preparing food for dinner. Usually people in the South then ate three meals a day—breakfast, dinner, and supper. They didn't have anything called lunch. Dinner was the heaviest, and, of course, the men that worked, and probably worked at the mill and the compress, their food was carried to them, the midday meal. It was cooked and carried out to them by the children, piping hot to them. I had to take my father his. We had large baskets and we carried complete meals. And he was proud to show his because I would take time to fix it. In the evening they had a lighter meal than the noon hour.

The house I had with my husband had a little more room. We didn't have a very large house at all. There were two houses on the property. As a child, we had our grandmother in her house. It was much larger than my mother and father's house.

I didn't know anything about childbearing. They didn't talk about those things. Not any information. It (my son) appeared before I had any information. Which I didn't know what to do at all. But when it appeared, then I was instructed about it. My son was born at home, at the house. In a small town like that they hardly had a small hospital, but most of the babies were born at home. The doctor came and then the neighbors. The doctor came to the house. They didn't know anything about office calls in those days.

I thought my instructions were pretty good. I appreciated it. Because they did teach me to be honest and to work and to be clean. That was one thing that was impressed upon me to keep yourself clean and, of course, that meant the baby clean. So I had already had quite a bit of instruction on that.

I think a child will fall into the category he wants to learn about, you know, and not rush them into what I want. I did start my daughter in music very early hoping that she would like that and would carry it on to high instructions, but then she married, too, and didn't carry that through. So my son very early knew what he wanted to do. He wanted to be a doctor and he is. So he was already set.

I moved to Phoenix when I guess I was about twenty-two or twenty-three. I separated from my husband. It wasn't a usual thing in those days. A few did it, but it wasn't…just many at all. They (my family) just left it alone. It was a mutual agreement. I made the decision to move.

I came out here to Phoenix…I had always studied and read about it, so it was on my mind to come out here. I don't know (what I thought I'd find). The man I married came out here and we got together and married out here. He left Louisiana, he came from another part. He wasn't there in Minden, but I met him at another place in Louisiana. A little country town, and we had summer instructions and I met him there. Instructions is teaching. So he came out here and he asked me to come out here and I came on.

I knew Phoenix was a desert and a town. I knew that much. That's where it got its name Arizona. Arid Zone. I was always glad to go to a new place anyway. I still am like that. I always liked to go to somewhere I had never been.

I thought it (Phoenix) was beautiful. Very much so. That was in 1919. I thought it was a fine opportunity to do most anything you could do here. It was wide open and there wasn't too many streets then. Prices was high but not as much as it was in Louisiana. I liked it very much; I'm still here.

I lived right up here on the corner of 15th and Jefferson. There was a two-story building there and they rented rooms. So I lived there. A family owned that. They (Negroes) were very much restricted. Negroes hardly lived above Van Buren. I don't think we had over one or two families, and that was in the later years after I came here. Most Negroes live on the west side.

I lived different places. On Monroe and East Jefferson in the 1700 block, and then we bought here. I think we were here four years (before we got this house). My husband worked as a cotton sampler. Cotton brokers. They sample bales of cotton to determine the fiber. If it's short or long staple. This country is like Egypt. It's noted for long staple cotton, Arizona, just like Egypt. Cottoners moved out here to get that long staple. It was worth more than short. Now, he had to go to the bales of cotton and get samples from those bales and usually they were on the yard near the cotton mill and he'd get samples and take them down to the office where he worked. And then they had a man in there to determine the length of the fiber.

There were very few opportunities for Negro men. Most of them were janitors, elevator men. Loads (of opportunities) for cotton pickers, cotton choppers. So, they had lots of people come out from Oklahoma. Years ago in Oklahoma they really come out in large droves and people from different parts of the South. They came out and they could do that kind of work and they chopped the cotton, that is, to thin it out. You can't have it too close together. And then in the fall, they would start to pick it. So there was a lot of that to be done. There were a number of school-teachers here. Men and women.

We had one or two Negro women back then that were typists in a lawyer's office. I know two. That was just about it. The barbershops was done by Negro men and they had young ladies in there to do manicuring. But they were very few in number. It was open to whites. Yes, it was open to whites only. All downtown there were Negro barbers. I don't know that they had any white barbershops downtown or not. I don't think so. Later on there was.

I didn't work outside the home. I had to take care of the children. I think a child should have special care at least for three years. They really need that, and they need a mother's love and care to help them be healthy and strong. So, I was glad to stay home and take care of mine and when they were a little larger and they hadn't any trouble with them.... Clarence Jr. was the weakest child I had, but he grew out of it. We could get a doctor most any time because they all came out to the house, white or black, physicians. They come to the house.

We went to the Christian Methodist Church. We had ordained ministers. They were trained in Negro colleges. They have them in the South. Some were well prepared. Others were not. The AME Church did not allow pastors unless they were educated. He had to have an education and, of course, that did mean college. They are very strict.

Women were in other departments in the church. Missionary societies, Sunday school, and various clubs that were organized. Those who were not schoolteachers or missionaries…there were other departments.

They (women) usually did missionary work. Visiting the sick, whatever they could for anyone, and then they would have different meetings. They would usually meet once a month, at least, and they would plan their work for the year. The conference year.

Some (women) were stewardesses. They had work to perform at the church with the sacrament table setup, the tablecloths, and the instruments, whatever they had to have. The stewardesses always did that.

I worked as a missionary. As I said, we had to visit the sick and prepare meals, or see after someone that was disabled if...whatever we could do—maybe we would have to go and clean the house for someone that didn't have anyone to help. It hasn't been too long that they sent out people from the different social departments of the government to take care of people that were sick and disabled. So, in those days we had to do it from the church, and missionaries did that.

We would have various functions, programs, and maybe a dinner, and things to raise our monies, but we were too poor because we had to report to the general treasurer as well as the local. So there were various activities we had to raise money.

Usually in our meetings, anyone in the meeting had the opportunity to suggest something and usually they agreed with it because it usually was a good plan. Maybe it was a pie sale, maybe it was a dinner. We would have activities like this. You would have to pay ten cents for every inch of your girth or how much you weighed. You would have to pay for that. Well, we had a lot of fun with all of that. We knew some were cheating on it and that made it even funnier. So we had little things like that.

I had taken training in hairdressing, and, of course, I went into that after my husband passed, into hairdressing. I had to make money for my children and myself. So there wasn't any profitable thing I could do then because I wasn't prepared to accompany the different artists that I wanted to. So I chose the hairdressing as my way of working.

Well, I was out here, I had no family, my husband died, you know, he died in 1929, and I had no relations at all. Left heavily in debt, I didn't have a dime. Didn't have anything but just the determination to work, and take care of my children and educate them. All I wanted was life, health, and strength. I felt I would come out of it, but I had fifty cents cash the night my husband died and it wasn't mine.

I had nothing to do but work. And manage. That management means so much. That's for anybody, rich or poor. If you don't manage then you won't make it. You have to manage that money. So the few dimes I had I did just that. The children, the three of them got ten cents a day for lunch. All that tickles my grandchildren. They don't understand that at all. I'd give them ten cents apiece for their lunch and sometimes that would be all I had. I didn't have another penny. But I got my money every day with the customers, so I started to work the beauty business, and I worked up to six operators and myself.

This elongated room you see out here was the beauty shop. Now that's why it's jutting out there, it was the beauty shop so I had to put on another living room back here for the new addition. So I worked it up to a very good thing. I had to have six beside myself. So we worked here…some nights it would be eleven o'clock or twelve o'clock before they'd finish.

I had the beauty shop for twenty-five years, and I've seen a lot of changes. The first thing: Negro people don't have an oily scalp. It is perfectly dry, and it has to have oil added to it. It's not like the Caucasian or some of the other races where the scalp produces oil, and it makes it straight. So, the Negro women wanted theirs straight and we had to use oil. We had a special preparation called a pressing oil and we had to use hot irons for that after we gave the shampoo, then we pressed it straight and then they wanted it curled after that. Later on, the Marcelle came, they wanted that and then the next style was the Cocono curl, which was very hard and it was very taxing from the wrist because you really bear down to give a real Cocono, but it would last a long, long while and very beautiful. They have changed now, they have preparations where they don't have to go to the beauty shop only about two or three months because of the Jerry Curl and different other styles that they have. And that's produced with special oil. So, now those that get the Jerry Curl have to have it pressed. They just put this special preparation on it, and it makes it curl and stay that way.

We had a comb called a straightening comb. It had a wooden handle and metal teeth and we would heat the metal part, and then press the hair with this oil on it. And then if we wanted it even straighter, we had something, it was very scissorslike, but on the end it had a flat surface like a fifty-cent piece, and, of course, it made the hair perfectly straight, and a lot of people wanted that. We had to use that, and then after the straightening, then we curled as they wished.

It took about two or two and a half hours to complete that. That was the shampoo, the press, and the curl. It took all of that to put it like they wanted then you would have to style it after it was curled and some of them styled it themselves. So, with the girls in the shop now the time was cut in half. They take about one and a quarter hours to do what it took me about two and a half hours to do. So, they make faster money and don't have to work as hard.

This was in the early thirties, but it lasted years. Some of them do it now. Because the shop I go to, they do a lot of that pressing now. Only they don't make it straight. They just run the comb through slightly.

We had gas heaters, very small. Just long enough to heat the comb. And we used gas. The electricity isn't as hot as the gas. So, we used gas stoves, special kind of stoves.

And back then we only got $2 or $2.50. For two and a half hours work? That's all we got. But that was a lot of money at that time. That was during the Depression. That's really right. We could go to the store and buy enough for one meal for a family of four or five for $1. You could get stew meat very cheap—ten cents a pound—and if you had a pound, you had enough to make a big pot of stew, potatoes, and other vegetables and make some cornbread up, biscuits, and have salad. So the money went a long, long way then. And we could get fruit, about fifty cents for a lug; peaches, different kinds of fruit for fifty cents a lug then. So, you see the money covered quite a bit.

I didn't have over five or six people to actually cheat me out of the work. That's true. Most of the ladies were working people, they worked out in service, that is, out—domestic work in the homes of white people, and they were my clients. I had all classes. The sporting class, the working class, and a few women stayed home. And, of course, I stayed busy most of the time.

Then when the 364th Infantry came, the government stationed them out in Papago Park. That was quite an overwhelming group of women that would come here to stay here with the husbands, sweethearts, they would send for them to come stay a while. At that time, the shop ran almost all night. We would start early in the morning and maybe be two o'clock in the morning before we finished. It was just that rushed. They didn't even care because in those days they had a lot of parties to go to and they didn't care.

The 364th Infantry didn't come until the late thirties and early forties. We had quite a business. So, I didn't really suffer during the Depression because I stayed busy. Sometimes I didn't make but $1; those who just wanted a shampoo and press—that was just $1. So, we managed. Maybe we always have to manage no matter how little or much we get, we have to manage it, and I was very good about that.

We had the working class and then we had (what we called) the sporting class. There were three classifications there. We had—I call them the alley bats. That was the don't care, goof—they would go from time to time on paydays. And they would talk about all their experiences and it wouldn't matter if it was the same man or same men, they just discussed all of that, and I just learned quite a bit. You know, very loose life. Then we had the working class, then the sporting women who catered only to the business white men downtown. We had some of the richest and most respectful businessmen that catered to those women of our class. They rented their little cabins downtown, and, of course, these men would cater to them and these women were very, very smart. Some of them were highly educated, and they tell me that they came—or some came over from California to do that kind of work to pay for a home. She says, "I can pay for my home and take care of my mother in two years. I can be through and then I'm through with the life. I'm going back to teaching." And we had those that kept up with all the news because they had to discuss these current events with these businessmen and they kept a leg on that. So, it was quite interesting to have those different types of people. I learned quite a lot because I didn't get any worldly experience at a young age at all and it was very interesting. So, I enjoyed and all classes respected the place. That is one thing I demanded of anyone, but I didn't have to say it in words because they had a respect for the place. So, I had quite a time.

I enjoyed the changes very much, there was always something to learn about whatever you were doing. Of course, I enjoyed the entire twenty-five years that I worked in the beauty shop. I started there in Minden, and, of course, after I came here Marcelle waving came out and I went down to the Adams Hotel. I had to have special instructions in the hotel instead of the school because the students, the other students were white and they did not want any Negroes in it. But the lady that ran the school was French and she wanted me to have this so she had me come to the hotel and her husband taught me himself how to Marcelle wave. I had to add on to my training—training for Negro hair, not for the white race because it's quite different.

Mine was the first Negro shop. I was very glad to stay at home to be with my children at home, and I made home comfortable and happy for them so they'd want to stay here and the other children come here and play. It was open house. We had no key. No key to the house at all.

That's really true. We didn't have any key. And I allowed all of the children to come here whenever they wanted as long as they respected the place. And, of course, the food, it went out just as fast. But I enjoyed it. So I made home very comfortable for them. They can never forget home because it was very pleasant and I made it that way for them and for their friends. So this was headquarters. I call it city hall #2.

At all times. Front door and back door they're coming in. They'd come here and study their lessons with my children and play the piano and enjoy themselves. They were glad to come here and they'd meet and talk and have fun. I'd put a music box in there at one time and the music would get good and they'd have to stop and dance it off. We enjoyed it very much. I assure you that, twenty-five years of service there. And I appreci-ated it. Well, it did help me to get all of my children educated as far as they would go. Howard didn't finish college, but he did high school. He went to the war two years or more. He was halfway through college when he went and then he finished after he got back. And then he had a grant from the government to go into medical training.

I launched out into the political field (myself) because I saw where the Democratic Party would help poor people. I know the Republicans were always for the rich, and the Democrats really were down to earth with the poor people. And I worked very hard on that, very hard in registration and in campaigning and anything to help the Democratic Party. I really went into it full force because they really helped the poor and I'm always for the underdog. Someone that really needs.

I started that way back in '32. That was the year President Roosevelt ran. Of course, he just enlightened the whole country with his plan. And I really started and have continued to work up until this day with the Democratic Party because it would help so many poor people. That's the only way they have improved to where they are now, is through the government. It wasn't individuals, the rich people that had it, they didn't bother about it, but the government did and it opened up so many high positions for income that the Negroes never would have had in any manner. So, I have always stuck with the Democrats. And I was appointed with my work because there wasn't any money in it at all. I wasn't (in it) for money. Then our county chairman realized the work I had done and he went to the convention and he talked with the heads there and sang (praise for) my work. And finally he went to the recorder's office and asked to put me on in the office, and they let me know that I was only to be there for six months. That was for registration. So, I gladly accepted. I was the first Negro appointed there, you know. So, I knew when I went they would last longer than six months. I never discussed it with anyone, but within there was something that said I would be there longer. So, I worked very hard and did all that I could to make myself as pleasant as possible with the public and for workers. And before the six months was up one of the men in the recorder's office said, "Mrs. Copeland, why don't you speak to Roger (his name was Roger Levine) about putting you on regular? You've made good. You are liked and you do your work well. Go to Roger and speak to him." I thanked him, but I never did go.

I didn't say one word to him. Not at all, but before my six months was up he sent for me to come to the office, and he told me that I had been highly recommended to be put on a permanent position as a recorder, deputy county recorder in the office. So I knew it was coming because I just felt it within.

He says, "Now there is a Baptist preacher said he has a lady that he wanted for this position."

I says, "Well, I was sent here by our chairman and I have also written to you."

He said, "I threw all those letters in the wastebasket."

But he says, "With the record you've made with the party, we will certainly give this to you." So he says, "You come back to my office about 1:30 and I'll have you to sign" because my chairman had called me that morning and said—I'll never forget the time—it was 11:15 in the morning. I was in the act of general cleaning, furniture and everything in the backyard, the rugs and all to be cleaned, and so the phone rang and I went to answer. It was the chairman, and he says, "Copeland, you get down to Roger's office by twelve o'clock."

"At twelve o'clock. Oh," I said, "Thank you."

So I stopped everything—left everything out in the yard, took a bath and I caught the quarter to twelve o'clock bus. So I was in his office at twelve o'clock and I had this interview. I had prayed for something to do 'cause I had worked in the beauty shop for twenty-five years and did the hard work. It made my wrist very weak giving Cocono curls, and I knew I couldn't do it any longer unless I would ruin my wrists. So I was going to clean up, rent the house, and go to San Diego, California, and work over there because I couldn't work in a beauty shop anymore.

And I also had gone out to the American Legion, the white American Legion; they were just moving out on Thomas Road, so the idea came to me to go out there and ask them would they allow me to serve meals on the weekends only. Just the weekends, and he said, "I'm glad you came, for we have no one. We haven't even opened the kitchen and we won't have our opening for about a month, and we would be glad to have someone to serve the meals on weekends."

I prayed, fasted and prayed to the Lord to help me to find some work because I could no longer work in a beauty shop, and I fasted and prayed for three days, and on the last day the telephone call came from downtown to go to Mr. Levine. So that was it. That was my work instead of preparing meals, it was downtown. I was so glad. I was the first permanent deputy county recorder, Negro county recorder, they had. So I was very happy to go and stayed there fourteen years. So it was quite an experience. I still work in the party because that's the only one for the poor people.

After World War II, the opportunities were opening up gradually more and more. Negroes were getting positions that they had never had before, and it just helped all the way around to have these things open up to them because they had never made any money, and there was a chance to progress that way. Well, they worked in government positions, the OEO and housing. They had a number of them, but I can't recall now in detail, but they had a number to open up for Negro men and women could work. So, it made it nicer.

Discrimination has abated, you know, it's quieted, but it's still there. I think it will always be here until the Lord turns everything to heaven as he said he would. I think it will always be here, but we don't have anything like as much as we used to have. Not anything like it. Well, they have it in most all areas. They have opened up, you know, to allow Negroes to hold offices and run for election, but there's still enough of it here. We'll never get out of all of it. I'm just thankful that progress has happened like it has for them. Because there are always some white people to help us. That's how we got it. They opened the way for us. But the large number don't believe in that at all. They sure don't. We can go to any hotel, any restaurant. That used to be unthinkable, completely unthinkable, but now it's open for us to go.

When prejudice was really strong, Negroes were separated, definitely. You could only sit in the balcony (in public theaters), and only a certain section of the balcony. It stayed that way for a long, long time.

President Truman did quite a job (to change things). And, of course, back in Roosevelt's time, they opened the gates wide open, and they had a lot of citizens that helped, too. They were for it, and it made it much easier for the minority races. The Mexicans were segregated just like Negroes. Of course, some of them got jobs because they could speak Spanish, and they wanted the Spanish trade, that was the cause of so many of them being hired long before Negroes were. So, for that reason, they got a number of jobs.

Changes for Negroes were very gradual. I know when a few worked at the NAACP we picketed a lot of places. We picketed Woolworth's and the Rialto Theater that had all that segregation there, and all of those stores, ten-cent stores, they were picketed. I was involved in the NAACP, but I was in kind of a little band. I say that because we were sincere. There were some in that were not sincere at all. They were really working both ends against the middle.

We were trying to work for jobs and to go to these businessmen and ask them to hire the Negro girls, but, of course, some couldn't hire them because the girls had never had any training in typing. They were not allowed to go to the business school at all, and what typing they could do they learned it in high school, and we were successful in getting some in the different offices to work in the files. And then in the ten-cent stores they first started with the lunch counter. They didn't serve you at all there, and, of course, we just kept that up until it was broken down. As one of the Negro ladies told the head down there at Woolworth's that we just bought something over here on this side, buying merchandise—why can't we buy food? Well, they couldn't deny it, you know, because after all they were serving customers all over the store and, of course, that was broken down.

There was trouble out to the airport; they would not serve Negroes, and that was run by the city. So, I have a very dear friend and the two of us went down to the mayor's office as soon as it came out in the paper where they had refused to serve Louis Jordan and his wife. He was an entertainer, they refused to serve him, and, of course, we went into the mayor's office and told him the story about it. And as we said, it's run by the city, and we would like to have it open so that all races can go because all races are supporting the airport. He said, "I'll let you know at five o'clock this afternoon my decision."

So, we left and promptly at five o'clock he called, he did, right on the dot of five o'clock, he called and said he had made the change. It would be open. So, I said to her (my dear friend), I said, "Let's not hurry," I said, "They may put something in the food. Let's wait a little while. They may be so mad they want to make us sick." We had a lot of fun with that.

I picketed just a very little bit because I was working mostly inside. I was really going directly to the businessmen and a lot of them I knew because I was a Democratic Party (worker) and I was always busy with it. I knew a lot of them and some of them I did not know, but I went to them anyway. Sure did. I didn't do any picketing to amount to anything, but I went directly to the offices of the businessmen.

I was out working in the flower beds one morning and I had to come in the house to get some more flower seed, I think, and when I got back there were two white men and I didn't know what on earth they were here for. And they pulled out their cards, they were from the FBI.

I said, "Well, what on earth do you want with me?"

"We came to tell you not to run against this doctor here."

He was the president of the NAACP, but I was stunned because I didn't even know the FBI even knew we had an NAACP club. They never did appear or try to work at anything. I was stunned and I always looked on the FBI as just a Lord from heaven. I said, "Those are law-abiding people. They know their law and they want you to do right."

I really looked up to the organization but those men started getting after me about going against this doctor. I was so stunned at that. I couldn't imagine, and they said to come on in the house, they didn't want to be seen too much outside.

So, they wanted to know, "Do you think that the Communists have something to do with the NAACP?"

I said, I don't know, I don't know anything about communism. Not the first thing do I know about that. And, of course, I said, "You know the thing, you should be helping us uphold the law. Really and truly, President Truman just announced all prejudice must go in housing and different things."

I said, "You should be helping us work. What are you doing out here getting after me?"

I was really stunned. I was followed quite a bit. I was followed and really had quite an experience. Hard experience with it because they seemed to have thought that I was against the government or Congress or something. And I said I didn't know anybody would do anything like that, but I was truly American. I don't know a thing about any other country, Africa, or Germany, or Russia, or anything. All I wanted was for Negroes to raise out of the horrible condition they were in because they were held down and couldn't make the progress of the white race.

So, we worked hard to try to get jobs, and try to improve the conditions among our race, and we were kind of an offshoot there. We were not even recognized and they planned to have the election of officers and they asked the members to be there at four o'clock. Do you know when we got there? This other group had met at three o'clock. They met at three o'clock and had elections.

And Dr. Phillips's wife, Louise, she was about as dishonest as anybody I ought to know because he made her the chairman of the membership drive. And they had a big meeting, and the Negroes flocked up there like everything and (signed up for) membership. But they haven't received a card till this day. Didn't have any membership. Their money was not there; they kept it. So, it was quite a confrontation you're going to have when you're fighting for the rights. You are going to really have steel nerves to stand up against some things that you come up against because they'll test you in every way. I was tested in my church, my lodge. I never wavered and I never was afraid because I knew I had done nothing but work hard for my poor race to come out from under the cloud they were under. So, I didn't ever bother about them.

I came to Phoenix in 1919. And I had never voted prior to that time. That was unthinkable. Oh, yes indeed. In my hometown, I tell you, Negroes would rather stay home, even, because the white people would be mad if they saw you on the street. Think you come to try to vote. My first voting was for President (Franklin) Roosevelt.

Arizona was a suffrage state. Women had already had suffrage. I didn't have any particular reason (to vote). I sure didn't. I was in childbearing days then. My attention was drawn on babies. I had nothing at all against it. So, my husband said, well, this is where I came to registration because he was Republican like most all Negroes were until Franklin Roosevelt came then, and I registered Democrat and voted for him.

(When my children were growing up the schools they went to) they were all Negro. Very much so. Right here at Booker T. All three finished grammar school....Well, Booker T. right here, and then they went to the high school. They built one down there on Grant Street. Well, anyway, it was down across the tracks. They built one there so they all finished high school down there at this school on Grant.

And then my son went to college, first in Arizona, and then he went to Berkeley. He went to the state university up there. I don't know whether it was Oakland or Berkeley but he finished college there before he went east to go to medical school. He really prepared himself for it. He was very studious. He wasn't smart, brilliant to catch on to everything at once, but he studied hard. So he stayed back east until he was prepared and he would not even start surgery until he had special lessons for a year or more under one of the experienced doctors in Philadelphia. And then he had his internship in St. Louis, so he would not hang up the shingle until he felt prepared, That's what he wanted to do. And thank the Lord he made good and is very successful at Oakland. I went up to the graduation of the last daughter of his in May, and he is just busy all the time.

My daughter also went to college. She hasn't finished the entire course, but she's halfway. She said she was some time later on. She works for slow readers. She works with those. She seems to be making good with that and they are keeping her there. She has seven children.

I have twelve grandchildren and about eighteen great-grandchildren. I'm eighty-six you know so I have great grandchildren. I'm very proud of them.

INTERVIEW BY MARIA HERNANDEZ, JULY 21, 1981
COURTESY ARIZONA STATE UNIVERSITY
DEPARTMENT OF ARCHIVES AND MANUSCRIPTS

Herbert Cowens

Jazz drummer and U.S.O. bandleader
Life dates: May 24, 1904–January 23, 1993

Herbert Cowens was from a musical family. Two brothers played drums, one sister was a dancer, and the other sister was a singer. Cowens started as a shoeshine boy, and with the money he earned at street dancing, he bought his first set of drums. He played with the Satisfied Five until 1926 and with other local jazz bands. In 1927, he left Dallas with Cleo Mitchell's "Shake Your Feet" Company. From 1927 to 1980, Cowens lived in New York City and worked in vaudeville, Broadway shows, musicals, and for several notable bandleaders, including Eubie Blake, Fats

Herbie "Kat" Cowens playing as part of The Kat and His Kittens. (Herbert and Rubye Cowens Collection, courtesy Texas African American Photography Archive)

Waller, Stuff Smith, and Fletcher Henderson. In addition, Cowens led his own band, The Kat and His Kittens, and made annual overseas U.S.O. tours to the Far East, Japan, Europe, and the Mediterranean. Cowens married Rubye Houston of Dallas in 1936.

When I was a youngster I had quite a few brothers and sisters and it was a little rough at times. We were living in a place called Frogtown in the 2500 block of Cochran Street in what was then called North Dallas. So, when we went to and back from school, we had to cross McKinney Avenue. And in so doing, the white kids would throw rocks and we'd have to fight to get to where we were going. We'd have to fight to get to school and we'd have to fight to get home. But as far as grown-ups were concerned, we never had any trouble.

I was born May 24, 1904. There were thirteen kids altogether, though I lost a baby brother in my younger days and I lost a sister. We all went to Booker T. Washington and then to North Dallas High School.

In school we didn't have any instruments. So, we had to march out to the beat of a drum. A young man before me played the drum, but he gave it up and I took it over. Just beating the drum for them to march up and down the stairs. And after that I started listening more to the drummer at the movies. He was named Jessie Atkins and he was one of the greatest. Every time I'd go to the movies I would sit there near the drummer and it just came on me that I should be a drummer. And that's the way it started. I must have been about twelve or thirteen.

When I got into high school I worked as a "blackjack." I shined shoes and with the extra money I earned I would buy a piece of drum. Of course, I got quite a few lickings, but I took the lickings and kept on buying the drums.

I worked two different shine parlors and if I didn't like one, I was privileged to go on. I worked one on Main Street and one on Elm around the corner. And I also worked in another little place at Harwood and Elm. That was where the cowboys used to come in for the weekend.

In high school I started a little band called the Rainbow Jazz Band. We were just school kids and we got a few jobs around Texas. It was a great thing to see, these five young guys trying to make a living. We had to walk just about everywhere.

Two of my brothers were also drummers, Alvis Vernon Cowens and Cardin Augustus Cowens. And I had two sisters who went into the business. I should say "three." Beatrice was a singer, Louise was a singer, and Lorraine was a dancer.

We used to go the live shows at the Park Theatre. The first time I went I must have been about ten years old because I went there with my father. (My father's name was Fred Douglas Cowens, and my oldest brother was named after him, Fred Douglas Cowens Jr.) We went to the Park Theatre to see a blues singer by the name of Ida Cox. They had different shows every week. Ida Cox, Bessie Smith, Ma Rainey. The TOBA, the Theater Owners Booking Association, brought in shows one after the other. Dan James was in charge of the Park Theatre.

What I remember about Deep Ellum is the way the train passed right down Central Avenue. I liked going down there to walk by the hotel where all the musicians congregated and to listen to them talk. That was at the Delmonico Hotel, right at Swiss and Pacific. I saw Blind Lemon Jefferson at the Delmonico Hotel the first time, and the second time I saw him, he was crossing Central Avenue going over there to Fat Jack's, which was the movie house. I couldn't understand how Blind Lemon could play so good and still not see. He was wonderful, but I didn't ever talk to him. I just saw him go back and forth. I didn't know he couldn't see until I saw one guy help him across the street one day. That's the only time I knew he was blind. He'd start to playing and put his hat down and it wouldn't be long before it would be full.

Another group I remember was led by Coley Jones. He had what we call a band. He had four pieces and they would play anyplace that they could pass the hat. Everybody knew him. He not only played there out in the village under your window, he'd take his group and play in the drugstores downtown and out in Dallas. Most of all of them that he played were blues.

I used to play in front of the Tip Top Tailors every Saturday. That's the place where they made clothes. We played out in front and people would come out to hear the music and go have clothes made. Most of the time, I'd be with Frenchie. He was a trumpet player and he had a band with three or four pieces in it: trombone, saxophone, trumpet, and drums. We played any kind of music that we knew at the time. Frenchie was a kind of heavyset fellow and he could blow his horn. They say you could hear it from Elm Street to far North Dallas. His real name was Potite Christian. I don't know how he spelled it, but he was from New Orleans.

I met Buster Smith in front of Tip Top Tailors. He used to come to hear the band play. He was about my age and he'd talk to me and I would talk to him about music.

We used to go dancing on Central Avenue. They used to call it down on the track. There was a skating rink that turned into a dance place. They called it the Skating Rink at first and then they changed it to The Rink when they started the dancing.

Sometimes we'd go by the Green Parrot that was on Elm Street right beside McMillan's Cafe. They had music at the Green Parrot, but I was too young to get up close to really see anything about the musicians and so forth.

R.T. Ashford had a shine parlor on the track near the corner of Elm and he sold records. He had three daughters that worked in there with him. Sammy Price worked at Ashford's, but I didn't know him then. I was raised with Sammy. He lived across Leonard Street from where I lived. He lived on the west side of Leonard and I, on the east side. Sammy and I grew up together. We knew each other in Dallas and got to know each other again in New York. Sammy went on the road and I left Dallas in 1927 with one of them TOBA shows, and when we got to Kansas City it closed. So, then I was there and didn't have no job and didn't know anybody. But I got with a circus and worked with the circus for a while and eventually I made my way to New York.

Interview by Alan Govenar, April 19, 1987

Leon Davis

Policeman's son; U.S. Air Force colonel (ret.)
Life dates: 1866–1955

Leon Davis is the son of one of the first black policemen in Tulsa, Oklahoma. His
father, A. D. Davis, had moved from Mississippi to Oklahoma, where he financially
prospered but encountered more racism than he expected. Davis's mother was the
daughter of Tama Franklin, a relative of the historian Dr. John Hope Franklin.
His mother's family was black Creek Indians, who donated the land for the first
school for blacks in Haskell, Oklahoma. Davis was a retired colonel in the Air
Force and was active in Black Creek Freedmen's meetings held in Tulsa.

In my research, I have found that there was a lot of discrimination in the
Tulsa police force in the 1920s and 1930s. The black policemen were
given their jobs as political plums for services they had rendered to white
politicians. That was the case of all black policemen then. There was no
such thing as a merit system then. There was a lot of friction and bicker-
ing. White policemen wanted black policemen investigated because they
said the blacks were too lenient on their own race, especially toward bootleggers who whites said were allowed to cook their liquor in "Chockhouses"
all over North Tulsa! Black policemen wanted white policemen investigated because they felt there was a double standard (just as there is today),
which resulted in harsher treatment of blacks for the same infractions that
were overlooked when committed by whites.

I always heard my dad talk about those days when he was one of
Tulsa's first black policemen. Dad was one of the "foot patrol" policemen.
He knew and admired Roughhouse McGill, who was one of the elite motorcycle squad cops. That motorcycle squad was started by the police department so policemen could run down bootleggers who were driving
cars. The foot patrol couldn't outrun them on foot, so the motorcycle
cops were entrusted with the duty of tracking down those lawbreakers.
Back then, The Strip—Greenwood—where the black policemen patrolled
was only about a mile. Now, what we call The Strip covers about seven
miles.

My father was well respected as a policeman on The Strip, and he
was also respected as a businessman. He had come to Oklahoma from
Mississippi in search of the Promised Land. When he was sixty-nine years
old he married my mother and started a new family (four sons, including
me, the youngest). He didn't find Tulsa to be a Promised Land, race-wise,
but he did prosper financially. He started by buying up real estate property in North Tulsa. We lived in the main house at 520 North Elgin Street

Fires pour smoke into the sky during the 1921 race riot in Tulsa, Oklahoma. (Corbis)

and Dad rented the other houses. He also had the largest shoeshine stand in Tulsa at 4th and Main in downtown Tulsa, where the shoes of Tulsa's elite white citizens were shined! When he died, when I was ten years old, my father left his family well provided for. We lived in the original family home until Urban Renewal took it over in 1975, and there was even enough money left by my dad to send all four of us children to college. I think my dad would be proud of us if he could see us today. The oldest, A. D. Davis Jr., is a retired full-bird colonel in the U.S. Air Force, M. B. is employed at American Airlines, Ernest D. is a teacher, and I am a freelance writer and businessman.

My mother, Bertha Townsend Davis, was an interesting person, too. She just died recently at the age of eighty-seven. She was the daughter of Tama Franklin, who was kin to B. C. Franklin and Dr. John Hope Franklin; she was a Black Creek Freedman who gave the land for the first school for blacks in Haskell, Oklahoma. She also had 160 acres of land that overflowed with oil. Some kind of way, she and her heirs were beaten out of their oil rights. I am active in Black Creek Freedmen's meetings, which are being held in Tulsa. Scott McIntosh is the chief of our organization, and I am the chief spokesman for the group. We hope to reclaim our lands and our oil rights, which were taken away from us by greedy whites.

My brothers and I treasure the mementos we have of our dad's days on Greenwood. One brother got Dad's service revolver, which in those days was a .44. Another got his (Dad's) field Winchester rifle, and all of the 32nd-degree Mason materials went to a third brother, and I got the family photographs, including a long, long picture that shows all of Tulsa's black policemen who served at the same time as my dad. I think Tulsa can be proud of the record those policemen left. Though their jobs were political plums for past services rendered to white politicians, they took their positions seriously and most of them served with great courage, dignity, discipline, love, respect, and loyalty in the North Tulsa community, the only part of the city where they were allowed to patrol.

INTERVIEW BY EDDIE FAYE GATES, SEPTEMBER 29, 1994
COURTESY OKLAHOMA HISTORICAL SOCIETY
ARCHIVES AND MANUSCRIPT DIVISION, ORAL HISTORY DEPARTMENT

LaVerne Cooksey Davis, L.P.N.

Licensed Practical Nurse
Born: May 24, 1904, Royse City, Texas

Mrs. Eddie May Faye Gates conducted this interview with LaVerne Cooksey Davis under the auspices of the North Tulsa Oral History Project and the Tulsa Race Riot Commission. This oral history is one of many conducted with residents of the Greenwood section of Tulsa who survived the Tulsa race riot of 1921. Greenwood was an African American community that flourished after World War I despite the dominating presence of the Ku Klux Klan. The Tulsa race riot started after a black man, Dick Rowland, apparently jostled a white woman, Sarah Page, in a crowded downtown elevator on May 30, 1921. After Page accused Rowland of raping her, the Tulsa Tribune published a fictitious story the next day with a headline that stated that Rowland was likely to be lynched. That night a white mob gathered around the courthouse where Rowland was being held and the police did nothing to disperse the crowd. In a short time, a group of seventy-five blacks arrived to help protect Rowland, and in an ensuing argument a shot was fired and the riot began. The blacks retreated to the Greenwood section of the city, but the rioting intensified. Whites surrounded the area and began shooting guns and igniting fires. At 11:30, the mayor declared martial law, but by the time the National Guard arrived the next morning, many African Americans had been killed—estimates range as high as more than 300. Nearly all of the 11,000 people in the black community were left homeless (half were arrested and interned in tents outside the city). During the riot, the Greenwood African American community was completely leveled, and according to some reports, two airplanes flew over the neighborhood and dropped bombs. After several weeks the tensions resulting from the riot calmed: All of the internees were freed, and Rowland was released, as were twenty-seven other blacks arrested on murder charges.

We left Texas and moved to Oklahoma in 1916, settling in Pawnee. Three years later, we moved to Tulsa. We left Texas because conditions were just terrible for black farmers like my dad. We heard that things were better in Oklahoma, especially in Tulsa, which was a booming oil town then. We heard that there were many good jobs for black folks in Oklahoma, what with all those oil people coming in from the North and from the East. But I didn't find Tulsa to be much different from Texas. In Texas, my first job, when I was eleven or twelve years old, was washing dishes for a white lady in exchange for piano lessons. In Tulsa, the only job that I could find was being a maid for a white doctor in South Tulsa. After the Tulsa race riot of 1921, I left Tulsa. I just couldn't face the prospects of spending my life being a maid.

Oh, that riot was such a terrible thing. It left its mark on me; I just can't ever forget it. When the riot started, it was in the wee hours of the morning. I had gone to bed and after midnight, I got a telephone call from the doctor who was still downtown. I wondered why he was calling me at that late hour. He told me not to go into Little Africa. That is what people called North Tulsa in those days. I thought that was strange for him to tell me that. I wouldn't have been going into North Tulsa at that late hour anyway. Well, later on the doctor called me again, and this time he was more urgent in telling me not to go into Little Africa. He said, "Hell has broken out in Little Africa. Don't go down there!"

I was safe in my maid's quarters in South Tulsa, but many of my friends in the Greenwood area had their homes burned to the ground. Before their homes were burned, some of the people were taken out of their beds. They went to detention centers in their pajamas and housecoats because the police wouldn't give them time to dress. I was so disturbed. I didn't know where my friends had been taken. Later I found out that most of them had been taken to the Convention Center. Five or six days after the riot, blacks could get passes from the militia to go down into the Greenwood area to try to find friends and relatives. That riot was a tragic thing, and it has stayed on my mind all these years.

After the riot, the job situation in Tulsa didn't get any better. The only jobs available to blacks were either in the service industries—in hotels, restaurants, lounges, etc.—or as maids and housemen in the South and West Tulsa mansions of oil millionaires. That's why I left Tulsa. I first went to Pittsburgh, Pennsylvania, where I worked seven years in the millinery business. Then I moved to Kansas City, Missouri, and improved myself by going to nursing school and becoming a Licensed Practical Nurse. I enjoyed my career in nursing, but I returned to Tulsa in the 1970s to be near my sister, Katherine Butler. I worked thirteen years for the Tulsa Red Cross and retired in 1984.

I have seen a lot of changes in my lifetime. One thing that I wish is that people would listen more to what elderly people tell them. These people have lived longer, they have seen so much, and they can give so much good advice if only people would listen to them! Americans need to learn to respect older people more, and to respect people who are wise even if they are not formally educated. Too often, they listen only to the educated, to the "high leaders." Uneducated people are not "ignorant." Many of them are good, wise, intelligent people who just may not have had the opportunity to get a formal education. We could learn a lot from them if only we would learn to listen. I've read that in other cultures, there is great respect for the elderly; unfortunately, that is not true in the United States. Here, they are often viewed as just a burden on society. That need not be the case. I'd like to tell people, especially young people, to get back to being more loving, caring people. Then we would have a more loving and caring nation like we used to have. Families were more together then and they reached out and helped others in the community. We cared about each other. We were raised to treat others as we would want others to treat us, barring none. We were taught to work for the betterment of all people, barring none!

INTERVIEW BY EDDIE FAYE GATES, MAY–AUGUST, 1994
COURTESY OKLAHOMA HISTORICAL SOCIETY
ARCHIVES AND MANUSCRIPTS DIVISION, ORAL HISTORY DEPARTMENT

Virginia Clark Gayton

Power machine operator; descendant of Lewis E. Clarke
Born: 1901, Nashville, Tennessee

Virginia Clark Gayton is a descendant of Lewis and Milton Clarke, slaves who escaped to freedom (see page 28 for excerpts from the published Lewis and Milton Clarke slave narrative). Gayton was raised in Spokane, Washington. She graduated from Lewis and Clark High School in Spokane and attended Howard University in Washington, D.C., for two years. In 1919, she went to Vancouver, British Columbia, where her family had relocated because her father was able to find a better job. Gayton moved to Seattle, where she worked as a power machine operator. In 1926, she married John Clark, who was employed at a haberdasher shop. Clark recalls her experiences in Washington State, including education, marriage, discrimination, and black community life.

My mother and father were married in Spokane, Washington, in 1901. And nearly a year later when I was about to be born, my mother, having come out here to a raw country, wanted to go back to her mother to have the baby where she could have the care of her mother and family, because Spokane, Washington, was quite a raw community. Of course, hospitalization was almost an unknown thing as far as childbirth was concerned in those days, and there were few Negroes there. So my mother was rather homesick and she went back to Nashville, Tennessee. So I happen to be born there, but returned to Spokane about two months later, in early 1902.

I finished my schooling at Lewis and Clark High School in Spokane. I had an aunt, my father's sister, in Washington, D.C., and she had had no children. She was a librarian in the Library of Congress, a clerk in the Library of Congress. My uncle, her husband, Henry Baker, was a patent office examiner. He was in the patent office for about four years and he gathered a lot of resource materials as far as Negro inventors were concerned. He gathered the blueprints and wrote a pamphlet about Negro inventors. My aunt had started to teach stenography at Howard University when it was still a high school.

Henry E. Baker. His name is on the resource material, and you can find it. He was the third Negro to attend Annapolis in the year 1874. There had been two Negroes previously who stayed two months and six months and he was able to stand it not quite two years; the treatment was so rough. So he left there and finished in law at Howard University, although he didn't practice. He took an examination and was an examiner in the patent office, the second assistant examiner. He often remarked that if he had been white, why, he would have progressed higher.

I lived and went to school there, at Howard University, for two years. The summer in between, I was fortunate enough to get a job as messenger in the Library of Congress, where it happened that Mr. Jones was the senator from the state of Washington. There weren't many people from way out in the Northwest, where they thought the Indians were still prominent. I worked there for about four months. My aunt's health became poor, and she didn't feel able to continue to send me to school, so I came back to where my family was now living, in Vancouver, B.C. They had moved there in 1919 from Spokane.

My father had gotten out of, for some reason, his job, discontinued in Spokane, and he was doing maintenance work. He had finished high school and taught school in Nashville, Tennessee, as had my mother. But there was little opportunity for that kind of work, and, in fact, even the Post Office paid so little and Spokane in its history hasn't had many employed in the Post Office there. It paid so little, the railroad was about the best paying job that Negroes could get, and so that's what he worked at in Spokane. And any other labor jobs which he could get to support the family.

He heard that in Canada, where he had been born, there was opportunity to get work up there. Soon after he got there, why, the railroad had a strike up there, and he was unemployed for some time. So, in 1922, I came from Washington and came to Vancouver to live with my family. The employment for young people, especially, was very poor there and as usual, all the Negroes could get was menial and housework. I had a friend there who had graduated from the University of British Columbia, and she had applied and was admitted to the University of Washington, the School of Pharmacy. She was staying here in Seattle at the Phyllis Wheatley YWCA, which was on 102 21st Avenue North. It was an old home that was being made to serve as a YWCA Center, and it was quite an active branch. Much of the social activity of the young people especially and the Sunday afternoon vesper services, and any affairs of women and concerts and other club meetings were held there. I roomed with Clara James there until she finished in pharmacy at the University of Washington. And then she went on to get work. She went to Providence Hospital, I think that's the name of it, in Kansas City, Missouri.

Later she went to Chicago and married a man there, and they had their own pharmacy. I haven't heard from her for some time. So, then I was here in Spokane and Seattle. I was looking for some sort of employment. I didn't know enough about housework to apply for a job there. I did apply at Mr. Stone, a caterer, who had a very nice catering shop, but at that time he had no vacancy. So I eventually got a job as a power machine operator and worked for them for about two years. It (the machine) was for hats. Men's hats and caps. It was the Seattle Cap.... I don't know whether it's still in force or not. I worked there until I married. My husband at that time was employed at one of the haberdashers in town here. We were married on April 25, 1926.

Now his father was a bailiff at that time in the county. He was a librarian at that time. He may have been a bailiff. He was employed at the U. S. Court as a bailiff first and then later as librarian at the...and Judge Neever was the judge for whom he worked.

Looking east on Riverside Avenue, the principal business street of Spokane, Washington, ca. 1920s (Underwood & Underwood / Corbis)

When I was first married, I tried to continue on with the job at the power machine work, but it was too little pay when I would have to pay a baby-sitter and expenses. The big salary I got at that time was $15 a week, and for a time it paid low. That was supposed to be a pretty good salary for that type of work.

In those days the Post Office, where my husband eventually went to work, paid very little. Although there were several early-day employees, clerks, or carriers in the Post Office, and there was Mr. Fork and Mr. Harris. I know there were several, but there were a few. I don't know why there were so few, whether they thought there was anything...but evidently, as some of them got in, there must have been the opportunity there. Of course, the salary was small and the entrance examination was supposed to be rather difficult.

There was discrimination, as far as I can understand, perhaps not as rigid. It certainly wasn't as rigid as some places, but it was there, and the attitude of the majority of the population, as most Negroes did, they didn't want to go to places where they were not wanted and would be insulted. Although in several specific instances where it probably hindered their mode of living, or their life, like perhaps buying property or getting a job that they thought they were qualified for. Clarence Anderson was one of the lawyers that I remember especially. He won, they say, every case that he defended... so he was notable for that.

This would have been in 1920. And there was a lawyer previous to that, Black, Andrew Black. I don't remember whether he was dead or died soon after I came. I don't know too much about him, but he was practicing here in Seattle. There were very often several avenues of business that, for the early times, could compare favorably with the present times. There was a well-built hotel down in the railroad station area, a brick hotel. There was a very nice drugstore.... And there was the E. I. Robinson and Tutt drugstore. We had a very good drugstore and there was a very good delicatessen and grocery store.

It was a mixed clientele. There wasn't anything segregated about them, they were mostly mixed—at least the grocery store—I don't know about the hotel. But there were a lot of people who lived out, who lived in sections where perhaps now it would be hard to get into. There were several around the Green Lake and the Ballard area. Stone, the caterer, was black.... He was also a stone mason, and I think...his home was up in the Mt. Baker district. And his wife just recently, not too long ago, died. But there are no members of his family...there's a granddaughter. He has a granddaughter. She lives in the city.

We had some excellent newspapers. Mr. Caton started *The Republican* and there was *The Enterprise*. I especially remember when *The Enterprise* had an editor named William Wilson. I think he must have been trained in journalism from the type of newspaper that he had.

Mr. Caton came here and was able to build up...make a good living here and accumulate quite a bit. But the minute he started to write and defend the Negroes' rights, why, all the white people who had supported him with advertising, why, they stopped. Let's see, Mr. Norris, he had a father...he came from Nashville, Tennessee, I believe, and had a good job there. He started a freight, or, what is it called, like we would call a trucking now, but drays. The Peoples, Sam Peoples, he and his brothers, I think Margaret Peoples, her name was—they were quite active and they still have some of his grandchildren here.

When my husband and I went, I don't remember whether there was any segregated seating in the movie theater. But I remember some, like they had two, two confectioneries....They used to have these large ice cream and confectionery places. One was called the Pig and Whistle, and I think it had been known not to want.... I think they must have made some...there must have been some enforcement because I think we could have gone but we didn't particularly want to go when you didn't know how it would be. Those that felt like taking up the fight and going on...

being young I think people who felt their legal...would know their legal rights and wanted to be really definite, I think they did through lawsuits.

I don't remember too much about the black migration to the rural sector of Washington, only secondhand. There are other families whose families came from that area who would go to Yakima. Charles Taylor came from the Yakima area. His mother and his father are the ones, they still have relatives there. I was talking to someone who said that many of them came because, as up in Alberta, in Canada, they put ads in papers in Arkansas and Oklahoma and those places where perhaps Negroes were accustomed to farming. I don't know what the enticements were to get them to come, but some still are in Alberta and Yakima. Here in the Seattle area, why, they did the same thing in regard to bringing Negroes up to work in the mines.

Black Diamond and New Castle. My husband says that as a boy and even in his teens—it must have been before he was going to Franklin High School—he had to cross the lake on a boat every morning to get to Franklin. He lived over there near Hazelwood, near Kendall.

Now there used to be a dock there where the boat was, but that has gone now and he used to make his extra money....They had to move over there from Seattle because of his mother's health. The doctor thought the country would be easier on her, so they built a house. It was rather primitive but the children always remember it with affection because they were young there. And I remember the wonderful food the mother cooked and the people. Their friends in Seattle loved to come over in the summer and picnic there. They remember the dog they had, my husband especially. He was the oldest and he tells about his father getting off the boat and having to walk, I forget how many miles, with his bag of groceries over his shoulder, to bring to the family. Although my father-in-law wasn't much of a...they used to kind of kid him about his ability as a farmer...but they enjoyed it...had a cow, and a little kind of a garden. They enjoyed it, they were happy...they were hospitable people and had a nice enjoyable time. My husband earned his money by working in this New Castle coal mine. He was just a boy. They moved over there when he was twelve, and they moved back to Seattle when he was seventeen.

I don't know how long he worked in the mines, I don't know what hours, but he mentioned coming home in the dark, so he must have worked swing shift. He had a bicycle, and he said, "I don't see how anybody ever made their way in the dark with no lights." He said he was as scared as he could be, riding his bicycle back in the dark.

When my husband arrived in Seattle at age seventeen, he stopped soon after that, I believe, but he was practically graduated. I don't know for what reason. His mother had poor health about that time, and I imagine that must have been a time when jobs were hard to get. He wasn't in the First World War because just as he was supposed to be drafted or had been drafted, the war ended. Then he went to E. N. Brooks, the haberdasher that he worked for for many years. He was a very good man. He was from Maine.... He was there as a messenger, a stock boy. I think he did some of the cleaning up in the store.

All our Negro schools, the majority of them, were founded by one religious denomination or another. Fisk was founded by the American Missionary Association and Howard was founded by Congregationalists, Spelman (by the Rockefeller family) and I think Morris Brown College in Atlanta was a Baptist school. There's another Baptist school, Oberlin, that was the first college to admit Negroes, and it was Congregationalist.

Of course, we know from history, the AME Church, how it happened to be founded. They were Negroes in Philadelphia trying to participate in the Methodist Church—and we all know this story, how they were—while they were praying, they were aroused and told that Negroes couldn't worship there. They wouldn't wait until they got through praying to stop that. So that was the origin of the AME Church.

When I grew up in Spokane, my family were Baptists where they came from, so I grew up there. I also, as young people will, I went where there were a larger number of young people as far as Christian Endeavor was concerned. So, I went to that. Then in the afternoon there weren't many places to go. It was terrible to be caught in the movie theater at that time, in that era, so I visited the Episcopalian Church in the afternoon, that was practically our social activity.

When the family moved to Vancouver, there were no Baptist churches, but my father, and the way I had been raised, they were open-minded and they thought to belong to a Negro church, whatever denomination, was more important than denomination. There was a Methodist AME Church in Vancouver, and we joined that church. My father was an intelligent man, and any organization he was in, they always wanted him to be the treasurer or the secretary. He had beautiful handwriting and he used to read papers to us and we had a family history. His grandfather was an escaped slave up to Canada.

Lewis Clarke was the grandfather, and he ran away up to Canada and he helped to get some of his other brothers and sisters out. They had thought they were free because Lewis Clarke's father was a white man and had married a mixed Negro slave, and they thought they would be free. When the father died, the master sold all his nieces and nephews back. So that's how Lewis and Milton Clarke came to run away. I believe...according to the little booklet that the family has, it says twenty-five years of slavery and poor treatment they had.

There were nine children in my father's family. Lewis Clarke and his brother went around lecturing, telling of their experiences, and then…trying to get help for other slaves through the underground or one way or another. They wrote a little booklet of all their experiences. Then in 1846, I think, the book was published.

My father was especially proud of the education and appreciated it. Our older generation of Negroes did. I know my father—and he could hardly walk—I don't remember him missing a voting time; he made every election. Mr. Gayton also. Mr. Gayton helped train immigrants as far as passing the test for immigration, that's one of the things he did.

Anybody who wanted to become an American citizen, and especially Italian immigrants. I believe the neighborhood where they lived had a number of Italians. So, then my father…when they were up in Canada, it was in the country and the mother died. They moved to Oberlin. I don't know whether the mother died after they had moved to Oberlin or before, but the children had to then be on their own mostly. I know my father speaks of working on a farm for somebody. My aunt, that I lived with, another family raised them. They all apparently got good educations because…one reason, I guess these men escaped was because they had some education. They had gotten it from their father.

So we were fortunate in that way. But as I have said, I don't know whether it was a true assumption or not, but so often coming out here to the West, the Negroes without any formal education had better chance of getting jobs, I think, than those with education.

My father really couldn't get a decent job. He never…as long as I remember did he have a job that was of any standing, and yet I see so many who had jobs who certainly didn't have the qualifications that he had. The best kind of job that he could get was on the railroad as a porter at that time. Perhaps he was an impatient person because, of course, he had taught school in Nashville and then when this political …after the Reconstruction, he thought he would be—as many people have in political times—thought he had a job promise, but when it came up, why, he was disappointed. So out of the disillusionment and need of more money, why, he went on the railroad. I think he was on the roads maybe four or five years before he settled in Spokane, and I think he went back to Chicago.

So, in the church my father, in Spokane and in Nashville, was superintendent of the Sunday school as a young man, and in Spokane he was the clerk of the church. He had beautiful handwriting. You know, they used to write, it looked like script. I have some of the letters that he wrote and it looks like script. He wrote like you read in stories. I mean, the language was nice, but, of course, those were times when people had more time to be gentler, I guess, and nice. He had a slight stroke there and had been out of work for a year in Vancouver. Although he was active in the Masons and the church had a debating society, he always took part in civil affairs. But then he got ill and moved here when he was partially crippled. He died here. That's the way. On both sides of the family, I think my children have been fortunate in having backgrounds where both families were luckily, neither on each side, from broken homes.

I was showing why we felt constrained to join the Methodist church, because of its history. Now it's a different thing, things are integrated. It's a good move to be members of white churches if you care to; they're integrated. That's the way the movement is that we hopefully have been working for all these years from during slavery time through DuBois, Frederick Douglass, and all those times, that's what we've been working for.

INTERVIEW BY RICHARD BERNER, JUNE 16, 1970
COURTESY SPECIAL COLLECTIONS, MANUSCRIPTS AND UNIVERSITY ARCHIVES
UNIVERSITY OF WASHINGTON, SEATTLE

Anita Hairston

NAACP volunteer
Born: November 5, 1907, Port Gibson, Mississippi

Anita Hairston left Mississippi looking for better educational opportunities. She attended Langston University in Langston, Oklahoma, and moved to St. Louis, Missouri, where she studied to become a teacher. In St. Louis, she met Everette Hairston, a young dentist, whom she later married. She relocated with her husband to Tulsa, Oklahoma, where she became a volunteer for the NAACP.

Access to education has never been easy for me. In my native Port Gibson, Mississippi, public education for blacks went no further than the tenth grade. So my parents sent me to Southern Christian Institute, a private black boarding school in Edwards, Mississippi, to complete my high school education. Then I enrolled at Langston University in Oklahoma. When I graduated from Langston, I moved to St. Louis, Missouri, where I had to go back to college for a year because the St. Louis school system wouldn't accept some of my Langston credits. After that year of remediation, I got a teaching job in the city, where I was very happy with my career. But my career was cut short because I met a young man.

I met Everette Hairston, a young dentist from Virginia, through the Disciples of Christ Church in St. Louis. Later, when he asked me to marry him, I said yes. But when he asked me to leave St. Louis and my teaching career to join him in Oklahoma, where he was going to set up his practice, I was very reluctant. But I did quit my job and come to Oklahoma with him in 1946.

I joined the Tulsa branch of the NAACP and served on its Education Committee. I attended an NAACP meeting in Los Angeles in 1948, and when I came back to Tulsa I was on fire to do something to help my own community more, to help the city provide more opportunities for black people. I had been thinking about going to graduate school. I didn't think that it was fair that black Tulsans had to leave the city, the city where they paid taxes just like everybody else, and go out of the city, and out of the state, to pursue graduate study. So I decided that I was going to go to the University of Tulsa, but, first, I would have to integrate it! I didn't think I would have much trouble. After all, the U.S. Supreme Court had ordered the University of Oklahoma to admit George McLaurin and Ada Lois Sipuel. But that Court ruling had no effect on the University of Tulsa. The university rejected my application for admission to school for the fall term of 1949! I just couldn't believe it. I tell you, I was mad. I was simmering.

Still simmering, I confronted Dr. Harry W. Gowans, then dean of the University of Tulsa's Downtown Division. This time, I met with partial success. Dr. Gowans said the University of Tulsa would provide classes for "colored students." The catch was that the "colored" students couldn't attend classes on the campus; the university would provide the classes in George Washington Carver Junior High School in North Tulsa. I had mixed feelings. On the one hand, I was glad that I could be a University of Tulsa student, at last, but I was disappointed that I couldn't go to class on the main campus. I longed to stroll that beautiful campus, to have classes in those classic buildings such as Tyrell Hall and in Kendall Hall, and to study in the magnificent McFarlin Library (named for Tulsa oil man Robert McFarlin). But that was not to be at that time.

I was asked to recruit other black teachers to study with me at Carver. Twenty signed up, but they let me down. Only one black teacher from Tulsa, Algerita Jackson, and five black teachers from Wagoner joined me in my graduate studies. It wasn't all that I expected. Still, I was grateful for the progress that we, as blacks in Tulsa, had made. It was a first step toward integration and full equality. My grandfather always told me, "One step is better than no step."

In just one year, black students were allowed on the main campus. The spring of 1950, Dr. Sandor Kovacs, a University of Tulsa sociology professor, put me in his class on the main campus. Years later, Dr. Kovacs was asked why he made that decision, why he became the university official to integrate the TU campus. He said, "I just felt that she (Hairston) would get more out of her studies on the main campus. I asked my students how they felt; not one objected." I instantly became a part of that class. The teacher was beautiful! The students were beautiful! It was a wonderful experience. Once the class went on a field trip to a house in Sand Springs (a little town just outside Tulsa). The entire class rode a bus to the home of a Sand Springs family who was host to the class. We had dinner with the family. We had the best time. Everyone was just as nice as could be.

When graduation time came in May 1952, some blacks in the community were apprehensive about me marching. They felt that there might be trouble if I marched across that stage and so they suggested that I have my diploma mailed to me. But my mind was made up. If that class of 1952 marched across that stage, I was going to march across it, too. I was part of that class and they were not going to mail me anything! And so I did march across that stage.

Things have changed so much. In 1952, blacks were fearful that I would be mistreated if I marched across the stage with my class. Now the University of Tulsa couldn't be nicer to me. In 1987, I was an honored member of the class of 1952's thirty-fifth reunion. They made such a fuss over me. Now the first thing you see when you walk into the TU Alumni

Center is a picture of me in my cap and gown on that day in May 1952, when I made history. Some people call me a human rights activist; some call me a hero. I'm pleased when my friends call me those things. But I wasn't trying to be a hero. I spent my whole life just trying to make this world a little better for all people. When I see students of all colors strolling over the beautiful TU campus today, I thank God for making me the vessel that made that possible.

INTERVIEW BY EDDIE FAYE GATES, MAY–AUGUST, 1994
COURTESY OKLAHOMA HISTORICAL SOCIETY
ARCHIVES AND MANUSCRIPT DIVISION, ORAL HISTORY DEPARTMENT

Erma Hadrey Hayman

Window dresser
Life dates: not known

Erma Hadrey Hayman's family moved around a lot when she was growing up—to Seattle and Boise and back to her birthplace, Nampa, Idaho. Her parents were farmers, but her father also worked as a custodian. When she was young, she was shocked to find that racism in Boise was "worse than the South for awhile." Hayman recalls that her parents and others had moved to Idaho because they had heard there were "better times" there. For most of her adult life, Hayman was employed as a window dresser.

My parents moved to Nampa in the early 1900s. They were there when Nampa was just beginning…they were there before there were any sidewalks. My father, I think, came to Montana for his health. My sister, she lives on South 13th, she was born in Missouri, and I was born out here many years later. My sister's name is Leona Horton. Andrew Horton is her husband. She doesn't like to talk about those days, I guess, because she's a lot older than I am, and she just doesn't like that. She said she can remember things that happened a long time ago.

My father, they used to live in Missouri—mother and father, and his health was bad there. And they heard of Montana. They needed men in the mines there, copper mines. He came out to Montana and I think he met this man that he later worked for and this man was coming to Idaho and I think that's where my father got the idea of coming to Nampa.

In Nampa he did a lot of things. My folks were farmers to begin with. My mother was a real farmer. My father wasn't so much of a farmer, so he went to town. There wasn't much for anyone to do then because the town was just beginning to build up, so he did whatever he could, which was mostly custodian work.

My mother was a housewife and like I said, we had a farm, a dairy farm to start out with. Yeah, she was a housewife and she loved to farm, too. Lots of people did. We had more people that were farmers then—in fact, most everybody then had just about spent part of their life on a farm. Now people know nothing about a farm, don't want to know anything about it.

I lived in Boise a long time ago...in 1928, 1927 and 1928. Then we moved to Seattle and I lived there for a while and then I came back. I lived with my parents for a while. They were beginning to get up in age then, and I stayed with them for a while. I decided it was time for me to get on my own, and that's when I moved to Boise. Well, my husband was a disabled veteran, my kids were little, and he spent most of his time in a veterans' hospital. A number of years.

Unidentified. Photo labeled "Tom" on back. He was a cook for the railroad along the Salmon River, ca. 1908-1910. (Idaho State Historical Society)

In Boise I lived on Grand Avenue. There were houses all along Miller Street; there were houses down Grand Avenue. Where I live now (617 Ash Street in Boise) I'm pretty sure is one of the older parts of Boise. I forget how many houses they took down around here. And people that rented, those houses were bought out from under them and then they'd have to find another place to live. That's why my neighbor here, there was a lady living in the house next door, she got wind they were trying to sell that property, so while she had a chance to get an apartment, she did. So it's vacant. Because that's what happened to people down here. If you didn't own your home, you better start looking for someplace because realtors and other people that knew this land was valuable—they began to sneak in down here and buy up the property.

I think this was the oldest part of Boise. I think it was when Boise first began to grow. This perhaps was where people lived then. It's always been mixed up (racially) down here. I'll tell you one thing that no one ever talks about, is this was the only part of town we (blacks) could live in. That's why we're down here. They won't talk about it, but it's the truth. Because I have tried to buy property other places a long time ago, before I bought here, and when they found out I was black, the first thing they'd say was that it was sold. I know they don't want us to believe that, but it's really been done. They just wouldn't rent you any house in any other part of town. If you did it was something that, you know, wasn't—if you got a place to live in any other part of town, it was kind of a run-down house. I know they don't like to hear you say that, but it's the truth. I've been here all my life, and I bought here. I could have bought some other places if they would have sold it to me.

I remember back when they couldn't even go in pool halls uptown. If they were going to have any pool hall or anything like that, they had to have it right down in this neighborhood. And that's why, that's why they had them. And anything else that went on.

I remember back when...you wouldn't be served in a restaurant. It's really been segregated here. I mean, it's worse than the South for a while. In the early days of Boise, now, the people uptown must have been here for very long; they don't want you to talk about that, but it is the truth. I remember back then. I'd say back in the twenties. I don't remember, like I say, I was out of the state for a while. I don't remember when it began to change, but even restaurants uptown didn't want to serve you.

Yeah, it began to change. There was (a few black families around here). But most of those people have died. I guess (they came to Idaho) for the same reason that my parents came. Maybe they heard there's better times out here. Maybe they just wanted—and maybe they came with some-one to work for, to work for them. That might have been the way some of them got out here. But yes, there was a few families. I know my parents and about a couple more families were the only black families that was in Nampa. And then really there was a few more in Boise. But most of those older ones, the ones that were here many years ago, back in the twenties, most of them have died because they would be quite old now.

There used to be a (black) lady lived down on South 14th, and her husband was a railroad man, and he stayed in Salt Lake (City) and she stayed here. But she would go visit him and he'd spend time here. I don't know. I think the Pullman porters used to come out here at one time.

The Pullman porters, they stayed overnight here. I think that's why she was here. Then after a while, they didn't do that. They'd just go back to Salt Lake. So I think that's why she stayed. And her niece is still here, but she's in her nineties and she's in a nursing home.

I guess there were problems, but to just remember everything that has happened and what went on, it's kind of tough. That's been a long time ago. Times have changed. You try to forget about those things.

There was a problem here for a while. I think it's been in the last ten years that they've been able to get better jobs here. Because again, you're really segregated from better jobs—you worked for someone in a home, at least most of them did. Of course, the younger generation has better jobs now. But when I was young in Boise, it was tough to get a good job. You didn't do anything but housework. I never have done housework, but

I did most of the other things. In fact, I worked for Lerners for about twenty years. It's a ladies' dress shop. But most of my friends did housework, things like that.

I was in display, and that's very hard. That's harder than housework. Lerners was a chain store and I don't think other stores had that kind of job available. Then later I trimmed the windows. But a lot of the other stores, one of the saleswomen would do that part of it. But Lerners wouldn't. I think they still do have a person to just take care of windows, display. Because that helps to sell their ladies' ready-to-wear.

Even the salespeople made a better salary than I did. It was one of the lowest-paid jobs in the store. I don't know what it's like today. But I hope times will get better, and I hope young people will get better jobs. I don't know why that is so, when you go to apply for a job and they think, well, you're just not qualified. They don't give you a chance; they just say you're not qualified.

There's always been black ministers here. But I don't remember them. I know they were here. There were two churches, but the main one was St. Paul's. Because finally the Methodist church folded because they didn't have enough people. The last minister I remember being there was Reverend Warren, and I think after he left, they didn't have a church anymore. I'm neither Methodist or Baptist, so I don't know much about the church. Like I say, I can't tell you too much about this part of town because I worked all the time.

There used to be a county hospital out on Fairview Avenue, and I think part of the hospital was for people who, when they got older, couldn't look after themselves or was sick. Because I remember a few people that were out there and then finally they did away with that. I don't remember what year. Now I suppose each hospital has, maybe a ward where people go that can't afford to pay their way. I think that's the way it's handled. I'm not sure.

A lot of people would just stay in their house until they died. You know, they did the best they could until they just got to the place where they needed to go to the hospital.

We had several neighbors as they got older they just stayed in their house until they just couldn't look after themselves and then, of course, it wasn't long then—they didn't live long after they put them in the hospital. My neighbor, Mr. Gillie, he was dependent on a man that lived across the street, and on me, to get his groceries to him, to pay his bills, and anything that needs to be done, we had to do it. And this neighbor sold his property and moved away, and so then it was just left to me. It was quite a lot of work. Then he needed to go to a nursing home because he was getting to the place where he couldn't get in his shower, he couldn't do anything for himself, and so one day I went over there and he was just talking about airplanes buzzing around the ceiling, so then we called in the medics and they took him to the hospital, and from there he went to the nursing home. I think you find people like that all over Boise.

I lived up on Pioneer because I wasn't able to find any other place to live except right around here. At that time, Senator Borah was living and he used to come down in this area. I remember a number of times when guys would just sit on your porch if you had a porch and they'd just sit there and talk in the evenings. A lot of times Senator Borah would be out there talking with them because that little short street up there is named Borah Street—used to walk from Owyhee down in this area. I think he stayed at the Owyhee (Hotel).

He used to come down and sit on my front porch and talk to the guys that lived there in the area. He'd discuss things—maybe politics, for all I know. You wouldn't think of him as being a senator because he was common with people. Just talked to everybody.

It was a very comfortable street. That must have been why they named it Borah, because he loved to walk down in that part of town. That's why I say, it must have been one of the first neighborhoods in Boise. It was an easy street for people to wander from town and I guess that's why they put what's called now Pioneer Walk. I walked on that street for about twenty years, going to town. I do it now; it's just a habit. When I go to town I don't want to drive. It's just as quick to just get on that path and go uptown. They've been talking about making a brick walk out of that for many years. So they finally did it.

Everybody, even from down in that part of town, they would come this way and up Pioneer, or cross at 13th, and 13th got to be kind of dangerous because I think a couple of people got hit there. I can just see a lot of people walking to town going up Lover's Lane because it was an easy way, a quick way to get to town. You can walk uptown in about five minutes going that way.

Interview by Mateo Osa, December 17, 1980
Courtesy Idaho Oral History Center, Boise, Idaho

Minnie Lee Haynes

Housekeeper; descendant of Samuel D. Chambers
Born: March 14, 1881, Mississippi

Minnie Lee Haynes is the granddaughter of Samuel D. Chambers, who migrated to Utah in 1870. Chambers was thirteen years old and a slave in Mississippi when he became a Mormon in 1844. After his emancipation in 1865, he labored as a sharecropper until he earned enough money to move his family. Chambers prospered as a producer of currants and small fruits in Utah and was a highly regarded member of the Mormon community. In 1927, he sent for Minnie Lee Haynes, his granddaughter by marriage, to come to help him. Haynes was living in Memphis, Tennessee, at the time and decided to relocate her family to Utah. In the following excerpts from the interviews conducted by William G. Hartley as part of the Church of Jesus Christ of Latter-day Saints oral history program, Haynes recounts her memories of Chambers and discusses her life in Mississippi and the circumstances that led to her move to Memphis and then to Salt Lake City.

My mother was a sharecropper with a widow woman with the name Miss Jennie Calhoun; she was in Mississippi. We sharecropped two years with her, then we moved to another place. We moved with the Jack Cottons then. We moved from Jack Cottons's to Sam Avery's. And the next place we went to was Clarence Weaver's. I stayed there four years sharecropping. He was a big plantation man, had 200 to 300 head of people living on his place. Now Bill Weaver and Clarence Weaver was brothers and I don't know who had the most people on their place, their plantation, Clarence or Bill. But we lived with Clarence about six years. Well, when we was through sharecropping with him we come to Louisville, Mississippi, and sharecropped with Mrs. Rosie Armstrong. That was our little town, Louisville, Mississippi. And after we left Louisville we come to Memphis, Tennessee, stayed there four years and come from there here to Salt Lake and been here ever since, and the year we got here was 1927. That's as far as I can go.

I lived in Arkansas before I lived in Louisville. 'Course we was sharecroppers and this colored man told my husband what he'd do for him if he moved up there. And we was so far in the country, I always did want to get close to town with my kids. You know, it was more fun to see than it was back out there in the woods. And some places, you lived so far out in the woods, 'course there was a road that come in there and one to go back out but then you never did see nobody pass there and come in like you see cars pass people's houses now, and I just didn't want to stay there. We had

*Amanda and Samuel
D. Chambers, Salt
Lake City, 1908
(LDS Church Archive)*

so many places, 'course we was sharecroppers mind you, we'd move there and if we liked you and you liked us, we'd stay there and we raise our chickens, our cows and calves, horses, pigs, sheep, anything we wanted to raise; we didn't have to pay for that. No, we didn't have to pay for that.

I left Dr. Kirk when I went to Louisville. Champus Kirk. His brother's named Clem Kirk. Well, I lived with Albert Liddell; when I left him we went to Dr. Kirk's and when we left Dr. Kirk we come to Louisville. Before Dr. Kirk I lived with the Averys.

It was about twelve or thirteen miles from Louisville. It was just a country town, but people out in the suburbs would always come to town every Saturday. Bring milk to sell and cream and butter. That's the way he made his money for the church. My husband and me and my sister and sister-in-law, all the neighborhood people down there, did that. And Louisville, you see, that was the only town we could go to, and you know in lots of places everything have to be sterilized in this and that and have to be inspected. Well, we never did have it inspected, but the white folks bought it. And that's all that we cared for. Sometimes we would be building the church and they would want to enlarge the church and buy land. We sold butter and milk and eggs, chickens, enough to put $125 in our church. And we had gas lights like we got electric lights now. We just always put our money to good; we raised everything we needed.

Well, Calhouns weren't so close to Louisville. That was way out in the country. It would take you a day to drive from the Calhouns' to Louisville. You'd have to leave before day to get there by noon.

It wasn't no town, it was just the country. A lot of people lived out there and farmed out there, sharecroppers. Now Shugualak was the next close town where you carried the cotton and the seed to sell down there. They could get more money for the cotton and seeds in Shugualak than you could in Louisville, so they just always go to Shugualak.

Well, we'd start like this evening and get there at crack of dawn in the morning, it was just that far apart. Just like you was going from Provo to Idaho; it is that distance apart.

When I was like five, six, seven, eight years old, I was baby-sitting for Annie Whitfield. She was a Missouri woman. I stayed with her more than I stayed with my own mother. Me and her oldest daughter Jennie were the same age. She had Jennie and little Annie and Joe, she had three kids. Two girls and one boy. Her husband, he was the store man, he run the store down there, country store. Me and her oldest daughter was the same age, Jennie and Minnie. And she wanted all the other of Mother's kids to call her daughter "sister," so these other two kids would say "sister" and wouldn't say "Jennie." And that's the way we were all raised, just like a nut in the shell. We was all raised right there. Mother washed for her for years, my mother washed and ironed for her. And her husband was named Seymour and she was named Annie, and her second girl, she's a doctor. She had two girls and one boy, Joe. I don't know where he is. They may be living and they may be dead.

Well, there was a line, you know, you'd be on your side and the other farm is on this side. Way down here going on the Heber "Creeper" Railroad from Heber, Utah, to Provo Canyon. The farms down there remind me of there: the old wood fences, the rail fences, boards around, old-fashioned barns, and the things what they put the cows in. Partitions you know, way down there, that's on the other side of Provo. We've been down there twice this year, the senior citizens.

My parents grew cotton, they grew peas, they grew peanuts, Irish or white potatoes, sweet potatoes, they had three kinds of sweet potatoes; they had white yam and yellow yam, then these here others was Spanish taters, but they was a purple tater, grew so big (eight inches to a foot). Big around, that big around and so long (over a foot). Great big taters. Watermelons and peas and cane. Now ribbon cane, they called that blue cane. Then the sorghum cane, that was just the sorghum, but it had a dropped top, a crooked top to it. That's what they made the syrup out of. You raised everything and made the sugar out of molasses, and you never have to buy no sugar. Never. The biggest thing you bought at the store was flour and rice and coffee and like that, but the rest of the stuff, chickens, turkeys, guineas, pigs, and everything was raised right there for this house. Everybody had it. In places they raised their own horses down there, too.

Our house was nothing but a log house. With the boards nailed over the cracks, from end to end and on the top. They didn't have no roofing for the cover of the house. Had to cover it with the shingles and pieces of plank and you could look up and see stars through the top of the house when you was in the bed. And when it rained, you'd have to get up and get the tub and set it down and catch the water. That's quite a house when you live there.

The houses were different; the further up toward the west we come, the better the houses was. Now when I moved to Louisville I didn't have but my three kids—that was before this boy Robert was born—three girls, and we farmed up there but we was in a good house. It wasn't but three rooms and a shed room and a porch, but it was a good house to live in. Kitchen stove, and wasn't no dining room, you just had to put the table on one side of the kitchen and cooking (things) on this side.

I reckon it could have been around 1913 when we moved to Louisville. I had all them papers, but moving and packing up and throwing away things, things I ought to have kept, I throwed them away, and I've been up there on Goshen Street, over on 3rd North and there at 7th South, round on Blair South, on 8th South, here on Salt Lake. And I lived on Washington Street and 8th West over here. So I'm going to move away from here if I can find what I want.

The first house I remember had two rooms. Shed room and a bedroom. That's all. Just them two. Me and my sister and mother slept together, and them boys slept together. Just like pigs in a pen, piled up together, you couldn't do no better. Just couldn't do no better. Did you know that some men in the country is awful holy about it? If your wife go and tell Mr. So and So about your condition, why he'll live right with her, but if she wanted to stay here with you and didn't want to move, why he'd go and leave her and get him another woman and move off and get from around her, and she's still hanging on to you. That's the way it is in lots of places in the South. The woman would have to go first. And then he'd come and take over after. And that's the reason I wouldn't never marry no more, God knows, never.

Oh, we stayed there I reckon near three years. I don't know. I could have been thirteen or fourteen years old. I was born in 1881, so you can figure. That's as far as I know about that. It's just been so many turns around and turn up, you know.

With sharecropping now, like you got a farm. And you want me to work with you. Well, I work with you and everything is raised on your lot, you get half and I get half. That's the way it'll be. Half of the corn, half of the cotton, half of the seeds, half of everything that's raised there. I get half and you get half. That's what you call sharecropping.

We always got together. And we done have rooster fighting and I seen one on the TV the other night and I was laughing to Robert and I say, "That's the way folks used to be, have roosters, one was a game rooster and the other one was a Rhode Island Red, and these here other speckled chickens, I forget the name of them, but anyhow, they'd go miles to see these two roosters fight just like you'd go to see a prizefight, to see who had the best chicken. They wasn't nothing but just roosters. And that was all the time, you know, recreation you know, for the community, for the people. And you didn't hear talk of no shooting, no killing, no running away and kidnapping day and night like they doing now. And everybody had one pair of shoes they wore to church every Sunday. When them shoes wear out, they'd go barefoot. Yes sir, I know that myself, for I've had to do it many and many and many a times.

When I was young, they'd have log rollings out in the country. Cleaning up ground, you know, for the farm. And they'd ask people to this log rolling, sometime there would be twenty men there, just men outside of the women what was cooking the dinner for this log rolling. Louis Floor, we was living there. And he had such a pretty place down there in Kemper, and he said he wanted to get them there logs sawed in two, and they was going to have dinner at his house for to have the log rollings. And had two acres of logs for to pick up and pile up and burn up. And they all called me "Bob" all the time, just like all them here in Salt Lake call me "Grandma."

"Well," he said, "Bob, you and me going to work together today."

And he's a big man. Look like he'd going to have twin babies, his belly was so big.

I said, "You want to lift logs with me?" I was pregnant. "Because you're stout." I say, "I ain't going to be lifting no logs with you. That there stick might slip out of your hand, it might hit me in the stomach and kill my baby, and I want my baby to live. Oh no. Oh no." Well, it'd be four to the log, two in front and two behind. Just like the casket, to put it in the morgue or something. And bless your soul, me and him hauled logs all day.

Mrs. Eldredge says, "Lou, who did you lift logs with today?"

He say, "With Bob."

She said, "No you didn't. The woman's pregnant, and you lifting logs with her?"

He says, "Why sure, she lifted it." And when it's pigtail, it's just two in the front, one on that side and one on this side, and the other one is holding the log by hisself, just that one.

And she says, "I'm going to get after her." And she told Mary Hudson to tell me to come down there. Mary a little bitty short woman. I went up. She says, "What is you lifting logs with my husband for?"

I says, "We cleaned up the grounds so we could have some farming this year." I said, "You ain't married is you?"

She said, "No I'm not married, Minnie." I bought her coat from her. And she says, "Now listen, don't you be lifting and straining after these logs with them 'cause they say you strong because you might lose your baby."

I said, "I ain't going to lose my baby. The more work I do before the baby come, the better time I have when I go to have the baby." And I know that, I didn't dodge nothing. I went in digging ditches, plowing with these here old steel plows that throwed the dirt both ways, busters, I done every bit of it. Plowed with the busters, harrows. Drag the ground off and go back and make center ridges, make the rows for to plant the stuff. I did all of that. And God has blessed me to see and to talk about it, and if I had to do it again, if it wouldn't be too heavy, I'd try it again.

We had ball games, baseball games. My husband was the umpire for eleven years. That's the reason I love ball games so much now. I sit and look at them. Not thinking about eating. Just look out and see who's the best in the game, you know. And we'd go to the ball games and then they'd have parties from one house to the other. Well, next Friday night it's going to be something over at Jim Rogers's, then when it goes from Jim, it'd go to Shep Shed's and it would go from Shep Shed's, the corner 'round to King Bird's, there's the neighborhood, you know. But after King come to be a minister, he just stopped the partying, you know. Oh them was good old days then, oh boy! We was having a lot of fun in the country and out in the country, too.

Well, they felt just fine (about sharecropping), if they knew you was a good man, they fell in line for you. We going to live with Mr. So and So, he won't let us go hungry while we work and we're lots of the people.

Now a man, Gib Clark, his oldest son was a doctor. He was over in Sunnyside. He was a plantation doctor over there. He had three slaves with him. And ole Miss Betsy, she was old man Gib's wife, and they cook this old, hard pone bread meal. Just put salt in it, cook it. And you know she'd put it in this wheelbarrow and them old people would have to get that bread out of there to eat and they was setting up to the table with peach pie, apple pie, and Jell-O and jelly. Something else, you name it and they had it on the table, but they didn't feed them slaves and they done all the work. And this one he called this boy, his name Nick, little colored boy.

He said, "You come and I'm going to whip you tomorrow." Now if he tells you he is going to whip you tomorrow, he wouldn't whip you today, he'd wait till tomorrow come. And he said, "You come up here to me," make him pull his shirt off down to his waist and then every time he'd draw back, why kick, he'd run back.

He's says, "Oh, they didn't get me in the ditch." It was just so funny. It was just bad to see him like that and they'd slip around at night from house to house and they'd come back and speak with him, living with old man Clark right there on Main Street, it was just a little suburb place with a lot of beer and stuff around.

But old lady Betsy, ole hussy, I says, "Oh Fannie" (Fannie was this ole lady, Betsy's daughter), and I've told all these many a day. I've said to put lye in her coffee. "How come?" And she's mean, too. When you find one of them white women down there was mean, it was just unmanageable. And they was mean to the colored folks. They wasn't mean to the white, their own color. It wasn't that there was no white slaves no how. It wasn't nothing but them. And I've told Fannie many a day, put lye in her coffee and give it to her. And she'd taste it, "Oh, and bring the coffee, it's too hot. Bring the coffee, it's too cold." This one gal would just keep a going all the time, to and from until she'd get through. And I just hated her so bad. I reckon I got to ask God to forgive me for hating that white woman like I did. But if I'd had a chance and had been around her using her food, and that's something like I never had thoughts of doing to nobody, because your life is just as good to you as mine is to me. But I know I'd a put something in her food to get shut of her. I know it, ain't no need a lying, I know I'd a done it if I'd a been there, but I wasn't there.

She was just a neighborhood woman. All of us lived there together. One would go to the other's house and get meal, and get salt, and get something to go in the food. That's the way we lived. We just lived that close together. When one didn't have it, if you had it, I'd come and get it and if I had it and you didn't have it, you'd come and get it. That's the way we lived. For years and years and years.

Oh, there (were several families that sharecropped). There was Jim Rogers and his mother had his own family, and old man Robertson, that's two. And Robert Marshall was three. John Marshall was four. Jim Patey was five. Let me see. There's some more. Then there's another set of Dougans, that was my auntie's husband, Charlie Dougan. That's all of us that worked with him and lived with him. There was colored Dougans and white Dougans, you know. Well, in slavery, reason the colored had the white man's name, because the parents was slaves of his, you see. And so they just called him Uncle Charlie. Charlie Dougan. But he was named after Jim Dougan, his daddy. Jim was named after his daddy and Charlie was named Dougan after him. That's the way that come around.

Well, they didn't have nowhere else to work. They had to work somewhere to make a living. And Dougan had pretty good houses for them, you know, for them to live in. They work in the fields all day and then work flower yard work at home at night. And they had the prettiest yards down there out in the country ever you walked through. Do the washing at night so they could make a full day tomorrow in the field. Now in celebration days, like a birthday now, and Fourth of July and those, they'd give us these days. And they'd make this old molasses bread. Oh, it was good. Everybody'd come and they got these great big huge pines, these old pines, and lots of places they baked the bread in these kilns like you see the Italians make their bread. Now over in Sunnyside you can't see nothing but kilns, brick kilns, and you can just bake so much bread. You can bake 100 pounds of bread at one baking in them kilns. I worked over there for eighteen months with a man what owns Sunnyside. Went over there to pick cotton and I wasn't making much out at picking cotton, so they take me in the house and so I was the cook and I stayed over there eighteen months. In Sunnyside, Arkansas. That was before, I reckon two or three years before I come here.

Sunnyside is southwest of Memphis. You know the Mississippi River cuts Arkansas and all them places right in two. Mississippi on the southeast side. I was in Sunnyside, I stayed there 18 months. I went over there to pick cotton. But the man what owned the plantation, his wife liked me so much, and I could cook, I just went in the house, and there I stayed eighteen months, till I come back home. My kids wasn't nothing but babies, but my mother kept them and I paid her for keeping them.

The boats (on the Mississippi River) would land there every day, three or four boats a day would land there at the landing. It's just out of walking distance where I was living on the south side of the levee, walk about as far as from here down to the river, be to the landing where the boats landed.

In Sunnyside they had a great big plantation. Hundreds of acres belonged to one man. Horses and cows, he'd have two riders. One riding to see about his end and the other one riding to see about that end. It sure was nice over there. But you know, a mother got kids regardless to the money in which she gets. Them kids come first. All three of them girls was with my mother, and she cared for them, done for them a whole lot what

I wouldn't do for them. She'd wash the little dresses at night and dry them and iron them, kept them clean. That's the way I'd do but when I got tired I'd quit. Anyway, that's where I was at, in Sunnyside, Arkansas. Old man Eldredge, Eddie Eldredge, he was an old man but he married this redheaded young woman, and she was just a lover of colored people. I stayed with her, she was sweet to me, give me more of her whick-whacks (knick-knacks), what she didn't want to throw out she would give to me. She hated to have me go, but I done been away from my kids so long, it wasn't five years but it was just eighteen months, but it was long enough. I had to come home and see about my kids. They was in Noxubee, Mississippi.

Well, they had everything, they had soy beans, they had cotton, they had cane, blue cane, and sorghum cane, and corn and peas and peanuts and potatoes, they haul them like they haul them in Idaho, just by the tons. And I'm telling you, just like I told my boy here a week ago last, says, "You know, you been talking about getting me a house, I want one out on the west side of Redwood Road where I can have me a pig and some chickens."

"Mama, you know that's too much work for you to do, you can't work like that no more." I said that you wouldn't have nothing to do but get the feed and set it in a dry place and feed them when the time comes to feed them. I'd like to do that right now. But I ain't got the strength now that I used to have. Working all day in the fields, and coming to the house, washing, hanging the clothes up, four or five lines of clothes, but they don't do that no more, they got washers now and dryers, too, you can wash your clothes and dry them and iron them and get through with them.

I picked cotton for one week. And I stayed there the balance of the time. I separated and sold milk and cooked, done general housework. I got $24 a week. And all the food I could eat, because I was cooking at the time. And we had a houseboy there named Joe Anderson. He'd been with Mr. Eldredge and them, oh for years. And he thought he was white, but he was just a light boy. And anybody that just didn't know him would take his stuff. Mr. and Mrs. Eldredge, the red house, the store, everything he thought belonged to him. And he come on in there, he done all the milking but I done all the separating, milk you know, they got them things you separate the cream from the milk. He brought a big bucket of milk in, sat it there, turned around.

"You better separate that milk before the cream rise up." I say, "You can separate it if you want."

"Well, I ain't going to separate it, and you going to separate it right now."

And when the right-hand door rolled up, it would lock. And Mrs. Eldredge had some knives in there and cleavers, they was always killing something and having something to cut with. I slammed that door and grabbed that cleaver there. He jumped up in the sink, he broke that in, broke all the front off her china closet and the cabinets up on the east side of the kitchen. I had him so hot with that knife he turned loose and fell, and when he fell he run against the door and that's what opened the door for him and he got out. I tried to cut his head off.

Mrs. Eldredge heard all falling and them dishes and she come in there and says, "What in the world is the matter?"

I say, "Ask Joe when he comes back."

She say, "What is that?" I say, "He gone outside there somewhere."

"Did you hurt him?"

I wasn't much of a woman when I was young, stout as a man. I ain't saying it was 'cause of me, but I had nine big brothers. And what those boys did, I was so much of a tomboy that I had to do it, too. And my sister, she was so much ladylike, she just didn't take sides with nothing I did. I didn't rob nobody and I didn't kill nobody but I just didn't take no stuff off of nobody. You talk to me, I talk back at you. And that is me today. When they talk to me at senior citizens, I talk back to them. If they want to fight, I don't know how long it will last, but I'll fight, too.

My daddy's daddy was a slave. And his mother. I don't know whether they have any Indian slaves or not. But anyhow, his mother was Choctaw Indian. I don't know whether she was ever any slave or not. Made no difference how you cooked and fixed it. She wanted that pone bread when you make it with all the print of your fingers on it, you know. And she just liked that bread all the time.

That was my daddy's mother. And I remember her, her braids laid that far on her lap. She was a little short woman, broad. I declare I always just wanted her hair, but the Lord didn't give it to me. But she sure had some beautiful hair.

All I know about the Civil War was that my husband's mother, Martha Harris, she said that she was a girl twelve years old when the Civil War started. And she died right over there in my house on Goshen Street here in Salt Lake. I got a pair of her eyeglasses. I'm going to try to find them. They're silver and they are gold-frame glasses all over. Just the little things is just half as large as the glasses is now. And she says them were her glasses and she started wearing them glasses the day the Civil War started. And she broke them and wrapped them up and put them in a case, and I've moved that thing a dozen times and I'm so afraid they are going to get throwed away in taking out boxes of paper.

Now the woman I what raised me, Annie Whitfield, now she was from Missouri and she didn't never talk anything. Some of the people would talk to their kids and some of them wouldn't.

I reckon my grandfather must have worked on the Dougan plantation as a slave because I wasn't old enough to know and big enough, too, but he worked on there. He worked right along with the rest of us. Dougans, I tell you, it's just like Murray, Utah, down here. One man on Murray, one here, that the way Dougan was. He just owned a lot of people and owned a lot of land and had a whole lot. He'd go from one to the other. But he didn't do like old Dan Pickett. He had a lot of young, nice, pretty colored girls. He didn't take up with them. Aza Lee, Richard Craig's daughter, that was the girl that old Dan, he wouldn't marry her, because the whites is against the colored and the whites marrying; they couldn't marry there like they do here: colored man marry a white woman and a white man marry a colored woman. They don't go for that now. No. Now but Dougan, he was just a gentleman to everybody. He was just a nice man. And he tried to feed everybody out of the same spoon. Wouldn't make no difference in the people, you know. Some he liked all right. But he never would do that (like Pickett). If he did there wasn't none of us that knew anything about it. But old Dan, there is so much dog in him. Had some of the prettiest kids. Great big old chunky, round-faced, brown-eyed gals. They didn't have Aza Lee's hair at all. They had straight hair just like their daddy.

Down there had a baptizing place, 'course it was in the creek, but nevertheless, Dougan always let them baptize in his certain spot. And there's more water moccasins and snakes in that place than ever I've seen in my life. It was just a snaky country down there, that's what it is. I don't know where the snakes come from. And we had a place up there in the field, they called it the "snake graveyard." That was when we was living with Clarence Weaver. We'd plow and just like you see that line all looped up and down (points to the extension cord on the floor), you can plow them up and look back and see snakes laying in there, that was coiled like that line. They'd bite you, too, if you didn't get out of the way. You'd done plowed them up, but they'd sure bite you. Let me tell you, you walking behind the plow, when you plowing, you can't walk to the side of the plow, you got to stay in between them handles, and hold that plow just right for to make your furrow like you want to make it. And then you plow up a snake, and he is as long as from here over there (five feet) and about as big around as that coffee can, what you going to do? I just turned the plow loose, and when you go to run, what you plowing—the horse or the mule—he'll run, too, because he ain't got nothing to hold him back. Oh, Lord, I made such a roar one day I was snakebit, I plowed a whole lot and I was coming up. I just made so sure I was snakebit, I throwed this plow down and held to my lines and pulled the horse out, and come on around. Those snakes; you could just see the dust behind him. He's making a dust trying to get to the woods. We was right over from the woods. And that's since I met my husband and was married. And he always called me "wife."

He says, "Wife, where you going?"

I pointed back and he went on up and he sees these two great big old snakes.

He said, "Them's guinea snakes, they won't bite you, to hurt you."

I say, "I don't want nary a one them damn snakes to bite me. I don't care if them don't."

Mr. Dougan was a fine man. His wife was named Mary. Mary Lou. She's just as white and blonde. Hair as long as a cow's tail. I've combed and brushed her hair many a day. Oh, yes. They was good people. You can find good white people down there and then and you can find…when you find a wretch you done found one. He's wretched.

I came to Salt Lake to Samuel D. Chambers in 1927. And I've been here ever since. I was in Memphis, Tennessee. He sent for me to come and stay with him and wait on him and his wife and I did. His wife passed and I took care of him until he died; washed, cooked, ironed, cleaned up for him.

I've done everything needed to be done. I had my whole family here, my daughter, and her baby, my husband and my baby, that boy was here, Robert. I weaned him right here in Salt Lake up there on East 20th. Dr. Aura O. Johnson weaned that boy from my breast. I been here ever since.

We taken care of the fruit trees and their farm. We made as much as $250 a year over his fruit, but he turned it in to pay his tithes in the church. That's what he do with it. I didn't get nothing but just what we ate. We had a granary there, with everything in it. You name it, he had it. And we didn't buy nothing, only just staple stuff like flour, sugar, and rice every now and then from the store. Mr. White was running the store there on 33rd and Highland Drive, and he furnished our groceries. His boy was our grocery boy. He'd deliver our groceries every week. Dude was his name. Dude White and his wife: Dude's mother, she named Dot. His sister's named Cornelius White. Mrs. White and Joe White and John White, all the Whites are still over there now. I can carry you to their houses right now.

I used to work for Mrs. Neff. She lives straight up Evergreen. On the corner, on the right-hand corner of Evergreen going east. I worked for her three years just on the farm and in the flowers, milked cows, and changed the milk. I just worked. All the white people out there knows Minnie Haynes; everybody knows me. I worked for them a long time.

So, Grandpa Chambers...he just wanted us to stay there and work and get just what we needed to eat, but no clothes, no shoes, no nothing. I thought at his last days he would give me a house.... They said when I come there, "Well, Grandpa's house is very nice." He had it built for him and Amanda. But it was so filthy. She wasn't no woman who could have anything nice, keep it nice; she just loved to be outside all the time. That was his wife. She had a bleeding cancer.... I had to wash her every day from Monday morning till Monday morning. Sunday didn't make no difference. I had to wash her to keep her clean, keep things for her to change in. Then the blood when it passes is just like water coming out a pipe.

And Bishop Fagg, he was the bishop then, Charles Fagg.... I went down to the church, but bishop get after me about joining the church and being baptized, in the Latter-day Saint faith. But I said, "Christ wasn't baptized but once. Why should I be baptized twice?" But I just as well went on and did it because I was baptized in the church I'm in now. And that's the Holiness Church....We got colored bishops, just like you all got white bishops.... I went to Wilford Ward Church. I can't tell how many times I been there. I stayed out there in that neck of the woods six years and I went to the church and up to the Mormon Temple...Tabernacle I mean. I went a solid week with Bishop Fagg; he was minister up there, and he'd come.

"You wanta go to church, Haynes?"

I'd say, "Yes, I want to go. I'll go get ready."

"Crawl in the truck with me."

It was a cattle truck for the butcher shop. Me and my husband worked up there, and he had a butcher shop way out up there where he killed sheep and the pigs and everything and brought them into his brother's shop down there on Highland Drive. We'd go up there and, oh dear Lord, he had gave me 200 pounds of lard off of the pigs and sheep. And got all the chitlins, that what they called them, and some called them ruffles. We called them chitlins, the pigs and sheep bowels. We'd go up there and the snow was a foot and a half deep.

And we carried Grandpa up to the Zions Saving. We went to ZCMI's first, that was where he had his clothes and shoes made in the basement at the ZCMI store.... You name it and they do it because I stood and looked at them cut out Grandpa's shoes that day. You know, whenever I see anything, I never forget it. And so we got his suit and his shoes and six pair of socks. He got his wife a print dress and a fifty-cent hat with a great big border of roses to the front part of it. We were getting them ready to go to the old folks' day down at Liberty Park, and that was the day he throwed his real bank book up over that thing, that partition, but it's got an opening to it.

Thomas says, "You going to get any money out, Grandpa, while you're up here where you can get change?"

He looked at me and rolled his eyes. He says, "No."

He throwed it up over there. He said, "What I've got, it from the white man and it's going back to the white man." That's what he said. He'd taken the book from Tommy and just throwed it like that and Mr. McEwen, he got the book. That was his lawyer, William McEwen. You can look in there and tell what money, and this here's all I got when I stayed with Grandpa. You can go all the way through that book.

Well, he give his son, Sam Davidson, a $1,000 before he died. He give his daughter $1,000....That's Martha, my husband's mother. He gave her $1,000....And Minnie (Mrs. Dennis Pipsin) was uncle Sam's (Davidson) daughter. He give her $1,000. She lives in Denver, Colorado, now. And so after Grandpa died, they were going to get up the money, get them a lawyer here to see how much Grandpa had. Well, the interest on the money was $5,000 then.

I don't know what year it was, but anyway, that was after he died and was buried. They were going to get it (and prevent other members of the family from getting any). Well, they got D. A. Oliver, I reckon I knew him, he was a colored lawyer.

He said they were going to have a suit about this money. Well, they got Oliver up there. They all met early and someone paid Oliver off, and that just cut everybody else out. Oliver got his money for working for these here three people, for Minnie, Sam, and Peter....But didn't none of them come there and do nothing for him when he was sick! Before he got sick, they didn't come and clean up and wash and scrub and wash the woodwork and keep the house. But I did that.

Dot White, she come there and she'd stand and look. She says, "Minnie, this house is cleaner than it's ever been since Brother Chambers had it."

She said, "You done nice careful work here, keeping this place cleaned up."

I always like a clean house and nice yard. He didn't have any objection to me putting flowers around, bordering the year with flowers, and cleaning. But he didn't give me what he ought to give me, because I done a lot of work there. Lots of work. He'd just get to thinking, just sitting, thinking, talking to himself. I said he's going crazy. I'd always tease him. He'd call me "Mattie" all the time, he never would call me Minnie.

I say, "What you sitting out here, what doing, counting your money?"

"No, Mattie, I ain't counting my money. I'm just thinking."

I say, "What you thinking about, tell me so I can help you think."

I teased him all the time. He liked me very much. And I liked him, but he didn't like me well enough to give me an acre of ground for a house. He didn't do that. And after, he give it to the bank. As long as he was here, he had 100 acres of land in Idaho.

And what did they do with that land? Everything Grandpa Chambers had went to the state and to the church. Well, after all of that, why didn't they get somebody to come there and do what I did? Why didn't they? They was getting it for nothing, how come I couldn't get some? I was working for what I got. But I didn't get nothing. And I ain't got nothing today. I need a home today.

I was talking last night with my teacher. I said, "Mr. Mac, you know. I'm going to ask the Latter-day saints for me a home."

He said, "Up there they will give it to you, anywhere you want it. Ask them for it."

I go to school two nights a week, Monday and Wednesday. My teacher here, Mac Isabell, he says, "I think the Latter-day Saints should give you something." Because Grandpa's money will never run out, exists as long as Salt Lake is in this valley. Now, he's the founder of the Sugar House. Grandpa Chambers is. And he's got 100 acres of land up in Idaho.

But I reckoned it went to the church, too, and me, I ain't got nothing.... If I don't live but two days, I want a house of my own.

He says, "What sort of house do you...."

And I say, "I want a two-bedroom house."

I belong to the Holiness Church. When I lived over in Goshen, 448 Goshen, I stayed there thirty years. People from California come in, the missionaries and ministers going to Chicago, going to St. Louis, they come to Mother Haynes's house. I'm known from coast to coast. Bishop Clark, his wife was first cousin to my husband.

Every time they come in to Salt Lake from Arizona, they'd come to Mother Haynes's. And I had had so many preachers and missionaries there. I wouldn't have no place to sleep. I give them my bed to sleep in, trying to be nice to them. But God has blessed me for what I did. He really has, and I know he's blessed me and he going to bless what I want. He's going to bless me to get. I don't know how long I'm going to live after I get it, but I'm going to live to get it.

Yes, I come from Memphis, Tennessee, here. Samuel Chambers had written to Martha ever since he had left the South. The Hayneses, she and husband and kids, they worked the farm and peddled Samuel's fruit in his last years.

Samuel Chambers's house had a living and dining room, kitchen; upstairs had three bedrooms. There was a granary to the northeast. Furniture not fancy. Hardwood bed and an iron bed. Maybe a partial basement. The farm was maybe eight acres. Was long, running east and west and maybe one acre wide.

Amanda lived longer than Samuel…they come in Brigham Young's day. She told me they come in covered wagons. Brigham Young and them, and brings Brez Leggroan (Edward). He's dead. Lou's dead. Ed's dead. All the Leggroans is dead.

Grandpa (Chambers) was my husband's mother's daddy…. Samuel D. Chambers was Martha Harris's daddy. Her last husband was a Harris but her first husband was a Haynes.

And so they all come there together, and stayed together. Now Brigham Young's wife…she was the first woman in the state, hit the spike. They called it the spike something (Golden Spike Monument—where the train tracks from the East and West were joined in Promontory, Utah).

Amanda laughed and talked about it (life before they came to Utah). They farmed. All of us farmed down there. It was in Mississippi, and they worked on shares. Half was what I made, and you got half of it.

Grandpa Chambers once had been a slave. And he went by the white people's name. But he was so white. Just an old white man. He wife…he wanted to marry my husband's mother's mother, and she was so white they wouldn't let them marry, you see, or the kids be white. They was this mulatto people, one-half white. The whiter a man is, the blacker the woman is, the whiter the child. When white man marries a brown woman, the child is not as white as when he marry a dark woman, That's how it works, anyway. So he said they wouldn't let him marry Mary. Mary Vann. That's Thomas's mother's mother. They wouldn't let Grandpa Chambers marry Mary Vann but he did slip and get this baby by her and raised her. She had one child and that was Martha. And she was as white as woman needed and still in the colored race. Well, her mother was colored. I don't know how they met. They could have been on plantations. Just like this (block) is a plantation and cross over there and there's a plantation. And they could have. Now, he said he crawled a half mile through the cotton—you know the cotton grows tall—to get with this woman. He found her out there waiting for him.

In Mississippi they plowed oxen down there in place of plowing the horses. They mill the corn. But when they all got up, all they was going over the plains to Utah. Everybody sold out and give out and come to Utah. They had covered wagons. They have them there in the parade every July (when they all come out). His monument's right there on Temple Square right in the center of the street. He said, "Boys, this is the place."

They was six months getting here but God did bless them to get here. They (the Leggroans and the Chamberses) come from Mississippi.

They would see one another every Sunday or two going to the Baptist churches. But they come to be Latter-day Saint people after they come there and went to going to Brigham Young's church. He made Mormons out of them. Maybe they joined the church in Mississippi. But I know he (Chambers), he joined after he got here because he was a real Mormon. He didn't drink coffee, he didn't drink tea. I know what I'm talking about because I stayed right there in the house with him. Seeing him every hour of the day for three years.

I went to his church all the time. Sunday school. Carry the kids down there. Meet with them in Sunday school. Went on to have here, let's see, ward meeting. I went there. I love to go to church anyway. I just love it regardless. I just love it.

The ward teachers...I would come there (to Grandpa Chambers's house) and administer that healing oil on Grandma and Grandpa and put it on me, too. I was here with them. I'd draw up from it. They would come sometimes three and four times in a month. I had a notion one time, if I had went and joined the Mormon church, I'd been living a whole lot better today than I'm living. I know that. But I just couldn't see, and I don't see it yet. It ain't (discrimination). The same man made you, he made me. The same man made me made you. All of us working for the same place. Try to get there if we can. Well, I don't know. I just wasn't ready to join the Mormon church, and I ain't joined it yet.

Samuel? He was all right, but he just wanted everything to be there for him and his wife. If you was hungry, he believed in fixing something of everything in the house for a meal for you to eat. But when you got away from that, you was through. That's what he said.

I told him. I say, "You know one thing. I got a house from Auntie Jane." I always called his nephew's wife Auntie Jane.

He said, "Well, where you going?"

And I said, "I'm going to move up into Auntie Jane's house."

He wanted me to give the kids this and give them that for their breakfast and cook a whole lot for dinner, and if they didn't eat it, he say I was wasting his food. I did what he asked me to do. He say cook it, and I know I was a good cook, and he'd sit down and he'd eat. I tell you I know I was a good cook, and he'd sit down and he'd eat.

"I tell you Mattie, I want you stop cooking corn bread."

I says, "Why?"

"I'll be so big directly I can't walk."

And Lordy, he would go right back to eating it again.

There was Sammy was my baby, Robert was my lap baby. Ruthie, she was, oh, eight or nine years old, my oldest daughter, and then Connie, she's named Cornelius, well, she was there. My whole family, all six of us, come when he sent us one of these yard-long tickets to get from Memphis into here. And then when I got done with my family, well the family got big with him and Grandma in it. I just had more work to do. Wasn't nobody living there but him and her.

Samuel's son Peter was living in Idaho, he had a wife. Well, he did move down there. He was married to an Indian woman, you know. I knew her till she died. She's named Mary. She sure was pretty. He had, let me see, Al is one, Roy is two, Rose is three, Hazel four. He had four kids by her. And they all is dead. Peter's dead and Mary's dead and all the kids. Oh yes, they (the kids) grew up, and he's got one girl. She was in Pocatello.

And the last time I heard from Rosie, she sent me a card with two kittens on it and you squeeze the card, it goes "mew mew." That was back in the thirties. I ain't heard from Rosie since, and I've been going out up there. I went to Pocatello to the Convocation, I went all across Ogden to all the churches over there. And when the Convocations is going on, it runs weeks, you know, eight days and nights. But I never did see Rosie to know her. But she grew to make a big stout...you can tell she was an Indian.

Peter lived in Idaho. But he moved down and lived just north of Grandpa's house. And that's where Mary died. I don't know whether he met her in Idaho. There was a lot of Indians here you know. Mary was a white Indian, had long, black hair, hung down across her lap. And thick as it was long and so pretty and black. And all Uncle Peter's children had hair just like their mother's. Sure did.

Peter was a Mormon and she was a Mormon. She was Indian but she was a Mormon. At least she went to the Mormon church all the time. My daughter Sammy joined the Mormons. She's been here all these years. I reckon she's two months old in the Mormon's church now. She's been going to the Mormon church a whole lot more than she's been going to her own race church, you know. And her dad was deacon of Calvary up here in Salt Lake. And her uncle, he died in East St. Louis, he was a minister up there; and I joined the Holiness Church, but I was here twenty years before I joined the church. And you know there is just so much going and coming and so much doing, I just didn't know. I just got tired being on the outside. When you are a widower, you stays widower, some people, you know what I mean. And I just got tired.

Now, my grandson, Paul Perkins, he was a boxer. I have followed him everywhere but to California and seen him fight. Win fights. Here in Salt Lake, down at Murray, down in Lehi. I've been all around. And so he's sick now. He's still alive, but I think he's got cancer and I don't know what Paul did, might have been drugs, but regardless of his sickness, they carry him up here and keep him a while in the veterans' hospital. He's a war veteran, you know. And so they carry him back out to the point, then he gets sick, and they bring him back up here to the veterans' hospital. And he was very sick. They say that cancer is nothing to be cured.

I heard a man talking on the TV, said everything people wasn't born with can be cured because the scientists have found out what's the cause of it and all. I said, Lord I have such pain in my breast sometimes, until I just wouldn't know what was the cause of it. I ain't had the pneumonia but once. But nevertheless God has blessed me and I know it. I've got fourteen grandchildren and forty great-grandchildren.

INTERVIEW BY WILLIAM G. HARTLEY
AUGUST 22 AND DECEMBER 1, 1972
COURTESY LDS CHURCH ARCHIVE

Fannie Ezelle Hill

Civil rights activist
Born: August 8, 1904, Americus, Georgia

Fannie Ezelle Hill moved to Tulsa, Oklahoma, after teaching school in Georgia and Mississippi for ten years. Hill's grandmother was a slave until she was emancipated at age thirteen. Hill had experienced considerable racism in Georgia, although her family did form good relationships with some white people, most notably President Jimmy Carter's family. After moving to Oklahoma, Hill had a difficult time adjusting to "Tulsa's form of prejudice and discrimination." She was active in the civil rights movement and participated in the 1963 march on Washington.

I have had a long and rewarding life, and I thank God for that. I was born and raised in Georgia. People ask me how I could be so loving and kind, and be from Georgia, too! Well I credit that to my loving parents. I had the most wonderful, loving parents in the world and my grandmother on my mother's side, an ex-slave, lived with us. I was taught to love everybody and not to be bitter no matter what bitter experiences you had suffered. My grandmother was a slave until she was thirteen. She didn't like slavery, but she never let that experience poison her mind. She was precious and she was not bitter at all. Another thing that people do not know is that growing up in Georgia was not all prejudice, racism, and bitterness.

There was such a paradox in the Deep South. Even though there was rigid segregation and oftentimes cruelty and violence directed against black people, there were also acts of kindness and genuine friendships between people of the different races. An example of this was the friendship between my family and President Jimmy Carter's family which flourished right during this terrible period of segregation in Georgia. My brothers had played with the Carter boys when they were growing up in Plains, Georgia. The friendship between our families was solidified during a crisis which occurred in my immediate family. When I was a young wife and mother, my nine-month-old son George became gravely ill, and the doctor who had been summoned to treat him informed us that the baby would probably not live through the night. I was heartbroken and distraught. In fact, I was mad at God and I said to God, "If you are going to take my baby so soon, why did you send him to me in the first place!" My mother was shocked by my outburst and sent me to my room to rest and pray. But I couldn't pray, I couldn't sleep, I couldn't eat. I couldn't do anything but think about my precious baby and how I feared that he would be dead in the morning. Miss Lillian, Jimmy Carter's mother, a nurse, was aware of my baby's illness. When she finished her duties that day, she rode out to our house that evening by horseback and brought a remedy for the baby. My mother followed the directions religiously and the remedy worked! When I awoke the next morning (somehow I had fitfully slept), I was afraid to look into my baby's room because I thought he would be dead. But I was drawn to that room. I slowly crept into the room and went over to my baby's crib. He looked up at me and gave me a little grin. I grabbed him up into my arms, squeezed him tight, and wept tears of joy. That was the happiest day of my life. From that point on, the Carter, the Johnson, and the Hill families were as united as blood relatives. My "baby" is now a retired U.S. Air Force officer.

There is nothing I wouldn't do for the Carter family. When I learned that Jimmy was running for president, I joined his campaign trail. When he was in the White House, I accepted numerous invitations to join the family for various activities in the capital. Yes, mutual respect, friendship, and love will always exist between our families. The bonds are strong enough to withstand any so-called human factor such as race.

Actually, I found Tulsa's form of prejudice and discrimination more difficult to adjust to. When I came to Oklahoma, I had taught school for ten years in Georgia and Mississippi. My poor husband had sure had a rough time adjusting to the South. You see, he was born in Nova Scotia, Canada, and raised in Colorado. He wasn't used to segregation. In Georgia, I had to train him how to deal with segregation. He would drive up to a gas station pump and sit there expecting the service station man to put gas in his car for him just as he did for other customers. He just couldn't understand why he was being treated differently because of his color. But that was the way it was in Georgia for black people then. But in Georgia, (and elsewhere in the Deep South), there were provisions for black people, unlike in Oklahoma.

I was used to attending the best movies in beautiful movie theaters. Even though we had to sit in the balcony, we got to see the same current movies that white folks saw. In Tulsa, blacks were not allowed in white theaters, not even in the balcony! North Tulsa had only two movie theaters, and they showed poor-quality, out-of-date films. When "The Ten Commandments" came to the Orpheum Theater in Tulsa, I was determined to see that film. I went down to the Orpheum every day that movie showed, but the answer was always the same, "Now Mrs. Hill (they knew me well because of my husband's work at Vernon AME Church and as an activist in the community, and because of my own interfaith activities to promote peace and brotherhood in the community), you know we can't allow you in because of the law." But I kept going every day just to show my indignation over Oklahoma's unfair segregation laws.

Tulsa was so segregated then. There were no stores, restaurants, movie theaters, no public accommodations open to blacks. We used to see the white women meeting in tea rooms to discuss issues, but you wouldn't see a black face there, though black people were most often the subject of the "issues" being discussed! Seidenbach's was one of the nicest stores in Tulsa then. Mrs. Seidenbach and I were among the first to begin the process of breaking down racial barriers in Tulsa.

The women of different races did begin to meet together, in their churches and in their homes. I had a conversation with Mrs. Seidenbach. She was receptive to making changes in their store by hiring a black clerk, but she was fearful of what other whites would think. I told her, "Do what you feel in your heart is right. Just follow your heart!" She did, too. She hired the first black saleswoman in a white Tulsa store. Whenever a black person would come into the store, that black clerk would be called. 'Course, Seidenbach's still had a floor on which the elevator would not stop if a black person was aboard. Tulsa was so hung up on race. I remember I once had an interfaith tea in my home and one of my dear white friends came. Her husband drove her to my house, but she said he wouldn't come in. He was afraid his white friends and neighbors would label him a "Communist." Well, I went out to the car and said to him, "Come on in, we won't bite you!" He came in and we later became very good friends. Most people are good people and mean well. We just have to love them and help them overcome their fears so we can live together as brothers and sisters.

It is better today. Accommodations are open to all races, there is interracial exchange between the churches, people go to school together, go to the same hospitals, and socialize together today. So we have come a long way. My generation did its best to speed up this process. In the forties, fifties, and sixties, we called ourselves "Salt and Pepper" (black and white) groups, and we did our best to smooth the path with our religious dialogue groups. That opened up thought to an equal society. Then we proceeded on to active civil rights protests to bring "the cause" to full fruition. Those were some exciting days—the civil rights protest with Tulsa's wonderful religious and secular elements coming together, young and old, black and white, for justice and equality in the city. My participation in the 1963 civil rights march on Washington was the highlight of my civil rights activism days. I will never forget that day as long as I live. Yes, we have come a long way. People still think too much about race, though. Like the man who had been trying to locate Vernon AME Church. He said he had been looking for the black church. I told him, "No wonder you couldn't find it. It's not black, it's red brick!" The next day, my comment, and a photograph of me, appeared in the *Tulsa Tribune* newspaper. That is the way I feel. We need to stop being so hung up over race, over the color of someone's skin. We need to be busy about God's work. We need to just love everybody!

INTERVIEW BY EDDIE FAYE GATES, MAY–AUGUST, 1994
COURTESY OKLAHOMA HISTORICAL SOCIETY
ARCHIVES AND MANUSCRIPT DIVISION, ORAL HISTORY DEPARTMENT

Hugh Hollins

Barber

Born: November 2, 1913, Gilmer, Texas

Hugh Hollins grew up in a farming community in East Texas. When he was eight years old, he began cutting his friends' hair. In time, he became a professional barber, a career that afforded him a steady income and a stable livelihood. He moved to Tulsa, Oklahoma, in 1946.

As a young man in the little colored community of Gilmer, Texas, I was a farmer like my daddy, my brothers, and most of the other black males in that part of Texas. And I was a pretty good farmer, if I do say so myself. But it was always barbering that I loved best. When I was growing up in our little farming community, I was a leader among the poor black

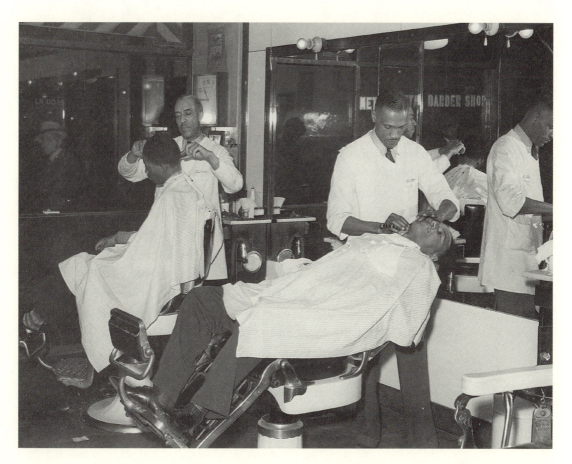

African American barbershop on the South Side of Chicago, April 1941. (Corbis)

farm kids. For some reason, I always had the knack of talking and making others listen to me. The other boys always looked up to me and listened to me.

When I was eight years old, I talked one of my little playmates into letting me cut his hair. I charged him a nickel for doing it. I can't put into words how happy I felt when I finished that haircut and when I put that nickel in my pocket. Something just clicked in me, and I felt that someday I was going to be a famous barber! I kept practicing cutting hair and I kept getting better. By the time I was twelve years old, my reputation as a hair-stylist was spreading. By the time I was fourteen, I was earning good money giving "style" haircuts to all the black boys in Gilmer. (I was also earning money helping grownups do carpentry jobs. That is why I called myself a "Jackleg of all Trades.")

I kept trying to learn all I could about barbering. I began to pay attention to the hairstyles of whites in nearby Mineola. I was curious about how they cut their straight hair. There were two colored boys in Gilmer who had what we called "good hair" in those days, hair that was straight like white folks' hair. One was my brother, who had fairly good hair; the other boy was a neighbor who had dark skin, but he had straight hair, hair just as straight as any white person's. I begged both of them to let me experiment with their hair. I told them that I wanted to start a style in the community. And they let me cut their hair! I cut my brother's hair first. I cut his hair just like I had seen the whites cut their hair, but I added my own touch, like using the razor all around, knocking the line in the back with a razor. I called it "box cutting." Then I cut the other boy's hair, adding my own special touches. My reputation spread, and soon all the colored boys were coming to me for "box styles." And wouldn't you know it. Those white barbers in Mineral Wells stole my style and never gave me no credit for it. They renamed my "box cut" "The Longbranch." But that Longbranch was nothing but the style I had created, and they never gave me no credit for it, no credit at all!

When I grew up, I had other jobs before I became a barber full-time. First of all, I was a farmer and helped my dad and brothers bring in many a good crop. I was also a pretty good jackleg carpenter. I went to Texarkana, Arkansas, to work in a bomber plant in 1942. Then I came back to the Mineral Wells area of Texas and worked as a barber and as an inspector of cookware at the Army base there. Then in 1944, I went to Oakland, California, and worked at the naval yard there. I came to Oklahoma in 1946. First, I worked in Hugo and then in Oklahoma City. In Hugo, I met Alonzo Batson, who had moved to Tulsa. He kept telling me what a good place Tulsa was for barbering. He wanted me to come and set up a nice barbershop in a safe place in North Tulsa. He suggested that I locate further up on Greenwood, not down on Deep Greenwood. He felt that there were too many shootings and stabbings down there, especially on Thursday nights and weekends when black people got their days off, and their wages, from their South Tulsa employers and headed to Greenwood for partying. And usually, during their partying, someone got shot or stabbed. I did set up my shop further on up like Alonzo had suggested, and I had thirty years of happy barbering there. When Urban Renewal came through there and bought us black businesspeople out, I had to move out to the 46th and Cincinnati area of Tulsa. It was all right out there. I had a nice little shop, but it was nothing like the shop I had on Greenwood all those years. I sure did love Greenwood in the old days.

INTERVIEW BY EDDIE FAYE GATES, MAY–AUGUST, 1994
COURTESY OKLAHOMA HISTORICAL SOCIETY
ARCHIVES AND MANUSCRIPT DIVISION, ORAL HISTORY DEPARTMENT

Eunice Jackson

Funeral director
Born: August 27, 1903, Lake Village, Arkansas

Eunice Jackson describes the conditions under which African American funeral homes were forced to operate. She recounts her experiences working in Tulsa, Oklahoma, and provides a distinct perspective on the Tulsa race riot of 1921. (For more information on the Tulsa race riot, see the LaVerne Cooksey Davis oral history, on page 173.)

Racial discrimination affected black people from the cradle to the grave before the civil rights movement of the 1960s opened up accommodations to blacks. In the old days, even in death black people had to take care of their own. White people wouldn't embalm black people in Oklahoma then. When a black person died, Mr. McBirney and other white funeral home owners wouldn't pick up the body. If they went to a place and found out that the body was that of a black person, they would say, "What's the matter with Mr. Jackson? Call him!" They just wouldn't touch a black body.

Our first funeral home was located at 639 East Marshall Place, just off of Greenwood, where the funeral home was downstairs and the living quarters upstairs. That building was burned down in the race riot of 1921. We relocated several times after that. Our last move was to our present location on 36th Street North.

That riot that destroyed our first funeral home and so much of North Tulsa was a terrible thing. When the riot began that evening, we were sitting out in the yard and people were just running toward us and hollering. Mama yelled, "What's the matter? Where are you people going?" Somebody replied, "There's a riot over on Brickyard Hill (the Greenwood Avenue area). They're just shooting everybody they can!" More black people came running by. So we joined the running crowd—men, women, and children—all just running, running for our lives! We were stopped by the police at Pine and Greenwood, a place that was called "The Section Line." It was a big crowd of us black people by then. We were marched to the Convention Hall on Brady Street, where we stayed all afternoon.

Later, people who had a home were allowed to go home. We left, although we didn't know if our house was standing or not. My mother had a bag with my brother's gun in it. On the way home, a policeman stopped her and asked, "What you got in the bag, Auntie?" All the black people were staring at the white policeman; they were just scared out of their wits. My mother slowly opened the bag. The policeman took the gun out and kept it. All he said was, "You don't need this." We went on our way, and when we got to our house, which was on the corner of Marshall and Elgin Streets, oh Lordy, it was still standing! We later found out how our house was saved. Every time a white mob would put a bucket (of burning debris) into our house, and go on to set a bucket in another house, some poor white neighbors of ours would go in and take out the burning bucket. You hear a lot about the white mobs during the riot; you don't hear much about good white Samaritans, but they were there, too. I will always be grateful to those white neighbors who saved our house during that riot. Most black people weren't as lucky as we were, though. Most of their homes and businesses were just gutted, just burned to the foundation!

After the riot, black people rebuilt. They just were not going to be kept down. They were determined not to give up. So they rebuilt Greenwood, and it was just wonderful. It became known as The Black Wall Street of America. Of course, it was a little on the wild side. Greenwood was always wild. When Mama used to bring us kids up to Tulsa, before the riot, we'd come by train. The conductor always announced the Greenwood stop (at the corner of Archer) with a little song:

> All out for Tush hog town,
> Greenwood Street, the battling ground!

There was a lot of battling (fighting) on Greenwood, too. There was always some knifing or shooting down on Greenwood. But people also took great pride in the beautiful homes and businesses in the Greenwood area. That's why it is so sad to see what's left of Greenwood today. Urban Renewal and the highway just took away our Greenwood. First the riot took it away, and we rebuilt. Now Urban Renewal and that highway (I-244) took it away, and we haven't been able to build it back.

The funeral home business has changed, too. For one thing, black funeral homes have many more supplies than they had in the old days. In fact, in the 1920s and early 1930s, the bodies of black people were embalmed right in their homes, where they had died. The mortician would put the person on an ironing board or something flat like that and embalm the body right there. The deceased would be placed in the coffin that the funeral director had brought, and the families would then be ready to receive visitors. The selection of coffins has changed, too. Then, people bought simple, sad-looking coffins. Now they want elaborate, satin-lined, padded, elegant caskets. Behavior at funerals has changed also. In those days, preachers preached long, sad funerals and relatives would just cry, scream, jump, and fall out during their grief. We would stand around with bottles of smelling salts, handkerchiefs, and fans. Funeral directors taught

us how to catch the falling, stricken people so they wouldn't hurt themselves or us. Some of the changes in the funeral business are good. In fact,
most of them are good. There are better and nicer supplies. Preachers
don't preach funerals to make people fall out and have fits like they used
to, and black people are no longer discriminated against from the cradle
to the grave. That final trip—to the funeral home and to the cemetery—
is integrated now. And that's a good thing for the American democracy
and for human beings no matter what their color.

Interview by Eddie Faye Gates, May–August, 1994
Courtesy Oklahoma Historical Society
Archives and Manuscript Division, Oral History Department

Herb Jeffries

Actor and entertainer
Born: September 24, 1911, Detroit, Michigan

*Herb Jeffries, the son of a dressmaker and an entertainer, began his career as a
jazz vocalist in Chicago in 1933. Jeffries became interested in acting a year later
while he was touring with the Earl Hines Band in the South. He was repulsed by
the segregated theaters where blacks had to wait in long lines to see white Western
movies. After numerous investors rejected his idea to introduce the black cowboy in
Westerns as a positive role model for young African Americans, Jeffries approached Jed Buell, who had produced* The Terror of Tiny Town, *a Western
starring midgets and dwarfs. Buell liked Jeffries's idea immediately, and together
they made four Westerns:* Harlem on the Prairie *(1937),* The Bronze Buckaroo *(1938),* Harlem Rides the Range *(1938), and* Two-Gun Man from
Harlem *(1938). In the 1940s, Jeffries joined the Duke Ellington Orchestra and
recorded the hit song "Flamingo" for RCA Victor. In the 1950s, Jeffries moved his
family to Europe and opened a jazz club in Paris. Over the years, Jeffries's career
has been characterized by perseverance and determination. During the 1990s,
Jeffries recorded a CD entitled "The Bronze Buckaroo," reviving the music of his
Westerns of the 1930s. He currently lives in California.*

I'm a mongrel. I come from a very mixed racial family. My mother was
100 percent Irish, born in Port Huron, Michigan. My grandfather and
grandmother were both Irish, from County Cork, Ireland. And my father
was a mixture of Italian, French, Chippewa Indian, and Ethiopian. That's
what I am. I'm that mongrel that came from that many different nationalities, and so I celebrate all of them. I celebrate St. Patrick's Day and I

Sheet music for "Love Me" (1951) features Herb Jeffries. (Courtesy John Slate)

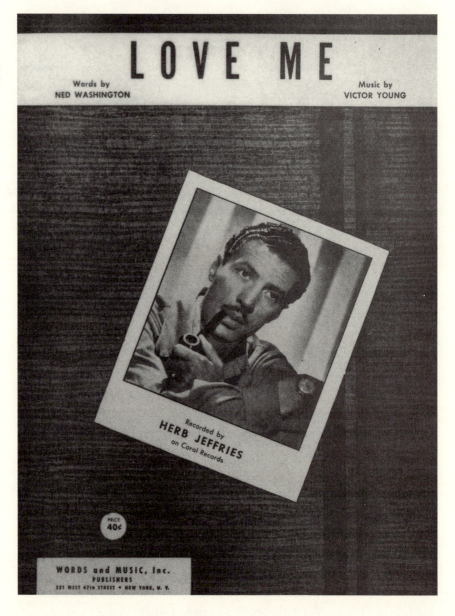

celebrate the Indian holidays, the American Indian. I celebrate the Italian holidays as well as the Afro-American holidays, although I'm an American. I prefer being an American. This is my nation; this is where I was born. So, however, what I chose to represent was Afro-American. I felt I had the right to do it because, you know, on the Italian scene, there was a man by the name of Hannibal who came over the mountains and conquered all of the Mediterranean area, clear down in through Spain and parts of Ireland. That's where the black Irish come from. So the Moors were called black, and so I feel because of that in the Italian blood of mine, plus the Ethiopian blood, which is a part of Africa, I felt that that entitled me to represent that part of my family.

At any rate, I lived in a neighborhood in Detroit that was very well mixed. We had Jewish, a high concentration of Jewish neighbors. We had some Italian neighbors. And then we had Polish neighbors. My neighborhood in Detroit bordered on Hamtramck, which was a Polish neighborhood, totally Polish. The Polish people who migrated in here in those early days migrated up into a section of Detroit called Hamtramck. My neighborhood bordered on that. And so, we had Polish neighbors as well as many of the Jewish immigrants who came in at that particular time. There were many of them who came in from Germany, and, of course, they spoke with a German accent. And, of course, they also spoke Yiddish. There were many of them, immigrants, in my neighborhood, that had come in after World War I.

My mother's name was Mildred. My father's name was Howard. My mother was a costume designer. She designed costumes, a dressmaker who did a lot of costume designing for many shows that came through at that particular time. And my father was a singer, entertainer who sang around through our small area, regional area, such as Saginaw, Bay City, Flint, places like that that were near around. He entertained and sang around places like that.

My neighborhood had many cultures and many nationalities, and we did not know discrimination. We shared our cultures in our neighborhood, and we were very close. The immigrants coming in were very happy to be accepted, and, of course, we were learning things from them as well, that they brought from the old country. Of course, my relatives were Irish immigrants. So, we didn't have the problem that they have today in the neighborhood, and it was not a very wealthy neighborhood either. We were a little bit below the middle class at that time. We weren't ghetto, but were damn close. We all had to work in our family in order to support it and to keep it going, and there were five of us, two sisters and two brothers beside myself and my mother. My father died when I was around seven, so I didn't get a chance to know him very well. All I know is what I've heard about him and what people told me about him.

My father sang all kinds of music—classical music, and music of the times. He was not a jazz singer. Jazz was very popular in Chicago, it was coming up from New Orleans, but we didn't have any great exposure to that kind of music around my place, my neighborhood. I heard classical music and pop music and singers as I was growing up like Russ Columbo. Some of the recordings that I heard of popular singers at that time, I became interested in and learned from. My father sang more classical type songs, things like "The Road to Mandalay" and "Never Had a Sweetheart Till I Met You," those great old songs that were being played and published during that particular time, from World War I on up into the twenties.

Herb Jeffries, photographed by A. B. Bell, Dallas, Texas, ca. 1973. (Courtesy Texas African American Photography Archive)

I started my career about sixteen, seventeen years old, singing around in some of the carnivals and wherever I could sing. Well, I was around music all my life, my mother making costumes for theatrical places, my father being a singer, entertainers coming to our house. We had a home with a piano in it, and many different entertainers would come to visit, such as they do today, knowing each other. They would play piano and sing songs. We had piano rolls that we would pump on the player piano, and there were all kinds of wonderful popular tunes that you could get on a piano roll. So it was things like that that I was influenced by. And when I started singing, there were songs like "Stormy Weather" and "Sweetheart of Sigma Chi" and wonderful pop songs like that that were around that I would go sing. And then at the age of about nineteen, I started singing in cabarets around my local area in my hometown.

My mother did things for the Shubert Theater, the people who played for places like that. I couldn't remember the names of those shows if my life depended upon it. I know there were many of them that came through at that time, but I was too young at that time. I was more concerned about what was happening with my career and singers that I could hear on records. I collected records and played them on the phonograph.

My brother next to me, younger brother next to me, yeah, got into singing, and he was a very good singer. His name was Howard—Howard Jeffries. He never did record, but he did sing around later in life when he became an adult, in some of the nightclubs around, and he tried very hard to follow in my footsteps. But that's very difficult, as you can see from many other families. Sinatra's son didn't do too well trying to fill those shoes that were as large as his. The Crosby boys didn't do too well. They did all right, they were recognized, but they never did become big stars. You can see that's sort of a rule of thumb. It's very seldom that in the singing business—in the acting business today, it's a little bit different—but in the singing business, during that period of time. So my brother did all right, but he never had a recording contract and never became very successful as a singer, even though he had a very fine voice. My younger brother Don did not make any effort to be musical or to sing, other than he was interested in the business as a road agent, as a road manager, and things like that, but he never got into performing.

Well, I went to Chicago in 1933 to spread my wings. I had been as successful as I could be in my hometown, and I wanted to get into broadcasting. And so I knew that there were some opportunities during the World's Fair to get exposed to some of the big bandleaders. And I went into Chicago, and I sang with a bandleader there called Erskine Tate, who had the orchestra pit band for the Regal Theater, which was one of the big theaters in Chicago in the South Park area. Then there was a dance hall next to that called the Savoy on South Park Way next to the Regal Theater, and he played there on the weekends. And so I got a job singing with his band, and that gave me a chance to be seen, and then Earl Hines came in and caught me singing with his band one time and offered me a job at the Grand Terrace. And he was broadcasting over the national networks, and that gave me some exposure. And I recorded several songs with his band, which gave me my first recording exposure. At the Grand Terrace, 1934, in the year after the World's Fair, when I joined his band, I recorded two songs with his band; trying to think what they are right now. And then I recorded another thing with him that made some noise called "Blues for You, Johnny." That was one of them, along with Baby Dodds on drums, who was Johnny's brother, and I believe there was Earl Hines on piano, and Sidney Bechet, one of the great-grandfathers of the soprano saxophone.

Jelly Roll Morton was in and out of Chicago a lot because, at that time, music was coming from everyplace. It was coming out of Kansas City, St. Louis. It was coming out of New Orleans, heavily out of New Orleans, into Chicago at that time. That was right at the very beginnings of the swing era. There was a lot of different kinds of music going on. A lot of blues, Dixieland, and then, of course, the new music, which was jazz, and it was becoming more sophisticated all along because there were great arrangers such as Fletcher Henderson, who was doing a lot of charts, and the things that Hines was arranging himself. So, of course, you know it was really an exciting period, new innovators coming in and out all the time.

There were many little after-hour places in Chicago. It was right after Prohibition, so there was a lot of celebration. Plenty of people were drinking and having the freedom to go to clubs and drink because it was legal.

By the time I got to Chicago I was ready for the entertainment business. Growing up, not much of the music I listened to really turned me on. I listened to the Canadian band there in Detroit; that was Guy Lombardo. And it was fine, but it wasn't anything that really gave me a quick jolt of energy to say, "Well, now, I want to sing with that kind of band." But after we got out of church on Sundays, our younger group of teenagers would meet down by the Detroit River at some of the soda fountains down there. And back then, jukeboxes were starting to become a very big thing, and most of the jukeboxes had bands like Lucky Millinder and Cab Calloway, had Duke Ellington, Count Basie, Jimmie Lunceford, bands of that class that were swinging. And we danced to that kind of music, and I was highly influenced by it.

Around that time I was starting to get some sense of the discrimination that black people had to face. I sensed it around the perimeter of where I lived. There was a migration coming up from the South to go to work for the automotive companies. And many of these people were blacks and some were whites coming up from the same place. And they hated each other down there, and so when they got to Detroit those kind of hateful feelings were beginning to drift in and leak into the outer perimeters of our community.

You see, these people brought the problems they had with each other; it came from class discrimination. The fact is that when I did go down south, I found out that most black people—animals were treated better than blacks, that a black dog could sit on the porch of a white place in Tulunk, Mississippi, or whatever you want to call it. They'd be out there in their little community cities, their little city halls, and they'd be sitting around the cracker barrels and the spittoons, and the dogs would be sitting beside them, black dogs and brown dogs, and they were well treated and well fed and well kept. But a black person had to walk off the sidewalk so that a white person could pass by. Black people were looked upon as some kind of a domestic animal, like a cow or some horse that was doing a service for them. And certainly (blacks) weren't paid any amount of money whatsoever, because if you look at their communities and see the way they lived, you would see that they didn't live too much better than animals. Some of their homes had dirt floors, didn't even have flooring on it. I saw those places. I've seen people living in hovels that were unbelievable. And they had no political representation, plus they couldn't vote. They had no political representation, and, therefore, they had no hygienic education whatsoever. So, of course, a disease doesn't give a damn who catches it. It doesn't care whether it's white, black, green, yellow, pink, or blue. And so, here were people living in these conditions and certainly some of them were disease-ridden, and that disease can be transmitted on to anybody. And I guess a lot of these people were kept in abeyance because the syphilis was in a great flurry down in the South at that time, and was heavily amongst blacks because they had no doctors, or very few doctors that could care for them, or treatment that they could go get for it. So that only made the matters worse. It put fuel on the fire because signs went up, "Don't drink out of this fountain," "Don't use this toilet," "Don't do this and don't do that." And here were these poor people.

It was unreal. And when I saw it, coming from where I came from, it infuriated me. And it made me want to represent them (black people) even more. You know, I said, "Hey, this shouldn't be." And it should have never been in this country. This country, by the Constitution of the United States of America, it says, "All people are created equal." You know what I mean? The animals were treated better than the blacks were treated in the South, and I'm sorry if this offends anybody, but I'm being honest, and the truth will set you free. I don't mean to bear down with a militant attitude against any other race. I'm not saying that the people who did this were terrible and bad people. I think they were ignorant.

Well, I got the idea to make black movies when I was traveling through the South in 1934. Even in the capital of the United States, blacks could not sit on the first floor with whites. They had to sit up in the balconies. And these balconies were very tenderly called by people "Nigger Heaven." And I'm sorry, but that's the way it was. And when I saw that, I was repulsed by it because I'm a kid who put my hand over my heart in school and said, "I pledge allegiance to the flag and to the republic for which it stands. One nation indivisible with liberty and justice for all." And then when I saw this going on down there, I said, "What have I been doing here? This is not true. Maybe in my little section of the town, I saw it, but down here, I didn't see it." So, all of a sudden, I just said, "Wow! You know, here are these discriminated theaters."

And the further I traveled south, I began to see that blacks could not go to any theater, that they had to have their own little tin-roofed theaters, and they had thousands and thousands of them. What were they playing? White cowboy pictures. I said, "Well, wait a minute. This is not what I read in my hometown. This is not what I studied in school." I studied that blacks after the Civil War, those who had escaped, and there were thousands and thousands of them, escaped and were taken in by the Indian reservations. Indian camps; they weren't reservations then. They were taken in by the Indians, all over the place. The blacks went with the Chippewa, the Sioux, the Mohawks, the Cherokees. They all took the blacks in because they were in sympathy with them and they felt that if they were ever captured, they would be made slaves, the same as the blacks were. And they were right; when they were captured, they made slaves out of them. So, of course, they were very compassionate and sympathetic with the blacks. They could relate to the slave because when slaves went into the Indian camps, they were at home. Why? Because it reminded them of Africa. In Africa, what did they use? Bows and arrows and spears, and what was their dress? Feathers. And what was their war dress? Their identification, whether they were hunters or warriors—they wore paint on their faces. And the hunting tribesmen, tribesmen like the American

Indians, they worshipped the elements and they had witch doctors and medicine men just the same as the American Indian tribes did. So, the black slaves were right at home with the Indians They could assimilate very easily.

And when the blacks came out after the Civil War, they were fabulous riders. They could ride bareback, and they made great cowboys. One out of three cowboys who helped to pioneer our country were black, one out of three. And the blacks were great drovers because the cattlemen preferred using them in many instances because they could wheel and deal with the Indians, and they could speak their tongue. And so they could get their cattle through with the black drovers a heck of a lot easier than they could with the white ones. So, you see, when I saw thousands of black theaters all throughout the South playing white cowboy pictures, I said, "Wait a minute. Here's a chance to take something bad and make something good out of it. Let me see if I can find someone that'll finance an all-black cowboy picture." And so it took me two years to find the backing to make the first black Western.

That was in 1934, 1935, I was traveling through the South with Earl Hines. We were playing at tobacco warehouses and immediately after the engagement and the dance was over, the concert was over, there would be two cars of sheriffs heralding us out of their community, making damn sure that we were in the next community and out of theirs, a bus of black musicians. And I can't tell you how many times I saw signs that said, "Nigger, don't let the sun set on you in this community." Big billboards. So, you see, that was enough to give me the driving force to say, "Wait a minute. You know, let me make a picture where a black man is a hero." We didn't have that. Even with Bill Robinson and men who were making big money— and mind you when I say that, I have great love and respect for Bill. I knew him very well. But even then he played subservient parts for Shirley Temple. So we (blacks) didn't have national distribution of motion pictures that showed a black man as a hero, that little children could identify with.

Who'd I go to? I went to everybody. I went back to Chicago to the "policy" (gambling) barons. And I talked to the policy barons back there, who paid as much as what it would cost me to make a picture for one race horse: $80,000. They'd buy a race horse for that. And I spoke to several of those guys back there who I knew. I had met them when I was working at the Terrace with Earl Hines. They came in there to, you know, to show off their wealth and their popularity and power. And I met them, and they weren't interested. They said, "Don't know nothing about motion pictures, and that's not our business. We're not interested." I went to see two playboys (two brothers) in Chicago that were Oklahoma multimillionaires. I spoke to them. And they pretty much passed their money around in luxury, playing with big cars and things. And I tried to raise money in the black community. There were these two black men. Both of them were Afro-American, but they weren't Afro-Americans then because they didn't have any what we call Afro-Americans at that time.

No one wanted to give me a chance. So, finally I read an article in a magazine about a man who had produced a picture called *The Terror of Tiny Town*. It was made of all midgets, little people. And I figured if this guy would do a picture made with little people, an entire Western, that he might be interested in doing a black motion picture. And I came to Hollywood and walked into his office. His name was Jed Buell. In fifteen minutes, we had agreed that it was a good idea. He called to Dallas, Texas, and spoke to the man who owned Sack Amusement in Dallas by the name of Alfred Sack. And Sack said, "I'll take as many as you got. How many you got?" So we were in business, and we started on the first picture, which was called *Harlem on the Prairie*.

Well, Jed Buell asked me, "Who's going to write the script?"

And I looked down on the floor and saw a bunch of scripts piled up there, and I said, "What is that?"

And he says, "Oh, those are some scripts we did about six or seven years ago."

I just yanked one out and I said, "What's the difference? Why don't we use this one?" I said, "By the time we put black characters in there and have someone write some black humor in it, nobody's going to recognize it anyway."

And he said, "Gee, that's a good idea." I mean, this guy was right on the ball. Any suggestion, he was ready for any new ideas, and so he said, "That's a good idea." He says, "Who's gonna write the black humor?"

I said, "Well, I know some guys down on Central Avenue who are comedians," and I said, "I think that they could take this script and write the black humor in for the sidekick and the comedians in there, and we'll just use the same story line." It was called *Sunset on the Prairie*. And we called it *Harlem on the Prairie*. Using the word "Harlem" would definitely let everyone know it was a black film.

This movie took us about eight days to make. Movies like this were called "quickies."

I loved it in California. California was mild on its discrimination. There were places in Hollywood at the time where they may have frowned upon blacks fraternizing, but they did play in the clubs there. The head of the Chamber of Commerce, he frowned upon it, but it didn't do much good because the black bands were very popular bands out here. They were more or less black and tan. There was some discrimination, but not like I had seen it in other places. And then the weather, of course, the climate was so wonderful, I loved it out here. I saw some good possibilities. At first, I lived in the black neighborhoods, and then after I got moving fairly well in the picture business, then I moved into the west side of the city, which did not have too many blacks, but blacks were starting to move out in the areas around Western Avenue.

Central Avenue was wonderful. It was like a small Harlem. They had some wonderful clubs. They had the Club Alabam, which was a big club that had chorus girls and a big band and was sort of our Cotton Club out here. Then there were little mushrooms coming up, nightspots and after-hours spots, and many of the movies stars, the big movie stars, came down to see the entertainment, black entertainment, the black shows and the clubs. It was quite black and tan. Many of the big stars came down; the Gables came down. Oh, I saw people like Buck Jones, he would come down to watch the shows. And there were a lot of Texans in that area around Central Avenue. As a matter of fact, when we made the Western pictures, we had a good choice of some of the black Texas cowboys that were around.

I made the first record of "Angel Eyes." Yeah, it came to me, and at that time, Buddy Baker, he was out of Kansas, I believe, he came out to spread his wings. He was a brilliant arranger, and we put a big orchestra together, big, lush band with strings, and we recorded "Angel Eyes." It was brought to me first. But we were with a small company that was just beginning called Exclusive. It was owned by Leon Rene, who wrote "Sleepy Time Down South," "Someone's Rocking My Dreamboat," "Swallows Come Back from Capistrano." Leon formed this small label, the first, I believe it was the first, in my mind, the first independent black-owned major-category label, first ever. And certainly the first in California. And if anybody's name should have been on the sidewalk as a pioneer of the independent record company, it should be Leon Rene. I don't think it's on there, though, but at any rate, yes, I made the first record of it, and because we were a small company, why, we were covered by several major companies, and Sinatra, of course, covered it, and he was with a big major label that could really do a great job of publicity on it. I don't think Sinatra needed too much help because he was the rage at that time.

I guess my shepherds into the film business were Tom Mix and Buck Jones and Ken Maynard and people like that that I went to see in the movie theaters in my local environment as a youngster. I would go into the movies on Saturdays about eleven o'clock in the morning and then my sister would have to come and get me out at eight o'clock in the evening because I'd watch the same picture over and over four or five times. So she'd come and get me at seven, eight o'clock to come home and have dinner. And these were my heroes, and so, of course, I had always had that desire inside of me, as most youngsters do, to ride off into the sunset with the fair maiden. Most young kids have that same kind of dream. And, of course, it was my tenacity, I guess, and then I should say my anger, to make it happen.

I think that once you're a performer on the stage, you're taking acting lessons, because you have a live audience in front of you, and that's why we call our performance an "act." You say, "What is your act?" My act was singing. And so when I was on a stage, I was always performing for a live audience. In nightclubs, I had a different type of an emotion to deal with. I had to deal with people who came not only to hear the music and to see the show but to drink and to maybe make contact with the fair maiden or vice versa. And so that was a different audience. Then there was the audience who came to just sit in the theater and listen, and they didn't drink and they didn't do anything but maybe have popcorn and pop. And then there, of course, was the concert audiences, the larger audiences. So, I think if you'll take Frank Sinatra, Sammy Davis Jr., people like Dean Martin, why they went into the acting business and were successful at it, without having to go to a tutor, that they had already had that experience in trial and error. I think that's what makes a good actor. And then life itself, the trial and error of life, of falling down and getting up and falling down and getting up in many of your efforts, in your career. And especially if you have the lows and the highs, you learn how to perform any of those emotions. You know how it is to be hungry. You know how it is to be drunk. You know how it is to be high. You know how it is to be rich. You know how it is to cry sadness. So, you experience all those emotions as you try to become successful in whatever your career may be. And I think that's what makes the better actor, rather than the canned ones, the ones that come out of a can.

I never knew Jed Buell until I walked into his office for the first time; in fifteen minutes, he bought my story. And later on I did finally meet that other wonderful man, Alfred N. Sack, out of Dallas—Sack Amusement— who when Mr. Buell spoke to him on the telephone, he said, "Yeah, great, I'll take all you got." So, that was encouraging, and he was always a great supporter, and this, of course, was a man who had national distribution.

I don't mean to take anything away from Oscar Michaux and Spencer Williams, who were great pioneers of the black motion picture business. I have a great deal of respect for them and I love them very much. I never met Mr. Michaux, but Spencer, of course, I worked with. They were brilliant men. But unfortunately, in their earlier days, they didn't get on the track because they were making small-budget pictures with low finances, probably black financing or whatever money that Michaux could get out of his own pocket. His distribution in those days, as I recall it, was in churches and small theaters that he could set up any kind of contact with. And, at the same time, Sack Amusement had national distribution to all these theaters and was putting his white cowboy pictures and white pictures in these black theaters all over the United States.

Well, I was fortunate enough to strike it rich the first time my ax went into the mine, through Jed Buell. Of course, that was a great atmosphere to be around because it was totally professional. Mr. Buell had made numerous white cowboy pictures and was good and accurate at it. And our locations were good locations. The first one was at Murray's Dude Ranch in Victorville.

The other ones we made in different locations. Some at Murray's and then in Saugus out there in the rock country. Yeah, Murray's Ranch. Murray was an Afro-American who owned that particular ranch in Victorville, California. So Mr. Buell was a learning tree for me. We had Sam Newfield as our director; he was a wonderful director, had done many, many, many white Westerns. And I sat at his shoulders, and then learned how to go in and use a Moviola and learn to cut and to be a film editor. And, of course, film editing is really the true way to learn directing. So through Sam Newfield, I was able to have that environment around me, of learning, and he was a wonderful man and a good friend, and I took good direction from him because he was a very understanding person. And so, any success that came from my performances certainly came through Sam Newfield, the director.

Another actor I worked with was Clarence Brooks; he was wonderful. He was from New York and from the Lafayette Players. He had had a lot of experience working in New York onstage. He was a fine stage actor. And, as a matter of fact, he was very light-skinned, and a lot of people thought he was Caucasian. In many instances, I'd have people say, "Well, who was the Caucasian that was working in the picture?"

Then again, we get into another element of the criticisms against Oscar Michaux, which I'd like to defend. Michaux was criticized by the fact that he used a lot of light-skinned actors all the time in his films. Well, I'm going to tell you how that was. Because, see, during those times, the light-skinned people had greater opportunities for education, and also you know, some of them could pass (as white) and go into schools to be educated. And also, their job opportunities were a little bit better. It's like putting cream in coffee, you know, to lighten it up a little bit. And so, the prejudiced man would be more acceptable to the light-skinned Negro than he was to the black, to the darker skin. And, of course, these (lighter-skinned) people had a better opportunity for education; therefore, a lot of them would go to the drama classes and learn drama. And so it was that more of these (lighter-skinned) people had a better understanding of drama.

And when you would cast for a movie, you wanted to cast somebody who was more articulate and who could play the part. And so it seemed that you found that there were a lot more light-skinned Negroes who were interested in drama than darker-skinned Negroes. You see, so it wasn't that Michaux preferred the light-skinned Negro, it was that they were more available to do the parts he wanted them to play. And it wasn't really that he used them to an excess. When he found an actor, he picked them for their ability as an actor and not because of their skin color. It just happened to turn out that way.

Look, take me for instance. You know, I'm a mongrel. I have many, many races. I have preferred to represent myself as a black man because of my ethnic DNA, I guess. I chose it. But many times, I've been places where people have no idea that I have any black blood whatsoever.

When I went to make this cowboy picture, Mr. Buell did not want me to play the lead part. Absolutely not. He said, "No way." We screen-tested around twenty different people, dark-skinned actors. But either they couldn't ride a horse or they couldn't sing. Or if they could sing, they couldn't act. If they could act, they couldn't ride a horse, scared to death of horses. So we just couldn't find the actor that would have been able to play that part and not hold down production with somebody teaching him how to do it. You see what I'm saying? So of course this was our problem. He didn't want me to play it.

I finally went to him and said, "What are we going to do about the picture? I can sing, I can ride, I can act, I can do all this."

He said, "They'll never buy you."

I said, "What do you mean, they'll never buy me? I've been down south with Earl Hines, singing in places, they bought me down there." I finally said to him, "May I ask you a question? Have you ever lived in a black neighborhood?"

He said no.

I said, "Well, you're an Irishman. You know that I could take you right now down to Central Avenue and tell them you're my brother, and you would be accepted? Nobody would question you. I'd say you're black; they'd say, 'Okay, cool.'"

I said, "First of all, what you don't understand is that black people, or Afro-Americans, or Negroes" (which they were called at that time). I said, "They come in a bouquet of colors." I said, "Obviously, you have never lived amongst them, so you wouldn't know this."

And he said, "Well, I don't know."

I said, "Well, let me say this to you. Did you ever see a picture called *Good Earth?*"

He said, "Yeah."

I said, "Well, there's a man by the name of Paul Muni from the Jewish theater who played a Chinaman. He played a Chinese part. And also, an Austrian lady played his maid." So, I said, "If they can play Chinese, if I'm an actor, why can't I play any part I want to play?"

And on the basis of that, he called on the phone and said, "Give this guy a screen test and get him out of my hair."

So, I took the screen test. I didn't know a cowboy song to my name. And I sang "Way Down Upon the Sewanee River" for my screen test. And they accepted it. And we used it in the picture, opened the picture up with me riding a horse and the guitar, singing "Way Down Upon the Sewanee River."

I learned to ride at my uncle's place in Toledo, Ohio. I spent my summer vacations there when I was a young boy. And my grandfather had a farm, he was a dairyman, up in Port Huron, Michigan. I brought many cows in when I was eight, nine, ten years old on my summer vacations. I had early experience in riding and knew animals very well. And then later on, I became very serious about it, when I went to live up on a ranch up there in California. I learned what cowboys really were about as far as branding and as far as going out on the trails. This was during the time after my first picture, right after I made my first picture. '37, '38, '39. I have a ranch right now up in Oregon called the Flaming O Ranch.

I worked with cowboys, and I worked with some very good actors. One of these was Maceo Sheffield. He was a policeman. Well, Sheffield was very important in the first picture because he really was the guy who helped to cast that picture. Because he was a policeman and was very well known, he knew all the actors and all the people and everybody around there, and he was a fairly good actor himself. Later on, he was a cafe and club owner. Yeah, he got into that later on, after he got into the club business. But his main character when I first met him, he was a cop. He was a detective. And he, I think, was responsible for the first all-black rodeo in California. He was a man who was very much interested in Western things, and he was interested in the handling of firearms, being a policeman.

Of course, youngsters who desired to become a cowboy or Western man, you know, always have this consciousness about guns. And it was to show that there were other things entertaining about the cowboy besides him just being out on the range, branding and bringing in the cattle and saving the girl from somebody who wants to buy her ranch or steal it from her. There were cowboys who could ride broncs and who were great bull riders and bull handlers and clowns, and so, of course, it was likely that Maceo would be the first guy that would bring a rodeo to California—a black rodeo to California.

Oh, I enjoyed working with him. I had a very good relationship with him, a very good communication with Maceo. We liked each other much. I found him easy to work with as a heavy when we would do our choreographing for our fight scenes. And we didn't have any doubles in those days; we couldn't afford them. And, as a matter of fact, there were no stunt associations around at that particular time, like there are now. So we did all our own stunts and we choreographed all our fights through our director, Sam Newfield. And many times, I took one on the chin, you know, that didn't come off the way we choreographed it. And vice versa. He took a couple of blows from me, too, you know. That happens in the best of routine layouts in fighting. And in the stunts, in any kind of stunt.

Another actor I worked with was John Lawrence Criner. He was in, I think, *Harlem on the Prairie*. He was an older guy who had been acting starting in the twenties. He had been a Lafayette Player. My uncle was also a member of the Lafayette Players. Romaine Johns. And that's how I know about the Lafayette Players, the original Lafayette Players out of New York. Yeah, John Criner, that's right. Well, as I said, you know, I had a flashback into my long-range memory. And we're now talking over fifty years, sixty years ago. And I think there are some people of my vintage who are not able to remember six years back.

In '37, I made *Harlem on the Prairie* for Associated with Jed Buell. Well, as best as I can remember, we made these pictures in five and six days, you know. Seven days at the most. A week would be over budget, really. They were quickies. So you must realize that when you do something and you got seven days of memory on it and were working like, say, out at Victorville at Murray's Ranch, and were occupied maybe fourteen or fifteen hours a day. In order for us to push a picture through in a five-day quickie formula, we were working from the time the fog lifted and we got the first ray of light coming over the hills until the last light, and that would put our reflectors out of business, and then we went into arc lamps to do interiors. And sometimes we would work from six or seven o'clock in the morning till eleven, twelve o'clock at night. And so we were really pushed and occupied in our stunt routines, our dialogue memory, and things like that. Now I can't tell you too much about the location, other than the fact that in Victorville, there's a lot of rocks. There was a ranch house there. When we shot, a lot of times, day for night, with our filters on, and then when we did interiors, there was an old house there that didn't have a roof on it, and we'd arc it up with the generators at that time, and we would shoot interiors right in this old house. We did our bunkhouses and our things there, with arc lights at nighttime.

Oh, we had several real black cowboys, yeah, that came out of Texas. And we had, oh, two or three of them. Then we had another black cowboy that came up from just beyond Santa Barbara and the ranches that there were up there. And they groomed all the rest of our guys in the posses, you know, teaching them how to ride. Sometimes they would go out with these guys so that they'd get the look of being real cowboys. These guys were Central Avenue people. Some of them, you know, had never been on a horse.

There probably were some of them (real cowboys who sang) when we were out there at the ranch. There were several of them that would sing some songs. I don't recall any of them ever having any great voices, but I don't think you're going to hear too many great voices on cowboy records even today. You're not going to have any you're going to compare with Johnny Mathis or Frank Sinatra. I'm sorry about that. But cowboy songs don't necessitate you having a good voice.

Songs of the range. Well, not any in my group, but I've heard a lot of songs of the range in my travels because I'm sitting here with a pair of cowboy boots on right now. My closets are full of cowboy boots. I've always been a cowboy. I will die being a cowboy. I love the cowboy world, and it came into my life in my early stage, and it's still a part of my dream. I was sitting here in my room looking at this with a light picture I have on the wall which has two guns in harness and the hat over the top of it. I was inducted into the hall of the fame of the International Western Music Association. I have that plaque. I just received my commemorative gun of the original gun that I used in *The Bronze Buckaroo*, and I'm looking at it here on the wall. The duplicates of them are being made by a company called America Remembers. They are making that gun, and it's called the Bronze Buckaroo, and it's engraved in gold. So my room is pretty well filled here with Western stuff. It's an atmosphere I live in because I'm a cowboy at heart. So I've heard a lot of range songs.

But do you know why cowboys sing and that they were not invented in the singing movie pictures, as everybody wants to say, that singing cowboys were invented by Hollywood? That's the biggest lie that was ever told. Do you know how cowboys and why cowboys sing on the range? It quiets the cattle down. And do you know who brought that into the cowboy world? The black cowboy brought it in because he would get out there on the range with his guitar and sing the blues, and they found out that it would settle the cattle down. That's why you hear a lot of great white blues singers who have learned it from the black blues singers. And that's why the blues influence is still in the cowboy business, whether they're black, white, Indians, or whatever. But that's how it started, and they'd notice that one of those cowboys was out there singing the blues, and playing his guitar, and the cattle settled down. This has been more years way back than I can remember, but I know in my research that that's what I found out.

The three pictures I made prior to *The Bronze Buckaroo* were all called "Harlem." *Harlem on the Prairie*, *Two Gun Man From Harlem*, *Harlem Rides the Range*. I was sick of "Harlem." And they did that because they wanted to identify it as a black picture. But moreover, a guy by the name of Bob Blake, who was a character in the picture, was well known and well recognized. And I didn't think that, with a character named Bob Blake, they needed to use "Harlem" for the rest of these pictures. So I decided I don't want to use "Harlem" anymore.

They said, "Well, what do you want to call it?"

I said, "Call it *The Bronze Buckaroo*. " So that's how the name came to be—but I wrote a lot of the music for the pictures, a lot of the music. And what we didn't have I wrote it. For the first picture there was a guy named Lou Porter, who did a lot of writing. And there was some other guy they brought into it. But the latter pictures, I did a good deal of the writing of music in the pictures, because we couldn't afford great musical scores in those pictures. Our budgets were too low.

Dick Cohn was another director I worked with. Well, yeah, let me tell you that story. See, Jed Buell made the first picture, but he was so busy with the success of the first picture, which not only played in black movie houses but also was playing in white movie houses, through Sack Amusement, because of its entertainment value, and because of its uniqueness, and he was so busy that he forgot to sign me for some other pictures. Well, all of a sudden, these things started to break loose and become successful. Richard Cohn got in touch with me and said, "Listen, I'd like to sign you for three more pictures." And he got to me with a better deal than I got from Buell. He didn't have to twist my wrist.

And then, of course, I had an opportunity to own my own horse to make a deal where I said, "Hey, if you want me in this picture, I don't want a rental horse, I want a horse that can fall in love with me and I can fall in love with it, and this could be my buddy horse, like the rest of the cowboys." So part of my deal was that he bought this horse for me, which was Stardust, which I used in all of my pictures thereafter.

Dick Cohn was with Hollywood Productions. He was a terrific guy, just a wonderful man, very compassionate, and understanding. He felt that he was doing what needed to be done, that these pictures needed to be out there so that other little children—not just Afro-American children, but there were Indian children; there were Puerto Rican children; and there were Mexican children out there who were also getting bad treatment and had no heroes to identify with. And so we were trying to create an image that these youngsters could identify with. And, in the pictures, we had moral standards. In none of my pictures did I drink. I faked drinking in one of them. I pretended to be drunk in order to get upstairs and get to the guy who I wanted to get to and get some information. I never shot a man unless it was in self-defense. I didn't smoke any cigarettes in the pictures. We had moral standards, which I must say we did not create. These were the same things that were being used in the Roy Rogers and the Gene Autry pictures. We sort of tried to copy the moral principles.

I made a total of four of the black cowboy films. And then what happened after that was a very interesting thing. I went back to my hometown to make an appearance at a theater where my picture was playing. In Detroit. And while I was there, the great Duke Elllington was playing at one of our well-known ballrooms, there on Woodward Avenue. And, of course, I had met him before on several occasions. I had gone backstage to congratulate him some years prior to this appearance. We shared a professional respect for each other. Well, he was playing at the ballroom. And so I thought, well, I'll just keep these cowboy clothes on. I'll just go to that ballroom that night. I'll stand in the front of the bandstand and maybe Duke Ellington will see me and remember me and that way, I might attract some attention to my personal appearance at the theater I was playing at. I was really on a sort of an advertising campaign. And when I went there, I had all my Western regalia on, the big hat and all that, which, of course, created a focus of attention because nobody else was wearing that kind of clothes. And then, too, people recognized me, as well, from my pictures, and it was a black affair. And when I walked down in the front of the bandstand, Duke looked down and he saw me. He not only recognized me but he stopped the band and he said, "Ladies and gentlemen, I have standing in front of me the Bronze Buckaroo, Mr. Herb Jeffries, whose picture I just played with for the last week at the Apollo Theater."

He had been playing along with the *The Bronze Buckaroo* in New York at the Apollo Theater, doing the stage show in between pictures. You know, a picture, and then a stage show, and then another picture and another stage show. So, he was well aware of me and he announced me and asked me if I would come up and sing a song with the band. So I went up and I sang something, I don't recall what it was. It probably was something like "Stardust" or something like that. Anyway, he had an arrangement in my key, and then after that he said, "Don't go away."

He says, "During intermission, I'd like to talk to you." So I went back in his dressing room during intermission, and he asked me, he said, "I'm doing this series of stage shows, and I'd like you to come and perform on our stage show and join my group."

So I went with him and he introduced me as the Bronze Buckaroo, and I didn't wear Western clothes; I wore a tuxedo and I started singing with his band. And then he asked me later on if I would record with his band and make some records with them. And we selected some songs to record, one of which was "Flamingo." Needless to say, "Flamingo" was a multimillion-record seller. And so I had another career going for me. You recall that most singers such as Dick Haymes, Frank Sinatra, Dean Martin, they were band singers who became movie stars. I was a movie star who became a band singer. I went the other way because I realized that I was performing with one of my heroes and a man who I believed would go down in music as a Mozart, Beethoven of our times, Mr. Duke Ellington. No question about it. No question in my mind's eye.

Once upon a time, in England, I was asked on BBC if I had been influenced by Duke Ellington. I said, "Absolutely not. I was cloned by him." He was one of the most wonderful human beings I have ever met in my whole life. He was not only a great inspiration as far as education and articulation was concerned, but he was one of the ten best well-dressed men in the world. And besides that, here was a man, if you spent one hour with him, you forgot epidermis. You became brain-conscious. He did not have a color. And one day that is what is going to break down the (color) barrier. We have another man who just proved that by the name of Colin Powell, who proved that education is the answer for discrimination. This is the man who not only was the head of the Joint Chiefs of Staffs, but turned down being president of the United States.

I came up with so many people who helped to break down so many of the barriers that black people faced. In Detroit there was Jesse Owens. I knew him very, very well. He was a great, great guy. Well, I can only tell you that this was a man, Jesse Owens, who was a great uplift to me, because when I saw that he could become a champion, it only made me know that I was on the right track. A champion like that becomes a hero.

Jackie Robinson was the same way. He was a baseball champion who went through his trials and tribulations. That is a part of success, trial and error. But he became a hero, not only in the eyesight of his own ethnic group, but he was a hero to all people. And so was my friend Joe Louis. I saw him fight many times. And I went to the Brewster Center, where he would go train. That's where I used to go, too, to take my athletic training. He was another great inspiration for me, to see the Brown Bomber become a man who was not well educated but still was a scientist of great intelligence as far as the science of the art of self-defense was concerned and who became one of the great heroes, not just to his own ethnic group but to the world.

The greatest Joe Louis fights, for me, were the two Schmeling fights. The Schmeling fight that he lost and then came back and took it away from him. For me. Now I'm sure he may have had greater fights, but those were greatest for me. You know, so many hopes and aspirations kind of rode on every one of those fights. Absolutely.

I heard a man, just the last week I was at the stroke center where I usually go every week as a volunteer. We do a rap session with the stroke people here. I usually do it with a good friend of mine. He's an actor by the name of Richard Harrison. And Harrison and I were there doing our rap session with these people. Anyway, he said something that kind of bemused me. He's a Caucasian. And he says to all these people, who are disabled through paralysis. It's a rehabilitation center as well. But anyway, he said something that kind of really amused me, and I've mused over it ever since. He said, "You know, Herb, I'm beginning to think that black people are special people. My God, there are no athletes like them in the world. They're champions in everything they do. Look at these guys in basketball; my God, man, they produce nothing but champions."

I said, "Well, it's not that they're a super-people, not at all. But what creates the super feeling, the super emotion, which is in me, is the tenacity it created. And that tenacity is not to take no for an answer. I'm gonna be in your hair. I'm gonna bug the hell out of you until you say, 'Do something with this guy. Get him out of my hair.' This is the way to forge forward. And this is what creates champions; it's that you have to do it. You must do it."

I think the civil rights movement started with the freedom riding. Freedom riding down through the South. And there were many people who also assisted in this. Now, we're going to talk about a man who happens to be one of my champions. I don't know if you like him or not, but he's a champion of mine. We're talking about Adam Clayton Powell, who tricked the president into the integration of the federal government. And he's been sort of forgotten about. I knew Adam very well. I wanted to do his life story. I wanted to do the ACP story. And so when I was at Universal doing a picture with a man by the name of Jim Drury, I was doing *The Virginian*, and so Jim said to me, "You know what," he said, "I think I can get Universal interested in doing Adam Clayton Powell's life, and you should do it."

And I said, "I'd be interested in doing it. He's a very dear friend of mine."

He said, "You think you can get the rights?"

And I said, "I'm sure I can if I can get ahold of him. He's in Bimini." So through one of his aides, who was teaching up at a university, who wrote a story called *The Kingfish*, I was able to get ahold of him and I said, "Get ahold of Adam for me."

He said, "I'll get ahold of Adam. But you're going to have to be at a telephone booth someplace at a certain time where he can call you back, because that's the only way you can communicate with him in Bimini."

So I was at the Mayfair Hotel in Washington, D. C., and I gave them the telephone number at the bar downstairs, and at seven o'clock, that specific time that night, the phone rang. I went into the booth; it was Adam, calling me from Bimini. And he said, "What can I do for you, Herb?" See, I had known him from Paris, because he had come over to Paris many times to visit with his son and with Hazel, and I was living in Paris at the time. I had a big jazz club there, a successful jazz club, called the Flamingo. That was from 1950 till 1958 I owned that. It was just off the Champs-Elysées a block from Pierre Charon, about three blocks from the Georges V Hotel. Half a block off of the Champs-Elysées.

I had a very successful jazz club, and Adam Clayton Powell came to see me and talk to me about some things. And we became very close, and when I'd come to the city, New York, I'd always get together with him.

Well, Adam tricked Eisenhower into making a statement (after World War II), and then he released it to the newspapers the next day. He told Eisenhower that he was a man who had dealt with races successfully in the services and that the federal government should be integrated, and it was time for us to stand behind the Constitution. And he said, "I think you could make yourself a very big man." And so Eisenhower agreed to it, and he released to the paper the next day, that Eisenhower was going to up-hold the bill of integration in the federal government.

It was actually Truman who initiated the administrative action to integrate the armed forces. But Eisenhower was the guy that started the ball rolling…you know, who completed the picture. Adam Clayton passed about fifty-two bills. He was an incredible congressman and an incredible man. But unfortunately for him, he never was really able to represent the race because he was too fair. And the militants came into the picture at that particular time and overshadowed what he was doing. But neverthe-less, what's the difference? The difference is, it was done.

Look at me; I was eighty-one years old before I signed a contract with Warner Brothers. And they came looking for me because of the black cowboy pictures.

I went to Europe in 1950. I went over to France. I tried to get agents to book me there. They wouldn't book me because they didn't want to split commissions. I was with William Morris at the time, had big success here. And records were playing all over the world. And I was known, but they wouldn't book me there. They didn't want to split the commissions. So I woke up one morning, my wife and my child, and I said, "We're selling everything. We're going to sell the house; we're going to sell our cars; we're going to sell all the clothes and everything; and we're going to go and get educated in Europe. I want to go." And we sold everything, and we got on a ship. We had booked it three months ahead of time, so that I'd have to leave. And we went to Paris. And we got a flat in Paris and we lived around there for a while, and then finally I decided to go take a look at the south of France. I took a look at the south and then came back. We came back to Los Angeles, but I had no intentions of staying because I'd sold my house. And so we rented a place for a short period of time, and I had analyzed the whole situation there and decided I'm gonna go back and I want to open up a club. So I did. I went back in '51, found a spot, opened it up, and it was an immediate success. Parisians love jazz. And everybody came.

I knew Richard Wright living in the south of France. I didn't live very far from him. I had a villa there. And Richard lived very close. He was brilliant. Then he opened up a club, he went into a business in Paris and became an investor in a club called the Ringside, which Eartha Kitt worked. The stage was built like a ring, like a fighters' ring. And it was quite successful.

Richard was a very intelligent man. Here again is the way, the only way we're going to get rid of this thing (racism and discrimination), and believe me when I tell you I believe that it's promoted. I believe the whole damn thing is promoted by the hierarchy. Because it's an old formula called divide and conquer. As long as they can keep us divided, racially, class, sex, age, think about it. There's not a living ass on the face of this world, regardless of his epidermis, that is not going to suffer discrimination. Because I don't care if you're white, I don't care if you're Oriental, I don't care if you're an Indian, or if you're Mexican, or French, or German, or Spanish, or whatever you are, you're going to get old, if you live long enough. And if you get old, you're going to be discriminated against. Age discrimination is the largest form of discrimination on the face of this earth. Even among your own family. Your own family's going to say, "Hey, let's put this guy in a home, man; he's starting to bug me."

So, you see, now we have what we call sex discrimination. And then we have racial discrimination. And we have class discrimination. My God, man, I mean, I'll tell you. And the hierarchy loves it because it's divide and conquer. They can manipulate you and push you around and move you where they want.

Richard Wright was angry. Angry. You get angry about the situation which you know is hypocrisy. It's hypocrisy, and it's the greatest trauma for you to look me in my face and tell me you care for me and you care about me and what I'm doing and then behind my back say that I'm not good enough to belong to your golf club, or I'm not good enough to belong to your social structure. C'mon. So when you go to Europe, you don't have that problem. There's no such thing as that in France, not even in England today. Even along with the discrimination they have. But you are not class-discriminated.

It's always been that way in France, and even from the days that I can recall and the days I've read about. That's the way Josephine (Baker) felt. Josephine, whom I finally met, in Italy for the first time. Oh, I loved her. I loved her to pieces. I mean, how can you not love intelligence? She was a beautiful woman. And she spoke French fluently. Here's a woman who became a part of the French underground. I mean, here's a woman that was loved by the French, who was adored by the French and who is still adored by the French. When you met her, you met class, you met elegance, you met nobility. When you looked at her profile, she looked like some kind of a queen from a lost African tribe.

For me, California was a frontier, and then Europe. In Europe there was a great sense of possibility. Exactly. California was a frontier because the motion picture business was in its infancy; it was beginning, and the movie czars were building it. Still, as I looked about and observed then, being interested in history all of my life, I was curious about other countries. I wanted to go to them. I went to Paris, and then Paris satisfied a certain part of my life. And then, you know, I needed Italy, and I went to Italy for three years. And then I went to England for a while.

I was in Rome for three years. I studied in Rome, studied music there. And while I was living in Rome I traveled around Italy, but I headquartered out of Rome. It was my home. Then I went to London. I spent about a year in London. And then London is where I met a man who interested me in India, a man who was an Indian. And he was a guru, a teacher of the yoga philosophies. And then I became highly interested in the yoga teachings. I am ever grateful to it because I learned that I could not stop the aging process, but that I could slow it down, and that's what I've been able to do. And I still practice yoga. Every moment of my life. I'm practicing it right now.

I came back to the United States in '58, '59. Then I went back again. I would sometimes go and stay maybe six or eight months and then come back because I would miss the culture. And here in this country, we're suffering from cultural anemia. I've lived all over the world. I spent time in India. I came back, then I wanted to see what the East was like. And I went into Malaysia, Singapore, Hong Kong, Philippines, all down through the archipelagos, into Australia, New Zealand. You know, when a man is eighty-six years old, he can go a lot of places during that time.

The wiser a man becomes, the more he knows how little he knows. And so, I'm hungry for knowledge. What I'm searching for is results. And I get to see the results, that would be my reward. I want to help make new frontiers, or be part of the new roads to be paved. I've only touched the tip of the iceberg. What keeps me going is that I'm curious. I want to know more. I've got places to go and things to do.

INTERVIEW BY ALAN GOVENAR AND JOHN SLATE
JANUARY 7, 1998

Irene McClellan King

Teacher

Born: September 11, 1911, Oklahoma City, Oklahoma

Irene McClellan King grew up in Phoenix, Arizona. Her parents left Oklahoma looking for a better life, but Arizona posed a new set of difficulties. King went to segregated schools. When she graduated from Carver High School, she wanted to go to the University of Arizona, but was unable to afford the tuition. She enrolled at Phoenix College and then transferred to Arizona State University, where she received a teaching degree. She began teaching in 1936 and was an active member of the Maricopa County Teachers' Association and the Arizona Teachers' Association. King taught school in Arizona for more than forty years.

We moved to Arizona from Oklahoma when I was eight years (old), going on nine. My father wasn't satisfied with the condition he was having to live under because he realized that they wanted his land, so he eventually traded his five-acre tract just north of the state capitol to buy ninety-eight acres of desert land out of Laveen, Arizona.

We went to Arizona by train. There was (step) mother and father, four children; then my mother's sister and her husband and a baby. My mother died when I was two.

Laveen was nothing but a farming district with a store and a post office. So we came to Phoenix for practically everything we wanted. Even sometimes to school. We drove that distance in to the old desert school here in Phoenix.

My father was a farmer. And my stepmother worked (outside the home) sometimes. She worked at the old St. Joseph's Hospital for a while. Then did farming. We ran a dairy out at Laveen. My brother and I discovered that we could have a dairy and get up in the morning and milk the cows and go to school and come back and do that work in the evening, and we didn't have to miss school. We didn't have to stay out of work.

We lived in a mixed neighborhood where you were with the black children if you came to town to church and at school. Other times, most of your friends were other farmers' children. If you wanted to go horseback riding or like that, you went with one of them.

You were with children when you went to school or you went to church school or occasionally someone could drive out from town. That was in the early twenties, '22, '23, and you had a horse and buggy, and that was your transportation. And dad trusted us. He would let the three children come to town to Sunday school and church. We sang in the choir, and then we'd go visiting. They would go and invite you over for dinner, and by three o'clock you were ready to start back home.

Well, they didn't have as many cars back then. Dad didn't get his first car until 1924. Oh yes, he had the trust in us. We grew up being able to do for ourselves. At age five, I thought I was as big as any of the rest of them and washed dishes, put me a little stool up there. And I loved to sweep, straighten out the house. And they just let me do it.

We were shown certain things. By the time I was ten, my mother was working here in town at old St. Joseph's Hospital, and I did my brother's washing and my sister did my father's. And I did my brother's ironing.

Well, you had your certain things and you didn't bother hers. And she had hers, and you knew where your things were and you had your own drawers to put your clothes in and you just didn't bother her things and she didn't bother yours.

There were some things I wanted. If she (my sister) knew I really wanted it badly enough she would say, "You can use it, bring it back."

She had the most beautiful tissue, gingham dress. She wouldn't give me the dress, but she let me use it.

I never had to fight because if I got into it with my brother, my sister defended me. If I got into it with my sister, my brother.... And they didn't play games, and if they were really ribbing me and I wanted to cry, dad took my place.

We had a problem with segregation. If they didn't have a school for us out at Laveen, we had to be transported, and that's why I went to Roosevelt School two different times, two different years, because they didn't have enough children, black children in Laveen, to have separate schools. The Laveen District transferred us up there (to Phoenix). I was the only one from the Laveen District to be transferred. Laveen school was a one-room, and the strangest thing about it, until I left the second grade up till I was in eighth grade, I was the only one in my class. There was no one else in the class. We had a one-room school with one teacher with a number of grades in there.

For high school we had to drive to Phoenix. I believe they called it the Phoenix Colored High School, which later became Carver High. (In Phoenix), it made it hard getting used to getting down to doing the work. You didn't express yourself or speak out unless you knew what you were going to say. And when you spoke nobody was supposed to challenge you.

Arizona State University, ca. 1930s (Arizona State University, Dept. of Archives & Manuscripts)

And to a point, I'm that way now. I don't speak unless I know what I'm talking about. And it doesn't give you a chance to challenge. Even all of these years. Forty-one years of teaching. I got to meetings. I served seven years on the board of directors of the YWCA and you didn't speak unless you had something definite to say, and when you said it, everybody stopped and listened.

My parents (told me), "Be prepared to earn a good living." And in order to do that, you have to have an education. Out at Laveen, the white families want to know how did you do it. My dad's nickname was Cocomoh. And Cocomoh had two children (go) through college. They (whites) couldn't get any through, and we had to finish college. They just couldn't see how we did it.

My brother insisted on getting an education, and we were very close together; so he carried me right along with him. He had a job at nighttime and, between my brother and sister, they helped me and I was able to finish school.

Now, where I really found it hard was at Phoenix College. I had a friend, a doctor over in Berkeley now, and we were in several classes together, and to hear the white students discuss something that they had in high school that we hadn't had, it kept you continually going back and getting things that you knew you didn't get. And you spent extra time going places, doing things to improve yourself.

I kind of wanted to go to the University of Arizona, but I never had enough money. But all the way through Phoenix College I followed the University of Arizona course of study. I had four years of science. ASU (Arizona State University) had a course out there, biological science, where you'd go out (work) with some calves, chickens. I grew up on a farm and I didn't need that so I had to get a special permit from the head of the department to be excused. They asked me why don't you and I said I don't need it. I had general science, biology, chemistry, and physics. I only wanted to be a teacher. The only reason I would say to take some more science is if I were going to be a nurse or doctor.

Well, they accepted it. As I say, when I made up my mind, I knew I had grounds to stand on.

Most of your businesspeople had their children go two years at Phoenix College, and then they sent them off to school. They did not let them leave that young. And they could get adjusted to college life, then they could go off to school. And that way it gave you the chance to know the most important people in the city because you went to school. And when I started working with them in the Y and the Junior Red Cross, through the Red Cross, Camp Fire Girls. I was director of the Bluebirds for fifteen years. And you knew the people because you had grown up (with them). And the minute that someone asked for someone to do something, they would immediately think of Irene King.

A principal (once) told me, "Mrs. King, you would be the best person to do it because you have lived through it. Do the history of our school."

And he asked me to write a history because I could go all the way back. Even now I could almost give you the names of all of the retired teachers. I was very active with the local teachers. I served on the board of directors with eight districts, different school districts, under my supervision. Well, that gave you a chance to really know what was going on in the education field in Maricopa County.

The Maricopa County Teachers' Association was made up of delegates from the different local associations. They had the board of directors. One of the experiences that I had was I served on the ATA (Arizona Teachers' Association), which was the state teachers' organization. I served on the insurance committee. And then Phoenix Elementary was going to select insurance for the district; they had a professional board come in and did the planning and drawing up the rules and regulations for the teachers. And I served three years on that. It was an experience, and you just don't forget it.

I began teaching in 1936. I graduated from ASU in May, and there was one job open and a fellow had gotten there before I knew it. There were no vacancies. So a week before school was to start in September…they didn't hire married teachers, and if you were married you were automatically (out)…and a friend of mine married and I got the job that she had. So I taught one year at Booker T. (Washington). They needed someone to organize and someone to take those children who were not ready for first grade, so they chose me to do it. The state didn't pay for those kindergartens. For years they didn't pay for them.

Many of the districts didn't get kindergartens until here recently because the districts were not able to pay for them. They were going to combine the kindergarten and the first grades. So then, I finally taught kindergarten from the second grade back. And in '51, Eleanor Ragsdale resigned and they needed a first-grade teacher. So, I said, "Here I go again." And I taught forty years and one at Booker T.

My method of teaching was quite a bit different than the other teachers'. It was noticeable. And my last year of teaching, I had a group of students from ASU who were visiting the school. So after the others had gone, I had three students who slipped back over to my room and asked me how did I do it. They noticed that even my room was different from the other classrooms.

And I said it's my method of teaching. And I had parents clamoring to get their students in my room. They knew I'd give them a good start, and if you check the number who have graduated from high school and college, you'll say they must have gotten a good start to be able to have gone on. And I meet them, parents and students, even now. They're doing a good job.

I've taught children of my former students. Third generations. Well, the first thing that I would tell them, "Wait a minute. You are in trouble now. I can find out who your parents are." I'd say, "Well, you'd better go home now and check with your mother or check with your father and ask them what Mrs. King is going to do." And usually didn't have much trouble.

See, I started out teaching the children of my schoolmates and class-mates. I started out with their children, and that was one reason why I didn't want to leave that area because I had become well acquainted with the parents. And you didn't have to work out a new problem. You usually knew the parents and you knew what to expect. Now, once in a while you did get disappointed in a child.

I taught forty years at Dunbar School and one year at Booker T. That's lots of classes and a lot of children.

What has happened to Phoenix proper...the older people are still here, like I am. Well, I don't feel like moving someplace else. So as a result, I'm right here. I moved here in 1937, my second year of teaching. As they told me when I retired, "We'll look up and see King coming over to Dunbar."

I said, "No, you won't see me coming over. You might see that Chevy coming over here. That Chevy has been backed out of the garage for so many years, it might automatically back out. But I won't be in it." And as a result, I haven't done any sub work or visiting the school, and I've only seen about four children from Dunbar School. And the reason for that was the principal asked me to write a history of Dunbar School and I wrote a history of Dunbar School and what shocked him was I included a list of so many of these students who went through Dunbar School who had fin-ished college. And all I had to do was go through my files. They can stay at the housing project, but that shouldn't keep a child from advancing. To me, the house in the project was an advantage. I could name a number of teachers, Morrison Warren (for one) whose article was in yesterday's pa-per. Now Morrison was married and lived in the project when he taught at Dunbar. He was living there in the projects. You see, I taught Morrison Warren when I was doing my practice teaching. I taught his wife. Morrison was in the seventh grade, and his wife was in the sixth grade.

And, of course, we had this come up once. My sorority always would give...we called it a walk, contest. And no matter who they had running for queen, they said, "Well, no matter, who Irene King is supporting is going to win. She knows everybody but the governor." I sent word back to the teacher that made that statement..."You tell her that I know the governor."

So that's what I enjoyed about the broad spectrum of working in the community. Not only your school community, you knew the community as a whole. You knew the important businesspeople, and you attended affairs with them. You kept up with the times.

INTERVIEW BY MARIA HERNANDEZ, JULY 29, 1981
COURTESY ARIZONA STATE UNIVERSITY
DEPARTMENT OF ARCHIVES AND MANUSCRIPTS

Gwendolyn Knight

Artist

Born: May 26, 1913, Barbados, Caribbean

Gwendolyn Knight came to St. Louis, Missouri, from Barbados when she was seven years old. In 1926, she moved with her family to Harlem, where she took art classes in public school. She attended the School of Fine Arts at Howard University from 1931 to 1933, when she could no longer afford the tuition. She returned to New York and studied with sculptor Augusta Savage. While studying with Savage, she met painter Jacob Lawrence, whom she married in 1941. She continued painting but received little recognition. In 1960, she enrolled at the New School for Social Research in New York and studied art there until 1966. She then went to the Skowhegan School of Painting and Sculpture in Skowhegan, Maine (1968–1970). For most of her career, Knight has been a figurative painter of portraits and still lifes, utilizing oil, charcoal, and ink in her work.

We lived in the Caribbean until I was seven. My father, Malcolm, died when I was two. He was a pharmacist. I was an only child. My mother's name was Miriam. She died in 1984. She had a good life.

My early childhood was very pleasant. I remember going to a little school and passing the walls overgrown with flowers on the way. Just everyday life; things come back to me once in a while. I don't really think about them that much.

The Caribbean was a British colony. And it wasn't like the South or anything like that. It was quite different than the United States, I think. The people, the white and the black people, lived peacefully, I think. I wasn't there till I was an adult and grown up, but as a child, I don't remember any discrimination.

A family adopted me, and we moved to the United States. We went to St. Louis. It was amazing to me. There was cold weather, and snow, and different kinds of holidays. And so it was quite different and very wonderful, as far as I thought. But in St. Louis there was discrimination. I went to a segregated school. And there was lots of discrimination, because that was almost like a southern town. I think you could ride buses and things, and sit anywhere, but it was a segregated town. It didn't really bother me at the time.

My foster sister was the one who adopted me. She was practically as old as my mother, I guess. My mother stayed in the islands. She had been crippled in one of the tornadoes. So I don't even know if they would have allowed her in at that time. But I kept in touch with her all the time. And so there was no missing Mother.

We went to St. Louis because my foster sister was working as a dresser for an opera star—Dorothy Francis. It was white opera. In St. Louis and Forest Park every summer, they had opera. So she came with Dorothy Francis to St. Louis, and she met and married someone there.

To me, it (St. Louis) was fine. I had lots of little friends, and we lived in a nice neighborhood. And I had good teachers. Our school was wonderful. I have no idea how I got interested in art. From the time I can remember, I've been interested in doing that. I always liked drawing and doing portraits. I loved to do portraits, even as a little girl. But everybody thought they were ugly.

My mother would say to me, "Oh, I'm not that ugly."

But anyhow, I really enjoyed it. Then I used to see some very glossy calendars that had maids with water jugs and all that, standing by the fountain, something Italian, and I thought they were gorgeous.

I read a lot. And I was very nosy and bossy, but when my friend Sarah Turner—she was younger than I, so I was sort of the bossy person with her—and it wasn't that there was any antipathy or anything like that, I just assumed that since I was older, I would know better than she would know how to act. So when they had a show there, I asked everybody if Sarah Turner was still there, and then we found Sarah Turner, so she told me that after I moved to New York, I wrote her letters telling her how to behave.

I think that my foster sister had been in the United States for some years before. Then her family came. We arrived in 1920. And we went to live in New York in 1926, I guess. I finished junior high school in St. Louis.

When I got to New York, it was exciting. I had been living in a segregated city and going to a segregated school, and all my friends were black. In New York I was amazed at all the different kinds of people, like Italians and Jews.... So, I was fascinated by that and loved the Italian names and thought it was wonderful.

We lived in Harlem. My sister had been here before, so when we first arrived, we lived with a family in a private house on 126th Street until my sister found an apartment. And then she found an apartment on 114th Street. And from there, we moved to 1851 Seventh Avenue.

Gwendolyn Knight and Jacob Lawrence, photograph by Alan Govenar, Dallas, Texas, 1997.
(Texas African American Photography Archive)

I went to high school in New York. I went to Wadley. Wadley High School was the girls' high school, and had a good reputation. It was mixed, and that was on 115th Street. Well, when I first came, Wadley had two annexes, and one was on 77th Street and Amsterdam Avenue, and the other was on 103rd. I went to the one at 77th Street and Amsterdam. And I met an art teacher there. She was a typical art teacher. She had short hair and wore long beads and she was very interested in what I was doing, so I continued with my art there. I spent my freshman year at the annex. And then I went to the main building, which was on 115th between Seventh and Lenox.

While I was at the annex, I had the really good support of this art teacher. I can't remember her name. But anyhow, she made a great impression on me. She was white. She was very involved and very helpful to me, so I felt that I could do something. But at the main high school, it was a little bit different to me. I didn't know it at the time, but I think I ran into some people who did not favor blacks. So it was a little bit different.

After I was an artist and got to know the artists in Harlem, I had a sense of the Harlem Renaissance. Of course, I used to read a lot, so I had read some books by black writers, Langston Hughes and Claude McKay, so I knew the writers just by reading about them. I spent a lot of time in the library, too.

After high school I went to Howard University. This was 1931. I was a student in the art department. I had Lois Mailou Jones, and Mr. Porter was head of the art department. I only stayed at Howard two years because that was just at the beginning of the Depression, and the money was not available after two years.

So, I went back to Harlem. That's when we were living on 124th Street. Through Dorothy Francis, my sister became a housekeeper for a very well known psychiatrist.

Well, after I came back from Howard University and was not going back to school again, I met a lady, Mrs. Welch, a black woman, and she got on my case and asked me what I was doing and all that kind of thing; why wasn't I doing something? So she took me up to Augusta Savage's studio, and I began to go there and study and meet the artists.

Mrs. Welch was a fine dressmaker. She thought that I was interested in art, and Augusta Savage's studio was well known in the art world at the time. And so it was the place that I could go and do the things I liked to do.

Augusta Savage had had some recognition, so I would have thought at the time, she must have been in her thirties, but now that I look at it, she must have been older than that. But you know, as a child, you either think somebody is ancient—or as a young woman, anyhow—or if you like them, you think they're close to you.

It's really incredible when I think about it because it was only for one year, and I'm always surprised when I think of it, because she had an influence on my life as an artist. I mean, I don't think that had I not known her, I would have persisted in doing what I'm doing.

Augusta didn't give lessons. She got models for us, and we drew and she did her sculpture, and I guess she must have done some teaching because she was there, you know. She would come and say, "This is good, or that," but she was a sculptor, and I was a painter or graphic artist.

I was working from the model at the studio and at Augusta's place and doing charcoal drawings. And then I did little opaque watercolor works and things like that. But I did not really work very hard, I tell you.

Then, the WPA, the art program, came on. And I got a job as an assistant to one of the master artists, who was involved in the Murals-in-Harlem project. Her name was Selma Day, but the head of that project was Charles Alston. He was kind of a mentor to Jake.

I met Jake at 306. That was the place where Jake worked and also the place where all the mural artists signed in for work. It was on 141st Street between Eighth and St. Nicholas, I believe, Number 306. That was what, in '33, '34?

I knew Jake all the time. I'm not sure when we started actually dating. We were married in 1941.

I thought Jake's work was wonderful, and he had the stick-to-it-ness. He just worked more than anybody. I thought he was a very good artist, and he was a nice man, too, young man.

I am absolutely sure that in other places, you wouldn't have had that kind of community (that we had in New York) because there was everything going on there, and especially at that time, the WPA time. Orson Welles's *Emperor Jones* played there, and all the arts were being followed in Harlem. I don't think any other place would have given me this opportunity. And on top of that, I began to know other artists because in '41 and '43, Jake became a member of the Downtown Gallery.

The place I remember most is East 51st Street. And she had taken Jake as one of the stable in her gallery. It was Edith Halpert. So I got to know all those gallery artists, and there was Ben Shahn, all the well-known artists. There was a kind of mixing that went on in New York that couldn't happen someplace else

Before the sixties, before the (civil rights) movement, everybody was in Harlem. All the (black) intellectuals, all the professional people—the doctors, the lawyers—everybody lived in Harlem, and I guess we all cared about each other. So it was a rich community. It changed at the end of segregation. There was a wider opportunity for people to live places other than Harlem. And I guess people who could afford it moved out. And that was too bad, I think. And that left people who were not as able to defend themselves, to try to better themselves. And children didn't get the same sense of knowledge and truth in their community.

When I got there (Harlem) in '26, I was too young to be really involved in the arts scene; I didn't know anything about it, for one thing. So I think the twenties was the time of the Renaissance. I knew these other people because Augusta was one of the Renaissance people. I don't know whether she entertained people like Langston Hughes, but she did know a lot of people who were—Aaron Douglass, Claude McKay. She knew them, and the community was a small community, so you knew everybody. You knew all the artists. We could meet the writers and the painters. There were all these great jazz people. Duke Ellington, Billie Holiday. All the big bands. We used to go to the Savoy, and all the big bands came there. And we went to Small's Paradise. If you wanted to dance, you went to the Savoy. That was it. And Small's was fine. And there were several neighborhood places that you could go. I've forgotten the names of them.

I think it (Harlem) was a Mecca. That was the place to go if you were an artist. There weren't many opportunities for black artists elsewhere. I didn't expect that we'd be here (Seattle) this long. I had never really thought about the state of Washington. If I thought of the West Coast at all, I thought San Francisco or Los Angeles, where the movie industry was. And I just didn't think about it. We had a friend who was a dancer, Perry. And he had gone into the service and had been stationed at Fort Lewis out here.

And we met Perry one day on the street and he said, "I'm thinking about moving to Seattle."

So we said, "Oh, isn't that nice." And then I said to Jake, "Why does he want to move to Seattle?" We were surprised, you know. But it's a very nice place, and it's been very good for us. Well, now it has a very vital arts scene. But it wasn't always like this.

I can't put my finger on the group of artists who are as cohesive and close as the ones I knew in New York. Well, it's a different time. I guess people are different.

I met one young woman on one of our trips, and she wanted to re-create that. She was so taken with the Renaissance and Harlem as the place where the art flourished, and there was so much going on, and where it was so joyful at times. And she wanted to know how she could start back to that time.

Jake and I are quite different artists. I think I'm more spontaneous, in a way. He's interested in history and very controlled—he knows more or less what the painting is going to be like when it's finished. You know, he plans it, and it's done, and it comes out exactly as he was thinking about it. There may be some small changes, or maybe not. But I never know. So I find that doing a monoprint suits me fine.

I don't work very much because I get involved—we're busy all the time. But I do work. I just had a show of monoprints in the spring, and Jake has a big exhibition here at the Henry Gallery. And they have two portraits that I did: one a self-portrait and one of Jake.

I think it's the art (that keeps me going), it's the music, it's the paintings, it's the dance, it's all the arts. It's wonderful. We got the Sunday *Times*, we get the *Times* every day, and it's just wonderful to read about what's happening in the arts. And every time we get to New York, I visit a museum. So I think the arts is really what keeps me involved.

INTERVIEW BY ALAN GOVENAR, SEPTEMBER 3, 1998

Jacob Lawrence

Artist

Life dates: September 7, 1917–June 9, 2000

Jacob Lawrence grew up in Harlem during the Great Depression. He was raised by his mother, who had separated from his father soon after the births of his sister, Geraldine, and brother, William. Because his mother was a domestic who was often on welfare, Lawrence was forced to work in a printer's shop and in a laundry to help support his family. He attended night classes in painting between 1932 and 1937. He received training in the Harlem Art Workshops, supported first by the College Art Association and later by the Federal Art Project of the WPA. Lawrence attended the American Artists' School in New York City from 1937 to 1939. He had his first one-person exhibition at the Harlem YMCA in 1938 and achieved national acclaim when his "Migration of the Negro" series was exhibited at New York's Downtown Gallery in 1941. New York was a frontier for him and other African American artists, providing opportunities that did not exist elsewhere in the United States in the 1930s and 1940s. Throughout his career, Lawrence has focused on scenes from his Harlem background and the African American experience, creating historical series, including Toussaint L'Ouverture *(1937-1938),* Frederick Douglass *(1938–1939), and* Harriet Tubman, *as well as thematic works, such as* Theater *(1951–1952) and* Wounded Man *(1968) about the civil rights conflicts in the United States. In 1941, Lawrence married Gwendolyn Knight; they live in Seattle, Washington, where Lawrence was a professor of art at the University of Washington from 1971 until his retirement in 1987.*

My family was a part of the migration. That is, my mother, my sister, and my brother. My father and my mother were separated. I was born in Atlantic City, New Jersey. They were moving up the coast, as many families were during that migration. And I was part of that. We moved up to various cities until we arrived—the last two cities I can remember before moving to New York were Easton, Pennsylvania, and Philadelphia, Pennsylvania. And then we finally settled in New York City. So that was my upbringing. My young years were spent just doing that: traveling as part of the migration, and that was it.

I was aware of people moving, older people like my mother's peers— I would hear them talk about how another family has arrived. And these were the people who would mention the fact that they had been here a few years and they were seeing the new migrants coming in and settling or moving on. And I didn't realize what it was at the time, of course; it's only in later years that I realized what was going on.

For me, there were bright lights, the excitement, the movement, the texture, the vitality. I didn't know it in those terms then, but it's only in remembering my subconscious feeling of moving into this great metropolis or into this great Harlem community, which was a part of New York City. And that's remained with me. In fact, much of my work is based on that experience.

My mother's name was Rosalie Armstead. She was born in Fredericksburg, Virginia. My father's name was Jacob, and he was born in South Carolina. And he worked as a cook on the railroad. I was very young when they split up. We arrived in New York in 1930 when I was thirteen years of age. And we didn't arrive in New York direct from Easton, Pennsylvania. I must have been six, seven, around that when they split up. My parents were on the move, like many of the migrants were. Maybe I was like two, one or two, when they left the South.

It's only in retrospect that I can realize the significance of the migration to my own work. I couldn't analyze it like that. Not at that time. I could only see it from a child's point of view. I didn't realize the significance of it at the time. When I did the "Migration" series, of course, I realized it. But prior to that time, I did not know the significance of it. There was so much going on. The lynchings were at their peak in the South; people were talking about this; there were the Marcus Garvey people; there were black nationalists. There was just so much happening. There was so much going on that I couldn't analyze it. I wasn't a sociologist.

In New York my mother was able to maintain us. We lived in an apartment in Harlem. I think we arrived at 137th Street, right near Harlem Hospital. We always lived up around that area. I had one brother and one sister. Geraldine was my sister, and William was my brother.

We lived in a railroad flat. When you say "small," it had two bedrooms and a kitchen and a living room, like many of the places in the Harlem community. Much was going on in that part of Harlem. You'd walk up and down Seventh Avenue or Lennox Avenue. There were so-called soapbox orators. I didn't always understand the content of what they were saying, but it was full of life, full of vitality, full of energy, and it was only later that I realized that many of them were the Garveyites, or the religious people, the Communists, and they were all very active. It was a very active community. And the churches played a very vital role in our community. I was baptized in the Abyssinian Baptist Church. That was Adam Clayton Powell's father's church, and then the younger Powell took over. And that was a very big church in the community. A very important church in the community.

I got placed in a foster home right after my mother and father were separated. That must have been seven, around there. That wasn't in New York. That was before we got there. My brother and sister were placed separate. I didn't know enough to be scared. You don't realize these things as a youngster, you don't realize what's going on.

But when we got to Harlem, we lived with my mother. She was a domestic. I know she didn't work in the Harlem community, because the people in the Harlem community for the most part didn't hire domestics. They were all blacks. My mother worked like most domestics, she worked, I guess, throughout the city, in the Bronx and Manhattan and wherever people could find work.

I didn't realize that I had gotten there at the end of the Harlem Renaissance. It kind of teetered off in the thirties at the beginning of the Great Depression. But the important years, I think, took place in the twenties. And after the Great Depression, what we know of the Renaissance started to phase out.

I went to Public School 68, elementary school; Public School 89, which is a junior high; and the High School of Commerce. I didn't get interested in art until I was at the Utopia Children's Center, Utopia House. My mother enrolled us there when she was working, and you could go there and get lunch for a dime, the children, and there was also an after-school center that offered a program in arts and crafts. And that's when I had the opportunity. I was encouraged to work with paint. I loved color. I must have been about thirteen or fourteen years of age.

The most influential artist for me was Charles Austin. When I was thirteen, he was twenty-three, which is quite a difference when you're young. And he was taking his graduate work, I think, at Columbia University, and he was also hired by the Utopia House as a counselor, as a person who taught arts and crafts. He knew I liked color, like most kids; that's not unusual. And he encouraged me. And that's when I was encouraged to work with color, to play with color, and had a wonderful time.

My first paintings were abstract. I didn't get interested in figurative kinds of work until I started telling stories of the community, seeing people in the community, the pool halls, the churches, the people on the street, the soapbox orators, and so on. And that's what stimulated my interest to try to portray this life.

I was encouraged in my art when I was in high school, but not to the same degree as I was encouraged outside. Let's go back a moment. You know, during that period is the Great Depression. The Roosevelt administration established arts centers throughout the country, which gave people work, like teachers and counselors and people like that, to run these centers. Augusta Savage was one. Charles Austin was another. And I was encouraged to attend. After I left the Utopia House, Austin got his own place on 147th Street, and I was encouraged to come in and join the group—people of all ages. And these centers were wonderful because they gave us the opportunity—we met people of all ages. Of course, they were completely free, and if you were interested in music, dance, theater, any of the arts, performing arts like this, you attended one of these centers. And I went into one of these centers during the early thirties when I was about fifteen, sixteen years of age. I met all kinds of people, you know: not just people from the Harlem community, but people outside the community, people of all ethnic backgrounds. It was just a wonderful thing.

It was an inspiration to me. I realize it more now, I think, than I did then. Oh, I think there were many artists who got their start there and who are actually working now. Many of them are dead, of course. My wife came up during that period. There was Ronald Joseph; there was Romare Bearden, who was not a member of the center because he was a welfare worker, but he attended the center. And so there were people like that who had outside jobs. They would congregate and meet in the centers in the evening, so it was just a wonderful experience.

I didn't graduate from high school. I just left school. That must have been about the second year in high school. I sold newspapers, I worked in hand laundries, just did anything, like many young people of my age did.

But I did receive a scholarship at the American Artists' School, which is now nonexistent. It's been nonexistent for years. And I think it was a left-wing school. That was the school I attended—outside the Harlem community. Because when I went to the Harlem Arts Center, that was a school, too, but it was in Harlem. The American Artists' School was on 14th Street in Manhattan between Fifth and Sixth Avenues, I think. I was in and out of the American Artists' School in a couple of years.

At the Harlem artists' school we had several teachers: Augusta Savage, Charles Austin, Sara West, William Johnson, Ronald Joseph. Many active artists. And it was free. This was under the Federal Art Project.

The first opportunity I had to show my work was in the Harlem community. It was at the James Weldon Johnson Literary Guild. And the name means just what it says. Women who were very interested in the life of James Weldon Johnson, they set up this program. And they gave me a show. It was at one of the Harlem art centers. There were about four of them. Augusta Savage had one on 136th or 137th Street. My wife went to her center. Then there was Austin's center. That was on 141st Street. And then there were two others in the Harlem community that I remember. I can't give you the streets.

Harlem was very active at that time. There were so many people on the streets. People played music just like you see them play on the streets today. But then they played instruments up from the South, washboards, harmonicas, and things of that sort.

I was a young fellow then. I never thought of nightclubs or anything like that. I lived at home with my mother until I began to work on the Federal Art Project. And that would have been about when I was twenty-one years of age. That's when I established my own studio.

I was invited to sign up for the project, to get a job on the Federal Art Project, which many people did. I was twenty-one years of age. And Augusta Savage was responsible for that. Augusta Savage was very well known, very highly respected in the black artistic community. And she was just a wonderful person. She took me down to the hiring office. She was a mentor in the community with many of the young black artists. And she took me down in 1936, to sign me up for the project. They told her I was too young, to come back next year.

Well, I went back to Harlem; I'd completely forgotten about it. But she hadn't forgotten. And she took me down again in 1938, when I was twenty-one years of age. And I was signed up, and I made a fabulous salary of $23.86 a week, which was a lot of money then. I also served time in the CCC, Civilian Conservation Corps. I worked on a dam up in New York State. It was the first time I remember going into the countryside. It was nice. I was around people my own age. It was a good experience.

My first studio of my own was on 125th Street, between Lenox and Seventh Avenue. It was a loft apartment. I was able to get that after I received a fellowship award. At that time, my work was figurative. But first, before doing people, I just did designs, like arabesque designs and things like that. And then I moved on. I did masks. Just not representing any particular person or persons; I just did masks. And then I started doing street scenes. That was it.

I started thinking about the Migration series about 1939. That was completed in 1941. I was inspired by the people talking about people coming up from the South. That was a big thing on people's minds. The lynchings that went on in the South were at their peak. The *Amsterdam News* reported that almost every week, a lynching was taking place. And I was doing people on the street even before that, and then I decided to do a series, and that's how the "Migration" things came out. And it shows people, North, South, North, South, North, South, with the panels alternating like that. This was happening in the South, and then we moved north, happening in the South, we moved north, happening in the South, we moved north, until the sixty panels were completed.

New York represented a frontier for these people that were coming. The opportunities, jobs, and we were going to war.

The Migration series brought me attention outside the community, outside the Harlem community. But I got my first attention, I'll always remember this, from the people of the Harlem community, and that's something I'll never forget. That was a very important thing, like the James Weldon Johnson Literary Guild. My support came from the black community. The life of my work was that community.

I was drafted in 1943. I went into the U.S. Coast Guard. And my first station was aboard ship, the USS *Seacloud*. That was the name of the ship. And I was stationed in Curtis Bay, Maryland. But you know, that's many years ago, so I can't remember exactly. It was segregated in the service, but this ship, the *Seacloud*, was an experiment, one of the first experiments to have an integrated ship, during the war. The segregation was beginning to break down throughout the Army and Navy, throughout the services.

I was in the service twenty-five months. I went overseas aboard a troop transport. I went to the southern port of England, Southampton. And then we went to France, and to a part of India, then Egypt. On a troop transport, you really got around. It was a new experience for me. If you had to be in the war, then Navy or Coast Guard, any of those services, was a very good place to be. You always had clean bedding, clean clothes. And I didn't really see much warfare. When I went out on ship, the Atlantic was more or less cleaned up of submarines.

When I came back to New York, I just picked up my painting and continued to paint, got fellowships, received a Guggenheim to do my War series. And I've just been painting ever since.

The War series was done in 1946. And after that, I did a theater series, and then, a series on the civil rights business in the South. It was in the sixties. And I did a piece called "Struggle," a history of the American people. These were three of the series I did after I left the service.

I never thought I'd leave New York. But I did briefly in 1941. I got married, we went to New Orleans, and then to Virginia, near Richmond. From there we came back to New York, and that's where we lived until 1971, when we moved out to the West Coast. I was invited to teach at the University of Washington, and we thought we'd be out here for three to five years, and we've been out here since then. We've been out here for about twentysome years.

I miss New York, but being out here, it's a nice experience. There was a big migration, of course, out to Washington, too, during the war years, when so many blacks moved from places like Texas into the West and California. But this migration never attracted my interest enough to want to make paintings about it. I guess I said everything I wanted to say in the Migration series. There was nothing else I could add. I mean, I couldn't do it. And I was interested in painting, but not doing that again, I'll put it that way. It would have been repetitive, it would have repeated itself.

I like storytelling. I always liked that. I like history, and so I put the two together, my painting and my interest in the historical scene. And it's very exciting for me. Painting. The excitement of painting, the excitement of working with color, hoping that I'm growing, that I'm developing. And the encouragement I receive constantly. I constantly get this.

I love tools. When I was a youngster, I was around tools. I was around three brothers, the Bates bothers. There was Addison Bates, John Bates, and Leonard Bates. And they were brothers, and they were cabinetmakers. And I was around them, and I didn't realize what an impression they were making as cabinetmakers. I didn't realize at the time, that this would be one of my basic subjects. And that's how that started. I just love tools; they're beautiful. I paint them.

Artists must be committed. What is the commitment to the community, to the world community? I think to show beauty, to show your insight, always searching, always looking for something.

INTERVIEW BY ALAN GOVENAR, SEPTEMBER 3, 1998

Bruce Lee, Ph.D.

Biologist
Born: November 16, 1921, Buffalo, New York

Bruce Lee grew up in the Cold Spring area of Buffalo, New York, in a community he defines as people of mixed Indian, African, and Anglo-Saxon descent. Lee calls this region of upstate New York the Niagara Frontier, where colored professionals came with their families to live without having to be constantly reminded of the limitations imposed by racial segregation. Lee recounts childhood meetings with W. E. B. Du Bois, Eugene Kinkle Jones, Mary McLeod Bethune, and other African American leaders who were involved with the Niagara Movement and the struggle for civil rights. Lee attended a predominantly white school through the eighth grade and then went to high school in downtown Buffalo, where the colored teachers worked, although the classes had students with different ethnic backgrounds (the children of Jewish, German, and Irish immigrants). After high school, Lee enrolled in the Brockport Normal School; he received a B.A. degree (1947) from the Tuskegee Institute and an M.A. (1948) and a Ph.D. (1952) in biology from the University of Michigan. After working for many years as a biologist, he moved in 1970 to California to accept a position with the Department of Health, Education, and Welfare. Lee retired in 1983.

I was born into the colored community of Buffalo. The African American community of Buffalo did not accept readily the term "Negro" that was given to us by the white world before and after the Civil War, nor did they accept the term "African American." They preferred to be called colored—"colored" meaning they knew they were the descendants of African American slaves, who came here in the seventeenth and eighteenth centuries, and also they were proud of the fact that they had European ancestors, and also a rich heritage from the American Indian communities. The region I came from in upstate New York was known as the Niagara Frontier. That was the area bordered by the lakes of Ontario, the Niagara River, and Lake Erie.

One Sunday morning in 1952, after I had finished my doctorate at the University of Michigan, I was invited to have breakfast with Charles S. Johnson, who was the distinguished president of Fiske University and who was also a great researcher of African American history in the United States. In the early 1920s, Johnson went to Buffalo to observe the colored community. And he characterized the colored families, and the white families for whom they worked, as "peculiarly friendly." He noted that the whites sometimes attended the African American social events, which were patterned after those the whites had. These coloreds were quite familiar with the social gatherings of the aristocrats because it was their responsibility to serve at their society affairs. Colored families had a presence in political campaigns, municipal celebrations, and the reception of visitors to the city. Except for the Irish, whites seemed to tolerate these colored families. Coloreds and whites attended the same parties, where everyone spoke German.

I can concur with Johnson's observations. My father was fluent in German, and many of the people of his generation were, because in the schools German was taught along with English in the early grades. The children became fluent, and they developed that peculiar relationship. I speak to it because it has influenced my life.

I came up in Buffalo, realizing that every summer, we would have large arrival of the colored professionals from the eastern United States. There would be the physicians, the dentists, the doctors, the lawyers, and people who had other status away from manual labor and service. Many of them were graduates of the finest colleges, and they took great pride in their accomplishments. And the older colored families of Buffalo opened their homes to these people, not as roomers, but as visitors and guests.

My mother was a New York woman. She was born in Jersey City, but she was socialized in New York. My mother was a Pratt graduate from

Leaders of the Niagara Movement gather at Fort Erie, New York, in 1905 in answer to the call of W. E. B Du Bois (second from left, center row) to "organize thoroughly the intelligent, honest Negroes throughout the United States." (The Granger Collection)

Brooklyn, New York, in haute couture, and she designed the clothes for some of the families on Fifth Avenue, Riverside Drive, and the East Side of New York City. She knew these people, and when they came to Buffalo, we were taken to meet them. All these people came to Buffalo because they were able to go to the theaters, go to the stores, use the public recreational facilities, and move without segregation. Buffalo was one of the few cities, maybe the only city in the North, which had practically open access for colored people.

As a child, I used to hear that Mother was not ashamed of the word "Negro," but in the world of Buffalo, we seldom heard it. People referred to themselves as colored people. And I came to look upon myself as a colored person, which I still do. It's very difficult for me to understand how people can call themselves black, which is an adjective. You don't hear Chinese people referred to as yellows, or Indian people as reds. This is only group in the country that is labeled black, an adjective. Use a term which describes them. They are colored people. "Colored" is an adjective, but the "people" is a noun. They also speak to the fact that they are a group of three races. That's what the African American is. It's the amalgam of three races—the African, the European, and the American Indian. And it is something that I am proud of. And my family is proud of. And the people I was raised amongst are proud of. There is nothing to be ashamed of. It's not trying to be anything different. It's what we are.

In Buffalo, the only things that were segregated were the Christian things. The churches were segregated. We went to colored churches. The white YMCA was closed. They gave us a black YMCA that was miles from where I lived, and so I used to go over to the white YMCA with my white friends to watch them recreate. I was a spectator to sports, not a participant. They could use the pools. They could use the tennis courts. And I'd wait for them outside. They often wondered why I was never admitted. It was a question of pigmentation that kept me from participating. The Boy Scout troups, you could join, as long as you remained in your own packs. You were never allowed to choose the pack you wanted to be in. They assigned you to your pack, which was segregation. The Boys Clubs were also segregated. So, I took it upon myself to say, if that's what they want, they can have it. I made my own way. I looked out in the world above me. Having a father who ran on the railroad. He was the chief waiter on the Empire State Express—those crack trains. He used to go to New York and bring back the papers. And he and I would assemble scrapbooks. And he also opened the world to me.

I'm a descendant of one of the first of the colored families in western New York. My father was Edward David Lee, Senior, and my mother was Florence Randolph Jackson of Jersey City, New Jersey. They were married in Niagara Falls in September of 1915.

There were five of us in my family, my brothers, Voyle (1918–1995) and Edward (1921–1946), I'm the middle child, and my two sisters, Harriet Agnes Louise and Florence Lois Jane. The three of us younger ones are still surviving. Voyle and Edward died in the last two years.

My family was in western New York, and that means a lot because they were people who were there during slavery. The earliest reference in the family is 1789 on my mother's side; the gravestone is in Niagara Falls. The earliest reference in my father's family is to his great-great-grandfather, Henry, who was brought over as an Ibo slave to Baltimore, Maryland. Henry escaped his captors and joined the Indian nation outside of Baltimore and married an Indian woman called Patty. And my great-grandfather, Edward Cook, was born in 1815, and he was baptized a Catholic at St. Charles Cathedral in Baltimore. I have his baptismal certificate with the names of his parents and grandparents on it.

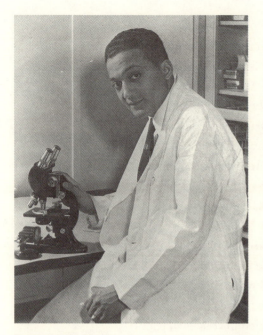

Dr. Bruce Lee, Chief of Microbiology Lab, Detroit Arsenal, Ordnance Corps, U.S. Army, ca. 1953 (Courtesy Bruce Lee, Ph.D.)

Edward Cook was declared free because he was of Indian heritage; his father was Ibo and his mother was a Menneponi Indian. The mayor of Baltimore issued him his free papers in 1837, and this allowed him to leave Baltimore with a passport. The passport is a written statement from the mayor: "Edward Cook, behaving himself in an orderly manner, colored man, is allowed to be out until ten o'clock P.M., behaving himself in an orderly manner." Signed by Mayor Smith. He used that, and he joined an overland train which went over the Allegheny Mountains, and he came to Buffalo. He established himself in 1837 as a barber at the Mansion House, one of the finest hotels in Buffalo (on the site where the Statler Building now stands). And he was there until he died in 1906.

One day in 1840 or 1843, Edward was down at the terminus of the Erie Canal, and he saw a very lovely Indian lady getting off the canal boat. He looked at her and he said, "That's the girl for me." And he started to court her. She was a Mohawk lady called Phoebe Lansing. She was born in 1821 in Fort Plain, New York, which is outside of Albany, and they were married October 29, 1845, at the Vine Street Methodist Church in Buffalo, New York. I have in my possession the silk wedding slipper she wore. It was made in Lynn, Massachusetts. I also have the wedding blanket, which is homespun and was used on their bed.

Phoebe and Edward had eight children. My grandmother, Harriet Emma, was born in 1850. She married my grandfather David Moses Lee in 1870. Grandpa Lee was the child of a Madagascar native who was kidnapped into slavery from Madagascar and brought to Niagara on the Lake, where he was a slave until he was freed by the Canadian government about 1837, many years before the Emancipation Proclamation in the United States. Barnard Lee was his full name.

Barnard Lee was a bitter man because he could never develop the means to get himself back to his native land. In 1840, he married an English-Irish girl called Eleanor Jane McCormick. Some people call her the name McCornish. Her family came from Tipperary, Ireland. She sailed (with her family) to Canada from County Cork. And I have in my possession the blanket, the biddy blanket, which she wore on the voyage over. It's a Jacob's coat of many colors, made of Irish homespun. She brought with her some peasant mourning jewelry. It's made of basalt, a black material, and she wore it when people in our family died. I also have some the cameos she had sewn onto her as buttons on her waistcoat, as well as some of her dining china.

Eleanor was an interesting woman. She loved Barnard Lee, but she had a hard time living with him because he was so bitter about his status. I remember that there's a story in our family that he always resented the fact that his race was enslaved in America. They were living in Niagara on the Lake. And yet, I was told as a child that often people would see Eleanor out in the yard, washing his dirty drawers, and he'd say, "You see that, don't you? They've got my folks in slavery down South, but you see that, don't you?" And after a while, she decided to leave him. But before she did, they had three children. George was the oldest son. Now, George appeared to be a white man, and in the 1860s, he left Canada and sailed to England, where he settled in Liverpool. He sent three letters saying he was doing well, and that's the last we heard of him. He took the name of George Cotton.

David Moses Lee, my grandfather, was born in 1847, and in 1870, he married my grandmother, Harriet Emma, who was the daughter of Edward Cook and Phoebe Lansing. Edward and Phoebe had another child, who was known as Anna. We called her Auntie. She appeared to be an Indian, although she was Malagasy-English-Irish. When she grew to her maturity, she left her family and joined the Kiowa Indian nation. We learned by word of mouth that she married a man named Douglas Harvey and settled in Oklahoma. And that's the last we heard of her.

David Lee was born in Branford, Ontario, and he came to the United States. He married my grandmother in Buffalo, New York, and they had two children: my Aunt Jennie, her name was Cora Jane Lee (1873–1953), and my father, Edward David Lee (1877–1954). Aunt Jennie was the second colored person to finish the Buffalo High School, which is known as Central High. She graduated in 1894. That was unique because in that year, the New York State Regents Examination in algebra was so difficult that the city had a hard time finding people, who passed the examination, to graduate. She was, I think, one of three people to pass, and she graduated.

My grandfather Lee was a male nurse. He worked at Dr. Pierce's hospital in Buffalo. Dr. Pierce advertised "Dr. Pierce's Golden Medical Discovery." And that Golden Medical Discovery was a medicine that was supposed to cure certain venereal diseases. It's particularly amazing because the leading courtesans from Europe used to come to Dr. Pierce's hospital to get cured. My grandfather used to say they got "boiled out." Apparently, what he did was to immerse them in hot water to raise their body temperatures to kill off the existing spirocete, which caused syphilis. And they felt well for a time before they went back to their professions.

In the 1890s, when David Lee was working with Dr. Pierce, a courtesan and a large retinue came from Europe, and David Lee was assigned to be their nurse to look after them. When they left, the courtesan said, "Dave, I appreciate what you've done for us. I'm going to give you something." She gave him a sunburst-of-diamonds stud and a single solitary diamond stud for his formal outfit. You see, the colored community often had formal balls in Buffalo, which were attended in exquisite clothes and jewelry.

The marriage of my grandparents foundered in the 1870s, and my grandmother separated from Dave. They did not divorce, but she lived the remainder of her life alone. My father came into his maturity in the early part of the twentieth century. And in 1915, he courted and married Florence Randolph Jackson of Jersey City and Niagara Falls. Florence Randolph Jackson was the daughter of Charles Kersey Jackson, who was born a slave around 1846 near Roanoke, Virginia. He was the grandson of John Randolph, who was a cousin of Thomas Jefferson, the ambassador to Russia and a member of the House of Representatives from Virginia. Randolph was supposed to never have had children, but when I heard this, I said that was incorrect. He had one child, but they often said, he didn't have any white children. He had one child by a slave. We never knew her name. But Martha Randolph was the child of this slave. Martha Randolph secured her freedom when Randolph died. He manumitted his slaves, including Martha, and she was the mother of my grandfather.

For some reason, Martha's children were never free, and they were sold into slavery. But she kept up with her children. I don't know how that happened: why she was manumitted and not the children. Martha appeared to be a white person; she was very fair-skinned. And when General Grant took Richmond, she sought out her children, gathered them, and posed as a white woman, saying, "I'm liberating these three slaves." They were in their teens. And she took them to New York City.

When Martha was growing up, her white relatives in the Randolph household did something which they were not supposed to do. They taught Martha to read and to write and to do figures (math), and in New York, she became a very astute businesswoman. Within two years, she owned her own house at 220 Whiton Street in Jersey City, and the house is still standing. She set up her house with business as a modiste, making clothes for women. She taught her children that the key to success in life is to get into business and to always own your own home. And this lesson was well known. Martha had three children, James and Charles, and a girl. James and Charles grew up and owned hotels. James went to Saratoga to run a hotel, and my grandfather, Charles, owned the Falls House and later the Robinson House, a large hotel, in Niagara Falls. They were large hotels for white tourist trade. African American trade was impossible because of the social customs of the day. Now, my grandfather was a very astute businessman. He always resented the fact that he'd been a slave. He was barely literate; he wrote phonetically, but his speech was astute and he was alert to any opportunity to make money. And every fall, at the end of the season, he would take a trip through the South, after closing the hotel, to visit the "Negro" colleges, looking for fair-skinned Negroes, in those days, who could pass for white persons. And he would offer them jobs the next year working for him in the Robinson House. So the Robinson House was a hotel for white trade staffed by so-called white people who were African Americans passing as whites and who were able to give him the standards of services that he required. They worked on the desk, as concierge. They worked all through the hotel in various occupations. Domestic work, unfortunately, was done by dark-skinned African Americans.

When we came along, my brothers, Voyle and Edward, myself, and my sisters, Harriet and Florence, some of us were fair, and some of us were brown-skinned. I remember as a child, trying to use the front steps of my grandfather's hotel and being taken by a maid off to the side down to the park to watch the Falls. I think I knew more about the Falls than I did anyplace else as a child.

And, in spite of his success, my grandfather had a feeling of inferiority about himself. In his will, he said he wanted no colored man to handle any of his affairs because they knew nothing about business. And as a result, his lawyer cleaned the estate. He died and left a huge amount of money. In those days, it must have been over $150,000 in cash and the hotel and the properties that we owned. But by 1932 during the Depression, practically nothing was left. My grandmother's last days were not what they should have been.

They had three daughters, Paulina, born in 1882; Florence (1884–1965) my mother; and Ethel (1895–1985). Now, my grandfather, even though he was born a slave and did not have education, was a stickler for education. And he dressed his daughters elegantly. Their clothes were from the finest shops in New York City. He was able to give them a background which you didn't ordinarily find with the colored society of that day except in New York City. The society at the turn of the century was an elegant colored society. There was a tremendous respect for education. My mother was a member of the Scotia Scholastic Society. The Scotia Scholastic Society consisted of young colored men and women who stayed in the metropolitan area for education. They went to Columbia. They went to Fordham. The girls went to Barnard or they went to the normal schools there. They took advantage of the local education rather than going south. And they would give affairs during the year to try to raise money to help people who wanted to do the same things they did: Stay in the North and get educated.

My mother told a story that in the early 1900s she dated an African prince. She said he had a strange name: Prince Icaca. It was about 1910, and he gave a dinner party at Columbia where he attended. And he served strawberries in January. Well, that was in those days before there was refrigeration and freezing. You can imagine, that was considered the height of elegance.

These were the stories of my background. I try to characterize this colored world. It was a world of people who thought themselves apart. You had to be born into it and you died out of it. They were the descendants of people who were freed before the Emancipation Proclamation. Many of them were freed in the eighteenth century and they came to Buffalo and they formed their own community. Out of a city of about 500,000 people, there might have been 5,000 colored people. They lived downtown in the older part of the city. I grew up in an area known as Cold Springs. In my day, it was considered the outskirts of the city, but now it's the center of the city. They numbered about fifty families. We knew each other. We associated only with each other. And, unfortunately, they never told us the true facts of life, of our relationship as African Americans to the world about us. We thought that everybody lived as we did, with all its advantages.

When I got into the Army, I was shocked to find that there were African Americans who had never been allowed to use a library. They had never been into a store. They had never been into a theater. They never had the advantages I took for granted. Almost everything was open in Buffalo. It was one of the few cities in the country you could shop. You could go downtown to the theater, or you could eat out. In the summertime you could take a boat ride. You could go to Canada. The Niagara Frontier was filled with the colored professionals from the South who came to the North to live without having to be reminded every minute that things were not open to them, simply on the basis of their skin color.

Many of them came to Buffalo for vacation and then they moved to the city from the South. They came to western New York. They loved to go shopping downtown. During summer vacation, people would say, "Well, where are you staying?" They never said they were rooming. Instead, they were the guest of such and such a person. To me, they were the most elegant people. I remember being taken out to meet these people. I met W. E. B. Du Bois, Eugene Kinkle Jones, James Weldon Johnson, Mary McLeod Bethune, Mordecai Johnson, Rasmun Johnson, and his brother (who wrote "Lift Every Voice and Sing"), you name it, anybody who was anybody in the colored world from about 1900 to the 1950s came to Buffalo. Anybody who was for civil rights or pressing for the improvement of the race, they would come to town and my mother would march us kids in there, the five of us, to meet these people.

Years later, in 1948, when I was a student at the University of Michigan, I attended a rally in Detroit to help Dr. W. E. B. Du Bois fight the monstrous charges concerning his loyalty pressed against him by our government. I was a veteran, and I was called to help with this meeting. And he and his wife, Shirley Graham, were there. They were traveling about the country, and a group organized a mass meeting at Bethel Church in Detroit. Shirley Graham was trying to raise money for his defense. And after the meeting, we went back to the minister's quarters to meet them. There was W. E. B. Du Bois, looking like a polished new Buddha of fine ivory. He was in his eighties then. He died in 1963; that was 1948. Oh, to see this person, who all my life I had revered, and to shake his hand. And I told him who I was, and I saw this smile come to his face.

The people of the Niagara Movement came through Buffalo. I have in my possession the loving cup given to my great-grandfather by the colored community in 1868 because of his work as a conductor on the Underground Railroad during the years of slavery.

The Niagara Movement was the precursor to the NAACP. That's the reason Du Bois was in the Niagara Frontier. My family was involved. They served as hosts for the people who came to town, and they would ferry them to Canada. They all had to meet in Niagara, Ontario, because the customs of the day made it nearly impossible for them to meet without difficulty.

They came to western New York; it was picturesque. The summer season was a time when you could spend your time being elegant. The homes of the society were thrown open to these people.

When Marcus Garvey started his improvement association in the early part of the century, many of the colored people looked at him askance because, first of all, he was dark-skinned. This colored world, I'm sorry to say, was often composed of those people who were there because of their color. I also realize that I had my own prejudice about many of the people who came at that time. Was there prejudice among the colored world? Of course there was. It was based on your family background and your skin color, and sometimes your hair quality and how you looked. And as children, we were amazed to hear one family member, when she was growing up, told not to bring anybody home who was darker than her. When my son heard this, he was appalled. And I told him, "I never practiced it."

My mother was fair-skinned, and coming from New York City, she thought that the local attitudes were atrocious. And she never allowed any of us to do anything like that. But with my father's side of the family, there was an emphasis on physical features. I recall being told this old adage, "If you're white, you're right. If you're yellow, you're mellow. If you're brown, stick around. If you're black, get back." And, tragically, it happened. Also, within our community, it extended to where you went to church. In my youth, there was only one church to be attended, to be socially accepted and that was St. Philip's Anglican Episcopal Church. It was the high Episcopalian Anglican. Also, it was a church, they used to say, you were born into and you died out of. And the whole time I was there, the twenty-one years I lived in Buffalo, very few people joined the church because they weren't welcome. The congregation didn't have to worry about paying our bills to the diocese because the white churches didn't want us as members of their church. And they'd given us our church to keep us out of their church. My mother was easily aware of what that meant. Also, there was a succession of ministers until there was the arrival of an outstanding man, Osmond Henry Brown, who was West Indian. He came there in the twenties and he stayed until the fifties. He was an amazing man, and he had the most wonderful, wonderful wife, who was a New Englander. But she said to my mother, "Florence, I'm not fish nor fowl." She wasn't a West Indian and she wasn't a Buffalonian. And she was practically crucified by the viciousness of many of the people in the church. But she turned out three wonderful boys. Alan is now a physician in Georgia. And Junior, Osmond Henry Brown Junior, became a priest, and he's dead. And the last one, John, became a federal employee and he's dead.

My mother was very much aware of what was going on and was constantly angry and doing battle with the locals. She was never really accepted into old Buffalo society, and she didn't give a damn because she came from New York society. She was very proud, and we were very proud within our family. But in the world we lived in, it was difficult, because my father also kept these scrapbooks. It wasn't concealed—the colored versus the new Negro situation. The colored people lived in Cold Springs. The new Negroes, often called blacks, lived downtown. And it was not on the basis of color, it was on the basis of culture. Is your culture white-oriented, or is it Negro-oriented? The church you went to, Anglican Church, was high church, English in origin. Many services were attended by white people who wanted to enjoy the high Anglican service, which they couldn't get in their own Episcopal churches. Yes, there were many mixed people. One woman, a new member, said to my aunt, "I visited one of your old members. I come to your church, but I feel like I have a strange disease. No one will speak to me, and I've been coming for years."

So, my aunt had her to tea. And she said, "Now, dear, where are you from?" And the woman said she was from Alabama. And my aunt said, "Have you told that to anyone?"

She said, "Yes." And she said, "Well, that's your trouble. You'll have to reinvent you. You were really born in New York, Rochester, Olean,

Salamanca, and you were taken south as a child. Now you've come back to reclaim your heritage."

The woman said, "I think you're crazy," and left. And she joined the Roman Catholic Church. In my day, the Roman Catholic Church maintained a separate church for Negroes called St. Augustin's, which is downtown. And if you were a colored Catholic, you had to go there.

When I was in the Army, down at Tuskegee, every church was closed except the Roman Catholic. On Sundays, you'd see the people going up to worship their God without fear of being arrested. And as far as the local colored population, many went to the Michigan Avenue Baptist Church. The Michigan Avenue Baptist Church was the center of the Underground Railroad in Buffalo. It was the stopping place for hiding many of the runaway slaves. And many of the older residents of the city went there, and many of the newcomers, because when they went to the Episcopal church, they were not accepted or they were insulted. They had a minister called Elder Jesse Nash. He came there in 1892, and he stayed until 1952—a huge span of years. He was ancient. And the church is still there, but it's moved to a different location. But the building is still there. During slavery, during all the civil rights of those days, it was there.

In Buffalo, there was Bethel AME Zion, of which my great-grandparents were charter members, back in the 1840s. And my brother returned to that church, when he married a Methodist girl. And he was buried at that church. In fact, the first Methodist service I went to was his funeral. I never knew my brothers well, but as I sat there during the funeral and I listened, I learned who my brother was, by the testimonies these people gave. He found his heritage back in the church that his ancestors founded.

Deceased people were laid out for people to see in many of the Protestant churches. We called it the "Last Look." But we were Anglicans, and the casket was closed when you left the home or funeral home, and that was the last you saw of the person. That was sort of social distinction, we're not like you, in other words. And the "Last Look" was not in the Anglican church. When the body leaves the home or where it was laid out, the funeral parlor, the coffin is closed, and that's that for eternity.

My brother Voyle was buried Anglican, but Eddie was buried Methodist. I watched, aisle after aisle, people would go up for an hour looking at his body. And I wouldn't go, because that was not the way I felt. I remembered him as he was. I did visit homes where people used to have pictures taken of people laid out in their coffins. And I visited homes where people had the "Last Look" of people laid out.

In our church, I was often asked to sing at funerals. I was a boy soprano. And we'd have a High Mass. The services in our church were rigidly formal, whereas in the Protestant churches, the Baptist and the Methodist church, there's a lot of emotion. And people would express themselves and cry out. But that's typical African, and there's nothing wrong with that. That's one of the vestiges which came over from slavery which still survives. And after the "Last Look," they'd close the coffin, and I think they used to sing, "If I Can See My Mother Pray." They'd sing those songs that bring the tears falling. And the ministers would get up and they'd read telegrams and they'd read testimonials, and people would get up to speak what they remembered of the deceased. But you never saw that at the Anglican church. The Anglican church would have the credo and the Agnes Dei, and Sanctus, and then it would be over.

Buffalo was one of the few cities in the country where blacks are buried in the best cemeteries. My great-grandfather bought our lots at Forest Lawn Cemetery in 1846. There's forty of us buried there. You just bought your lot and you were buried there, and nobody said anything. But in many places, like Detroit and Cleveland, it's difficult to be buried where you want to be buried. Those cities have these black cemeteries, and I was amazed to see how poorly they're kept. Well, when you're dead, who gives a damn anyway? But the fact remains, Forest Lawn is maintained beautifully. And every time I go home, I go out and talk to my folks for a whole day. We're buried in three cemeteries in Buffalo. We're buried in Forest Lawn in two sections, and in Niagara Falls and Oakwood, where my grandmother's and grandfather's people are.

It was the colored world, but our interface was with the white world we lived in. We moved into an area before the whites came. The home was built out in Cold Springs in the early 1870s, and then the Germans and Irish came and settled around us. Buffalo was the frontier in the 1870s. Buffalo was part of the Underground Railroad. Escaped slaves were rowed by people across the Niagara River. I wonder how it was done, seeing that current; it's ten miles an hour. But it must have been done by some skillful boatmen.

In 1852, there was one night when there was a roundup of runaway slaves. And the people who were helping them run away emptied the city overnight.

All during slavery until emancipation, my great-grandfather had to carry with him a shillelagh, and I've still got it hanging on my wall. It's a knob. It'll brain you by hitting you. And these were things which were part of the world in which he had children. And he had to constantly be on the alert. His kids had to be aware that they lived a precarious existence, to be weary of strangers, although they were free people. If they were not aware, they could be carried back to slavery.

One of the things colored people don't want to admit is their Indian heritage. They are proud of their white heritage, but their Indian heritage is looked upon askance by many people. My Indian heritage is Mohawk Cherokee, Menneponi, and Naragansett. And these are the groups which make—and I'm not unique. Most of the people I knew, the colored people, were these mixtures because when the Trail of Tears happened, many of the Indians joined black families and black people. And many Indians even adopted black runaways into their tribes. Osceola, the famous chief of the Seminoles, was half-black. Some of the Indian tribes were also slaveholders. And they had families with them, too. And, of course, the genes are immortal. And for that reason, you often see these high cheekbones and hair quality.

When I was growing up, discrimination was really twofold: one recognized, and one not recognized. We just assumed white values were right. The black doctors in Buffalo had a very difficult time getting clientele because the colored people went to white doctors. You went to white hospitals. I went to completely white schools. I was one or two of the colored kids in my eighth-grade class. And in high school, I had all these wonderful advantages, and I didn't realize what an enchanted life I was leading.

I went to PS 8. It was built in 1919, and architecturally, it was a magnificent building, built like the Parthenon in Athens. The interior had the frieze of the Parthenon around the auditorium. And I went back there a couple of years ago; it was a class day. The school population was totally black. And the principal was this older lady, and she gave me a few minutes. And as we walked through the auditorium, I said, "Do you know what that is up there?" and she said, "That's the frieze of the Parthenon." In my class, each room had Greek names. I was the room called Athens, and my brother was the one called Sparta, and area where the rooms were located was called the Peleponnesius. We put on plays which emphasized the Greek heritage, apparent all over the building: the Ionic, the Doric, and the Corinthian, all the way through the school. Everywhere there were these motifs. The Acanthus was everywhere. And we were proud of it. And I was so amazed, when I walked through the building a couple of years ago, to see an oil painting on the side of the auditorium. And I said to her, "That picture's by Jean Francois Millet, the French painter."

She said, "Do you know that picture?"

And I said, "Yes, my class gave that to the school in 1932. And when I was in school we used to have art contests to describe the picture. One month I won the prize. Do you still have the contests?"

"Oh," she said, "well, we have very little time. We have so many pressing problems here. I don't know where to start."

In Buffalo, the inner city is now called Spring. When I lived there, it was one of the outskirts of the city. The people came there in the 1850s and they made their way. But now we're living in a world filled with the problems. There's drugs, there's overpopulation and the various things which go along with economic displacement, and the various things which didn't exist in my time. In my time, the school was a middle-class school, and you never thought of yourself as anything different. The only thing I did notice was when I was trying to play on sports teams, my classmates would not accept me. When the baseball season came, they'd choose up sides and say, "We don't want him. We don't want him." And the teacher would assign me to a team, and they'd say, "We don't want him." So, I'd play the best I could, but when I told my mother about, "Well, baseball, football, and basketball are un-American sports."

"Un-American?" I asked.

"Un-American, yes," she said, "If you can't play them, they're un-American." And so we stayed away, and, of course, in my day, it was the school that mattered most. We had fantastic teachers. They were mostly older people. And the same with the high school. We went from one to eight in PS 8, then you went from high school, from freshman to senior. The colored teachers in Buffalo taught downtown at PS 32 and 41 and 7, and those were not black schools, but there were many colored students attending. Now, the schools there were full of immigrants. Mostly, there were Jews, and when the Ashkenazi (Jews) first started coming to Buffalo, the older Jews were Sephardim. But when the Ashkenazi first started coming in, they settled down there around Williams Street, where my family first lived. And my aunt told me that the older Ashkenazi women would come door-to-door selling things, and that's when they first became aware that there were new immigrants coming to town.

The descendants of the Christians and Jews, who made their way into the city, became the teachers in the schools I went to. I started off for college when I finished high school in 1939. My father had gone blind in 1933 during the Depression. It was a very difficult time for the family because we had a fourteen-room house, and my mother was forced to go to work. And she found work in the WPA, Works Progress Administration, under Roosevelt. My mother used to say to us, "We're not poor. We're broke. There's a big difference." And the people who were our social workers were our friends, and my mother would always have tea ready for them when they came. And it was sort of a social visit, trying to work out a budget for seven people to live on $15 a week. How could you do it? Well, we had learned to put up a front. The people where we traded when we had money. My father made a good living on the road. And the grocery man took the welfare check and gave my mother the money, saying, "Trade where you wish." And my mother said, "We're going to trade right here. You're giving me dignity." This is the way we lived. Nobody knew we were on relief, because my mother had money to spend and not the welfare check.

I went to school with kids who were very well off. My mother would give us Ann Page peanut butter sandwiches. I hated them. At lunchtime up at school, there'd be a chap named Noel, and his mother gave him a pound cake, sandwiches, and he said, "I don't want any of this stuff. You want it, Bruce?" Every day I sat with Noel, and I had his lunch, because he would buy his lunch at the commissary; he had money. And he didn't realize I ate off of him for two or three years. When we graduated, I guess the saddest day of my life was September 5, 1939, when I had to go down to the station to watch all my friends from high school go to Harvard and Yale and the various places I wanted to go. I was accepted by the University of Michigan, but they wanted $400, and there was no way I could afford it.

If it wasn't for Lethia Warren, I might have never been able to go to college. Lethia was a fair-skinned person who came to Buffalo and she ran a nightclub at the Vendome Hotel. She spotlighted people like Sammy Davis, Senior and Junior, and Jimmie Lunceford and his band and Bill "Bojangles" Robinson. All the people in town came to her establishment. When she left that business, she became a supervisor for the National Youth Administration (NYA) under Roosevelt. That was my salvation. I worked for a check of $18 a month. I think I gave twenty hours of work a week on the project. Well, they had what they called colored projects in Buffalo, which is the first time I ran across that type of thing. It was run by a minister who didn't particularly care for these older colored people, who thought nothing of him. Now he was in charge of their children. He gave me a job emptying ashes at a police station. I didn't go for that. I was breaking my back. So, I went to Lethia, who was my supervisor, and I complained, and that started sixty years of friendship with that woman. She gave me a job. I had been a member of the Junior Education Department at the Buffalo Museum of Science. That's where my interest in birds and nature came from. I worked in the NYA program of the Museum of Science, and I learned how to do taxonomy, the naming of mollusks in the shell collection. At that time, I was sixteen or seventeen, and I was doing this professional work, and it was opening me to the world into the world of science. And it was considered quite a thing because I was a colored boy working on a white project through that door Lethia Warren opened for me. And the door never closed.

So, I went back to high school, PG (post graduate) the next year, because I couldn't afford to go to college and didn't want to waste the year lacking any education. I took courses I didn't need, but that interested me—in music, literature, and subjects such as that.

Later, Lethia arranged for a scholarship from the Alpha Phi Alpha fraternity (which is the colored fraternity), and I went downstate to a small normal school called Brockport Normal, which is now a state university. It's a big school now with 20,000 students, but when I went there, they only had about 1,000. And she said, "Now Bruce, you're going there, and they don't want you down there. Now, don't tear your ass. But remember, call me if you need me." I never had to call her. It opened doors, and there were three colored men: Dr. Edwin Harris Mitchell, who's now chief of radiology at Meharry Medical College; Dr. Jimmy Singleterry, who's now dead, but was in the State Department at Washington; and myself. We all got our doctorates. I got mine from Michigan, Jimmy got his from Chicago, and Ed went into medicine.

When I went to Brockport, there was also a colored girl, named Norine Anderson. The school was small, in a small village that looked at us, didn't want us there. We had no place to stay, so we stayed at a farm on the outskirts of town and found what you might call one of those living saints. A farmer's wife, a Mrs. Burlingame, took us in and said, "Use my cold cellar." I'd never heard of a cold cellar. It's a hole in the ground which freezes and was filled with vegetables and fatback. We learned to live very well on the produce that she put down for us. All I can say is that she was a living saint. And I stayed there a year, and I would have finished there, except that it was so difficult to find anything to do in the town because the Christians didn't want us around. So I came back to Buffalo and entered teachers' college. Then the war came.

I was sworn into the Army as a white man in those days because of the fact I'd been a museum kid. I'd been awarded medals (for achievement) from the Buffalo Museum of Science and the Junior Education Department. The head of the museum knew my grandmother. She'd worked for him and his family. His name was Chauncy Hamlin, and he gave me a card to give to the chief of the induction center. And when the person in charge at the induction center saw that name, he said, "I'm going to help you. I'm not to do anything illegal." And when my class was called up, I went down, and there were twenty-nine people from my class at teachers' college. We went through the induction. I raised my hand and was sworn into the Army. And then, he said, "Now I'm leaving here, and whoever succeeds me is going to figure out what to do with you as a colored person."

Well, they called my class up in six months. I went down there that day. There were crying mothers. My mother was down there. They took everybody away but me, because they didn't know what to do with this colored boy who had come into the Army as a white man. I was sworn in as white. And somebody said, "Well, there's Tuskegee." And I went down to Tuskegee as a flying cadet at the Army airfield. Well, the first day, that man asked me if I drove a car. I said that I never learned to drive. I was twenty-four years old. So I washed out the first day there in training.

My roommate at Tuskegee was killed. And I realized, also that day, the paper *PM* came out and had pictures of Helen Gahagen Douglas (a representative in Congress) and one of the other people who pushed the GI Bill of Rights through. I said, "That's for me. I'm going to reactivate my application to Michigan." Well, I did it and it was approved, and I washed out on purpose to keep alive. And I'm glad I did that. I'm still here.

When I was down at Tuskegee, P. H. Polk, who had a photographic studio on campus, made my portrait. And I still have it. I didn't realize what a fine work it was. Polk was thin and tall. And the thing I remember most about him was that he had bins that were about twenty feet long and had these long, open, glass negative bins filled with the work he'd done over the years. It was just captivating for me to see his work.

Tuskegee in those days was living on a name long since past. If you've read *The Invisible Man,* you know what I'm talking about. Fred Patterson was in charge, and he was trying to fit into the twentieth century with attributes of the nineteenth. And all of us boys who'd been to northern schools were just appalled by the quality of work and the lack of understanding. We knew we were in a second-class outfit of a segregated Army. We were in something called Negro Military Personnel. And when people said, "Well, I won't get into that," I have very strange feelings about this country. My first night on a Jim Crow car was like *Schindler's List.* We rode in wooden cars behind the engine with upper windows out. The coal dust blew in. I was in a car that was built to hold 80 people, but there must have been over 150 men jammed into it. The toilets were broken down and there were mice and bed-bugs all around. This was my first experience with Jim Crow, and these things opened my life to the fact that I lived in a world of illusion in Buffalo. My parents had carefully protected me from knowing that anything like that was out there. I had heard about Jim Crow, but I didn't know what it was really like. It was bad chasm that is filled with the ghosts and the refuse of what had happened to people who had aspired to dignity.

One day, coming back from furlough, I got off the train in Nashville, Tennessee, and I made the mistake of walking with the white troop into a white waiting room. Suddenly, an MP came up to me and before I could say a word, he hit me over the head and I blacked out. When I came to, I was laying on a baggage cart, and this lovely, older colored lady was leaning over saying, "When will you northern boys learn?" And she had a broken cookie and a jelly jar full of water. And I tried to stand up. I had a concussion. And I had to stand on the train with a concussion from Nashville to Cincinnati until I could get some competent medical help. That was my welcome to America in October 1943.

I never had a gun in my hand. I never had any basic training. What I did when I was in the Army, I collected butterflies, which are now at the University of Michigan and quite valued. You see, there were flying MATS, military air transports, planes that went from South America to Alabama. They didn't fumigate them, and we'd get these exotic, tropical species breeding for one season in the Tuskegee area and then dying out when the winter came. And the ones I collected were from there, and they're now in the University of Michigan collection. So, I did do something. I didn't waste my time. I was an intelligence clerk and I served there from 1943 until 1946.

On the G. I. Bill, I finished my bachelor's (degree), got my master's and my doctorate in biology at University of Michigan and I realized, whoopee, old Helen Gahagen Douglas and people such as she have opened the door. Plus, there was Lethia Warren and the two of my high school teachers Drew Stengal and Dorothy Pearman and people like Thelma Burner at the Buffalo Museum of Science, people who realized that I had potential. And that my potential was being stifled, and then they opened doors. Thelma Burner now has Alzheimer's in Santa Barbara. Lethia just died. And Dorothy and Drew died several years ago, and they left me their diaries and their medals and their stories and their poetry, and I read these things and it's like seeing yourself in retrospect. They're very wonderful diaries and they're wonderful memories, which made me realize there were people who cared for me and loved me and are the people who made me as I am today.

Well, I came out in '47 (with my bachelor's degree), over fifty years ago this year. And I got my master's in '48, and doctorate in '51–'52, from Michigan, earned in '51, awarded in '52.

When I came out of the university, my professors wanted me to go south to teach. And I said to them, "Look it, I've lived there. I'm not going to raise any children down there. There's no opportunities." So, I took a job as a riveter-porter at Kaiser-Frazier. I told them I'd finished the fifth grade in Alabama. They hired me immediately.

The plant is in Ypsilanti, Michigan. I went over there at four o'clock in the morning to get the job. I stood in line until eight o'clock because I had a child. My wife was going to medical school. I didn't worry about it. And I stayed there until I could make some money.

When I was at the University of Michigan, I had befriended a young black man who'd come north for his master's degree. The black students who came from the South had never been allowed to be in libraries because blacks couldn't use libraries in the cities where they lived. And when they came to Michigan, they were given assignments to use the library, and many of them asked, "How do you use it?" So I said, "I'll show you."

And I took groups of them to the library and showed them how to use the card catalog, the encyclopedias, and the basic reference tools that they were going to need for doing their master's degrees. And this one man I helped never forgot me. And one Christmas morning in 1951, he called, saying, "There's a job at the Detroit Arsenal in microbiology and it's yours." I said, "I've only had four hours in that." He said, "Don't tell them, fake it." And I went there. And I spent the next thirty-five years going from job to job in government, always moving upward, moving toward one thing: dignity, learning on the job, and holding responsible positions. I worked all over the world, and I have no regrets. When I walked out the door and retired, I said, "Well, you did it, Bruce." And like many people, the blacks of my generation, all of us knew when we got our doctorates, we'd never work in our field, the field in which we got our doctorate. You worked where you could, and I saw that. But I was not going to reproduce what happened to my father's generation, when I saw these people who had educations doing porter work and doing demeaning occupations. And yet they never let you know they were demeaning. They were people who maintained their dignity, in spite of their status. I had an aunt that used to go to work every morning carrying a violin case. They thought she was playing it at the Gypsy Tea Room. She wasn't. She worked as a maid downtown and she carried her stuff in it. She posed as a musician with her case to keep her dignity.

I moved to California in 1970, '71. There was a job posted out here, and I had befriended a person back in Washington. When she sent me the announcement of the job: "Grants Officer, Region 9, HEW," I said, "That's for me." I went for the interview and I was hired. I was supposed to go to Chicago, but San Francisco interviewed me first and I was offered the job. I went and my life changed. I took the position as Grants Officer, and I was promoted in a year to be the Assistant Regional Director for Human Development of Health, Education, and Welfare. I had five years in that office. I was in charge of the programs, for the states of California, Nevada, Arizona, and Hawaii, and the whole Pacific—Polynesia, Micronesia, and a bit of Melanesia. It was a headache in many ways, but it was also a learning experience for me because it taught me the extent of need, the extent of having to have an objective, to be a caring, compassionate person doing public programs, able to deal with the society's needs as they emerge. I had a staff of over a hundred people. And I did it.

I retired in 1983. I had a wonderful boss, a Nixon appointment, but what a wonderful man. He was one of the finest people I'll ever know. George Miller. San Francisco is a very difficult region because everybody wants to come here. And they come with different agendas of why they want to be here. And it made it wonderful for me because I was able to live in a city where you can love who you wish and do the work you love. And that's an amazing, amazing, wonderful place.

Western New York was colored; the Bay Area is black. And you've got the people in the Bay Area from the Deep South, people who you would never know in Buffalo. They're here in large numbers, and I found friendships I never knew possible, people from Louisiana and Arkansas and Texas. Their stories, there's one from Texas, Ruth, she's ninety-two years old now. She's fantastic. She's marvelous. And she'll talk about her experience. She was raised in the cotton fields, and she has on her mantelpiece—you know what a pea is, for measuring cotton? And she has that right above her mantelpiece in a beautiful home. She says, "I started out with that." And here she is with a beautiful home, and she has her own life. And she still drives her own car. Then, there's my friend, Cora, and their friend, Sally, who died. All of these three women have become important in my life, people I would never have known. And these are people who have come there. And there's another woman, who was partially blind, but who had an elegance about her that makes me realize that I'm blessed to have people such as these to work with, to fall in love with, and to know these are my friends.

Most of the blacks came during World War II and went to Richmond. Ruth said she lived in Dallas, and was working in a white beauty shop. She got on a train, and when it pulled into Pasadena, she saw them flowers and said, "You know, I never went back. I called my landlady, and said, 'Send my things.'" And the landlady sent her things, and she said, "I worked at Lockheed for thirty-some years." And then she moved up and married a man in Berkeley, and he died and left her this house, paid up. All these people, they lived in paid-up houses. And Sally was this wonderful woman who came from Louisiana and during the war and as the people came in, she'd take them into her house as roomers and she'd say, "Look it, I bought a house for you today." "What do you mean?" "I put $500 down. Now you pay me back. But you got a house." And when she died, the church was filled with over twenty people, who got up and said that she got them into being homeowners.

Every time I take these ladies out, it's a learning experience. We go to the housewives' market in Oakland and I see people. I'll say to them, "Louisiana? How do you recognize it?" There's something about the dignity of the older people that I recognize. They carry themselves with great dignity, and each one of them has a story. What I do, I go up to them and say, "I'm cooking greens today. What do I need? How do you cook that? How do you cook that?" And before you know it, you're deep into conversation with them. And you get the story of their lives. They're amazing, amazing.

My mother, when she was a young woman in New York City at the turn of the century, worked as a deaconess at Ellis Island. When I was at the Tenement Museum with a friend, the man said, "Any of your parents come through this house that is now a museum?" I said, "My mother probably worked here." The young colored girls who were college students from, say, 1905 to 1915, they didn't have what they call social workers, they had deaconesses. Women on the weekends would work with the Eastern Europeans as they came over. And the man said, "Well, I can't believe that. Colored people?" I said, "Yes, there were. If you come to my house, I'll show you pictures of them, the five girls. They called themselves Les Cinque—the five. And they worked down there on the East Side, when they used to move the people from the island to the Lower East Side as they started their march through American society to where they are today."

These people I've met, the people from Texas and Arkansas, have the same history. Mr. C. Taylor was one man from Arkansas who worked for me as my yardman. Some of the stories would curl your hair as he'd talk about escaping as a twelve-year-old boy, falling off a train and being left for dead. And this older woman picked him up, called "Auntie." He said, "Auntie took me in and brought me back to life." And he said, "And you see that line of trees, dark leaves, that goes from the Bay Bridge out to Richmond? I planted every one of those trees." He's Man Mountain, a big, strapping black man, and you look at his old age. When he went through my yard, all I could see was this man mowing this yard, grabbing things up. He cleared out my backyard. When I came to the house, they hadn't kept the backyard. Within one day, all I could see was this man, grabbing, grabbing and creating. And to hear his stories. I said, "What's your name?" "Mr. C. Taylor. I don't want any white person calling me by my first name." So, he's Mr. C. Taylor. His name is Cal. He said, "But when I'm away from this house and away from home, I'm Mr. C. Taylor."

I work in a shop as a volunteer where we get discards from many of the fine homes in San Francisco. The things we can't use, we send to a shop out in Richmond, where the three ladies, Ruth, Cora, and Sally, and others work. It's a wonder to see how these people take these things, which I give, and give love when they sell these things to the people who come to that shop. It's a type of charity, and I'm just amazed. It makes me feel good to see people who have humble beginnings living in dignity and greatness. What keeps me going is the fact that each day I'm on borrowed time now. I'm nearly eighty years old. And each day, I celebrate. I'm not a Christian, but I look upon myself as a very fortunate person, to have had, if you had been born as I was, to be raised in Buffalo, where there was the charm, even though it was deceptive. And then my Army experiences and my first chance to really get to know black people and to know them as personal friends. And the academic experience and the wonderful years in the government, traveling all over the world, being sent to Paris and London and working there and finding that there was a Mecca on the West Coast, the Bay Area, San Francisco. I moved there, and I've never regretted it. I say, well, you can check out, but you can never leave that city. It's true. I consider myself to have good health. The only thing I got now, since I'm older is my health. Money can't buy health. And I find also—memory. Nabokov said, "Speak memory." You mine your memory. And I think of these memories. There are tons more of them, but it's basically where I am, and I'm grateful.

INTERVIEW BY ALAN GOVENAR, JUNE 22, 1997.

Tony Lott

Ranch cowboy
Born: November 4, 1906, Powell Ranch, Texas

Tony Lott grew up on the Powell Ranch in southeast Texas, where his parents and grandparents had labored before him. His grandfather, Isaiah Weathers, was a slave who stayed on the ranch after he was emancipated. Lott started working as a cowboy when he was eight years old, "throwing calves all day long." Lott recounts his experiences as a ranch hand and recalls the songs that he heard in church and the fragments of blues that were sung by older cowboys.

I was raised up on the Powell Ranch. I was about eight years old when I started working. And when they started to work, I'd ride the boss's horse and gather up the milk cows and stuff like that. And when they start to work the cattle, I got to holding the remuda. I was getting twenty-five cents a day holding the horses together, holding the remuda.

And I remember once I was riding a horse named Revolution. I had an old piece of saddle and the horse got loose, went running off. And I finally overtaken it and brought him back and put it back in the herd. And that's the way we started out cowboying, you know. My daddy was riding the pasture. His name was Henry Lott.

My grandfather's name was Isaiah Weathers. Grandpa was a slave. Reverend Mack and I are first cousins. We all kinfolks. We all related.

My mother was named Julia Weathers before she married. And Reverend Mack's was Emma Weathers. I didn't hear too much stories about slavery.

When I was a little boy about eight or nine years old, I went to get those horses and I was running a cow down the side of the fence and this old bay horse, he turned the other way to meet the cow. It was a great story. And we used to throw calves all day long. Calves go one way and the cows go one way.

At noon we eat dinner, and we throw those calves all day. It'd take about five or six hours to throw them calves. Mug them, you know, put the hot iron.

At the ranches, every ranch had a night horse. And that night horse they kept in the pen all night, of course, he was fed and fat. And, uh, that horse they used in the mornings to get up the remuda with. Get up the other horses with. Bring them in. And so after they bring their other horses in, they turn that old night horse out. But that old night horse come lazy, so Mr. O'Connor wanted to go fishin' 'cause he was going to ride his other horse. He had a fast horse named Lightnin', Mr. O'Connor did. And so he and Grandpa went down from the river ranch on down to Twenty Mile Lake, and that Twenty Mile Lake was an artesian well there, that was the oldest…that was the first well in Texas. And so in going down there, well, Grandpa got on old Darby, that was the night horse, bareback. So Mr. O'Connor said, "Why don't you put a saddle on that horse?" He said he don't want to go now and put a saddle on him, he gonna get more lazy. Well, they got down there and just about the time they tied the horse, well, what the people did, they rode their horses there and a little piece out when they were going to leave from there and go to Victoria or come to Refugio or different places, because the Indians, you know around this part, they get out, well, the horse was all ready to run. And they had two gaits—slow walk, slow lope and a fast run. And they could move. So they got after…they got the lines out, and they hear something—ya, ya, ya, ya! He said, "My God! Thornton, here come the Indians." So Mr. O'Conner went out there and got old Lightnin' by the reins, and that old horse was just coming around. He stepped up on that horse and went on, and Grandpa out there untying that little stake rope and put that on him, and stepped up on him and when he did that, he took off. And Mr. O'Connor had to run from Twenty Mile Lake over to Brush Tank. And before he thought about Grandpa and he had on his forty-four, he said, "My good God! Say Thornton!" and just as he went to pull up, Grandpa passed him on old Darby. He said, "Don't stop now, they're right behind you." From there to the ranch, you couldn't catch Grandpa and ol' Darby.

Once we was down in Angelino. We had a great big herd, about 800 or 900. They left me there, and said, "Tony, you stay here and watch these steers. We going back and get some more." I stood there and watched the steers, and they all bedded down. Then I got off my horse and tied it to a

Tony Lott,
photograph by Alan
Govenar, Corpus
Christi, Texas, 1994.
(Documentary Arts)

fence, and I went to sleep. This is true. I went to sleep. And I don't know how long, but when I woke up, all the steers were gone and the horse was gone. A long, long ways from me. So, I started walking. And they seen me walking, and they come over and brought me my horse. I got sleepy, you know, I was just tired and went to sleep with the steers. Yeah, that's true.

On the ranch, we had a little old church house out there, a little old house that would sit about fifteen to twenty people. The preacher was named Isaiah Weathers, my grandfather. He'd come out there and preach. He'd come around and preach, and we had no money to give him; we'd give him eggs and butter and stuff like that. He'd come horseback. From San Antonio. Then we finally bought him an old T-Model car. The old T-Model car cost about $600, and we all pitched in and bought it for him—it had a crank to start it. He'd go from his church, from his home to the church in that old T-Model car. Then he come to Corpus. He was preacher at Mount Zion Baptist Church. He would just preach. His prayer was—"God that heard our mothers and fathers pray in the day of slaves, you are the same God now you were then. Now we want you to go with us, keep us in your care…. These blessings in Jesus' name, amen." He said that prayer. I remember that prayer. And one day he was preaching. We raised watermelon then. He was preaching when I walked in the church house, I was a little boy. He said, "Son, did you bring my melons?" I says "Yeah." And I gave him his watermelon.

In church, he'd sing:

Jesus getting' us ready for that great day
Oh, Jesus getting' us ready for that great day
Jesus getting' us ready for that great day
Oh I shall be able to stand

Well he got my mother ready for that great day
Whoa-o-o-o, he got my mother ready for that great day
Well he got my mother ready for that great day

Whoa-o-o-o, the sinners will be runnin' in that great day
Whoa-o-o-o, the sinners will be runnin' in that great day
Whoa-o-o-o, the sinners will be runnin' in that great day
Oh, who shall be able to stand?

Songs like that we sang. Some old songs.

I started singing when I was in church, you know, I started singing at church and then at school. Singing church songs. I was about twelve years old, started singing in school. Well, the old cowboys songs, I don't remember too many of them. My dad used to sing:

Time, time, time
Time has made a change
Oh, time, time, time
Time has made a change
Oh Lordy, time, time, time
Time has made a change Whoo-o-o,
Time has made a change Whoo-o-o
Deacon don't pray like he used to pray
Time has made a change, Whoo-o-o
The deacon don't pray like he used to pray
Time has made a change, Whoo-o-o
The deacon don't pray like he used to pray
Time has made a change, Whoo-o-o
Time has made a change.
Well, it's time, time, time
Time has made a change, Whoo-o-o
Time, time, time
Time has made a change, Whoo-o-o
Time, time, time
Time has made a change, Whoo-o-o
Time has made a change.

My dad used to sing this song when we were little, and I'd walk right behind him. Or, if we were riding a horse, or buggies or watching buggies. Watch them cows, he'd sing that song.

Sometimes he'd sing this old song:

> Whoo-o-o the Word of God is right
> Hallelujah to His name
> Whoo-o-o the Word of God is right
> Hallelujah to His name
> Whoo-o-o the Word of God is right
> Hallelujah to His name
> Whoo-o-o the Word of God is right
> It will make you shout sometime
> Hallelujah to His name
> Make you shout sometime
> Hallelujah to His name
> Make you shout sometime
> Hallelujah to His name
> Oh, the Word of God is right
> It will make you love everybody
> Hallelujah to His name
> It will make you love everybody
> Hallelujah to His name
> Oh, the Word of God is right.

He sang that song working in the field. We were picking cotton. He sang that song and he got me to sing that song: "The Word of God Is Right, Hallelujah to His Name."

And he sang old songs:

> Miss Angelina, I sure love you, I sure love you
> There's no other one so good and true, so good and true
> Miss Angelina, oh black baby's you
> She's a daisy, run me crazy....
> Miss Angelina, oh black baby's you.

That's all I know of that. That's an old song. I don't know where he got that from. We didn't sing too much. My daddy used to sing that song. Let me see, I'm trying to think of another song he sang. This is a song I sang every Sunday morning at church. I get up, I said, "Well, this is God's house. We gonna have a good time here this morning. I want y'all to join in and help us sing this song."

We gonna have a good time
Come on in this house
O-o-o-oh, we gonna have a good time
Come on in this house
Whoo-o-o, we gonna have a good time
Come on in this house
Whoo-o-o, come on in this house
Said the Lord,
You don't need no invitation
Come on in this house
Whoo-o-o, you don't need no invitation
Come on in this house
Whoo-o-o, you don't need no invitation
Come on in this house and serve the Lord
O-o-o-oh, come on, come on, come on church
Come on in this house
Whoo-o-o, come on, come on, come on
Whoo-o-o, come on in this house
Whoo-o-o, come on, come on, come on
Come on in this house
Whoo-o-o, come on in this house and serve the Lord.

I sang that at church sometimes. Here's one my mother sung the last summer I heard her sing. It's called "Mother's There."

Take a stand, take a stand, take a stand, take a stand
If I never, never see you anymore, anymore
Take a stand, take a stand, take a stand, take a stand
I'll meet you on yonder shore
Keep the faith, keep the faith, keep the faith
If I never, never see you anymore, who -o-o-o anymore
Keep the faith, keep the faith, keep the faith
I'll meet you on yonder shore
Oh, Mother's there, Mother's there, Mother's there, Mother's
there
If I never, never see you anymore, who -o-o-o anymore
Oh, Mother's there, Mother's there, Mother's there, Mother's
there
I'll meet you on yonder shore.

That was one of her songs. My mother was named Julia Lott. She sang it around the house, she sang it at church. Here's another one she would sing.

Gimme that ol' time religion,
Gimme that ol' time religion,
Gimme that ol' time religion,
Lord it's good enough for me
It was good for Paul and Silas,
It was good for Paul and Silas,
It was good for Paul and Silas,
Lord it's good enough for me
Whoo-o-o, gimme me that ol' time religion
Gimme that ol' time religion,
Gimme that ol' time religion,
Lord it's good enough for me
Whoo-o-o, it will make you love everybody
It will make you love everybody
It will make you love everybody
Lord it's good enough for me
O-o-o-oh, gimme that ol' time religion,
Gimme that ol' time religion,
Gimme that ol' time religion,
Lord it's good enough for me.

That's an old one. But I never heard the cowboys singing much. A little whoopin' and hollerin' but they never did no singing. What we would do at night, we'd be cutting out yearlings from the herd. And we be yelling coming back to the herd. And the boys had to ride to keep them yearlings from going back, you know. "Why'd you let that yearling get back in the herd?" "Yeah, so and so got back in the herd on me." That's what we'd be hollering about, something like that.

To calm the herd down, we'd sing:

Whoo-o-o, doggie, whoo-o-o doggie, calm down

We'd sing something like that to them. Sing same verse, over and over. They'd be walking. That would calm 'em down. Then, sometimes we'd have to whoop and holler to get them going again. But we sing to them.

When I was coming up, they used to have these country dances. Be a fiddler and guitar. A fellow by the name of Will Sample. They had them at people's houses that had a place for it. My brother-in-law was a fiddler, was a guitar player, you know. They sing those old country tunes.

Well, I'm out and I'm down and I haven't got a friend
Haven't got a friend, I'm all out and down and haven't got a
friend

My brother-in-law, Henry Rice, could sing, play the guitar.

> Tisket, Tasket, green and yellow basket
> Wrote a letter to my honey, and on the way I lost it

Drop a handkerchief behind you, and they pick up the handkerchief. You gotta run all the way around and if they catch you before you get back here, they put you in the ring.

Oh, I heard people singin' blues. Papa used to sing a song:

> Uncle Bud, Uncle Bud, Uncle Bud don't rob
> Uncle Bud don't steal, Uncle Bud ride around in his automobile
> Uncle Bud, great God

> Uncle Bud got the cotton, gonna sell it in the seed
> Gonna buy Henrietta everything she need
> Uncle Bud, great God

My daddy, my daddy used to sing that. When he would sing those songs, he sometimes just sing pieces of them. Wouldn't sing the whole song. We'd be riding, ridin' out there. He's singing that song. Uncle Bud.

I remember that song. That was back when I came up on the Powell Ranch. We had all black cowboys, all eighteen of them. And they all dead but me and my brother, J. Y. Lott. In 1919, I left the Powell Ranch and started work for Mr. James Welder.

One time, Mr. James had a horse name Squito. And old Squito was a good horse. I used to ride old Squito myself and he'd take me with him. And the boss tell me, "You take that old Squito."

Well, Squito's a good horse, a good cuttin' horse, he's a good cuttin' horse, but he'd get hot and he'd get riled and walk out of the herd. And Mr. James would carry him out there and give him a good whooping, hoping to put him back in the herd. And Mr. James Welder was a business-man when he wasn't working. He whooped old Squito out there and made him go back to the herd and stop him before he went into the herd. He'd be just like one of us boys when we were working. He'd laugh and joke with us, something like that. But when he was working he was all a differ-ent man altogether.

In 1924 came a great big freeze, great big freeze. We had a bunk-house about 200 yards from the kitchen and we got up in the morning and it was sunny. And he (Mr. Welder) was already up. We didn't get up early that morning. I don't know, we slept a little late. We'd all dressed and walked on that ice to the camp house and he was waiting on us. He said, "I want a volunteer to go to deliver something for me." That's twenty miles, everything was froze over, ice everywhere. He said "I want a volunteer," and the third time he said, "I want a volunteer." I said, "I'll go, Mr. Welder." He said, "Come on in the house."

Where they lived was a big white house. He said, "Come on in the house." So, I went on in the house. And he put a soldier suit on me, wrapped my legs good, put a little short coat on me and then put a big, old coat on me. Then he give me some gloves and he said "Catch that sorrel horse."

I said, "I'm riding the boss's horse." So I got on that horse, walked that horse two miles, just walking, couldn't ride, the slopes were too icy. You'd slip up. Just walked him. I got to the gate and had to unlock the gate. I got off that horse, my hands was like near froze. I got off the gate, run down the fence. That horse run. Got back on that horse again and just walk on that solid ice. Then I come to a creek. I knew it was coming because, oh, I remember this creek. So I got off the horse, that horse was sliding. That creek was icy, and I wanted to help that horse some. Then I got back on the horse, and all along that side of the fence that cattle was piled up frozen. So I walked on, 'till I went to where I was supposed to go. He had a big farm. Some went thisaway, some went thataway, and we drift all the cows to the bottom. I stayed all night. Slept on some hay, put hay all over me, and that man give me an old quilt. Got up the next morning, ate breakfast, and had to go back to the ranch, some twenty miles away.

When I got to the ranch, a boy there named Boone, me and him hitched up his horses, that had the camp wagon on it, and we had to go work together cutting trees down. We take our ax, we didn't have no chain saw, we take our ax and we cut. We cut up about fifteen, twenty trees a day. Because everything was covered with ice. We had another cow, and we had to put hay down in the tent. We put the hay down on top of the ice about four or five days; then, when we moved camp, and that ice was still underneath. We had hay on top of it, we didn't know. So bossman come down there, Mr. James come down there, and said, "You boys come in this evening." So we saddled up and got all the stuff together and put it in the wagon and go on back to the ranch. That was a pretty big ranch.

When came time for dippin' the cattle, we'd be two days at this ranch. Then we go to Taylor Ranch, about two, three days over there. Then we come back and go to Angelino. That's sixty miles. At Angelino we'd dip down there, and by the time we get through dipping down there, it'd be time to start over. Just ten to fourteen days over there, and we have to start somewhere else.

We never did sing much for songs. We told jokes mostly around the camp. But Mr. James make us sing one song he liked. That's a long time ago. I'm eighty-seven years old, that was a long time ago.

When my life's work is ended and I cross that swimming tide
In that bright and getting' up mornin'
I shall see, I shall see,
I shall know my Redeemer when I reach the other side.

I left Mr. Welder in 1924. I said, "Mr. James, I want to go to Corpus Christi to see my sister, I'll be back Monday." He said, "All right, Tony," says, "That'd be a good thing, there ain't much to do now, that'd be good." So, he probably give me $3 or $4, I don't know. I went home, taken a bath, wrapped up a shirt, a pair of pants, underwear in a paper bag, and tied a string around it, and went down there to Corpus, got on the railroad track. Twelve o'clock, if the train's coming, you had to flag the train down. You step right there next to the track—toot-toot, he stop. You get on. And I went into Corpus and stayed.

Back then, I had a meeting with my brothers and sisters. That was on Saturday. On Saturday night my brother-in-law said, "Tony, why don't you stay down here and go to work at the compress?" But I didn't want to do that.

He said "Yeah, they hiring over there. You can get a job. I'll carry you there in the morning." So Sunday morning he carried me over to the ranch, over to the compress. A man named Johnny Simpson, he just died about two years ago. "Mr. Simpson, here's a boy that want to work."

"What can you do boy?"

I said "Nothin.'"

He said, "You the man I want."

Compress is where they bale cotton. Where they make big bales and they bale cotton. They bale the cotton and tie it and bale it.

So, I went to work at the compress, trucking cotton. He showed me how to catch the bale. So I caught the bale as he pulled the bale, and I'm trucking and dumping. Then the man give me a hook to pull cotton down. I pulled cotton down. Then he give me a job riding a trailer to the docks. They put six on a trailer. So I rode at night. And the first week, I made $30. Three tens, I never will forget it. Open the envelope and Oh! three tens, good night! Three tens, I was getting' $7 out there on the ranch, $7.

Three tens, I said, "That's too much." So, I backed off, my number was 360. Six hundred men working there. I'll never forget it. I backed off, and he paid all the other people off. This is true. I went to him and said, "Mr. Simpson, you make a mistake in my money?"

"Let me see, Brother Lott, let me see, Brother Lott." He said, "Monday night you went to the dock with Charlie Dean. Tuesday you went to the dock with Ezra. Wednesday night you went to the dock with Ted."

I said "Oh, yeah, yeah, yeah." He thought I wanted some more money, but I wanted to give some of that back. $30.

Where I lived was about two miles from the compress, and I broke into a run. I broke into a run. I says, "Sister," I said, "I made $30!" She said, "Well, you take your bath, and we'll carry you downtown to get you a suit."

So, I take me a bath in the number three tub. And she carried me downtown to this tailor. I never had a suit before. He measured me up, said the suit would be ready soon.

I paid him $15, that suit was $30. I paid him $15 down on that suit. I never will forget it, I paid him $15 down on that suit. Gray finished, gabardine, double-breasted.

I said, "When will it be ready?"

He said, "I'll be ready next Saturday, Tony."

He called me Tony. I said okay. Next Saturday I went down there. I owed $15. Next door there was a store that sold Thom McAn Shoes, cheap shoes. Get a good pair of shoes for $5, $8, they didn't have no name, just shoes. I bought me two-tone black and white spat shoes. Sunday morning I put on them shoes and that gray suit and went to church. I was all dressed up.

I worked at the compress about seven, eight years. Then I went back to the ranch. I went back to the ranch on a Monday. I been in soup lines four or five blocks long. It was the Depression. I went back on a Monday. It was seven years (from the time I left); I went back on the ranch in the spring. And they looked up to see me get off the bus out there on the highway.

"That look like Tony, old boy. That look like Tony coming yonder."

I had a suitcase then. I had some clothes, I had a suitcase, and Mr. James, he met me and he said, "Tony, you said you was coming back Monday, but you didn't say what Monday!"

I said, "No, I didn't say what Monday."

He said, "Get in that pickup there."

They had a little old country store down there. "Go down to the store and get a roll of rope." So I got in the pickup, went down and got a ball of rope. And I worked there back at the ranch about another three years. Then I come back to Corpus. I was a chauffeur for a man who raised quarter horses. He hired me because I knowed horses. Then I started cutting grass, doing yard work, and I still do a little yard work.

INTERVIEW BY ALAN GOVENAR, JULY 21, 1994

John McLendon

Basketball coach
Life dates: April 5, 1915–October 8, 1999

John McLendon moved to Kansas City after the death of his mother when he
was three years old. McClendon recalls his family history and talks about the
"Exodusters" who fled Kentucky for Kansas in the 1870s and his grandparents,
who were homesteaders in Colorado. McLendon attended elementary and
secondary schools in Kansas City and enrolled as a physical education major at
Kansas University. He attended Kansas University from 1933 to 1936, and
studied with Dr. James Naismith, the inventor of basketball. In 1937, he began
graduate school at the University of Iowa. After receiving an M.A. degree in
physical education, he was hired as an assistant basketball coach at the North
Carolina College for Negroes (now called North Carolina Central). McLendon
is credited with desegregating basketball by challenging white-only teams to
compete against his champion African American players. For McLendon,
competitive sports presented a frontier where racism could be confronted and
overcome.

M y dad was a mail clerk on the Rock Island Railroad after having
spent a year or two in Kansas, after his exodus from North Carolina, where he was born, in Clemsonville. On my dad's side, I was fortunate enough to be able to talk to my grandmother. She was a slave for five
years. She was born in 1860. And she was a slave for five years, from 1860
to '65. That was in Washington, Georgia. And the family came from two
Scotch brothers who owned the slaves in Washington, Georgia, where all
the McLendons came from, even those with two C's rather than one. My
name has one C. I'm a one-C-McLendon. My grandmother said they were
all from the same family, and the same plantation owned by the two Scotch
brothers named McLendon.

When I was at the hundredth-anniversary-of-basketball celebration
at the University of Kansas, I met a man going to school there, working on
his doctorate degree, who has the same name I have, except that he has
two C's in his name. We got together and had a great time talking about it.
And I asked him what was his version of how he had two C's in his name
instead of one. Neither family could spell, so one took the name like they
heard it, and the other one just put another C in it. So that was about all
there was to it.

My grandmother's name was Julia McLendon. My dad was born in
Ansonville after my grandmother moved and granddad moved from Washington, Georgia, to North Carolina. This was right after the Reconstruction

John McLendon
(Courtesy John
McLendon)

because the Reconstruction period was ending when Dad was born in 1881, in Ansonville.

I went to meet my grandmother in Ansonville the first time I went to North Carolina myself. But anyway, my father left Ansonville after he graduated from North Carolina A&T University. He went to school to learn contracting. And he did build some buildings and houses in Kansas, but he became a mail clerk on the Rock Island line after he moved to Kansas. The Rock Island line ran from Kansas City to Caldwell, which is right on the Kansas-Colorado line. He met my mother on the train, going back and forth to western Kansas. And they married. And my brother and I were born in Hiawatha, Kansas, and my sister, my younger sister, was born in Kansas City. And my older sister was also born in Hiawatha, Kansas.

My older sister's named Anita. She's living in Hollywood right now. And my younger sister is named Elsie, just sent me a birthday card yesterday. My brother's named Arthur. He's an attorney, Arthur McLendon. He's living in Kansas. My parents were John and Effie McLendon.

Now my mother's parents met in Hiawatha, Kansas. Her parents' names were Jim and Mariah Hunn and he had come to Kansas from Websterville, Missouri. And her mother's side of the family was part of what was called Grandpa Baker's family. I don't even know what his full name was, but everybody knew him by that. Because he led a large number of blacks from Bakersville, Kentucky, to Kansas in 1879. And one of the history books that I saw about Kansas, northeast Kansas, had a little short chapter in it, "The Coming of the Colored." That was the name of the chapter. There was a large number of black people came from various places. I've read the book, *Exodusters,* and they talk about this delegation from Kentucky.

Incidentally, I was on the stage one night waiting to talk to some high school kids, and the governor came in and sat beside me and asked me how the team was doing. I was coaching at Kentucky State College.

I said, "Fine."

He said, "Where'd you come from, Coach?"

And I told him, from Kansas.

He said, "Were you one of those people that left here? Was your family one of the families that left here?" He said, "I'm from Bakersville myself. And all the black people in Bakersville went to Kansas. Were your folks in that group?"

I said, "Yes, they were." Because that's where Grandpa Baker, my mother's father, and his wife, they came from—Bakersville.

They left Kentucky because they just felt like that since slavery was over, that they should have a different status. They felt that they should be free to vote. See, staying where you were a slave made you a sharecropper, and that wasn't much better than slavery. Fact is, as a sharecropper, you were indebted to the master, and, of course, you had to work it off. And the way they had to work it off, by working and farming the master's land, you never would work it off, in most cases. Very few slaveholders freely gave up their slaves.

They left for Kansas because Kansas was the only state in the Union that invited former slaves to come to their territory. That was in 1879, and that marked the beginning for most of the exodus from Louisiana and Mississippi. In places like Louisiana and Mississippi, blacks got out in a hurry because the white folk were bulldozing their cabins and even shooting them. Some 2,000 or more were hurt in two or three years. It was pretty well documented by newspapers. It's not a fiction.

Life was much better in Kansas. My parents owned a piece of property in Hiawatha, Kansas, on 11th Street. But when my mother died, the family got split up. I was only three. My brother was a year and a half younger than I was. Sister, she died right after her birth with my mother in the influenza epidemic of 1918. So after my mother left us at that time, my grandmother and granddad took me and my brother in. My two sisters were sent to other relatives. My younger sister, Elsie, went to live with some family members in Omaha, Nebraska. At that time, southern Nebraska and northeast Kansas seemed to be the places for blacks to go in the Middle West. My oldest sister, Anita, I never saw her again for forty-five years. But my younger sister and I and my brother were reunited as a family when it was time for me to go to school, and my dad had remarried a woman named Minnie Jackson. And so that was when we started living in Kansas City, Kansas.

But before my dad remarried, my brother and I were sent to Los Animas County in Colorado, where my grandfather and his five sons had gone to homestead the land there. That's in southeast Colorado, a few miles northeast of Trinidad. They went west, like a lot of black folks, after the Homestead Act was passed, somewhere around 1912. You could go west and stake out land, and if you stayed on it for five years, it was yours.

So, after my mother died, my grandparents, Jim and Mariah Hunn, took my brother and me with them out to Colorado. But I don't know exactly how long they had actually been out there before they took my brother and me out there. We were more or less sent out there to "prove" the land. That was what it was called. You had to stay on the land, or some member of the family had to stay on the land for five years.

Well, when my brother and I were in Colorado, my grandparents tried farming, but they only did a scant amount of it. The main thing my grandfather did was to put his sons into what he called the 5H Ranch. He built the 5H Ranch out there. And he called it that for Five Hunns. That was the name of the family. My grandfather was named Hunn. My great-great grandfather was Grandpa Baker, on my mother's side. But my grandfather was named Hunn. He had the 5H Ranch. It was registered and everything.

My grandfather did mostly horse wrangling. They'd go out and catch wild horses and break them. I remember, even though I was a little guy, sitting on the fence, watching them ride these horses until they were tame enough to be sold. And he did that, and they had cattle, but that wasn't their main occupation. Little farming and horse wrangling. They rounded up horses and led them to the corral and my brother could barely remember, but I remember. I was old enough to remember watching them. And my brother remembers when granddad gave us a mule of our own.

When I was about four or five, I remember how he'd have to go clear over to the land. We were in sight of the mountains. Fisher Peak is one of them. You could go from Trinidad through the pass over to New Mexico. One of my uncles moved over to New Mexico. That's the way you go from Colorado to New Mexico on Interstate 25. Anyway, you can go over there.

My grandmother and grandfather were married 76 years. And my Uncle Bernie and Aunt Mira left southeastern Colorado and went to Denver, and they were married 75 years. Before Uncle Bernie passed away. And I have my Aunt Grace and two uncles still living. They're past 100 years old. And one of them's in Northridge, California.

It was tough for my grandparents in Las Animas County because they were harassed all the time by the white folks out there. I remember some of that. I remember jumping off the buckboard and running and getting between the corn rows to hide because I thought there was going to be some trouble.

Now my brother and sister and I, we still own our land. All the rest of it's been sold. We do have 320 acres out there in the middle of the prairie; we pay taxes on it every year and had it surveyed. One time, somebody else appropriated part of it. We went down to the courthouse in 1973 or '74, and looked at the land records and went over the land itself. We found that it was encircled with a big marker. And written inside of this big circle was "colored land." And that kind of explained the reason my grandmother was harassed so. After my grandfather had died, they dynamited the windmill and pulled the barn down by taking the ropes and putting it on the posts and pulling it down with a truck. They harassed my grandmother and Aunt Grace, who stayed on the land with her, and they also harassed Aunt Clara, right down the road. One time somebody got lynched in Marysville, Missouri, and we heard about it then. We heard about it just in passing. And we just knew that the South, that great big space out there, was nowhere to go.

So when my dad remarried, we were all brought back to Kansas City, except my older sister; the relatives with whom she stayed would never reveal where they were. Nobody knew where they went. And that's why we were separated for so long. Finally, we got back together when I was coaching the Cleveland Pipers. Met her on the West Coast.

The people that took in my sister Anita when my mother died, just took her to Idaho, a ranch out in Idaho. We never heard from her anymore. Well, we only knew that Anita was out on a ranch out there in Idaho. They never did have any address that I know of. We found her, my sister and my brother, we searched for her when we got old enough to. And a lot of our friends were railroad workers in the summertime and vacation time. And so we had heard that she was out West. So one of them finally came up with where she was. She had come to California, to Los Angeles, with her foster parents, and married a man named Williams. She had been looking for us, too. So we got together, and we still haven't finished talking to each other about what happened in our lives.

I came back to Kansas when I was six; I only stayed in Colorado from age three to six. I came back to Kansas—my dad had remarried and I started school at Dunbar Elementary School in Kansas City, Kansas. And my brother came back with me. Well, later on, my younger sister was reassembled with the family, about a year or so later. I never referred to my second mother as stepmother, because that may connote a feeling that she was less than a mother should be. I don't know how anybody could have had a better mother.

My father worked for the railroad until he passed away at age ninety-two. Well, he retired before that. They gave him ten more years than he was supposed to get. They did away with the sixty-year retirement thing. He was a railway mail clerk, and then he finally got to be railway mail clerk in charge. They sort mail on the train. And you got all this mail in the mail car and then put it in certain slots. They'd take examinations all the time. You'd have to know every town in Kansas. Post office, now they have the ZIP code. They didn't have that then. That might have made it more difficult.

I thought it was great growing up in Kansas, but I found out since it wasn't so great after all. Well, we went to segregated schools in Kansas City, where for years before I went it had been an integrated school

Ho for Kansas!

Brethren, Friends, & Fellow Citizens:
I feel thankful to inform you that the
REAL ESTATE
AND
Homestead   Association,
Will Leave Here the
15th of April, 1878,

In pursuit of Homes in the Southwestern Lands of America, at Transportation Rates, cheaper than ever was known before.

For full information inquire of

Benj. Singleton, better known as old Pap,
NO. 5 NORTH FRONT STREET.

Beware of Speculators and Adventurers, as it is a dangerous thing to fall in their hands.

Nashville, Tenn., March 18, 1878.

system. In fact, when my second mother, Minnie, went to school, it was integrated. But then they separated, and I went to a segregated school, Dunbar. Then I went to Northeast Junior High School, Sumner Senior High School, and went to one year, Kansas City Junior College, Sumner branch. All of these schools were segregated. I never had a white teacher until I went my first year to Kansas University.

My second mother had gone to Wyandotte High School, and then she went to Emporia State because about that time, that was about the only school in the state that would accept black students. And by the time I went to school, everything was segregated. But that turned out to be one of the best experiences that I could have had at that time. Because, I'll tell you this, I worked hard and made the highest award; they only gave doctorate degrees to seven blacks when I was in college. And five of them came from Sumner. I'm one of the five. But, understand, I'm just saying this as a tribute to the background and education that we got. We didn't know it—well, we thought it was the way things were, I guess. I never thought about it much. We weren't led to think about it, in our house. We passed by Longfellow School on the way to Dunbar, but we just passed by all the time. We never had any social relationship with anybody (who was white). So I was brought up in that. But, on the other hand, we had other experiences that included other people. And my family was one of the families, I don't know, most of them were like ours, I think. They never did preach anything; they always said that there were better things that we could be doing, things that we should achieve, and so forth. But they never made a big issue of being segregated or separated. I don't know of any time that they ever tried to even integrate the schools. Not during my time.

I studied physical education when I finally started at Kansas University and all the subjects that went with it. Dr. James Naismith started the degree for the physical education program. He was the inventor of basketball. And the first year I went there, he started the degree program where you could get a degree in physical education if you combined it with health and some other minor subjects. My minor happened to be education and sociology.

He didn't talk too much about inventing basketball. But he'd talk about it when we asked him to. Oh, he just said that he started the game because the football players were unruly in the dormitory at night and they needed an indoor game after the football season ended to kind of wear the players out so when they went to their rooms to study a little bit, they'd go to sleep instead of staying up all night, being boisterous. So, actually, basketball was invented for football players. He invented basketball in 1891. Now he was my teacher when he was in his seventies.

I went to Kansas University from 1933 to 1936. Kansas University was mixed. There were sixty blacks there out of 4,000. Now when I went there, Dr. Naismith had just started the physical education program through which you could get a degree. And he kept seven of us together, tried to, keep us all together, so we could—we did all graduate with our degree, and I think six of the seven stayed together the whole time. He got the university to approve the degree, but he had to use other colleges and schools in the system to get us through because we took our anatomy in the medical school. And he even required us to have a cadaver so we could learn the muscles. The medical students would do a section and we'd have to go look at it and stuff. Anyway, his main subject was anatomy and kinesiology. Although he taught me gymnastics. The only letter I made in high school other than a basketball student manager was in gymnastics.

Dr. Naismith was a football player; he and Alonzo Stagg invented the football helmet. He was a football player when he was in college. But after he invented basketball, it began to catch on through the YMCA system. Well, a couple of years ago, they had a placard going all over the country. "Basketball is a YMCA invention." So Dr. Naismith came from Canada, McGill University, at the age of thirty. Went to Springfield College and started basketball. Springfield College is in Massachusetts, Springfield, Massachusetts. He started basketball at the age of thirty when he was also a doctor of divinity.

See, when he got to Springfield College, they told him what his job was, to find something for these players to do. So he came in with this game. He tried indoor soccer at first. It was too rough, and so he came up with basketball. And then the YMCA spread it all across the U.S.A.

So, by the time I went to school, there was competitive basketball. Oh, yes, that was what they were celebrating out there in Kansas a couple of months ago. The hundredth anniversary of basketball at the University of Kansas. See, around 1898, Kansas started their basketball program. Yeah, Kansas was one of the first. But one other school says it started it first. Naismith had started his career in Denver, Colorado, in the YMCA in Denver. But then he left Denver YMCA and came to Kansas University as an instructor, and also as a basketball coach and a physical education professor. See, he coached basketball there for a few years. He was followed by Phog Allen, Forest "Phog" Allen, who's considered the father of basketball coaching.

I didn't play basketball at Kansas University because they wouldn't let blacks play anything. I just went there because Dr. Naismith was there. Me being a basketball coach, my father didn't have money enough, and I didn't either, and even after working and putting aside money for college, we didn't have enough to get to Springfield College in Massachusetts. But in the meantime, he researched where Dr. Naismith was. He said, "Why go where basketball was invented when we can go right up here at Kansas University?" He made that discovery, he found Dr. Naismith, found out, luckily for us, that he was only forty miles away.

I never saw an indoor basketball court until I got to seventh grade. And that was when I fell in love with it. We were touring the new junior high school, to which all of the black kids in the city were going to go the next year. And they had already gotten their staff together in that other school, and when we were touring the building, in the middle of the floor was a man shooting a basketball. And I just couldn't get over how anybody could make that. From where he was shooting, it would be about a four- or five-point shot. And he was making them. And it fascinated me, to the point where I decided I'd like to do whatever he was doing. He was a physical trainer. He wasn't even called a basketball coach.

His name was P. L. Jacobs. And he'd come there from Washington, D.C., and was going to have basketball in the junior high school. Well, the senior high school, Sumner, always had it. You know, they had it earlier. But the junior high school was incorporated into the senior school league. I'd never heard of that before, but they held their own. In fact, they won it one time. But P. L. Jacobs was my first coach, and when I went out for the team, he told me I'd do better in gymnastics. So I went out for gymnastics and made a letter in that. But I was student manager in basketball, and then when I went to Sumner High School, A. T. Edwards was there. He was one of the most successful coaches in Kansas, only in the segregated league. Kansas-Missouri Athletic Conference. I became his student manager. After I couldn't make the team, I had an agreement with him that I'd be his student manager. So I had a good time being the manager, but I always sat next to some of the best coaching that was going on at the time and trying to learn everything about the game. So, when I got to the University of Kansas, I knew about the game pretty well. But now here was the source of it all, and the main thing I got from Dr. Naismith was how to coach, the psychology of coaching, anatomy and kinesiology, of course.

Well, actually, the philosophy of coaching is to get an understanding with your players, what your goals (are), and merge their goals with yours. And also, to teach the game. He didn't really believe in coaching. You know, for years, you couldn't have a time-out where you could come to the sideline. Because the players were supposed to have been instructed beforehand what they were going to do, and when they called time-out, you couldn't go out on the court, nor could they come to the sideline. You had messages that you sent, signals and stuff, and even sometimes on little packs and little boards.

He discouraged the coach being such a big part of the game. He believed that the players were supposed to have been instructed thoroughly and that they should have a game plan that you gave to them. And they went out there and carried it out. Well, Dr. Allen came along and said, "No." It took a long time for them to follow his advice, that you could have a time-out and the players could come over to the side so you could reconstruct the game or decide on different strategy and so forth. And so he was the one that first started that. And they were in the same building, right down the hall from each other. I took classes from Dr. Allen, physical therapy and athletic administration, and I took principles of physical education from another fellow there in the building, another teacher. So I got the whole business. I was very fortunate, really.

When I graduated from the University of Kansas, Dr. Naismith asked me what was I going to do. He told me I was going to graduate school, but I said I'd have to go back home and go to work. I had been working at the packinghouse, Cudahay's packinghouse, in the summertime. And he told me then it wasn't a good idea. He said, "You shouldn't discontinue your studies, and it's hard to go back and go to work and then come back to your academics."

I asked him what could I do about it. I didn't have any way to go to school.

He said, "Step in my office here a minute."

He called up a guy, Ed Schroeder, was his name, up in Iowa. They have a building on the University of Iowa campus named after him. But anyway, Dr. Naismith called him and told him there was a young fellow here. He said, "He'll make a good student for you." Well, they knew each other, apparently, because he said for him to send me on. And I went to Iowa University because of a telephone call. But mainly, I went because there was a man there named C. H. McCloy. He was the leading research person in physical education during that time. This was during the thirties. Dr. Naismith had talked about him in class, about his research work and so forth. And so that was one of the reasons when he said, "Where would you like to go?" I said, "Iowa. Because you've talked to us about Dr. McCloy." But when I went there, I met Dr. McCloy, and we became very good friends because he had very special people in the graduate class. It was an opportunity to be friends and at the same time have a top-notch instructor working on you. He chose my thesis for me and everything, and helped me implement it. So that was all because of a call from Dr. Naismith. The only thing I had to pay to go to the University of Iowa was room rent. And that was $10 a month. That was in 1937.

I went to college through some difficult times. Those were the years of the Depression. Well, there was a lady there named Lemmie, and she took in black students because they didn't have any provision for black students on the campus in Iowa, no more than they had at the University of Kansas. You usually had to stay in somebody's residence. So I stayed with Miss Lemmie, who they named a school after. Of course, she carried such a load for years. Practically all the black students came to her house. She had a big old house with about ten, twelve rooms in it. So that's where I stayed. And all she charged was $10 a month per person. My roommate and I, that made it $20 a month.

So, I got my master's degree. And I met a fellow named—well, he became Dr. William F. Burghardt. But we were classmates and we got to be great friends, so much so that that's how I ended up at North Carolina. He was a distant relative of W. E. Burghardt Du Bois. Because he traced his ancestry back to 1700-something. And, of course, that name was the key to you know, being able to do that.

He got a job at North Carolina College for Negroes. Today it's North Carolina Central. And he sent for me, and I came out there as his assistant from 1937 to 1940, '41. And he left to pursue a doctor's degree, which he finally got, and I became head of physical education and head basketball coach in 1940, '41. I stayed another twelve years, total of fifteen.

Well, North Carolina was heavily segregated when I got there in 1937, and we were all members of the Central Intercollegiate Athletic Association, which in those days was called the Colored Intercollegiate Athletic Association and changed its name in 1945 to Central Intercollegiate. But anyway, we were in that league. Well, we operated within that league, and that was it. We never saw anybody else play. Nobody ever saw us play. We had about sixteen colleges in the Central Intercollegiate Athletic Association. And it stretched all the way to West Virginia. West Virginia State, and Bluefield State of West Virginia, they were in the Central Intercollegiate Athletic Association (CIAA). On the North, Lincoln University of Pennsylvania and the University of Maryland Eastern Shore, they came in later, but Howard University was one of the schools. And five others in North Carolina, the largest of which was North Carolina A&P State University, and so we were all in the league conference. But at that time, playing games between races was forbidden. It was against the law. But I had been trying to get my team to understand that basketball was a game that really needn't be segregated or anything; the main thing being that it was so separate that you would think each of us was playing a different game. The other side (the white league) was always in the newspaper, and the players were big heroes, and we didn't have any publicity. I won the CIAA championship and never even made the newspaper at one time.

So, that led me to a game in Washington, D. C., in 1942, when I challenged all the teams that I could think of to come to Washington, D. C. Washington, D. C., was supposedly a neutral ground, and I challenged any team to play my team because I had just won the CI double-A championship my first year of coaching. We had a 14-0 record in the CI double-A conference and won the conference championship, which was the visitation championship at that time. So, the only response we got was from Brooklyn College, who had defeated all the schools in New York, all the schools that had a record of any kind, and they had beaten them. But they said they would play us in Washington, D. C., since it was neutral ground and so forth and it wasn't against the law there. So I invited Eleanor Roosevelt and she couldn't come, and she sent Harry Hopkins, her State Department representative. He came to the game. We played the first integrated college basketball game in the District of Columbia.

So, then it became known to students that came to North Carolina that I was interested in integrating the schedule someday. One of my things was to stay as ready as I could so anytime it ever happened, we'd come off pretty good. In the meantime, this player of mine, he was at a YMCA meeting—they were rather covertly held. They didn't hide it or anything, but they just had YMCA meetings. Whatever, in this meeting, one of my players, George Parks, he's still living, in Orange County, California, heard one of the players from Duke Navy Medical School say that they were the best team in the state because they had beaten all the teams in the state. And Parks took exception.

He said, "Well, you haven't played us."

So out of that, they came back and told me that they, we, our team, had challenged them. But they didn't have anywhere to play. They needed to play in our gym at a time when nobody would notice. And that turned out to be at eleven o'clock Sunday morning. Just about everybody in Durham was in church on Sunday morning. So, the Duke Navy Medical School team came over, and we played a regular game and we won. But the spectators were outside the building. And, of course, they hadn't seen the spectators when they came in because they hid until they got inside, then they got on boxes, barrels, crates, and ladders, and everything to look in the windows. The windows were so constructed; they were six feet off the ground, almost. So anyway, we had spectators outside the building. They never paid any attention to them, as I recall, and I said, "Well, we saw them up there, but never thought anything about it that they were looking in the windows." But the main thing was that we thought that if we played the game without spectators, at least they thought that that might not be so hard on us if we were discovered playing. But whatever, nobody ever discovered it.

Fact of the matter is, Scott Ellsworth was the first reporter who ever asked me about it. When they had the fiftieth anniversary of the CIAA tournament in 1996, he came up and said, "What does this mean?" I had down there "523 victories," and in parentheses, just facetiously, I had added, "plus one, if the secret game was counted."

The Klan was pretty strong at the time we played that game—that "plus one." In fact, our student manager recalled that the Klan had had a meeting there on the outskirts of Durham just the week before. Furthermore, it hadn't been very long since a bus driver had murdered a black soldier for not moving on the bus. The jury only debated twenty minutes and freed the guy. So it was a pretty tough time. One thing though, in our favor, was that there was a black guy who was a colonel that was stationed there at Camp Buckner, about twelve miles north of Durham. That was something for us to be very proud of. We didn't know anybody was going to be that far up in the armed services. But he came in there about the time this soldier was shot. And so he sent his entire company into Durham to ride the buses. They rode the buses all over for a day or two. And nothing happened. But they were ready. They were going to counter with promised drastic action if anybody was not treated fairly. Anyway, it was at this time, that these white guys said, "Okay, we'll play you." And they came over, and since that time, I've counted them very special people. I think they were. They were very special to even take the chance, because they would have been penalized worse than we were. They would have been socially ostracized and everything else. At that time, that was the thing. That was the main punishment, ostracism and name-calling and stuff.

The only thing that might have happened to us was, and I never even thought about it at the time, our appropriation might have been slashed, from the State Department of Education. And I always will think that I got drafted into the Army illegally. They weren't taking anybody twenty-nine years old with children. They took me. I have always thought that the story leaked out. Because that was one way the draft board had of clearing a community of integrationists and people that didn't want to act right. They used to draft them into the Army to get them out of the community.

But as it was, I got out of it. Actually, the president of our school, when it looked like everybody was going to be drafted, he objected. I was one of the few people left in the department. In fact, I ended up being a two-man physical education department, of which I was the head. And did everything. And when I left, they got five people in my place. I was in North Carolina from 1937 to 1952. Head coach from 1940 to '52.

In 1949, I played the first public integrated game in the state of North Carolina, when we played Camp LeJeune Marines. That was around about the time of Executive Order 8802, integrating the armed forces. Executive Order 8802 was put forward by Harry Truman. And about that time, the various military bases around the country entertained sports on any level, any sport, including colleges. So we contacted Camp LeJeune Marines, and asked them for a game, and they gave it to us. So, in 1949, we played Camp LeJeune Marines. All that's getting to the point that I started a committee, called the National Basketball Committee, which later became the National Athletic Steering Committee. Its main purpose was to integrate sports on a national level.

I left North Carolina and went to Hampton in 1952. Now Hampton was where the first black college basketball program existed. That's out in Hampton, Virginia. They started in 1909. There was a man name of U.V. Henderson, and he got the colleges organized enough to play and engage in competition.

I stayed at Hampton for two years. Very nice, enjoyable time. But I went there by choice because after I left North Carolina, I wanted to coach in a school that didn't give scholarships, to see how it would be. At Hampton at that time, you couldn't get in without a B average, and you couldn't get in without the proved fact that you had enough money to go there. In other words, you had to pay to go to school, and I think their initial fee was $342. But you had to have that. There were no scholarships or grant aids or anything given until you paid that money. Anyway, I enjoyed it. I went there because one of my best friends was athletic director there, and another friend was head coach. He said he'd give it up if I'd come in with them. So I went to Hampton. Of course, it was one of the best schools you could go to, and still is.

But while I was at Hampton, Tennessee State's athletic director and president contacted me and said, "If this is going to be the mission of your life, you better come on out here. Because we have the athletes, we have the government behind us. Here, you can manage this on a national level, and this is the place for you to be." Well, Tennessee State was practically number one in sports. So I left Hampton and went to Tennessee State. And that's where we integrated sports on a national level when the NAIA finally granted us an opportunity to play in the tournament in Kansas City.

That was a National Association of Intercollegiate Athletics tournament. And it's a long story, but we put the proposition to them, that we should be in sports on a national level, and we had tried the other organization, NCAA, and they declined to get into that. However, when the NAIA invited us in, two years later, the NCAA started the college division tournament in Evansville, which was then open to everybody. The NCAA started it in 1956, where the NAIA had its first black team play in the tournament in 1953.

Clarence Cash was the coach at Tennessee State then. And the NAIA opened its doors first, but the conditions were that you'd have to decide among yourselves—you're talking about eighty-six schools who had basketball—which one team can come to Kansas City and take one place in the thirty-two-team bracket. So that wasn't really total integration, but it was the beginning.

Well, when you reflect back on it, if you think like we do today, you might say, "Never mind, we're not coming," but that was the first foot-in-the-door thing that we could deal with. And furthermore, it created within us a great spirit of competition which improved our team because you had to win the Negro National Championship to get to that NAIA tournament in Kansas City.

I think a number of organizations around the country, a number of communities, were influenced by the executive order (that integrated the armed forces), coming on the basis of the war and the experiences in the war, where black soldiers were fighting without full rights of citizenship. And this was actually the beginning of the social revolution that extended on to the sixties, in my opinion.

That was the catalyst. So the part athletics played was when they integrated that tournament, on the national level, even their membership. And when the NCAA found out what the NAIA was doing, they then created the tournament in Evansville. And besides that, there were several hundred schools that didn't belong to any organization. And they built their membership up from that beginning, when they opened up the doors for their own schools.

I went to Tennessee State in '54, and the year I went there, the NAIA had a Christmas tournament, which is like the NIT (National Intercollegiate Tournament). And they chose the teams that they felt had performed well in the previous spring tournament. And Tennessee State was one of those teams. Clarence Cash's team had performed what they considered very well in Kansas City, although they didn't win the tournament. I received the invitation that was for Clarence. Clarence had left Tennessee State. But when they called and told me that I was in the tournament, that was when the integration of Kansas City, hotels and restaurants, took place, because I refused to come unless they did that. And they just said, I just had to come or I wouldn't be able to compete, but I wasn't coming unless they let us stay in the same hotels and eat at the same restaurants as the other teams. See, we had to be the best of all the Negro schools to get one place in a thirty-two-team bracket. But in the invitational tournament, they only asked for eight, see. They just had an eight-team tournament, which is like a preseason Christmas tournament. At that time, I talked to my assistant coaches, and I also talked to the team, who had been to Kansas City. Most of them had been there, to Kansas City, twice before. Tennessee State won the Negro National Championship in '53 and '54.

And they said, "Well, we're with you, Coach. If you don't want to go till we can do better with our accommodations, well, we'll be with you."

See, I never did take this up with the administration. Because I knew one thing: If they said no, that would have been an impasse. If they said yes, then they would have gotten in trouble with the state authorities. So it was better for me to do it and get fired or get chastised or reprimanded or something than for the president to get involved because he could always say, "Well, I didn't know anything about it. I didn't have any idea he'd do something like that." And when he heard about it, that's what he said he would have said.

The late Al Duer, who was executive secretary of the NAIA at the time, was the one that called me and told me that my team was supposed to take part in this tournament. And I told him, yes, I knew it, but I wasn't planning on coming. Good thing he called me.

He said, "What's the problem?"

I told him.

So he said, "How long will you be by the phone?"

And I told him, "All day, if necessary."

He said, "I'll call you back in twenty minutes."

In twenty minutes, he canvassed the chamber of commerce, junior chamber of commerce, and his committee, who had apparently been studying this anyway, and called me back and said we could stay at the Hotel Kansas Citian and we could eat at any of the restaurants that the other teams do. So that's how Kansas City was integrated. That was 1954. Up until that time, even Lena Horne couldn't stay downtown.

Well, I stayed at Tennessee State for five years. I went from there to the new opportunity in basketball, which gave black guys a chance to coach beyond the college level. I joined the Cleveland Pipers in the National Industrial League. This was the league that stretched from coast to coast and was sponsored by big corporations and industry, like Goodyear. Semi-pro, they called it.

I left Tennessee State to take that job. It was a step forward for all of us, and it was quite challenging, so I went. And one of the conditions I had then was, I had to bring some of my own players with me, so I took four players from Tennessee State into that experience. The Industrial League was integrated. That is, they were integrated to the extent that they could be if they wanted to. I think one team had two black players, and another six didn't have any.

I stayed with the Pipers about two years. I won the championship in the second year. And that league broke up because the pros didn't like it. There were better players in that league than there were in the pros at the time. So they took all of them. They just came around and took them all and broke the league up. My team won the last NIBL (National Industrial Basketball League) championship. Then I also won the AAU championship the same year. The team was bought by George Steinbrenner. And we didn't get along very well, so in midseason.... Actually, they had two separate seasons; the championship was one-half of the year, and then start over and have another one the second half of the year. At the end of the first half of the season, my team won the Eastern Division championship. Then a situation came up that I don't even care to talk about it; it was kind of ugly. So, we parted company.

But I was then quickly called by the State Department and asked to teach basketball to the coaches of Southeast Asia. I went to Malaysia for six months. And it was a great experience. Then, I came back to Tennessee

State, but my two assistants there had played for me before. For years, I wouldn't have any assistants unless they had played for me. Saved a lot of arguments and problems. Anyway, they were being successful with the team in my absence, and even though they asked me to take it back, I told them no. So the president made me head of everything, graduate school, undergraduate school, for that year. And then the president of the council, athletic council, and also one of the leading professors in the school, was called to Kentucky State to be its president. So I went on up there with him.

I was at Kentucky State for three years: 1963–1966. Well, I had very good, great success there. Fact is, I took the team to Kansas City. Won one game and gave me the record, which hasn't been broken, seventeen straight victories in the national tournament. That's not likely to be broken anytime soon. But anyway, then I left Kentucky, and I went back to Cleveland, because Cleveland State, where I am now, had a new president. And when he came in and found out that no predominantly white school in the United States had ever hired a black basketball coach, he said, "This has got to end." He called me up on the telephone and said, "You've got to get up here to Cleveland. It's very important. I want to talk to you." So I went up there, and that's what he said. "You've got to be the new coach."

And since then I've been at Cleveland State off and on. I left Cleveland and went with the Denver Rockets in the ABA, '69, '70. Then I went with Converse for one year and stayed with them twenty. I was their national basketball rep, and international rep as well. They sent me everywhere, all around the world, teaching basketball and coaching all-star teams. I became a member of the basketball Olympic committee, Olympic Basketball Committee, for ten years, did all the scouting for the Olympic team during that time.

I came back to Cleveland State in a year; I got here around 1990. This is my seventh year back. And for the last six years, I've been either athletic adviser or teaching in the athletic department. But the last five years, I've been teaching in the history department.

I'm teaching a course that nobody knows anything about, believe it or not, the history of sports in the United States and the role of minorities in their development. I just yesterday started teaching at Tri-C. There are three community colleges here, all under one administration. So they asked me would I teach the same course over to their place. So now I'm teaching at Tri-C and Cleveland State.

I've had some great players. They've told me. One of them calls me up every now and then, says, "Don't forget who put you in the Hall of Fame." Aubrey Stanley. He's a member of that team that played that secret game. His nickname was "Stinky."

Some of the other great players I've coached are Sam Jones and Dick Barnett, although on my 1959 team, four players went in the NBA: John Barnhill, Ben Walley, Dick Barnett, and Porter Merriwether. The Boston Celtics were the first NBA team to integrate, when they took Charles Cooper in 1950. But that year, two other teams also took black players: the Washington Capitals, who soon went out of business. The Washington Capitols today are an ice hockey team. Then the New York Knicks followed. There were four blacks that went in the NBA in 1950: Freewater with the Knicks, Harold Hunter with the Capitols, Charles Cooper with the Celtics, and Bob Wilson with the Hawks.

I coached Sam Jones in '50. In fact, I recruited and coached him in '50, '52. He went in the service. He went in about '56 or '57. Sam Jones was one of my miracle players. But it took him about eight games to make the starting lineup on my team. Of course, there were a lot of guys nobody ever heard of. But they could play ball.

Teaching and dealing with people, young people, keeps me going. I think it helps.

INTERVIEW BY ALAN GOVENAR, APRIL 6, 1996

Brownie McGhee

Blues musician
Life dates: November 30, 1915–February 16, 1996

Walter Brown "Brownie" McGhee left his home in Knoxville, Tennessee, at age eighteen to perform his self-taught blues in medicine shows and juke joints around the South. He made his first recordings in 1939; stylistically, he was influenced by the Piedmont blues of Blind Boy Fuller, and for a brief period after Fuller's death in 1941, McGhee was billed as Blind Boy Fuller No. 2. He moved to New York in the early 1940s and teamed up with harmonica stylist Sonny Terry. Together, Terry and McGhee joined with folk blues legend Huddie "Leadbelly" Ledbetter to perform with the Woody Guthrie Singers. In 1948, McGhee started a blues guitar school in Harlem called Brownie McGhee's Home of the Blues. In the 1950s, he was invited to perform in films, as well as in such plays as Tennessee Williams's "Cat on a Hot Tin Roof" (1954) and Langston Hughes's "Simply Heavenly" (1957). Throughout the 1960s and 1970s, McGhee and Terry toured extensively as part of the blues and folk music revival, appearing at festivals across the United States and abroad. In 1982, McGhee and Terry received a National Heritage Fellowship from the National Endowment for the Arts.

I didn't want to become a musician; my father was a guitar player in front of me, and I liked what he was doing. I never dreamed of becoming a musician. I had polio when I was five. My ideas of life was in not knowing what it consisted of. I wanted to be a lawyer or doctor. I don't know why, but I never would be able to work that hard. I had polio, which was called infantile paralysis at that time. And I think a good education is what I wanted. I wanted an education to become a lawyer or doctor. That was the only two things I could think of, and then I used to read a lot. 'Cause Mother and Father separated when I was five. So, in between all of that, financial difficulties and family affairs got in the way, but I got a high school education. I picked up the guitar and took a walk. I went looking for a school because down south there weren't any black colleges. So I finished high school, and I didn't have any money.

My daddy said, "You have to make it on your own now, son."

So I thought you could go to school until you got tired of going, but I found out about tuition…and my family had financial difficulties. They didn't have it. So I went out searching for a school, and religion come in it. And I got disappointed about religion. Methodist blacks had money. Baptist blacks didn't have much. And the Methodist people had Methodist black colleges. And so if I become a Methodist, I could go to college. I was too independent to change my way of thinking because I felt there was something funny about religion. If there was a God, and he separated like that, I didn't want no part of it. So I didn't go to college, and I say that's why I picked up my guitar.

A guitar was my companion. I figured I could find a school somewhere. And, everywhere I went I got, "Tuitions, tuitions." Then I studied that word, and that was money. That's what they wanted, money. And I was singing at the time, and so I was picked up by a talent scout, and that was the beginning.

My father played his kind of music. What I mean, I thought my daddy made guitars. I thought he was the originator of a guitar. You know, I only saw my daddy play. He had one. He played bluesy, what you might call our music. His daily life, his happenings. I know it had to be his now. Because I'd never heard it before until I got big enough. And then some of the things, I heard other people sing in later years.

Growing up with my father, well, it was marvelous growing up with him, because my father wasn't a highly educated man. He was a common laborer, and he only played his guitar on the weekend. And then when he'd have problems on the job, or wherever he was working, he'd come home and (I knew that in later years, but I didn't know then), but he'd come home and play his guitar, and out of that guitar would come something. He'd sing a lot. And I remember now, it didn't rhyme at times. But what

Brownie McGhee (left) plays on stage with an unidentified man in New York City, 1947 (Archive Photos / Frank Driggs Collection)

he would sing, it was like he was talking, you know. And it was really. I was so impressed with what he was doing. I liked to hear him do it, but my daddy played more guitar during the time he was drinking. And I really enjoyed seeing him drink because he would take up a lot of time with me when he drank. And he'd show me things because I'd grab the guitar. And he was very friendly with me, and tell me what wasn't right, or what wasn't wrong. There was one thing about it, people says, my father didn't abuse me when he drank.

I play like him. Yeah, I remember that, because he said you cannot strum a guitar, you got to pick it. That's what I remember, and that's what I do. I started on guitar; I got it from my father. No matter what else I got, I knew I'd never end up playing (exactly) like him. So, I developed into my daddy and Lonnie Johnson. Those are the two fellas—my daddy was my biggest influence, and then Lonnie Johnson I heard on records.

Lot of lyrics that my daddy did, I put them into my songs—the way he talked to me is what I wrote. See, what my daddy talked to me was parables. And when he talked to me, I'd say it couldn't be possible. It couldn't be possible. You know what he taught, he taught me to remember, he taught me how to be obedient. And it was things that you don't get nowadays so much from a father. And I learned "John Henry" from my daddy, "Betty and Dupree" from my daddy. And I learned a lot of lyrics from my father that make sense now, to live by. And the things that he talked to me about, I wrote it down and called it "My Father's Words," and those are the tidings that are my ethics of living.

One of these lyrics is, I didn't know what he meant when he said, "The longer the road, the shorter the turn." You know, you're a young kid, and you talk to a kid, talk to me like that, way he talked to me, I didn't know what it was. "The taller the tree, the deeper the roots." That was pretty strong stuff. And when I began to realize what he was saying, it followed me through the years, those words: "The longer the road, the shorter the turn, and son, you, no matter how long you live, you'll never grow too old to learn."

"Taller the tree, the deeper the roots; blacker the berry, the sweeter the juice."

"If you want to be loved," he'd always say, "you got to love somebody if you want them to love you, but don't never let your right hand know what your left hand do." A thing, I just got a call on, they want to use it on the radio. I called it "My Father's Words," but it's my last album that I did, it's called "Blues Is Truth." It comes from that whole record. And so I did that, and I used that as one of my things of my father. As I say, I lived with that.

It wasn't that tough (growing up in Tennessee) because I can't say that, because I had a roof over my head, and I had plenty to eat. I never had to go from door to door. One thing about my father, if we had beans, we had a lot of beans. If we had potatoes, I had plenty of potatoes. And I always had clothes. And so it was with shoes. And I had to go to school. I never played hooky. And if I was late, I got a whipping for it. If I was disobedient at school, I got a whipping, because the teacher come by and said, "Walter was bad," and I got a whipping that day, not the next day. You got to obey the teacher, you got to go to school, and you had to know, learn something. That's what you had to do.

I was brought up on discrimination. That's what my daddy was talking about. I was taught that I was the best, I was the greatest thing, I was the biggest thing, nobody as good as you, son. You are it. You're good-looking, you're intelligent, and you everything. And you all it is. Love yourself, and then you can love the world and everybody that's in it. But you must love yourself first. Give away a little bit, but keep the big end. Don't ever give it all to anybody. Keep you some for yourself. Love yourself. That's the main thing he taught me, to love myself. And today, I'm as good as any man in the world. Better than some men that don't have—I don't even realize it, I have polio.

I went through all the changes. I get up, and I had an operation. Walked with a crutch and a cane until I was nineteen. I sang my way a cappella;

state of Tennessee gave me three operations, didn't cost me anything. I threw my crutch and the cane away and took to the road. You know, those things. My life is built on experiences of reality.

I started singing at eight. Whatever I heard, I'd sing it. I could learn myself. And what my daddy sang, I could sing. But I wasn't to do when he did, I had to do what he told me to do. See, children come up now, and they do what you do. But you don't do what I do, do what I tell you to do. My daddy cursed every breath he drew, but I never cursed until—now I curse when I want to. Not because I have to, because it's not a demand, but my father, I thought he had to. I heard that from my childhood. But I did not curse. Because I wasn't taught to curse. My daddy did it. I got to where I liked it. When he didn't do it, I thought there was something wrong. And so, it's just one of those type of things.

Yeah, everything I sing about today is from my childhood. (Sings): "From my childhood to where I am now/ I ain't gonna worry/ I'll get by somehow/ My mama had 'em/ My daddy had 'em, too/ You know I, I was born with the blues."

And I used to sing spirituals. "How sweet and a-happy seems, those days of which I dream/ When memories recall them now and then/ And with what a righteous feat/ My worried heart would beat/ If I could hear my mother pray again." I think that was, I sang that far back as I can re-member, that song. And I don't think I ever heard my mother pray. But I remember her very well. My mother and father separated when I was five, and I never saw her no more after about the 1920s. She died in New York State.

I was discovered by a talent scout—J. B. Long, in 1939, in North Carolina. I was still looking for that school. I had my high school diploma in my pocket and I was singing in a black ghetto in Burlington, North Carolina. And some black washboard player went and told him, says, "Man, I hear a guy down there singing something. It's different than it is here in North Carolina." And I was singing a song, a poem that I had written. It was called "Me and My Dog." And I didn't know anybody had ever told anybody about it. I was picking up nickels and dimes, and was gonna buy me some wine.

And this black boy, Washboard George, says, "Hey, Mr. Long wants you to come down to his store, man."

I said, "Who is Mr. Long?"

He says, "A white fella, man, takes you up to make records."

"Oh, "I said, "man, I ain't got time to bother with nobody. You see this crowd I got?" I said I was picking up the change. I was making some money. Had my cap laying down in there.

But he says, "He's gonna stay…" He went off and come back and said, "He's gonna stay in the store tonight late; he wants you to come down."

So I said, "Well all right, if he's there late, I will."

But anyway, after it was all over, and after midnight, this guy was still hanging around, says, "It's right down the street here, Mr. Long," and I went down.

Mr. Long says, "What's that song you're singing up there about this dog?"

Ha, ha, ha, tickled me to death. That was my first song I ever wrote, myself. "Me and My Dog." "Oh," I say, yeah, "Me and My Dog," He say, "Yes, well, sing it for me." And I sang "Me and My Dog" for him. And he said, "That's nice." And he asked me a few questions 'bout records. I didn't know nothin' 'bout records. What you talkin' about, records? But everything, I'd say, "Yes. Yes." You know, how it is, black boy talkin' to a white man in the South in the thirties. "Yes, yes."

"How'd you like to make records?"

"Fine." But anyway, I'd never made a record, and never dreamed of making any records. I wished, if he'd said, "School," man, it would have been my best deal.

And he said, "I'd like to take you and make some records…"

I said, "Yes."

He said, "Well, come down here tomorrow, bring your guitar, come down, and we'll see what we gonna do," and I did.

I didn't even know what in the world was going on, making records. I never dreamed I'd ever make a record. I didn't study music. I had four years of voice in school, you know, singing, as I say, a cappella.

Well, he thought I was great. He took me up to Chicago. I made a record. And I had never heard myself.

So, he said, "We're going to play this one back. Listen to it." Here I come on, never heard myself. I didn't know. People was judging, I didn't judge. I would just play and sing. I was singing, you know, but it didn't dawn on me that that's what it was. And it was "Me and My Dog," with guitar behind it.

"How'd you like that, McGhee? Yeah, that was you."

I said, "Me?" I said, "No, I can beat that."

He said, "Well, that's good, we think that's pretty good, we gonna keep that one."

I said to him, "Man, I can beat that." That was 1939. And I been trying to beat that. Competing with myself. Because I'd never heard myself. See, I was so outdone that that's the way I sounded when I wasn't, when I was listening. People accepted that, and so that was the way, and he thought that, the thing that he said to me has come to pass. And I thought what Long said to me was a white man talking to a southerner. He was trying to lift me up, you know, give me some support or something. I don't know what he saw, but to me, I was thinking, what's he telling me all this bull for? Because I had went through some changes with him. I'd flashed my diploma on him. I told him I finished high school. Got my diploma, had a driver's license. You know, Tennessee driver's license, little card about that big: "You're eligible to drive." And he said a lot of things to me, and it went in one ear and out the other, but what lodged up there was what he was saying. I never heard about commercials. I never heard about writing, you know, what it was, music, I didn't study this, but what he said to me, everything that he said to me, it wasn't him, it was me. Everything he said come to pass. Now he foreseen this because I didn't know nothing about it.

He says, "You the first guy that I ever heard sing the blues that could read or write." And he done picked up many of them. He says, "I'm from Georgia, but I got my store here in North Carolina." And heh, heh, heh, and that was another thing, you know, I couldn't believe that he was talking to me, says, "You're the first black guy I ever met that could read and write."

Quite natural to me, I'm looking at him, him talking to me, how much of that he thought I believed. And so he said, "Now what you can do," he taught me what I know about writing my songs down. I didn't know a bit more about writing, how long it took and what it takes. I learned more, and so I went along with him.

He didn't take no deal. He was my life at the time. He was all I knew. J. B. Long is the man that caused me to be sitting here, that man I'm talking about. J. B. Long. That was OKeh Records, which is Columbia.

I heard him talk to that man on the telephone. I heard him tell J. B. Long, "I don't want any more of those country blues singers. They make good records, but they don't sell."

J. B. Long says, "I think this boy's got something. I'm going to bring him to Chicago anyway."

So up to Chicago I went with J. B. Long. I say I didn't have a deal because whatever I made, you understand, I was rich. Because I earned it, and it wasn't no big money deal. I signed a deal, but the point of it was, I didn't read it. And he didn't beat me out of anything. I loved J. B. He's dead. I know his children, I knew his wife, and I knew a lot of people around him after that. But if it hadn't been for J. B., I could have been sitting on a corner in North Carolina or standing on a street in Tennessee today. But I went along with him, and I went back home, and my daddy was a little smarter than I thought he was. When I showed him the papers, I signed for them, too, used my name, anyway it would fit to sell records, publicize me. And I didn't read this thing. I just signed. Piece of paper. And I made, I got a hundred and some dollars for my first record session. And was I happy? A hundred and some dollars in my hand? And singing then on record was just, "What did I do to get this?" I'd been singing all day and didn't make $2. But here I sing six or seven lyrics, I call it, six or seven times, and the man say, "That's it."

Because I didn't know how to make records, they just cut me off. All of my first records was just stopped. There wasn't no endings because I didn't know nothing about it. I'd just sing. So they cut it off. And J. B. Long give me a hundred and some dollars, transportation to Chicago and back, a hotel, and a meal ticket. And I thought I was rich. I was rich. A hundred dollars. That's the first hundred dollars I had in my life, and I earned it. But I didn't know that I had money coming because I didn't have a Social Security card. Well, all this comes to be facts because I went on and left J. B. Long and went on, he said, "Now you go on, man, and I'm going to take you up. You know, we'll do some other things, but write down your songs."

He says, "Write them down, your lyrics are great. Write four verses and sing three and play one and then sing two more and out, and you've got a complete record. Make it about three minutes."

But I couldn't count, but as time went on, I learned the skill of it, and then Long began to call me and write me letters. I got them in there in my scrapbook. And so and so selling the record says it's coming out today. "Me and My Dog" is out. Now "Me and My Dog" was a song.

Well, I kidnapped a girl. I didn't kidnap her, I took her away from her mother because she bragged when I was in the hospital with this leg, it's: "Nobody can get me away from my mother." And at that time I was a shrewd guy because I'd been studying public speaking, because I figured I'd be a lawyer if I had a chance to go on to school, but as I said, it was financial difficulties and family affairs. But laying in the hospital, and I heard this girl, beautiful girl, and I said to myself, "I can get you away from Mother." And I did. I didn't have a quarter. I had a guitar in the hospital. Singing to myself, you know, riding around in a wheelchair. I come out of that hospital, that was my girlfriend, and a few months after I got here, man, I went and bought my brother-in-law's car, and went back, threw her suitcase over the fence, and put it in my brother-in-law's car and we lit out a hundred miles from my hometown, Knoxville, up to Kingsport, Tennessee. And I took her up there and kept her. I didn't have no money, but anyway I got her away from her mother. And this song was about her after she left and went back to her mother, was that Victor dog. You seen that dog singing in that horn? That dog was on (78-rpm) records. And what was that he was in? He had his face in this horn. But anyway, that dog was a picture on the wall. And that's what I had in my room. And after she left me and went back to her mother, I used to lay at night and sing, set in the little room and sing: "Just me and my dog, we don't have no friends right now. Just me and my dog, we don't have no friends right now. The woman I love may be living like a queen, but I'll get along somehow." Well, that was the first stanza of it. That was after she left me and that dog used to be at the foot of our little bed that we had, and seemed like that dog was saying, "Now you're by yourself. Nobody here with you." And I'd pick up my little old guitar, and I wrote down these lyrics.

Just before I started to singing it, I sat down and I wrote about this girl leaving me, see, and it almost drove me out of my mind. And I wrote this down, and this dog was looking at me and I used to say, "Just me and my dog, we don't have no friends right now. Woman I love, she lives like a queen, but I'll get along somehow." And then I started to singing it, not knowing that I'd ever be, you know, playing it on the guitar, and everybody thinking it was something real great, and I did, too. And I just sang about the things that happened in our lives, and that's what I was singing, went along: "Just me and my dog, we don't have no friends right now. Just me and my dog, we don't have no friends right now. The woman I love may be living like a queen, but I'll get along somehow."

He said, "That's great, that's fine." But he didn't know that I was singing about that paper dog. He thought I was a lover of a real dog. And it was years before the war broke out that I told him what it was, and then he just really asked me, says, "What happened to that dog?" Me and him was driving along, you know, on the highway I used to drive.

And I said, "Aw, man, that dog, I left that dog on the wall." It was funny. Then I told him the story, and he thought it was marvelous, and that was the first record, the first song I wrote, first record I recorded, in 1939.

Then I began to write. He says, "Write it down, you just write it down." Now he never did copyright any of my things. I didn't learn to copyright my songs until I got to New York. And Long didn't have me, I was under contract to Long, but I wasn't under contract to OKeh Records and so I didn't know. I thought I had a contract with OKeh Records. But the war broke out, and I got into New York, and they said, "We're not doing any more songs."

Long says, "I ain't got nothing on you. I ain't got no papers on you."

So I went down to OKeh Records, and the man says, "We don't know anything about you. Who are you?"

"I'm Brownie McGhee."

"Brownie McGhee?" They thought I was one of them crazy New Yorkers. They said, "Come down," this girl in the office says, "Come down, it's one of these crazy Harlem guys down here talking about how he works for OKeh Records."

Well, the man come down, "Who are you?"

And I mentioned J. B. Long. He said, "Oooh. Get J. B. Long's file."

See, I didn't know that existed. "Oh," he looked, said, "you one of J. B.'s boys. North Carolina. Yeah, but we don't have a contract with you. We not even buying J. B.'s boys anymore." Says, "We don't have no contract. We had a contract, but we bought you from J. B. You're as free as a bird, far as we concerned. You don't do us no harm. We don't have Long's boys, so automatically you have no contract with us. But I'll give you a copy of everything you ever did with us."

So I got the copies. They give me a copy. It looked like, "Well, J. B. made a couple dollars." But I wasn't mad with J. B. because he made some money. It was stupid if he hadn't have made some. That's where I learned my lesson. If he hadn't made some money, then I'd have thought it was a trick game. But he didn't give me all he made because what he spent on me is more than what he got. Educational, nice as he was, up to Chicago and back, I know it cost more than 600 bucks, man. I've had a fine hotel, I wasn't, didn't sleep in no car, I didn't sleep in no second-grade hotels in Chicago. I wasn't dropped on the street. And I had a meal ticket. That's one thing I had. And I had cigarettes, and money for a drink. J. B. Long had saw to that.

And I couldn't understand people saying that you got picked up by a talent scout and got beat for money. Now, J. B. Long, if he, if it had lasted long, he might have made some money because I might have got wise and told him, "What are you doing?" but he didn't. And when I found that out, J. B. Long got $600 or $700 a session for me and he give me a hundred and something. I didn't owe him anything, and I got clothes from his store, and I got cigarettes from his store. He had a store in Burlington, North Carolina, and he didn't charge me for that. He advanced me money. So J. B. was my life.

Brownie is my name. Brown. My name is Brown Walter McGhee. "Brownie" was given to me at school. My daddy didn't like "Brownie," but the kids called me "Brownie," and my daddy couldn't do nothing about it. And I accepted "Brownie." I answered by "Brownie." He always told me "Brownie" was a dog's name. "Brown" is a man's name. "Brownie" is a dog's name. But anyway, I liked "Brownie."

Now, for J. B. Long, I was playing under the name of "Poor Brown." I wanted to be called "Poor Brown."

J. B. Long says, "Let's do this. Anybody can be Poor Brown. But there can't be but one Brownie McGhee." And that's why, he says, "I like that better anyways. Why don't we stay with 'Brownie McGhee'?" And that was it. And I changed my birth certificate, you know, I was grown then, but after I got up and got to New York, I wrote home and got my birth certificate changed from "Brown, Walter" to "Walter Brownie McGhee." Officially known, signed and sealed, in Nashville, Tennessee, in the archives there. I am Walter Brownie McGhee. There's nobody dead, nobody—I'm the one, I'm the only. And so that's what it is. And Brownie McGhee is my name. Walter B. Walter B. makes the money, Brownie McGhee spends it. No, Brownie McGhee makes it and Walter B. spends it. I tell a tale like that. So it's all real, that's the way it was.

There were no clubs in the South. People should realize that. A black man hardly had a place to hang his hat. The ghettos was very narrow and small. And if you played anyplace, it had to be a whorehouse, a roadhouse, a whiskey joint, or a gambling den, or a medicine show. And I did medicine shows. Just to get around there, you know, hustling a little, two quarters and things, which wasn't a fair deal anyway, but it was just one of those things. But after my first record in 1939, I went back home to sit down to write my songs down after I heard my first record come out of "Me and My Dog" and some more sides that I'd made.

Then I made "The Death of Blind Boy Fuller." Blind Boy Fuller was a black blues artist. And then they called me, J. B. Long called me "Blind Boy Fuller No. 2." Which my daddy resented. And which I never thought about it, because it was a big seller. And I still, they give me a couple or $300, Long did, give me some money to put in my pocket and travel around and boost the record in North Carolina. That's why people think I'm a North Carolinian. But I'm not. I'm a Tennessean. And I didn't play any clubs there 'cause there wasn't any clubs. I'd just played joints and the street corners.

(Years later), I went to Washington, D.C., to the Library of Congress with Sonny Terry. Take him up there, they asked me, "What you doing with that guitar?" J. B. Long told me to take it with me, says, "Why don't you take Sonny up?"

So I said, "Well, I won't need no kind of guitar, I'm going up with Sonny."

He said, "No, take your guitar."

I went up there in last of '39 to record for Alan Lomax. At that time, yeah. John (Lomax) might have been there, but Alan was beginning to do it. So, I went up, and Sonny was making some stuff for the Library of Congress, he heard me sing, and said, "Why don't you do something, too?" Because I had got a few dollars for taking Sonny up. Because me and Sonny hadn't played together.

J. B. Long had found Sonny Terry also. J. B. Long had Sonny and Blind Boy Fuller and Old Red, Mitchell's Christian Singers and some more artists, he had there, and Buddy Moss. J. B. Long had all those artists. He had those Georgia and Tennessee and North Carolina artists, and I met these people all through J. B. Long. I was introduced to them.

I found out about the Library of Congress through J. B. Long. Because they called Sonny, and they wanted—Blind Boy Fuller was blind, and Sonny was, couldn't see. And J. B. just thought I could do anything, which I could. I could read, I could pick Sonny up. I could catch a train, I could catch a bus, you know what I mean, I could buy the tickets. And all that was a helper. He didn't have to do that. But I didn't know that until later; he explained to me. I didn't charge him for it. I didn't know to charge him. I thought it was a great deal.

"Well, Brownie, you catch a train. You can pick up some tickets at the L&N station, Southern train station, you pick up two tickets and you get off at such and such a place, and call this man."

That was a responsibility. I was qualified to do that because I had finished high school. And then after he found out I had a diploma. Anything that come to do, why, and I did it. I'd do it. And so I learned all that and met these people. And I was introduced to a lot of good people. I hung in there.

Sonny was marvelous. Yes, he was marvelous. I met him and Fuller at the same time. And he was a harmonica player, too. I started playing with Sonny in '43, but I had played around Durham, North Carolina. J. B. Long created this Sonny Terry and Brownie McGhee thing, because he asked me would I go over and see if I could be of some help to Sonny cause Fuller was dead. And that's how me and Sonny got together. It wasn't no choice. Because I didn't need, Sonny couldn't see good, and I was handicapped to a point, not that I had relied on it, but I took care of myself, see. I'm going to look out for Brownie McGhee first. And I went over to look out for Sonny and played around Durham, North Carolina, and people began to hear us playing around there, you know. We made a few dollars, and I stayed there in Durham with Sonny for a while. We never made any records until '43.

Sonny was an individualist. He was on his own. I didn't, wasn't any problems. And I had a harmonica player when I met Sonny. I had a fellow by the name of Jordan Webb, and Webb was a good harmonica player and piano player. And so when I met Sonny, I thought Sonny was, he'd been backing up Blind Boy Fuller. And so me and Sonny's friendship lasted thirty-five years until he died in the 1980s.

Sonny was in New York. We come to New York at the same time. We were sent for there by Millard Lampell, a writer, California, Hollywood writer. And Alan Lomax and Millard Lampell suggested that I come to New York and be introduced to Josh White and Leadbelly. They were there, so automatically, I went on back home. I dropped Sonny off in North Carolina. I caught me a train and went on to Tennessee. And they was going to send for me, and I just thought, ah, they just talking. What they want me in New York, hell.

Sure enough, I got a wire: "Come at once. Sonny's already here. He didn't know how to get you a ticket. We sent the ticket to Sonny in North Carolina, and he didn't know how to get it to you in Tennessee, so he brought it back to New York. So we got the ticket."

So I called up. And they wired me some money instead of a ticket. At that time, I could get on a Greyhound bus from Kingsport, Tennessee, for $10 or $15, go to New York. In the thirties. And so they sent me a ticket, sent me $100, and I caught the bus. And that's how I got to New York. And when I got to New York, I met Leadbelly. I had met Leadbelly in Washington. But I knew he was in New York. And then I met Lee Hays, Pete Seeger, and Alan Lomax, and Alan's sister, Bess Lomax, and then I met Millard and Josh White. But clubs wasn't my bag, because I was a street player, but anyway, I developed into a club singer. I had never played a club before. I was pretty rough when I got to New York.

Sure, I went into clubs, but I'd blow them out of that club. I had a steel guitar and steel picks. I'd wham down on it, and I didn't have no sense of microphones, because, you know, I didn't pay a mike no attention. And they'd move it back. They couldn't get the guitar. They'd have to move the mike so far back, the guitar distorted. I just didn't have no club technique, period. And I had to develop technique. I could make it. I would listen. I learned.

Oh, I played everything for a dollar. I played everything. I did a lot of charity work. I wasn't a politician, but what did I care if there were politicians with some money involved? I played on shows with Leadbelly, Pete Seeger, and Alan and Bess, and all the people back in that day, in the forties. Unions were just beginning. They had these functions. They were just big singing functions to me. I mean, it wasn't nothing, and they were talking Communist, but didn't mean a thing to me. Communist—I'd never heard the word before. I thought they was talking a word that I missed in the dictionary. We didn't study it in school. And anyway, it was just singing, and I sang my same songs, I didn't change my songs.

Leadbelly was great. I never met a warmer man than Leadbelly. I started living with Leadbelly after I got to New York. 604 East Ninth Street, that was the first place, in a cold-water flat, him and his wife. Me and Sonny lived down there with Leadbelly, him and his twelve-string. Ah, boy, he was marvelous to live with. I mean, to be around. I wished I'd have known more about him. I lived with him about a year. Almost a year. You know, on and off. Him and Alice, but at the time I was there, he was strictly a professional. According to Hoyle. Yeah, he was great.

I started (recording with the Savoy label) December 12, 1944. I picked up an agent in New York, West Indian fella, Sam Manning. And I was singing on the street there.

The most money I made on the street was the night that Roosevelt died. And I was walking Lenox Avenue, singing a song, people throwing money out the windows, wrapped up in newspapers, and paper bags, and, "How long will you wait till I come down and sing it again?" I laughed...I was surprised. That was some of my hometown people. They wasn't New Yorkers. Mostly all southern people.

And I got invitations to people's houses and things like that, and I got this invitation for Savoy, to make some records, and I took it. But I had to pay this guy twenty-five cents out of a dollar. I didn't care about giving him twenty-five cents out of a dollar just to get some records, make some records...You know, easy money singing, and I had wrote a few songs for Savoy Records. I never will forget it 'cause I've got it down somewhere, December 12, 1944, WOR studio in New York.

I didn't have a big hit until 1948 with Savoy, but I had some good sellers, smooth sellers, but my lyrics used to be real shoddy. I used to do a lot of risqués. "Bad Blood," "Let Me Look Under Your Hood," and "Big Leg Woman." You know, them things couldn't be sent; they sold, but they were just southern records. They didn't get east. If a record went south and didn't sell, it didn't come east. It didn't come back. If it went south and became a hit, you'd find it in New York. I learned that after I got there. It had to go south first. All blues went south. It wasn't played in New York, it wasn't played at all. But my biggest song for Savoy was "My Fault," in 1948.

"I'm beggin'. It's all my fault. Just give me one more chance, and I'll correct it all. I'm beggin', babe, it's all my fault. Just one more chance, and I'll correct it all. You know it's my fault, just one more chance, and I'll correct it all." That was from a misunderstanding from a girlfriend, right down the street where I lived. She left a letter for me to read, so I might have a better understanding of her life before I met her. I took it jealously, threw the keys in her face, because I was living with her. And I saw a mistake that I'd made and I went back to get the keys. I said, "Give me my keys back."

She says, "It's your fault, Brownie. It was your fault. I won't give you my keys anymore. We'll always be friends, but we'll never be lovers no more."

I went and sat down and I wrote this song, "It's my fault, give me another chance, and I'll correct it." I just got a call from her—Christmas.

That was 1948. And that was my biggest seller with Savoy. My biggest seller. Oh, it made money, $2,000 royalties, and I was getting half a cent. I didn't even know what royalties were, because I never got any royalties from OKeh for records at thirty cents apiece, thirty-five at the most. And might have made some money, but I got money all right. I got some money from J. B. Long. I don't know where Long got it from. I never saw a royalty statement from OKeh Records.

In the forties records went for seventy-five cents, then they moved up to a dollar. Well, in the forties, yeah, thirty-five cents down south. J. B. Long sold my records at thirty-five cents apiece. My 78s, "Me and My Dog," came out at thirty-five cents. In a sleeve and all. But records moved up to seventy-five cents, 78 rpms. When you saw a record for seventy-five cents, it was a band, you know, big band record, something like that. Which I didn't buy. And I didn't see no royalties until I signed with, I had a gentleman's agreement, with Lavinsky. Lavinsky's the man who put me in (Musicians Union Local) 802. Because I was recording under my same union card that J. B. Long brought me to New York to record under. He stopped in Jersey and got it because they had offices there. Local 802 was in Newark at the time, and he picked me a transfer card, a permit to come to New York to record. In Chicago, you see, they had a split union there, black and white. So I wasn't in the union. I just got up and picked up a recording session card, and I still have that in my pocket. And the man walked in and called Lavinsky and said, "This man is not going to record for you because you know better than to have him in the studio. If you want him to record, you better get over here and get him a card. That was December 12, '44, I joined the union.

After I recorded with Savoy, I recorded for everybody, five alias names, went to England and recorded. Yes, I made records for every company in New York. I recorded as Blind Boy Fuller No. 2, Big Tom Collins, Spider Sam, Tennessee Gabriel, Henry Johnson, and there's another one, Blind Boy Williams, I played piano and my brother played guitar. I made records under all those names. Well, I could compete with myself. Because I was voice-wise, singing, I could sing with a sixteen-piece band and strum my guitar, and you wouldn't even know, unless you knew me very well, and which I had a way of doing it. And then I fixed my guitar, was a different style. I didn't play orchestration chords, so automatically, Brownie McGhee was the thing I was under. So if I made a record, and Spider Sam sold, Brownie McGhee would come along and do it. I got switched. And by that time, I had a family. My first kids was born, I was just trying to make a dollar. That was easy money, because I'd make, I'd get an advance from a guy, record signature, go cut the same song for somebody else. Until I got to England, and people was over there trying to find out was, is this Brownie McGhee, or who is this, it sounds like him. You know, his guitar, "I think it's him." Now then that's when I let the cat out of the water, in 1958. Nobody in the States knew it.

When I got to England, I just, I told it all to them, a writer over there, and he put it out, that, "Do you want to know who Brownie McGhee really is?" and I did that one after that, and then I made money. I mean, I got all the records I have made, every company I recorded for, I know.

I had my own label and sold it out to the Mafia. My label was called Atomic. It was just getting under way when they discovered me, and when the ban was on. You wouldn't remember the ban, when the union ban was on. They made no more records. That was in the forties. And Petrillo was master of 802 then. And nobody made records. They stopped making records. They put the ban on recordings, and so everybody was buying then, because people was trying to get records that couldn't get them, and I was in New York. Somebody says, "If you want to get a blues artist, a southern blues singer, Brownie McGhee." And they come and got me with money. And you be the artist, and we'll be the company. Now how much money you want? And that's the way it's done. And any songs that you don't know, buy the record and learn it, we want to record them and ship them down south. They begging for them.

The ban was because of the shellac (during World War II). That's right. Now you're talking. And the record (at that time) was, you play it twice, roll it up, and put it in your pocket. It was cardboard. Some of mine was like that. You play it four times on the jukebox, and that was it. And so I started to making records, and everybody was looking for me. I was a gimmick, but I didn't know how to be a crook. See, I always figured I played fair. I didn't sell out.

I married before in '49. I got with my wife in '48. After "My Fault." My first kid was born in '50. My oldest girl. And my wife died in '74, right here (in Oakland, California). I bought this house for her. In '74. My wife had three open-heart surgeries. Her name was Ruth. Wasn't she a pretty girl? Sweetest girl in the world, boy. Her maiden name was Ruth Dantzler. Too good for a bum like me, but we were together about thirty years. She was from South Carolina. I met her in New York. Yeah, I got the guitar that I had when I met her. It's sitting in there in the closet. I had four kids by her. She had two small kids at the time. I raised them. One of the boys, he lives out with my daughter. Out there, and the other one's got two kids, and she's in South Carolina.

I'll be seventy-five this year (1990). Everything is still like it was with my wife. My house is just like it was. I got my family; all my children are grown. I've got twenty-two grandchildren and six great-grands, and I'm a proud old man. Happy old man, too, you know, I'm not the type of guy, I'm not greedy and I'm not worldly, you know, I've had a good life. Not a bored life. I haven't looked back. Nobody did me so bad that I hate anybody. I love everybody; see, I love myself, that's why. That's what makes me love people, 'cause I love myself. Money has never been an obstacle. I've never let money get between me and happiness. I can't take it with me. I can't buy no passport to heaven, and can't ship it ahead and have no fun where I'm going. So I stay here and enjoy life as long as I can, and forget the rest of it.

I played in Harlem. Down to 59th Street and back up to, on 55th. In Harlem. And I made good money from Madison Avenue over to Eighth, St. Nicholas. And I'd go up and down on them avenues. Cross streets. Make good money. After I made myself known, they knew where I was, and I was from the South, and I met so many southern people there, I didn't have to worry about nothing. I made enough money in two days to last me to the next week and still have money in my pocket. Because I, as I said, I was just partying, sitting in bars drinking, and anybody would: "Play me a piece, give you a drink, man, you want a drink? Buy you a bottle." Didn't have to run from the police, so why you gonna buy whiskey when somebody's gonna give it to you? I got smart. I got New York smart. But I wasn't smart enough to relax until I got married. See, I kept saying there was something missing in my life in New York, and I didn't stay there until I tried to turn out the lights, and I wasn't getting anywhere. So I got married and I met my wife, that was it. Oh, boy, I thought, the whole world blossomed. Because she was a guiding light. She wanted me to play. She liked to hear me play—she loved to hear me play. And she liked to hear me write. My kids are getting royalties, now, from songs I used to write, because she okayed them. I stopped writing bad about women. And she says. "You know, I'm a woman, I ain't gonna buy that. You have to say something good about women." And you know, she'd say, "I don't like that verse." Certain things you say about songs, and I started changing my lyrics, and she said, "That's great," or, "That's beautiful," and I'd sing a song, she'd say, "That's beautiful. Be sure to record that." And everything she ever said to me to do, I was successful. She got me on Broadway. She caused me to come to California. She caused me to go to England.

"Do it for me," she says. "Now, when you don't want to do nothing for yourself, do it for me."

We'd sit down and talk, me and my wife would sit down and talk, you know. I loved her, too. She didn't know how much I loved her. I couldn't tell her how much I loved her because I always go on. I don't think you can love nobody and let them starve to death or let them suffer. And I knew I could make it when she wanted me to make it. But she felt that I could make it, too. And I used to say, "Oh, I've tried that, honey, you don't know," and she'd say, "Listen. You try it this time for me." I'd tried Broadway. And she says, "Go down. They want you to come down now. You go down for me now. 'Cause you didn't have me then."

I'd call her and say, "I got the job." You know what she gonna say, "I told you. You do this for me, didn't you?" And I come to California, and we eventually moved to California. She said, "Just go out there. They ain't offering you no money. They going to give you a place to sleep, and they offer you some money, take it. Go 'head. I'll be all right till you get back. You'll be back." And that's the way my wife was with me. She kept, "You can make it." And I wrote a song. She didn't get to hear it. I wrote it. I never recorded it until '75, and she died in '74. "Blues Have a Baby."

No, the blues had a baby, and they called it rock 'n' roll. See, that was before rock 'n' roll. Me and my wife was together before rock 'n'roll come out. And when rock 'n'roll started, I wrote this song, and we was up in the Berkshire Mountains, had the kids with us. And I said, I got an idea, and I wrote it.

She said, "Oh, Honey, why don't you record that? That's great." She always said, "That's the best idea you've had in a long time."

I said, "But Honey, if I record it now, and then, rock 'n' roll don't last, it's a dead idea."

She said, "Well, anyway, preserve it." She kept telling me, and I said, "Ah."

And I told her, I said, "If it lasts fifteen years, I'm gonna record it. I'm gonna give rock 'n' roll a chance. I'm gonna give the baby long enough to get fifteen years old." Blues had a baby and called it rock 'n' roll. I say, "I'm gonna let rock 'n' roll get fifteen." And that was my plan. And so I copyrighted it. And in '75, I recorded it.

"The blues had a baby. Blues is the mother, don't forget it, brother. It's been having sex with the world a long time. It's been underestimated because it was segregated, now the story must be told. You know the blues had a baby, and the whole world is calling it rock 'n' roll."

And she said, "Oh, God, that's beautiful." "From Bessie Smith to Janis Joplin, the blues has been a poppin'. Lady Day, she sang 'em, too. From California to Japan and other foreign lands, that's the way the story goes. The blues had a baby, the whole world's calling it rock 'n' roll. Listen everybody, don't get excited. It ain't no secret anymore. The blues had a baby, and the whole world is calling it rock 'n' roll."

So Muddy Waters made it number two; he wanted to do it. Said, "Brownie, I like the idea. How about me doing it?" So I sent him a sheet of it.

He said, "But I can't do those lyrics...." I didn't know that Muddy had a speech impediment, I didn't know, that Muddy had a style.

Like anybody else, you have a style of doing things. And he says, "I want to write and do it my way."

I said, "Well, just do 'Blues Had a Baby No. 2.'" So, they sent me a copyright, sent me a sheet, and I signed it. So we sold "No. 2" to Motown. We leased it to Motown. It's making money. It's making a few; it ain't gonna make you rich, but I enjoy a check coming in.

I went to England (in about 1958) for a friend of mine that was dying. Let me tell you. I didn't go to Europe for Europe. I didn't go to play for people over there. But what it was, I just figured that America didn't know me, why should I go over there and them understand me? They don't understand it. America don't. But my wife says, "Go ahead." I said, "Well, I'm going for Bill." She says, "I don't care who you go for. Go ahead." Bill says, "I'll have an operation." Big Bill Broonzy, I'm talking about.

I went to England for Big Bill Broonzy because he had lost his voice with cancer or whatever it was between the vocal cords. And anyway, he was losing his voice. He couldn't sing anymore, and he says, "Brownie, I'll have an operation if you and Sonny will go to Europe and represent the blues for me."

I said, "Bill, you know I'll do anything for you if you have an operation." So I drew up the deal with Bill in Chicago, come back home, and told my wife about it. She says, "All right." I called him back, and the agreement was set. And we went over in April of that year. And I went over and got off of the ship, and the red carpet was down. And I couldn't understand what in the hell it was for. I was embarrassed because I didn't know, I didn't go over to meet anybody, so I went over for Bill, I had Bill on my mind. I knew Bill, and I liked him. You know, he was an old pal of mine. He introduced me to a lot of people in Chicago. And when I got off in Southhampton, this red carpet, and the bands were playing, washboards and harmonicas and kazoos and all this crap was going on and cameras flashing, and I was moving out of the way, you know, and stepping back. Nobody told me what was gonna happen.

And I said, "Excuse me, please," and, "No, you." "Me?" Talking to a camera. "What in the hell do you want with me?" You know, I'm very, "What you taking pictures of me for? You don't know me, I've never been here before." You know, and all this. "Oh, this is for you. This is for you. You, you," and cameras. I never saw my guitar and my suitcase and nothing else I took over there. I was stupid, I didn't know what, I took trunks and everything, amplifiers. And I got to the hotel and I got over there and I didn't even know the people. What was I doing with a red carpet? And the people seemed to love me. And I got over there and it was an altogether different ball game. And I'd never been appreciated. But I hadn't done anything. But I didn't know my records were there. When I got there, my records had been playing, "Sporting Life" was a big thing, and you know, all this kinda stuff, and they were talking about me, and I couldn't understand it. In every magazine and newspaper, there I was on the front. And singing to people, and I didn't know. I ain't never played the electric guitar until I went back two or three years later. 'Cause it wouldn't play over there. And I loved the people. I fell in love with it.

I went over there so much, I told 'em, "Please, don't, I don't want to go," I went twice a year, and I used to go over at night and do a concert and come back the next day. They're calling me now. They just told me five weeks ago and trying to get me to come over there. I just really, I don't know, you know, it's just got to where, every time I looked up, I was there. It was marvelous. I made a deal with a guy in New Orleans. Come back and told the agent to cancel it. I didn't make a deal with him. I told him to get the agent, and the agent drew up a deal, and I said, "No, I don't want to go. I ain't going. I'm going to relax awhile."

What do I want to retire for? I'm the boss. I can play when I get ready. You know, I play piano, and I play my guitar. You see them sitting here? And I play all the time. No, I'm not retired. I don't have to. Now why should I get in the young people's way? I don't want to prove a point. I ain't got no points to prove. You know, I did it. I paid my dues. And I said something. And I've still got a lot to say. I don't want to get in their way, because people have things to say, and there's things coming along, and I know I'm it. Can't leave me out. I'm the captain. I'm what it is. I'm the blues, see. I'm America. And I know, I don't care who plays it, who does it, how they do it. It ain't me. I know who I am. I am the blues. Blues is America. And the blues is me. I'm an American. I'm not an import. I'm real. And so, why should I beat my head against the wall? Let them try and try. There's jobs offered to me. Plenty things. I do plenty things. But it's not the money. It's not the money. I don't feel like I should be sitting in the schools. I don't feel like that I should go out here, and I don't have to, financially. Mentally, I don't want to degrade myself to a point that I'll drop dead on a stage. I'm not seeing as well as I used to. I don't drive, and I'll get to be a nuisance. I'll get to be overbearing, I want things done my way, but they think I'm doing it because I'm old. And don't tell me that I'm old. I'm not. So I stay home and you can't abuse me.

That's what the blues is. Blues is truth. Blues is not a fairly tale, it's not an imagination. Blues is real. Because I say that it's a living thing. It's me. Blues is people. Blues is a people. It's a living thing. You know, you can't get rid of it. If you get rid of the blues, America's dead. And America will never die because of the blues, it has made America, and America has made me. I'm affiliated with this. I'm affiliated with this. I'm in it. I'm it. It's truth. You can't tell a lie about it. And you get away from it; you can't go around it. It's too wide. You can't get over it. It's too high. You can't go under it. It's too deep. See, I don't care what other people do and say about it. It doesn't insult me at all. You're only preaching my philosophy. Rock 'n' roll is, I say the blues had a baby and they called it rock 'n' roll. I love them for that. Name the children after some of my stuff. I love that. And if you feel like implying yourself with it, I love you. I love you for that. I know what it is, see. It's another one of those, they call my stuff everything. They call the blues everything, but really what it is because they don't know that it's truth. And so I don't mind. And when I know what it is, I'll sit back and listen as people do, and don't you know how happy I am? Keeping it alive. Blues will never die. And it's truth because no matter what you say or do, it's not fancy. You can only like yourself because you know yourself. You like the blues, you feel it, you enjoy it. You eat bread, it's a part of you. My life, my living, my job, everything.

I'm not a musician, I'm an entertainer. People got confused. I didn't study any of this here stuff. I haven't lost any sleep of preparing myself to go out here to tell people I had time. This is what I got out of life, is the way I feel. I know what I'm talking about. I'm not afraid to make an error because there's no errors in the truth. You just don't know it's truth because you haven't dealt with it thataway. I know who I am. I can look at myself with my eyes closed and know I'm good-looking. I know I'm happy because I am. It's not money. Nothing worldly makes me happy. Just me. I got plenty to eat. I got a couple of bucks. I got good cars. What good are they? I can't take them nowhere. I can't go nowhere. A man, well, you know, all of this is my philosophy. I live with this. You're born to die. You have to get out of somebody's way sometime. Can't live forever, otherwise the world's overcrowded. Now as it is, you only prepare to keep going. I left footprints in the sands of time. I can look back. I'm not ashamed to look back because I left footprints. I can turn around, and I can go back the same way I come. And I'm not ashamed. That's news to some people. I haven't did anything in life that I regret. Happiness. That's what keeps me going. I have made it this far. It's the sunshine that makes me feel good every day. I can go to two or three banks and get me some money, but that don't make me happy. You know, I'm so glad that I'm alive. I may not even get to the bank, but they'll say, "You know, McGhee was smiling." That's my life. That's where I am. Right here in this chair. This is heaven on earth to me.

Interview by Alan Govenar, March 17, 1990

Jay McShann

Jazz bandleader

Born: January 12, 1916, Muskogee, Oklahoma

Jay McShann learned to play the piano as a child in his parents' home in Muskogee, Oklahoma. At first, he played church songs, but after listening to a record (he thinks it was Mamie Smith) on the family Victrola, he became interested in blues and jazz. McShann attended the Manual Training High School and began performing professionally with the Gray Brothers Band, a six-piece family group that came through Muskogee. After graduating from high school, McShann moved to Tulsa and got a job with Al Denny's big band. He eventually settled in Kansas City, where in time he was able to establish himself as a bandleader and pianist. McShann has performed the big-band swing sound throughout his career, touring around the United States and abroad.

I grew up in Muskogee, Oklahoma. It was a little small town that was the county seat of the Five Civilized Tribes. It was kind of an Indian town. The population wasn't over 30,000. I never did know it to go over 30,000. In fact, after all those years have passed, I think it's lucky if it's 40,000 now.

My dad's name was Jesse McShann, J. S. McShann. And my mother was Leona. Her maiden name was McBee. My mother was from Alabama. And Dad's folks came from Mississippi and settled in Dallas, Dallas County. My dad brought the family to Oklahoma; I guess he was looking for work. Dad drove a truck, a furniture truck, and worked for years there in Muskogee.

When I was in school, they wanted my parents to buy me a horn, and my folks were too poor. They didn't have any money to buy me a horn. And we had a piano there at the house, and I couldn't get a horn. So, I just started fooling around on the piano. I was just a kid around the house, probably around seven or eight years old. Nothing else for me to do, and neighbor kids would come over, and they would bang on the piano, and then I'd turn around and bang, too. Kids in the neighborhood, those that did have instruments, sometimes they'd come by the house, bring their instruments and, you know, toot on their instruments—just something for kids to do. I think that's the way it started.

Then the way my folks were, they were very church-minded, and I can remember my mother playing a few church songs. She gave my sister lessons, and my sister would play for the church choir. So then, I listened to my sister; I just listened to her, and when she couldn't get to church to play for the choir, then they'd send me along to do it. Well, I hadn't taken

Jay McShann (at piano) and his band in Dallas, Texas, in 1941, with Charlie Parker (third from left) and Walter Brown (second from left). (Archive Photo)

any music or anything, but I could hear; I guess I had an ear. And things that I'd heard, I'd play for the church. I'd just tell them, "Number 86," or whatever it was, and I'd play it because I'd heard her play it, and I'd just watch what she was doing and would do it.

I remember one time, I noticed (at the furniture company where my dad worked) there were some broken records in the big old truck outside. So I picked these records up and brought them inside. We had a little old Victrola that had the old bulldog and the horn on it, the megaphone. And so I brought one of these records in, and it was either Bessie or Mamie Smith. And the name of the song was "The Backwater Blues." And I put that on, and when I put that on, I knew that I liked the blues. I put it on there; it was a half-broken record, but I put it on, and I knew right then, because I liked what they were doing. It was Bessie Smith, either Mamie Smith or Bessie. I don't remember which one it was. But I tried to do the same thing that I heard. Just trial-and-error method. I just tried to play along with it.

Then eventually, after so long a while, I started to kind of get a little bit of a sound. And I just continued, and the next thing you know, I started to sound a little bit more like the record. And that's what happened. I think that was a turning point. I'd say I was about ten or eleven years old.

There was one guy around Musgokee named John Maddox who played, but he wasn't a bluesman. He just played the piano, and played songs like "Molly and me and the baby makes three" and that kind of stuff. And a lot of stuff that they were recording in New Orleans. He had a piano. They had a piano. They stayed across the street from us. And I used to listen to him. And they had a player, too, as well. And he'd play the player piano sometimes. I could tell the difference when he wasn't playing the player piano and was playing himself. I was training my ear all the time, and I didn't realize it. I was getting a lesson in ear training. It just happens naturally, but you don't realize it at the time.

I didn't see too much discrimination in Muskogee because I can remember back when a lot of the white barbershops always had black barbers. I remember that way back. And I used to wonder, but I never did know, but I do remember that blacks used to cut whites' hair all the time, you know.

It wasn't a bad relationship between the Indians and the blacks. In fact, it wasn't a bad relationship at all. They got along pretty good. I think a lot of times, those old Indians, they liked the taste of that stuff (whiskey). They liked that lightning, and every once in a while, they'd get to acting up, that stuff would get to working on them. And I often thought about it, and I used to hear people talk about too many Indians. But I think the reason is, how that thing got started, I mean, too many chiefs and no Indians. I think how that got started because when they'd get full of that mess, it'd make him feel good when they call him "Chief," you know. He'd be just an Indian, he wouldn't be no chief, but all Indians they called chiefs. And I think when they called 'em "Chief," that gave them a big feeling, you know, and they liked that. That's why they said no Indians, all chiefs.

I got started playing music professionally with a family group named the Gray Brothers Band. And they used to come through Muskogee, and they would, the old man, their dad, used to be an old music teacher, from Carolina, somewhere out in North Carolina, or South Carolina, and they settled out from Muskogee in another town called Haskell. And they would play dates all over the state. They did dates in Tulsa, Harmony, just all over the state of Oklahoma. And sometimes they wouldn't have a piano player. So when they didn't have a piano player, they thought I could play piano, and they'd come get me to come play with them. And they'd probably wind up with about a six-piece group. They'd come get me to play with them, but I didn't know that much about playing. But what little I did know, I got that while I was in school.

I went to the Manual Training High School right there in Muskogee. They'd bring a music teacher maybe two times a month or something like that. And before that I went to grade school in Muskogee at the Douglass

Grade School. And then I left Douglass and went to Dunbar. And when you leave Dunbar, that just goes to the sixth grade, when you leave there, then you go to junior high, which was Manual Training Junior High. And then when you hit high school at the ninth grade, nine through twelve, high school. Junior high and high school were all together in the same building.

So, they'd bring a music teacher over there, this particular guy—I can't think of his name. He used to just come in and out of there. But then finally, they brought some guy from Texas, and he would teach a few elementary subjects, as well as music. And then music was on the side. And he taught guys to play the horns and things like that. I guess that was on the side as well as subjects like English and things like that that he taught. And so he was really the guy that really, I guess, kind of started me.

He told me one day, he says, "I'd like for you to play in assembly."

And I said, "No, no, I don't want to play in assembly. I can't play. First of all, I don't play well enough to be playing in assembly."

He said, "Well, I want you to. I just want you to do it." And he asked me, he said, "Just do it for me."

And I didn't want to do it. And I kept telling him no, I didn't want to. But anyway, I finally decided I would go on and do it. But I asked him, I said, "Well, what can I play? I don't know anything." And actually, the only thing that I knew was to try to play that blues thing that I'd heard Mamie Smith do. I'd try to sound like the piano that was backing her up. I said, "If I play that, I'll be in trouble in school."

He said, "No you won't. I'm behind you." He said, "Play whatever you want to play. Just play that," he said. "Play that."

So I played that, and you know how kids' emotions are. When I'd hit that old blues sound, ding, ding, ding, de-ding, de-ding, de-ding, ding, ding, then the kids squalled, they hollered. These kids hollered. I figured I was in trouble. I said, "I knew I shouldn't have done it."

Sure enough, the next day in school, my teacher was giving me hell all day. I had a teacher, she was giving me hell about playing that low-down stuff in assembly hall. And it was one teacher, mostly, that gave me all that trouble about it. And she spoke about it in class.

She said, "One of our members in our classroom here got up and played some undesirable music, and blab, blab, blab, and blab, blab, blab, and I really felt insulted. I felt bad about that. Because I didn't want to do it in the beginning, and this other teacher begged me to do it for him.

I said, "well, I ain't gonna never play and do nothing concerning it no way of nothing." It was a kind of disheartened feeling. So I wouldn't. They'd always try to get me to play after that, and I never would.

Anyway, later on, they kind of loosened up a little bit. And there was a gal who used to play, called Lovie Bryant. She would get up there and play when we were having football games, like when we were playing Tulsa or Oklahoma City or McAlester or some town. They'd have what they call a pep meeting before the game. And the first thing, I never did understand it, she'd play anything she wanted to play and they never said nothing about it. I guess it was because of the game and it's supposed to be a pep meeting. But nobody never mentioned a word. And she would get up there and play anything that she wanted to play.

So finally, this guy that was teaching band, he finally got a little old group together and he had me playing piano with them. He played trumpet and he had a saxophone player and he had a trombone player and a bass player and a drummer. And he had me on piano. And we'd get together and play on days like Christmas and dates and things like that come around, or private parties—well, sometimes he'd take me with him and we'd go play these things.

Anyway, he would take me on little old gigs, and we'd make gigs. We might play a breakfast dance; the breakfast dance started at five o'clock in the morning and we'd go until about eight or nine. And then if we played some town in football; well, that night after the game, they'd have a thing down at the hall, the dance hall, convention hall, or whatever it is. And then they'd bring a band, and he'd bring us in and we'd get up there and play a few things. And I never will forget. See, I hadn't had any training. I didn't know what to do. I remember one time, I think it was the first gig that I went with him on, and he kept telling me, he'd always turn around and tell me, "Complement the blues." Well, I didn't know what the heck he was talking about, because I thought he was talking about it as a compliment, you know what I mean. He said, "Complement the blues." But he meant accompaniment. I did know what accompaniment meant. And he'd get up and blow the trumpet and maybe a sax player would blow, and he'd turn around, and while he'd be blowing, he'd say, "Complement the blues." Lean over in my ear.

And I said, "What in the heck is he talking about?"

He said, "Complement the blues."

I was just thinking. Did he want me to say this is a nice blues, or what? And after a while I just started to play comp; you've heard them talk about comp, that piano players play behind horns. I just started comping. I didn't know whether I was comping, what I was doing. But that's what they call it: "comp."

I'd accompany him. I'd play behind the horns. See what I mean: We're going along with him, we're playing along with him, but we're not taking the lead. He's got the lead. He's the man that's telling the story. What we're doing, we're helping him to tell the story. But we're staying out of his way. So I just started doing my hands, one hand down, another hand up. One down, another, and he said, "That's what I've been trying to get you to do all night."

I said, "My goodness, why didn't he tell me to do that?" You know, play with one hand up and the other hand down. But I found out what "accompany" meant. So I said, "Well, spell this thing for me. You talk about 'complement the blues.'"

After I finished high school, I wanted to go off to college, but I didn't have any money, I didn't have nothin'. I was poor, poor as Job's turkey. And so, what I did, I got a letter from the Gray boys. They was playing in Tulsa at a club named La Joanne. And so they told me, they said, "Come on to Tulsa, Mac." They says, "We think we can get you a job over here." Say, "If we don't get you a job here where we playing, we'll get you a job somewhere else."

So, I came on to Tulsa, went over there, and I walked around there for about two weeks, just trying to find a job. I had an uncle in Tulsa, and I was staying with him. Wasn't nothin' happening. I was just ready to give it up. And so these guys, they'd been trying to get me jobs, but they couldn't find nothing. Things were just bad then. You talk about bad times. Times was tough then. So one day I had been out looking for a job and couldn't find one, but I heard a band rehearsing, and I followed the sound. Then I realized they were upstairs somewhere rehearsing. Well, I seen people just walking up the stairs, going up there; so I did the same thing, went on up there and walked over and sat down. I listened to the rehearsal. Then I heard these guys talking about how they needed a piano player. So I waited till they got through rehearsing before I'd said anything about how I could play, because see, I couldn't play any of their music. They had an orchestration sitting up there on the piano. And after they finished rehearsing, I told the guy, I said, "Y'all still need a piano player?"

He said, "Yeah…Man, why didn't you say something about that, you play piano?"

I said, "No, but I think I can do what you want to do. I think I can play what you probably want."

"Well," he said, "Okay." And they called a number and they put this number up on the piano, and they stomped it off, and I just went on and played what I'd heard them doing. Played on along. And so they put these other tunes up there that they had practiced. And I just went on with them.

Then they said, "Play something and take off on something." You know, that just means play something by myself. So I played something by myself.

They said, "Man, this cat, he can read and fake." But I couldn't read nothing. And wasn't faking that much, just enough to try to get by. And so they said, "Well, look, man, I think you can do the job." They says, "We're playing Saturday night." And they gave me the job. So that was with Al Denny's band. Al had about a twelve- or fourteen-piece band. He had a big-band sound, see, because he had three trumpets, four saxophones, three trombones, bass, drum, guitar, and piano. And they would get these orchestrations, and they'd play them.

Al Denny put me to work with his band. And then by being around there, I got a chance to work with other groups off and on. Then finally I went up to Kansas, because there was a lot of work up in Kansas, the southern part of Kansas. In fact, all over Kansas. Because Kansas was dry, it made it good for private clubs up that way. There weren't too many musicians hanging around up that way. But the nightclubs that would open, they wanted musicians. They were always wanting musicians in these little small towns, like Ark City and places like that, these small towns all around Wichita. Out in eastern Kansas, western Kansas, southern, southwest Kansas, all those little places. So, I went to work up there in Ark City, Kansas. That's Arkansas City, Kansas. I went to work up there in a club. And the Gray Brothers, they was working up there in another club. I worked up there until the club closed. The Gray Brothers, when the gig ran out, they left and went to Shawnee, Oklahoma. Now that's right out of Oklahoma City. They were playing with another group called Eddie Hill. And while they were with Eddie Hill, I decided to go to junior college.

I went to junior college in Ark City. And I did about a year there at junior college. And then there weren't any gigs happening up there, so they called for me to come down and join them in Shawnee. So I left school and came on, joined them in Shawnee. There used to be a place around there called the Old Bluebird in Shawnee, Oklahoma. It would be open about four nights a week. And we'd work there, and on the other nights that we'd be off, sometimes we'd book somewhere around, oh, other little towns, for one-nighters or something like that.

This was all before World War II. We'd book little old towns like Wewoka, Seminole; these were all oil towns down there in Oklahoma. And in them little oil towns, people are always looking for somewhere to go. And we'd go down there and make a little noise for them. So we stayed there, oh, off and on, until we got a chance to go to Albuquerque, New Mexico.

We went out to Albuquerque. And we played out there at a place called Selves Resort. That was, I'd say, about twelve or fourteen miles east of Albuquerque right in the mountains. It was a white resort. We worked there, at this club there, until the club manager and his wife, they divorced and they broke up. And after they broke up, he got on a rampage and came out there and shot her. He shot his old lady. And then her mother was living out there with her, and her mother went and cut her throat. And then the lady's dad had been somewhere, up in Colorado, somewhere, and they contacted him and told him about the tragedy. And he came there.

Well, he knew us. And he said, "One of you boys...."

Somebody had stole the money out of the club. He went in there, checking to see if the band had done it. He said, "Well, I know you guys well enough, I don't think you guys done it." That let us off. But the thing fell on this Mexican guy that was bartending half the time. He and I had been pretty good buddies. So the old man just swore it was him.

I said, "No, no, it's not him."

And told the old man, "Of all the things, I just want you to know that this guy did not get that money." Well, I knew that the bartender didn't get it, because one of the guys wanted to pay my way back to Oklahoma City. That's the way life goes. And I knew he didn't have any money. But I stayed there and worked with some of the local guys around there for about a year and a half. And then I heard about this club back up in Ark City, and I went back to Ark City and went to work. And then when the club in Ark City closed, I decided I'd go to Omaha. I had an uncle in Omaha. I thought I'd go up there and see what was happening, music-wise. And on my way to Omaha, I had to change buses in Kansas City.

I asked one of the guys there at the bus station about how far the Reno Club was, where Basie had been working.

And he said, "Well, it ain't that far. It's just about a couple of blocks."

So he told me where it was, and I said, "Well, I'll run around there and holler at some of the musicians." And I went around there and hollered at some of the guys, and at that time Basie had gone east and Bus Moten had the band there. That was the nephew of Benny Moten. Benny died during that time. I knew some of the guys I had played with around Tulsa and other places in the band.

They said, "Mac, what are you doing in Kansas City?"

I said, "Man, I'm on my way to Omaha."

They said, "No, no, no, no, don't go no further. Stop right here in Kansas, 'cause man, it ain't nothing happening in Omaha like it is in Kansas City. Man, you'll get a gig here in a minute, in a day or two."

I said, "Buddy, my money's too low."

He (bassist Bill Hadnott) says, "Well, I tell you what. You take my key. You take my room and keep my room, and I'll stay at my girlfriend's house." So I couldn't turn that down.

I said, "Okay." And sure enough, within a couple or three days, I did have a gig.

The old-timer called Elmer Hopkins was around Kansas City, and he was always good for a gig. He always got a lot of jobs during that time. I ran into Hop, and old Hop says, "Man, you that new piano player in town?"

He says, "I think I got a gig for us." He played drums. And he did. He had a gig for me. And he took me on this gig. And the gig that he took me on was a neighborhood gig. See, in the neighborhood gigs, you only played from eight till twelve or nine to one or 1:30. So that's the way we were working. But the rest of the musicians in town, all the happenings in the clubs and things, they were going to work, some of them, at eight o'clock at night and working until six in the morning. And where Basie and them had been, they'd go to work at nine and get off at three, sometimes get off at four. And those were the kind of hours that musicians were putting in around here then. So by being on this gig with Hop, this neighborhood gig, the hours weren't bad.

Well, I got a chance to get around and meet a lot of the musicians and the club owners in Kansas City because when I'd get off at say, one o'clock or 1:15, they were just getting started good. And I'd go to this club one night and another club another night, and then that's when I found out how things were happening. They used to have what they called a "spook breakfast." All the clubs in town go to the spook breakfast, wherever it was designed to be. It'd be Monday night at one club, Tuesday night another club, Wednesday another club, Thursday, Friday, Saturday, over and over, different clubs in town every night. So then I really got a chance to get around and find out what was happening, you know. The first spook breakfast I went to started at five, maybe, or six, and was supposed to be over with by nine or ten. And so it was always people that ain't ready to go. They're still partying. So it was always some singers around there, and these singers say, "Man, hey, come here. We can make some extra change. These people still ready to party. Come on." So I'd go on with the singer and I'd play the piano, back him up with the piano, and we'd stay there and make us an extra $10 or $12. And I liked that.

Kansas City was everything, just like the guys said. And I decided then, I said, "No, no, I don't want to leave Kansas City." Kansas City was wide open, and you could get action twenty-four hours a day. They didn't close the clubs. The guy that was cleaning up, he'd come in there and clean the place up, and the guys all over at the bar, he'd move them over there to the other side, and he'd clean up the bar, all down the bar, everything. When he finished that, they'd go back over to the bar, drinking, and he'd finish cleaning up where they just left. It was interesting to me.

After I left Hop, I went with a guy named Dee Stewart. Well, they called him Prince Stewart. And he had about an eight-piece band, and he had some good musicians with him. And I liked that because I didn't have any experience, and every time I could get a chance to get around some guys who were good and had the experience, I could always try to learn something.

Basie had just gone east when I got here. He had gone east, Basie and Andy Kirk's band. Both bands, both were big bands. I mostly stayed around Kansas City until after I got a band, and then I left and went east. Jay McShann and his band. I had about twelve pieces.

Well, I didn't actually leave Kansas City. A whole lot went down before I left, you know what I mean. What I'm trying to say is this: It was 1940 before I actually left Kansas City and went to New York. But we did one-night things all the way into New York. We played right out of Chicago, I remember it was on a Christmas. That was in Gary, Indiana. We did Gary, and then we did, oh, I think, Battle Creek, Michigan, then we went into Detroit. We did a week in Detroit at the theater there. I guess we got to New York, I'd say in January of '41, and we had left Kansas City around Thanksgiving, 1940.

Well, we stayed in New York at least six months before we ever got back out, I think. We had recorded before we went to New York. Our first recording was in Chicago, but it was a disaster, because, see, at that time, I didn't even know that you had to have a contract to go in there to record. We just went on up there to record, and when the union found out we were in town to record, boy, they jumped right down our throat. And they stopped everything. It was on the Decca label. And so then this guy realized, he come and told me, "Man, I didn't know you guys didn't have a contract. I'll tell you what, next year, I'll be going to the West Coast to do some recording. So I'll set you guys up for that time in Dallas, have y'all meet me in Dallas, and you won't have no problem. And you get straight with the union and everything, so you won't have no problems like this one in Dallas."

So the first place we actually recorded was Dallas. That was early '41. Well, I'll say '40, last of '40. That was for Decca, yeah. Oh, we recorded "Hootie Blues," "Confessin' the Blues," "Vine Street Boogie," and "Swingmatism." I had a singer then. That was Walter Brown. He was the blues singer.

Well, quite naturally, after we left New York, and during the war years we got on the road. Ain't nothing else for you to do, you got a band, you get on the road and do one-nighters and whatever you can do, whatever they book you.

I never played with Basie. Basie played piano, and I played piano, too. But Basie and I knew each other because the same fella that used to help Basie out when Basie was in Kansas City did the same thing for me when I came to Kansas City. He was a rich white fella here that had money. He liked to play the piano himself, and that's how he and Basie met up. His name was Walter Bales. In fact, he helped him when they sent Basie east. He was a big help to Basie.

Buster Smith was with the Basie band. Buster was a hell of a musician. And then, see, what happened, they made some changes in the band and Buster came back, and that was the first band that I was telling you about that I worked with in Kansas City, that Dee Stewart. Buster was playing with Dee Stewart then when I joined Prince Stewart. And I was glad to get around guys like Buster, because Buster had all that experience. And he could write, he could do anything musically. He could do it all, and so Buster was doing a lot of writing for Prince Stewart at that time. And then Buster also played three or four instruments. He could play the violin, he could play those stringed instruments, the guitar, he could play the piano, sax, and clarinet. Sax and clarinet, he was just out of sight. And when we'd be playing, we'd tell him to take a solo, and he wouldn't take but one solo. You'd have to keep after him, make him take them. "Take another one, take another one. Blow another one." You'd have to stay on him. But he could just—his ideas could come so fast. And he was so full of good ideas. And we would like for him always to take solos, because he was full of ideas, and he inspired the group.

Yeah, Buster Smith, that was my man. I thought there was nobody like Buster because I always felt that Buster didn't know his potential. Yeah, he didn't know what all he could do. It was just a shame that…. I know that every time we'd call and try to find out where Buster was, or what was going on, they'd say, "Man, Buster's down in Texas, down there at a place right out east of there where they built all that fishing and stuff out there." He liked to go fishing out there, yeah. That's out around Rockwall (Texas).

I never made any moves, particularly, to organize a band. But we went to work…they came down from Chicago and wanted me to take a trio in there at the Three Deuces. And so, well, there were three musicians going in there. But they didn't know who the bandleader was going to be. So we went into Chicago again and didn't deposit any contract. And so then the guy from the union come down there, and he was raising hell with the guys. It was just the bass, drum, and piano. So he thought the drummer was supposed to be the bandleader.

Drummer said, "No, no, no, hell, no. I wasn't supposed to be no bandleader." So then he asked the bass player.

Bass player: "No, no, no."

So they said, "Well, there ain't but one left. And that's you, McShann, so you the bandleader."

And they said, "What in the hell you think you're doing, coming down here in our territory and not bringing a contract? And you think you'll get on this job and play."

So they raised all that hell with me, and so after they got through, then they said, "Okay now, tell you what we're gonna do. We're gonna straighten you out. We're gonna get you straight. We're gonna issue a contract, like what should have been done in the beginning. Now you're the leader, and here's your sidemen. Put your sidemen's name on the back."

They showed me all that stuff, the things I should have known but I didn't. Somebody should have known. Anyway, they made me bandleader. And I've been the bandleader ever since.

Well, I keep going; ain't no need of stopping. I've been all over the country. And the place I liked playing the most was the one that paid the most money. I used to go to Europe every year. From 1968 up until last year. I haven't been to Europe this year. Last year, we spent more time in Europe. We went all over. We had a ball in France. France was good. England was good. Let's see. All over. Spain was good. In Europe they usually paid more. In the States, they just figure, "Well, here's another band."

My sound has changed as I've gotten older. It changes, but I don't know how to explain it. Well, I might play more blues now than I did then. When I was coming up, it was the big-band thing. See, Kansas City always did swing. New Orleans had a two-beat sound, and Kansas City had a four-beat. And a two-beat sound sounds like marching music, see. If you notice, most of that Dixieland sounds like marches. It was two beats, whereas, in Kansas City it was four beats and it swings. That was the difference. The four-beat was swinging more, far more than the two-beat. The two-beat sound, on a good two-beat tune, it sounds great. It's hard to beat that two-beat sound. But for swinging, Kansas City had it. And Kansas City musicians did swing; there's no question about it.

INTERVIEW BY ALAN GOVENAR, JANUARY 6, 1998

Martha Nash

Community worker; doctor's widow
Born: September 26, 1925, Sedalia, Missouri

Martha Nash grew up in Waterloo, Iowa. Her father, Steven Furgerson, was a physician, who left his home in Austin, Texas, after graduation from high school to pursue better educational opportunities in Iowa. Nash recalls that "racism wasn't formal" in Iowa, while segregation laws in Texas were strict and readily apparent. Nash's father attended the University of Iowa, where he earned an M.D. degree. Nash went to high School in Waterloo, Iowa, and then enrolled at Talladega

College in Alabama, where she was awarded a B.A. degree in history. While at Talladega, she met Warren Nash, whom she married in 1948. After her husband received his M.D. degree from Creighton University in Omaha, Nebraska, they relocated to Iowa.

I was born in Missouri, but that was just for two or three months, and then my mother came back to Iowa to work while she was waiting for my father to finish his internship. All except for about three or four months of my life, the early years were spent in Iowa, except for the time I went to college and the time my husband was in medical school in Omaha.

My maiden name was Furgerson. Martha Ann Furgerson. And that was spelled F-u-r-g-e-r-s-o-n. And my last name is Nash. My mother's name was Lilly Nina—her maiden name was Williams. And my father was Lee Burton Furgerson. And we spelled it that queer way. The rest of his relatives changed theirs to F-e-r-g-u-s-o-n, but he kept it that way be-cause his school records and all were spelled that way.

My father was born November the 23rd, 1898, and my mother was born October the 10th, 1902. My father died in August of 1948. And my mother died in October of 1973. My mother was born in Des Moines, Iowa, but grew up—she split her time between Des Moines and Sedalia (Missouri) and then finished high school in Cedar Rapids. My father was born in Navasota, Texas, and when he was about ten, they moved into Austin. He went to high school at Tillotson, which had a high school there and was located at Austin. His oldest sister had a house there; he grew up under the shadow of the University of Texas. His sister's name was Sara Manor. And, in fact, I think her house was where Interstate 35 goes through the Johnson Library. It was in that area.

His mother sent him north to college (because of the racial condi-tions in Austin). When he finished high school, the war had started. The United States had entered World War I. So she thought that if he got drafted, he'd have a better chance of staying in school if he were in Iowa, rather than staying in Texas. And he had an older brother, named Steve Furgerson, who had moved to Iowa City. So that's why he came to Iowa.

His father's name was Steven Furgerson, and we have no idea when he was born because he died when my father was about ten, and I don't know if my father knew much about him. He was an itinerant preacher, he fancied himself, so he did some preaching. But they worked in the cotton fields around Navasota, too. My grandmother, her name was Martha Holmes. We don't know when she was born. She said she could remem-ber waving at the soldiers. She thought she was around three or four when the Civil War was ending. The man that owned her supposedly sold her mother while she was still a small child, a very small child. We've never

Martha Nash (left) with her friends Gloria (middle) and Josey (right) at Talladega College in Alabama 1943–1944 (Iowa Women's Archive)

been able to figure out who she might have stayed with. My brother-in-law has it pieced together that maybe there were some people that they considered almost like relatives, that they may be who she grew up with. And she didn't want to have much to do with the man that was her father. Evidently he was some kind of merchant because this story is that one time after she was grown and living in Austin and he was in Austin, he wanted to come and see her, and she wouldn't. So there was some bitterness there. Maybe it's about their mother. I don't know. But he was supposed to be her father. He was Irish, I guess, and he lived in that area. What is it, the 1890 census records that are the ones that got burned? They were kept in Kansas, and they had a fire and a lot of them got burned. So it's hard to trace down, we don't know because in the 1860s, they didn't record by name in Texas. They just said "female slave." So we don't know, and then in 1880, she was married and living with her husband, I guess. So we don't know—those years, it's hard to trace her. Then her husband, my great-grandfather, all we know is that supposedly he and his brothers were born and grew up in Mississippi, and when the Union soldiers started approaching the place where they were living, the man who owned them sold them into Texas. And we don't know what their names were. Somewhere they adopted (the name) Furgerson, and she lost track of any brothers she might have had. One time (two of my sisters and me) we came down to Texas and were checking the census records, and my brother-in-law has delved into some of the records of Navasota and all, but we haven't really been able to locate them, and nobody's ever gone to check to see if there was anything in the Freedman's Bureau.

So, during the war, my father was assigned to the Student Army Training Corps. He entered the University of Iowa. I think he had a football scholarship, but he didn't play football. University of Iowa was integrated. Iowa had had public accommodations laws. They weren't always enforced. Before the Civil War, I think they had something about education...about not having separate schools. I think it grew out of the incident in Danville, Iowa, where they tried to lynch somebody or something. The only places that were separate—you know they were, because George Washington Carver went to school in Iowa, in Ames and so forth. So there were several who came up to Iowa from Texas along with my father. That continued—even when I was a little girl, there were quite a few who had come from Texas to Iowa to school.

Racism wasn't formal (in Iowa). But it still was there. They (my father and other black students) didn't stay in the dorms. They had black fraternities—there was women's clubs. It wasn't until my sister next to me, after she went to the university that they integrated the dorms. So it must have been about '46, '45 or '46 because someone came and talked to my father about why we went to Iowa. I was going to Talladega then. In Talladega, Alabama. One of the historical black colleges.

I was born in '25, we came to Iowa in '27. To Waterloo. Waterloo has the highest percentage of blacks. Most of them came around the end of World War I. There was a strike at the Illinois Central (Railroad). A lot of them were brought up from Mississippi, Holmes County and those counties that were between Chicago and New Orleans on the Illinois Central line, to work on the railroad. And then some families came in the twenties and so forth.

My father was a doctor, so some of the things that a lot of people had, we didn't have. But there were places in Waterloo that had signs that said, "We reserve the right to solicit our patronage." So we didn't have free access to restaurants and so forth. Education was no problem. They didn't want to sell or rent houses to blacks, so most of them were confined to an area that was bounded by the Illinois Central yards, and not too many blacks beyond that. It was kind of a narrow district. They began to break out of it at the end of World War II.

My father got his medical degree at Iowa. He went all the way through undergraduate and graduate. And when we came to Waterloo, he was the only black doctor. There had been a couple, but they didn't stay. In fact, there was a fellow who was a lawyer. When he was looking for a place to practice, he had written the people in Des Moines to come to Waterloo, set up a practice.

My father had about half and half, white and black (patients). He used to say it was a funny thing. If you were a professional person, if you were good and did a good job, you were accepted. There were other black doctors in Iowa. There were several in Des Moines. There was the Harper brothers in Fort Madison, and one of them was in Keokuk, two of them in Fort Madison. There was Dr. Scales in Des Moines. Dr. Bush, who was a dentist, in Sioux City.

There were some things (that made you feel there was discrimination and racism). But you know when you grow up in the North, you had some hidden things and then, because my father was a doctor, my family was regarded as somehow different from all the worker blacks. So we didn't run into it openly. And I used to go places, because of my color, I'm not very dark, and my mother was light. I used to go when I was in junior high, the junior high was close to the downtown. I used to go in restaurants. A white could take me for Hawaiian, anything but black, so I used to go a lot of different places. But we didn't eat out much in those days because most of us didn't have that much money. I grew up in the Depression.

In fact, health insurance didn't begin to come in for people with some of the big employers, John Deere and Rath, until around 1940. Blue Cross and Blue Shield came and did this. So up until then, nobody had a lot of spare money. We created a social life with friends in Iowa City and Fort Madison and Des Moines; we had a social circle.

We used to have Emancipation Day there on the first Monday in August in the Electric Park. Now you didn't go to the Electric Park any other time of the year. The NAACP used to have that big dinner. We were always fighting housing. And it was hard for blacks to get loans for home improvements, so my father and attorney Fields started a savings and loan in order to try and get that—my father was very active with the NAACP on and off. He felt he owed it to the community. When people would come, like Marian Anderson and things like that, he always invited people to our house. Nobody expected to stay in hotels. Iowa had a public accommodations law, but it wasn't enforced until they instituted a series of sit-ins at a drugstore in Des Moines. And I think we had a sit-in here, too, at one of those big department stores. They had a tearoom, and they didn't want to serve you up here. A friend of mine, she was an older lady, but she and a group of NAACP had a sit-in. And that would have been in the '40s. So race, you know, it wasn't de jure, but three was de facto segregation.

I went to high school here in Waterloo, and college at Talladega. I had a B. A. in history. Then I got married in 1948. My husband's name was Warren Nash. He was from Birmingham. And we met in Talladega. Then we moved to Waterloo. And then he went to medical school, started medical school in the fall of '49. He went to Creighton in Omaha. My father started practicing medicine in '27 and he died in 1948, August of '48.

The leadership of the NAACP was strong, you'd have monthly meetings, but they weren't always so strong. We used to have, when we had the Emancipation Day things, speakers like William Hasty and Thurgood Marshall used to come out. They were with the NAACP then, you know, in the national office. My father spent one term on the national nominating committee for choosing board members. He had a trip to New York. He went to several conventions. I went to two of them, one in Richmond, Virginia, in '39, and the one in Houston, Texas, which was in '41. And the branches were in Waterloo and Davenport. We were working for anti-lynching laws, and then the whole thing with education started. I remember when we went to the NAACP convention in Richmond, my father had somehow known Roy Wilkins as a boy, because he worked out of St. Paul when he was in school, on the railroad, you know, during the summers. He had known Roy Wilkins when Roy Wilkins was a young boy, but I know we met people like Dr. Louis Wright; he was a surgeon. But there were those kind of people that we were constantly getting to know. Some of them stayed at our house sometimes, like Thurgood Marshall.

Thurgood Marshall had a great sense of humor. He was always telling tall tales, stories. We didn't know they were famous then. Like William Hasty. He later become a judge and all, but he was just a staff person with the NAACP. We had a lot of people who were famous as musicians. They didn't expect to see that, these black folks in Iowa—any black folks in Iowa. Well, we had Duke Ellington, almost all the fellows in the band, at one time or another, Clark Terry.

Well, when you got to know Duke Ellington, he was very friendly. At first, he had a way of protecting himself from slights, and so he didn't let you see the real self. He was very easy to know, very comfortable.

Oh, there were clubs, I don't know if you'd call them nightclubs. I don't know (their names), because we didn't go to any of them. We met the musicians when they came to play concerts—Duke Ellington and them. The first time I got to know them, they came to do a concert at what is now the University of Northern Iowa, which is in the neighboring town of Cedar Falls. And I was taking some classes up there, and they were wandering around on campus, some of them, and I first got to know one of the horn players—I'm bad on names today. Anyway, he played clarinet and he played saxophone, and those were the first ones we got to know. And gradually, my sister and all, we got to know everybody in the band. And we met Clark when he first started playing with Duke.

I had been an AKA when I was at Talladega. There weren't that many in Iowa when I was growing up. My mother had been a Delta. Delta Sigma Theta. And my father belonged to Kappa Kappa Alpha Phi.

In Iowa there was also a black Elks group, and there was Masons. And there was Eastern Star. After we became Catholic, you really didn't join Masons then—the so-called secret whatever it was. And there grew up some social clubs later, and there were the churches.

Well, I was really brought up Catholic. There was a mission here in one of the parishes, and they really didn't want us (blacks) to come to school there or join. We didn't think much about it then. There was the other church, but whites came to the church because of the neighborhood because it was closer. But I didn't really care—they had bought enough land that they were going to build a school up there. My father said they're only going to build a school because it's going to be segregated, so they never built the school. And the church closed because most of the children left, and by the time my younger brother and sister came along, by that time, they had decided they should go to St. Mary's. So they closed the church, and then we got a neighborhood center when that War on Poverty thing started. Money came through for a neighborhood center, so it was turned over by the diocese to be used as a neighborhood center.

I had seven children myself. I've got one that lives here with me. None of the others do. I've got one that lives in Switzerland. Then there's Jeanann; her husband is at Fort Hood, so she lives down there, whatever that town is. Jeanann was born in '49.

My daughter Theresa is the one who lives in Switzerland; she was born in 1950. Well, right now she isn't working. But she's got her master's in finance, an MBA. She has worked for Chase Manhattan, and then when she went to Europe, after a while she went to work for Digital, their finance division. Then her last job, which she just quit last spring, she was working to head up an office for a fellow from the Ivory Coast who did rice importing.

I have a boy, Warren, that lives in D. C. He's an attorney. He was born in '52. Mary, she was born in '53. She lives in Columbia, South Carolina, and she's a social worker. And Lois, she's forty-three, because there's exactly thirty years' difference in our ages. And she's with a bank here as a finance executive. And the last two are twins, there's Michael, he lives in Haywood, California, and he works for some kind of cable thing. He's a purchasing agent. His twin sister Moira, they were born in '58. She works as a supervisor for supplying temporary help, but I think she's a placement person. And she lives in California, too; both of them live in the Bay Area.

My husband died in '79. The last few years have been tough. In '88, I had to have my left leg amputated above the knee. I went to work after my husband died, '81, and I worked until '95. I was executive director of a community-based organization. And then retired in '95. Then the last year's been kind of tough. I've got a problem with my hip, too. My right hip. I haven't been downstairs since the end of July just because I can't get back up. Until I went to work, I did a lot of volunteer work.

Well, I was every active in the fifties and sixties in groups here in the state. Anybody that spent four years going to school in the South, you'd notice the difference. Especially if you had to go through Birmingham. You sort of got used to it, but I did some short stories and wrote some stuff, and I realized how bitter I was in the journal that I was keeping, the little bit of time I took some creative writing courses.

Although (my husband and my father) they were accepted and everything, there were things that happened to them. I know when my husband wanted to borrow money to set up practice, he couldn't get what he really needed to set up a good practice. They were general practitioners. And there were people in the hospital, you know, who'd run into them in the hospital, didn't think they were doctors, they acted like they were janitors and so forth. There were always little things you'd run into.

The black population of Waterloo, it's about 12 percent of the total population. It's probably about the same (as it's been). You know, we went through a big downturn in the eighties with John Deere—well, first of all, Rath Packing closed. Illinois Central was sold. This was division headquarters for the Illinois Central, western division. And with the diesels, they didn't need all the repair work here.

And when John Deere went through its downturn, we went through a real depression, economic downturn, in the eighties here in Iowa, and John Deere went from a company that had hired maybe 14,000 to 15,000 people to almost half. And John Deere was our main employer. But you noticed things changing in the fifties, with the beginning of what was happening in the South.

I think, after World War II, things changed. The difference was the fellows who came back from the service, who came back at the end of World War II. Even though they weren't always integrated, they had experienced something entirely different, and that's when some of the movement began because they weren't going to come back to the United States and put up with it. There were some demonstrations at Talladega after I graduated. And then the thing with Montgomery.

We have a very close family, my sisters and brother. I have one brother and three sisters. My sister next to me is Betty Jean Furgerson, and then I have a sister in Cedar Rapids; her name is Lileah Harris; her husband is a doctor in Cedar Rapids who grew up here. He came here when he was in junior high because his family was from Mississippi and Memphis. He moved here after his mother died and grew up with his aunt. Then he went to Howard for undergrad and medical school. And then I have a brother, whose name is Lee; he's a junior. He's retired now on disability; he worked for Blue Cross Blue Shield as an executive. And my youngest sister, Rebecca, works at the University of Northern Iowa in the education department. I think she handles their finances.

I had a family that encouraged us to do things. And I don't think my father ever thought that girls weren't as capable as boys. And my mother was active as a volunteer. My father hired extra help so she could be a volunteer. And then when he died, my mother went back to finish her education and then taught school almost until she died. I think my parents took advantage of the opportunities.

INTERVIEW BY ALAN GOVENAR, SEPTEMBER 18, 1998

Earl W. Rand, Ph.D.

Educator and college president
Born: August 13, 1911, Lodi, Texas

Earl Rand grew up in Cass County, Texas, near the Louisiana border. His father was a farmer, timberman, and cross-tie inspector for the Texas & Pacific Railroad. After finishing the seventh grade, he attended Jarvis Christian College in Hawkins, Texas. Rand earned a B.A. degree in history from Bishop College. He received an M.A. degree from Atlanta University in 1942 and a Ph.D. from Indiana University in 1951. He taught at Alcorn University (Mississippi), Southern University (Louisiana), and Texas Southern University (Houston). In 1976, Dr. Rand was appointed president of Jarvis Christian College and later served for one year as president of Wiley College in Marshall, Texas.

Lodi is in Marion County, but I was born across the line in Cass County. Lodi is a part of East Texas. Cass County and Marion County border on the state of Louisiana. My parents were Mote and Idella Rand. Grandparents were Richard Rand, grandfather, and grandmother, on the father's side, I never knew. And my grandmother, the only one that I knew, was Mrs. Lockett, the mother of my mother.

My grandfather, I am told, was brought here when he was about six or eight years old, from Alabama. His old slaveholder brought him here with him. Well, my grandfather was the son of his slaveholder father. I don't know about the mother, but I do know that they had at least four boys that were the sons of this gentleman. His name was William Harrison Rand. And he had at least one daughter that I knew of. Incidentally, she's the grandmother of Mrs. Nancy Smith out here, west of here. They came to Texas and settled in Cass County. In fact, settled in Cass and Marion.

My parents were farmers and my father was a timberman, cross-tie inspector, logger, both of those put together, and a pretty good farmer. That was all that—they had about a third-grade education. I grew up as a farm boy. So I start out with that. My father had a farm, and there were about four of us boys that were there that were farmworkers. And we actually did the farming. He did the planting. But he was a cross-tie inspector operating from Woodlawn, Texas, to Queen City, Texas, for the Texas & Pacific Railroad. And we did the work on the farm.

The educational opportunities at that time were limited. We had five- or six-month school. And, of course, the facilities and equipment were virtually nil because when I began school, we had to buy our books and so forth, and parents who were farmers and workers, daily workers, could hardly take care of their families, to say anything about buying textbooks. However, that did change. Were it not for a good teacher, which I had in the sixth and seventh grades, I would not be here, perhaps, today.

My teacher that I speak of as a good teacher had neither a high school diploma nor a college degree. But in my judgment over some seventy-five years, or eighty, I haven't found a better teacher in terms of getting it over to the student.

I went for the ninth grade, when I finished seventh grade, they had removed eighth grade from the curriculum in Texas as a part of high school. So I went to Jarvis Christian College. They had an academy. In fact, all of the colleges in Texas that I know of had an academy at that time. And I went there at the ninth-grade level and completed high school and junior college while studying there. I didn't obtain a degree at the junior college level. I just went to school and got a diploma, finishing two years of college.

I was encouraged tremendously. In fact, when I went to Jarvis, it opened my eyes to the value of education and what I had not seen in the backwoods of East Texas. I dropped out for one year and then went back to Bishop College for the bachelor's degree, with a major in history. And this enthused me to go further, and, of course, as I grew in experience, I sought better preparation to do a better job. And I might say again, I always remember the man who opened my eyes to the need for being able to do a good job whenever you're called upon.

Well, after finishing Bishop College, I attended summer school at the University of Colorado. Then finally I went to Atlanta University and completed my master's degree there in the field of biology. I taught biology for some ten or twelve years, but always looked forward to going into the teacher education field. I don't know why, because it wasn't the difficulty. But it was my ambition to help prepare teachers if I could, to do a good job. Upon completing my college work, I got a job, I don't know what you'd call it, at Jarvis Christian College. I think I taught one class, and began the building of the biology department at Jarvis Christian College. Then I went away to Atlanta University for my master's degree. Received it in 1942. I'm not sure whether it was '41 or '42, but I completed the work in '41. When I came out of there, I was requested to take over the deanship at Jarvis Christian College. And there I remained until I went into railway mail service.

I was talking with a lady today. I saw her brother the first night I worked in postal service. And it was at that time that I decided in my own mind that I wouldn't stay with this the rest of my life. I don't know what the problem was. It wasn't anything about the work because that's all I knew.

The postal service offered a real opportunity for blacks. I earned more in two weeks in the postal service than I earned in a month as dean of the college. You can understand. I needed that job because I had mortgaged and borrowed from every person I could while I was studying for the master's degree. A master's degree in 1942 was like a Ph.D. degree or more so now, for a person to have it. I remember we used to count the master's degrees on the faculty where we were in school. You could count them. But that has changed.

So this encouraged me to go on. And then I decided, after three years in the postal service, to go back to Jarvis Christian College again to work. And then I began my doctoral studies at Greeley College; I believe it's called the University of Northern Colorado now. That was my first experience there. But at the same time, I had made arrangements to go to Indiana University at Bloomington. But at the time that I went to Colorado, there was no housing available following the war at Bloomington. So I arranged with the dean there that I should take courses that would be of transferable nature at Indiana University. And then in 1948, I went to Indiana University and began my work on the doctoral program. Studied three summers, then spent a year and completed the work. I was at that time teaching at Alcorn A&M College, University now, in Mississippi. From there I transferred later on to Southern University, Baton Rouge. And I spent six years at Southern University, Baton Rouge.

I made my return again to Jarvis Christian College in 1957 for two years. I was filling in for someone, and to be honest with you, I was trying to get back to Texas. So that was my opportunity. Then I ended up at Texas Southern University in 1959 and remained there until I retired as director of teacher education, finally as the dean of the graduate school.

After I had retired from Texas Southern University, I came to Wiley College to work. And while I was here, I was asked to assume the responsibility as president at Jarvis Christian College in 1976. I didn't have much trouble finding my way around. I suggested to someone who was participating in the search for president at Wiley this year. I said, "If you can get one who has had the experience on the campus, that background of experience will put him through. But if he hasn't, he's got to learn his way, it'll take him more years to learn his way." I served as president of Wiley College for one year.

I didn't see that much difference between being an administrator and a teacher. Oh, you have greater responsibility as president. As a teacher, you can finish your class, lock your doors, and go home. But the president can't go home so easily. He carries the institution with him wherever he goes.

The life span of a college president is usually about five years. I'd say give him three to five years to find what he's about. Now, I'm speaking from experience. If I had any success, I had the advantage of having worked in both institutions and knowing something about the fabric of their operation. And, of course, at Jarvis, I had been there from the time that I was in high school, in and out of there. Therefore, I was pretty well situated with its mission and purpose and so forth.

There is a difference in HBCUs (Historically Black Colleges and Universities), especially in terms of finance. But in terms of mission, I'm not sure that there's a great, a wide span of difference. That's what I was basing my position on. They serve the same or similar clientele.

I remember Dr. Douglas sat right over there at that little table. It was a different table there then. When he came here, called up about seven o'clock in the morning, or eight, and told us he wanted to eat breakfast with us, well, I knew it was something wrong. And he came in here and he was on the board of trustees of Jarvis. And he came in here to ask me if I would accept the responsibility at Jarvis if the board gave it to me. And he turned around and said, "They have requested that I get you." My wife didn't want me to go at that time. But, of course, she knew I was going. Both of us were graduates of the school, her from the college level and me from the junior college level. But she just didn't want to be torn up, but she went along. I had one of the finest women as a wife. Had to be to get along with me. But she was marvelous.

Of course, there have been low points in the life. You know you have that. I guess the lowest is when I left Jarvis and went into the postal service. But if you'll excuse the term, the gut level of my ambition was not satisfied by the money. Now it helped me to pay my debts. And mind you, I didn't plan that. When I got through with my debts, I got right out of the mail service. It was purely for expediency. That is what happened. So I presume when you owe everybody, you don't want to meet anybody. That's a low low. But, of course, when I received the top degree, in fact, all of my degrees, I was pleased, because you see, I worked my way up after I finished Jarvis junior college; I made it myself from there.

I was a freshman at Bishop College when 1929 hit. And it dropped right down on us. And that old house standing on the corner of Bishop and Burleson, that's where I lived with Mrs. Thompson. And it was tough times, meaning at $10 a month I would pay to stay and eat. But I made it through. If you look at my transcript, the lowest grades that I made while I was in school were made during those two quarters. They were on the quarter system. So I guess you could call that the lowest, because as a child, I wasn't a boy, I didn't, I had lows and ups every day. But it was just play lows and play ups.

I think my understanding of discrimination started in the graveyard. Some of my family who were slaves were buried. They didn't have but one graveyard, but they moved over behind somewhere in the bushes and put the black folks. Those were, I would say, the first evidences of slavery. I had known it was there all the time, but I didn't know it had black people over behind in it. I never felt that we were able to come and be a part of it. My mother had a brother. See, her father was a slaveholder, too. My mother's father. And he had a brother that used to come to see her every year at least once. But he'd never go in the house. He'd sit on the porch and talk to her. But my mother was older than he. And he knew her, but he'd come to see her. To me, that was demeaning. Yes, he came to see her every year. Sit on the front porch of the house. Well, I don't imagine it was very common. Last time I saw him was in Linden, Texas. And he recognized me. Came over. He didn't know my name. But he came over and identified me as my mother's son. Which meant that he had seen me enough to know, and I imagine she had told him enough about it.

There are other experiences that have taught me about discrimination. See, when I went to school here (Marshall) in 1929, you couldn't get a hamburger in this town. You couldn't in any of the places that considered themselves important. You couldn't get a hamburger there. Certain areas you weren't supposed to go. Marshall was terrible. Marshall seemed to have its own unique brand of racism or discrimination towards blacks. To the point of when Social Security was voted in, and home workers were recognized in it, we had people here that went all the way to the Supreme Court to try to keep from paying Social Security for their housekeepers. They live right here now. They're teachers.

I knew of a case in Port Gibson, Mississippi, where the girl worked in the post office. And the black boy, I don't remember what he did. But they both had to get out of there. She went because he went. And he was ordered to go, or else. Those are the kinds of things that show me the depth of this. I listened this morning to a discussion that took place yesterday, I believe, on welfare. And it looks like in every law that they've passed, they weave into it somewhere where they can cut us a little harder. Because they know if they turn the money over to the states, without direct guidelines, when they talk about big government, to me, that's what it means. "Get the government off our back." It's to set us up like we used to be. That's right. States' rights.

I took the examination for mail carrier in Texarkana, Texas, in 1937, I think. Might have been '36 or '37. Passed it. And was called up by the office in Washington. But when I entered that door, for my interview, the man turned as red as that. And you know what he told me? "These jobs are for people who need." And that was bold discrimination.

Yes. I passed the exam. I think my score was number six in the exam. Took it right there in Texarkana. But I was called to carry mail. Glad I didn't get it because I might have stayed with it at that time. But that to me is the essence of bigotry and discrimination. Now mind you, when I went to work in Texarkana in 1942, there wasn't a Negro working in the main post office except the janitor. Of course, that wasn't just true in Texarkana. You know, President Roosevelt had to issue an executive order for a Dallas boy to let him work in the window and sell stamps. That really wrecked the train. That to me was the essence of discrimination. Yeah, I'd taken the examination, passed it, and got certified, and he sent me home.

The South is a little bolder with discrimination. The North is subtle with it. And if we aren't thoroughly oriented, intelligent on the matter, you'll not sense it. For example, I went to Indianapolis. This is before I went to Indiana University. And man, I couldn't find anything there that represented any different from what was here, in terms of us: where we lived, how we lived, what we were doing at that time. Now it changed tremendously in the time that I went there, which was in 1937, to 1945, it tremendously changed, when I went back. However, I don't think even now it's thoroughly safe.

I have to be careful not to revert to the way I came up and, you know, watch my language. See, we have no problem with you calling me "nigger." *You* doing it. It just says, strongly, of course, how deep the problem is. I remember a story my daddy tells about he and his brother. My dad's about your complexion, and his brother's about my complexion. They were little fellas, playing around in their house, where their mother's sitting up, patching or doing something. And my dad looked up—he was younger than his brother—looked up at his mama and he came back and touched his brother and said, "Son," that's what we called him, "Uncle Son." "Ain't we got a pretty Mammy?" That's what they called her. He looked up at her and he said, "Yes, but she's black, though." Well, the little fella's lying on the floor, playing. But that's how deep the thing is—of course, that was a hundred years ago. But we have not overcome. We've got to do a whole lot of what you doing now. And we got to get more people together. We got to hem up these white folks. We've got to hem them up. What I mean by that, we've got to come to the point where we sit down and face up to the issue.

America's got to find a way to get its leaders together so that they can first identify the problems. You can't do much teaching if you can't identify the problem that you're dealing with. And then go to work. What will resolve this? See, we pass civil rights legislation and so forth, all of that's good. But implementation can be problematic.

I ran a desegregation institute in Houston where the superintendent of schools would not—at least the school board, I presume, and the superintendent—would not allow the teachers—I won't say he wouldn't allow them—but he did not encourage them to attend. Yes, public schoolteachers. They came from about eleven counties, I think. We had a structure that said, "We'd like to have a superintendent or an officer of the superintendent, a principal, and two teachers, a black and a white, that would go all the way through." We had eighty-three people involved in it. But we ran that thing. I think all the TVs were on that morning, when we opened up. I guess they thought we were going to be a Farrakhan. Somebody like that. But here, I'm in charge of it.

I'm concerned about finding a means of implementation, helping the teachers and the administrators to get it going. Two things happened that to me were significant. Lady from Trinity, Texas, principal of the high school, had a system to keep us from congregating. See, we had white and black. To keep us from congregating all together. We reserved tables in a cafeteria downtown every day, that is, Monday through Friday. We set up, we saw what was happening, so we set up a system whereby I couldn't eat at the same table every day with the same leader. For example, I could be at the head of one table. You couldn't eat with me every day. That forced them to get around.

Well, it paid off, I think, in some respects. This is what I call implementation. But this old lady came that day and sat down at my table. "I want to eat with Dr. Rand." And you know what she said? "This is the first time I ever sat down to eat with a Negro."

She was bragging about it. And I heard her tell an evaluator that came in, almost the same thing. She was really enthused about it. The other thing that happened, the old superintendent who wouldn't let them, by the time we were through with it, and we went for evaluation, we invited all the superintendents to come that day. We had a luncheon out at

Houston Baptist College. While at the luncheon, I don't know what came up. But naturally in that setting, it would come up. The superintendent of Beaumont schools told about their decision in that athletic district to integrate the schedule.

Well, they made their first mistake. I didn't think about it till way later. First mistake, they didn't invite the black coaches to the discussion. Had only the superintendents and the white coaches and perhaps principals. Well, that was historical.

But he said, "You know, even so, that school is state champion in football. Charlton Pollard."

And both of these schools were right there in his hometown.

"Charlton Pollard is at the top in basketball in the state." So, he told that at the table."

And that afternoon when we came back, the last session, Mr. Fletcher, the superintendent, told me—I was in charge of that session, said, "Dr. Rand, when we found that we had to integrate the faculties, we were greatly concerned about the black teachers going into the former white schools. The problems they would have. But we have found exactly the opposite."

That was a surprise. Yes, but I knew it. I knew, right there. They didn't stay until noon, gone. They wouldn't stay there. Well, I said to him, see, he was at the luncheon, and he heard the man tell the story, I said, and I just reminded him of it. I said, "Mr. Fletcher, sometimes we assume truths that are not in evidence." And you see, that was the historical background of the white man, that he's better than the Negro, no matter what, how many degrees you've got, but you just aren't as good as a good white man or a good white woman.

Incidentally, when I was at Indiana, that year that I spent there, the first black that ever played in the Big Ten basketball played. He was at Indiana. Bill Garrett. He's dead now. I understand cancer got him. Yeah, he was a fine fellow. He was a senior that year. But that was the first time. They wouldn't let him play. He wasn't good enough to play in the Big Ten. Now the blacks have taken over the Big Ten.

INTERVIEW BY LLOYD THOMPSON, SEPTEMBER 2, 1997

Clarence Ray

Gambler

Life dates: February 28, 1900–December 1, 1993

Clarence Ray has mixed racial ancestry; his paternal grandparents were Creek Indians, his maternal grandmother was a slave, and his maternal grandfather was a British subject from Barbados. Ray's parents, Inez Smith and Floyd Oscar Ray, owned land in Oklahoma, but didn't farm it themselves, preferring instead to rent "shares" to sharecroppers. Prior to Clarence's birth, his parents split up, and his mother went to California. Clarence was born February 28, 1900, in Fresno, California, and when he was a child, "moved around a lot"—to Arizona and New Mexico. When Clarence was about ten, his mother remarried; at eighteen, he enrolled at Western University in Kansas City, Kansas. While in Kansas, Clarence tried out for Negro League baseball and was hired by a team based in Spring Valley, Illinois. As a baseball player, he traveled around the country. In Mason City, Iowa, he met Rosie Dorsey, whom he later married.

Clarence's uncle introduced him to gambling in Fresno, and Clarence soon became involved in the business, working as a dealer in Chinese gambling houses in San Diego, Los Angeles, and San Francisco, as well as in Mexican establishments in Mexicali and Tijuana, Mexico. In 1922, Clarence visited Las Vegas, Nevada. He returned three years later, and stayed for the remainder of his career.

The following excerpts from the Clarence Ray oral history cover his early years and his move to Las Vegas. The interview was conducted by Helen M. Blue and Jamie Coughtry and is provided courtesy of the University of Nevada-Reno oral history program.

I don't know very much about my paternal grandparents except that they were Creek Indians, but I knew my grandparents on my mother's side well. My mother's mother, whose first name was Fanny, was born a slave, but she didn't talk very much about her time as a slave. My mother's father's name was Henry Swinger. He was quite a talkative person. Grandfather Swinger was never a slave; he was a British subject who was born in the Barbados Islands and became a seaman when he was seventeen.

My grandfather went to sea, which was a common thing for a lot of the blacks down in that area to do. About twenty-five or thirty of them got on a ship that was going to Canada. They jumped ship when they got up in the Canadian waters, and then they came down into the United States to fight in the Civil War. (They had heard all about how there was going to be a civil war and that we were going to free the slaves!) My grandfather said they got down to Massachusetts, which was the first place they could join the National Guard. Right away they went and fought in the Civil War. My grandfather fought in the war for two and a half years.

When the war was over, they were at a place called the Chickamauga battleground right out of Chattanooga, Tennessee. My grandmother, Fanny, was there. She was one of the ex-slaves who was there who had no place to go. She just kind of took up with the troops and followed my grandfather around. She didn't have food, so he would divide his food with her. When he was ready to leave, they asked, "What are you going to do, Fanny?"

She said, "I want to go with Henry."

They asked Henry, "Will you take her?"

He said, "Yes." She wasn't quite fourteen years old. Then came the time when he said, "But I don't know if I can take her or not."

A guy said, "Why not?"

He said, "I'm not an American citizen. I'm from the Barbados islands."

The man said, "You fought all during the war?"

Henry said, "Yes."

He said, "How long?"

"Two and a half years," he said.

The man said, "You're a citizen. You can take her."

After it was all agreed, my grandfather got papers saying that my grandmother could go with him kind of as a wife or a companion after the war. My grandmother was already pregnant by another slave when my grandfather took her as a wife. Her first daughter was born when she was fourteen. (She eventually became mother of seventeen more children, so my grandparents had eighteen children altogether. My mother, Inez Smith, was the first child that my grandmother and grandfather had together.)

My grandparents walked from Chattanooga, Tennessee, to Muskogee, Oklahoma. My grandfather used to tell my cousin and me about that; he liked to talk to us. He said most of the walking they did was across Arkansas. He knew where he was going: He wanted to go to Indian Territory. Since he had been told that he was a citizen, he wanted to go write a claim on some land, which he did; when they got to Oklahoma, my grandfather got 160 acres for himself and 160 acres for his wife. As each of their children were born, he'd see to him getting land. My mother was born there in Oklahoma. My grandfather was commonly known in that part of the country as a freedman.

My grandmother, Fanny Swinger. I'll never forget her. She was 104 when she died. She would always say, "You always go out to your other grandmother, as you like her better than you do me, because she's an

Clarence Ray,
photograph by Helen
M. Blue, Las Vegas,
Nevada, May 1991
(University of Nevada
Oral History Program)

Indian." But I didn't. I liked one as well as the other one, but my mother's mother, she just wasn't like my father's mother—she didn't do nothing but clean up the house and the yard and everything else.

My Indian grandmother's name was Edie Ray. I don't remember my grandfather's name, because we only called him Grandpa. They lived right out of town on what they called a farm; they call them ranches now. There was a big pond where they watered the horses and cows, and it had fish in it. And she'd go down on the stream with us and fish, and we'd clean the fish and fry them out, just like we was way out somewhere. We got a kick out of that. Beyond that, I don't remember too much about either one of them.

Where our family grew up, it was the Creek Nation. There were five tribes of Indians in Oklahoma called the Five Civilized Tribes. In Oklahoma the Indians didn't live on reservations like they do in most other places. Instead, they claimed their lands and owned them. Our family was considered as Creek freedmen because they lived in Indian Territory.

Though they had quite a bit of land, my family didn't farm. (But they were fortunate enough that some of the land had oil on it.) My grandfather Swinger would rent the land out to sharecroppers, who worked the land. He furnished the land and the seed and the animals, and the workers got a certain amount of whatever the land produced. As near as I can understand it, mostly everybody who worked got a certain amount of the profits.

I was very close to my grandfather. I'd ask questions, and he didn't mind answering. I wanted him to tell me about the war and about how he came over to the United States. He would tell me about slavery so I'd be sure to understand the difference between working as a slave and working for a salary. He said a great thing had happened to all of the blacks in America who had lived in the slave states. After emancipation, they would have to be paid and they were promised land and animals. But my grandfather also told us right away that the government didn't live up to its promises: They didn't give very many blacks land, and very few of them got any help to raise crops. They went from one type of slavery into another—into what we now call economic slavery, I guess.

This grandfather of mine had a certain amount of education, and he talked all the time about segregation and black history. One man he admired a lot was Booker T. Washington. He was the founder of Tuskegee

Institute, an all-black school in Alabama. He also told us who Frederick Douglass was. My grandfather was the only real influence I had other than my mother. He died when I was twelve.

My mother, Inez Smith, was married to my father, Floyd Oscar Ray, in Oklahoma. (He was a Creek Indian from Oklahoma.) It seemed as though they were both kind of high-tempered. They had some kind of misunderstanding, and during a little scrape, she shot him. She got scared! This older half sister of hers was married and lived in California, so my mother left Oklahoma and went there. Her half sister's family had a farm and raised grain and cattle. (That was before cotton came to California.) My mother stayed in California until I was born, February 28, 1900, in Fresno. In fact, some of my family still lives there on that land. I was four or five years old before I went to Oklahoma at all.

My mother moved us around when I was young—California, Arizona, New Mexico. We lived in Phoenix a while, and then Yuma. We traveled by train; it was before the car days. (I remember when we bought our first car we could travel in—this was about 1917.) Wherever we were, we usually lived in town, although most places we lived, we did own a farm. As near as I ever came to living in the country was later in a place called Malaga, just four miles from Fresno. My mother would sometimes go as she wanted to and leave us kids behind, because she got good at handling her own money.

When I was about ten or twelve years old, my mother was married to a man named McDaniels, and we moved to California. McDaniels was my first stepfather that I remember and was the father of my brother, Jack McDaniels. He was a farmer, as near as I can understand. He and my mother eventually separated in Arizona. After that, my mother married a fellow named Frank Smith. He was the father of my three sisters, so there were five of us. He was a Baptist preacher. Though he was a minister, my mother wasn't much of a churchgoer, so I didn't go to church. But we did read the Bible at home. All preachers moved around. Frank Smith moved around quite a bit until he settled down during his last twenty-five years and made his home in Fresno.

I was close to my stepfathers, especially to Frank Smith. We were very, very close. He lived eight or ten years after my mother died in the 1940s—she was in her eighties. Then he stayed on with us until he died. He and my mother are both buried in Fresno, California.

I think it was probably my mother who influenced me the most, because she seemed to be the boss of the family at all times. She was the one who insisted on us going to school, and she tried to tell us all the rights and wrongs that she knew about. She didn't have too much education herself, but she was kind of self-made.

My mother always tried to acquire land, so we lived well. I guess it was because of some of the teachings from her father that she always did this. She had farmland up around Fresno, which is part of the San Joaquin Valley. There was a lot of fruit, alfalfa, and corn. It was not unusual for black families to own land in that part of California.

Education was very important in our family—it was then, and it still is. Although my mother didn't have much education, she tried to see that the rest of us did. My mother learned to read after she was grown. She knew a little bit about reading, but to just sit down and take a book and read a story or read the newspaper…she learned that after we started going to school. I guess I was more of a teacher to her after I was in school than any of the rest of my family.

I started school in Oklahoma, but I later attended public school around Fresno. That was back in the days when they had a book that was just ahead of the first grade; they called it a primer. That was the first book I tried to read anything in. We had complete segregation in Oklahoma—all-black schools. The next school I went to was around Fresno. I also went to school in the Imperial Valley in El Centro. Then I went to seventh and eighth grade in Los Angeles. I finished high school in Fresno when I was eighteen. I graduated from Edison High School in 1918. (A lot of people think it was the first high school in Fresno, but it wasn't. Fresno Union

High was the first one, and then there was Edison School. It was put there by a big electrical corporation in the central part of California.)

I never knew much segregation in California schools, because we all went to the same schools back then. The only thing I remember about segregation of blacks concerned a black schoolteacher in the 1920s in Imperial County. This black schoolteacher had moved from Arkansas. Instead of trying to get a job as a schoolteacher in California schools, he began to ask for an all-black school. He probably felt that the only way he could get a job teaching school was if there were a separate black school. Eventually, they carried it to the courts, and they said there would be no segregated schools in California.

As near as I can remember, the only trouble we had in school in Fresno was with the Mexicans. There was quite a number of Mexicans; California was very thickly populated with Mexicans when I was young—more Mexicans than anything else. There weren't enough blacks going to school to have any beef about it, but they were having some kind of trouble with the Mexicans. (I had quite a few Mexican friends in California. Part of my family speaks Spanish. I now have Mexican members of my family among the younger ones, because I've got some nephews and nieces who are married to Mexicans. Some of my older family members had Creek wives that they brought from Oklahoma, like my uncle, Bradley Swinger—my mother's brother—married a Creek woman.)

Fresno is where I first started reading newspapers that amounted to anything. Of course, we got papers from both San Francisco and Los Angeles. They'd be a day late, because everything traveled by train in those days. Though it was late, my people always took the paper. There were two black papers printed then: one in Philadelphia and one Chicago—the *Chicago Defender*. We read them all the time. Wherever we moved, we had them sent to us.

There was a big ranching outfit around Fresno called Miller and Lux. They were like cattle barons. They already owned a lot of the land, which they used for grazing purposes. When these cattle barons got ready to sell their cattle, they needed to fatten them up. The few people who had farms that they were really working just raised grain to sell to Miller and Lux. They'd raise oats, wheat, corn, and other stuff of that kind. They also bought all the hay you could produce, so people always made a good living.

The first place they planted cotton in California was in the Imperial Valley, right on the Mexican border, in 1925. Then they put cotton over in another valley called the Palo Verde Valley. The main town over there now is Blythe, California. They had cotton there as far back as I can remember, but I didn't go down there until I was about eighteen or nineteen years old. When they put the cotton in, it seemed like it was going to be a big thing. They started buying up all those small places, and the big farms up there owned a thousand acres of land that they would raise cotton on.

When I was eighteen, my family sent me to this all-black Methodist school called Western University. It was kind of an agricultural school in Kansas City, Kansas. I think the reason I got sent there was because my grandfather, Henry Swinger, was a Methodist—at least he used to talk about Methodists all the time. That's the only all-black school I have ever gone to. (It was founded by W. T. Bernard, and it's closed now. The school had quite a bit of land, and I think the state bought it and did something else with the land.) I didn't really want to study anything in particular. Of course, it was a kind of a trade school, and I took up automotive engineering. I guess I figured I was going to be a mechanic, but that didn't work out, and I only went one year. My excuse for quitting was because I didn't make the football team my second year, so I went home. I kind of lied to my mother and told her I was going to go back the next session. She finally told me if I wasn't going back to school, to tell her. So I did, and she told me, "Your room rent and board bill starts today." That's when I was nineteen years old.

I had been a good athlete when I was in school. They didn't have mixed professional teams then, but we had mixed teams in school. All the schools up through Iowa and Illinois had mixed teams. Kids went to school together and played together, but after we got out and turned professional, we played in segregated teams. I played in the Negro League.

My first team was the Wichita ABCs in Wichita, Kansas. They changed their name from the ABCs to the Monrovians after I was there two years. Then I tried out for the Kansas City Monarchs. That was the best-known black team in America at that time. I didn't make the team, but instead of going back to Wichita, I went to Spring Valley, Illinois, to play.

I came back to California every winter, because the baseball season was just during the summer. In California, we played in what they called the winter league. All the teams would be mixed. I played for Soaper's Giants in Los Angeles, which had whites, blacks, and Mexicans. (The man who organized that league was named Joe Soaper.) We had the best semi-pro team out here. The Soapers eventually got to be kind of a big thing, but not while I was with it. I played about four years, altogether. But you couldn't make any money at it, so I quit...I had nothing but gambling on my mind, anyway.

I met my wife, Rosie, while I was playing ball. Her maiden name was Dorsey. She was from Rockford, Illinois. Being a ballplayer on the all-Negro team, I was moving around and I met her in Mason City, Iowa. She was there visiting somebody. I got acquainted with her and she gave me her address and telephone number in Rockford. I was quite young—about twenty—and she must have been seventeen. Rosie and I were married in Rockford, Illinois. That's the only way I could get her away from there. I had to be married to her, or people wouldn't let her leave. We left there and went to El Centro, California. We were together off and on for nine years, but it wasn't continuously. I'd leave places and go back and get her. I thought I had a lifetime contract on her, I guess. After we separated, she married Orion Stevens, who worked for the railroad in Las Vegas.

My mother had always talked about me being a professional man of some kind, because she felt that I had the makings for it. I always said that I didn't want to be a doctor, so she would talk about the law a little bit. I think what really kept me from being interested in school after I got to be about twenty years old was this: In Fresno, there were only two black professional men—one was a lawyer and one was a doctor. But they never seemed to have enough money to buy food for their wives and children. (Both of them had two children.) They didn't really get clients, because hardly anybody would go to them. Even the black families that lived there didn't go to them. This race issue would still come up among them. All of the blacks were from the South, and they'd say, "What does he know?"

At that time, my uncle, George Taylor, often fed these two black professional men. He wasn't much older than me. Uncle George had some gambling going in Fresno. He got me into gambling when I was a young man, and taught me all about it. He had a poolroom and he always had crap games and poker games in the back of it. I worked with him and he'd give me a percentage out of whatever I made on the games. So I told myself, "These men went to school until they were twenty-five or twenty-six years old, and they can't even make a living. Here I'm making a hundred dollars a week!" One hundred dollars a week was a lot of money in those days—that was more than the average person got in a month! And that's one of the reasons why I wasn't too interested in furthering my education; he's the cause of me not continuing school! But I've been very sorry every since—I live well, but I still have been sorry.

At my Uncle George's place, they played all the games—dominoes, all kinds of cards, checkers. This uncle of mine was supposed to be one of the best checker players in the state of California, because he went to Pasadena and played in the tournaments and wound up second. People always said that he had learned out of a book, but he said nobody ever taught him. He just made up his own combinations and things and knew how to play. He won a lot of games—there wasn't too much money in checkers, but I've known him to win as much as $2,000 at one time.

I ran the crap game for my uncle. We'd shoot craps on the table. Back in those days when they were running crap games, if the crap shooter wanted to shoot $2, he had to put a nickel in, and the house took the nickels. That's what I would do: I'd take what we call the "take off" now. My uncle would take the nickels and put them in a locked box. At the end of a shift, I had to count the money. If there was $50 there, 25 percent of it was mine.

Uncle George first made a cheater out of me when I was gambling, because I was young, and nobody... Since I was only eighteen, we figured nobody would pay too much attention to me. He would set me up in games to try to hustle people—sometimes it'd be a game that I'd like to play; sometimes it'd be a game he'd play. Both of us made money off it—enough to keep me from going to school, all right. I also played pool pretty good, but cards and dice was my game.

Uncle George never was involved in the Nevada gambling, no more than just to come up where I later worked sometimes. He owned a little place in Fresno, and then he was in with one or two that I worked in up here. But he was a silent partner; he never put his name on a license.

My uncle George Taylor was originally named George Swinger—he just changed his name! He was my grandfather Swinger's youngest son. He got into trouble, so he just changed his name. My uncle grew up in California. My mother helped to raise him, and wherever she went, why, he would follow. (Of course, my uncle's dead and gone now; he died a few years ago.)

Besides working in my uncle's place, I also worked in Chinese gambling houses in San Diego, Los Angeles, San Francisco, and in Mexico. It was common for the Chinese to employ blacks, more so than anybody else. You hardly ever found any whites working at a Chinese gambling house. They hired a lot of blacks because they usually set up their operations in black neighborhoods—they couldn't get legally licensed to operate in white neighborhoods. But the Chinese were always willing to pay more shakedown than anybody else. So the authorities would look the other way.

In California there would be Chinese dealers, black dealers and Mexicans—of course, there were a lot of Mexicans in California. When I first went to work for the Chinese, I went to work in Mexico, over in Mexicali, right across the border from Calexico, California. I was living in El Centro, California, then. I was about nineteen years old. I just kind of followed the gambling from place to place. Where the gambling closed in one place, we'd all go to another place. I also worked in Tijuana; this was in the late 1920s and early 1930s when I was living in San Diego. They gave us a salary of $20 a day, plus a small percentage of the take. Most people then were making $25 a week! Since gambling was legal in Mexico, working in the Chinese gambling houses was a good business for the Chinese as well as us workers. I worked in them off and on from my early twenties until about twenty-five years ago, when I decided to stay home all the time.

The Chinese had the same type of gambling as the white places, except for one game that they only played among themselves. It was called Pai-Yu or something; I never could understand it, so I never involved myself with it. I was paid by the day. You had to be able to work on all the games, because they always had two or three different types of games—keno, blackjack, and poker. They had the numbers game, what we call keno here now. Back in those days, they called it Chinese lottery. When I was a boy, they were playing that.

I've always considered myself a professional gambler because I've always made my living in or around a gambling house. Gambling was illegal in California, but there was always some official who liked money. That's the way it was. The people who had the gambling houses where I worked always had somebody to pay off, so I never had any trouble. But later, I did get arrested a few times in Los Angeles for what they called floating crap games. You'd go to jail and stay a half hour or something like that, and then somebody would get you out. But I never had any trouble at that particular time, because I wasn't even old enough to be operating a gambling house. I just knew enough about it to always get a job.

I made my first trip to Las Vegas when I was living around Los Angeles in 1922. Nobody was making any money. There were three or four of us around there who were pretty good pool players, but it was all hanging around the pool halls and shooting craps, and nobody had any money. Ralph Simpson, Henry Wilson, and myself were all pool hustlers, and one day a guy came down and asked would we be interested in working. All of us said, "Yes!" We thought maybe it was just one of those one-, two-, or three-day jobs.

He said, "You got to go to Las Vegas. All the work you want's up there."

I said, "What kind of pay? What are they paying up there?"

He said, "Oh, you'll make about $5 a day," which was real good pay in 1922, because the money was getting tight again right after World War I. Being young and excited about maybe making two or three paydays at $5 a day, we left for Las Vegas.

We came on the Union Pacific Railroad. But when we got here, we went over to the railroad shop and found out there was a strike. The man who had told us about the jobs didn't tell us he was looking for strikebreakers! That's what he was doing, but he didn't tell us he was.

I said, "What time do we go to work?"

They said, "Seven o'clock tomorrow morning."

I said, "I'm going out and look at the town. I'll be back before dark."

They said, "You can't go out looking at the town."

I said, "Why not?" The first thing that came to my mind was that the town was so segregated that blacks couldn't go out.

He said, "You're a strikebreaker! If they catch you out there, they'll beat you up."

I said, "Oh, I didn't know that."

From some of the guys working around there, I found out there were only two buses a day running through here: one from Salt Lake to Los Angeles and one from Los Angeles to Salt Lake. The buses would get here at night. As soon as it got dark, I slipped out and caught a bus and went back to Los Angeles. I left Ralph Simpson and Henry Wilson in Las Vegas, and they stayed on.

At the time we didn't know too much about strikes and things of that kind. I knew that I liked the idea of unions, because I felt the working man needed some protection. Without the union, the bosses tell you when to work, when to quit, and how much you get paid. I knew I wasn't going to try to protect these guys' nonunion jobs. I was only twenty-two years old, but I did know that I liked the idea of the union. I had been reading the story about the coal miners' union. It was the only kind of union that was being supported. It was in 1919 when they had a big commotion about that. I was nineteen years old when Lewis headed the miners' union. The miners' union was the only worthwhile union at that time. Even the railroad companies didn't have a union. I knew quite a bit about that, because I read about it. I always knew that the working class of people didn't get a fair shake. That is what Lewis [labor leader John L. Lewis] said.

I had gotten this idea about the working class earlier from my uncles. They never wanted to do any labor for others; they always worked for themselves, because they said they couldn't get the proper pay otherwise. My uncles had their own little farms and things of that kind, and I had one who talked to me a lot. He was called the teaming contractor. He had his own teams, and he hauled, and when trucks came in he started buying them. At one time he got the trucks and worked for the garbage department in Fresno. He had to hire the people who worked, and the city paid him a certain amount. He would always try to get somebody he knew to work for him, so he got his own people. He said he'd be glad when the laborers got a union.

When I returned to Las Vegas the second time, I came on my own in 1925. Between 1922 and 1925, I had been in El Centro, California, where my mother had a grocery store. The story had broken about money being appropriated to build the dam. (They called it the Boulder Dam in those days, and some people still do.) I read a long story in a Washington paper about it, so I started coming back up here. In 1925, I just moved back up here to stay. I was going to stay at least until they started on the dam. (As it turned out, Las Vegas has been home since then, though I voted away from here one time in 1940 in Tulare, California.)

When I first returned, I thought I could probably get a lot of experience because I didn't intend to do anything but gamble. Las Vegas had always fascinated me because of the legalized gambling. They had what they called the mild form of legalized gambling and legalized prostitution in this town. This was before the wide-open gambling came. Slot machines were already here when I came in 1925; there were slots in all the places. The legalized gambling was going on, but it was just so small.

The first job I had was in a gambling house called the Miner's Club. It was owned by a Mexican fellow named Lopez down on First and Fremont Street. I ran a poker game, and back then you could make better than the average salary doing that. Each player had to pay so much per hour to play—at that particular time, it was sixty cents; they called it table rent. Players also had to buy their cards from the house. After supervising the poker game for a week or ten days, the guy found out I really knew what I was doing, and he gave me another job as an assistant shift boss. Then I could sell chips, and go from table to table and get the sixty cents. Because so many people didn't last the hour, we broke down the table rent—that way, players paid twenty cents every twenty minutes. That was my job.

The next job I had was at a gambling house called the Exchange Club, which was owned by whites. Everybody called them the McCarthy brothers, but I didn't know one brother's name from the other. The Exchange Club was on First Street between Carson and Fremont.

I lived on Third Street in Las Vegas in a house owned by a woman named Mary Nettles; I rented a room from her. Mary Nettles was originally from Alabama, and she moved all of her family out here. She owned quite a bit of property and was wealthy. Most all of Second Street and all of Third Street was owned by blacks, and some black families also lived on First Street. Mrs. Nettles had a building she had built on the side of the house. It had eight rooms with kitchen facilities in the back of the house. Mrs. Nettles also owned a couple of houses on the alley. I don't know how she paid for them; I never did hear her say, but this was back in the bootleg days, and I've heard people say she used to make whiskey and sell it…but I don't know that for a fact. This downtown property still belongs to Mrs. Nettles's family. She never did sell it; she just let out long-term leases on it. (Unfortunately, very few Negroes who owned property held onto it long enough to realize the increases in land value which have taken place.)

All the people who rented from Mrs. Nettles were black. They worked in the railroad shops; there was really no other kind of work for anyone to do except for in the railroad shops. They worked as machinists and electricians and everything, and some of the families are still here. I can't remember any poor blacks in Las Vegas back then, because if you didn't have a job, you had no incentive to stay, so you'd just move on. Everybody had some kind of a job. Some of the black children that were born here left for California, Salt Lake City—bigger towns. But some stayed, too.

I remember when I first came to Las Vegas, there were a few black families who lived on A Street; they had two or three lots. Most of them lived over in the town when I first came. There were not many blacks on the West Side; they lived downtown, mostly. Blacks did not live on Block 16. Block 16 was just a place where all the houses of prostitution were. Blacks owned some of the property, but they rented to the people who ran the establishments. They never mixed up on Block 16; you might as well say it was segregated, and most of the girls who worked the prostitution were white. I can recall maybe one or two black girls going over there in a matter of the ten or fifteen years that I lived close to it. Once or twice you'd see one come and stay a little while and then leave.

Blacks owned property in Las Vegas. Most of our people worked in the railroad shops, and the railroad company owned a lot of the land. They would encourage the employees to buy, so almost everybody had their own properties. Since blacks could buy property anywhere, every one of these people I remember owned more than just one house.

I recall a lot of the black people who lived in Las Vegas in the 1920s. There were thirteen or fourteen black families—perhaps as many as 100 individuals. Blacks were just like the rest of the people and had the same types of jobs, though there were never many black miners. Sam Nettles, Mary Nettles's husband, was a machinist in the railroad shop. Their son, Clarence Hodges, had a shoe-shine business combined with a newsstand on First Street, just off Fremont. There was another black family named Pullom. Ike [Isaac] Pullom was a machinist in the railroad shop. His wife was Nancy Pullom, and she was a housewife. They had two sons. One was named Ike, and the other was named Ernest, but he was commonly known all over the state as Babe Pullom. Nobody ever called him anything but Babe.

There was another family, the Levi Irvine family. Levi was a machinist for the railroad, and his wife was a housewife; I don't remember her name. Henry Wilson—who I came to Las Vegas with in 1922—worked in the railroad shop. Then there was the A. B. Mitchell family. Everybody called him Pop. He was a carpenter, and I later worked for him. He homesteaded forty acres in Paradise Valley with a man named Wash, who started the Fresh Air Club. Pop Mitchell had a wife and a daughter. His wife was a nurse in the local hospital, and his daughter, Natalie, was the first black child of record born in this town, followed by Cecile Mason. (Natalie is still alive and now lives in Seattle, Washington.) Pop Mitchell's sister, whose last name was Logan, owned ten acres on Industrial Road behind the present Stardust Hotel, which was once the location of the Sweet ranch. She was eventually paid $10,000 for her property. Cecile Mason and Juanita Stevens were probably the first black girls to graduate from high school in Las Vegas. Juanita Stevens was the mother of Juanita Barr, and she lived at Second and Stewart. She once owned about ten houses, near where the bus station is now.

Then there was Robert Jones, who was also a machinist for the railroad. His wife was Coreen Jones; she was one of the few black women who had a job doing domestic work. They had two children, Ruth and Robert Jones. Both of them were raised here and finished high school and then moved away to Los Angeles. There also was a Negro man who ran the express office; he was from New Jersey.

There are other people I remember: Ernie Stevens was kind of a handyman; he could do everything. They were still burning wood at the railroad, and he'd cut wood because he had a saw. He had one son, Orion Stevens, who was called Buster. He's still around Las Vegas, but he's very sick now. Buster retired from the railroad after fifty years. He was what they called a hostler helper. A hostler moves the engines and cars around to get them ready for the people to use. Buster advanced from a hostler helper and became a hostler. He took four years out to go into the service and came back, but he had forty-some years' seniority with the railroad company. His two sisters, Susie and Juanita, are still here. Juanita is quite a historian. Sue lives on Elliott Street, and her sister lives with her, but they both own their own homes.

Ralph Simpson, one of the men I came to Las Vegas with in 1922, stayed here as a machinist in the railroad shop. (They use the term "machinist," but they could be electricians or what-have-you.) Ralph Simpson married a woman named Georgia, who was a schoolteacher, and they had one daughter. She's still in Las Vegas and retired from the Motor Vehicles Department last year. Ralph Simpson homesteaded in Paradise Valley along with Bill Jones, Henry Wilson, Jimmy Turner, and some others.

Then there was the Hoggard family. (David Hoggard remembers that a black woman who looked East Indian used to own the Bellevue Hotel between Ogden and Stewart on Second Street.) I always argued with the people who said that Mabel Hoggard was the first black teacher in Las Vegas. About twenty years ago I put up an argument about that, but I found that they were right and I was wrong! I thought that Georgia Simpson was the first black schoolteacher. We had a little black paper here called the Las Vegas *Voice,* and I put a story about Mrs. Simpson in the newspaper. It showed a picture of Georgia Simpson and me talking over a fence. I had a chance to talk to her and she said, "Clarence, I was the first black teacher here, but I was working for the railroad company. Mrs. Hoggard was the first black teacher who was working for the Clark County school system." At that particular time there were a couple of railroad sections out there ten or fifteen miles from town. If they had as many as five or six children, they had to have a teacher, so that's how Georgia Simpson got to teaching. During her first full five years as a teacher, she was working for the railroad company, and Mrs. Hoggard was the first black teacher to work for the school system. So I had to write a retraction and apologize for my mistake.

There was a black man named Johnson, who was kind of a contractor. He could do a little of everything, and he took a contract to build houses. He could also lay brick. He lived here for a long time and owned a lot of property on First Street. He had two daughters and a grandson named Richard Courtney, who owned property at First and Stewart Streets. Since we were the same age, Richard and I did a lot of things together. We played ball together, and we used to fish and hunt and swim around the Colorado River. We'd hunt all over the southern part of Nevada. We hunted birds, rabbits, and, of course, deer. There were quite a few deer; you could kill deer out around what they call Mount Charleston now. Then they made a reserve out of it, and nobody could kill the deer up there but the Indians. The Indians could go and get one deer without a license or anything. Richard and I usually hunted close to town. We used to ride up in the Moapa Valley, because there were all kinds of birds and game. There were quail and doves, because people raised grain up there. Richard Courtney was hot-tempered; he was quick to fight. When we'd get into things, he would always be right. But Richard Courtney and I were very good friends. He stayed in Las Vegas and worked for the railroad company until he died.

Mr. Washington, another black man, had been a farmer in Iowa. He had a pretty good-sized family. He had a son named George and one named Howard. He also had two daughters, but I don't remember their names now. The daughters were both married to white men, and each one of them acquired some property around town. The two Washington boys worked in the railroad shop, and Mr. Washington had a place out in the country; it was small, and he had a truck garden. He died kind of early, just about the time I came here. Howard was the last of the Washington family that I can remember. He was a World War I veteran; he just died last year. They brought him back here from Detroit and buried him out where they had a plot.

Joe Lightfoot was another person I remember. He was black. There were three Lightfoot brothers: Art, George, and Joe. Joe and his wife were cooks, and they set up kitchens for the big mining operations out around Eldorado Canyon and Searchlight, which was a big gold mining center. Joe Lightfoot brought in black cooks to do the cooking and so forth. He'd go set up kitchens where they had big strikes. Sometimes Joe would have to leave one of his brothers to operate the kitchen until they brought in another cook. He made quite a living at it, and bought quite a bit of property around Las Vegas.

I recall "Mammy" Pinkston quite well because I used to live in one of her apartments. (Her real name was Ginny.) Ginny Pinkston was kind of a con woman. She had these big dinners and charged high prices, and the guys that was handling the money wanted her to cater the parties; they called her Mammy Pinkston. She didn't have too much to do with other blacks—I guess she just kind of isolated herself. She was here when I first came here.

I understand that the way she came to the state was that she was a maid in one of the houses of prostitution, and she knew quite a bit about operating one. (In fact, I heard that she later became an operator up around Ely or someplace.) She came to Las Vegas and opened a cafe, and that's what she was doing when I first came. Whites went to her cafe. She was married to an Englishman by the name of Wilshire; he was quite sociable. She never called him anything but Mr. Wilshire, so we all called him Mr. Wilshire. No one called her Mrs. Wilshire, though. Mr. Wilshire...I knew him! He was a real fine man. He'd just go around and take care of his apartments and collect the rent. They had gone to Utah to get married, and they came back here. Blacks and whites couldn't marry in this state at that particular time. When he passed away, he left all of his property to her. When he passed on, I guess he had people who were way over in England someplace, because nobody ever come to visit him, to my knowledge.

We had some people who came from Utah who were intermarried: for example, the Stevens family. Mrs. Stevens's first husband was white. (I don't know his name.) They had three sons. When he died, she married a black man, Erne Stevens. There were some mixed marriages and there were some who lived as common-law marriages on both sides: white women and black men; black women and white men.

There was a black barber in Las Vegas, but I can't think of his name. He was the only black barber in town. He'd take white customers or anybody who come along, but I don't remember seeing any blacks go to the white-operated barbershops. We only had one funeral home here, Palm Mortuary, and it was owned by Mrs. Parks. She was a white woman, but blacks used her funeral home, too.

Of course, when they later started building Boulder Dam, mainly black people came to Las Vegas. Orion Stevens's mother owned a lot of property downtown. She bought some property from Joe Lightfoot. She let people put up tents back there, and they started calling it Tent City, but nobody lived over there but blacks. This property that Mrs. Stevens owned was one-half the block going behind Stewart Street quite a way. (There were no more streets after Stewart Street, because the fairgrounds were there.) The other half of the block belonged to a white fellow named Frank Ryan. I think they got together and sold out at the same time.

I knew a lot of black men who worked on the dam. There was "Uncle" Jake Ensley and his son, Boysie Ensley. Jake came in 1931 from Muskogee, Oklahoma, right when they were building the dam. (All of the work on the dam was mining—digging through those rocks.) Jake had a cafe business on First Street. Later, he opened a club on First and Ogden. His son finally wound up with the gambling and rooming houses and all his other property. Boysie just passed away about ten years ago. Jake's been dead about twenty-five years.

Harvey Jones was a dam worker. He worked there until they completed the dam. He had quite a bit of property around town. He had two or three apartment houses—mostly rooming houses. He passed away about five years ago. He has a daughter named Anderson. His wife and son wound up with most of the Jones property when he died. Most all the guys who worked on the dam have now passed away.

Most of the Indians who stayed here in town lived in this little place they called the Indian village. It's still there. As you go to North Las Vegas, you cross the street where the big Indian smoke shop is on Paiute Drive—that's the entrance to the Indian village. It was created so they'd have some place to stay in town, because you know how funny they are about staying together. They all like to stay together, sort of like the Mexicans and the blacks. When they'd come into town, they'd want to have some place to stay. So the government gave them that land, too. That's why they have a store of their own.

In the 1930s the West Side became the black part of town. Before then, it had quite a number of whites, Mexicans—about a fifth of the population was Mexican—and a very few blacks. It was called Old Town in the 1920s. Blacks moved to the West Side because they bought lots from the railroad company for nearly nothing. People started to talk about $20,000, $30,000, $40,000 for a lot, and some of them already had lots over here on the West Side. Some had two or three fifty-foot lots. There was a black family I remember at the West Side whose name was Russell. The mother and her two sons, Eli and Harrison, lived on A Street. They had property there, I guess, up until the last one of them died. I remember one of the Russell guys got in a little trouble around here. He went away, and he had his brother just sell the property then. I don't know what happened to them, but I know they all died out. The Gilberts were here, too. Chet Gilbert operated a store on Bonanza Road on the West Side.

People wanted to move to the West Side from the downtown area. When they first came over, it was just like a desert, and the streets hadn't been laid out. It was really just a small community that hadn't yet been developed. But between the 1930s and the 1940s, it changed quite a little bit, because as a small amount of the blacks worked on the dam, they bought homes and built homes.

The only black businesses we had on the West Side during the 1930s was a couple of cafes downtown, and one two-storey hotel built by a lady who come out here from Pennsylvania. One of the cafes was called Uncle Jake's Place; his name was Jake Ensley. Then there was another cafe owner, Mrs. Harris. She had a place right on Stewart Street, across the street from where the old post office is. There was another fellow, too, named Johnson, who had a cafe on First Street right across the street from what they called Block 16, where prostitution was legal. Then there were barbershops. There was one just off of Fremont Street on First Street. That shop was owned by a black man named Harry Garrett. The other barbershop was on Stewart Street. There was a card room that was owned by a black fellow named Eli Nicholson; they called him Big Nick. That was on First Street just off Fremont. See, all the gaming that they had in town was on Main Street for two blocks. It was right along in there—except the gaming that Bill Jones and I put up on Stewart Street across from the post office.

The only thing that's been in business a long time in this community is owned by the Hewes family. They just have the liquor store now, but they used to have a grocery store, too. They've been there for thirty years. The rest of these businesses just come and go. Many people owned small lots here on the West Side that they weren't doing anything with. Although she never lived on this side of town, Mrs. Nettles had a house and lot over here, and she had been renting it for years. When blacks got to where they could sell their downtown property for a big profit, they sold it and came over here, but not because they were asked to move or anything like that. It was because as land prices went up downtown, many people couldn't afford to hang on to their property. In fact, many of them made a lot of money on properties which they had acquired for little or nothing. But Mrs. Nettles never did sell her downtown land. She kept it and rented it out. The Mitchells kept part of their land; the Pulloms had several lots; Tom Harris and his family kept theirs; the Irvines kept theirs and rented it out. (Mr. Levi Irvine, I think, was the first black guy who drowned in Lake Mead—he was out fishing. In the early days he worked in the railroad shop. When Mr. Irvine died, Mrs. Irvine moved over here onto some property that they had.)

When blacks started selling their downtown properties, it was said that they were asked to move out. That's not true. A lot of the things that they said about Ernie Cragin was mostly street talk. I never heard him say all these bad things, and I knew him quite well. When I first came to this town, I had gone to work over at the railroad shop for a little while, and Ernie Cragin was a bookkeeper over there at that particular time. There was a man by the name of William Pike—we called him Bill Pike—and Bill Pike liked Ernie Cragin, so he picked him up as a young man and took him in as a partner. Eventually they opened the El Portal theater and an insurance business, Cragin and Pike. Though black property owners downtown were not really forced out, Jake Ensley also said that the police commissioner in the late 1930s told black businessmen that their license would not be renewed unless they moved to the West Side. Chet Gilbert's father may have been the commissioner involved.

I owned property both on the West Side and in what they now call East Las Vegas. I bought the property in East Las Vegas in 1931. People had been living there, and the property had a well on it and a house. The owner came to see me and said, "My stepson says that you might be able to buy this land that I want to sell. I'd like to sell it to a black man because my wife was black, and we were together clear up until she died. She's buried here in this town." (This man and his wife had come here from Kansas, and I knew his stepson because we had played ball together in Kansas and Oklahoma.)

I said, "Well, I'd like to have it." I had seen the property, because his stepson showed it to me when he was here visiting. He had it fixed up real nice—a little garden spot and fence around it and everything. He said he wanted to have at least $5,000. I bought it, but I never did live on it; the guy who rented it raised chickens. I'd give him a part of whatever he could produce, and he had an acre that was under cultivation. I owned that property for probably eight years, but I continued to live in town in a house I rented from Joe Lightfoot. Joe had three or four houses right on Stewart Street just a block from the post office.

When I let the property go, I bought some other property over on West Washington Street on the West Side about 1934 or 1935. Nothing was here when I bought it, but people lived on the block. The Mendoza family lived on part of the block, and I bought what was left. There were just four 25-foot by 140-foot lots, and I bought them. That was on the original Las Vegas town site. That's where I live now, and I've still got all of the lots. I have just the one house that I built in 1942. I had a carpenter build it. This has been my home, but I haven't continuously lived here.

When I thought I was going into the Army, I put it into my mother's name, because I wasn't married. My mother put a cousin in there, and he stayed until I came back in 1947. When I came back, I never did take it out of her name. When she died, my sister had it probated back to me. I have a yard and trees and what-have-you. I guess why I like it so well is that it faces three streets, because it's a short block. I have 100 feet on Washington, 140 feet on H, and 100 on Allen. I bought another property in 1942, but I never lived there. An investment was all it was. I sold it while I was away, about 1945. In fact, my mother sold it for me.

This side of town would have been better if people could have just made the investments where they had their property, you know, built nicer homes, apartment houses, hotels. We did have a hotel in the 1960s that was built, but they let it go broke. It never really did get off the ground, because they never did no big gambling. Then the hotel was a little bit too far away; had it been two or three blocks closer downtown, where the white and black parts of town met, it would have been a success. But our problems in this part of town...we made them happen ourselves. We just didn't reinvest our money over here; we'd do something else with it. That's still true now, because they're doing the same thing.

I lived away from Las Vegas from 1942 to 1947. When I left, we only had this one little gambling house, and there weren't many other black-owned businesses. I moved to the San Francisco area, and I stayed up there four years before I moved back. Before I left, I had already built a house on the West Side in 1942. (Many blacks had moved to the West Side in the 1930s and 1940s.)

When I came back in 1947, there were four black-owned gambling houses operating on Jackson Street. That was the main business street among the blacks over here, and by that time the West Side had become known as the black community. One of those gambling houses was the Cotton Club. Another one was the Ebony Club, and there was the Chicka-dee. There was also the Brown Derby. So that made four gambling houses. By the time I got back in 1947, some of the streets had been laid on the West Side. Some people say that the living conditions were so bad on the West Side, but that's not true.

When I first came here, they had never had a regular city baseball team, because they had the railroad teams. (We were here four or five years and had nothing but the railroad teams.) If you worked in the rail-road shop, you could play; if you didn't work, you could still play! They called it a Union Pacific team. After about eight or ten years, they came up with a little city team, and eventually, there turned out to be white teams and black teams. Some of the Mexican kids who were raised and schooled around here were good athletes. They would just play with either team that they wanted to. I don't think we ever had an all-Mexican team, but I guess maybe the blacks segregated themselves. I don't recall what kind of a name we had, because we were just always in Las Vegas.

At one time there were two teams down here and they never did know which one was the best. Finally, the railroad company had what they called the inter-mountain championship from all the different railroad teams: Ogden, Salt Lake City, and all that. We split our team up, and all of us got on what was called the Union Pacific team from Las Vegas—whites, blacks, and Mexicans. One time we won the inter-mountain championship, but we had a little beef about getting the trophy, because some of us didn't work for the railroad company. We didn't get the trophy that time, because they were supposed to be playing a railroad team, and we were just a mixed city team.

When I first come here, the schools were not segregated. But they came up with redistricting in the school system after I moved here to stay in 1925. But there never was a race issue to my knowledge in the schools. Everybody just went to school together.

Back in the 1920s and early 1930s, blacks and whites in Las Vegas got along fine. They were just one big family. We had traveling bands come to town, and we could have a dance and everybody got together...we knew each other. Whites and blacks danced together and drank together, and we went to all the prizefights together. (There were some good fights here during the construction of the dam, but all the big fights that we ever had in this state were staged in Reno.) We went to everything together, and we would all sit together. There was a movie theater called the Majestic, where the Golden Nugget is now, and it was not segregated. Of course, there was only one grade school and one high school, so everyone went to school together, too. The high school was where the federal building is today. We never had any trouble until later.

The NAACP got popular out in the West in the 1920s. It had started in New York and worked its way out here. My family have been members of the NAACP ever since it started in 1910, and everywhere I went—Kansas, Oklahoma, California—people were NAACP members. They'd talk about the NAACP and said we needed it because it was a champion for the black folks. In Las Vegas, we knew about the NAACP, so some of us got together—this was in 1928. There was Mary Nettles, who I roomed with, and two or three others. We put $350 to organize an NAACP chapter and gave the money to A. B. Mitchell. We kind of made him the president, but instead of him taking the money and sending it back to the national office in New York, he took the money and left town! He went to San Diego and didn't come back for a long time. By that time I had seen him, so I told everybody, I said, "I saw Mitchell down in San Diego." (I had gone down to Tijuana to the races; when I was there, I saw him.)

Mrs. Nettles said, "What'd he say about our money?"

I said, "He wanted to press it. He wanted to borrow $50 from me!"

She said, "You can kiss that money good-bye. Let's have another meeting."

So, we had another meeting with the same people…except for A. B. Mitchell. Arthur McCants, who was a barber, was there. He had been the president of a local NAACP chapter up in Wyoming. He had resigned and came down here, so I talked to him. I said, "Would you be willing to help organize this thing? I've been trying to organize it, but I don't really know what I'm doing."

He said, "Yes, I'll be glad to help. It's needed very badly." So we set it up and put the money together again: Mrs. Nettles and me again; Bill Jones (one of my partners who ran a little gambling venture with me); and a woman named Zimmy Turner. It took the four of us to make the money up. At that time, it had to be four-hundred-and-some dollars to get the charter. Arthur McCants said, "Nobody's going to run off with this, because we're going to set this up right! We're going to send the bank draft back to the national." We sent it right away, and in less than a month, we had a charter. Arthur McCants was our first NAACP president of record.

INTERVIEW BY HELEN M. BLUE AND JAMIE COUGHTRY, JULY 1989 AND MAY–DECEMBER, 1991
COURTESY UNIVERSITY OF NEVADA, ORAL HISTORY PROGRAM

Archie Reynolds Jr.

Gospel singer
Born: December 13, 1921, Gulfport, Mississippi

Archie Reynolds was born in Gulfport, Mississippi, but moved often to different communities along the Gulf Coast when he was a child. He was influenced at an early age by the singing of his mother, who performed in a family gospel group called the Davis Sisters. While Reynolds was a student in secondary school in New Orleans, he sang with various groups, including the Gospel Bells and the Humble Queens. In 1943, he left New Orleans for San Francisco, following the advice of some of his relatives, who called California "the land of milk and honey" because there was less racism and many more opportunities. In California,

Reynolds organized his own gospel group, the Sewanee River Singers, and later formed the Symphonic Harmoneers. In 1951, he joined the Paramount Singers, a successful gospel quartet, and toured extensively, although most of his income derived from outside work, the most successful of which was his own business, Archie's Hickory Pit barbecue restaurant and catering service.

My father was Archie Reynolds Senior. He was a chef cook. And he cooked at some of the great hotels down there in Gulfport, Mississippi—Edgewater Gulf Hotel and others at that time. From there we went to New Orleans, and there he cooked at the Monteleone Hotel and Ursuline Convent. Then, we went back to Mississippi, Bay St. Louis, where he was cooking at St. Stancil Arts College.

My father could cook anything; he'd cook a lot of French dishes. French food, that was his specialty, really. He came from Biloxi, Mississippi, actually. That's where he was born. I don't know how he became a chef, because I heard my mother say, "Well, I taught you how to cook." You know, "I taught you how to cook, and blah, blah." But I think it was just something that he picked up during the time, and then he read a lot. He read a lot of books. Now if he went to school, I don't know about that. All I know, he was well qualified and well thought after.

I only knew my grandmother on my mother's side. Chloe Davis. And I remember as a little boy, I was playing in the yard and she was washing clothes and they had during those days, a scrub board and she was out there. And they had a little shed built, and she was out there under that shed. And then I was playing, and she fell. And when she fell, I ran. I called her and she didn't answer, and I ran next door and got one of the neighbors and when they came over, she had died. She had an aneurysm. Yeah, my mother died with an aneurysm. I had it, see, I had an aneurysm, but I survived it. So far.

When I was little we moved around a lot. We were back and forth, but during that period of time, my mother was a good singer. She sang solos in churches. And everybody admired her voice. So I think I probably followed her in this singing field because when I was a little boy about four years old, they told me they used to put me up on a stool in the church so I could sing. This is where my career started.

My mother's name was Clozella Reynolds. Her maiden name was Davis, and her and two of her sisters and another relative of ours, they called themselves the Davis Sisters. Now you got to visualize this. This is back in Hansboro, Mississippi—little old, small town, and they included me in this one appearance. They say that I rehearsed with them, and I was supposed to sing this song, "Little David, play on your harp, hallelu, hallelu, David, play on your harp, hallelu, hmmm, hmmm. It ain't but one train that run this track." I was to be the little train, running the track. You know, "runs right to glory." I was supposed to run out in front of the audience and sing, "and it runs right back." But everything I was supposed to have done, I didn't do. And I rehearsed for it.

My mother said, "When I get you home, I'm gonna run your little track."

But my father, he pleaded my case. He said, "Ah," he used to call my mother "Hon." "Ah, Hon, he's just a little boy, he didn't understand everything. You guys didn't rehearse him enough. So please, don't run his little track."

So, that was my first solo, my first indication I was going to be a singer with a group, I guess. From then on, we moved, we were in New Orleans again. We were back in New Orleans. See, wherever my father went, that's where we had to go because he was the breadwinner.

I remember that they had a church in Algiers (section of New Orleans) and the pastor there was named Billy Sunday. You've heard of Billy Sunday? They tell me he was a great white preacher. But this pastor in Algiers was named Black Billy Sunday. And he saw me there in the church, and he knew of my reputation.

He said, "Well, I think we have a surprise for you this morning. We're gonna let 'Toots' (that was my nickname) sing before I deliver the message this morning." So he called, "Toots, will you come up and sing a solo?"

Well, I was just energetic to go up there and sing a solo. And I decided I was going to go up and do what my mother did. When she was out washing clothes and hanging them up on the line, she was singing this song, and just enjoying it, making up her own lyrics. So on this particular Sunday, I said I'm gonna sing this song. "At the cross, at the cross, where I first saw the light and the burdens of my heart rolled away. It was there by faith I received my sight and now I am happy all the day." But you see, my mother had put her own lyrics in it. She said, "At the bar, at the bar, where I smoked my first cigar and the change in my pockets rolled away. It was there by chance that I tore my Sunday pants and now I have to wear them every day." And you know what happened? You can imagine what happened. My mother whipped me all the way from the church to our home.

And finally, I said, "Maybe solos are not too good for me to sing." I wanted to sing with a group, and that's what I did. I began singing with different groups. I started with the Gospel Bells. That was in New Orleans. Then there was another group, they called themselves the Humble Queens or something like that.

I gained quite a bit of recognition in New Orleans from singing because I was a tenor singer. I was a tenor singer my whole life until the bass

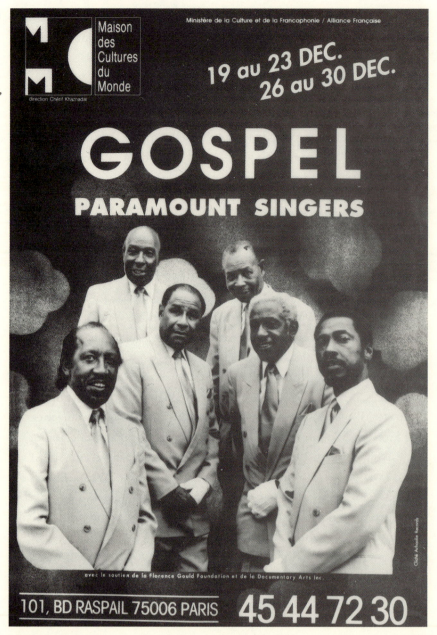

Left to right: Archie Reynolds, J. B. Williams, Clyde Price, Rev. Oddis Brown, Joseph Dean, William Johnson (Arhoolie Productions)

singer died with the Paramount Singers. We could not find another bass singer to fit the style of singing that we sung. So I said, well, you could find tenor singers, but you couldn't find bass singers. So I said, "Well, I'll sing bass." If you notice, tenor singers and bass, they're on the same scale when you're singing. One is high and the other one is low. But they are (essentially) the same voice.

I left New Orleans for California because in New Orleans during that time, you couldn't make a living singing. In Louisiana, there was quite a bit of discrimination. There was always discrimination, but my father had some stature because he was a chef cook. For us, it wasn't as bad because we didn't live in the—I hate to say low-class area—you know, we were always well taken care of. I know he made enough in those days. We had three cars when people were walking. And there were five of us. I had two brothers and two sisters. My oldest brother was named Robert Reynolds. And coming on down the line, I'm next, Archie Reynolds. My sister, oldest girl, Evelyn Reynolds. The next was my other sister, Esmerelda Reynolds, and then the baby was my brother Henry Reynolds. They came to California after me. I was the pioneer.

Things were happening here so fast in California, I didn't have time to really concentrate on it, you know. In 1943, I came here from New Orleans. I came individually on the Santa Fe Railroad. Paid my own way out here. But the interesting part is that it was summertime; I had on a straw hat, white shoes, white suit. And when I got to San Francisco and got on the Market Street streetcar, that wind was blowing. It was cold like Alaska in August, when I came here. And people were looking at me as to say, "I wonder where he came from." But I felt very, I felt really embarrassed. I don't think I owned a white suit or straw hat until I started singing recently to make it a uniform. But to own a white suit, no. Not here in California.

I picked San Francisco because I had some relatives here. They came a little before me. They came like maybe three months before I did, and they called me and said, "Archie, this is the land of milk and honey, almost." Say, "Why don't you come out?" Says, "Plenty work out here."

And during that time, I had just two kids. And so I told my wife, I said, "Well, I think I'll go out to San Francisco." And that's how we came out here, to San Francisco. I got married just before the war. The war started in 1941; my wife and I, we got married in 1940. July the 20th, 1940. My wife's name is Cora Lee Reynolds. Her maiden name was Cora Lee Hill, and she was from New Orleans. After we got married, I didn't go to the (military) service. I had bad eyes. My vision, I had bad vision, so I didn't make it.

My first cousin was here, Lillian Winfield, and two sisters' children, and her husband, Herbert Winfield. And then there was Martha Wilson, which was my mother's sister. And then her son was John Wilson. So they were here before I was, before I came out here. They encouraged me. They all came from Louisiana. They worked for the Navy and then I got a job working for the Navy. I was an electrician. I was doing electrical work for the Navy. It was fun then because I was making plenty of money. I think, in '43, I must have been getting about $5 an hour, $5 or $4.25, about minimum wage, I'm thinking, then. Five dollars, in '43. Minimum wage for today. That's right. That was a lot of money.

Yeah, it was good. I just cannot really tell you how it looked out here at that time. People were like ants building ant beds. People doing so much work. I mean, shipyards, work, just work, work, all kinds of work, night and day. It was like something I had never seen before. Night and day, twenty-four hours a day, people were just like passing each other going to work, or down, don't go to entertainment, because the place be full. Everywhere you went. Churches were full.

I was living over in the Fillmore District when I first came here. That was called the location for the blacks, in the Fillmore area, but it was always mixed. It was always mixed, but predominantly the blacks lived in that area. And now the Japanese have it, mostly.

The Fillmore extended from, let's say Hays Street all the way out to approximately California Street. But this is a long area. And this is where blacks had predominantly all the businesses. In that section of the city: clubs, stores, everything in that section. But they never bought, they never owned anything. Because when the Japanese came back out of the service, they took that area over.

Then I moved out here to Bay View. They call it Bay View-Hunter's Point. When I first came here, it was Italians, mostly, in this area. And to tell you, I was the first black businessman. You see that plaque up on that wall here? I was the first black president of the Bay View Business District. I came out here in '57. And I had a hickory pit (barbecue), we called it Archie's Hickory Pit.

My business flourished. I had the respect of the whole Bay View District. And so they voted me in as the first president, black, of the whole business district, never had been a black holding that position. They have twenty-four districts in this city, and I was the first one. I've met practically all the mayors, the senators. And I was the second black on the CMC, Community Music Center. I was the second black on that.

The discrimination wasn't visible at the time. Because so many people—whites, blacks, Asians—everybody was just working. They didn't have time to concentrate on discrimination, and things opened up. I understand some people had some incidents. But everything was open, you know, the hotels, motels, the clubs, the restaurants. For example, the Fisherman's Wharf was always open to everybody. It was great. And that's what made people want to stay here. Because it was cosmopolitan. It wasn't just like in the South where I left from, where it was just black and white. Here, you had Asians, you name them. We have all nationalities here. And that's why a lot of people love this area here.

California was also good for my music. When I got here, I organized a group called the Sewanee River Singers. You know, different voices. I'd go to church and hear different voices, and I'd put these voices together.

Later on, I figured out that with other good singers coming out to California from back east, my group was not comparable. And I sort of got a little bit discouraged with my group competing against others.

Then, I met Cy Hartman, a Jewish fella, who had heard us sing, and he asked me, says, "Archie, would you like to do some little pop songs? I can guarantee you you'll get more money."

I said, "I'll try."

So he said, "Do you know anybody?"

And I got a few more guys. One of the guys was named Louis. Another was R. B. McLendon, and a guy named Hamilton. So, there were four of us and we called ourselves the Symphonic Harmoneers. And we did a few things with Cy; we worked nightclubs, and some state fairs. We did clubs and whatever else, you know.

But my heart was always in the gospel field, always. So my wife, she said, "Archie, you know, I'd prefer you singing gospel, you know. You like gospel."

Well, the Paramount Singers heard about me. They had heard me before, and they were coming to my home, asking me to sing with them. They needed a tenor singer. So I said, "Okay. I'll think about it." And that's how I joined the Paramount Singers, and left the Symphonic Harmoneers. I told them, "I'm gonna do gospel, because that's in my heart."

The Paramount Singers came to the San Francisco area from Austin, Texas, and they had a huge reputation. A lot of the Soul Stirrers came from the Paramount Singers. You heard of the Soul Stirrers.

Jenoa Terrell was the founder of the Paramount Singers, and the group included his brother, Kermit Terrell, Ben Williams, and Haywood Medlock, the bass singer, who later went to the Soul Stirrers. The Paramounts' main lead singer was named Sam Reese, and he went on to the ministry. They were all from Texas. Then Victor L. Medearis, who has a church here, too, he's pastoring, he was in the group because he was a tenor singer. At the time, they had two tenors. That's why they wanted me. Two tenor singers because their voices weren't strong enough for one. But Medearis, he's now pastor of the Double Rock Baptist Church. So when he started pastoring the church, I became the manager. He was the manager then. I became the manager of the Paramount Singers. I think it was around 1950 or '51.

In California at that time, there were a lot of black musicians—gospel, R&B, pop, many from Texas. There was T-Bone Walker. A lot of good artists. John Lee Hooker was out here, came out here, and people came from all over the South. They had artists come out from Chicago, too. Because, see, let me sort of go back just a little bit. They had black hotels in the Fillmore District. They had one on Fillmore, the Manor Plaza. That was across that on Fillmore between McAlister and Fulton. And across the street, Mr. King, before I went into the barbecue business, they used to call him King. And he had a barbecue business. But not of my magnitude. It was small, but he made plenty of money. And he opened this club for his daughter, who was named Leola King. She had a club around there in that same block where the Manor Plaza was. And that was during the time that Joe Louis was fighting and champion. And all the celebrities would congregate at this club she had. And it was a beautiful club. She kept good artists. She kept real top-notch artists coming in here. You know, Flip Wilson used to live at the Manor Plaza, too.

Blues, jazz, gospel. This place was just loaded with music. That (gospel) quartet sound was popular, but let me tell you , they didn't sing it like we are doing now. For instance, I'll give you an idea. When we went to Paris (1994) and we sang at this theater for two weeks; that was not heard of, not for gospel singers. Gospel singers were confined to churches and to an auditorium, maybe. But it has expanded because now gospel singers are in theaters, clubs, nightclubs, you know.

My mother's group was the first quartet I ever heard. Yeah, they made themselves a quartet. They called themselves the Davis Sisters. When I came here, there were a few, but not relatively known. They had the Rising Star, they had these guys from Richmond, Richmond, California.

When I came here, I belonged to the Third Baptist Church. It was located downtown on Taylor—no, it was on Jones, not Taylor. It was on Jones and right off California. Downtown. It was a black church. And then later on, they moved to where they are now, back on McAlister. Big church, but downtown, it was kinda small, it wasn't as large as it is now. But that was the first church I belonged to. And then when Madearis started pastoring, I joined his church. Double Rock Baptist Church. Then after, well, a couple of guys left Medearis and went over to Providence; so I just joined, went over to Providence. I joined Providence. And that's the only three churches I've ever belonged to.

With the Paramounts we did some big shows. We did some things with Doris Day at the Golden Gate Theater. And that just came in later years, you know, when we went to Salt Lake City, Utah. We did a thing up there. And just started working festivals. See, gospel groups years ago didn't ever work festivals.

For years, the Paramounts just did churches. That's right. Just take up donations. But the churches would be full at night, you know. Every night in the week, you could have a good, solid gospel program. Because, you have to remember, this was right after the war and people were really kind of frightened. I think when things like that happen, the churches begin to have more people. But then it seems like after they find out it's not happening, they scatter again, you know what I'm saying? They scatter, yeah.

The first recording opportunity we had with Decca because of that song "Peace in the Valley." That was in the forties. Decca had heard about us through, I don't know, some source. They had heard about us, but at that time, we were not available. We were gone. And so when they found out it was a public domain number, they just utilized it and got Red Foley to do it, and he made millions off of it. So that was the first big opportunity we had. We still did stuff for Decca anyway, but they put it on the Coral label. They told us that they could release it faster on Coral than they could on Decca, so we went for that. We weren't record-wise, you know, at that time. Then later on we recorded for Peacock. Don Robey. In the 1950s, he had heard of our reputation. This guy named Tiny Powell, who was from back east, that was with the Paramount Singers at that time, he had a reputation from back east all the way out here. And Don heard about him being with the Paramount Singers. He was looking for talent. Don Robey had the Blind Boys, but he didn't have the Soul Stirrers. He had the Blind Boys and the Bells of Joy, who recorded "Let's Talk about Jesus." Bobby Bland was on his label, too.

We went to Houston to cut about, I think we did about six or eight songs with Robey. Oh, he was a nice guy, very businesslike. He loved gospel music; he got excited when he heard that song we sing about "Jesus Is All This World to Me." And it was so short and compact until he stopped his whole staff from working. Robey said, "I want you to hear this song." "Jesus Is All This World to Me." And then the song that I wrote was another one, he put that on the other side. "Mother." I wrote that song. And then we did some more with him. "Work and Pray On," and quite a few others.

We did pretty well with him. But we didn't follow up like we should have, you know. During those days, we were excited just to let it get out and so people could hear it. But as far as the business end of it, we just got our front money and that was it. At that time, I'll tell you about the Paramount Singers. We never did go back east because, like I said, we all had families. We were working, and singing on the side. And you couldn't leave. We had families to support.

I had thirteen employees at the Hickory Pit, and I was the largest hickory pit in San Francisco. I used to deliver all over the city. Even to Fantasy Records. I used to do all his picnics. I used to do Bell Records out of New York. I had ribs, chicken, hot links, potato pies, beef, apple pies, lemon pies, and all kinds of barbecue. I was delivering all over the city.

I wanted to educate my kids. I wanted them to have a decent education. So I said, if I go into business for myself, I think I can possibly do it. But I couldn't do it when I was working for the post office. And so that's what inspired me to go into my own business. But I never knew it was going to grow this big. You know, up to that magnitude. Archie's Hickory Pit. And it was, if you'd see the phone directory in those days, I had an ad. It was a picture drawn in here with a truck, and the truck had wings on it. So that meant fast service. Take it and go and deliver. We delivered all over. So when Hunter's Point, when the shipyards were working, I would do $1,500, just for lunchtime. And then after lunch, I didn't close until three o'clock. And then after the clubs closed, during dinnertime, I delivered all over the city. Oh, I was big business. Plus, I also had a record shop. Right on Third Street, too, right in that same area. But I named it after my daughter, Paulette's Records. That's the way I had it. So I was in the record business for quite a while.

During the same time I had the Hickory Pit, I started Archway Records, and I recorded a comedian who's active today. And incidentally, he's in Dallas. Howard Eubanks, I don't know if you ever heard of him. He lives in Dallas. He was out here, and then he moved to Dallas, Texas. I did an album on him. I did an album on Jacqueline Jones and on the relatives. I didn't follow through because distribution was tough at that time.

I have six kids. Two boys and four girls. Six kids. Archie Jr. is the oldest. He's actually Archie III, but after my father died, he was just Junior. And then I have Ursalander, she's the oldest girl. Paulette, who used to have the record shop. I named it after her, and she's a sheriff now; she's been with the sheriff's department a long time. Lucius is my other son, Lucius Reynolds. And then there's Janeth Reynolds, and my baby, Leora Reynolds. She's not a Reynolds now. She got married in September last year. They're all here in California. In fact, Janeth is living with me now, and my other daughter, Leora, the one that just got married, her and her husband, I gave them this apartment upstairs. But they're buying a place now. They're buying their own place. So my daughters are well off.

Archie Junior, he plays music. He plays bass. I don't think he has a band right now, but they had like a five-piece band. Hip-hop. He tried to help me one time. He wanted to sing gospel, but he's not into it. He's more into the pop side of life. Lucius, he's a barber. And the rest of my kids, they work for the school system.

Moving to California was the right choice for me. And for my relatives. It was good for them, too. Most of them have passed, and the ones that haven't, they're in Oakland. They live on the Oakland side. So I don't see them that much, as I should.

A lot of people were working in Oakland at the naval supply depots and you know, whatever. Seemed like they had a lot of work over in Oakland for people that wanted that type of work. But you can look at my hands. I never did nothing like that but cooked, you know. And I did clerical work, and that's all. I had a big business until after the shipyards closed about 1970, then my business went down. I couldn't get people to deliver because they started robbing the drivers. That made things a lot tougher. So I sold the hickory pit place I had and I bought a club. I bought the Horse and Cow, which was a bar in '73. It was just a regular bar—didn't have no live entertainment. Jukebox music.

The Horse and Cow was very successful until my bartender got killed. And when he got killed, I just felt, well, I'm still a gospel man; I can't get away from that. Still a religious man. Him and some other guy got into it. Shot him in the head. And I seen that and I said, "No, this is not for me." I sold that. I said, I'm outta here. I was in there three years and I sold it.

Then I went down and opened up a travel agency down on Gary and Paul. I had Archway's Travel Service down there. I've always been an entrepreneur. I have. But after I had the aneurysm, I just retired. That was about '78. I think it was, yeah. So far. I've been blessed. You can look at my family and tell, you know. You haven't seen that many of them, my kids are here. They're very supportive of us. They're very good to us, close-knit, you know, close-knit family. We're not a distant family.

INTERVIEW BY ALAN GOVENAR, JUNE 7, 1997

Herman Simmons

Pullman porter
Born: September 21, 1916, Violet, Louisiana

Herman Simmons grew up in New Orleans and aspired at an early age to be a Pullman porter. For Simmons, becoming a Pullman porter offered the frontier of travel and the opportunity for financial security: When he was a child, the Pullman porter he knew in his neighborhood had a "nice home…his kids were neat….Most of us were renting. He was buying his home." Simmons was hired by the Pullman Company in 1943 and moved to California, but he only worked five months before he was drafted. During World War II, he served in the Navy. After his discharge, he returned to the Pullman Company, where he worked until 1969. In this oral history, Simmons recounts his experiences in New Orleans, including a discussion of racism, Mardi Gras, brass bands and jazz, and he provides an overview of his career as a Pullman porter and his memories of union organizers C. L. Dellums and A. Philip Randolph. In addition, Simmons recalls his life in the African American communities of San Francisco and Oakland.

Unidentified Pullman porter, 15 September 1940 (Culver Pictures)

I was born in a little town about ten miles below New Orleans called Violet. Like the flower. But I was raised in New Orleans. As a baby, my mother moved to New Orleans and I stayed there until 1943. And then after 1943, I came to California to work for the Pullman Company. I was twenty-seven years old at the time. And I worked for Pullman from July 5 until December 15. Then I was drafted into the Navy. At that time, they gave you a choice, Army, Navy, or Marines. So I went into the Navy. I stayed in the Navy two years. I was sent to Great Lakes. Then I went to Hampton Institute for diesel training. At that time they were giving blacks a chance at just being messmen in the Navy, you know. And I had four months of training at Hampton Institute; then from there they sent me to Minneapolis, Minnesota. There was no diesel engine nowhere on the base. So I stayed there for two years.

When I first enlisted in the Navy, we went to the Great Lakes. And when we got off the train from Chicago to the Great Lakes, we had our civilian clothes on. We just got into the Great Lakes, and we walked into the big auditorium with guys coming from all over the country, white and black sailors coming into the Great Lakes. And as you walked into the main drill hall (that's where they interviewed you when you went in there) a loudspeaker was saying, "All the white mates will get to stand to the left, and all the Negro mates, or the colored mates, will move to the right."

Then they come over with the big boxes to put beside you. Big pasteboard boxes. And tell you how to undress and how to put your clothes in that box to pack them. They were going to send your clothes back home. And then they sent you to another section of the hall there and issued Navy clothes. Like, say, for instance, a white cap, your Donald Duck cap, your blue trousers, your dress trousers, your white trousers, your shoes, so many pair of shoes, the underwear and everything, and a little bag they called a ditty bag, which was like a toilet kit. You carry your toothpaste and your soap and everything in that. And then your sea bag, which was the big bag where you pack your clothes up in that.

The whites and the blacks stayed in different camps. I was in Camp Robert Smalls, and then I was in Camp Lawrence. But now when I got sent to Minneapolis, we still had separate barracks, but there weren't too many of us up there. See, because we were going to service school. We were supposed to be the elite. In other words, we weren't just ordinary sailors. When I came out, I was discharged as a fireman first class. But I never went overseas at all. The only action I saw was in the ring. I used to like to box around New Orleans.

We used to box in the streets like that, not no professional or nothing like that, no. I was twenty-nine when I got into Golden Gloves. And I believe I'm the oldest man to go into Golden Gloves. Now, boxing was not very segregated. Yeah, Joe Louis took care of a whole lot of it. I once got to see Joe Louis train. I never seen him fight, other than in the movies and stuff like that. Well, he was an easygoing guy. Nice, quiet. And he had a sense of humor. Well, he had character. I mean he wasn't flamboyant or nothing like that. Boxing was more of a sport than it is now.

I boxed in the Golden Gloves in 1945, and lost. And then by that time, the war was over, and I was sent down to Corpus Christi, Texas. I was discharged from there in 1945, November 5. Then I returned back to California with the Pullman Company. They said my job was still open for me with my seniority. And I worked for Pullman until 1969, when they went out of business. And then Southern Pacific knew that I was a sleeping car porter. I used to make beds on the train. And when Pullman went out of business, Southern Pacific needed men to operate their sleeping cars. So I went over to Southern Pacific and worked for them for about two years. Then they decided to give up passenger business altogether. All your railroads, your major railroads. Then that's where Amtrak comes in; the government comes in. Now they take over the passenger trains. Now when Amtrak took over the railroads, it was an overnight thing. They had no employees. So, the railroads kept us on to instruct new members. See, they started hiring people left and right. And I worked as an instructor for several months. And then I stayed on as a porter with Amtrak until 1980. I retired in 1980. I caught the first Amtrak train from Seattle to Oakland.

I grew up in the Seventh Ward area of New Orleans. There are different wards, you know. I lived in the Seventh Ward. I lived in the Ninth Ward. I lived in the Sixth Ward. And there's another place they call the Treme. My mother was named Elizabeth. Elizabeth Lenares. That was her maiden name. She was born in 1900. I won't forget that. She passed in 1949. At that time, I was living in Richmond, California.

My father's name was Augustus Simmons. He was born and raised, and he passed, in Violet. That's where he lived all his life. I don't remember my father's birth date because my mother and my father separated while I was still a baby, a little kid. He passed in 1926. I saw him every now and then. My mother would take me down to visit with him, you know what I mean, but I never knew too much about him. Oh, far as I remember, he was working at the sugar refinery in New Orleans. The American

THE POSTAL ALLIANCE

AN ORGANIZATION OF ACHIEVEMENT ★ ORGANIZED IN 1913

OFFICIAL ORGAN, NATIONAL ALLIANCE OF POSTAL EMPLOYEES

Future Status of War Service Employees Under Civil Service (see page 2)
$300.00 *Pay Raise* vs. $748.00 *Loss in Overtime* (see page 4)

A. Philip Randolph (see Cover, page 5)
Dedicated to the Cause for a Permanent F.E.P.C. (see pages 18, 19, 20, 21, 22, 23)

FEBRUARY   PRICE 15 CENTS   1946

A. Philip Randolph, 1946 (Texas African American Photography Archive)

Sugar Refinery. And he got sick. And when he passed, I went down and stayed in Violet for about a short time with my grandparents. Then my mother came to get me and brought me back to New Orleans. So every now and then, every year or every two or three years, I'd go down and visit them because they really liked me quite a bit. And they gave me almost everything I wanted. And, as a matter of fact, they helped support me because my mother wasn't able to do too much for me.

My mother worked around, washing, domestic work, washing and ironing, and house cleaning, in New Orleans. Both of my grandparents were farmers. George Simmons was my grandfather on my father's side. His wife was called Henrietta. We used to call her Ietta, you know. That's his wife. That was my grandmother. And on my mother's side, my grandfather was Claudino Lenares. And his wife was called Ernestine Voltaire.

I remember when my grandfather died, but I don't remember his birth date or anything. On my mother's side, they spoke French. My mother never knew her mother. She never remembered her mother. She was pretty young. She was the baby out of four sisters, she was the smallest; she was the youngest one.

There was quite a bit of racism in New Orleans. I can give some incidents. But I'll tell you one thing about New Orleans. The working-class people, the poorer class of people, there wasn't no segregated neighborhoods. They all lived together. So it was integrated neighborhoods. Now some neighborhoods may have had more whites than blacks, and some may have more blacks than whites. But now, the middle class and the richer people, those were the ones that had they own neighborhoods and everything, like up the Garden District, up around St. Charles Avenue and up around Napoleon Avenue and all them places there. But they had groceries, grocery stores like was mostly run by whites, on each corner like that. And some of them was Italian, and some were Irish. The kids, we all played together. All day we played together, and at night, we'd fight. They'd call us that N-word, and we'd call them the W-T word, you know, which meant white trash, and we'd fight. The next day, we was out there playing again.

Well, when they built this project, when the government started building projects, I moved into the Lafitte project back in about '41. About in the forties, they started building those projects there. Then they built white projects and black projects, and that's where they separated. But I worked in a pants factory. I used to go to work at six o'clock in the morning, get off five o'clock in the evening. Six dollars a week, and I even had a family. You look at it like this: You used to be able to buy bread for a nickel. Nickel loaf of bread and get beans and rice for a nickel, half and half, you know. And you buy some shoes, you're going to buy a pair of shoes or a trousers or a suit. You pay so much down, it was maybe $4 for a pair of tailor-made trousers and you pay fifty cents down, pay five cents a week. And we had streetcars; public transportation and things, they were segregated. You had blacks in back, whites in the front.

The grocery store where we went kept two sets of books when you went to buy groceries. A ledger; there was theirs and then you had yours. Now they'd mark whatever you buy. You buy rice, red beans and rice or something, they mark it in the book. And when you go to pay it, on Saturdays, you look at your book and at their books. And there was usually ten or fifteen cents more in their book than you had. That wasn't much, but in those days, that counted for a lot, you know. So, I'd say, "Well, I didn't buy that. My book says so and so."

"Yeah, but…" So if you didn't pay them you didn't get credit the next week. But they'd give you something when you'd paid your bill you call lagniappe. That was like a thank-you. A box of cookies, candy bar, something, you know. In other words, "Thanks for dealing with us."

There was one guy who had an ice truck. He used to deliver ice back in those days, in big wagons and trucks. So he'd tell the kids, like on Saturday afternoon, "Run, everybody run. You go out and run the kids out. Tell them we're going to leave at six o'clock. We going to the theater." And we'd leave from the grocery store, going to the theater. And we'd all get in the back of the truck, boys and girls, black and white, laughing, talking, joking. You know how kids like to do, playing. And when we get to the theater, we'd get out of the truck. We'd go to this door, and they'd go around to that door. See, there were two entrances. And he'd leave word, say, "Now I'll be back for y'all at nine o'clock," or eight o'clock, whatever time it would be. "Now who's not here, I'm going to leave you. I want everybody out here at that time." And we'd be looking around, near nine o'clock, near eight o'clock, be looking around the theater say, to the other kids, say, "We'd better go because he'll be back here for us after a while."

Now blacks had little shops, like wood shops, coal, and stuff like that, little small shops, snowball shops that sell candies and cookies, like that. They had a little business going on there, too. And so, as I grew up, when you got to a certain age, the white kids, when they start courting, going out to see boys and girls and stuff like that, they want you to call them Missus or Mister. And you know, we were not going to argue with them.

We used to have a lot of fun, but we had some bad times, too. Hard times, like on the streetcars. You get on the streetcar, and if it was full, they had a screen—it was a little border, "For colored patrons" on one side, an on the other side, "For white patrons." Now underneath that board, you had two prongs that went to a hole on the back of the seat. So, I'd get on the streetcar in the back, and they got a lot of vacant seats up ahead, and a white person sitting back to the last seat. I'd ask him, "Do you mind moving up a seat or two," something like that, you know what I mean. Sometimes they'd move, sometimes guy would say, "I ain't going nowhere; you stand up," like that, you know. Well, in that case, we'd pick the screen

Interior of Southern Pacific's Oakland Mole Terminal where about 40 Redcaps were employed in the 1930s (San Francisco Maritime National Historic Park)

up, put it in front of him, and sit. Now he's sitting behind the screen, too. Eventually, they'd get up, and you'd move.

I noticed when they showed what happened in Montgomery (Alabama) the black passengers would get on the bus in the front, pay their fare, come down, go around to the back and get on the bus through the back door. We didn't do that in New Orleans. We all got on in the front. Only when we got on, we paid our fare, and we went to the back, automatically. But that didn't seem to make sense, to get on, put your money in there, then get back, walk around, and get in the back door. Now, Rosa Parks—there could have been a whole lot of people who did what she did—but she was just lucky to get caught, because she was tired and she happened to be in the wrong place at the right time.

We had quite a few skirmishes. People would get into fights sometimes. I don't remember being spit on, but I mean, I've been insulted, and, of course, I've insulted some of them, too. Oh, they'd say, "Get right back where you belong. Get back in the back where you belong!" And I'd say, "I belong anywhere I want to sit. You gonna move me?" Things like that, you know. It usually didn't mean much, it didn't move to anything.

In the wards in New Orleans we had music. I was too young at that time to go to a lot of those places, but I used to see them street bands. You see, the bands would come on, like Louis Armstrong, Buddie Petit, all those different guys. They'd come around and they'd have a ball or something going on, so they'd come around on the truck, on the back of a truck. And every corner they'd get to, they'd play music. And everybody come out in the streets and start clapping their hands and dancing at the music. Then they moved to the next block and played. It had a big sign on it, say, "We gonna have a ball tonight" at such and such a club. I was a small kid.

And I remember the Mardi Gras Indians. At that time, they only had two of them down there, two. We call them tribes. You had one called the Yellow Pocahontas, and one was called the Hundred and One Ranch. And they had another one, but I can't think of the name of that one. But now you got a whole bunch of them out there. And they were some of the most different things you went to see on Mardi Gras day, but they raised so much hell that when the police come, they say, "Here come the cowboys." Those guys would get out there, they'd fight and put on a beautiful show. Now they've all organized so it's one of the prettiest things you want to see down there.

Oh, they had beautiful costumes. Like they making a costume for next year now. Right after Mardi Gras day, they start making a costume for the next year. I've gone back to New Orleans several times. Last time I was down there was about two years ago. My wife and I went down for the Mardi Gras, but every two or three years, I go down.

Everyone went to see them Indians when I was growing up. Yeah, they'd say, "Here come the Indians, down there." "Where?" "They over on that street, and they coming this way." Well, they were dancing. And I guess it was Indian songs they were singing, but they were dancing and they had tambourines. They had queens. Women, they called the queens, with long, long wigs hanging off the side of their head. And they had beautiful costumes on, too, and they'll be dancing. They had one they called the Spy Boy. He'd go about three or four blocks ahead.

I knew some of them Indians Some of them I went to school with, you know. Oh, they liked it. They looked forward to it every year. I mean, it's one of the biggest things down there, especially among blacks.

And on Mardi Gras day the Zulu parade was always a big one. But it wasn't as big as it is now. See, now they got beautiful floats. Now they got some floats now, about twelve, thirteen floats. Before, they used to have, it was a comedy thing. They used to have the queen, riding on an old wagon with a horse pulling the wagon at her wedding. Had an old raggedy white gown on with a bouquet of wilted flowers in her arms, and the groom was on there with an old busted-up beaver hat on and an old tuxedo all full of holes and everything. And that was a big thing. You see, it was a wedding ceremony. I mean just the queen and the bride and groom. That was the king's daughter. Now the king sat on the only float they had, which wasn't too much of a float. But the king sat on the float with his grass skirt on, his scepter in his hand, and his crown on. And the thing about it that got everybody really going was that at the end of the parade, they had this Dixieland band playing music. Then they had what they called the second line. Now they're playing music, jazzing it up, and behind them is the spectators behind there, dancing behind them, called the second line. And when we were down there, the upper class of people, they'd look at it, and say, "Look at them, look at them down there, they embarrass us. I mean, isn't that bad? Isn't that bad?" Now it's a big thing, they look forward to it down there now. Everybody dances and they have umbrellas and everything.

They used to go on Washington Avenue, start up around Washington Avenue, and then the parade would go all around Claiborne. There were certain areas they used to go. But everything had to get out of the way for Rex, when Rex come through. See, they'd go out through mostly black neighborhoods. And that's where they'd do all their playing. When you get around Claiborne and Orleans, and when everybody's gathered round there, that's where they start doing their dancing—the old Congo Square, a place they call the Congo Square. They used to go over there with their beautiful costumes on and do all their dancing.

Well, when I was coming up, I used to like Louis Armstrong for jazz, but we had a group back in the thirties, when I really got interested in music, called the Ink Spots, the four Ink Spots. They used to be my favorite. I got almost every record they made. Ella Fitzgerald and Chick Webb. Duke Ellington, of course, you know he had to be in there.

In the Treme, I liked some of the brass bands. We had the one called the Tuxedo Brass Band and the Olympia Brass Band. They used to also play for funerals, you know. There was organizations they called benevolent associations. If one of the members died, they'd have music behind him, you see. Everybody didn't do that, but it was just for those organizations. I went to those funerals. Oh, they'd be playing. But if they got a long ways to go to the cemetery, too far to walk, they only go and play on certain blocks. And the band would be playing hymns, sad music, walking slow, everybody walking behind. And those that did go to the cemetery, after they go into the cemetery, and after the body was interred, they'd all stand around, crowd outside the gateway for the band to start. Then they'll come outside and hit that big drum. Boom, boom, boom! Then they start playing songs like "When the Saints Go Marching In." They jazz it up now. And everybody goes out in the street dancing. Men and women, children, everybody dancing behind the band.

Well, I liked living in New Orleans, but a friend of mine got a job with the Pullman Company. And that gave me the opportunity to get out of New Orleans myself. The Pullman porters were role models for us kids. All the kids, everybody wanted to be a Pullman porter if they got a chance, but it wasn't easy to get the job. So, when World War II broke out, they were hiring everybody they could get, because they had troop movements to be made. They were moving troops. They were moving troops all over the country. And a friend of mine got on, and he asked me would I want a job. I said, "Yeah, I'd like it." He brought me to see the instructor. And he also did the hiring. He gave me an application and told me to bring it back as soon as possible. About a week later, I had the application there, all filled out and everything. I was out of school then, because I came out of school in 1934. See, I dropped out of high school, Albert Weekly Junior High. I went to elementary school at Valena C. Jones and then to Joseph A. Craig.

Craig was the first stucco, first modern-built school for blacks in New Orleans. I was living in the Sixth Ward when I went to Craig school. You had to go to whatever school, whatever ward you was living in. And the next year, 1927, I think it was, I was moved. My mother moved down to Seventh Ward, and by that time, they had just completed Valena C. Jones, I went to that school.

Well, the application to be a Pullman porter was, "Would you be willing to stay away from home?" Would I be willing to leave home and work out of another city? And he told me that they needed men in San Francisco. All these Army camps and guys coming from overseas. This was before I went to the service. This was in '43. And they gave you two weeks' training. The training was right in the city, in different railroad yards. You see, you had five stations in New Orleans. You had the L&N station, the Southern station, which was called the Terminal Station, you had the IC station, the Union Station, the TP station. You had the L&A station, Louisiana and Arkansas Railroad. So we'd go to each yard. They showed us how to make beds, how to take care of your (train) car; they work you up. See, we'd operate everything on them cars. It was just like a home away from home when you left home. Everybody wanted to be a Pullman porter. His kids were always neat. He lived in a nice home. Most of us were renting. He was buying his home.

When I started, I was getting forty cents an hour. But I was hired in New Orleans to work in San Francisco. And the more you worked, the more money you made. So I worked out of Oakland. Oh, I got homesick; I came out in '43, July of '43, and I had no place to stay. They told us before we came out that there'd be no place for us to stay now or later. But they did take some of us to different projects (public housing) out there to put applications in for the guys so we'd have a place for our families to come out. Some of the guys knew some fellows that came out here before them, and they had a place they'd rent, or they lived with some friends of theirs and their families. They had two old cars out in the yards: Pullman cars, stationary. They made them stationary, and there were thirty-six beds to a car. And if you got in off the road, you came in off a trip, if you got there in time, you could sign and get a bed. But every morning, you'd have to get up and go re-sign again for the next night for the bed if you stayed in town some more. We'd try to stay on the road as much as we could, because when we were on the road, we had our food there, and we had our beds. Although we paid for our food, we got a little discount. The Pullman porters, that is. The waiters and the other guys on the railroad, they got theirs because they were working for the railroad, see.

At that time, we could get breakfast for about $2 and something, you see. You pay a dollar and something for breakfast, and then we leave a quarter tip for the waiter. And we made beds for everybody plus the passengers, but they had dining car stewards. At that time, they all were white. They just started hiring black maître d's and black stewards just before they went out of business.

Well, the steward slept in a sleeping car because he handled the company's money. And so he had to have a room with a door on it. So we'd make a bed for him, and the next morning, we'd get our meals free. In fact, as long as we were with him, we'd get our meals free because he only went as far as that regular line went. So when the SP cut out, then we got the UP. Now SP cut out, the SP employees, the waiters, the diners, the bartenders, and all that, they'd get off with the SP. But Pullman went all the way. Like, we leave here going to Chicago, we change to three different railroads: Southern Pacific, the Union Pacific, and then the Chicago Northwestern.

It took us three nights to go from New Orleans to Oakland. They sent us on the slowest train. They had two trains coming from New Orleans to LA. One was the Argonaut; that was the three-night train. That's when they put eight of us on there, sent us out, you see. In other words, we were working with some elderly porters, and they were showing us how to work, breaking us in for coming out here. We had three nights in Los Angeles. And one more night to Oakland. They put us on the train they called the Owl. Ran between Los Angeles and Oakland. Then the Sunset Limited was two nights, from New Orleans to Los Angeles.

They worked us out. We had two student trips in New Orleans. They sent me on two trips to Houston, Texas, and back. One guy went to Tennessee. All overnight runs from New Orleans. One guy went to Nashville, one went to Knoxville. One went to Shreveport and back. One went to Birmingham, Alabama, and back. Gave us two trips like that with another porter. That was a guide to break us in and show us how to do the work.

I really loved it. In Houston, they had quarters for us: Everywhere Pullman went, they had quarters. If it wasn't in a YMCA, they had a car sitting somewhere out in the yard for you to sleep in. Or maybe there was a lady whose husband had passed on, and the Pullman Company helped her by giving her some compensation for letting the company use, maybe four or five rooms in her house. The Pullman Company would put maybe four bunks in each room for the porters to sleep in. That was their quarters. They'd go there and check in with her, and the guys would work around there, they'd help fix things around the house that need to be fixed, and the Pullman Company supplied the linen, the sheets and towels and soap and everything we used. In the morning she may have fixed breakfast for the fellows there, and the guys would eat and pay her and tip her. And she made a nice living off of that.

Now, when I left New Orleans, the guys told me, "Now, when we get to San Francisco, the first thing you do is look up Mr. Dellums, C. L. Dellums." He was the head of the local chapter of the union, the Brotherhood of Sleeping Car Porters (founded in 1867). And he let us know what it was all about, you know, what to do, what not to do. He told us to get out there and keep our nose clean and do a good job. And if we had any kind of problems, come and see him right away.

Dellums was the head of the local union, but the real man at the union was A. Philip Randolph. He was based in New York. I met him several times. And I had dinner with him once. Mr. Randolph was a socialist. I had dinner with him on Jack London Square at Slim Jenkins's restaurant. I was by myself. Slim Jenkins was the big man in Oakland, far as blacks were concerned. Nice restaurant, he was the first black to own a restaurant on Jack London Square. And, as a matter of fact, he had been a Pullman porter, too.

Every year, Randolph would get a chance to go around to different places, different districts, and see how the districts were doing, how the fellows were making out, any complaints, any grievances they had against the company. And at this time, this was one of his trips when he was out here. So Jules Brown and Dellums was out of town. Jules Brown was having dinner with Milton P. Webster out of Chicago. Mr. Webster was the head man in Chicago.

Well, when we had these dinners, we used to sit down and talk, old casual conversation, let them tell you what they're thinking on doing with this district or what this guy did in that district. In other words, they'd keep the job in front of you.

Now, Mr. Randolph, he'd come out to make a talk to everybody at a certain day to tell you what progress they made with the company. But any grievances you had, you'd talk to him about that, you know, and he'd tell you if you were right or if you were wrong on different situations.

I'll tell you how Randolph started out. He used to preach on the streets of Harlem for unionizing different jobs, stuff like that. He was like a self-made organizer. But Dellums was a Pullman porter, and he got fired; the Pullman Company fired him because he was trying to help form the union. They say they weren't gonna pay him to fight against them. They thought he gave it up. But he didn't give it up; they fired him.

They started trying to form that union in 1925. They tried. It took twelve years, from 1925 to 1937. It took that long for them to get a contract with the Pullman Company. But they had tried to get a contract long before that. See, but the Pullman Company wouldn't give in to them. And we had a strong organization of women following us, backing us, the ladies' auxiliary. Mrs. Lavinia Tucker was in charge, and it was quite a fight there. They'd hired all blacks. And so when the guys were first trying to form a union against the Pullman Company, the Pullman Company wanted to form their own union. So the porters wanted to form a union with Randolph backing them up. Even some of your newspapers, like your black newspapers, like the *Chicago Defender,* well, they were against that. They said it was going to cause a whole lot of black men to lose their jobs, because they were gonna get rid of them if they fought the company too hard. But Randolph used to have that Harvard accent, you know, and he'd say, "Well, who do they think they are? We'll show them."

They was threatening to go on strike. I don't know what year that was. But I'll tell you what happened: The railroads were going to make a march on Washington, too. That's the first march on Washington they was gonna make. That Martin Luther King, that was Randolph's brainchild, that march on Washington. But far as the union's concerned, the railroads went on strike. And every time the railroad would go on strike, the guys would get a raise, whatever it was; we would get that raise, too, you see. We were going on strike. They had all the placards and everything made for it.

Well, I had been out here quite a while. That was after I came out of the service. It was about '46, '47, somewhere in there, because we used to have our meetings on Seventh Street. The building is still there on Seventh Street. Right here in Oakland. I think it's a liquor store now, downstairs there. All the building in front is all stuccoed now. See, the trains didn't even go to San Francisco. They ended in Oakland here. They went to the pier. We got off the train at the 16th Street station. There was eight of us. Mr. Barksdale, now he was the instructor out here. I don't know if you know anything about basketball, but his son was one of the first black professional basketball players, Don Barksdale. Don had the radio station, too, and he had an ice cream parlor, and he had a nightclub.

Well, Mr. Barksdale (his first name was Argee) picked us up in a station wagon, and another fellow, Mr. Drivers, had another car, and they brought us to the yard, to check in at the yard. When we came out on Seventh Street, that's where the office was, and it was also where the SP yards were.

Well, I know you have heard of Rampart Street, 18th and Vine, Harlem and Central Avenue, one of those kind of streets, you know, a ghetto area. Seventh Street was no different. Lot of gambling and lot of noise, lot of hell-raising. When I came, on Seventh Street, all you had out there walking around, mostly, was people working the shipyards that came from back home, and some of them didn't have no place to stay. You couldn't find a place to stay with a pocket full of money. You couldn't find anyplace to stay. We used to stay in the yard, the railroad men, when they had a space for us in that car there. Otherwise, I remember lots of times I went down to the old T&D Theater, the Broadway Theater, the Paramount Theater. It was open all night during the war. And you could go in there and buy a ticket and go sit in the theater and sleep. In the morning, the police would come in, clubbing on the seats with their clubs, wake up everybody and say, "Okay, let's go, got to clean the theater out for it to open again at eleven o'clock." You know, everybody'd get up, starting wiping their eyes, go to the rest room, or go to the railroad station or the bus station, somewhere to kind of freshen up a little bit. I'd go back to the quarters and change clothes or take a shower. But some people were paying, were renting out garages, and you had people working the different shifts, three different shifts. You had night shift, midnight shift, and a day shift. All they wanted was a place to lay down and rest. You come in, they want a cot; that guy come in, he go to bed, next guy come, he go to bed, that's the way it was. People just worked. Everybody was making money.

My family didn't come out here until 1946. When I came back out to live, I, too, was looking for a place. All my buddies that had been out here, when I left to go to the Navy, they lived in the projects. Lot of them lived on Portrero Street in Richmond out there. Around Pullman Boulevard. And they had places for their families. But I had to start all over again. So I finally got a place.

My wife was named Carmelita. That's my first wife. She passed in '72. She was born in 1919. They're from New Orleans, yeah. But her mother had passed, her mother and father; when I met her, they were deceased. And I had three children with her. I have Natalie, that's my oldest girl. She's at Children's Hospital, in the office. And I had Herman, that's Junior. And I had Cyril. He just left here not too long ago. That's my three kids. And I got, oh goodness, I got so many grandkids, I've lost track of them, and great-grandkids.

When my family first came out here, we went to Richmond. We got some projects out in Richmond. I don't remember how much we paid, but it wasn't too much. We was able to get along comfortably because everything was covered. I mean, whatever you paid, your rent covered everything. They had beds and furniture. You got a Frigidaire. You had a stove and a heater. That's all you need. All that was supplied with the projects. I lived in a place they called the Canal Projects. And we had a lot of guys, we'd come in like, this guy's coming in today, if he went on a regular run, we knew when he was coming back in. So if I was in town when he came in, I went to pick him up, see. If he was in town and I came in, he'd pick me up. But now if we left on an extra trip, didn't have no regular run, you didn't know when you was coming back. So we could always call some guy, see if he was in town, he'd come pick us up at the station, bring us home. We used to carry each other back and forth. That's when we got cars, you know. When we first came out, you didn't have no automobile. I didn't have no car then.

Most of them projects out there were built for the shipyard workers. The Canal Projects are all torn down now. Back then McDonald Street in Richmond, the main street down there, looked more lively then than it does now. Lot of buildings are all boarded up and everything. It was a booming area. It was like Seventh Street was in Oakland.

And they had a place they called North Richmond. That was a place out there where they built homes for people that was out there. And they were some pretty pitiful-looking homes. It was something that you wouldn't want to go back to.

There was a lot of music out there, bands come out there, and they had jam sessions. Rhythm and blues and jazz and blues: T-Bone Walker, Lowell Fulsom, Jimmy McCracklin. In Oakland we also had some nice clubs. But you see, I'll tell you, Seventh Street had some nice places, and you had some bad places. You had to know where to go. They had a place they called the Swing Club. And Slim Jenkins's was about one of the nicest places you had. And then in later years, well, the railroad men used to go around to Esther's, Esther's Orbit Room. And you had the 49ers Club.

They had one place they called Seventh and Adeline. I forgot what they called it. You'd go in on one street and come out on the other street. Big, wide place, big, long bar and everything. And San Francisco had a long bar over there. And you had places over in San Francisco. We used to go over there a lot of the times. Like Jack's Place, Sullivan's Club, and Texas.

The black section of San Francisco was around Fillmore Street and Sutter, all up in there. And they moved further out east in Oakland as the years rolled by. And after the war they moved out here because when I first came to Oakland, there wasn't any blacks out here. At least not in east Oakland out here. After I left Richmond, I moved to Berkeley then. They had some projects there they called the Cordonices. But that belonged to the University of California. That's located on San Pablo Street. Some of it's still left. The University of California let the government use that for the war workers. And after the war, they wanted the land back for the college students. And then we had to move to that housing project that's still down there. Right off Harrison Street there. Harrison and Gilman.

I left Berkeley in 1954. In 1950, I had moved to the Cordonices. And then we had to move in '54. Then I decided to buy out here in Oakland, over across the ramp in an area they called Brookfield Village. Now it's called Columbia Gardens. And we'd walk up and down Seventh Street, back and forth, one end to the other, go in one bar and out the other bar. We were away from home, away from our families, didn't know anybody. And longshoremen, railroad men, sailors, soldiers, Marines, all going up and down there. We came to east Oakland in 1954.

Oh, my goodness, I can't think of all the miles I've traveled by train. I wrote a timetable that I kept back in the garage. All the places I've been. Not all of them. There's so many of them I went to before I started keeping tab of them.

I ran to Chicago off and on for two or three years. That's about 2,000 and some odd miles to Chicago. And see, you consider that every two weeks, making a trip like that. And I went cross-country lots of times. I couldn't even begin to tell you how many times. We had run to Washington, D.C. And that was four nights. That was the Southern Pacific on an old train we used to call the Overland Limited. We used to leave out here on the Overland Limited, and out of Chicago, you get the B&O, going into Washington, D.C. Sometimes I'd be gone two nights, and then I'd be back home for a week. Usually, it was a week on and a week off.

Now, when you went to bed on a train, see, the Pullman men, we only slept four hours a night. Well, let's put it like this. The first man was off duty between every two cars. I got some equipment around here, I can't get it out now, it's too much trouble to get that out. What they call a car bell connector. You hook it between two cars. I'd go to bed, say from ten to two. The guy in the next car; at two o'clock he'd wake me up and he'd go to bed and I'd get up. In other words, between every two cars, there was one man on duty at all times in case somebody wanted anything. Now some of our duties were like, a woman get on there, she'd give you some baby bottles, formulas. You put them on ice. Sometime during the night, she may ring the bell for a bottle. You go get the bottle, turn the basin on, the water get hot, let the bottle get warm enough, bring it back, test it out to see if it's warm enough, and you give it to her. Somebody may be getting on the train during the time you're in the sleepers. Somebody may be getting off, or somebody's got to be up at all times to see that these people get off or had to get on.

Well, we used to deadhead a lot. On a job, we didn't fool around playing cards too much. Oh, that's when they send you to pick up a job, like you may get a troop train, say, they want you to go to Bakersfield, California, to pick up a troop train. Well, you get on, they'd send you on the train, they send you there. That's called deadheading. Anytime you ride on a train without paying, you're deadheading. We used to call passengers deadheads, too, when they was on a pass.

I enjoyed it. I didn't care too much about retiring, but when Amtrak took over, you know, they came out with these double-decked cars up there, upstairs and downstairs. I made one trip to see what they looked like, how they would work. I used to leave home, I'd take the newspaper and some magazines, some books or something to read en route. And I left out of here one morning, and I never got a chance to open a newspaper or magazine or a book. I was busy all the time, trying to familiarize myself with the cars, you see. The bell would ring, you'd go upstairs and check, come downstairs, up, down. Forty-four beds to make every night. When they were full, there were forty-eight beds, instead of the thirty-six on your regular sleepers. You see, you had different types of cars. You had so many different types of cars. You had all section cars, which had thirty-two beds.

We had all kinds of passengers, like we had soldiers, we had movie stars, we had politicians. We had sports figures, we carried all them. They all used to travel by Pullman then. And the one that stands out the most, I didn't meet him, but I carried his luggage. I never did see him in person. And that was Clark Gable. Yeah, when he got married, they were coming from Hawaii, I think it was, and he had a reservation on the Lark. Now the Lark was a train that ran between Los Angeles and San Francisco, all Pullman train, first-class train, one of your finest trains in the country. And when you get on the train, you go to check your linen out, see how your linen is on there. If you got a celebrity guest on there, a special person on there, they would always have a note in your locker. "Mr. and Mrs. Clark Gable will be occupying Bedroom D on your car from San Francisco to Santa Barbara. Please see that he is not inconvenienced in any way."

At the last minute, before the train left, his baggage came down. Some guy brought his baggage down there and say, "This is Mr. Gable's baggage. They decided to drive down. When you get to Santa Barbara, there'll be somebody there to pick up their luggage." And he gave me a $20 tip. So, I got to Santa Barbara in the morning, and another guy came to pick up his bags. And "Mr. Gable says to give you this." He gave me another $20 tip.

Well, I once had Ralph Edwards's wife, not him; his wife was on the train. She rode less than a mile. Glendale, you get on at Glendale and go to Palo Alto, most of them. And I had Rex Ingram. I don't know if you know him. He's the one played as De Lord. And I had Bob Newhart. I've had Earle Stanley Gardner. I had three Academy Award winners: Jane Wyman, Cecil B. De Mille, and Peter Finch.

You see, the trains were segregated. Black and white couldn't ride together in the coach. The only time a black person got in the front of the coach up there was if he was an invalid person, or maybe an invalid white person, or a kid with a caretaker. They segregated them. They might eat in the same dining car, but the black person had to sit behind a curtain. Had curtains on there. Now they made a distinction. I don't know how big you had to be, but all the blacks I know rode back behind the curtain down in the South. And they had a way of doing it up here, too. They gave blacks a compartment, a bedroom—a room and adjoining room.

Well, I got a nice family. See, I love my family, got a nice family. I go to church sometimes. My wife goes. She goes to church every Sunday. She's in church, and in the week, too. Well, I'm Catholic, you see, and I go 'round the corner 'round here. But she's Baptist. She goes to Haywood Baptist Church. And I go with her sometimes. Everybody out there likes me just as much as they like her at her church. When I'm not there, they all say they miss me.

Well, there's a lot more to say about the railroad. I never did tell you too much about the railroad, the things we did on the job. Because we had a pretty rough time on the job. But one thing I'd like to let you know is that when we went to bed at night, when we retired, when we got off with the job, we had a smoking room. Randolph worked and worked and worked to get us decent working facilities on the train. There was a big room where the men did their toilet in the morning. And they had a sofa in there. And they had a little mattress on each about that thick, blankets and a pillow. And that's where we slept. We went to bed. Now if the passengers were in the smoking room, smoking, holding a conversation, talking or reading, anything like that, you couldn't ask them to move. When they left, you went to bed. Now, in a case like that, you had the Pullman conductor. Now he was over all the porters, the Pullman porters. But your train conductor was head of the whole train. Most of the Pullman conductors were white. I saw one black Pullman conductor, and that was just before the Pullman Company went out of business in 1969. He was out of Salt Lake City.

Randolph, we used to call him the Big Chief, when he came to Oakland, we used to call him the Chief. A. Philip Randolph. He died in 1979. He was a brown-skinned man, who in later years, was kind of heavyset, but he used to be a little slender fellow. Dellums was another leader in the union. He used to wear a big hat, big wide straw hat, used to wear a beaver all the time. We used to go in the back of his office, there, he kept a stove back there, and the guys would go back there, they'd play poker, they'd play cards all day long and everything. And they'd cook. Some of the guys that could cook, they'd cook some beans and rice, pork chops. When they was in town, that's where most of the guys went on their off day. And then leave there and go around to Harvey's and different places and get a couple of drinks, like that, and come on back home.

No one messed with Dellums. He was a pretty strong man. You joked about some of them, some of them had jokes about them, but I don't know of any jokes about Mr. Randolph. Now I'll tell you about history. I don't want to lie about this, because I really don't know. But I understand it to be a fact that the Pullman Company offered him a check to get off their back. He was giving them such a bad time, trying to organize the porters. Now some say they gave him a $10,000 check. And some say they gave him a blank check and said, "Write anything you want on it, under a million dollars." But the thing that I'm proud of, he never accepted either one of them. They tell me he had his check hanging up in his office, on display in his office in New York.

I could be here talking about this for a long time. There's so much I haven't told you, like I was in two railroad wrecks. Two wrecks and one where eight people got killed. On the Owl. Broken rail. 1948. '47. Down near Bakersfield, on the Owl, going out to Los Angeles. But nobody got hurt on that one. When the people got killed, the train jumped a rail. It jumped your broken rail. I was in the second to last car on the train. My car was leaning. The last car didn't even leave the track, but all the people were killed in them coaches up ahead. About seventy, eighty miles an hour. And when the train veered over this broken rail, it threw the people from this side of the car over to the other side, clean through the window on the ground. The train just ground them up underneath there.

Anyway, I've had the golden spike in my hand. The golden spike is from when they made their cross-country, transcontinental railroad. The last spike they drove down was the golden spike at Promentory Point up in Utah. I had read about that in school, when I was going to school in grade school, and I finally got to hold it in my hand. I was so thrilled it's hard for me to explain it. It was in 1969 that they celebrated the centennial at Promentory Point.

At Sacramento, we picked up some politicians, I don't know who they were, but they were going there to make speeches at this celebration up there. And they had the golden spike with them. And he told me, one of the guards, says, "Porter, have ever seen the golden spike?"

I said, "No, I have never seen it."

He said, "You want to take a look at it?"

I said, "Yeah." So he got up on a chair, it was on a box on top of the rack. Brought it down, slid the top back, there it was.

I said, "Wow!"

"Pick it up."

And I picked it up. I don't know, I can't describe the feeling, but I said, "Whee! I studied about this when I was a little bitty kid in school. And here I'm holding it in my hand." It's kept at the Smithsonian Institution.

I've had a good life. Hard work, long hours. It was just routine. But we ran across some dogs out there, now. Once, we were going through on the troop train through Columbus, South Carolina, when they had that riot where they tried to keep those kids out of the school during the civil rights movement.

And the conductor told us, "We are not gonna stop at the station. Keep your shades down, keep your lights out."

We could hear them out there, raising all kind of hell. We laid down listening. That's around the civil rights movement, trying to get those kids in school, in the sixties or the fifties. Trying to get the kids to go to those schools.

Other times we had special trains, leave out of here, be gone for twenty-one days. We had a porter went with the Goldwyn Girls. The old Goldwyn Girls, used to be at Metro-Goldwyn-Mayer when they used to make all them musical movies. Well, he had all them on the train for fifty days. They were going around different cities, putting on style shows. They were all just living in the cars, until they completed their trip.

I've had Ronald Reagan. He's been on the train, after him and Jane Wyman had divorced. He used to ride between Palo Alto and Glendale. She did, too. She had a compartment. When I caught him, he only had a roomette. He was by himself. See, I never had him with Nancy, his wife, but they say whenever he traveled with Nancy, he had a compartment, two of them. That's when he was breaking into politics. He had just left the movies, you know, had gone into politics.

Get me started, and I can't stop. We have a club they call the Retired Railroad Men's Club. We meet once, twice a month: once, executive board members and once for the regular floor meeting. Oh, we got a very few left now. We had about, I don't think we got 30 guys left yet. We were looking at the roster the other day. We used to have about 200 men. But this club wasn't for Pullman porters, it was for all railroad men. All black men.

Well, here's a joke I want to tell you. You've probably heard it before. Everybody's talked about it. It's one of the favorite jokes about a Pullman porter. He woke up the next morning, got himself ready for his passengers when they get up. And so the first passenger up walked to him and didn't say anything to him. The other porters told him, "Say, good morning, sir. How did you sleep last night?" He told the porter, he said, "Huh! What the hell is it to you how I slept?" The porter say, "Well, I don't care. The company told me to ask you that."

INTERVIEW BY ALAN GOVENAR, JUNE 9, 1997

Charles Earl Simms

Attorney
Born: July 30, 1940

(For background information, see introductory note for Anna Mae Conley on page 139.)

My earliest memories are when I was about three years old. In fact, on a recent trip this year, to Dallas, I retraced a residence that we used to live at with my mother and father. And I took pictures. I took about, probably, a dozen pictures up at the old house where I can remember the porch, the concrete steps. The house is in pretty bad shape now, but it's still standing, and apparently it's occupied. It's on Octavia Street. Octavia and Metropolitan. And there is a CME church, where there used to be a theater. But it's the same basic building, I found out when I was there in April. I talked to one of the members and she gave me a little history on that church. It was converted from a theater many, many years ago. Same basic building is still there.

I never attended school in Texas. I remember when my parents migrated here to California. We stayed with my father's mother, my grandmother, and it was a fun time for us because I remember, my mom says it was about nine months. Seemed like about a year or so, but she basically looked after us. We lived with her those months. I can remember those years. I was only about five years old. And we came out here with my grandmother to join my parents on the train. And I remember the train station. It was a long, slow journey. I can recall waiting for what seemed to be hours at some station someplace, but we finally arrived. That was a fun trip. We had some good times with my grandmother. She was a very strict disciplinarian.

I don't recall that the trains were segregated, but I suspect that they were. My first awareness of segregation and discrimination was in Texas. I remember going to the theater in Texas, in Dallas, and we had to sit in separate sections. As a child, I can remember that. And, of course, I didn't understand what it was about, but I can remember that, that we had to sit in a certain area of the theater. It was a theater right across the street, as I mentioned, and I can kind of remember going there occasionally with my parents as a young child.

Well, it didn't impact me at that time because I was only about five or six years old, and that was the way things were. And so at that point I didn't know there was a different way of life. I've always attended an integrated school. Early on, in elementary school, I can remember, the blacks were the minority, sometimes maybe almost half black, because we lived in what we called the projects at that time.

When we first came to California and started school, we were living in the projects in Alameda, which was close to where my father was working at Alameda Naval Air Station. And it was a segregated housing situation at that time. I can recall the blacks pretty much lived in one section and the whites in another section. I mean segregated buildings, and although we attended an integrated school, we lived in the same neighborhood, but it was segregated. And that was just a way of life, and you know I had friends, I had relationships with blacks and whites at that time. In elementary school, the teachers were white. We got along, and it was just a way of life, but we knew at an early age that there was this separateness, you know, and that blacks lived pretty much by themselves. You mixed a little bit at school, but you didn't really associate with people outside of your own ethnic race that much.

All I know is that we just called them the projects because they were big, multifamily buildings, and I would guess probably maybe six families to a building. In fact, I'll say eight, because I can remember now, we were on the second floor. And there were four units on our side and four units on the other side of the building, one building. So, there were eight families. I don't know what the rent structure was, but I suspect it depended on how much money you made at the Naval Air Station.

I don't know what my dad's salary was at that time. My dad was, I would think, a training technician, working for the government at that time, and I would assume that the salary was competitive, although, let's face it, there's discrimination. My dad never finished high school, but he did a lot of technical study on his own, taking college classes, correspondence. I know he had some training when he was in the Army in electronics. But I can remember as a boy, that he would be taking courses at home, attending classes in the evening, studying on his own at home, a very astute man.

California was a great promised land for him. He had an uncle, my Uncle Charlie Simms, in fact, who was already here with his wife, my Aunt Minnie, who will be ninety-six in November. In fact, we're going to have a birthday party for her in Texarkana, Texas. We look forward to going there. But my dad had a family that he was able to come here to get started with. And it worked. I knew my dad and mom were coming here to look for better opportunity for the family, and, to be honest, I think it was successful. Because my dad was able to find a skilled job, had a lot of advancement and worked at the Naval Air Station in Alameda probably for, I'd say at least twelve to fifteen years and then he went on to work at the University of California Lawrence Laboratory in Livermore, and I'm trying to remember if he transferred to Berkeley his last few years. I think he did, before he retired. And then went on to teach at Laney College in electronics. So he had a very successful career, although he never completed high school, he never went to college, he had a lot of college-type classes. I mean he took all kinds of math, you know, algebra, trig, calculus, very astute man.

I'm one of four children. I'm the third oldest of four children born to my mother. My oldest sister is Caroline Stevenson; she is fifty-seven. She's had a birthday in May. Spencer remarried, and I'm the second oldest at fifty-six now, and I have a younger brother named Tommy who just turned fifty-five. And then I have a baby sister, Rosalyn, who lives in North Carolina, and Rosalyn, I don't want to misquote her age, she must be about thirty-seven.

We lived in Alameda for a number of years. And then my parents were able to buy a new home in what is now Richmond. It was San Pablo, California, at the time, but it is now Richmond. It's been annexed some years. And I would say we moved there in '51? Thereabout, '50 or '51? And we lived in San Pablo from about '51 to about '56. Then my parents separated, my dad remarried, and I moved to Oakland and lived in Oakland, attended Oakland High School, as did my oldest sister, Caroline, and my younger brother, Thomas. We all graduated from Oakland Technical High School.

I can remember a black photographer named Joseph when I was in high school. I can't remember the name. I just don't. But I remember in high school, in fact, I think some of my classmates, their dad ran this photography business. I'm not sure if that was his sole livelihood. But I can remember that.

I would say I had a very successful childhood. I'm thankful to my parents for that. I didn't have any real hardships. I had a paper route from the time I was ten years old. My brother and I both, I had a paper route from the age of ten, up to the age of sixteen, in fact. My brother and I were very industrious. We always had money in our pockets. We had our own bicycles that we'd deliver our papers with, and we had free rein. We could come and go when we wanted and, fortunately, we never got into any real serious trouble. A lot of the youngsters that I grew up with, a number of them, of course, got into some serious trouble and went on to jail and prison. But not all of them, of course. I know of people that I grew up with who are professional people, teachers. Many of them did finish college and went on to become very successful.

I started initially at San Francisco State, transferred to Fresno State, and then got a master's degree at UC-Berkeley in criminology. I was a criminology major undergrad. And I wanted to be, initially when I started college, something to do with science, kind of patterning after my father. But after about a year and a half of college, I realized that I didn't want to be a scientist. I wasn't that keen with the math and all, and it was just really overburdening me. And I decided I didn't want to work in a laboratory or sit inside working with figures, I'd rather work with people. So I decided I wanted to be like a probation or parole officer. So I changed my major and ended up getting a bachelor's degree in criminology.

I started with the Alameda County Probation Department at the age of twenty-five, right out of college, and just concluded almost thirty years with that office. And while I was working and got married, I went on to law school. Actually, I got married about a year after I graduated from college. Had a child who's grown now, gonna be thirty in September. She's a nurse practitioner. But I went to grad school at UC-Berkeley. While I was working full time, I attended in the evening and got my master's degree and then subsequently, after my brother finished law school, I decided I wanted to go to law school, and I went to the University of Santa Clara while I was working full time as a probation officer and commuted to Santa Clara, about forty miles from where I was living in Oakland. And basically, I have never practiced law. I wanted to stay and retire after working basically a full career as a probation officer. I decided it would be worthwhile to retire from that job, which I did. And I may practice law one of these days, but I'm not anxious to go back to work right now.

Black power salute is given to the casket containing the body of seventeen-year-old Jonathan P. Jackson as it is carried into St. Augustine's Episcopal Church, Oakland, California, August 1970. Jackson and William Christmas, killed in a kidnap-shooting, were eulogized as "courageous revolutionaries who made the ultimate sacrifice." (UPI Telephoto)

I don't know of any so-called traditional black colleges in California. I know there are a lot of them in the South. Offhand, I can't think of any in California. Not in the Bay Area, at least. There are a lot of very good colleges and universities in the San Francisco-Oakland Bay Area. And certainly in California. There are a lot. I mean, within a hundred-mile radius, if you include UC-Berkeley, Stanford, UC-Davis, just on and on, there are so many to choose from.

When I was growing up, there was a lot of tension. In fact, I look back now and I wonder how, as a group, blacks did as well as they did in some instances. There was discrimination. I know when I first got married, well, first of all, when I graduated from college and came back home to the Oakland area and got a job with the Alameda County Probation Department in Oakland, I applied for an apartment. And I learned later that the landlord was a little bit hesitant to rent to me. Took a credit application, inquired on my job. I hadn't been working that long. And sent me a letter. I have a copy of it. I ran across it recently in my keepsakes, saying that he had inquired and I seemed like a professional person, et cetera, et cetera, but it was a little unusual, I thought at the time. But he did allow me to occupy this particular dwelling. And then after I got married, my wife got pregnant and then we had to move because they didn't allow children at this particular residence. It's a multiunit building, probably about twenty-four units. So we had to relocate, and my wife was attending Cal State Hayward at the time, and so we found a fourplex right close to the campus. It was a brand-new building. Nice view and everything. And so I left Juvenile Hall, where I was employed at the time with the Probation Department, and drove out there on my lunch hour, talked to one of the tenants. There was a sign there that said, "For rent," et cetera, and I called the number, I talked to the tenant there and she says, "Yeah, I'll call that number and there's these two vacancies." There were two fourplex buildings right adjacent to one another. To make a long story short, I ended up talking to the owner by phone, arranging to meet him out there, I think, the next day or so, so he could show me the units. And I drove out there on my lunch hour. I had a hamburger, I was eating it in the car, and this guy pulls up in a car, and I got out and asked if he were Mr. Massa. And he says, "No, I'm just watching these places; we've been having a lot of robberies lately," as he put it. So, I went back to the office, after waiting about forty minutes. And I felt like that was the guy. And he stayed there the full time I was there. And I called his office, left messages, on and on, didn't get any response. And finally I called him at home. I got his home number from the job. He was a realtor. And I called him at home and I says, "This is Mr. Simms. I'm still interested in that unit." And he says, "Oh, I'm sorry, I won't be able to rent to you." And I says, "I beg your pardon." Because of my race he felt there that would be an uproar among the present tenants there and it wouldn't be acceptable.

On the phone, he said, "I'm sorry, I won't be able to rent to you basically because of your race. You're black, and I don't think my tenants would approve of that." So to make a long story short, there were laws against that in California at the time. This was in '66. Well, we sued. We went to court. I was appalled that the guy would just blatantly, a realtor at that, would just say it like that. And so I said, "Okay." And so we went to the Fair Employment Practice Commission at the time and we filed a suit. It was all in the papers, media and everything, still have an article from the *Oakland Tribune*. And to make a long story short, they got a restraining order that prohibited him from renting at least one unit. He had two buildings. They put a restraining order on one. And we went through a series of hearings, up to about a month or so before my child was born. And we won. The guy was gonna finally rent to us. He had no choice. We went out and looked at the place. And I told him I had changed my mind. In fact, we had found another place in Haywood, near the campus where my wife was going to be going to school. And it turns out that the landlord that allowed us to occupy the dwelling where we finally lived, he knew this realtor, Massa, and he had even read about the account in the paper. But he had no idea that it was me. And he was a little hesitant, he said, because he hadn't had a black man come in and ask to live in his building, but he allowed us to move in with no problem. We later became very good friends, and he told me later on that he found out that it was me that, uh, his buddy, his high school buddy, Massa, refused to rent and we won and decided we didn't want it. But we ended up getting a nice place anyway. So, that was one experience. And there were other experiences I've had where we've been discriminated against as far as housing. But fortunately, especially in the Bay Area, even though there is subtle discrimination, you can basically live wherever you want. We've had no real difficult problem moving from time to time. We've lived predominantly in, I would say, areas that are white, for the most part. But we've had no problem as far as getting along with the neighbors and that kind of thing. And it's interesting when I was denied residence in this apartment building, it was in the media, and no one at work ever said a word to me during this period of time. Even though it was in the papers and on the news, and finally the judge I remember once, in court, like two years later, asked me, "Oh, by the way, how'd you come out in that suit?" I mean, like two years later. But I could sense it, the Sunday that it came out in the paper, I went to work Monday, and I could just feel it. No one wanted to approach me and say anything, but I could sense the tension, and no one wanted to say, "Chuck, jeez, that's too bad, you know, is there anything I can do to help?" No one mentioned it. But I knew people knew about it.

When I was growing up, I remember pickets. I never engaged in any of that. I was not a so-called activist. I didn't have time to deal with that. In fact, I wondered, if I had to cope with all of that, I don't know if I would have been able to make it through school, because for the most part, I worked during my college years, even though I had help from my parents. But I had to kind of work my way through, and I would not have been able to endure the pressures of having to picket, for example. Look at the situations that happened in areas of the South, Medgar Evers and those kind of individuals who had to cope with just going to school and dealing with the discrimination. I don't think I could have done that, to be honest, you know. But no, I didn't have a lot of outright discrimination. I think perhaps there was some academically, just struggling to get through, and get grades and those kinds of things. I had just learned to deal with it, you know, and was able to overcome.

The Black Panthers were very powerful here in Oakland, as you know. In fact, it's interesting, on one of my recent visits to Dallas, I went to a barbecue place on Commerce in Deep Ellum, 2700 block of Commerce, walked in. Good place, too, I got barbecue the second time I was there. But I was there in April and I go in and get to talking and the guy says, "You're from Oakland, huh?" I said, "Yeah, I'm from Oakland, you know, just visiting here in Dallas." And he says, "Do you wear a bulletproof vest?" Just off the cuff, you know, he said that. And I said, "No, of course not."

You know. So, to make a long story short, he says, "Could you send me a hat that says 'Oakland'? You know, black and white, with black lettering, that says 'Oakland'?"

I says, "Yeah, I'll try to find something for you like that," but I end up finding a navy blue hat with gold lettering "Oakland" and sent it to the guy. He gave me a break on the purchase, like eight bucks. It cost about ten bucks. And I mailed it to him. And when I was there this last month, I asked him if he got it. I went back there, and he says, "Yeah, I got it." I talked to his brother actually, he says, "Yeah, he got it." It was kind of interesting. But he asked me if I wore a bulletproof vest in Oakland, it has the reputation.

Huey Newton was my classmate at Oakland Technical High School. Attended the same high school, the same year we graduated. I didn't know him, though, at the time. And, of course, he wasn't famous then. Not at that time, in high school. But he's in my yearbook. And he's obviously our most infamous classmate. We ran in different groups. I was in the more progressive groups, like the group of youngsters for the most part were college prep students. Some of the parents were successful, a few doctors, lawyers. Fortunately, I wasn't in that other group that he was in.

The Black Panthers were very radical. See, I'm in law enforcement. You kind of have to see where I'm coming from. I'm in law enforcement. I mean, we fought the drug element. We're still fighting it in Oakland and the remnants of the Black Panthers and many other radical groups that were outlaws. I mean, there's no other way to put it from a law enforcement perspective, you know. These were people caused a lot of harm to the community. Although they did some good things, too, now, they did stress education, health, of course, they had their own arsenal of weapons, which I think was detrimental to the community. There are a lot a firearms on the streets of Oakland, particularly, and I think for the most part it's very detrimental. Drugs are just devastating in the black community, especially crack cocaine.

I've been a city dweller for all my life, primarily Dallas, and then moving to the Oakland area. Although I like the so-called country. In fact, when I met my wife at Fresno State, Fresno is like midways between Oakland–San Francisco and Los Angeles. And it's a relatively rural area, even now, compared to Oakland. And at that time, when I met her, like I lived in Fresno when I went to school there, and her parents lived out in a little stick town called Helm. Like you could pass it with the blink of an eye. And she thought we could live there initially, when we first met. And I said, "Are you kidding? I'm from the city. I couldn't stand to live out in the country." But now that I've become older and I've gone through a career, I'd like to move to the country. Get a couple of acres and just be away from the major cities. So I would welcome the serenity of living in the country now.

I think often people are uptight, whites tend to live in segregated areas. Blacks tend to live in their own segregated areas. Even when let alone, people don't tend to mingle together and want to live in the same areas naturally. And I think that people, for example, coming up, living with my parents, we lived mostly in a segregated community. And we got along with people, but as you mixed and went to college and went to school and acquired friendships with people that were different from you, the different race, you learned that people aren't really any different. You all want pretty much the same. That is, a decent life, a good education, a decent place to live. And sure, you compete with each other in society, in school, on the job, the whole thing, but basically, you still want the same thing. That is, a decent life, the best life that you can acquire for yourself through hard work. But I think these barriers become less pronounced when you mix with people and you get to know them and you find out that your values are pretty much alike, based on your socioeconomic standing in life. So I think, sure, there are laws, that, for example, the segregation laws that are kind of being chipped away now. In fact, I just read recently where they say that the schools are probably as segregated as they've been in a long, long time. They're going back to being segregated with the advent of the courts' dropping the integration statutes and laws that compel kids to be bused and sent to schools where they mix together. There is a natural tendency for people, I think, of different races to want to be among their own kind, and they don't tend, on their own, to integrate naturally, for whatever reason. But I think as people do learn more about one another, they learn to respect one another, they can live together compatibly and they find out that you all really want the same thing. You know, that is, a decent life for yourself and your family.

INTERVIEW BY ALAN GOVENAR AND KALETA DOOLIN, JUNE 6, 1997

Katie Simms

Homemaker and domestic worker
Born: May 29, 1920, Dallas, Texas

(For background information, see introductory note for Anna Mae Conley on page 139.)

When my husband came home (to Texas) from World War II, he wasn't satisfied, and he thought going to California would give him a better chance on a job and education for the children. We had three children. So we came.

Tommy Simms was my husband's name. He was born in 1915, and he passed away in 1989. He was born in Louisiana. He came to Dallas sometime before 1940—I don't really know. I met him when we went to the same high school. You know, at that time, there was only one high school in Dallas for blacks, and that was Booker T. Washington. And we graduated from there. We had a split shift. But I didn't know him at the time.

We met in 1938, '39, and we married in '40, and we had three children. He went into the service soon after we were married. In Dallas it was tough getting a good job. In Dallas he was not doing very much of anything. He was working at Skillern's Drugstore as a delivery person when we got married. You know, at that time, the jobs for the African Americans weren't very good. And that's why he wanted to leave.

There was a lot of discrimination in Dallas, and segregation, very much so. Well, especially where this SMU is, where my son went to hear Cecil Williams. Have you heard of him? Well, anyway, he's a very prominent minister in San Francisco. And he went, he graduated from SMU. But at the time that we were living there, you didn't see blacks in Highland Park, and you didn't see blacks at all in that area unless they, the women, had on a white uniform and the men had on a chauffeur's cap during that time.

I grew up in South Dallas. I lived in several different streets because I was reared without mother or father and I stayed with an auntie until I was thirteen, and we lived several different places. My auntie's name was Tannie Roberson. And at thirteen, I moved in with my sister at 2817 Floyd. And this is my second child (Charles), and he was born at her house. At that time, the doctors would come to the house. We had a Baylor doctor, which was just across, maybe across the street, almost, from where she lived at that time.

Well, there were good times and bad times in Dallas, I guess, because see, like I said, I was reared without mother or father. And that was something I always wanted, you know, was a mother.

My mother passed away. I don't remember her. I was three when she passed on, and my mother's sister's the one who took me. And my father lived, I remember when he passed, but I was in high school before they told me that he was my father. My stepfather was a Lawson, and I married, I used that name because I didn't know that I wasn't a Lawson until I was up in high school.

I had some good and bad days. Anna (Mae Conley), I grew up with her and her brother and sister. We were like brothers and sisters. They only had one brother. But Anna and I were very close. We were like sisters at that time. School was okay. I wasn't actually an "A" student. Anna is smarter than I am. But I managed to graduate. I wasn't good in math. We had a split shift. One group went in the morning and one in the afternoon. We just had that one school, and we had to walk or get the bus, you know, across town to go to school. I met my husband, at the North Dallas Club, one Easter Sunday night. There was a dance. They had a band, but I don't know the name of the band or whatnot, yeah, but they had a live band. On Thomas and Hall, somewhere along in there, Thomas and Hall.

In Deep Ellum we had the Harlem Theater, and that was the only black theater at the time. And we used to go there for ten cents and stay all day, almost, at that time. Like holidays and different days, we would go there. And you know, at the Majestic at that time, we had to sit in the balcony. We weren't allowed to sit, you know, elsewhere.

Well, after we left Texas, we went to Berkeley (California), and they had this little station. I was disappointed; I thought there'd be a huge station. We came on the train. And it was just a little bitty station and whatnot, but we lived, we went to my husband's uncle. We stayed with them a while. But my children, their grandmother kept them from September to June. She kept them about nine months for us.

We stayed with my husband's uncle. See, my husband had no job or anything. But he was lucky; he worked with his uncle for a couple of weeks. And then he was hired at the Naval Air Station. And he was very successful. He was an electronics technician. He studied that when he was in service, and he retired from that. He taught at Laney College. He was a very smart man. And his children are smart, too. They really are, all three of them. Two of them are attorneys.

We didn't stay long in Berkeley. We moved to Alameda because the Naval Air Station was in Alameda, and we lived there for about four years. And then we moved to Richmond. We bought a house in Richmond.

For a number of years, that's all I did was stay home to take care of the children. Then, my husband and I separated after awhile. And I moved to Oakland, and I've been living in Oakland for quite a few years, since the mid-fifties, 1954-'55.

Well, I'm satisfied now that I've retired and I can do what I want to do when I get ready. For a long time, I didn't know anything but domestic work. And I did that for a while, and then I went to Laney College. My son insisted that I go. And I was in food service. So I worked at the schools in the dietary department and hospital, and I did that until I retired. Then I did volunteer work for a while.

The domestic work I did was all the way from cooking, housekeeping, and so forth and on serving. It wasn't so tough because there is a part of me that was a good housekeeper, and I never had no problems. They just turned things over after they found, you know, I had no problems. And I got references from the jobs that I had. The discrimination was still there, still is, as far as I'm concerned. Well, myself, I haven't had any problem. But it's still here. Definitely.

The world would be a better place if everybody could get along. And one is no better than the other, in a way of speaking. And money, as far as I'm concerned, can't buy happiness or health.

I go to church, but I'm not a church fanatic. I go to different ones. And my name is not on the roll at any of them. Because this building (where I live) is sponsored by a church, a Baptist church, but I'm not a member of the church.

INTERVIEW BY ALAN GOVENAR AND KALETA DOOLIN, JUNE 6, 1997

Rev. Wesley Sims

Minister
Born: 1921, Parsons, Kansas

Wesley Sims grew up in Lawrence, Kansas, where he attended segregated schools. He graduated from Lawrence Memorial High School and enrolled at the University of Kansas. Then he was drafted. During World War II he served in the Army and was trained as a chaplain. After his discharge he studied at Kentucky State College and then returned to the University of Kansas. In 1958, he moved to Austin, Texas, and became the pastor of the 12th Street Christian Church. In 1964, Sims relocated to Dallas, and in 1969 he was hired by the Parks and Recreation Department, where he worked until his retirement in 1986.

My parents were from the South. My mother was from Mississippi, and my father from Arkansas, and they both went to school at Southern Christian Institute in Edwards, Mississippi. And my father was a minister. When he finished college, he pastored in Georgetown, Kentucky. And then I guess that's where I was conceived, and I was born in Parsons, Kansas, and then we moved from there to Topeka, Kansas, in 1922, and we moved to Lawrence in '23. So I'm a native Kansan, and I've been in Kansas most of my life. I was there for thirty-four years.

My father was Wesley Sims, Wesley Sims Sr. He was born in 1893, on March 28. And my mother was born in 1898. And she was born on October 31, and my mother passed in 1990, and my father passed in '83. My father was from a little town, Montrose, Arkansas. And my mother was from Vicksburg, Mississippi. And they were classmates in school, and that's where they got married and entered the ministry. And my mother later was ordained to the ministry. So, my father and mother were both or-

The destruction of the town of Lawrence, Kansas, and the killing of more than 150 inhabitants by Confederate guerrillas led by William Clark Quantrill, August 21, 1863 (Library of Congress)

dained. That's the Disciples of Christ, Christian church. They went to Southern Christian Institute in Edwards, Mississippi, and that was one of the two, at that time, black Disciple colleges. That one no longer exists. That one went out in about 1964, I think. So we combined it with Jarvis Christian College, which is in Hawkins, Texas. So that's the only black college in the denomination left, Jarvis Christian College.

When my father graduated from SCI, he preached in Georgetown, Kentucky. And from there, they were starting a new congregation in Parsons, Kansas, so they sent him there to help get that church started. And then from there he went to Topeka, and then to Lawrence, Kansas. And he pastored a church in Lawrence for fifty-eight years after he left Topeka.

When he went to Kansas, most of those were small towns, and Lawrence, I think, was somewhere around 10,000 people, maybe a little less than that. And there were just very few black folks in Lawrence. But it was, for that reason, mostly integrated, the schools and most everything. Of course, the best jobs were still reserved for the affluent people. When we went to junior high and high school, the schools and everything were integrated in everything except athletics. In high school, we couldn't play football with the varsity team. Of course, we had our own black basketball team. About three years, we were state champions, incidentally. So we could beat the other team in their games. They weren't as good as we were, but they were the varsity team for the school. That was the kind of segregation. But we all went to the same classes and everything together.

It had to be integrated because I guess they couldn't afford a dual system of schools with the small percentage of minority people that were in Lawrence.

Most of the larger cities, certainly, had the racial tension, and they had segregated schools and all that type of thing. Topeka, for instance, was one of them. In fact, Topeka was just twenty-two miles from Lawrence, and we played them in basketball. Most of our competition was with Topeka, Leavenworth, Atchison, and all the different towns, Coffeeville and Kansas City and Hutchinson. And St. Joseph, Missouri, and the communities around, Sumner, Kansas City, different ones.

Most of our people were, well, like my father worked for the lumberyard. And he pastored a church. So he had a dual profession. He pastored and sometimes without salary or with very little salary. Most of his was the work that he did. And, of course, we came through the Depression years, too, in the twenties and thirties. And during those times, a lot of our parents worked on the WPA and the CCC camps and that type of thing. So we came through all of that.

One of the reasons I think a lot of people came to Kansas from the South was because jobs were supposed to be opening up. And then the flood of 1927 brought a lot of people from the South to northern cities. That was one of the big floods of the Mississippi basin or valley. In fact, a lot of my mother's people and my father's people, too, moved up north from Mississippi and Tennessee and all those states there.

A few people went to Nebraska. Most of them tried to disperse to the larger cities, Kansas City and Chicago and St. Louis, places like this where they were getting away from the Delta area.

There were just a very few people who owned farm property in Kansas. And some of them did have cattle, and some had horses and that type of thing. Yeah, there was quite a bit of that. Not too many blacks worked as ranch hands. Most of them just worked for industry and did waitering jobs, servitude jobs. They worked for people, doing yards and housecleaning and that type of thing. The women took in ironing, and they did washing, and they did nursery type of work. A lot of that was going on. We had maybe a few lawyers and a couple of doctors, maybe an undertaker who would have three or four cities that he serviced, and that type thing.

Back in those years, I didn't know a single black photographer. The only photographer I knew in Lawrence was a person my dad worked for. He was a photographer. And this guy was a white man. He was a white photographer. My father did his housework and cleaned his yard and planted trees and whatever gardening, stuff that he had to do. He did a lot of that type of thing for him.

There are very few pictures, professional pictures, of my family. But we did take pictures with old box cameras, so I have pictures of some of my parents and some of the older folks. I was impressed with one man there. When I was about seven or eight years old, he was in his nineties. And he was present at Lawrence during the Quantrill raid, and that was one of the things he used to tell us a lot about because he experienced it. He was a little kid, and he remembered when they came in and all the things that were happening with his folks, and how all the men left and the ones who didn't leave, they were shot. And how they burned down the buildings. It was vivid in his memory, this old man, and it really impressed me. He could tell us a lot of things about what was going on. That was back in about 1927, '28, '29, back in there. That raid was in 1863 and the entire town was destroyed.

Well, Lawrence, Kansas, was caught in the middle of the Civil War, and Union and Confederate forces ran across the land, often without suitable command. And one of these kind of brigands was William Clark Quantrill. Quantrill rode under both flags. And when he raided Lawrence, he sacked it twice.

Well, this old man I knew was a kid when the raid occurred, but he remembered it all his life. And this was in his memory. His name was Peter Jones. His father was one of the ones that got killed. And then his mother and some of the ladies survived. Of course, they had to hide when this was going on. Remember the Aldridge Hotel they burned down? It was the biggest building in Lawrence at that particular time. He was quite an amazing man. He survived it, and through the years he worked different jobs. He lived in Lawrence all his life. In fact, he probably never went over about twenty or thirty miles from Lawrence in his life, because he didn't know too much about anything else except Lawrence. Of course, everybody in town knew him, white and black. A lot of people would ask him a lot of questions about how it had developed.

I went to public schools in Lawrence, started at a little elementary school, Cordley School, and then went to junior high school. At that particular time, our junior high school was three separate buildings. Each one of them had been the high school, and they outgrew them and finally built a new high school. And, of course, I graduated from Lawrence Memorial High School. And then I started college, and the very year I started, two months in college and Uncle Sam drafted me. I went to the University of Kansas. And so I went in service, and I was in service three years. My freshman year at the University of Kansas, I was drafted. Most of my life I had been afflicted with asthma. So they inducted me at Leavenworth, Kansas, and so they examined me and they couldn't find anything wrong. And I told them, "I do have asthma." In fact, I was in the hospital with asthma when I got my induction papers. So for three days, every day they'd take me in and examine me and listen to my chest and that type of thing. And finally, they said, they wrote on my induction papers: "No asthma." So they sent me to Camp Breckinridge, Kentucky, for my basic training. Well, we were there about a week doing basic training. And, of course, they were reactivating the 92nd Division. And in my high school experience in Lawrence, we had done drills and this type of thing. The 92nd Infantry Division.

And so the company commander told me that I could get a staff sergeant position. I had more experience than those other guys, and I knew how to do the commands and that type of thing. But that was in November. And it was cold in Breckinridge. Every day, the guys would be out there drilling in the mornings, and the temperature dropped, and they were going to the infirmary with frostbitten toes and nose and ears and this type of thing. And the chaplain had put a notice in the company commander's office that he wanted to start a male chorus. So a bunch of us guys met over in the chapel on a Wednesday night, and no one there could play the organ. And I told them I could play a piano but I couldn't play the organ.

He said, "Well, you can learn to play the organ, if you can play the piano." He said, "I'll tell you what, if you will consider being the chaplain's assistant, we're reactivating the 92nd Division, and these positions are open and you wouldn't have to go through all these steps and stages."

And I told him, "Well, I think I'd rather go the other way." And when I went back out the next day, I think it dropped about ten more degrees, so I went back over and I told him, "I changed my mind."

So that's really how I got to work for the division chaplain. Now, when I did that, they told me that I would not have to do any charge of quarters. He said when I got up in the morning, just make my bed, come to his office and come to the chapel, and we'd go to work. Well, I ran into a little conflict a couple of times because the company commander tried to put me on charge of quarters or KP or something. And when he did, the chaplain finally let him know that I worked for him. And I didn't really do basic training. I got out of most of that. And every day, I mean, I would be in the chapel trying to learn to play that organ. I heard them out there, "Hup, two, three, four." They were out there working. And boy, I felt sorry for those guys. It was secure. But it was a good job and we had a lot of experiences together, the chaplain and I, because he took me into his confidence as an assistant. And then one of the unique things was the 92nd Division being the only black fighting division in the Army, we processed some seventy-two chaplains who were coming into the services. And they went to other units from there, but it was his job to train those chaplains, and so he trained me to help him train them. And so we had a lot of fun together. We all kept real close

Anyway, I met my wife there. When new troops would come in, we would always greet them as a chaplain, and sometimes we would look for talent to do programs at the chapel on Sunday and maybe find some ladies that could sing and that type of thing. And so, when they came and I met her, I made the mistake of carrying her bag up.

Being the chaplain, one of his jobs was to provide services for the troops. Okay, I learned to play the organ and I did typing and stuff for him and I helped him to do some counseling and that type of thing. So I got some experience in the ministry to start back in those days, even. And we went to all the little towns around Kentucky, Owensboro and Paducah and Henderson. The chaplain and I would go. He had access to a Jeep, his private transportation; I drove that. And we'd go around and we'd talk to ministers at a lot of churches, and what we'd do, we'd invite their choirs to come on Sunday mornings to render services at the chapel. And then on Sunday night, I organized a male chorus. And I had fifty-nine guys in the male chorus, and we'd take two big truckloads of them and we'd go back to those churches and have a little social affair for them. So the guys really loved to get in that choir because that gave them an opportunity to meet a lot of girls. So that happened.

Then we went overseas, and I was over in Italy and we got to meet a lot of people over there. I learned to speak quite a bit of Italian, so I did a lot of interpreting when I was over there. And was able to continue to communicate with those people. Then, in 1945, in November, I was eligible to be discharged. I got sick. And they sent me back to Staten Island Hospital. And I was there, and I had my wife to meet me in Colorado Springs, and that's where I was separated from service with an honorable discharge. I was discharged December the 22nd, 1945. And then I started back to school.

When I came back out of service, I spent the next year at Kentucky State College in Frankfort, Kentucky. There were quite a few black students at Kentucky State. I forget what the enrollment was, something like 600 or 700, I think. And then I came back to Lawrence and spent my next three and a half years at the University of Kansas.

When I was a kid, I know the population of Lawrence was about 10,000. And when I went in service in '41, it was around 14,000. When I came back from service, it had grown to about 30,000. Now it's close to 60,000. But during the war years, the population doubled.

After I was in the service, when I came back to Kansas, I was there for five years. I went to the University of Kansas, then when I finished there, I came to Texas. I pastored a church in Austin, Texas.

In Kansas I had some experiences, racial experiences. When I came back from overseas to my home in Lawrence, Kansas, one of the first things I did, my wife and I, it was the first time she'd been to Lawrence. We went to a theater and when we went in the theater, we purchased our tickets and we went to sit in the main floor of the theater. And one of the ushers came and told us that we couldn't sit there.

And I told him, "I don't know why." The seats were comfortable, and we were satisfied.

And he said, "Well, but you have to sit in the balcony."

I said, "No, I like these seats."

So he went and got the manager, and the manager came and told me the same thing. And I repeated that, and so he went and got the police. And they came and told us that we'd have to leave or go in the balcony. We could go and get our money back. Well, I told them I didn't want my money back. Well, that was one of the first experiences we had because in Kansas, we didn't have segregated schools. In fact, there were so few of us black folks, most schools were already integrated. Most of my rougher experiences in integration happened after we came to Texas in 1958 to pastor a church in Austin. That was 12th Street Christian Church. It was at 12th and Waller, right close to Interregional Highway. And when we moved, we moved further out on Webberville Road. I was there for seven years. After three years, we relocated. In fact, we moved twice after I went there. We had a pretty good experience there. The church we went to when we went there was a little small building, little small frame building on a 50-by-150-foot lot. And when we finally moved, we moved to another site with two and a half acres, and we had thirteen classrooms, a fellowship hall and sanctuary and a nursery. We grew quite a bit while I was there, and that was good experience. And then I came to Dallas.

I came to Dallas in '64, and it was as a result of my experience with the civil rights movement. The NAACP, right after the Kennedy assassination, decided that this was a good time, when Lyndon Johnson, who was a Texan, was elected president, for us to try to get some integration projects going in Austin. And so we announced that we were going to have a hot summer in 1963. We announced in '63 and we started in '64, which we did. And so we had those experiences, where we went through the siege of integrating hotels, skating rinks, I mean all the public facilities and that type of thing. And we gained a lot of support from people who were interested in it. Martin Luther King and all these other things were happening. And so this gave us added strength in trying to present our case. I remember we planned to do a march on the Capitol, a demonstration. John Connally was governor. When he heard that we were going to do that, he turned all the sprinkler systems on the lawn to stop the demonstrators.

Robert Whitby was a black photographer in Austin at that time. His wife was a member of my church. Well, she was a schoolteacher, too. And her sister was a schoolteacher, Betty Pool. He was also a teacher over at Anderson High School. And he taught at Huston-Tillotson College. Actually, there was Huston and Tillotson; they were separate. And then the two of them combined. And that made some difference.

George Givens was probably the most prominent black with the white people there. Some of the first experiences we had in Austin was integrating the Park and Recreation Department, city services, and this type of thing. They were so divided. For instance, in the park department, they had caretakers who worked with all those white facilities. And the gardeners worked for the black facilities, doing the same identical job. They were doing the same jobs, custodians and caretakers, or whatever. They had the same job, but the titles were different and the pay was different. And so we protested that. There was a big area in Austin where blacks lived. There were no sewer lines and this type of thing. Everybody used outhouses. And the streets were bad, and all that type of thing. And every year when the budget came out, there were, I think, five recreation facilities there. One was black. At the white ones, the managers, the persons who were in charge, were on salary. And the one that ran the black facility, he was on a kind of compensation thing where whatever concession they sold, he had to get his salary from that. So that kind of thing existed. I remember that an undertaker, a lawyer, and a doctor, several of us got together and we went to the city council and we began to protest the budget and just let them know some of the things that were not being fairly administered to the citizens.

And I remember the first time that I tried to present anything to the mayor, he said, "Well, have you talked to Doctor Givens about this?"

And I said, "Well, sir, no, I haven't, but I thought you were the mayor."

And he said, "Well, go right ahead, Reverend Sims." And he let me talk. But that kind of thing, you know.

Well, I was pastoring a church in Austin. I was associated with all the Texas churches, and they had a Texas Missionary Christian Convention. And I got to know all the ministers.

When I first came to Texas, Alonzo Smith was one of the older ministers who was going around selling suits to preachers. And he was an odd character. He went to school with Ronald Reagan, he tells us, and he was one of the first students at Jarvis Christian College. And anyway, Alonzo had a thing going where every time he would go and meet with ministers, he would always tell them that ministers don't wear black suits in the pulpit. And so he was trying to sell suits. And so he sold a lot of suits. A lot of ministers bought suits from him. So we got to know him that way. And we got to know him pretty well over the years, but he was more of a floater, going around from place to place. I understand that he did pastor a couple of churches before I met him. And one of them was in Tyler, Texas.

I started pastoring in Kansas when I was going to school. And my first church was Topeka, Kansas, the Second Christian Church there. And while I was pastoring that church, I got a call to pastor a church in Plattsburg, Missouri, so I was pastoring two churches at the same time. So what I would do, in the mornings, I'd get up early on Sunday morning, I'd go to Topeka. And then I'd leave that church and come back through Lawrence and go eighty miles east to Plattsburg, Missouri, and preach there. And then sometimes I'd come home at night, and my dad would have me preach. So I'd preach three times on Sunday sometimes. But that was my start. And I guess churches knew about me and heard about me and so I got calls from ministers who wanted to place me with congregations.

In fact, my preaching experience with that started with service. I was division chaplain, 92nd Division. I always required a salary everywhere I pastored. In fact, from about 1955 to 1986, I pastored churches consistently. I mean I wasn't without a pastorate at any time. If I left a church, it was to go to another church. I love the ministry. I love people, and I like to do the organizational part of the church, helping people to relate to the different functions of the church and get them working, this type of thing. That's part of it. And then in 1969, I started working for the Park and Recreation Department in Dallas. And I loved that work, because I worked with people and with children, and so I worked for them until 1986, when I retired. About three months, I worked as a recreation leader. And after that, I was a recreation center director at what's now Juanita Craft. And at that particular time, it was Wahoo Recreation center. Then I went to Exall Park, over in North Dallas. I was there for quite a while. I went back to Juanita Craft, then I went back to Exall, then I went to Martin Luther King. And those were the ones I worked with.

I knew Juanita Craft pretty well. She was a great woman. She was fine. She was a very community-oriented person; she was very concerned about cleaning up. She was a proud lady, and she wanted everybody else to be that way. And so she tried to do everything she could to inspire and to help people, to build character and that type of thing. So she was a very, very good person.

I met Barbara Jordan, but it was very informal. And I'd seen her and heard her speak several times, but I never did have real rapport with her. But I knew civil rights attorney W. J. Durham. I met Durham, and, in fact, we talked with Durham when we were doing our civil rights program in Austin. But at that particular time, he was remote from what we were doing in that, well, he was working in Dallas and we were working in Austin.

Now Martin Luther King, he was in Austin. I don't know exactly what year it was. The University of Texas. And we met him there. We had him as one of our principal speakers in 1966—I don't remember the year—here in Dallas at our general convention in the downtown convention center. And those are the two occasions when I met him. And I got to talk to him, not one-on-one but with a group of ministers. Yeah.

Arthur DeWitte. Well, the DeWitte brothers; there were several of them. Robert DeWitte and Arthur, they were real good during the civil rights time. And they worked with the press quite a bit, too.

Volma Overton was the president of the NAACP in Austin. He and I and several, well, there was an undertaker and a doctor and lawyer, got together and to strategize the summer we were going to have with the civil rights movement. I knew him very well, him and his wife and family, and, of course, being the president, he was kind of the catalyst for getting this started. In fact, when we actually started this program at City Hall, we knew that if we planned to do something, that you don't let everybody know, because a lot of times, when you do that, before everybody who's supposed to know knows it, then people who are not supposed to know, somebody will leak. And that's been one of the biggest problems and one of the biggest failures in most of the civil rights movements, is that people were able to anticipate and always set people up so that they can get somebody there that will tell them what's going on. And so this was a kind of a secret thing we did, because we told them that we were going to demonstrate at City Hall on this particular day, which we did. But we didn't tell them that some of us were going to come inside and we were going to interrupt the procedure and get on the agenda. So what we planned and we did, we had people—and this is what we told the constituency, most of the members of the group, is that what we were going to do, we were going to picket City Hall. And we were going to have people carrying signs. And we did. But only the five of us knew what we were going to do. We did the picketing before they opened the council meeting. And so we were marching, and a lot of people gathered around. And I remember I was carrying a sign. This one guy kept looking at us and kept calling us names, you know, all that kind of stuff. We just marched back and forth around the City Hall. And finally, one time he went like he was going to spit on me. And I stepped back, and I said, "Excuse me, sir, for getting in your way." And he cursed, but anyway, that went on. Well, Joan Baez was there. And she was playing some of her folk music, and so they thought this was the gist of it. But when the council session opened, Volma Overton, Booker T., and myself went inside, and when the council opened, the mayor looked at us, kind of strange, and he asked, me, "Reverend Sims, would you do the invocation?" So I did the little prayer. And then he declared the council meeting open and he started reading from the agenda, and he had some zoning things, two of them. When he started the second one, Volma Overton said, "Sir, I'd like to speak."

He said, "You want to speak on this?"

He said, "Yeah." He told him the area.

He said, "That's why I want to speak on it." And so he started talking. Basically, what he was saying was, these people get special treatment. And the other people don't. And I'm opposed to that, and I want to speak on that, blah, blah, blah, blah, blah. And so then he picked up a book. And the name of the book was "Black Like Me," written by Howard Griffin, from Mansfield, Texas. And he started page 1, he started reading.

And one of the council members said, "Damn. Are we going to have to listen to this?"

And the mayor said, "Well, Mr. Overton has the floor."

So he started reading. And the mayor interrupted, and said, "I'd like to interrupt. Mr. Overton, would you like to have a drink of water?"

"Yeah, I'll take a drink." He was trying to be nice.

So finally he says, "How long are you going to talk?"

He says, "Until we have justice." Okay. So he talked, and he talked, and finally, he read and read. And so finally, he said, "I would like to interrupt and let Claude Allen," who was a white professor at Huston-Tillotson College, "let him say a few words. Give you some statistics."

Well, Claude was great. Claude got up and he talked about the ghetto and how it was much more expensive for them to live in the ghetto because, he said, "Not only do you have to feed your family, but you got to feed the mice and roaches and you got to tear your car up on the bad streets," blah, blah, blah, blah, blah. They let him talk all day, all the rest of that day, and they adjourned the council till the next morning. He went back and he started talking again. And at that time, the council didn't have any ruling about any time limits. I mean, when they let you talk, then you had the floor. So he asked the mayor if he could yield for me to say a few words.

And the mayor said, "Well, we'll do that if Reverend Sims will only talk one hour."

And so, I stood up and I said, "Mayor, I'm appalled. Because you let this brother speak thirteen hours about my problem. And then when I want to talk about my problem, you're going to limit me to one hour. I'd be insulted."

He said, "Well, go ahead."

That's the mistake he made because I went on for three days. And did a whole lot of things.

Well, when this civil rights thing exploded and we protested the city council and we had a lot of problems there, and I got a lot of phone calls. People were threatening my family and my wife, and this type of thing. So I just started thinking about looking for another job. The Mississippi delegation of black churches asked me if I would consider a job in Edwards, Mississippi. And they invited me down there. So I went over to Edwards; that's where my mother and father went to school, and they would set up an office and everything. They wanted me to work over there. Well, there were some Mississippians got wind that I was coming there, and boy, they told me that if I came there, what they were going to do. So I had several offers, and I accepted coming to Dallas.

I went to the Bonnie View Christian Church. Bonnie View is on Loop 12 and Bonnie View. When I came to Dallas, I pastored Bonnie View, then went from Bonnie View to Romine Avenue Christian Church. And then I went to what is now Warren Avenue, Forest Avenue Church, associate minister for about a year. And then I got a call to go to East Side Christian Church in Longview, Texas. And I pastored that church down there for twelve and a half years. And then when I came back to Dallas, because I lived in Dallas all the time, I was commuting over there twelve and a half years, to Longview. I resigned that church, and I did interim for Canada Drive Christian Church in Dallas. And then my brother passed, and I did interim for almost two years at Community Christian Church in Fort Worth. And then I worked as associate minister in Waxahachie. And then I came back and I got a call to Denley Drive Christian Church, and from there I went back to Community for another year because they fired their pastor. And for the past four years now, I haven't been pastoring. I'm retired. I've been very active in church. I still work with the elders. I'm chairman of the elders, I've been chairman of the board and all that kind of stuff. I do preach. A lot of churches ask me occasionally to come down. In fact, Sunday before last, I was down in East Side Christian Church, where I pastored previously. And I get invitations to go to a lot of different churches to help them.

INTERVIEW BY ALAN GOVENAR AND JOHN SLATE, MAY 23, 1997

Roebuck "Pops" Staples

Gospel and pop singer
Born: December 14, 1914, Winona, Mississippi

Roebuck "Pops" Staples grew up in the Mississippi Delta region, the son of sharecropper farmers. In 1936, Staples and his wife, Oceola, moved their family to Chicago, hoping to find a better life. Staples took jobs in meatpacking, steel mills, and construction. In 1948, he formed the Staple Singers with his daughters, Cleotha and Mavis, and his son, Pervis. They started singing at home and then in local churches. The group made their first recordings in 1953 and had their first success with the 1957 release of "Uncloudy Day." The music of the Staple Singers reflected the social changes of the civil rights movement by writing and performing songs with positive and progressive messages. They released the song "A Long Walk to D.C." in memory of their friend Martin Luther King Jr., and in the 1970s they had their biggest commercial success with "Respect Yourself" (1971), "I'll Take You There" (1974), and "Let's Do It Again" (1976). In the 1980s, Pops Staples intended to retire, but instead began to pursue a solo career. He has released two solo albums, "Peace in the Neighborhood" and "Father, Father," which won a Grammy Award in 1994.

It was rough (in Mississippi). I didn't know much about it; I was young, but it was kind of tough for me when I did learn. It was pretty tough, but I made it through.

My father was Warren Staples. My mother was named Florence. My daddy was a genuine farmer. He loved that farming. He raised cotton and corn, potatoes, and he was good at it. They were the father and mother of fourteen children, seven boys and seven girls, and I was the thirteenth child.

Well, I'll tell you. Down in Mississippi there, we was farmers. And in those days, we didn't have nothing to play but our mouths. Didn't have no piano, guitars, or nothing, just clap their hands to sing by. So we'd go in the field and work all day and come home in the evening after we were through. Didn't have nothing to do till bedtime but to sit around. And sitting around waiting till bedtime, we got in the habit of singing. And everybody was older than me and the baby, so they would start singing. They had a big yard. We'd go out in the yard and start singing, and my sisters and brothers could sing. We'd get out there and start singing, and we'd look up and we'd see friends and neighbors coming from way around, far as our voices could be heard. We'd look out there and we'd have a yard full of people just singing, praising God. And that got into me. I've been a Christian since I was a boy. And that got into me, that singing. I loved it. So finally, I got married and started raising a family. When my baby got to be about three years old, I told them, I said, "When I was at home, we used to sing." I said, "Let's us sing like my family used to sing." So I started them out at an early age. And Mavis couldn't hold a note. I had to work with her about three years before she could even hold a note straight, you know. And we finally got together. In the meantime, though, when I was at home, we would have those chitlin parties, chiterling circuits, and they'd have suppers. We'd have to play. We'd have music for them. I leaned how to play the guitar. And I would play the guitar for some of those suppers and make $3, $5 a night. And that's what I would do. I learned to play. So when we got to Chicago, I started in to singing, and I did have an instrument to play better than we did at home. We didn't have nothing at home. Took me about five years, I guess, to get them lined up singing good like I wanted, and then we just sat around and sang and just loved it. Singing and praising God—we loved it. And one day my sister, one of my older sisters, her husband had passed and she wanted to stay with me. And she was staying with us, and we had a brother who was pastor of a church, Mount Zion Baptist Church. And we were going to have a little meeting that after-noon, and some singing would be going on. And she said, "Why don't y'all come on and sing at the church today?" And that's what we did. I didn't have a guitar case or nothing, no car. Got on the streetcar with the little guitar in my hand and went on and got to the church. We sung, and when we sung and got through singing, they wouldn't let us sit down. They just kept on, they loved us so well, they kept on clapping. So we went back and did an encore. And when we finished, and it was out, there was another minister from another church was there. And he told us, "If you come to my church and sing next Sunday night, we'll raise a collection and give you half." Oh, we was proud of that, so we went home and rehearsed. And we got through, we had a whole program lined out, so the next Sunday came along, we went over and we sang. We sung, I guess, about thirty-five or forty minutes, sung the whole program, and the collection that was raised was $35. And that was the first time we received money for singing. And that was our first payday, $17.50; we got half. And from that, before we started that, times was hard. I had a hard time raising four children, and my sister was there with me. She was a singer and she had a job, and she'd help me out every way. She'd loan me $10 every week to carry me along, so that's the way we made it with her. So when I got home that night, she was in bed, and first thing I did, I went to her and said, "You don't have to loan me $10 this week. I got $17." That's the way we got started.

I never did get to meet (Blind Lemon Jefferson). That was one of the people that caused me to be playing the guitar today. I loved his playing, and never did get to meet him, but we did have his records. Blind Lemon

The Staple Singers, publicity photo, ca. 1950 (Texas African American Photography Archive)

was a good artist. He was the leading man in those days, in my time. He was good. He knew how to make the chords. He could go from one to the other. I always wanted to be a good guitar player like that, but I never could. But being so good at changing from one chord to the other, that's what I liked about him.

Blind Willie Johnson was good, too. Blind Willie Johnson, Blind Lemon Jefferson, and Blind Blake. Blake was blind, too. And they was my favorites. And there was one in those days: Rosetta Tharpe. She was a player, too, and all those guitars I loved. I just love guitar music. And I'd tried to copy after them, you know.

I went to Chicago in 1936. Well (there were) hard times down in Mississippi. I never did like farming so much, because of quite a few different things. First, it was hard work, working in the sun. And the biggest objection I had of it was the money; didn't get much pay. Shoot. We'd make fifteen, twenty bales of cotton, sometimes my dad come out in debt. I couldn't figure that out. If we worked by the day, we worked for fifty cents an hour. I've worked many a day for fifty cents an hour. Worked a many a week for $3 an hour. And that's what I told him I didn't like about it. I thought he should have been doing better than that. We didn't do nothing, didn't burn no money, nothing but to eat on, from Christmas to furnishing time. Furnishing time started in March, and we'd eat from March to August from the big store, and charge it to us, and that's.... That was tough. And he'd come out in debt.

It was bad (discrimination) in Mississippi. It was bad. Black man had it tough there. If the boss man had a boy child, four or five years old, and I was older than him, we'd have to say, "Yes sir, and "No, sir." We'd go to town, little town, if you start meeting a white man on the street, street wasn't so wide, you wasn't given no room; you'd just have to step off and let him by. They really had things under control. Couldn't go into the restaurant to eat, none of that kind of stuff. If we went to a white restaurant, had to go round to the back and get the stuff and take it out. We weren't even allowed in the restaurant. It was hard. But we made it.

My daddy always taught us how to go round those things (discrimination). Humbling down, saying, "Yes, sir," "No, sir." Didn't make any difference what category they was in, or how poor. The lynching part, we never did run into none of that, but we did, oh Lord, hear about it in the joining places to us. And they'd mob up people, beat them up. My family, we did get in one fight there. My older brother. A Chinaman kicked him, and that's one thing. Go that far to hit you and not fight back, well, when he kicked him, my brother knocked him out. Then we had to run. My daddy was a hard worker. And if you were a good worker and tried to do right, those farmers, those landowners, they knew one another, and they found out that it was Warren Staples's boy that was fighting and they quieted it down. They wouldn't let it go. So we got through that without getting mobbed, by us living on a place with a good man, Will Dockery. And so we got by, by not getting hurt.

I started out (playing music) with the guitar. I was the first artist singing in the groups, in the band, that was allowed (to bring) the guitar in a church. They call it devil music. And I started out with the guitar, and after I started, all the quartets and singers then followed through my success with the guitar. And then they got bass and drums.

I sung in church a cappella. I was a singer before I came to Chicago. I was always singing. Always did sing, all my life, from about twelve up.

"How in the world do you think everybody's supposed to respect you? Oh, Lord. If you don't give a heck about the man with the Bible in his hand, just get out the way and let the gentleman do his thing. Oh, yeah. Respect yourself—da, da, da, da, respect yourself. De, de, de, de. If you don't respect yourself, ain't nobody gonna give a good cahoot yourself. Respect yourself." Need the group and music behind it, never sounds better, you know. Yeah. Yeah, we'd sing that. That was "Respect Yourself"—a million-seller. That was in 1971. That was our first big hit.

I love what I'm doing, and we love one another. We love people. We love trying to bring the world together, where everybody would be in peace with one another. I'm a Christian man. I believe that we should love one another and do unto others as we wish to be done by. That's what keeps me going in this business, and doing so, people have told me I have done a great deal for them and going the right way, what I call the right way, what we think is the right way, by doing this, they have been born again and learned to love Jesus Christ. Jesus Christ died for us, and I do believe I'm working now down here to have a better home when I leave here than I did down in Mississippi. And that's all right. He made everything right for me, but I want to have a better life when life is over here. That's what keeps me going.

The tradition of gospel is the beginning. I started out a new tradition of music when we started, but it come into the place where we sang tradition and sang message songs, come out of tradition. Everybody can understand tradition in the church and all. But the message song, we could go in places, in auditoriums, all where we sing message songs, telling a story, what we should be doing with each other, and we'd be singing the truth, and as long as we're singing the truth, we figure we're not singing no harm.

They let you know when you're connecting. Some people might not be like Pop, but I never go on the stage, I never go nowhere, I leave home with prayer. And somebody in that place where we sing is going to feel it, whether it be gospel or traditional. One way or another, somebody in there is going to be going through with what we're saying. That's the way, you know, we go like that.

I'm Missionary Baptist. That's the only one. When I was a boy, my father was a Methodist, he went in the Methodist church. And after I got up, I saw fit that I thought the Baptist was where I should be. And I went in there, and I been in there ever since.

When we started singing, we started driving cars. We went miles and miles to see where we could sleep because there wasn't no hotels for the black. We went miles being hungry because we couldn't stop and get nothing to eat unless we went in a grocery store. So we went through all of that. We had a hard time in coming through, made a little money, but the Lord fixed it. I don't have a Ph.D., nothing like that in education, but I've learned well enough to learn how to pray, and this situation that we're in, the Lord have been with us to go all over the world. My biggest education I got was from traveling, history, going all over the world to sing, God praise it, and that's what we've done. And I'm proud of it. I'm proud. So I'm doing okay, I'm eighty-three years old, I feel good, and want to go on as long as I can.

INTERVIEW BY ALAN GOVENAR, OCTOBER 8, 1998

Clara Terrell

Cloakroom attendant
Born: August 30, 1910, Rigby, Idaho

Clara Terrell was born on a farm. Hers was the only black family for miles. They moved to Boise, Idaho, about 1932, after her father developed rheumatism. She worked as a cloakroom attendant for country club dances and, despite the segregation of the time, had few problems with racism. She was active in community work and says she and her husband, Warren, taught their children to "earn respect."

My father was born and raised in Salt Lake City, and his folks moved to Idaho when he was four. His father told me that his dad liked to wander around, move around some, and one time they lived here in Boise, and my dad said, as a young fellow, he heard of cows here in Boise through the Franklin Smith family. And I guess they must have went from here up to Idaho Falls, but grandfather lived to be over a hundred years old, so he was up in years when I knew him.

My mother was raised in Salt Lake City and her father homesteaded in Idaho, first up at Ririe, Idaho, just out from Idaho Falls. In later years they moved to Idaho Falls. I think the families (mother and father) first met in Utah. My father's grandfather, Greenflake, came to Salt Lake City with Brigham Young's party.

I was born (on the farm) in Ririe, and my two (older) brothers were born in Idaho Falls. We were the only colored family for miles. Then we moved to Boise in 1932. My brother just older than I was working here in Boise at the time, and my father got rheumatism bad from working, from irrigating, being in the cold weather because he used to haul wood a lot in the wintertime from up there, from Raft River—haul wood, cedarwood, and sell. My mother used to card wool and make underwear, you know, with this wool, and make him gloves to keep him warm, and she'd make him warm wool quilts for him to take out with him in the wintertime, when he'd go after wood. He'd always stay busy at something; he wasn't around. But being in the cold weather so much and irrigating from the farm and all, he got rheumatism bad, so he moved to Boise, to where it was warmer.

My brother older than me, we called him Bud, and his name was James Steven—he worked at the Owyhee Hotel. He went to the Arrid Club first, but I don't know—Warner started working at the Owyhee first, and the Arrid Club, my brother started there first. My mother was just a housewife, and my father, he worked on farms for a while and then he got in the wood business for himself, hauling up near Idaho City—he and my mother would camp up there and he would take horses up there and take our kids up there in the summer so they could ride the horses and be up there in the fresh air and fishing and all that. He'd get wood out and then he'd come home and he would saw the wood up and he would sell kindling wood, other wood, self-employed. He had horses and wagons he brought down. He had a truck, too. It wasn't just wood for us—it was wood that he'd sell. Sometimes he'd have someone working and helping him, here in Boise, get the wood ready for sale. Not arranging the sale, but getting the wood sawed up and split and all. Some of it he sold by the cord, and the kindling, he'd bundle it up and sell it that way. I don't remember how many years he did that, but he stayed quite busy up to a year or two before he passed away—his health, he had a heart problem and had to give up the work. He passed away in 1950.

On the farm, when we'd have thrashers come—we had to hire men for sugar beet harvest, the potato harvest, and for thrashing grain, and there would be times when the thrashers would come, the neighbors would go help each other and there would maybe be twenty men to cook for, for breakfast, dinner, and supper, and that kept my mother really busy, and the other farm women, too, doing those things. On the farm my mother would raise—send and get maybe a 100 or 200 baby chickens and look after those. But she never worked away from home.

It was diversified farming—sugar beets, potatoes. Had hay and had to rake and stack. Sugar beets and potatoes were the main crops for selling. Forty acres. I used to pick potatoes on the farm. They would let school out for a week or two after, through harvesttime, so the kids could help their folks get the potatoes in. We had a large potato cellar, and through the winter the potatoes would be sorted and the number ones picked for shipping for sale. The neighbors helped each other a lot.

Being raised here, I haven't noticed any difference (being black) to speak of. Once in a while, you know, you might run into a problem, small problem. Once in a while going to school up there, where we were the only colored, maybe there would be one person—my brother maybe would be in a fight. I was in a fight one time and was expelled from school—it was a neighbor girl. That happened in Yukon. She was the neighbor girl across the street, and I guess she called me names and we fought on the school grounds, so we were both expelled from school. We were taken into the principal's room, he taught school also, and he was the bishop. He took us into his room, made us sit there for the last recess, we sat there till school let out, and then he expelled us.

We were supposed to apologize. I went back to school the next day, and I wouldn't apologize. The day after, my father went to school with me, he sat in a seat in the back of the room and he told me what to say.

Unidentified woman, ca. late 1800s (Idaho State Historical Society)

He said, "Tell them you're sorry that it happened on school grounds. You wished it would have happened down the street so you could have had it out."

When I got almost to that, he held up his finger for me to stop. She apologized. We were friends afterwards, 'cause we lived across the street from each other. I went to school in Yukon myself, my brother attended school some in Ririe. I went to school up to the eighth grade.

After we came to Boise, I worked at Kress's store for a while. I bagged candy in the back of the counters. It was next door, almost next door to where the Bon Marche is now. Kress's store was more or less like a ten-cent store. They had a variety of things in there. Candies and household things, just a general store, like.

On the farm there was a country store I worked at sometimes down the road from us. An elderly couple had this little grocery store, and they lived there also, and they would hire girls to help them because the woman was crippled and the man was up in years. He was mean to the other girls at different times when they'd work, and he'd curse them, send them home, but I got along with him fine, because everybody knew my dad and they respected him. So we got along fine. So, we'd go down there and work in shelves so we'd get hats, just the frames of ladies' hats, and then decorate them, and I would help do that and wait on people.

At the Kress's store I made about $10 or $12 a week, I think. It wasn't too much. It was going wages—it was back when you could buy a box of strawberries for five cents and a loaf of bread for ten; or fifteen cents worth of wieners would be a meal. So that's the way it went.

When my family first came to Boise, we lived at 124 Broadway in the Baptist parsonage. They didn't have a minister and that's where we lived at first, and then after that my dad and mother went out to White City Park, and they rented from Wanick Stein's father and mother. They moved from there to South Boise, and then their next move was 1313 North Fifth Street, here in Boise, and from there they built a home on North Thirteenth Street. There wasn't too many colored here at that time. Not too many associated with, I might say.

My dad and mother moved to South Boise, but I didn't because I'd gotten married June 27, 1937. Then Warner and I knew the parsonage was empty again, and Warner and I lived there at first when we got married. I guess it was the deacon we paid (rent) to, because they didn't have a minister.

I myself, I checked wraps at the Hillcrest Country Club for a number of years when they'd have dances out there. I checked wraps for years at the banquets and dances. I also checked wraps at the Arrid Club.

I enjoyed doing it. Got to know most of the people in Boise because it was people with money mostly that would come to Arrid Club and out to Hillcrest. But on the banquets at the hotel, it would be general public, more or less, when they would have business meetings there, and at one time, when the war was on, they had camps around Boise and they would have big going-away parties there for some of the fellows who would be leaving for overseas. I checked quite a number of wraps on quite a number of those parties.

Most of the time I didn't get a salary—I worked on tips. Sometimes it was good and sometimes it was different, but it balanced out pretty good. It depended on the type of party it was. Sometimes they'd tip better than other times.

Right from the start they tipped well because they knew my brother and knew Warner and they knew who I was. Had a problem one time, with one, I think it was at a party. The fellow come in, and he checked his bottle when he checked his coat, and different times he would come back and ask for the bottle, and the last time he asked for it, he didn't bring it back, but when the dance was over he come and asked for the bottle. Well, of course, I didn't have it, and he couldn't remember that he didn't bring it back the last time, so he got kind of ugly. So, I went off and got Mr. Kirkham, who is the manager of the banquet room and he told me. He said, "If a certain fellow was here tonight that is overseas, you wouldn't talk to this girl this way, and you're not going to talk to her now. You get your things and get out of this hotel and don't you ever come back." So that ended that. That was the only problem that I remember.

We tried to raise our family in a manner so they would be respected, of which they have been over the years. Because we were raised, that was both Warner and I.

Over the years I've worked with the YWCA. I've been with Booth Auxiliary, the auxiliary over at the unwed mothers. I was secretary of the auxiliary over at unwed mothers. I was secretary of the auxiliary there for about four years. I've been president of the American Legion. I've been chaplain in that. And I've done volunteer work out at the VA.

I would say that around World War II is when more coloreds started coming here. Before we moved to Boise, it seemed there'd been a pretty good number here, but they had moved away some and so then others started coming in about World War II.

Interview by Mateo Osa, January 13, 1981 (Courtesy Idaho Oral History Center, Boise, Idaho)

Jesse Thomas

Blues musician
Life dates: February 3, 1911–August 8, 1995

Jesse Thomas belied the stereotype of the hard-living bluesman. He rambled, but he also went to college and settled down. He continued to perform almost until he died, though a stroke limited his guitar playing. A quiet, dignified man, he lived in the same house in Shreveport, Louisiana, for almost thirty years. A list of rules for living affixed to a doorway included, "Never lose your self-control."

Thomas grew up in Logansport, Louisiana, near the Texas line, in the same country that produced Leadbelly. Thomas's father was a fiddler, and an older brother, Willard "Ramblin" Thomas, became a professional blues musician.

Jesse Thomas left home in his teens and took up the life of blues musician, staying on the move. He lived briefly in Dallas, where he made his first records in the late 1920s. He lived for several years in Fort Worth. He played on the streets, in cars, in alleys, in cafes—"anywhere they wanted to hear me play."

He moved to California in 1939. After service in World War II, he studied music in a junior college, though his public schooling had not gone beyond sixth grade. "Now if I write a song, I know where I'm going. I know what I'm talking about," he said. In 1957, Thomas returned to Shreveport, where he remained for the rest of his life. He worked at other jobs when the music business was slow. Toward the end of his life, he was popular on the festival circuit and played regularly with younger white musicians who treated him with kindness and respect.

George Thomas was my daddy. He was a sharecropper. My mama was named Laura. I had five brothers and three sisters. And not one of them is alive today. I was the next to the youngest.

My dad was a violin player. And he played for dances in houses and in dance halls. Most times he played by himself. They did what we called breakdown. It was something like a country dance. And a bunch of people danced around in circles. They would go first, join hands, hold hands, and circle round and the fellow on the head, dancing on the head, would get out of the circle and get in the middle of the circle and swing partners. He would swing all the girls and then get back in line, and the next fellow would get out of the circle and get in the ring and dance around, till we all danced, and then would go around the circle, and that was the end of that set. You would take the girl to the bar and buy her something, candy or an apple or peanuts, whatever. And then you were ready for another set. And that's the kind of dances he played. Quite a few people would come.

We used to have them at our houses, and I would participate in the dancing sometimes. I'd go to dances when I was about thirteen. My mother was a Christian person.

I had one brother who was a musician. Willard Rambin' Thomas. And I had one other brother; he was older than Rambling Thomas. He was named George Thomas Jr. He played violin and guitar, piano, mandolin. But he didn't take it as a career. He worked on the farm most of the time.

Rambling Thomas was nine years older than me. I think he became a professional musician when he was about twenty-two years old. Well, I learned from him and different ones. We always had a guitar around the house. I would pick it up and try to do what I saw him doing. Visitors would come and play a tune, and I'd copy what they did, until I got grown and I took music lessons. When I went to California, I was twenty-eight years old. When I was thirty-six, I went to college. I majored in music.

I picked up the guitar and music from different people. Then I heard piano. I always liked piano music and tried to make it sound near like a piano as I can. And then when I got around where I was playing in bands, I took a liking to saxophone, and that's where I tried string bending, pushing strings, try to sustain the note, hold that note.

When I was coming up, people still sang while they worked. It wasn't many words. A lot of times they'd just hum like that, all day. I used to have a cousin, he'd come to town. He lived in the country, worked on the farm with us, and when he'd leave, he sing, and we'd know what that meant.

Seems like he was telling us, "All right, I'm going. I'm gone." It seemed like we could understand that. I don't know whether he meant it or not. But to us, we were satisfied in thinking he meant this or that, you know. Sound good to us. That's the way it was. You know what they meant. At least you thought you knew. You were satisfied with what you thought.

That's where the blues came from. Yeah. Make up something. Carry a tune, same old blues tunes. And that tune was music. Bands didn't know that tune was music. W. C. Handy heard them singing that tune. And he wrote it down and put it with a band. And he played it back to them; they had already composed that melody, but it wasn't any words to it, you know. Wasn't no background, no form. Just melody. Duke played that melody and put words to it and background to it, a band and drums, and stuff, and it just swept the country. He made "St. Louis Blues," and you know what happened. It was a hit. It went everywhere. White people played it, recorded it. Black people. Came from that old song that people sang while they worked.

Some people had them record players. We heard different records. Bessie Smith sang blues, other people, Ma Rainey, Ida Cox.

Growing up I heard quite a bit of blues. There were people who would play in the houses, but in the barrelhouse, what we called the barrelhouse, where the people would go and dance and have drinks and have fun, but our parents didn't allow us to go there. But we would slip around sometimes to hear the piano player playing. But we couldn't go in. It was in Haslam, Texas, across the river from Logansport. It was a mile from Logansport.

I remember some of the musicians: Willie Ezell, he made records a long time ago. Bob Cole, he was a good piano player. Some women used to come to Haslam and sing the blues, but I don't remember their names. Elizadie, I don't know whether she sang in Haslam or not, but she used to come by Logansport, and she was a blues singer.

There were the traveling guitar players we would see on the medicine show. About every three weeks or so. They'd put on a show, and then the man selling the medicine would talk. And the guy that played the guitar, he would tell jokes and dance and play the guitar. And he would pass the medicine around. Some of the bigger ones had minstrel shows. They used to come in the fall when it was cotton-picking time. There was money in circulation, they would come in to get the money. They'd do the shows in a tent, like a circus tent. All of them were black, the performers were. The minstrel show was white. Some of the shows were good. A lot of girls would dance and sing, and the man would come out and dance and sing, tell jokes.

Some of the minstrel shows had white performers who would cork up their faces. And some of the black performers would blacken their

Jesse Thomas, photograph by Stan Carpenter, Shreveport, Louisiana, 1994 (Courtesy Stan Carpenter)

faces. Oh, yeah, most of them did that. The comedians would blacken their faces. To be funny. They'd have white lips to make it look like they had a big mouth.

I started playing guitar when I was about seven. I wasn't playing professionally. I liked music. My older brother George, he would always carry the violin somewhere. He carried the violin off and left it somewhere. My daddy was without a violin a long time. When he got a violin again, he just about retired from playing. When he got about fifty-five or sixty years old, he didn't play anymore. And they didn't allow us to play music much. We had to slip around and play. They thought that was the devil's music. The people talked to my dad and say, "You ought to quit playing that devil's music."

My daddy just quit; he got scared, I guess. They believed strongly in that type of religion. Right today, certain people, church people and a lot of other people, they think the blues is something else. Devil's music. A lot of good musicians, they're playing for the church. And I ask them sometimes to go and play a dance with me. I play parties and weddings. They won't even play a wedding or a wedding reception. Scared, I guess.

I know it's not bad. I started to play professionally when I was about sixteen. I was in Crandall, Texas, out from Dallas. I moved to Dallas when I was fifteen, or something like that. About 1926 or '27, yeah. I went on a cotton pick. I had been to Forney. I had a brother, my oldest brother, living there. And I went out there and stayed a few months with him when I was fourteen and went to school. Then I went back home.

When I was fifteen, I left home and went to Dallas. I came up here to Shreveport when I was fifteen and stayed a while, then I went on a cotton pick at Crandall, Texas. I went to Dallas and stayed with Rambling Thomas. He was staying in Dallas at that time. I lived in Dallas on Hall Street in North Dallas. Yeah, we were up and down Central all the time. That was where you played. I don't know how to describe it. There were cafes, houses, barbershops, things like that.

I heard Lonnie Johnson in Dallas at the Ella B. Moore Theater. He was playing acoustic guitar. And they had shows. It was like the minstrel shows. Only difference, they were in a building, inside, and the minstrel show was in a tent. That's the difference. I played for a man had me hired there, that might have been her (Ella B. Moore's) husband. I didn't ever know his name.

The Depression wiped a lot of them out. That's what hurt the musicians in a way, especially those that were playing on the street like me, for nickels and dimes. I used to make pretty good money, and I was beginning to make a good living. Then the Depression came along and cut that out. That's when they made the jukebox.

Before the Depression, I sometimes made $2 in a day, sometimes $5. I made $15 one night, I remember. Lot of nights I made $10.

When I lived in hotels or apartments, it usually cost $2 a week. You could get a meal for twenty-five cents. I've been in one cafe in Dallas I used to eat all the time, wasn't far from Ella B. Moore Theater. You would have a showcase in front. Pig feet and pig ears in a showcase, and a big pan of corn bread cut in blocks. I don't remember the name of it.

I played once at the Ella B. Moore Theater, on the corner there. And I didn't play much in Dallas because I was too young. I just played for the people who wanted to hear me play. I wasn't hired. I played anywhere they wanted me to play, but I wasn't hired. People would give me nickels and dimes and quarters. "Play me a tune"; "Here's a dime, play me a tune." On a street corner or in an alley or in a barbershop, in a cafe, anywhere.

Blind Lemon Jefferson was in and out of town. He was famous. He went to Chicago and places like that. I'd see him, and that's all. I never did talk to him.

I don't think I stayed in Dallas over three or four months. I went to Forney to see my brother again for a few days. And I had an aunt out in the country. I stayed out there with her a while. I went back to Crandall, stayed there a while, and I came home to stay a while. And I began to travel then. I went to Houston, stayed there a few months, went to Dallas for two months, went back to Houston. Went to Galveston, stayed a week. Came back to Houston and went to Dallas again. I was playing, yeah. On the streets. I made a living doing that. I stayed there in Dallas, then I went to Oklahoma City. Then I got a telegram from Dallas to come back, and that was from the RCA Victor Recording Company. And that's when I went and started making records.

I made my first records on Ellum Street, at a hotel. It was near where the track crossed Ellum. Yeah, I remember those Jews standing in the door on Ellum Street. "Come in, come in." I don't know how long Ellum Street was, or where it began, just that little section around Central.

After that, I was just traveling and wanted to make money and heard that times were good out there in California. I had lived in Fort Worth as long as I ever lived anywhere. Three or four years, at least, from the time that I was eighteen. I stayed where the colored people lived. I stayed out on the highway, the Dallas highway, in a motel where I worked and played music. The Broadway Inn was the name of that motel.

In Fort Worth I met Jesse Hooker. I played with him a lot. We would serenade the white people. We would go out in Mistletoe Heights and parade the streets, up and down the streets. We'd go up to the house and start playing. And they would come out and give us some money. We'd go on to the next house. Oh, they'd give us anywhere from twenty-five cents, sometimes a $1. $2. We'd play regular popular songs that you'd hear on the radio. We played some country songs, some standards. We were playing music. We wouldn't play blues for them unless they asked for a certain blues. There wasn't so many popular blues then. "St. Louis Blues," something like "Memphis Blues."

We had other musicians, other than Jesse Hooker and me, a drummer. We had them little trap drums. We called him "Frog." That's all I know. The last time I saw Jesse Hooker was in Fort Worth about 1957. Yeah, I came through there and went by his house. He lived over there on

Third Street. He was lying down. I don't think he was sick. He was just resting. He was quite a bit older than I was. I think he needed his rest, but he was still playing. He never did get up. I stayed there and talked to him, but wasn't sick. He was a light brown-skinned fellow. He wasn't tall. He was slim, about my height. He was good.

Well, I never did go back anymore. I would go through there all the time, coming back here. I didn't see Jesse Hooker again. I didn't have time to look him up.

Anyway, when I got to California, I first lived in Los Angeles, stayed there a few days, and then I toured the whole state. You might say I hoboed all over the state. A lot of times, we hitchhiked. We very seldom paid our fare, up until I went to work in Salinas. Then I settled there. I lived in Salinas, I guess, five or six years.

I went to work as a musician at the restaurant buffet on the main street. A restaurant and a bar. I played there for five years. I had a little old group: another guitar player and drums. We played mostly hillbilly music, country songs. That's what they wanted: "You Are My Sunshine," songs like that.

There were a lot of people there from Texas and Oklahoma. The people there were white. I began to learn a lot of different kinds of music before I went to California, in Texas. I played for white people most times; people with cars would pick me up sometimes. I'd play in the car. Sometimes I'd stand outside the car and put my foot on the running board and hold my guitar and play a song.

I never did play much with my brother Willard. I played two or three parties with him. But we played different types of music. He played slide and mostly blues. I couldn't play much blues then. I didn't know how to play blues on the guitar, melody. I played chords and sang.

I was twenty-six when Willard died; he must have died in 1937. He got sick in Memphis and he was sick a while, not seriously. And he wouldn't come home. Then he got seriously ill and he tried to come home. And he was too sick to come home, so I think he got sick on the way home and had to go back. A lady told us that he didn't have a wife, but he was living with a lady. He was buried in Memphis, I think.

I went to Salinas Junior College in 1947 to study music. I loved music. I could play good. But I didn't know about compositions. I didn't know how to write songs. I could make up a song, but I wouldn't know whether it was right or wrong. Now if I write a song, I know where I'm going. I know what I'm talking about.

I went to college for a couple of years. I was thirty-six years old. I really didn't graduate, but I told them I was graduated. I told them I graduated in Forney, Texas. I never went beyond sixth grade.

I guess I first heard about electric guitars in '38, when they first started making them. I ordered one out of a catalog. Charlie Christian was the first person I heard playing one. I remember T-Bone Walker; he was a slim guy, he wasn't very tall. We used to play together. He wasn't playing the guitar when I first met him. He was singing with bands.

That was in Los Angeles. He used to come in the places where I was playing around Central Avenue. Central Avenue was a long street, from about 5th Street in Los Angeles to 93rd. And there were colored businesses on both sides. And the streets that run across Central, there were colored people living on both sides. It was a colored street. A lot of clubs, hotels, several places. Dinah Washington used to work out there. Some movie stars used to come over there and visit.

In Los Angeles the segregation wasn't as bad as it was in Texas and Louisiana. Segregation was legal. They had passed laws that separated the colored from the white, but to make it equal, black people had equal accommodations with the white.

The railroad companies, they had a coach for the white and a coach for the black. And the station, they had a separate room, and it was just the same as the white. In a town like Houston, they had a big cafe, and this side was colored, and this side was white. That was where there was a lot of colored people. But in them little towns where there was a lot of whites, and maybe three or four colored, or ten, they couldn't afford to build a big place for the colored. So that made a difference. And then when the buses come out, instead of the train, they had one coach, and the colored people sit in the back, and you had to walk in the front. And that's what started all that stuff. And the schools, the colored people, like you had to build your own school. And the superintendent would give you a teacher. Well, where there's just a few colored people, what kind of school could they build? A whole town with a lot of white people, they could build a brick school, any kind of school they wanted, 'cause they had people to go to it. Where there were a few colored people, you couldn't afford a big school.

In Los Angeles everybody went to the same school. And they didn't build the schools. The state built the schools for them. Buses and streetcars, they weren't segregated. But you didn't mix and mingle together like you do now. Some places in California, they was segregated, too. There were little towns like El Centro, Barstow, few towns I know, they wouldn't serve colored. It's all over now. It was better, in a way. More jobs, make more money. Everything was better all the way around.

I was in California for twenty years, until 1957. And then I moved back to Shreveport. I wanted to be back where I could feel free to write my music, be with my people. They all died out now.

I've been a painter and a carpenter and insurance salesman. I would work all the time when the music business was dull. I didn't work during the time that I was playing in Salinas for that rodeo. I stayed on that job five years. For about seven years, I didn't do any work. I would do janitor work, anything.

I had been married once, when I was in Fort Worth. I married in 1968. I liked Fort Worth better than Dallas. It was more reliable, and they had a lottery (policy) and games. The black entertainment district comparable to Central Track was Ninth Street and Jones in Fort Worth.

The Jim Hotel was on Ninth Street. Jones Street crossed Ninth. There were a lot of cafes, barbershops, lottery, pool halls, and upstairs dance halls and all like that. I'd hang around that section and people would give me quarters and dimes. I made my living there for maybe a year or so. Then I went to work out at a motel. And I stayed out there. I had a job at the motel, and I made more money. In Dallas, I never had a job. And I didn't make much money in Dallas.

In Dallas, they had dance halls, but I couldn't get in there. I was too young, and they used bands: Red Calhoun, Blue Devils, Duke Ellington. Duke Ellington would play wherever the colored dance hall was. I don't know. We didn't go in there much. He would play for the white people. He would come there maybe two nights, and then he'd play maybe one night for the blacks. Duke Ellington was new music, he had a new style. We have bands playing like Duke Ellington today. His saxophones would riff, and the trumpets and trombones would riff, and they'd clash each other. Instruments was kind of different. You could hear the bass playing its part. It was modern music. He was ahead of everyone. Red Calhoun sounded like one instrument playing the melody, and the other people backing him up, something like that. Duke Ellington played a new style. The white people copied it, and black people copied what he was doing. He created a lot of stuff that Red Calhoun was playing, that he heard, what other people were playing. Benny Goodman and Tommy Dorsey and all of them, they hired arrangers to arrange their music kind of like what Duke was playing. But Duke could arrange his own music. He could compose it and arrange it and play it

Now, I play festivals. I played festivals here two or three times. Juneteenth, and I play at a jazz festival at LSU. I'm going to play at New Orleans at the jazz festival May 4. I'm going back to Dallas in April (to Muddy Waters again).

I have no idea how many songs I've written. I've never thought about counting, because all those old songs that I wrote, I didn't never count them, I just put then on record. I had forgotten a lot of them. Now they're coming back.

I'm still writing songs. I wrote a Christmas song: "Santy Claus, Is That You?" When I first start, I have a title. I good title. A write a rough draft from that title. Maybe write another draft, then I'll pick up the guitar and see how it sounds.

I had a stroke a few years ago. I can't execute on the guitar like I used to. I can't pick at all. See this hand? I just have to use this thumb. I used to use a thumb and two fingers. Just naked fingers. I also use a straight pick to play jazz. But I can't use it anymore. I can't hit where I want to hit. It's something else.

INTERVIEW BY JAY BRAKEFIELD, JANUARY 20, 1995

William Waddell IV, V.M.D.

Veterinarian
Born: August 9, 1908, Richmond, Virginia

William Waddell grew up in Richmond, Virginia, in a family of mixed racial ancestry. At age fourteen, he enrolled in the Manassas Industrial School in Manassas, Virginia, where he became interested in veterinary medicine. After graduation, he went to Lincoln University near Oxford, Pennsylvania. At Lincoln University he met Langston Hughes and Thurgood Marshall. In 1931, he became the first black student to attend the School of Veterinary Medicine at the University of Pennsylvania. He received his VMD degree in 1935 and was hired to teach at Tuskegee Institute in Alabama, working with George Washington Carver. During World War II, he served in the Army as a Buffalo Soldier in the same company as Joe Louis and Jackie Robinson. After World War II, Waddell worked in Alabama, West Virginia, and North Dakota before settling in Hawaii in the 1960s. He retired in 1973. Waddell is the author of two books on blacks and the veterinary medicine profession.

I was raised in a home that believed in values and discipline. My father was William H. Waddell III. And my mother's name was Sara. There were eight in my family, and I am the only living one. My father worked at one place all of his life. He went there at the age of eighteen. At Wingo, Elliott and Crump, in Richmond, Virginia, shoe company. He went there when the company was established, and he worked there until he died. My mother was a cook for the bosses of that company. One meal a day, at noon. And she did that for years. And she was an excellent cook for these people that my daddy worked for, as well as for her children as they grew up. She taught all the girls how to sew, wash, and iron. All the rich girls, she taught them how to do that. And the relationship at that time in Richmond, Virginia, among blacks and whites was very good in that everybody respected each other, and when you got sick, be you white or black, they would come and ask you, "Can I do anything for you?" And they would come and sit and bring you food or whatnot. And if people, black or white, would die, they would go to each other's funerals, although the blacks would have to sit in the back up in the attic. They would be there. They were invited. But it wasn't as bad as other parts of the South. Still, you knew you were in the South. The relationship, I think, was on a much higher schedule and level than further south.

Now, William H. Waddell I was born and reared in Wales. He never got married, but he lived with two women that were ex-slaves. However, he was very fertile in that he impregnated at least eighteen or twenty white women. All in a little town in North Carolina. These women had to leave town because in those days, when you got pregnant, and you weren't married, you left town. And I had the privilege of meeting them later on in life.

My grandfather was born and reared in Amelia County, Virginia. He was a tobacco farmer, sawmill man, and truck farmer. Amelia County is located between Richmond and Danville. My grandmother was a slave, but grandfather was not. He was born a year or so after slavery ended. His mother was a slave, who was impregnated by William H. Waddell I.

All that part of my grandparents' family looked white. And when my grandfather died, he left all of his land, over 800 acres, to his colored offspring, and they still own that land today, in Amelia County, Virginia. A lot of them have died off.

Of the children on my father's side, my father was the oldest. And there were four other brothers. And all of them worked and cooperated with each other. My father was the leader of the family, and if anything happened, they would not do anything until my father was consulted. My father had four brothers. My father's name was William, and his brothers were George, Edward, Joe, and Allen. And he had five sisters: Frances, Rosa, Louise, Helen, and Ellen. My siblings were Edward, Lorraine, Harry, Martha, Ellen, and Ophelia. Everybody's dead except myself.

At the age of thirteen and a half years, I was helped by a lady by the name of Grace Walker, who was trained in Boston, Massachusetts, at the school of public speaking, better known as Emerson. Her father was the first black lawyer to pass the state board exam in Virginia. Well, this lady thought it would be nice for them to get me away from Richmond, Virginia, because I was so much advanced over the students that went to the same school. Grace Walker did a lot to motivate me to go to the Manassas School—the Manassas Industrial School when I was nearly fourteen, located at Manassas, Virginia, also known as the Old Battlefield School because it was built on the fields where the Battle of Bull

George Washington Carver works with students in his laboratory at the Tuskegee Institute, undated photo (Corbis / Bettman)

Run was fought. That school was established by the daughter of an ex-slave in 1893. Most of the teachers at that school were from Howard University. The president of the trustees of that school was an outstanding white man from the North by the name of Oswald Garrison Villard. He was the grandson of William Lloyd Garrison, the abolitionist during the Civil War. He and John Brown were two of the greatest abolitionists of the North.

I had the opportunity of being exposed to some of the greatest black teachers in the world at that time. Such people as Alan Locke of Howard University. Carter G. Woodson at Howard University. E. E. Just, a biologist from Howard University. James Henderson from Howard University. Monroe Gregory, the captain of the Amhurst baseball team, from Minor Normal College. Sterling Brown from Howard University. Dr. Drew, the founder of the blood test. Kay Chambers, our coach. Bill Hastings, who wasn't a big lawyer then but turned out to be a big man later on in life. And W. E. B. Du Bois. As a matter of fact, Manassas ended up getting all of the people who came to Howard University as part of their program. Manassas was only thirty miles from Howard University.

At Manassas Industrial School, upon my arrival, they had training, military training, which is very good in the life of a child of my age. They believed in good old-fashioned training, which I will never forget. Now these people that were at Howard University, the outstanding people were not on the faculty. They did what we called in those days bootlegging. They would come down to Manassas once a month or twice a month because they had full-time jobs and they were professors at Howard. Strange as it might seem, in those days, they came down for $5 a day to lecture, $2 for gas and as much food as they could eat for free. It was only then that I found out that city people didn't eat as much as country people, because I've never seen people eat as much as some of those men at a meal.

I was very fortunate at Manassas that I met a lot of people who had gone out in the world and were not trained to do anything, but came back in later life to pick up trades. Those people served as big brothers to me, and, as a matter of fact, one of them recommended me to a job at the age of fourteen. I got a job as a porch boy at the Homestead Hotel, one of the most outstanding hotels in the world. And during those years, I worked hard and I met such interesting people as Marshall Fields and Anheuser Busch beer people, from St. Louis.

At the Homestead Hotel, I became the porch boy and the bellboy at the same time because I could realize more money. Everybody knew me as a porch boy and bellboy, and I got more money. This hotel was a huge placed that hired 3,000 people, employees. They raised their own food. They had the national tennis tournaments there, golf tournaments there, bridge tournaments, and bar associations all over the world would come there. So that's where I met the rich people. I waited on Roosevelt when he was the governor of New York. I waited on Warren Harding when he was the president of the United States. I waited on people like that. And I found out with the values accumulated in the high school and at home, plus the blending of the white world and my life, I learned a lot. It prepared me to be a better man because I found out, even back then, where these rich people came every morning and watched the papers for stocks and bonds and whatnot. I found out what it would mean to get into the mainstream of American life, that in order to be successful in life, you had to get into the mainstream. You just couldn't make a few dollars and say, "Well, I'm going to live myself, among my family, among my people." To be successful you got to get out there in the gravy, where the stuff is. And I learned that. And I learned how to get along with people and work with people, to communicate, to cooperate, to coordinate. And compromise. They're the things that I learned at Hot Springs and at Manassas and at home.

At the Manassas School, I watched the big boys. It was at Manassas that I became interested in veterinary medicine. A cow by the name of Minnehahah tried to calve. And she had difficulty. So the big boys came to my room and took me to the dairy barn and told me what to do. In other words, the neck of the calf was blocking the vulva so she couldn't get her head through. And her feet would knuckle under her. They couldn't get

Portrait of William Waddell in military dress (Courtesy William Waddell)

their arms in the cow to get them out, and I had a small arm. So they told me what to do. They gave me some small manila rope, they called it, and as the cow would stop laboring, I would push her back by the muscles on the chest. And I put a rope around each foot and brought the foot that would knuckle under her out toward the opening of the vulva. And after I got the legs straight to come out, then I put a rope around her neck, which was toward the right. I straightened it up to be parallel with the spinal cord above. And then they pulled her out, and we had a live, big, beautiful calf. And I decided on that day that I wanted to be a veterinarian.

During my stay at Manassas, the school didn't have a very good football team. Until I got to be a sophomore, we had hardly any team. Everybody beat us. But as time went on, and particularly during my junior and senior years, I was captain of the football teams that were never defeated in northern Virginia, nor interstate in that area. Also, captain of the baseball team. And in track I ran pin relays and we won at all the races. That's when we put Manassas on the map, those of my generation. And when I graduated, the day of graduation, Oswald Villard, the president of the trustee board, told me he had been reading about me and had written about me in his book, *Atlantic Life*. And he said to me, "Keep up the good work."

And the teacher who recommended me to go to Manassas shook my hand before a group of students, and told me, "I'm afraid that the colored papers have gone to your head. Well, if they haven't gone to your head, don't let them go to your head."

She said that because every time she picked up a paper, she read "Waddell this, Waddell that." She said, "I just got tired of reading about your name. I don't know what you're going to be. I hope you will be all right." So that was the greetings that she gave me.

My coach wrote a letter (of support) for me to enter Lincoln University of Pennsylvania. I had to write a paper about why I selected Lincoln, and I did, and I was accepted to be a student.

When I got to Lincoln University, I had no trouble. But when I got ready to take veterinary medicine, I had trouble getting in because the last black man who went there was from a rich family and looked like he was white. Well, he made it bad for everybody who followed him. But I worked at it. And I was the first black student to attend the veterinary school of

Pennsylvania since 1913, up until 1931, when I went there. Eighteen years, nearly, had passed. And they wouldn't accept another black because of the behavior pattern of this particular black who looked like a white man.

At Penn, however, before my time, John Baxter Taylor, the world's best, fastest quarter-miler, became one the first blacks to win the Olympics. And we had a man named Lushington, who was the first black to graduate, 1897, at Penn. Then John Baxter Taylor was a year later. Then, after Baxter, we had another man, and then this man who caused all the trouble. But he came from a very rich family, of Wilmington, Delaware, and his uncle married Marian Anderson, the singer. But Fisher was his name. He just caused a lot of trouble. And nobody in his class liked him. Of course, he was a smart man, too, because he'd studied veterinary medicine at Penn. But he wasn't too successful in life, I think, because he was a playboy, and he had too much money. He married white, which was all right, I have nothing against that. But they didn't find out he wasn't white until he died. They went to look for his body and couldn't find it till one man remembered that there was a bunch of Fishers that would look half white and owned the town of Wilmington, Delaware, nearly, so he recommended his wife go to that place, and that's where they found his body, at a black undertaker's place.

When I was at Penn, I had to uncover, break down, and build up everything that went wrong. Now those men before Fisher, all of them turned out to be very good men. All of them had wonderful jobs and did wonders for our race. But the little things that Fisher did stayed there all those years, and I had to break it down. However, I'm happy to say that during my tenure at Lincoln University, Pennsylvania, where I graduated, my record was terrific. All white professors except one. It was located near Oxford, Pennsylvania.

While I was there, I had the privilege of rooming for a while with Langston Hughes. And I had the privilege of knowing Thurgood Marshall.

Well, a lot of people—I've had over 2,000 people nearly, white people, write me and ask me if Langston was a sissy. Was he a homosexual? No, he was not a homosexual, as far as I knew. If he was a homosexual, he had the ability to make women yell at him, or holler, "Ow." So I figured he was no sissy. Or he could have been bisexual, but I didn't know anything about that. I would say the man was like anybody else. Just a scholar who had been exposed to an indifferent type of life and had a mama who had been harassed quite a bit in her life, and he was just different.

Langston wrote a book while he was there, *Not without Laughter*, a novel. And then he was writing all these other poems and whatnot. I don't remember them all. I remember some, but not all. But he was busy then trying to build a public relationship between the white and black worlds. He was going around speaking at white schools and going to football games and all. Trying to get recognition to Lincoln.

Thurgood Marshall was also at Lincoln at that time. I got along with Thurgood very well. But at Lincoln University, we had two classes of men. One we called "dog-ass" and one "chickenshit." But I didn't interfere. His behavior pattern didn't interfere with me. I got along with him, because I get along with people.

Thurgood was supposed to have finished Lincoln before I got through. But he came down with tuberculosis. And he stayed out two years. He was supposed to have finished the class of '29. But instead, they got him down as finishing the class of '31, my class.

Well, basically, I think, I was both dog-ass and chickenshit. But like I say, I got along with people. But now, if you weren't a regular guy, we'd call you chickenshit. And nobody wanted to be called chickenshit or dog-ass. So if you were in that class, you'd get out of it as soon as you could. But by the same token, we did a lot at Lincoln by bringing in an Alpha man, an Omega, a Kappa man, a Sigma man. Bringing in another fraternity known as Rho. Yeah, regular niggers. We were in a group that believed that you shouldn't waste all your time on your frat brothers, you ought to get out among everybody. We were the regular guys, Frank DeCosta, who has since passed. Johnson, who's passed. Baskerville, who's passed. Ted Hawkins has passed. But we formulated at Lincoln what we called Rho Nu—regular niggers.

From Lincoln, I went to veterinary school at University of Pennsylvania. I was there for four years. University of Pennsylvania was a Quaker school, white all the time. The oldest university in the world. In America. It's over 290 years old now. They gave me a medal ten years ago.

Well, they were nice to me when I was in school there. I respected myself. You got to respect yourself first. That's the first law of nature: Respect yourself. But when I got ready, when I applied to Penn, they wouldn't accept me because of what had gone on before my time. My benefactors that were rich; they got me in school. My rich white benefactors got me to the University of Pennsylvania.

I came out in '35. I graduated from Lincoln in '31. I graduated from the University of Pennsylvania June the 19th, 1935. That is when I became a second lieutenant, too. I became second lieutenant of the Officers' Reserve Corps of the University of Pennsylvania. They called it ORC then. Officers' Reserve Corps, but I met a man who was a captain in the U. S. Army. And he was telling me about it when he'd come to visit and lecture at Penn. He was telling me about the Ninth and Tenth Cavalries. So on the day of graduation from the University of Pennsylvania, I went down and

Booker T. Washington, ca. 1915 (Texas African American Photography Archive)

volunteered for duties with the Ninth and Tenth about an hour after graduation.

Well, that night, when I went to see Mrs. Bond—she was my chief benefactor, a rich Quaker lady. She said, "Well, what are you going to do now?"

I said, "Well, I've made arrangements to go into the Army. The Ninth and Tenth."

She said, "Well, I think it would be wise for you to break that because we made arrangements for you to go to Tuskegee Institute. We knew Mr. Washington, Booker T. Washington. And we knew him when he used to come to our churches and beg for money, and we gave him money and whatnot. And we feel like that with your training, and what we have done for you, you should go to Tuskegee Institute."

So, I got in touch with the people in the Army and told them that I'd be in touch, but I had to go to Tuskegee. Which I did. I worked there; I went straight to Tuskegee. And there I taught veterinary sciences. I was also working with Dr. Carver with peanut oil used to remove blemishes as well as to correct wrinkles in your face. I worked with him for two-and-a-half years, until he died. And then I drew up plans for the school of veterinary medicine.

At Tuskegee, I also met P. H. Polk. I got to know him well. He was the man who made pictures. He was a great photographer.

At Tuskegee, they made me the director of the veterinary division. And the veterinary division had about 400 or 500 dairy cows. They had sheep of all breeds, hogs of all breeds, beef cattle of all breeds. So I was in charge of all that. Not only did I do that, but I also had a hospital there, which was not to my liking. That's when I first had my trouble at Tuskegee, with the people. Not with the people, but the president. Because in those days all these black schools wanted me. Tennessee wanted me. A&T wanted me. Albany wanted me. And even in Oklahoma, at Langston University wanted me. But you know why they wanted me? The president of the schools would build a hospital or a place up for you to work with at the school's expense or the state's expense and then you gave them one-half the money you took in. That's the reason I didn't work at Tennessee State. They wanted me there. They gave me more money. They offered at least $300 more than I was getting at Tuskegee. And any outside practice I did, I had to share with the president. That was Hale, when he was there.

Edward Evans was at Prairie View at that time. He was in charge, and he was respected. Ed Evans was an educated man, a damn good veterinarian. But Ed Evans was a man that had forty-eight teeth. I mean sixty-four teeth, instead of thirty-two. He talked from both sides of his mouth. And we didn't get along too well.

But Ed Evans got in the program at Tuskegee when I was overseas, fighting for the country. They called him in. When I went back from over there, then I worked with him. Patterson called him in, saying that he was the best man. Right at that time, I was overseas. I had worked at Tuskegee from '35 up until I went overseas.

I had joined the Fifth Brigade, though my time in the Army was delayed by work at Tuskegee. The Fifth Brigade was located at that time at Brackettville, Texas. But as reserves officer, I had been also to this place Fort Riley. Out at Junction City, Kansas. I had been out there as a reserve officer. I went to Leavenworth. You see, when I took short courses, the Army prepared me to go all places. They were preparing me to be the first black brigadier general.

Being a Buffalo Soldier was terrific. Well, a man has not been a soldier nor any part of the U. S. Army in any division or any department unless he's been a Buffalo Soldier. Now I knew Bill Davis Sr., very well, played bridge with him and drank scotch with him, when he was at Tuskegee. In 1902, he served with the Buffalo Soldiers over in the Philippines. I got to know him; not only him, but some of the men that served under him. And, as a matter of fact, Bill Davis's son happens to be the godfather of my daughter.

My daughter's a doctor, too. But she is in political science and ethnic studies. Her name is Kathryn Takara. She spent four years abroad, four summers, each summer at a different place. She's had a Fulbright also for a year.

Well, to be a Buffalo Soldier it means, number one, that you had to discipline the men. It means getting out and riding horses every day. It meant having sham battles every day. It meant twenty-four hours a day of work, which they don't do now, because you had your horses to take care of as well as yourself. And we didn't have a lot of crap like you're having now 'cause we didn't have women. We had nurses, but they weren't at station hospitals. But we didn't have any trouble like you have now. You soldiered and you worked. And you had discipline. And you had values. You have culture with it, too.

My life at Brackettville was a hell of a life because we were up at 5:30 every morning, and we soldiered up until six in the evening. And you had to take care of your horses and you had to take care of your men as well as yourself. And you had to keep records of their families, to make certain their families were happy.

In those days, the cavalry, the morale of the cavalry depended upon money, food, and women. They encouraged that. Money, food, and women. And every company had its own cooking outfit, and every outfit had damn good cooks. You ate well. You soldiered well. And you never had any time off. Even on Sundays, when you were supposed to be off, you had to take your troops to Villa Cuna. That's off from Hondo, Texas. Right across the border. We'd take our men down there every Sunday for sex. They'd go down, and they'd spend a day, all Sunday. We'd get the money changed up for them, $2 bills, and they'd go over and have sex all day. You'd take them at eleven o'clock in the morning, and they'd leave at eleven o'clock at night. And still you have to be ready for 5:30 to get up those damn big-eyed horses the next day. That's what Brackettville was like. Armadillos. Rattlesnakes. Yellow snakes. Coyotes. Mosquitoes.

There were some black Seminoles around Brackettville. Some would serve as scouts. As a matter of fact, I saw one here two years ago, lectured at the universities. He lives down there now at Hondo, I think. His family served as scouts there. And I knew where the family lived and I knew where the graveyards were. But now it's a dude camp down there.

The black Seminoles were very close together. Much closer together than black people. Because black people as a rule, they're close together for a while, but some of them become educated, they forget all about where they came from. But the life at Brackettville, basically, was a rough, tough life: riding, bivouacking, going out, coming back, being eaten up with ticks all on your damn body. The first time I went out, I came back that night, I had about forty ticks on me. I was out for three days. And then I learned how to deal with them. You take chloroform and ether and put on them. And get them drunk and then pull them out. If you don't pull them out right away, you could get infected, highly infected, with so many of them on you. But then I learned how to take care of those. I learned how to fix my clothes and fix myself up that they wouldn't bother me, nor the men. Well, I was new the first time that happened. And I wasn't properly prepared for the bivouac I went on.

Life at Fort Clark, Texas, was a rough life. We'd eat well, we played hard. And Joe Louis was in our outfit. Yeah. So was Jackie Robinson. Jackie Robinson was a gentleman then and a gentleman all the way through life. He'd worked and gone to school. Whites, knew how to get along with them. And he'd beat the hell out of them at tennis. You talk about a man playing with a table tennis racket. I saw him sometime win as much as $500 from those young white boys.

And Joe Louis was a gentleman, too. Very nice, very refined. I even knew Joe before he went in the Army. I met him at a fight in New York. And I went round to his house, and I found out what he likes. He likes quiet. I went to a party they gave for him, and the house was just packed up with celebrities, both white and black. And you know where he was? Back on the couch in the den, eating an apple and looking at the funny papers.

The first woman Joe married wasn't for him. I met her, too, at the port of embarkation, or at San Antonio one night, coming back. I saw her there with another guy, and I knew. I had met her at her house. Ruth Brown was Joe Louis's second wife. She was a nice woman. She was a lawyer, educated. And she kept him straight.

When I started as a Buffalo Soldier, I was taking short courses. I was a Buffalo Soldier from the time that I started, after graduation from Penn because I was taking short courses here and there. Everything had to do with horses and warfare. I had to go to the Carlyle Barracks to learn how to put my ass on a horse—and about the use of gas in warfare and what to do about burns. And then at Fort Leavenworth I learned about the business of being an officer.

Well, Kansas was just a prejudiced damn town, just like up at Carlyle Barracks where I went. Carlyle Barracks was one of the worst damn places in the world. We couldn't even go to the officers' club in town. And those who went down there nearly got into fights and didn't go back anymore. And, of course, the people in Junction City, they were a little better because they depended upon that area for money, you see. However, even though they depended upon money from areas, they still had segregation. And it was that way at Fort Benning, Georgia. I was there.

I played baseball over there at Fort Benning with the faculty baseball team at Tuskegee. And I played baseball against Satchel Paige and all those guys, Jackie Robinson and Roy Campanella. I was a captain, manager of the faculty baseball team at Tuskegee.

When I was a Buffalo Soldier, we ended up going overseas, but we patrolled the borders of Mexico, too, to keep the Mexicans out. We kept them out. We chased them with horses, on horseback, and they had better damn horses. And they ran. And they wouldn't come back anymore when you chased them forty yards on a damn horseback. We were not trying to hurt them but just chase them enough to keep them off you until they got across the border.

Once when we patrolled the borders of Mexico, we went out looking for Pancho Villa's son or cousin, or relative, who was causing a lot of trouble on the border. He had been an officer in the Mexican army, but he deserted and decided to go out for himself and get rich. All I knew, he belonged to the Pancho Villa family. And Pancho Villa was the one that General Black Jack Pershing chased before my time.

I had met Black Jack Pershing when I was a porch boy at the Homestead Hotel. He was a fine man. The thing I didn't understand about him, I was porch boy when I first met him, he came over and looked at me and started smiling and asking me questions. I answered him and he rubbed his hand through my hair. Now my hair wasn't that good. Wasn't nappy, either, but it wasn't good hair, wasn't straight, you know. And he just said, "You're a nice boy." And I gave him his paper and thanked him. He gave me a dollar.

Now, when I was a Buffalo Soldier, we headed overseas. En route, however, we stopped at Patrick Henry, Virginia. We were supposed to be there for two weeks. And we got in a riot there. Well, our boys in my outfit, Company B, went up to the PX, just getting off the train. When we left the train, we went by the way of Waco and then all the way by Mobile until we came to Richmond. Then from Richmond to Patrick Henry down near Newport News. Well, when we got there, the boys decided they would go over to the PX and get something cold to drink and whatnot. And the paratroopers that were white, that we went on maneuvers with, and beat their butts down in Louisiana that same year, they decided to take the boots off our boys. They took the boots off a sergeant. And he walked back to his company and got his company and went up there and broke their damn place up. You didn't hear anything about that in the paper. But they broke it up. And we refused to go into the dining room to eat because they wanted to separate us up there, and we didn't go in. We refused to eat. And then they sent for a young man whose father was outstanding at Brown University by the name of Fritz Pollard that made All-American at Brown. Supposed to have been the first black All-American, followed by Paul Robeson later. He must have gotten through in 1914, round that neighborhood, 1913 or '14, in that neighborhood, made All-American at Brown. Fritz Pollard. So his son, who had graduated from North Dakota University, great track man and football player, too, was the liaison man for that area for blacks. So he came over and tried to get the boys—a division, now mind you, a division. the Ninth and Tenth Cavalry was a division. All of them were black. But we ate with our officers. And what they wanted to do was to separate us from the officers. So we wouldn't go in to eat.

Well, they finally made up their mind, after they had that riot there, nearly, and beat up the paratroopers, they let us in to eat. And we could eat the way we came there. That happened at Patrick Henry.

From Patrick Henry we went to Casablanca in Morocco. And we were there for two days, and then they moved us out the third day, because we had trouble there. We went down to the Casablanca club, the one that they made the movie *Casablanca*. We went down there, the officers did. And some white officers tried to stop the white officers in our outfit. We were with them. So we broke up that place. And they got us away the next day.

But we did get to see the prince of Morocco, who had a house where he had all of his wives. The house would hold 300 women. And what they would do, they'd have a woman, and they'd retire her after a certain length of time she spent being a wife. And then the prince would get another wife. And I got to see that place. They had these Senegalese soldiers on each floor, so nobody could get in there unless you were invited. We were invited in. And we stopped on our way out; we had trouble over by the University of Morocco. And we stopped there and one of the horses got sick, Arabian horses. And they came out to see whether or not they had a veterinarian. Well, we had met one or two people in Morocco during that time, and they, Moroccans remembered the blacks that they met because one or two of them were in the group that were thrown out, and he wanted to know whether or not they had any black veterinarians in the place. And we told them we had veterinarians, so they started looking. We were traveling forty by eight. That's the car to take eight horses or forty men.

Well, they finally found me. The general in the outfit recommended me. They had a horse, very beautiful horse, that they were having trouble with, and they wanted me to come over, and they were a quarter of a mile from where the railroad train was, and I went over in their jeep, in an American jeep that they had. And there were all these pretty women. I had never seen so many pretty women at one time as I did at that university. I mean, they were pretty women, Arabians. And crossed between all nationalities, but they were beautiful women. I went there, and this horse was there. And I got to go toward the horse, and the man told me he was wild and whatnot.

So, I reached in my pocket and got me out some sugar lumps that I generally carry around for those wild horses and just put that out. He ate that, and I started away, and I knew what was going to happen: He started following me. And when I stopped, he stopped and was reaching at me for more sugar, and I gave him and offered the sugar. And then I told the owner, or the manager, to hold the horse, let me look at him. So then, I gave him some grain and a pan for him to take over, and he did. The horse ate that because the grain was ground, and I gave him some corn to take to the horse, hard corn. And the horse ate some of that, and I saw he was having difficulty chewing. So then, I told them to bring me a bucket of water and some grease. And they did. And I soaped my hand, arm, down. And I went over to the horse. First I gave him sugar, and he ate that. Then I put my hand in his mouth, and the people started screaming. And I put my hand down because it was exciting the horse. And I looked, and they said, "Oh," in relief: They thought the horse was going to bite my arm off. But they didn't know that I put my hand on the side of the horse's mouth and the teeth were on the inside of my hand and my outside, the skin was on the mucous membrane of the horse, the horse couldn't bite me. And I found out what was wrong with the horse; its tooth was about a half an inch or more too long. And he couldn't chew. So then we opened up the bag I had there, and I cut that tooth off, and then I called that veterinarian over, who was from an Arabian university, or Morocco or someplace, and had him grind the teeth down, trim them, and make them even. And that horse was beginning to eat when I left and he came over and licked me. I gave him more sugar, and we left, because the train was pulling out. That was four or five hours. All this was traveling over mountains, going toward Oran, North Africa, where they were fighting. And we left. But that was the talk of the town. Nobody had ever seen a man put his hand in a horse's mouth. But it wasn't really in his mouth, too, but on the sides of the mouth. The teeth were facing the palm of my hand, and my skin was against the mucous membrane. He couldn't bite me then even if he wanted to. The only way he could hurt me was to rear up. And he didn't do that because I'd been giving him sugar, and he wanted the sugar. Horse had more sense than some people. So we left from there and went on to Oran, Algeria, and we started to fighting in North Africa.

Well, anywhere they're fighting and are being killed It's a bitch, man. It's terrible. But you've never thought about people dying. But I saw hard men who fought. Of course, in Oran, we were just running out the Germans and Italians that were there and got stranded and couldn't get out. So when we cleaned up fighting in Oran, North Africa, and Algiers and that neighborhood, then they put us on a ship and we went to Livorno, Italy.

In Livorno, we had to fight and drive the people from out of the hills there and make it possible for the citizens up in the hills that had gone up there to live to come back to their homes. We did that. And when we got people living in Livorno, then we went on over to Rome and in that neighborhood. And Salerno and Pisa. Then on up to France. And that's when we got there, they decided to break us up. Actually, we broke up the cavalry in North Africa, because in the cavalry you can fight on foot as well as on horseback. We broke that up because they needed the men so badly. And our men, we lost a lot of men in North Africa and in the Oran area. Then we went to Italy, and when we got there, I had two or three jobs. I was on the reconnaissance outfit to look and see how close the enemies were to us. The enemies, because they had two or three of them fighting us. I did that on a horse. And then I was with the mule pack outfit. And then I was with the battalion that unloads ships coming in and inspecting ships. I had three or four jobs because I was qualified. When you're qualified, they take advantage of you. And they took advantage of me when they had a lot of veterinarians. But they weren't trained. I have to say that. So finally, after we brought the Japanese from the 442nd in, to land near us to train for the battle, and then we brought in the 92nd that fought there. And we served as mule pack units for them.

I finally told the colonel one day—he was congratulating me for the fine job I was doing. So, I said in a very nice way, I said, "Colonel," I said, "I realize that," and I said, "the men up there"—incidentally, the outfit was white, the mule pack, mostly—and I was with that. So I can truthfully say that I integrated that to a large extent. But I told him, I said, "Now you say these men are not trained, and you call on me because I'm trained, because I had the experience, both at Tuskegee and at Penn. And most of your men that you've got in the cavalry now are dog and cat men or meat inspectors." I say, "You're right, they are. But why don't you let them go up with me up to the front and let me train one up there?"

Hell, I wanted to take some of that pressure off me, and he agreed to it. And, of course, those guys didn't like it. They were white, practically all of them. They didn't like going up there where they were shooting. But I showed them how to protect themselves and how to get up there and get back. That's what I did. But it was rough in Italy, because those Germans were smart as hell, excellent fighters. And they were much smarter than the Italians. The only thing you had to get accustomed to was the German 88. That was a type of cannon that they shot at you. But we fought up there, and we lost a lot of men.

Thanksgiving morning of '43, I never will forget. Terrible morning. They were dying around you like flies, man. And that was because—people wonder why that happened. That was because that French outfit down there—I've been to the place down there, in Central America. Martinique. Well, I was over there before and after the war. But their boys, a company, gave way and didn't know what to do, and ran. Now when you run (away from) the damn battle, you leave yourself exposed. And that's what happened. And finally, that whole outfit ended up, the 92nd, moving like hell to get out of the fire. They were given command to do that and regroup and come back. Then they found out what happened. That these guys couldn't hold where they were. Instead of notifying people to get air protection, they ran. Got the hell away from that fire.

Well, I got out of the Army after the war ended, but I stayed active until '54. I came home by request, special request, from North Africa, to start and be in charge of the veterinary school at Tuskegee, because Evans didn't know what he was doing. He didn't know the people there. And starting a school like that, you've got to have the original back there, and let them know what to do.

I went home when the war was over in Italy, that was the latter part of '45. I went home because Brigadier General Raymond Kelso, a graduate of the University of Pennsylvania, wanted me to come to Washington to be his successor. He was planning on retiring. And he had recommended me. However, Tuskegee had put in a request for me to come and work. They were in distress because the board of education in the South had given money to open up the veterinary school, and they wanted to start it. So I went in October of '45. I reported to Tuskegee and started work right away because I had to build up the outside of the clinic so they could have material to work with.

As I explained, I had my problems with Tuskegee, but I went back. I had originally gone to Tuskegee on a contract. But after the president of the school was in trouble financially with a lot of stuff, he brought up his brother-in-law to help him. His brother-in-law was a very dear friend of mine. His name was Bob Moten, and he told the president how much money I was making and that I had money in all the banks around there, because I was the veterinarian in four counties—all white. In that area, Negroes didn't do anything, veterinary-wise, so if they had anything, they let it die. By the time you get there, hell, they should have called an undertaker. But it was white people, rich white people, I did work for. And some of them I'm still very friendly with throughout the South. They were good, the better type of white person. Let's put it that way. But at Tuskegee, the president called me one day. Of course, I had a house I built from scratch, not myself, but I had the white people and black people to do it.

An eight-room house on eighty acres of land with big pecans all the way around it. And the president had a place about a quarter of a mile from my house where he had tried selling souvenirs from the school, but he failed. He tried the restaurant business and failed; he tried a nightclub and he failed. So then his brother-in-law wanted me to go into a veterinary business with him, and give him half of the money. Well, I objected to that very strongly; I didn't like the idea of working, doing all that damn work, and giving half of the money to somebody else not doing anything. But what happened was I showed him that I didn't like the deal and that I wanted to talk it over with my wife. My wife taught French there. So he told me he'd made up his mind. I was making $1,800 a month, and he agreed to take that up to $2,500. I told him I would do it, but I didn't like doing it. And he just smiled and said, "Well, do you have a choice?" I said, "Not right now." Well, in the meantime, being a reserve officer, when they called me, I talked to some of my white friends that were in charge, and they wanted me. They said, "You don't have to go, Doc. We're going to save you. You're going to stay here. We don't have a veterinarian." So I talked with them and told them I had to go. But I was also running the school's veterinary hospital, mind you, a clinic, for all of their animals. I was running my hospital on the side of the road. And Patterson had his building fixed up so that he could work with me, called it Tuskegee Animal Hospital, the first in the South.

And then I had a gas station where some Negroes worked and were stealing all the damn money. I thought I was going to have to kill them, but I got rid of them. Then I decided I had to slack down because I was doing the work in four counties. I didn't need the money then. My house was paid for, practically. My wife was working, and besides, she was pregnant.

After the war Tuskegee was different. They needed me and I went back and stayed at Tuskegee for four more years. Then I went on leave of absence from Tuskegee. I left there because I wasn't getting along too well with what was going on. In other words, Dr. Cooper, whom I brought there from Colorado as a teacher, was a gentleman and a wonderful man. He had practice and experience. But we had five men from Kansas City. None of them had one day's practice. Never saw anything but meat inspection. They came there. And they were getting the five men who had been practitioners down in the country and weren't cooperating, and it was in a mess that I didn't want to be in. So I told them that I hereby tender my resignation as soon as is possible, with one year's notice. I would work for one year. So after talking with Dr. Patterson and everybody, I started working for that year in back of my house, I built an animal hospital, which I sold later on as an apartment, built out of brick blocks.

When I finally left Tuskegee, the government wanted to send me to India to be in charge of a program. But I didn't. Evans did. Evans recommended me. I was under him then at Tuskegee. I was giving him so much hell that he recommended to the government that I was the logical man to go there or to Liberia. I had a chance to go to Liberia, India, and another place. But I refused to go because they called me also to go back to the Korean War. I said, "No. Life's not going to be that way." So the government told me they would save me. Kelso got me into government.

I went to work as a specialist. I decided to go into meat inspection instead of going to India or Liberia. I went to Morgantown, and they offered me protection to work in meat inspection. I was in charge of the shipment. I examined the meat that was being shipped to Korea. I grabbed that opportunity because I didn't want any more of that fighting and fire. Then I decided that I would open up a place. I decided I would open up a little place in Philippi, West Virginia, to have a little practice on the side, and they gave me the permission to do so. And then the practice got so big there, I decided I had to get away from that place or work myself to death. I went to Morgantown and built a hospital. It was one of the most beautiful places; I took care of a hundred animals. I stayed in West Virginia for ten or eleven years.

I've had a successful life. I became one of the first black Kiwanis in the world. I was president of the Junior Chamber of Commerce. I've been involved in many different service organizations. I've got 150 citations or awards on the wall here.

I came to Hawaii in 1963. My daughter was here, and I'd come here for vacation every year. Before Hawaii I was in Fargo, North Dakota. The U. S. government had sent me to do epidemiology work in the north-central states. It was quite a big job. I started there in 1963. And in 1973, I retired in Hawaii. But before I retired, I wrote two books. The first book was called *The Black Man in Veterinary Medicine*.

Before then, I was in Nebraska and West Virginia. I was in Morgantown, West Virginia, nearly ten or eleven years. And then the government borrowed me 'cause I opened my big mouth in Washington, D.C., where I was drinking some purple passion with the big boys up there. Right now as I talk to you, I have five pictures from Clinton himself here. But you'll see this in this resume I'll send you.

My wife, Lottie Young Waddell, died five years ago. She was in charge of French at North Dakota State, and she taught at Concordia. And she taught at Sorbonne, and she taught at all the black schools. And when I went to the north-central states, she followed me up there and taught at Concordia and Morehead and North Dakota State University in the French Department.

A man from Mississippi once asked me what keeps me going. He fellowshipped with me every day, and he wanted to know. I told him, "Hell, man, you're looking at an old man. You got to go back and start to eating raw, with vinegar, salt and pepper, pignuts. Raw pecans. Stuff like that." I was just kidding him. I just eat well. I drink what I want and eat what I want to. And I eat well. I do everything well.

INTERVIEW BY ALAN GOVENAR, MARCH 27, 1998

A. J. Walker

Cowboy and rodeo organizer
Born: March 7, 1930, Raywood, Texas

A. J. Walker was raised in southeast Texas, the son of a sharecropper farmer. He began riding horses at age four, and by twelve he was competing in local ranch rodeos. In the late 1940s, Walker left home to join the professional rodeo circuit and traveled around the country, struggling to overcome the all-too-prevalent racism that impeded his advancement as a cowboy. In the 1960s, Walker built his own rodeo arena on the forty-acre ranch he helped his father buy. Each year, from March to October, Walker organizes and promotes his own rodeos in which he works to provide opportunities and role models for young black cowboys. Walker is a member of the Anahuac Salt Grass Cowboys Association, a loosely knit association of black ranchers in southeast Texas.

I operate the Circle 6 Ranch Rodeo Arena. I was born and raised right here, lived here all my life, ride horses and bulls. My father's name was Thomas Walker, and my mother's name was Mary Walker. They was from Louisiana, Opelousas, and they moved out here in 1930, the same year I was born, and we've been here ever since.

Things got bad in Louisiana. I guess it was because of the flood. That was during the Depression. They come straight to the Raywood area.

My daddy worked as a three-fourths farmer. He was a sharecropper. At first he was a one-half. I imagine when we got over here we had to buy some horses and mules, but after we got going he became one-third and then a one-quarter farmer. He paid the boss man less. The boss man was Hubert Taylor.

We went to school over here at Raywood, didn't get much schooling, but the few years I did, we enjoyed it. When I was just starting school, we had a little school over there they called a Raywood school—right there—a little old school. We had to walk to school, and they built the other big school where we had to ride the bus, and it made it a whole lot better. But we walked many days in the cold and rain and hot weather and everything. It was tough, but we liked it and all.

My dad got forty acres of land right here in 1941, and I had to drop out of school to help pay for this land. I got up to the tenth grade at Woodson High School and I had to drop out. I made the ninth grade. There was a lot of work, build a lot of fences and everything. Then they made stock laws and you had to fence your cattle off. They drove their cattle miles and miles. They'd have to move them to feed them, and then they'd have to move to the train station to sort them out and sell what they want to sell.

I remember my grandfather; his name was Tom Walker, and my daddy was named after him. He was from Louisiana. I didn't know too much about him. He died about four or five years after he moved to Texas. I used to know what year it was in. He lived till about '47 or '49, the best I can remember. My grandfather wasn't involved in the ranch, my father was. He raised cattle, too, my father did, and we raised cattle and just worked around him, you know, built fast, but farm, too. We used to farm right here, cotton and corn, raise hogs and cattle and horses. We loved to keep our horses and mules around the place. We raised the mules and worked on the ranch. We had thirty to forty head of cattle. They feed on our land most of the year, but in the winter we'd make hay and feed them that way. My daddy used to say he'd cowboy until the cowboys come, meaning he didn't go to be no cowboy, but he'd ride till the cowboys got there. All of the cowboys in this part of Texas were black. The only whites out there was the bossman. Them white boys would get on them horses after you got them broke. The boss man or the boss man's son would take them.

They'd drive the rich man's cattle across the Intracoastal canal, put them up on the hill somewhere in that salt grass. Spring come, we'd have to move them back. They stay all winter in that salt grass. We'd have to swim them across that Intercoastal canal in Anahuac. They'd take a bulldozer and back the truck in there and unload before we drive them. We had a lead steer, and that lead steer would take them across. That would be thirty or forty miles. When we drive them, they would take a week, but then we put them in a truck and haul them. We do the branding in the spring and then again in the fall.

I started riding horses when I was four or five. I was riding horses before I ever went to school. We got quarter horses, just regular quarter horses. Some of them are mixed with a little mustang. We had some mustang mules; most of our horses were pretty good quarter horses, wasn't the best, but certainly could turn a cow back home.

There were just little ranch rodeos back in them times. The range was loose at that time. We didn't have no fences. They would turn all their horses and cows loose on the highway and in the pastures. They'd eat out

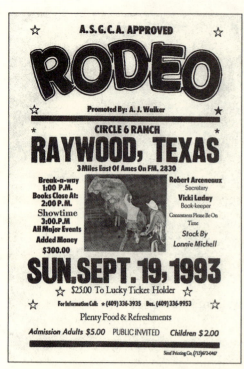

Poster for a 1993 rodeo at the Circle 6 Ranch, Raywood, Texas, promoted by A. J. Walker. (Texas African American Archive)

there, and a bunch of them would get out there and round them up in the open prairie. Some of them would hold the horses and bulls and cattle, and others would get off and ride them, rope and everything, just like in the rodeo. I was just old enough to remember them doing it on Saturday evenings about round up time. Just before it get cold, they round up them cattle. They have a ranch rodeo, and then they take them off to auction, or whatever you wanted to do. They'd do steer dogging and roping. They'd rope the head and heel. They didn't do bull riding like they do now. Mostly, they use them big yearlings. I never did compete in them; I was too young.

We raised mules, working mules. And I started riding them when I was about seven. I'd ride the mule while my daddy was working them. I'd go to sleep sitting up on those mules, and he'd hit one of them and wake me up, you know. As far as I can remember, I was near 'bout big enough to go to school. We had our general mules and stuff, and I just started riding them. Then I started riding calves. Not long after that, I started rodeoing and riding them heifers and a few of them bull calves and roping them calves. And that's something we like to do; me and all my brothers, we done the same thing.

By the time I was twelve, I was breaking horses. After I got started breaking them horses, my younger brother got into it, they'd take them and get all the jump on them. I broke horses back, and sometimes you get paid, and sometimes you wouldn't. I broke them and trained them. I've had about seven or eight horses tied up here at one time. Just tie them up—ride them in the evening, ride them in the morning before I go to work and ride them in the evening—just work them.

I got to where I felt I was good enough to compete on the rodeo circuit. My daddy didn't care much for rodeo, but I'd just take off and he didn't know. I just put my bull rope and rigging in a satchel and go off down the road. He didn't know where I was going. I got on my first bull in 1946 at the county fair in Anahuac. That was a real rodeo. Bull riding and bareback riding. I rode my horse and got bucked off the bull, but I had been riding yearlings around the house, little half-grown bulls and stuff.

I never went into the service during World War II. I already was married and had a bunch of kids. During those years, I worked on a rice farm, then later on I went to construction work during the fifties, after we quit farming. I got married the first time three days before my seventeenth birthday, seventh of March, 1937. All total, I've had two, three wives, and I've had twelve kids.

In 1947, we built a bunch of them ranch pens. I went to a lot of little rodeos, something to have fun with. We made a little money. There wasn't a lot of money to be made. You put up $5 and you'd make $15 or $20. They'd have five or six cowboys competing.

I started in professional rodeo in 1952. They didn't like the blacks and the whites to be together. We'd have to get on the bulls behind the chutes. They wanted us to stay in the back until after the rodeo. We'd ride after the rodeo. We couldn't go in the same places the white guys go in. We'd ride after the show. It would be the same prize money, but you couldn't ride at the same time as them white cowboys. We could ride after all the folks had left and after all the white cowboys were gone. You'd be competing for the same money as the white cowboys. They just wanted our entry fees.

In 1952, it cost you a $100 a rodeo and you could win $700 or $800. There was a lot of cowboys. In 1952, I went up to Madison Square Garden. I was working for a boss man, Everett Colbert out of Dublin, Texas. He was a white rancher and rodeo producer. We rode the train with the bulls up to Madison Square Garden. The bulls were on each end and we were in the middle of the boxcar. He was providing the livestock, he brought the bulls, the calves, the saddle horses, and stuff. We left Dublin and went to Fort Madison, Iowa, first. Then we left Fort Madison, Iowa, and went to New York. I kind of forgot how long that took, but it took us a week to come back. I went on the train and came back on a truck. We had three trucks, loaded with steers.

When we got to New York, we had to go to Long Island, to the stockyards, to unload all the stock there. We had to get them company, union trucks to take the bulls. We led all the horses. Each man had nine horses to lead from Long Island to Madison Square Garden, to go right downtown, all the horses. We led them horses on the street, and we had people watching from the time we left to the time we got there. We had 500 head of bucking horses and 500 head of saddle horses. I don't know if it was the first time they had a rodeo in Madison Square Garden. I never did find out.

We won money in the wild horse race. We won a saddle. There were three of us in it, and we flipped a coin for it, and the white cowboy out of Stephenville won the saddle, sure did. We were up in New York for thirty days. We stayed down in the basement with them bulls. New York City was nice, really nice. That's the only time I ever been there. In Madison Square Garden, we got to compete, but we had to ride after the show.

A. J. Walker,
photograph by Alan
Govenar, Raywood,
Texas, 1994.
(Documentary Arts)

When we got back to Texas, we just all come back home. I went out on the TRCA, Texas Rodeo Cowboy Association circuit. We were all black cowboys. We go around Texas.... We went to Louisiana, Oklahoma, Kansas, different places. We'd work during the week, and then we'd go out rodeoin' on weekends. They were all black rodeos. They were ranch rodeos, I don't remember all of them. They round up all the stock and you ride them out on the pastures. We went to Boley, all the black towns. We went to a Frontier Days rodeo in Kansas.

White cowboys didn't really like having the black cowboys around. They look at you crazy. They do anything they could to you. We stayed out of their way. We had a bunch of black cowboys around there, but we didn't want to have no trouble.

Rodeo didn't integrate until the 1960s. We joined the PRCA one year, in 1964. It was good, it was nice, but after that, I won a bareback riding buckle in Houston at the Diamond L Ranch. We could buy a permit and ride in that show.

I wanted to rodeo, and I wanted to build me some kind of old pen right here. Win a little money and have a lot of fun, train the young cowboys. All of them boys wanted to ride, try to ride. There wasn't a whole lot of money to be made, but it was lots of fun.

The Anahuac Salt Grass Cowboys Association started up just before the TRCA went out, twenty-five or thirty years ago. There weren't too many black landowners around here. There were the rich blacks, the Jacksons, and the Whites—a few more. Jacksons were half white, half black. The Whites were, too—half black, half white. The Whites and Jacksons put on the rodeo in forties in the park in Anahuac. I used to go down and watch them.

I imagine there are 500 to 600 members in the Anahuac Salt Grass Cowboys Association today. Now we have six or eight rodeos now. One in Lake Charles, two in Cheek, two in Anahuac, Easter Rodeo. Bobby Jason in Double Bayou. Elton Laday and his son built their own rodeo arena in Cheek. All of them rodeos are on ranches. They haven't got much land, but they call it a ranch.

I've been doing this now a long time. It's been tough, but I've liked every bit of it.

INTERVIEW BY ALAN GOVENAR, MARCH 4, 1993 AND FEBRUARY 23, 1998

Alice Mae Williams

Minister's wife; homemaker and mother
Born: December 2, 1921, Fagan Ranch, Texas

Alice Mae Barefield Williams grew up in Refugio County, Texas. She married Reverend Mack Williams (see oral history on page 494) when she was fifteen years old. Together, the Williamses lived in a two-room frame house on the Martin O'Connor Ranch. Alice Mae worked at home, taking care of her children and doing domestic chores, including cooking, ironing, washing, and gardening. In the evening she made "britches" quilts, sewn with patches from old pairs of work pants, and crafted pillows and comforters, picking the feathers by hand from the tame geese on the ranch.

I was born and raised on Pete Fagan's ranch. My grandfather was John Summers and he used to talk about how they used to drive cattle from here to Kansas City. But they didn't tell us too much about his life. And my other grandfather on my daddy's side, I didn't know him. Neither one. His name was George Barefield, and my grandmother was named Emma Barefield. And then my grandmother on John Summers's side, her name was Lizzie Harvey Summers. And she was from around Mission Valley and Wharton and around up in thataway.

My mother used to make quilts out of (Betty) Crocker sacks and old pants, and she would tack them. She didn't quilt them, she tacked them. She pieced a quilt and then she make the top part out of britches and then cover that. And she made some quilts with cotton. But most of the quilts she made them out of Crocker sacks. And she made one out of Crocker sack, and when she passed…I'm sure sorry that I gave it to my grand-daughter. I couldn't even cover up with it, it was so heavy. Very heavy.

We used to cut wood, pick chips, and get a whoopin' every evening for fighting. 'Cause we'd fight every evening on the woodpile.

We would take care of the children and cook and iron and wash. That's the way we did it on the ranch. We made pillows out of those, you know, those big tame geese, we made pillows out of that. I think I still have those pillows somewhere. We'd pick 'em. Pick near all the feathers out of them and make pillows out of them like that. They'd pick those geese while they was alive. You'd pick it off the breast, and what part, but you didn't pick them under the wing.

This Christmas we've been married sixty years (1996). I married Reverend Mack and we lived on the O'Connor Ranch. I was fifteen years old when I married, and he was twenty-two. I didn't want no preacher at first, but it's okay. It's fine. I don't know why. I just didn't want no preacher. And I had said, if I hadn't had my children, I still would have no preacher. 'Cause I didn't want no preacher.

INTERVIEW BY ALAN GOVENAR, DECEMBER 9, 1992

Arbie Williams

Quilter
Born: August 12, 1916, Clayton, Texas

Arbie Williams learned to quilt from her mother and grandmother in a small rural community near Carthage, Texas. Like many Texans of her generation, she moved to the San Francisco Bay Area in the 1940s. She worked a variety of jobs, including domestic, cook, and cocktail waitress. In Oakland she teamed up with Gussie Wells to make distinctive strip and "britches" quilts using abstract patterns of vivid colors and remnant fabrics. Williams and Wells received a National Heritage Fellowship award from the National Endowment for the Arts in 1991.

I was born and raised in East Texas, near Carthage, Henderson, in Begville. My father came to West Texas when I was about eight. I lived out there until I was twelve. Then he went back to East Texas. So when I was seven-teen, I got married. When I was twenty-two, I lost that husband. Then I met another husband, and I married him. And I come to California on my honey-moon, and I been here ever since. I was twenty-seven or twenty-eight.

I worked hard, but I loved to work. And my daddy was a farmer, so you didn't have no trouble. You had to work. You had to learn how to work. I been cooking ever since I was seven or eight. So I helped my mother raise the kids, then I got married, had babies one right after another one. Oh, well, here I am. Then three years later, after I lost that first husband, I got married to this Mr. Williams. And he was a railroad worker. So he said, "I'm going to carry you to California to see my sister." Say, "I been working for the railroad seventeen years." Say, "I can go there on my pass." We stood up all the way. That's when the war was going on. So we finally got to Oakland. We went to his sister's house. I been here ever since. I'm a Californian. I'm Texas-born.

When I got to California, it was different. Streetcars—I had never seen a streetcar before. And I always respect people. So I was on my honeymoon and I didn't work, so I stayed at home. And then I started another family. So I really was stuck at the house then. So when my baby was two, I went to work at a rest-home, and I worked until I retired about seven years ago. I did rest-home work, I did maid work, I did housework, I just worked. In Texas, I was a farmer. Plowed a horse. Raised chickens, cows, all that stuff. I'm just an old-time woman.

I started quilting when I was about ten or eleven. My mother said, "Here. If you lose this needle, don't come back to me." Times was hard then. You didn't throw stuff down. So by us being kids, two girls, we would lose them needles. So, she finally say, "Well, your uncle give you a quarter. You better send it off, get some thread and some needles because you're not using mine anymore." Been on my own ever since. She'd give me little pieces of scrap. And we'd sew them together. And from that, after I got married, it hooked on. And I come here and went to raising a family. That (quilting) was concentration to me at night. Put my babies to bed and maybe sit up until one or two o'clock (in the morning), getting to sew. All the children are grown now. I'm living with one of them. That's the third one out there. Or the second one, after I come to California.

My mother made real pretty quilts. But that's just one of them. It's a star—I don't know what you'd call that thing. But it's (the pattern) from a paper. But I really don't know the name of it. I done got too old. My mother died in Pecos, and my sister was in Pecos, so I didn't go up there to see how many quilts she had. And then my sister didn't live too long, about a year. Bless her heart. So I haven't been back.

Ooh, when you have a bunch of kids, you just strip them (quilts) together. They're going to tear them up anyway. This is one I just sit down at the sewing machine. Oh, man, I had lots of them, but they in storage and staying here in this little place. This is a star symbol. My mother taught me how to do it. But I just got into it after I come to California, so I finished this one. And I wished I had my quilt tops. But I don't. They in storage. This place is too little. So, me, I tell you, when you get old, you throw away lots of junk and then you forget where it's at. I just don't have nothing no more, really.

You don't pick your colors. Somebody come along with a piece of scrap, you take it. I don't know where I got the scraps from. But they all come in a sack. A lady told me that she had two boxes, that her mother did this kind of work. And she was going to bring me two boxes. She said, "So I got two boxes if you want it."

I just sit down and put my head together, do it. This is a pattern. But now what's the name of it? I don't know. All cotton. This was bought. Yeah. It's washable, and I would say it's cotton. I really don't know what kind of fabric, because there are so many different fabrics, or cotton. It's not gabardine. I really don't know. But I know we use it.

I wish you could see some of my granddaughter's quilting. I taught her how to quilt when she was little. Her mother was away in Washington, working. And I kept her until she was around eleven. And then they went up the hill and stayed about two years. And now, she still come for guidance: "Grandma, I'm on this new quilt. Show me how to put it together." She got some of the prettiest quilts.

I say, "Fina, what you gonna do?"

"Aw, Granny, I ain't gonna sell my quilts. I'm just gonna keep them."

But she takes the tape. See, that's the difference in people when they finish school. She takes all her tape and measures the inches and everything. And them quilts is put together. The tops. She hasn't quilted any. But I just wish you could see them.

She say, "I'm not gonna sell them. I just gonna pack them in this box."

I think she had twelve tops, queen-size. She don't make little ones. Her name is Ofina Parker. She's a single woman. She's about thirty-one now. Never been married. That's her hobby. But I raised her.

There are eight or more generations of quilters in my family—my mother, grandmother, great-grandmother, great-great-grandmother. Might be another grandmother. Because I have some of my great-grandchildren I haven't seen. Some of them are in Florida. Some of them in Ohio. Oh, I have children—some of them in southern California. I raised out eight children, and I've only lost two. So I got six living children. I don't know many grandchildren, great-grandchildren, and children. But they didn't have as many as I had.

I remember my grandmother on father's side and grandmother on my mother's side. Lutie Collins was my grandmother on mother's side. She was a stout, chunky woman. And my grandmother on father's side, she was a little bitty woman. I don't know what she was. She was cute. Both of them could sit on their hair. Now, I don't know what they was mixed with, but they were beautiful women. And Grandma Lutie was a fat woman: She was stout and plump. But my grandmother on daddy's side, she was little. Her name was Fanny; her husband had passed when I met her.

My grandma Lutie, that's my mother's mama, well, her husband was named George. George Collins. My parents' names were Joe Shepherd and Frances Shepherd.

Well, you had to quilt back then. You had to learn how to do that to stay warm. That's what my mother said. So when I was about nine, she wouldn't let us use her stuff.

She'd say, "You gotta learn how to make a quilt. 'Cause you'll be grown after a while. You gonna have to have cover to sleep under."

So they made the girls, in the wintertime, wasn't no cotton to pick, and you sitting around worrying Mama, playing dolls. She make you piece quilts and cook. I been cooking ever since I was nine.

Arbie Williams as a National Heritage Fellowship recipient in 1991. (Michael Bruce, Maguire-Reeder)

My sister was a blues singer from her heart behind my mother's back. So you just hum up a tune and you had a song. And we went to church every Sunday. And she was a church singer on Sunday. But you know how kids are. She was the dancer and the song singer. I was the drummer. I was on an old tub or something, beating it. That was your drums then. And she'd dance to that.

I didn't have a voice to sing. I talked. I don't mind running my mouth. But I never did have the voice to sing. There were three girls and two boys my mother raised. And I was the oldest, so I did lots of work.

My daddy used to go possum hunting back there in Texas and Louisiana. And coon hunting. And every house you'd go to, they had them dogs. My grandmother had, oh, I think about seven big old hound dogs. And my uncles, they had dogs. So we young people, we would get them dogs, in the fall of the year, and go possum hunting at night and get out in the woods way up in the mountains or somewhere. I don't now where I was. And they would sing the blues, just about anything.

I was always the speaker of the house, and if somebody new come, I always got up to tell them who they were and make them welcome and go cook them a good dinner. But my mother, she sung, oh man. Annie. She's dead and gone. I'm the only person living.

People didn't have nothing then. You were too poor to have a record player. We didn't. My grandmother had one, but she wouldn't let us play it. We'd tear it up. They wouldn't let us stand there and crank it. Wasn't nothing new then. Wasn't no lights. You had gas lights, I mean kerosene lights. You had pine lights. And you didn't have electric lights. You had to do everything by your hand. You'd go to the field and work and come home. You'd wash on a rub board. You'd wring them clothes and boil them. And you took them out of that water, and you'd rinse them and rinse them until Mama say, "Oh, well, did you rinse them in three waters?"

"Yeah, Mom."

"Well, hang them on the fence." Wasn't no lines.

My mother was a good-looking woman. She was, she say she was ninety-two. But I don't know. Like I say, they didn't have census then. And usually, so I understand, if she was born on a plantation, well, she never did go back there and get the real original birthday. You know, then, everybody was trying to get to the big time. And you'd move on maybe Mr. Joe's place, and all the kids born on that place would be named Joe's, and you wouldn't be no kin to him. And you'd just be born, and there wouldn't be no record of it.

You know one thing? I don't know what discrimination is. I run my mouth so. I loved everybody. I got along with the white like I did the black. And the Mexicans.

Mama once said (about some Mexicans), "Well, you don't eat her cooking because she cooks too hot for you to eat." So we didn't get to eat the Mexican food, and they didn't get to eat our food. But we knowed them.

There were a lot of problems in East Texas, though. Yeah. But I was in Texas and Oklahoma. Oklahoma City and Tulsa. My daddy went all over. Tulsa, Boley. He could pick 200 pounds of cotton, and somebody come through, "Well, we going to such and such a place, Joe, don't you want your family to go?"

"Yes sir."

"Can you pick cotton?"

"My wife can pick." And we'd get on that train and go hundreds of miles. That's the way we got all to Tulsa. We went way west to Paducah, Texas. Amarillo, Texas. Oklahoma City. Louisiana, name it. All around. We wouldn't be in a camp; we'd just be on some man's farm. One time we was in a tent. You know, we'd be out behind the barn somewhere in a big tent. We didn't get to play too much.

I don't know what my daddy did in the field, but we didn't get to go to the field when we was way west in Paducah and aw, what is that other little town? But anyway, I don't know, we didn't, like you say, we didn't mix, there wasn't too many mixing.

Now when I was way west, my daddy got up that Saturday morning. He was going to carry us to town to see a parade, and then he changed his mind. He said, "Oh, no, we can't go to town today."

I said "Why, Papa?"

"Oh, they say they gonna drag that boy. They gonna hang him."

And I said, "Well, I'm gonna go see it."

Papa, said, "No, I don't want to go."

So he didn't go in that day. But then Mama said, "No, we can go to town and stay on the edge of the town."

Well, when we got in town, we got right in the middle of it. And sure enough they dragged the boy by the head from the back of the wagon. Wasn't no cars. Maybe a little old T-Model, about as big as that chair. But I never did see no lynching. I don't know what he was hung for. I think he was insulting his boss man or something. I don't know. I was too young to hear about it. That was West Texas.

I tell you, my daddy would just leave. Man come by and say, "Joe, I got to farm." "Yeah, I'll go." And Mama, poor little thing, my mother was a little woman. Weighed about ninety pounds. "Honey, get the things ready, we're going to go to another farm." Mama would go in there, just grab up her quilts and one or two little dresses, and there we'd go, off to the next farm. So many little places we'd go. I couldn't name them now. I'm too old.

My second husband brought me to California. His name was Johnny Williams. He was a hard worker. He lifted ties and fixed the railroad. He was the big man. He worked for them for seventeen years. So when my first husband died, I went to Begville. My mother and them was living in Begville. And I went into town that evening, and he was getting off of work. So the first husband was dead and buried, and he saw me. So then we went back to the little honky-tonk, they called, that night. My sister was about sixteen. And we met, and about three years after I met him, we got married. Then for a honeymoon, he brought me here. Brought me to Oakland.

Lots of folks from Texas come this way. I don't know if it was better. I just think people was wanting to leave. Just wanted to see the world. Me, I always told my mother that I was. I said, "When I get grown, I'm gonna travel." And I must have been about thirteen. And I didn't go to school until I was twelve. Wasn't no schools.

So my mama said, "Gal, is you crazy?"

I said, "I'm going to Washington, D.C.," with my little hands on my hips one night. I said, "Mama," had my history book; papa had just paid $1.05 for a history book, and I was reading my history book.

She said, "What you learning in that book, gal?"

I say, "It tells you about the presidents of the United States and all the countries." Oh, I was crazy about my history. And I went on to name the presidents and the big men. I say, "And you know what?" See, kids was proud of themself then, when they got a book. I say, "I'm going to

Washington, D.C., when I get grown. And you want to know where I'm going next?" I must have been about twelve. In the second grade. First grade. You didn't get to go to school right. "I'm going to California."

"Gal, is you crazy?"

I say, "When I get grown, I'm going." And here I am. I've been to Washington, D.C. And I'm in California. My husband had a sister here, and we come here on our honeymoon. So he had worked for the railroad, for the Southern Pacific. He started when he was seventeen. So he must have been thirty-four. And he started working here. He got a little more money. He had never made $1.65 an hour. There, in Texas, you worked all day for seventy-five cents. That was 1945.

I couldn't get him to go back to Texas. He said, "Honey, I ain't going back." And he went to work. By the time he got here, he had brothers here, and they carried him to the Navy supply. The war was going on, and they hired him. And he come home that evening, "Come on, we gotta talk, Honey."

I say, "Why?"

"I ain't going back."

"What?"

"I ain't going back to Texas."

I say, "Why?"

"Well, you know, I got hired at the Navy supply. And they give you $1.45 an hour, and if you stay with them twenty years, you get a pension. And I won't have to work no more. I'll be a good husband."

I say, "I know you will. If you don't, you know I know how to work. I don't care."

So he quit his railroad job, and h e went to work in Navy supply. I been here ever since. He's dead and gone, God rest his soul. So, here I am, scuffling with one of his sons. But the world's been good to me. You know, I'm the mother of thirteen children. And I have, I don't know how many living. Nine, I think, living.

When I come to Oakland, we had been married about a year and a half, and he was working on the railroad. He went to work when he was seventeen for the Southern Pacific. And by me being in this little boxcar, you know, they furnish you little boxcars, they sit you with other folks. Well, there were three boxcars, and Miss Jones and Miss Hills and me were together. So they say to me, "What you do every day?"

I say, "I piece quilts."

"Oh, my God, I don't know how to piece quilts."

I say, "Well, I do."

So we pieced quilts in winter, and in the summer we would quilt. And that was our pleasure. That's the way I growed up in Texas. My husband would make me frames. Out of wood. Little planks like that. Four holes in it. They was easy to make. Yep. I've did lots of different work.

I pieced, I don't know how many quilts. And my neighbor, her husband was working on the railroad. So she said, "Williams, I don't ever see you outside. What do you do?"

I say, "I'm piecing quilts." I pieced my quilts in the winter and quilt in the summer.

She say, "I don't know how to do it."

I say, "Come on over; I'll teach you." And she was pregnant. So then she come over, and then the next woman heard about it. Well, before long, we had a group of women. A group of twelve women doing this. We'd piece our quilts in the winter and wouldn't let our buddies know what we was piecing. Of course, I was just there two years after I got married to Mr. Johnny. But we'd piece in the winter and quilt them in the summer. And that was our secret. So it was fun. I ain't never been lonesome. I come here and had my babies and, oh, I got friends here, all used to work in Piedmont, and all over Oakland.

They would come to your house and we would piece, like this week would be my week to have the girls over. The husbands were working. So we would cut quilt pieces, and we would piece them. Then when we go to quilt, we all would go to each other's house. Would be four of us, or five. And we could just about do a quilt in a run of a day. Oh, God, we talk about everything. How to raise the kids and whose husband got the drunkest...there was a lot of stuff going on then, just like it is now.

I never did believe in making up tales. I was just an old plain woman. If you did something wrong, I'd tell you. And if you did enough, well, we could have it out with our fists. But I never did tell tales. My sister was a big joker. And she could do the black bottom and the twist. I'd beat on the tub. So, I've just been a plain old housewife. And for a time, I went to work for the laundry. I worked for the laundry for eleven months until I got pregnant. Then I went baby-sitting. And then from that I went to taking care of old people in the rest-homes. And then I went to piecing quilts.

I used to stay on 14th Avenue. And I had to change to a 51 bus and get a 14 bus to go by my house. So when I got off up there on the freeway to catch the 51, I come under the bridge, I found a brand new pair of Levi jeans out in the middle of the street. And me, always be thinking for the worst, I said to myself, "Oh, God, some woman throwed him out of the house." Well, there was more than one pair of pants there, but there was one pair of beautiful blue jeans. I picked that bag of clothes up. I said, "Some woman got rid of him." And I carried them home, put them in my washing machine and hung them out. And I went to bed, brought them in, and I went to bed. But something woke me up about two o'clock. I said, "What am I gonnna do with them pants?" Lester can't wear them; see how big he is. And Johnny couldn't wear them. I didn't know nobody could wear them. And I got me a razor blade and slit them open. And next thing you know, I had joined them together, fixed them, turned them around. Then, I say, "I'm gonna see can I make a quilt top." And I did. I been a crazy old woman. I'm telling you.

I don't remember selling nobody no quilt. Maybe I do, or maybe I have. But if I see somebody need the quilt, I'd rather give him one than to sell him one. I've given many a quilt. I don't know. Like I say, I've worked all of my life, so I draw that little pension. And I've been pretty lucky. I do my quilts. And now, I get money for doing this. I've did lots of things to make money. I've had a happy life. I probably could have got married again after this husband died, and everything, but I don't want no husband. I done had a happy life, what I want to be tied up again, you know? So, I'm seventy-nine or eighty-one or whatever, let me be that. Go to church when I feel like it. I serve the old man upstairs. I never did believe in random. I never did drink. I was around it, but, "Arbie, don't you want a drink?" "Nah."

One time Lester (my son), him and his buddy was celebrating New Year's. That was about fourten years ago. He come in one night. He was young. "Mama, can we drink?" "You know this whiskey been under that sink in there ever since your birthday. Let me open it."

For about two years, it had been under the sink in the kitchen. So, I say, "Okay, come on now, you gonna have to help celebrate." It was the New Year's. I say, "Just fix me a little." They fixed me a little like that. I say, "Hey, you better carry me upstairs and put me into bed." This is all I could take of it. I didn't believe in drinking, but I served many a drink. I was a cocktail waitress. I was a dishwasher. I was a ballroom girl, served the cocktails, and back to the kitchen to get some more drinks, and then I was in the locker room. That was Walnut Creek…at a big country club, and I worked there for twelve years, until I got in a car wreck. I loved them women. They'd play golf. And then I went to serving dinners and drinks in the basement, where the women were at. I've done all kinds of honest work. Didn't catch me out there on the street, begging for money.

I'm just good with my fingers. I love to crochet, I love to piece, I love to use a needle. I don't know, I like to quilt, but I like to have somebody to run my mouth with when I'm quilting. I got whole boxes of tops, but no quilts. I need a group. Somebody to give you a backup. "Oh, Williams, you didn't catch this over here." "Oh, yeah, I see it." It's lots of fun. I've never been a lonely woman. Now I've lost one husband and then I got married again, had a bunch of children. We split up. I never was lonely 'cause I had my kids to keep me company. So I'm still here. I got a room in the back of the house (here in Richmond), so that's good enough for me. I tell him all the time, I say, "When I get too much, put me in the rest-home." I'd be good company there. Some of them old sisters sit up and worry over what they got at home. I could teach them a lesson.

INTERVIEW BY ALAN GOVENAR, JUNE 5, 1997

Francis Williams

Civil Rights Attorney
Life dates: April 23, 1922–August 22, 1993

Francis Williams was a prominent attorney in Houston, Texas. He grew up in Austin, Texas, the son of Pinckney Williams, an agent for the American Woodmen of the World insurance company. Francis Williams attended Tillotson College in Austin from 1940 to 1944, and was enrolled in Howard University from 1946 to 1950, when he received his law degree. In Houston, Williams helped to pursue desegregation suits against the city and the state, and worked with Henry Doyle, W. J. Durham, Hattie Mae White, Barbara Jordan, Thurgood Marshall, and other civil rights leaders.

I've been active in the NAACP since 1951, when I started practicing law. I'm originally from Austin. I went to law school at Howard University in Washington, D.C. When I applied to go to law school in 1946, there was no place to go to in Texas, being black. So, I started writing around the country to law schools. I got admitted to Howard and to a couple of others, but I chose Howard. I graduated with the class of 1950.

I was a reservist and I got recalled to active duty during the Korean conflict. I went back on active duty in September 1950, and stayed until October 1951. I bought a car and came to Houston to start practicing law with Henry Doyle.

I had a general practice years ago, but I have restricted that now. I spent a short period on the bench in the criminal court. So, now that I'm back in private practice, I restrict my activity to criminal law, probate, and family law. You cannot keep up with all of the law. Every time I try to keep up with law I get myself in trouble.

I was involved in several of the civil rights cases that were filed here in Houston. The two major ones that I participated in were the Court House Cafeteria Suit of 1953, and then in 1956, the day after Christmas, Mr. Doyle (who later became a judge) and I filed the Houston Independent School District Desegregation Suit, *Ross v. Rogers*.

Francis Williams, third from left, photograph by Benny Joseph, Houston, Texas, ca. 1960s (Texas African American Photography Archive)

In 1956, there were several parents who took their children to the closest school. Those close schools happened to be white schools, and, of course, their children were denied admission because the schools were designated white or colored. The parents called the NAACP and told what happened, "I took my child to such and such a school and talked to the principal and she said that she had instructions from the school board office that no colored were to be enrolled." So, I was quoted in the media as saying that the school board should follow the law of the land and admit children to the local schools. And one Saturday I looked out the front door. I lived in the Sunnyside area at the time. I was doing something in the house, and a cross was burning in the front yard. Where I lived was not in the city of Houston proper. It was in Harris County, so the sheriff had jurisdiction.

Several people asked me if I was scared. Hell no, I was mad. I ran and got my rifle, but they were long gone. As a matter of fact, when I went out the front door and looked, there was nobody up and down the street. They were gone. Of course, the neighbors and the volunteer fire department, we put the thing out with a water hose. And the sheriff was called and they came out and took it. I immediately began to get calls from newspapers and television stations. I remember one person called and said, "You Francis Williams? What's going on out there?"

"Nothing unusual."

"Okay."

They had called up all these stations and the night editor of the *Post* called and said, "They tell me some fool done set a burning cross in your front yard."

And I said, "They did."

He said, "Well, what are you going to do about it?"

"What do you mean, do about it?" I said, "Hell, they're gone."

And he asked, "What's your reaction?"

"It's racial bigots."

He said, "Did they come close to the house?"

I said, "I don't know, because I didn't see them."

And he said, "What would you have done if you had seen them?"

I said, "I would have probably shot them." I said, "Look, I don't want you to run that in the paper." I was president of the local NAACP from 1954 to 1959.

So, the other newspapers called. The *Chronicle* even had a picture of it in the paper. So, I went down to the sheriff's office to look at it and they had it in the closet with a lot of other things. It was made by a carpenter. The cross piece was not just nailed on, it was mitered. And there was a railroad spike in it to stick it in the ground. It had been carefully planned. Of course, it upset my wife very much.

I built a practice by going to civic club meetings and handing out cards. Almost every night I'd go to somebody's civic club and they would always let me say something because there weren't many black lawyers. I'd make a little speech. Well, being gone, my wife was upset. She wouldn't leave. She wouldn't go stay with anybody. So, a friend of mine, an electrician, came out and put lights on the corners of the house. The lights would light up both sides. I never had any problem. They never came back.

When I was preparing the Court House Cafeteria suit, my telephone used to ring. I'm listed, always have been. As long as I'm a lawyer, I'll be listed. Well, they called me up and cursed me out and called me, "Nigger, nigger, nigger," and I'd just hang up. And sometimes I'd get tired of that, and I'd cuss them out. My wife was horrified, but I'd cuss them out. I'll never forget one guy who called one Saturday. He was working at some kind of place that I could hear machinery in the background and he called. We were just talking about integration and he was saying how black folks shouldn't go to school with white folks. And I was trying to tell them that they're all children, and they all need to learn. Then he'd hang up. Every hour on the half hour he'd call. So, I told my wife, "Let's look at the late show," and so we sat up until about 1 o'clock and he called, but at 2:30 I was in bed asleep. I said, "Now don't call me anymore. I'm tired of talking to you. I've been talking to you all night. To hell with you, and you go on about your business."

He said, "We been talking all night, but you haven't cussed me."

I said, "I don't want to cuss you."

So, we had a cussing spree. You see, I was a child who went to school during the Depression. In Austin we used to have a lot of caustic rhymes we used to say with each other, very foul language. I started reciting some of those to him. And all he could say was "Why, you nigger! Why, you nigger!"

And I'd say something that insulted his female relatives. They used to call it "playing the dozens." And he never heard that, I'm sure. As soon as I'd say one, I'd think of another. I haven't thought of most of those in years, but he didn't call back.

Usually when they'd call, we'd have a discussion, although heated, about integration. They didn't call it desegregation. They called it integration. I used to get a lot of bad telephone calls when I was president of the NAACP.

In the first case, the Court House Cafeteria suit took about a year. The second case was filed the day after Christmas in 1956, and we tried it in 1957. But the case lasted almost thirty years on the docket. Mr. Doyle and I tried it, but after a period of time, we were no longer associated with it. You see, the NAACP was put out of business in 1957 in Texas.

The state of Texas alleged that the NAACP was a foreign corporation and not governing its business properly in registering as a foreign corporation and making reports to the state. There was a major lawsuit about that in Tyler, Texas. Why did they choose Tyler? I don't know why they chose Tyler, but I think it was because it was a hotbed of racial biasness in East Texas.

A compromise in the Tyler case came after about a year and a half. The NAACP was back in business.

People had not been meeting publicly. A judge had issued a temporary restraining order that forbade the NAACP to meet. So, there were other organizations that tried to assume the mantle, but most of them didn't get off the ground. They were not as viable as the NAACP.

The Courthouse Cafeteria case was one that got a lot of us to thinking in Texas. As the junior person in the office it was my chore to do the research on the Court House Cafeteria suit. I found two cases in 1953 dealing with public accommodation. One was a swimming pool case in Lima, Ohio, and the other was an NAACP-sponsored suit for Virginia Beach, Virginia. It seems that in the Virginia Beach case, there was a certain part of the beach set aside for coloreds (that's what we were called then. That was way before we were "black"). And the NAACP brought a lawsuit because of the city ordinance that they should be allowed to use the entire beach. That case I found in the federal courts. The other case I found was in the Ohio State courts. It was concerned with a swimming pool near a black area. If you have ever been in the North, there was residential segregation. Well, the city fathers decided to build an Olympic-sized swimming pool in a more affluent area. So, black folks went out there to swim, but they wouldn't let them swim. But you see, Ohio had an antisegregation law since the Civil War days, and that case was decided on state law rather than on constitutional grounds as the Virginia Beach suit.

Doyle and I talked about the research that I had done and we found out that everything in that Courthouse Cafeteria was bought by Harris County—the dishes, the plates, the pots and the pans, the seats. There was a concessionaire, a person who leased it, but everything there was paid for by the county. We sued the county judge. We tried that case for three days over in the federal court. That case was decided in our favor, but it was appealed by the county, of course, in the Fifth Circuit. I did not, however, at that time have my certificate to practice law before the Fifth Circuit Court in New Orleans. I did send in my money so that I could go to New Orleans to argue it. They heard it in Fort Worth, and that was a great comedown. Two judges from the circuit came and they affiliated one of the district judges and they heard the case. They decided to affirm the lower-court action. Again the county appealed to the Supreme Court of the United States. The Supreme Court of the United States denied it. They let the decision stand.

The *Ross v. Rogers* suit was finally dismissed about a year and a half ago, in 1986. All cases were under the continuous supervision of the courts to see that they complied. The basis of that case was that they denied entrance to black children to go to so-called white schools. White schools happened to be closer to them than the black schools. They had to travel a longer distance to the black schools.

Years later, there was a story in the local papers about the events of that time and how the case was finally dismissed. One of the papers found one of the plaintiffs, and she was grown and had children who were ten or eleven years old. She was a fifth-grader when she was a plaintiff with her parents, however.

Today you can go to the school closest to your home. Legally, the case was resolved because they eventually changed the rules. There were a lot of obstacles, and there still are some. People were pretty cohesive back then. We had a cadre of people who joined the NAACP and contributed money.

Let me tell you a story that I told the attorney general that came down to speak to the black lawyers' group about ten years ago. We had a dinner meeting and asked the attorney general to speak to the Houston Lawyers Association. We couldn't join the Houston Bar Association in those days. So, we formed our own organization. In any case, the attorney general was there and I was asked to make some remarks. I told him that we had trouble with one attorney general back during the 1950s. He was the one who initiated the NAACP lawsuit. They sent agents from the attorney general's office all over the state to seize the records of the NAACP in the various cities. That injunction was issued one day in Tyler, and the next morning when we first learned anything about it, some people went to the NAACP office to start looking through the records. Mrs. Adair was executive secretary of the NAACP at that time, and she called me. Of course, I didn't know anything about it and she said, "It's on the radio. Turn on the radio." And there was a flash every half hour that this action had been taken. They had done it all over the state. Everybody wanted to call Durham in Dallas. W. J. Durham was the leader of the NAACP lawyers in Texas. He was a lawyer with whom Thurgood Marshall associated in the Texas cases. And on this day no one could get through to Durham. The lines were so busy. Everyone was trying to call him. They wanted membership lists and contributor lists. Those are the main things they wanted, but they had to reckon with Mrs. C. D. Adair. Mrs. Adair was very feisty, but she was a horrible bookkeeper. Things were not that orderly. Her office looked worse than my desk. So, they said, "Where are the membership lists?"

She said, "We don't have any membership lists." And, of course, they didn't believe her. But she didn't type but hunt-and-peck, and she didn't keep a running roster. What she did was to keep the duplicates of the lists she sent to New York. If you put them together, you could finally figure out who was a member, but she didn't keep a running roster.

I found out later that they (the agents) were from the Comptrollers Office. And we decided that under no circumstances could we allow the Houston list to get in the hands of the attorney general. Not that we had too many white people in the NAACP, but we had some, and we had a lot of teachers, a lot of people who worked in jobs. And we figured that if that list became public, these people were going to lose their jobs. That happened in some places. So, after they had been there two whole days, we talked to Mrs. Adair. Every once in a while they asked her questions and she gave them a short answer. She was very uncooperative with them. I spent a half a day over there, the first day, talking with them, awaiting word from on high from New York (where the National NAACP offices were located), but the only word we got was that they had a temporary restraining order to proceed.

So, I looked at the attorney general and I told him that I got a key from Mrs. Adair and we went over there in the middle of the night. She told us exactly where those membership records were, exactly where the contribution records were, and we took them out in the middle of the night. And on the next day I burned them. I said, "I can tell you that, sir, because the statute of limitations has run against me." The lawyers there at the meeting went crazy. The statute of limitations had run against my action back in 1957. It was 1979, '80 or something, and they whooped it up.

Somebody told me that they had a photograph of me walking a picket line at Texas Southern graduation in May 1956. Photographs in those days could be used as evidence in court, for both sides. You see, I was president of the local NAACP branch, and we decided we should picket the commencement because Governor Allan Shivers was the speaker. Allan Shivers had expressed his opposition to the 1954 decision of *Brown v. Board of Education*. So, we labeled him a segregationist and picketed him.

We talked about it at the NAACP board meeting. We met every Thursday night, usually at a church somewhere, Third Ward this week. Sunnyside, all over the city. We had a cadre of about fifteen people who would come to the meeting irrespective to where it was. But we'd pick up people from those neighborhoods. We'd usually have fifty to sixty people, but when the issues were hot we had more than that.

We decided at the board meeting to picket, and we took it to the membership and they agreed with us. We sent somebody for some poster boards. I wanted to look at all the signs. I wanted to be sure that they were not in poor taste. So, they made signs that Saturday, and the word got out. Somebody said there was a law against picketing, and I had to hit the law books. I didn't know of any law, but I had to check, and all I found was something concerning the number of pickets at a union strike.

One woman was concerned about how it might affect her son. But we picketed and we had a parade of people along Wheeler Street to come to see the signs. We were on TV.

The signs said everything from "Down with Shivers" to "Segregation Must Go," and things that were related to his stand on public schools and desegregation.

There were lots of people taking pictures from the black media. The news services, AP or UPI, took pictures. But not much really changed because the (desegregation) suit was still in limbo. The school board tried a lot of "end arounds." For example, they established the brother and sister rule, that one child could not go to an integrated school if another child was going to an all-black school. In other words, brothers and sisters had to attend the same school. That had to be appealed. Henry Doyle and I were out of the case then. The NAACP had stepped in. They tried several devices. Finally, the school board changed and there was a lessening of impediments that were put in the way of students.

Hattie Mae White was the first black school board member, and that was in 1954. She and I were on television when the school board debated the integration issue. That was before she was a school board member. The school board was an entertainment once a month on television. They had a greater viewership for that than any other program, but they wanted to delete it because it got to be too much.

Weldon Berry was the black attorney who completed the school board suit. M. W. Plummer was the plaintiff in the Court House Cafeteria suit. We wanted him to be a lawyer, but he wanted to be a plaintiff. We honored him by putting his name first rather than in alphabetical order. So that the case is on the books as *M. W. Plummer and others v. Bob Casey*, who was the county judge.

Weldon Berry also represented plaintiffs in other small districts. Joe Reynolds split from that firm that had the school suit, and he made a specialty of defending school boards in desegregation suits all over East Texas. Joe Reynolds was very conservative. He said, "I don't know how many of you have money enough to send your children to private school, but I don't have any money. I'm going to have send my children to a public school because I can't afford to send my daughters to a private school." He was saying that his children would not go to school with black people. Well, his daughters didn't probably have to do that because the case was in court so long that they had probably finished. Nothing was done about housing segregation until the 1970s. And housing discrimination was rampant. I understand a lot of young couples would go beyond the housing projects in southwest Houston, and they would be told, "We don't have any apartments for rent."

The Sweatt case was one of the most important precedents for what followed. It was tried in Austin in 1946. At that time, the law was that suits like that had to be filed in state court. You had to exhaust your state remedy and then go from District Court to the Appellate Court to the State Supreme Court and then, and then only, could you file it in the federal system.

The local NAACP Houston branch initiated the suit because Sweatt was a postal carrier in the city. W. Durham was the attorney. He represented Heman Marion Sweatt. He just passed away. He became a social worker in Atlanta.

The case concerned his admission to the University of Texas Law School. I read about it in the *Austin American-Statesman*. I was thinking about going to law school. So, I strolled on up to the court house. I got there about ten. I saw a couple of people standing outside. I saw a big burly man. I just knew he was a police officer. There was a demeanor about him. I went to reach for the door, and he said, "You can't go in there!"

I looked and said, "Why?"

And he flushed and he said, "Because it's full." And I saw the other people looking at me. I don't know why. I wasn't trying to be testy with him. So, I just stood there, and at twelve o'clock the old double doors opened and everybody came out—Thurgood Marshall, and W. J. Durham and some other big-shot Austin, Texas folks. They all came out and went to lunch, and somebody told me it was going to be recessed to one o'clock. So, I went in and took a seat and when they opened back up I had a seat. It was very boring. They were reading statistics into the record, no flesh-and-blood testimony or anything. For example, they stated how many black people were in Texas, how many were going to Prairie View (A&M University).

I went to what's now called Huston-Tillotson. Sam Houston was a small Methodist school, and there was another small all-black school in Austin supported by the Congregationalist church, called Tillotson. The smartest thing they ever did was merge back in the late 1940s. I was an undergraduate from 1940 to 1944. Then I went to the war. I got deferred for about a year. I graduated, and I was going to be a doctor. I had applied to Howard and Meharry, the only black medical schools in the country, and didn't get in. My draft board consisted of one man. He told me, "We're going to give you boys at Sam Huston and Tillotson the same break we give to boys at the University in Austin."

I said, "Yes sir, yes sir."

And he said, "You're going to go to medical school. If not, you got to go to Raleigh." I didn't get in and thirty-six days later, I got my greetings and went into the service.

After I got out, I applied to law school and was admitted to Howard. The Sweatt case started that summer, and I was in law school at Howard when the Sweatt case was argued in the Supreme Court of the United States. It was argued in 1948 and the whole law school went there, but it wasn't finally decided in his favor until 1950.

Sweatt went to law school. Of course, they punched him out quickly. He failed. Well, I understand that some professors would call on him every day. It's difficult to brief cases for five professors every day. He was an excellent plaintiff by virtue of his personal history, no arrests. He was a graduate of Wylie College. He was a postman, paid his taxes. He was married. There was nothing on him. They wanted somebody who was squeaky clean in a case like that. He was mature, but he had been out of college for fourteen years and that made it very difficult.

Some of papa's friends urged me to wait for the Sweatt case to be resolved. One said, "You could live at home. It would be much cheaper," but money didn't bother me. I had the G.I. Bill. So, after I got admitted I got on the train and went to Washington.

My papa, Pinckney A. Williams, was an agent for a black-owned insurance company, called American Woodmen. He was also a real estate agent and a notary public. We lived in a mixed neighborhood, poor whites, poor blacks, and poor Mexicans all in the same block in Austin. But Papa was the only businessman on the block. Papa wore a white shirt with a detachable starched white collar every day. Papa always had a car. A lot of the people in our neighborhood didn't have cars. When they brought gas in, for example, in the late 1930s, we were one of the three people on the block who had gas.

Papa was what they called a "race man" because he had been active in a lot of civic affairs during his lifetime. We were taught never to trust white folks. We had no white people who came to our house to collect any money or anything. Papa got his own ice. He went to the creamery and bought his own milk. We had no deliveries from anybody. And so I grew up not trusting anybody. I never had a white doctor or dentist put his hands on me until I went to the Army during World War II.

Before I was born, Papa had been involved in what the NAACP called the Shillady incident. John Shillady was the secretary of the NAACP, and he was white. He came to Austin to fight against the city's order that a local NAACP chapter disband. Well, he was met at the train station by the law enforcement people. He was marched to the Driskill Hotel, and they beat him unmercifully, and then they marched him back to the next train. He didn't have a ticket on the train, and he died later from his injuries. There was quite a turmoil in the black community because the word was out that they were going to lynch these people who were going to meet with him. So, Papa, I'm told, found out about it and hid out for four days down on the river. They say he took a flour sack and canned goods, a can opener, his shotgun, his pistol, and he left home. Now, I was not born. This happened back in the early 1900s. I wasn't born until 1922, but my sisters all knew about it. Well, I didn't hear anything more about that until I became president of the local NAACP and was at a national meeting and somebody mentioned the Shillady incident. In the history of the NAACP there is a reference to what happened in Austin, Texas.

Three years ago, I got a call on the bench. I didn't take calls. I told the clerk, unless it's my wife (and I knew she would not call except for an emergency) or unless it was from another judge or another elected official in the county. I think it is the height of impropriety for a judge to be talking on the telephone while a case is going on, but I've seen them do it. After I got off the bench, they gave me the call and it was somebody from Austin. That evening I called her, and I didn't get an answer. Then my sister called and told me I was going to get a call from a white woman who wanted to know something about Papa. She didn't give her the time of day. She grew up with that attitude that we don't talk to white folks. We didn't tell them anything. Well, I found out this lady was from the historical society, and I got in touch with her on the next day. They were putting together a history of East Sixth Street and they kept on running across the name P. A. Williams. She wanted to know if I had any papers or pictures of Papa. I told her what I had, and she was interested. I called up my sister and said, "This is not a hatchet job they want to do a story about Papa. This is historical."

She said, "Well, you can handle it." In Austin they took what was the colored library and made it into a museum. They put together an exhibit on black businesses in Austin and featured Papa in a prominent manner. Papa was born in Brazoria, and his father, I understand, was a Reconstruction days deputy sheriff and he was poisoned with some milk. Grandma, I understand, took her three children and left immediately and went to San Antonio. They stayed there for a while, but then they came to Austin. My mother was a farm girl from down in Lockhart. Papa's first wife had passed away, and he met my mother at some meeting or association where she was teaching school. Her name was Buna Williams, and she died in 1964. Papa passed away in 1943 and at that time I think he was sixty-three years old. The NAACP was not an active organization in Austin when I was growing up. I think the Shillady incident and other things like that had affected people in an adverse way.

Thurgood Marshall came to Houston about once a year. Thurgood was a lively storyteller and he was much in demand as a speaker. Of course, he was busy raising funds for the NAACP.

We didn't have any political leaders, except persons with the NAACP. We didn't have any public officials outside of the people in New York and Chicago. We didn't have any public officials in California. There were no black elected public officials in Texas, and still there's not too many.

Barbara Jordan was very important during this period. She ran against Willis Watley in 1952 countywide for state representative and lost badly. She ran against the same man in 1954 and lost. Watley was a conservative, but in 1955, as a result of the 1950 census, there had to be redistricting mandated by the law. I sat on the committee. I was appointed by one of the commissioners. There were five blacks on the redistricting committee. At that time the eighteenth senatorial district was conceived, and we had a lot of union help. There were few so-called liberal Democrats and we carved out the eighteenth district for a black person, right down the middle of the county. We took in a lot of the Fifth Ward, some of the North Side, this area (Third Ward), Sunnyside, and we took in a majority of the black folks. We took in a great enough area so that a black person could win. Of course, Barbara ran for that seat. She was unopposed. No Republican would dare run. And Barbara Jordan won in 1956. She was from the Fifth Ward area.

Barbara graduated from the Boston University Law School, and from Texas Southern in liberal arts. She was on the debating team. After she left for Congress, Greg Washington ran for her seat in State Senate.

The year Barbara was elected state senator, a black, Curtis Graves, was elected state representative. That same year, a black was elected in Dallas. Three people were elected that year because of redistricting. Francis Williams has a theory. You see, we were bound together geographically and we supported each other because we couldn't move to southwest Houston. We couldn't go out and rent an apartment in southwest Houston. The young people rented apartments over here. Crime was not as rampant as it is now.

You knew the people around. Mrs. Adair was known and respected. They knew she was the NAACP lady. People might not know her name, but they knew who she was. We had a strong sense of community pride about us in those days. Nowadays, the youngsters can't wait until they graduate from high school and get any kind of job, girls and boys. Well, the boys want to get a car first, but the girls want to get themselves an apartment. They want to get away from home. They won't live over here in Third Ward. They won't live in Fifth Ward. They want to move out to southwest Houston. Well, the better apartments are in southwest Houston, because there have been no nice apartments built over here, that's for sure. The developers say they don't pay. So, that pride that you talk about was fostered because of segregation. We were lumped together. Black businesses thrived.

There were also Jews who lived in this area of Houston. There's a school on Palm that was a synagogue. The True Light Baptist Church was also a synagogue.

I tell you how that came about. In their haste to keep the black folks out of University of Texas, they were seeking some land on which to build a colored law school. And they found some vacant land over here on Wheeler Street. That land was a kind of buffer between the whites on this side of Blodgett Street. All of that was vacant land, and, you see, the blacks stopped at Alabama. Blacks didn't live on Truxillo. So, they stuck Texas Southern over there. I have mixed feelings about that, but I don't want to go into it. This caused the Jewish neighbors here some unrest, and they were just not used to having black people walk through the community, unless it was on the way to work, a woman getting off the bus with a white uniform on. So, I think the presence of TSU started white flight.

There was one act of violence. A fellow who had quite a bit of money, a cattle man, had a cross burned in front of his house on Wichita, over toward Dowling. You see, blacks were coming this way and there were "for sale" signs up all over the neighborhood. That's when Mr. Meyer went out and bought about a hundred acres of land in southwest Houston (it wasn't Houston then) and established Meyerland. He couldn't build those houses fast enough for the people to get out of here.

Houston, however, was unlike a lot cities in the South in that blacks were able to get loans to buy these houses. They couldn't do it in Atlanta unless they borrowed the money from the black bank in the city. In Houston blacks could get loans from white insurance companies, mortgage companies. They were able to get financing, like I did for this house. Houston was just one of the entrepreneur-type cities. They wanted money. Everybody got a premium price for these houses. I looked at many houses before I found one. This one apparently had been foreclosed on by the mortgage company. I bought this house from the insurance company that owned it in Austin.

There was not much violence, and we should be proud of that. My view is that we didn't have violence that they had in some of the other cities because black folks here could get a job. It might not pay but a dollar an hour, but they had a job. We didn't have a great unemployment problem like they did in some cities.

There were some very successful black businessmen. Don Robey was one of them. I didn't know him well. I went to his nightclub and I knew that he had his recording business and ties to a lot of gospel groups and blues. He was very successful.

The music was very popular because a lot of people listened to the radio. Radio was and is very important. I'm dismayed that no black person has been able to get into this immediate area with an FM station because all of these youngsters are listening to FM.

I used to do a little (legal) work for Lightnin' Hopkins, but when I met him his friends said he'd slowed down. That was in the early 1970s. Lightnin's friend and doctor, Dr. Cecil Herald, is an authority on him. He was Lightnin's representative, looked over his contracts and things. He was Lightnin's confidant. I remember when he bought his first Cadillac. He bought a Seville, and Herald talked to me about it. Herald was and still is a great collector and connoisseur of blues records. I used to, but I haven't bought anything in years. I've gotten away from it.

I remember one time Herald and I went to this place right off one of the freeway streets. There was an old theater and Muddy (Waters) was coming. And Lightnin' opened for him. I remember that 90 percent of the persons there were white, mostly youngsters. Right in the middle of the thing, Herald's beeper went off. He had a woman in labor at St. Joseph's Hospital and he had to leave, but I stayed.

Nobody had much money then. They were working hard. The wages were low, and the music talked to the people. You sang about the blues. I was a great blues man. Not too many white people liked blues then.

Once the blues musicians started going overseas, they were acclaimed in Germany, France, England, and so forth. And the major companies began to take notice of them. All of the older records, on Robey's labels, and others become popular. They called it rhythm and blues.

I went all the way from Miles (Davis) to Muddy (Waters). I skipped pop altogether. A lot of the social clubs featured the music at their dances. They'd usually have two a year, one that was public and one that was invitational. I was appointed to the County Criminal bench in 1985 and I spent about fourteen or fifteen months on the bench. And I left the bench in January 1987. I'm now sixty-four and I'm still practicing law. I've been practicing since October 1951. My steps are slow now. Somebody said, "Why don't you retire?" I don't know what in the world I'd do. I don't play golf. You see, I came along too late for golf. That sounds good, but I got a set of clubs over there in the corner. They're nice clubs. I went to the Oshman sale and bought some good clubs, shoes, tees, everything, and I've been out three times.

I got a friend who's retired and goes golfing every weekend or more now. Every time he comes over here and sees my clubs, he laughs.

INTERVIEW BY ALAN GOVENAR, SEPTEMBER 5, 1987

Rev. Mack Williams

Cowboy and minister
Life dates: November 16, 1914 – April 9, 1998

Mack Williams was raised on the O'Connor Ranch in the coastal plains region of southeast Texas, where his parents and grandparents worked. His grandfather, Thornton, a former slave, was brought to New England as a small boy and given the surname of his master, and later sold at auction in Louisiana to the O'Connor family. Thornton labored as a ranch hand and married a Cherokee woman, Fanny, who was captured in an Indian raid.

As a child, Mack Williams spoke Spanish, the primary language of many of the cowboys in the coastal plains region, and broken English. He later went to school in Conroe to learn proper English. In the early 1940s, he had a vision about preaching while he was riding in the pasture. Reverend Mack was pastor of the Mt. Gallilee Baptist Church in the town of Tivoli from 1951 until his death in 1998; he also pastored at the St. Paul Baptist Church in Victoria, Texas, and the Greater Dawn Baptist Church on the Welder Ranch at Vidaurri, Texas. In addition to working as a ranch hand, he was a park ranger at the Aransas National Wildlife Refuge. An oral history from Williams's wife, Alice Mae, appears on page 471.

The O'Connor ranches were started in 1836 by Tom O'Connor, who had come to Texas from Ireland two years earlier to work with empresario James Power. Empresarios like Power contracted with the Mexican government to settle a certain number of families in Texas in exchange for large grants of land. After Texas declared its independence from Mexico, O'Connor, like the other soldiers who fought with Sam Houston, was awarded a land grant. O'Connor continued to acquire land, and by 1876 had built his ranch to approximately 500,000 acres spread across Refugio, Goliad, Victoria, San Patricio, McMullen, Aransas, and LaSalle Counties. After his death in 1887, the ownership of his massive landholdings passed to his sons, Thomas Marion and Dennis Martin, who in turn divided the land further as it was passed on to their heirs.

I was born and raised right out there on Mr. Martin O'Connor's ranch. We were there for four generations, my grandfather, my father, me, and my two boys. Growing up around the cow pens and the horse pens and seeing the cowboys come out and riding horses and all that. Our greatest desire was to be a cowboy. And after becoming a cowboy, first they would give us these here old gentle horses, and we would ride them, some of them bareback. I used to leave from our house and get on, and meet an old herd out there and ride the old horse around in the back of the herd. And then from then on, they hired us and we become cowboys around like that.

There were ten of us: six boys and four girls. And all of us had a role to do. The girls, they helped around the house there with Mama. My mother's name was Emma Weathers. On the day that Mama was going to wash, we'd start out a bucket brigade.

I'm the third generation. My grandfather, Thornton Williams, was a slave. And my father was reared up there out on the River Ranch with Mr. Martin O'Connor, Mr. Tom O'Connor, old man Tom O'Connor, and old man Dennis O'Connor.

My grandpa, he won his freedom by running off. He ran off, and he laughed about that when my grandmother would tell me about those things. He ran off and said he was going to Mexico. Well, instead of going to Mexico, he wound up in San Antone. And he thought he was in Mexico, because of all the Spanish people around. I have to laugh when I think about him doing that. And when he went he told Grandma, "I'm going to

The Rev. Mack and Alice Mae Williams, photograph by Alan Govenar, Tivoli, Texas, 1994 (Documentary Arts)

run off, I'm going to Mexico." Grandma said, "You old fool. You don't know which way Mexico is."

"Mexico around by heap big water." And he said, "I don't care. I'm going."

And, of course, my grandmother was half Cherokee and she talked funny. So, he left.

Finally, a few months after that, Mr. O'Connor got a letter—"Mr. O'Connor, that fellow you put out a notice on, the runaway slave, say, we have him over here in San Antonio, and he's with me over here. And the day you want to come over here, let me know when you coming and I'll have him there."

So, Mr. O'Connor did. And the day that Mr. Dennis O'Connor was to get in town there, he met him at the train station. But the man who had found him, he told Grandpa, "Thornton, you go down there on the square with the other fellows there and act like you've been working hard." My grandfather was a real horseman. He could break a horse that you could walk on him and stand on top of him. And he told the man, "All right."

So, he went down and he dressed him up in a long tail suit, what we call them frocks now. And he got him a high beaver hat, high-crown beaver hat. Not only the high-crown beaver hat, but he put him on those button shoes and spats and those spats that come over on your shoe. And he went down there and gave him some change and couple of cheroot cigars. Well, that was a joke he was going to play on Mr. Dennis. So, when he met Mr. Dennis over there with that rubber tire buggy and everything, and take him on down, and Mr. Dennis says, "I don't see him out there nowheres." The man said, "Say, well, I say, I saw him down here a while ago. Say, call his name, maybe he'll be there." And Grandpa was there and he had a cigar in his mouth, and change in his pocket, rattling it around the old folks. And he looked like a wealthy man. And finally, Mr. Dennis called out and said, "Thornton!" right loud. And Grandpa recognized that voice. He turned around and he had his cigar in his mouth and he dusted the ashes off it. And he said "Well, well, Mr. O'Connor, what you doing over here in Mexico?"

Mr. Dennis said, "Now, look how you got him dressed. Say, when I get back to the ranch, I'm going to have trouble with him."

No, he didn't punish him. He just brought him on back there, and put him to work breaking horses again.

Yes, that's when Grandpa was a slave. I really don't know if it was before or after. I think it was right after the Civil War. Before the slaves were free completely.

Before it got down this far. See, up north, they had them all freed and then when it got down here, well, that was way down nearly another year. Things like that. Seems like they had a certain sense of humor about all that. They must have known that the Emancipation Proclamation had been signed in the North. That's the way things were.

That's right, you didn't have nothing but black cowboy slaves on all the ranches that had slaves. Well, they were the ones that did all the work. And so they weren't going to hire anybody else, Anglos or anybody.

My Uncle Henry, Papa's brother, was foreman on Mr. Martin O'Connor's ranch for nineteen years, until he died. My father was named Butler Williams, and he was the one that bought all the horses. See, the people used to go through the country with a big herd of horses, and the ranches would buy the horses from the fellow wherever he come from with a big herd of horses. That's the way they did that.

Some places they was cruel, and some they wasn't. Now, my grandfather had another brother named Butler. (In other words, the reason they called him Butler, the slaveholder that bought him was named Butler. And that's the name you go by. And so on down everywhere.) Well, they sold Butler to another fellow named Fannin, and Butler (Grandpa's brother) run away because he killed a man everywhere he went. He just wasn't going to be a slave. And he killed a man everywhere he went, and somebody else would buy him, and then it got on down to the Williamses. And so, when it was a Williams, that was the last name that they had after Grandpa and them. They kept that name Williams because when Mr. O'Connor had him here, they was just still Williams, because they bought from that Williams.

I never did know where they come from in Africa. The African name. And Grandpa didn't know either because he was brought over as a young man, well a boy. He didn't say where or how, and Grandma, she was half Cherokee and they got her through an Indian raid. When those cowboys, those black cowboys and the others was fighting the Indians back in those days. Well, they got them through a Indian raid. That's how Grandpa and Grandma got connected.

When they were picked up as slaves, they were brought up in the North country, up around France, and those places…New England, places out there. Well, the thing about it, the reason they got down into the southern country, was because they couldn't stand that cold weather. They came to New England. All through Boston and around those places. And then the northerners sold them to the South and they migrated on down through the South because it was too cold for them there. They couldn't stand that cold. They come from a warm climate. And after getting on down here, well, the first thing they did was sold them on the block at Louisiana and different places like that. And they auctioned them off. That's what you call selling them on the block. He never did say how much he was sold for. He never did talk to me because he died January 31 and I was born in November. I didn't know my grandfather. But I got all of this from Grandma, his wife. Her name was Fanny Williams. But age—she don't know her age. She didn't know exactly where she come from, and she said, "From them there hills." And I often thought about it when Mr. O'Connor sent us to Oklahoma that time taking us up there, and I looked at those hills and I thought, "Is there where old Grandma come from?" But she didn't know. All she knowed is that she came from them hills.

INTERVIEW BY ALAN GOVENAR, DECEMBER 9, 1992

Marvin Williams

Baseball player
Born: February 12, 1920, Conroe, Texas

*Marvin Williams was raised in Conroe, Texas, the son of a domestic and a sawmill
laborer. At an early age, he was interested in baseball, and by the time he was a
teenager, he was playing for a local team called the Pine Knots. When he was
twenty-two, a friend from Houston recommended him to the Philadelphia Stars
in the Negro League. He was asked to try out, and in 1943 he joined the team in
Philadelphia. In a relatively short time, Williams established himself as a
talented player, and in 1945 he went with Jackie Robinson and Sam Jethro to try
out for the Boston Red Sox. Despite their abilities, Joe Cronin, the manager of the
Red Sox, was unwilling to take the risk of hiring black players and trying to
integrate Major League Baseball. Disappointed, but not deterred, Williams
returned to the Negro League, where he continued to play until 1947. The Negro
League was phased out soon after Robinson was signed to play for the Brooklyn
Dodgers. Williams played for semiprofessional teams in the Arizona and Mexico
League, the Pacific Coast League, and the Texas League. In his oral history,
Williams talks frankly about his experiences in the Negro League, segregation,
and racism in Major League Baseball in the 1940s and 1950s.*

My father was named Frank Williams, and my mother was Eva
Williams. I didn't know my grandfather, but I knew my grandmother. I mostly lived with her until I was nine years old, because I could
have my way with her. And she passed away when I was nine years old.
Her name was Edna Nichols. She had remarried. I don't believe she was
born during slavery. She never talked about it, and I don't think so. But I
don't really know what her birth date was.

My grandmother was a wonderful, wonderful woman, I'd say, because she let me have my way. And we didn't live too far apart from her.
And when my mother and daddy gave me a bad time, I'd go to
Grandmomma's house, so I could have my way. And I didn't get any whippings there.

My daddy worked at the sawmill. It was pretty bad. Mother and
Daddy were real poor. My grandmother walked about a mile and a half to
work. And she worked for $3 and something a week. She cleaned up houses
and cooked meals for people. And the people she worked for didn't have
any car to come pick her up, and that's why she had to walk to get to the
job. There was plenty of discrimination. One race was way apart from the
other one, so they didn't have too much; you didn't see it too much. It
was there, but you didn't run into it like you do now, you know what I

Unidentified pitcher for the Dallas Eagles, ca. 1940 (Texas African American Photography Archive)

mean? Only thing different was that when you went to the courthouse, we had separate water fountains. One was painted white; other one was painted black.

Now when we were in Conroe, Texas, during the oil boom, there was a guy. I didn't see this, I was a baby. They're supposed to have burned a guy alive in the courthouse, right downtown. I think that's the worst. Some white lady said he was looking at her. He didn't touch her, didn't say anything to her. Just staring at her. And they made a big deal out of it. And that's what happened, now, and that's what I was told. I didn't see it.

Well, when I was coming up in Conroe, the superintendent of the sawmill liked to watch baseball. And we had enough guys there to play ball. And he liked to watch us play. In Conroe they had a white team, and we had a team. And so the superintendent said, "I'm going to build you guys a park. Give you enough lumber." And our team was named the Pine Knots.

I started to playing, and they thought I was good. And I kept playing and then when I got a little older, twenty-two years old, I had played against a guy in Houston. They had a team, too. We played against each other. Well, he was the first one went to Philadelphia. He was older than I was. And he recommended me to the owner in Philadelphia. The Philadelphia Stars. And so they come down and asked me did I think I could play Major League Baseball.

I said, "Well, those guys up there are playing. I think I can do what they're doing. I learn, I think I can do what they're doing."

They said, "Well, okay, we'll give you a try. You want to go try it?"

I said, "Yeah."

So, I went, and they said, "Well, you're not up here to play around. If you don't make it, we're going to send you back to Texas."

I said, "I understand. But I want the chance. You give me the chance, and then if I don't make it, I'm going to feel bad."

So I was lucky and good enough my first year; they thought I was good enough. And that's how I started to playing. With the Philadelphia Stars.

I had gone to the black schools in Conroe. We called it Booker T. Washington. That was the name of the high school there. But I never did finish, and I didn't go to college. I went through the tenth grade. Times were so hard. And my father was working twelve hours a day, I think, for a dollar. I tried to give as much help with the house as I could. And I know now that was a mistake, but at that time, I was thinking about helping my mother and father. And I just thought that helping them meant more than finishing school at that time. I know better now. But then I didn't.

During World War II, they called me to enlist, and I think one reason I didn't go, before I went up, I had an operation, in '42, for a peptic ulcerated stomach. And they called me to go in the service. When I went to do the examination, they wanted to know what that scar was from. So I told them I had an ulcer. And they put me in 4F.

They said, "We can't give no special treatment. You got to have milk and this and that, we put you in 4F. If the war gets that bad, that's the only way you'll go."

So, anyway, when the guy came to me and asked me to go to Philadelphia, he said, "I'm going to talk to your parents."

And he went and talked to my mother and father. And they didn't want me to go. And they said, "We're going to pay him $375 a month."

So my mother said, "I still don't want him away from home."

I said, "Well, I got to go one day. Let me go try." And I said, "I will send you some money on the fifteenth, first and fifteenth."

And she said, "No, I don't want you to go, honey, but we'll make it."

So, some of our neighbors and friends found out that they wanted me to go, and they insisted to her to let me go. And she told me, "If you get up there, don't get hungry. Let Mama know. We'll find a way to get you back home." And so I was lucky and I made it, stayed and sent her a little money on the first and helped them out on the fifteenth.

When I started, I played shortstop. And I spent my first winter in Philadelphia, in '43. And after my first year, they said, "I think you done made it. We going to give you a contract for next year. We're going to give you a raise. We'll give you $400."

I said, "Great."

And during the winter of '43, a few guys from the Negro League went over to the Panama Canal to play baseball. And when they came back, they started telling Eddie Godley, the owner of the Philadelphia Stars, about a young man named Frank Austin. So Eddie Godley sent Frank Austin a ticket. And he came to Philadelphia. And during the spring training, he was the shortstop. And he could hit the ball real good. So Eddie called me in the office and asked me, said, "We want Frank Austin, he can't play no other position. Will you go to second base and let him play short?"

I said, "Yeah, help the team. Don't make me no difference."

He said, "You hit good and he hit good; we have a good team."

I said, "Okay." So that's how I wound up playing second base.

I hit about three-something my first year; it wasn't that high of an average, but I was hitting pretty good and had a pretty good batting average. And that's when they gave me a contract.

Once I had a chance to see Joe Louis, but I didn't get the opportunity because this owner I played for in Philadelphia, Eddie Godley, he said he would get me tickets. But Joe never did fight in Philadelphia at the time I was there. He was always fighting somewhere else. And that killed it. If he had ever fought in Philadelphia while I was there, I would have got a chance to see him. But I listened to his fights on the radio. Not all his fights, just a couple of fights. There were two I really listened to—the first when Schmeling whipped him, and this other guy, a good fighter, Billy Conn. He was taking the championship away from Joe Louis in that thirteenth round. But he got cocky, and Louis knocked him out. He was ahead on points, though.

We had a little old transistor Zenith radio, I never will forget it. I lost it sometime. When we weren't playing ball, we used to listen to some of the different programs. We could turn it on and get programs from Louisiana and Texas. Yeah, we listened to T-Bone Walker; I even ran into him in Tulsa once when I was in the Texas League. He come up there to perform in the club.

In the winter of 1944, after the season was over in the States, they called me to come to Puerto Rico, San Juan, Puerto Rico, to play winter ball. So I would go to Puerto Rico to play winter ball, then come back to Philadelphia and play summer ball, that's what we call it. Winter and summer. And then that's the way it went the whole time. I was that good, and that's the way they wanted me. That's how I got to go to all the different countries. Venezuela, Cuba, Puerto Rico, and Mexico.

Well, I played in the Negro League through '47, then I went and played winter ball in winter of '47. And then I got a tryout with the Sacramento and Pacific Coast League. And then I went back and had contract trouble with my bossman in Philadelphia. There were two owners there, black guy owned it, and Eddie Godley, he ran the team. And they didn't want to pay my salary, what I wanted.

And so, I said, "Well, Eddie, you can't pay me. I can get paid in Mexico." I said, "Will you release me?"

In the confusion, he said, "Well, let me talk with them." So Eddie talked with the Pascal brothers, I remember, in Mexico. And he found out what they'd pay me, what they wanted to pay me, and so he said, "Well, I can't pay you that. We're losing money, and I don't think the league's going to last too much longer."

He said, "You go ahead and play this year and see how we're going to come out. And if we get started building back up, then you come back." But every year, they were losing money, and eventually, in '50, they just folded up. I was getting $600 in Mexico with all expenses paid. And even if you make $600 in the States, you had to pay your own expenses. That's the reason I played in all them different countries.

I never hit too many home runs in one year. The most home runs I hit was in the Arizona and Mexico League, after the Negro League broke up. They had games in Phoenix and Tucson, El Paso, and a little town in Mexico called Chihuahua. I hit forty-five home runs that year. The Arizona and Mexico League was made up of American and Cuban ballplayers.

I met Jackie Robinson—I believe Jackie started in either '43 or '44, with Kansas City. But I didn't meet him until we played Kansas City and Philadelphia. And when I got to know him personally a little better was in the winter of '45. The Negro League took an all-star team to Caracas, Venezuela. And Jackie Robinson was on it, and Sam Jethro was on it. Jackie played shortstop and Sam was in the outfield.

Not long after that, Jackie Robinson, Sam Jethro, and I got a chance to try out for the Boston Red Sox in '45. You see, they had this paper in Pittsburgh, called the *Pittsburgh Courier*. And they were trying to get the Major League to let the black ballplayers play in the Major League. Wendell Smith was the editor over that black paper, and he talked to Joe Cronin in Boston. At that time Joe Cronin was the general manager of the Red Sox, and he said he would like to have three players try out for the team.

So, I was invited to come try out with Jackie Robinson and Sam Jethro. That was in 1945. We had batting practice and took infield, ground balls, and that was all. And then we was going to have three days' tryout. But the first day we were there, President Roosevelt died. And that killed everything. That shut down everything. So we just had that one day. But they was real nice.

And Joe Cronin told us, he said, "There's no doubt in my mind that you guys can play Major League Baseball, it's just that, what owner's going to take the chance of putting all of you on the team?" He said, "That's the problem. See, there's sixteen teams in the league. Well, who's going to have the nerve to put you on the team?" He said, "You can play it, but that's the problem."

Well, it wasn't until a year later, that Mr. Branch Rickey had the nerve. I'd say every black athlete, I don't care what the sport is, has to give credit to Mr. Branch Rickey of the Brooklyn Dodgers. He signed Jackie Robinson. He took the chance and put Jackie in Montreal, in the minor league in 1946. And then brought him up to the Major League in 1947. And Jackie turned out okay.

Jackie Robinson was a great guy. But he wasn't the kind that wanted to go out and have a lot of fun. He would socialize with you. Don't get me wrong. But some of us, when we checked in a hotel, some of us would go one way and the others go another. Jackie always had those pocket books. He'd always read on the bus or read in the hotel. He bought all the Mickey Spillane books. And he just liked to read all the time.

The first year Jackie played for Brooklyn, I stayed in touch with him. And when they played the Phillies. You know, Philadelphia had two teams. And when they come there, I always made it my business to contact him. Jackie had some pretty rough times. But his wife, Rachel, was wonderful. She stayed right with him.

She said, "You're going to make it."

But I tell you, after what he went through, you can take so much. He took a lot. They went into Philadelphia, and they were trying to hurt Jackie in the game. Then it got kind of nasty. So the report came out in the *Philadelphia Inquirer*. Pee Wee Reese said, "Jackie, you took enough. We are with you all the way now." And I think this is why some people might say he got bitter. Because he had taken enough and you just keep picking, and when Pee Wee and the Dodgers got behind him, he might have got a little (satisfaction). He didn't take too much now. But he had to take a lot to make it.

But he had his wife, right there, you can give her credit. Because she said, "You can handle it. They don't want you to handle it. Show them you can handle it, and you can do it. I'm going to be with you. You can do it."

And he said, "Well, if you say I'll make it, I'll make it."

And she said, "I'm going to be with you. Every step."

When Jackie was signed in '46, and when he went to the Dodgers in '47, Eddie Godley told me that he believed the New York Yankee scouts were watching me. But no one ever did contact me. The Yankees wanted "Suitcase" Simpson when he was playing for the Black New York Yankees. But the owner of the Black Yankees wanted too much money. "Suitcase" went up for a tryout to see if he was worth that much. But he never did make it. That's why they called him Suitcase Simpson, because he didn't make it with the Yankees. And he went back to the Black Yankees, but he traveled quite a bit, different teams.

Josh Gibson was the greatest hitter I ever seen. He was a big guy, about 6'4" and 240 pounds. Josh and I were in Puerto Rico the same year, the first year I went down there. Josh was a catcher.

And the best pitcher I ever saw was Satchel Paige. I played against him. Knew him, too. He was real nice. He helped a lot of ballplayers. See, Satchel made more during that time. Satchel was making more money, him and Josh were making more money than any other players was. And those guys lived in Kansas City, where he lived, and he would help them out a whole lot, financial-wise.

In the Negro League we would play mostly four games a week. We'd start Thursday—and then play Friday, Saturday, and Sunday. Most of the time, we'd be traveling on Monday and Tuesday, trying to get to the next place. We went by bus, and we'd stay in either a black hotel or in someone's rooming house. Sometimes we couldn't all be together because the hotel or the house was too small for everyone. But we wouldn't be too far apart.

The living conditions were pretty bad. And actually, we didn't check in too many places. We slept on the bus. And let me explain why I mean on the bus. Say we play ball here in Dallas this afternoon. And after the game we would go somewhere and eat, you know. Not anyplace, just some barbecue place or go in the grocery store and get some baloneys or some stuff. Now if we had to play in Houston tomorrow, after we eat, we get in the bus. The pitcher is going to start a game tomorrow. He would get on the backseat, that's the long seat, and sleep. We'd have eighteen players. All the regulars would have a seat to themselves. They were kind of like a recliner. So we would just drive from here to Houston. By the time we'd get there, it would be just about time to play. So, that's the reason I say the conditions was kind of bad. We didn't have the money to stay in too many hotels because we wasn't making that much.

They gave you, I think, a couple of dollars a day to eat off. That's when you're on the road. You'd feed yourself when you're at home. And when I was in Philadelphia I couldn't afford an apartment. When they knew I was coming to Philadelphia, I had a friend of mine, Red Parnell. He lived with a lady had an apartment, a three-bedroom apartment. And when I got there, Parnell was going to retire. And he recommended that the lady let me live with her, renting a room. Rent me a room. And so I stayed there. She was a settled lady, and she didn't have nobody but her daughter and granddaughter living in the house with her. And she was kind of ill. And she welcomed for someone to be there, in the house. So I roomed with her.

Well, if we played Kansas City, we'd either play in the Polo Grounds or the Yankee Stadium or at Connie Mack Park. See, now that's how, only way we could make money. People were going to come out to see Satchel Paige pitch. So we had to be in a Major League ballpark in order to get the people to come. But now when we weren't playing Satchel, we'd go across the river there to Camden, New Jersey, and play a semi-pro team. And you wouldn't have too many people there. But they would guarantee us a certain amount of money.

I played semi-pro, too. We had a team in Brooklyn. The company had a team down there. And I forgot the name of that team. They had a good team, semi-pro team. They all had a job there at the factory; they didn't play anywhere else. And we had a good crowd; we'd draw a good crowd there.

Teams in the East and the West, we couldn't play each other too much, because there was too much distance, you know. From one team, you come up and play one game. And you didn't have the money to be staying two or three days in the hotel. And you could barely get a hotel. So what we would do, we would book Kansas City or Birmingham in their home city with the Philadelphia Stars, and we had a doubleheader. We'd play in Birmingham the first game; then Kansas City would play somebody the second game. That's how we'd get the people in the ballpark. We played different teams in a doubleheader. And the people go to see two games for the same price.

At some of our games, they had Jesse Owns to perform. He'd run against somebody before the game. That was another way to get the people to the game. They'd advertise Jesse Owens was going to be there. But after he raced, he would go home, leave the ballpark.

There were different leagues around the country where you could play winter ball. In the West they had what was called the Pacific Coast League. And we played in cities out on the coast of Mexico. Nogales and

Hermosillo and Obregon. They called that the coast. I liked playing baseball in Mexico, but the first year was kind of hard because I couldn't get used to the food. And I couldn't speak the language too good.

After the Negro League folded up in '50, I went with the Texas League for summer ball. The Texas League had Tulsa, Dallas, and Fort Worth. San Antonio, Austin, Victoria, Houston. There were the Tulsa Oilers...the Austin Senators. Oh, it started in March, and September, I think, it was over. Labor Day. Then I'd go to Mexico, Puerto Rico, somewhere to play in the winter.

I played three years in Tulsa, '56, '57, and '58. And I went to Victoria, Texas. They bought my contract from Tulsa. The Victoria Rosebuds. I played, I think, two years with them, and then when the Texas League broke up, I went back to Mexico and played until I retired in 1962.

After I was done with baseball, I went to work for Sears and Roebuck. I made deliveries, and then in 1981 I retired from that.

The best thing about the Negro League, I believe, was playing against certain teams and wanting to win, I guess. Like the Homestead Grays. Just to win, you know. It was fun to win. Yeah. And they would brag about them going to do us this way and that way, and we'd try to disappoint them.

Baseball's a lot different today. I never seen so many guys, the money they make, come up with charley horses. And pulled muscles and pulled groins. I don't understand it. I don't think they're in shape. See, you get in shape in spring training, that's what you go for. And if you get the kind of injury that keeps you out that long, there's something wrong. It wasn't that way when I was playing. I might have a little sprained ankle. But we didn't have a trainer. You had to miss a few games, but what it was, if you had a sprained ankle, we had a little foot tub. Fill it up full of ice. Put your foot in it. Put a foot in that tub, kill the nerve, and kill the swelling and the soreness, and tape it up real good. You could play some the next day.

I just loved the game. Just wanted to play. And it was the only thing I knew to do. So I just kept it up.

Interview by Alan Govenar, December 6, 1997

Liola McClean Cravens Woffort

Miner's descendant
Life dates: unknown

Liola McClean Cravens Woffort grew up in Roslyn, Washington. She went to
school in Roslyn through the eighth grade and attended high school in nearby
Cle Elum, Washington. Her grandfather was part of a group from Illinois
recruited as strikebreakers to work in the mines owned by the North Western
Improvement Company in Washington State. Woffort recounts the stories she
heard about the treatment of black workers and provides insight into the ways in
which moving west benefitted her family.

I am a descendant of one of the members of the group of Negroes who
came out to break the strike against the N.W.I. Company during the
years 1888–1889. The term N.W.I. stands for North Western Improvement Company, which is a subsidiary of the Northern Pacific Railroad
Company. My grandmother's name was Harriet Taylor Williams. She came
out with two children: Fred Taylor, who was later employed as an adult by
the Northern Pacific Railway, in the roundhouse in Yakima, Ellensburg,
and Nellie Taylor. They were young children when they came out.

The first group was recruited in Breakwood, Illinois, by Jim
Sheppardson. They came out on the train as far as Cle Elum, Washington,
and they were put on another train and sent up the Roslyn Spur. Rumors
were that strikers in Roslyn were to blow up the train, and if my memory
serves me right, being told by older people who come out at the same
time, dynamite was found along the tracks. The newcomers came through
Roslyn with shotguns, revolvers, and so forth, loaded to protect the families and other people on the train. The newcomers were allowed to stay in
Roslyn for a number of years but made their home at Jonesville, later
named Ronald, Washington, also known among the settlers as Number 3.
The reason was not so much that they were prejudiced against Negroes,
but just the fact that they were strikebreakers.

They had come out to break the strike, to work in the mines where
the Caucasians were unable to do this because they were on a strike. And
I started to say that also they would come down, and they had to be protected when they went in the mines and they had to be protected when
they came into Roslyn to buy their food supply. But in later years, and it
was a very short period of time, when the strike was over, the Negroes
settled in Roslyn. They bought homes; some of them continued to work in
the mines.

Mother often speaks about being told about how some people walked down there and they had to be out by nighttime. You know, they could come to Roslyn and you had to be out, and about one lady's husband (who) left her and how she come down there. She used to come down and work in Roslyn to make money so she could take care of her children. Then she'd walk back up the railroad and go back to, I call it Number 3. It will be Number 3 to me until I die…. It was called Number 3 because of the mine up there. The big mine was called Number 3 mine. They brought them down. They would come and protect them on horse and wagon.

And I'd like to say among the group that came out, there is one living member that I know of, and that is Mrs. Eva Strong. And she was a very young babe in arms when she came out, in her mother's arms when she came out. And she still lives in Roslyn, Washington. A group of people that came here, Negro people that came and settled here, in Roslyn, and eventually so many people that you will find that were here before the 1930s at one time passed through the towns of Roslyn, Cle Elum, seeking work. Then they have come to Seattle, Spokane, Yakima, and so forth. But their descendants, there are plenty of descendants living that descended from these people.

One thing I can remember about is that as far as going to school, I don't think she (Mother) encountered any more prejudice than you would now in school. The schools were open, and if you were willing to study, you would get a wonderful education. My mother went to the ninth grade and I think she was just as well learned as many a person as went into college. Because one thing you will find…that if you had the mind to learn they didn't pay too much attention to your color. As a matter of fact, we have one of the descendant's grandchildren come through and graduated as the first Negro valedictorian here.

I know her first name was Lillian. She is deceased now, but she graduated from what you call Central Washington College. It used to be called the Old Ellensburg Normal School at that time. So I do believe that, I mean, they could put their children through school, those that you know. But then again, there were quite a few Negroes and white children, about age of sixteen, because they had to go to school, they would work in the mine, you know, for their livelihood.

There were quite a few of them (blacks). And if you talk to her, you will find out that there were quite a few and, also, as Mother said, the people there were Italian and Slavic and Croatian and English, and they get along just like they do now. Matter of fact, Mother had quite a few friends among, you know, the different (groups) because many of their parents were immigrants and the children my mother's age were the first generation to be born here in the United States. So they had language problems; where maybe my mother's problem was being Negro, theirs was trying to speak English because they would speak the foreign language at home and then learn English....

And if you were English, you married an English girl or an English boy. And if you were Irish, you married an Irish boy or an Irish girl, but there were mixed marriages. And there were records of several that was there. And therefore they were kind of ostracized by both. And if you were Negro, you married Negro. And I think that this is what they wanted. Those few did pass, in later years, well, it wasn't so bad, I mean there were prejudices among the different groups there all the way around. And then you'll also hear this from my mother she'll tell you, because Italians had their dances, and nobody but Italians went.

Certain kids lived downtown, and as I said there was a group of children called the downtown kids. They were tough. There were the Brookside kids; they were tough. Then there was a group of Negroes who lived on Wall Street at that time, and they were tough. And they had, I can't remember this hill, up on Brewery Hill. It was called Brewery Hill because it had a brewery there. They were tough in Swede town. And, as a matter of fact, the kids just fought among themselves, back and forth. We laugh about this at our reunions, and even the people laugh at themselves about this. But as far as to say that it was just because you were black, no. It was just that there was the difference of language, and naturally with the Negroes, it could have been the difference of skin. And I mean everybody fought to get to school, they fought to get home. But when you got to school, no fighting was allowed. And as far as the schools were concerned, educational facilities, I think that they were good myself.

We started school in the late 1920s, myself, that's when I went. And I finished to the eighth grade there in Roslyn. Then I went to Cle Elum High School, in Cle Elum. And as far as learning, the prejudice there wasn't so much.

There were two blacks and about twenty others. Because South Roslyn had a school at the time. And there would have been more from the South Roslyn School. But it was several teachers who came to teach. And I can remember being asked to sing in the operetta because I was a Negro. So I got in every night free, but now I realize it was, you know, because we were Negroes. But the teacher that did this she come out of Portland. She come out of Oregon.

Well, there was room for us to go to these things, but we had to go down by bus, and the transportation was bad. You may not be able to get down there. Yes, and we'd go on the bus and you have to be back by a certain time to get on the bus. And people didn't have cars to put the children in, to carry their children that three miles (from Roslyn to Cle Elum). If there was something special Daddy would take us down to it. As far as that, I belonged to the girls' club. I was in the glee club, and that was about the only thing I myself was...participating in. At the assemblies, we sang, the girls who had very beautiful voices, we sang. And I can say as far as prejudice was concerned, some of it was there.

We didn't have the jobs, but by the time you cut your wood and brought your coal in and helped your mother bring out the clothes.... We had a big, three-story house. And then later Mother moved to a smaller house, in the late years. Then they moved down to where they live at now. I have four brothers and eight sisters. And there's one girl that passed when she was about two years old there.

You know during the strike, some of the things that would happen...the men wouldn't do so much, the women would come and, well, they would come in, well, they would come and bring men their lunch bucket and do things that wasn't right, and you know the average man, at that day and age, would not strike a woman. And so their wives would do a lot of these things, of, course, the men were doing enough. They would call them "scabby," because we used to be called "scabby kids" and things like that.

But, you know a scab is something that's been over a sore, so that is something they probably meant...scabby kids. And then we had names for them, you know, the same strike. I can remember them having a dance, and one man being killed and leaving his children without a father there to take care of them because he had to suffer for this. As a matter of fact, there's still some feeling right now concerning the strike. This among the whites. As far as the Negroes, they were on the western mines side then, and for a while the people that were working for the western miners were unable to get a job there for the Northern Pacific. You know, the Northern Pacific Improvement Company. But in later years, as wartime come along, and the coal was needed, some of these same people were hired. Some of them migrated away, they came to Seattle, Renton, and different places. But there are some hard feelings every now and then when it's Labor Day, you will hear some big discussions concerning this, you know, same strike.

Interview by Larry Gossett, February 2, 1968
Courtesy Special Collections, Manuscripts and University Archives
University of Washington, Seattle

Barbara Wood

Teacher

Born: July 29, 1914, Abbeville, South Carolina

In many ways, Barbara Wood embodies the frontier spirit of getting ahead through hard work in a new place. She moved from her hometown, Abbeville, South Carolina, to the Chicago suburb of Evanston, Illinois, in 1933, when she was eighteen. Wood was part of a black exodus from the Abbeville area that began with the 1916 lynching of Anthony Crawford, a prosperous black cotton farmer.

Wood's family stressed education, and that was her primary goal in moving north, though it took years to achieve it. Married and widowed twice, she has five children. Nonetheless, she continued going to school when she could earn a master's degree in education in her late forties. She became one of the city's first black teachers and taught elementary school twenty-three years.

In Evanston, she found a social life among the sizable community of emigrants from the area where she grew up. Church played a big role in her life. Overall, she is content, though she would have pursued her dream of becoming a college professor, given the opportunity.

I'm very fortunate, fairly good health, and my mental condition has not deteriorated measurably. I'm forgetful sometimes. Some of the people who were my peers are gone.

I came here (Evanston, Illinois) when I was eighteen, about 1933, and the World's Fair was going on up here, and that was so exciting for me. But I came here primarily to continue my education. My father wasn't well, and my mother wasn't either, and they had sent me away to Benedict College in South Carolina for one year.

Our background in the South is limited, so I've learned a lot here. I don't think I felt scared. I was always adventurous. People my age, Afro-Americans, were always somewhat restricted. There were things in Evanston that reminded me of the South because you were not allowed to shop; at least you were not accepted. There were jobs you could not hold because of your color whether your ability warranted it or not. There were many places, restaurants, especially, that blacks could not enter because you would not be served. Blacks in Evanston would have to go to Chicago. There were no black teachers in the schools. I was one of the first black teachers to cross the line.

Well, you know, Evanston is kind of small, and there were lots of people that knew me. I joined the church (Ebenezer AME), and I felt at home, kind of like a home away from home. A substantial portion of the people were from Abbeville, at least a third. A lot of them were from Abbeville proper, and then the surrounding area.

The reception there was warm, and you know, the excitement of being able to go to Chicago on the elevated. There was Riverview Park, and there were so many exciting things to do at that age, eighteen, going on nineteen, and I was excited with the bright lights. But a little later, I applied to enter school, and things worked out pretty well for me except that things were very tight, money-wise. Blacks were not able to get jobs, for the most part, other than domestic kinds of work, and I thought I was smart enough to get something else. People of my own race would invite me to dinner. I began to join clubs, organizations. Black people were great on having their own clubs because they had to for their social outlet. I became a Sunday school teacher pretty early on.

I came by train; that's the way we used to travel, by the Dixie Limited or the Dixie Flyer, two trains. When I went back to see my parents, they tried to get me to move, and I didn't. This woman in Montgomery [Rosa Parks] was not the first woman who refused to give up her seat. It's never that way, with almost anything, with research, with inventions. I was on the train, and it always left Chicago, going to Atlanta, and then we had to change to get to Abbeville. In Chicago, you sat with anybody, and I was sitting next to a white man, and we were talking. I saw all these people getting up. It must have been my first trip back, and I didn't know you had to move. I thought to myself, "They must be getting off." After a long time, the train was moving along, and then the little conductor, a little short guy, came in and asked me to move. He said, "You know, it's against the law for white and black to ride together." I don't think the Supreme Court had ruled, but I knew this was in the making, and I said, "Well, you know, the Supreme Court doesn't say that." I had been over here about four years, so it must have been the late thirties. There was some discussion about interstate travel. I said that, but it was really not true.

He came back several times, and I said, "I'm comfortable here where I am." I kept telling him I was comfortable. He was kind of nice; he wasn't too agitated. But then he went on back. And so the next morning, there were always these black guys working on the train, Pullman porters and all, and so one of them told me, "You know, we're really proud of you. We were talking about you back there. The superintendent said, 'Well, you really can't make her get off.' " And so I became a little frightened myself. I thought, "You know, they could have thrown you off that train." But I shall always remember it. I kept my seat, and nobody else said anything to me. It was in Evansville, Indiana. That's where the Mason-Dixon Line was.

When I came back that time my sister and I were together, we came through Atlanta and we were so hungry, we just wanted to get something to eat. We had a break. We went to a dime store, and we just wanted hot

dogs. And we stood and stood, and the people came and sat and were waited on. The people who were working behind the counter, they continued to wash their dishes and glasses and everything. They never did wait on us, and we finally had to leave. That was our experience then. I shall never forget that.

Now we couldn't have a place at the Eureka Hotel (now the Belmont Inn in Abbeville) at that time. My father worked there for years. He was head waiter and then he had a business, a dray business. You know, that word you don't hear anymore. I brought that out in my class one time, and nobody knew it. He worked at the hotel, and he hired a man to haul things around. They would haul trunks; they didn't have all these modes of transportation like they have now. His name was Allen McKellar. My mother's name was Essie Watt McKellar. And preceding them were my grandparents, Robert and Sally Watt. My grandfather was the blacksmith in the town of Abbeville. That was a very important trade at that time.

My parents told me about the lynching (of Anthony Crawford in 1916). But I came here primarily to continue my education. I continued to take courses here and there. I got married and became the mother of five children. My husband died, and I started my own little business, catering. Then I went back to school and got a job right here in Evanston as a teacher, and I taught for twenty-three years. I was teaching in elementary school. That was not my original idea. I was going to be a professor, I guess. But then I had to go the most sensible way that I thought would work out best for me because I still had children to think of.

I enjoyed teaching, I really did. I retired in 1982. I stayed on beyond sixty-five. I was sixty-seven, almost sixty-eight. The last time I went back to Abbeville was in 1981, for the fiftieth anniversary of our class. My mother, after my father died, she came up here and lived with me. I don't have any family in Abbeville itself, but my sister lives in Antreville.

There are a lot of people here now from the Cokesbury area now. And they meet throughout the country where people have gone. They were here this past year. Usually near summer. Well now, they can go to the Eureka Hotel.

All these things came very slowly. I was determined; my parents and grandparents, they all wanted us to be educated. It took me many years. If I had not been very poor, I could have gone further. I got a master's degree in education in my late forities. I has been a long trail a-winding, but it has paid off.

INTERVIEW BY JAY BRAKEFIELD, FEBRUARY 6, 1998

Wesley Young

Rodeo cowboy
Born: September 2, 1917, Beggs, Oklahoma

Wesley Young discusses the experiences growing up in rural Oklahoma that led him to become a professional cowboy. He talks about the African American cowboys who influenced him and the racism he endured as a competitor with white cowboys. In the 1940s and 1950s, Young operated a rodeo arena at his farm in Boynton, Oklahoma.

When I was twelve years old, my cousin Raynes Belton put me on an old roping horse named Levi, gave me a rope, and turned me loose to practice roping goats and I been roping ever since! When I caught my first goat I was hooked. It was such a thrill. I knew that I wanted to do this all of my life.

My mother supported me, but my daddy sure didn't. He never did like my roping. He said, "A horse ain't for rodeo playing 'round with. A horse is for plowing!" He didn't want me to have no rope, no horse, no bridle, no saddle! He just wanted me to plow. I sure wish that he had liked roping and could have supported me. I know I could have been really good. I could have been another Will Rogers. I just wish my daddy could have been proud of my roping.

When Mama died in 1929, I became serious about my roping. Oh, those were some good old days for cowboying! Us black cowboys stuck together like glue. There was Emory Metcalfe, Homer Silas, Jim Shoulders,

Unidentified black cowboy. Undated photograph. (Texas African American Photography Archive)

Jess Goodspeed, and some others. All of the Metcalfe family was into rodeoing. Emory's boys, Emory Jr., Benny, and Clyde, performed just like their daddy. But Benny got killed in a car wreck, and Emory Jr. got shot to death by his woman; she just shot him in the head during an argument! Clyde Metcalfe is still rodeoing and making movies and television shows out in Hollywood and in Tucson, Arizona. He was in that movie, *The Young Guns,* which starred Emilio Estevez and Kiefer Sutherland. Two Tulsa cowboys were also in that film, thirty-nine-year-old twins Donald and Ronald Stephens, who are also Tulsa firemen. Metcalfe and them Stephens twins were also in the television series, *The Desperados*. Metcalfe was a stand-in for one of the leads, Billy Dee Williams, and the Stephens twins played Buffalo Soldiers. That's the way it is today. In addition to rodeoing, cowboys also make films and movies, and some of them write articles and books about rodeoing, like Donald Stephens does. But in the old days, we just rodeoed.

It was rough for black cowboys in those days. There was so much prejudice and discrimination then. Blacks didn't get a fair chance then. We weren't allowed to participate in the main events. They let us pass the hats to collect the money or they let us perform in the unimportant opening acts. And when we began to break through and perform in the bigger events, there was resistance from some of the white cowboys and from the paying spectators. We were called racial names by some white people in the audience. You know, the big "N" word! That is why some of the black cowboys just stop trying to break into white rodeoin' and formed their own all-black rodeos, like the LeBlancs in Okmulgee. Rodeoin' was real popular with black folks. In the forties and fifties, I opened up my farm here in Boynton to accommodate Tulsa rodeo fans. So many Tulsans came to my weekend rodeos, you could hardly walk out here!

It's true that there was a lot of racism then and that some white folks mistreated us black cowboys, but there were some good white folks, too, and I have some pleasant memories, too, from them rodeoing days. For instance, there was Red Holmes, who sold cars and trucks in Henryetta, Oklahoma. Henryetta was an-all white town that was noted for its prejudice towards blacks. In fact, it had a "Sundown" law, which meant that blacks could not be in the town after sundown. Well, I broke that law all the time. I was always in that town talking to the cowboys who lived there. I didn't have no better sense than to be in that town any time of day or night. One time, someone jokingly said I was gonna get in trouble in Henryetta some night. But Old Red spoke up. He said, "Wes, if anybody messes with you, you just get to a telephone and call me. I'll have them rascals put away for good if they bother you!" Old Red was a good friend. He sure did like me. 'Course, he sure caused me a lot of friction with "Little Mama" (my wife Valdonia). You see, it was Red that got me on the rodeo circuit, which took me away from my wife and three children so much of the time.

Red got me on the rodeo circuit this way. One day we was just sitting around talking about rodeoing and Red said to me, "Wes, why don't you rodeo for me?"

I said, "Man I can't rodeo for you. I got a wife and three kids, and we're all on starvation."

He said, "You don't have to stay on starvation no more." He kept pestering me to go on the rodeo circuit under his sponsorship. He said I was good at calf roping and that I could make some big money. He said I could get started in Fort Worth, Texas, right away. I said, "Man, I ain't got no car, no truck for rodeoing. All I got is that old, beat-up secondhand truck setting over yonder."

Red said to me, "See those cars and trucks over there. I got acres of them. Go pick you one and don't worry about paying for it." So that's how I got the truck and trailer to carry my roping horse in. That's how I got into the rodeo circuit.

I went home and talked it over with Little Mama. She wasn't too happy about me going on the rodeo circuit, but she tolerated it if I wasn't gone too long and if I came home when I said I was comin'. Once she chewed me out good because instead of coming home like I had promised, I went and hooked up with another rodeo.

She said, "Now you look here. You're gone all the time away from me and these children. I'll tell you one thing, I'm not gonna put up with it. When you say you're gonna be back a certain time, I want you back then, or on the road coming back. I don't want you meeting someone by the side of the road and loadin' your horse onto somebody's trailer and going off somewhere else!" She was right. 'Course, even after her ultimatum, I just couldn't resist loading up my horse and hooking up with some other rodeo sometimes when I should have been going home. I still got into hot water with Little Mama sometimes.

Things have changed in rodeoing. Cowboys were more flexible then. We competed in many events; today, everything is so specialized. Performers compete in just one field. Then, we did everything! Cowboys are faster today due to faster horses, better ropes, and better-fed, healthier cowboys. Records are being broken every day. In the old days, ropin' a calf in sixteen or seventeen seconds was considered great; today it had better be done in seven to nine seconds. The first time a cowboy tied a calf up in twelve seconds, it was like a man going to the moon! Yeah, things sure have changed. But I liked it best in the old days. I sure do miss them days, and all of my cowboy friends, and Old Red. I even miss the little spats with Little Mama over my rodeoing. She was a good woman, a good wife and mother. And the children turned out just fine. Sometimes, I get out my rope and practice just like I did when I was twelve years old and Cousin Raynes turned me out to rope them goats. I still get a thrill every time I rope a calf. Rodeoin' is just in my blood. I'll be a roping till I die. There's just one thing I regret. I sure wish that Papa had liked my ropin'. I wish he could have supported me.

INTERVIEW BY EDDIE FAYE GATES, MAY–AUGUST, 1994
COURTESY OKLAHOMA HISTORICAL SOCIETY
ARCHIVES AND MANUSCRIPT DIVISION, ORAL HISTORY DEPARTMENT

Aaron. *Light of Truth and Slavery. Aaron's History in Virginia, New Jersey, and Rhode Island.* Worcester, Massachusetts, n.d. At Library of Congress.

"Adam Negro's Tryall." Edited by Abner C. Goodell. In *Publications of the Colonial Society of Massachusetts Transactions,* pp. 103–112.

Adams, John Quincy. *Narrative of the Life of John Quincy Adams, When in Slavery and Now as a Freeman.* Harrisburg, Pennsylvania, 1872. At Schomburg.

Alexander, Archer. *The Story of Alexander Archer, from Slavery to Freedom, March 30, 1863.* As related to William Greenleaf Eliot. Boston: Cupples, Upham, and Company, 1855. At Massachusetts State Library.

Allen, Richard. *The Life, Experiences, and Gospel Labors of the Right Reverend Richard Allen.* Philadelphia: Martin and Boden, 1833. At the Schomburg.

Anderson, John. *Story of John Anderson, Fugitive Slave.* Edited by Harper Twelvetrees, Chairman, John Anderson Committee. London: W. Tweedie, 1863. At Schomburg.

Anderson, Robert. *From Slavery to Affluence, Memoirs of Robert Anderson, Ex-Slave.* Hemingsford, Nebraska, 1927. At New York Public Library.

Anderson, Thomas. *Interesting Account of Thomas Anderson, a Slave, "Taken from His Own Lips."* Dictated to J. P. Clark. n.p., 1854 At Oberlin.

Archer, Armstrong. *A Compendium of Slavery as It Exists in the Present Day.* London: J. Haddon, 1844. At Massachusetts State Library.

Arthur. *The Life and Dying Speech of Arthur.* A Broadside. Boston: Printed and sold at Milk Street, 1768. New York Historical Society copy.

Aunt Sally; or, The Cross the Way to Freedom. Narrative of the Slave Life and Purchase of the Mother of Reverend Isaac Williams of Detroit, Michigan. Cincinnati: Western Tract and Book Society, 1858. At Schomburg.

_____. American Reform Tract and Book Society, 1862. At Schomburg.

Ball, Charles. *Slavery in the United States: A Narrative of the Life and Adventures of Charles Ball, a Black Man, Who Lived Forty Years in Maryland, South Carolina, and Georgia as a*

Slave. Prepared by Fisher from the verbal narrative by Ball. Lewiston, Pennsylvania: J. W. Shugert, 1836. At Schomburg.

_____. New York: J. S. Taylor, 1837. At Andover Seminary.

_____. Edited by Mrs. Alfred Barnard. London, 1846. At Harvard.

_____. Pittsburgh: J. T. Shryock, 1853. At Library of Congress.

_____. New York and Indianapolis: Dayton and Asher, 1859. At Schomburg.

_____. *Fifty Years in Chains; or, The Life of an American Slave*. New York: Dayton and Asher, 1858. At Library of Congress.

Bayley, Solomon. *Incidents in the Life of Solomon Bayley*. Philadelphia: Tract Association of Friends, No. 99, ca. 1820. At Harvard.

_____. *Narrative of Some Remarkable Incidents in the Life of Solomon Bayley, Formerly a Slave in the State of Delaware, Written by Himself, Published for His Benefit by Richard Hunard*. London, 1825. At Schomburg.

Bibb, Henry. *Narrative of the Life and Adventures of Henry Bibb, an American Slave, Written by Himself*. Introduction by Lucius C. Matlack. New York: Published for the author, 1849. At Schomburg.

_____. New York, 1850. At Massachusetts State Library.

Black, Leonard. *Life and Sufferings of Leonard Black, a Fugitive from Slavery, Written by Himself*. New York: Press of Benjamin Lindsay, 1847. At Schomburg.

Blake, Jane. *Memoirs of Margaret Jane Blake*. Related to Sarah R. Levering, Baltimore, whose father had owned Jane Blake. Philadelphia: Innes and Son, 1897. At Library of Congress.

Boen, William. *Anecdotes and Memoir of William Boen, a Colored Man, Who Lived and Died near Mount Holly, New Jersey. To Which Is Added the Testimony of Friends of Mount Holly Monthly Meeting Concerning Him*. Philadelphia: Printed by John Richards, 1834. At New York Historical Society.

Brown, Henry Box. *Narrative of Henry Box Brown, Who Escaped from Slavery Enclosed in a Box Three Feet Long, Two Wide, and Two and a Half High. Written from a Statement of Facts Made by Himself*. With remarks upon the remedy for slavery by Charles Stearns. Boston: Brown and Stearns, 1849. At Schomburg.

_____. Manchester, England, 1851. At Library of Congress.

Brown, Jane. *Narrative of the Life of Jane Brown and Her Two Children*. Related to the Reverend G. W. Offley. Hartford: Published for G. W. Offley, 1860. At Schomburg.

Brown, John. *Slave Life in Georgia: A Narrative of the Life, Sufferings, and Escape of John Brown, a Fugitive Slave, Now in England*. Edited by L. A. Chamerovzow. London: W. M. Watts, 1855. At Schomburg.

Brown, William Wells. *Narrative of William Wells Brown, a Fugitive Slave, Written by Himself*. Boston: The Anti-Slavery Office, 1847. At Schomburg.

_____. *Life of William Wells Brown*. Boston: Bela Marsh, 1848. At Boston Public Library.

_____. *Narrative of the Life of William Wells Brown*. Boston: Bela Marsh, 1849. At Harvard.

_____. *Illustrated Edition of the Life and Escape of William Wells Brown*. London: C. Gilpin, 1851. At New York Public Library.

_____. *Three Years in Europe; or, Places I have Seen and People I Have Met*. With a memoir of the author, by William Farmer. London: C. Gilpin, 1852. At Boston Public Library.

_____. *Clotel; or, The President's Daughter: A Narrative of Slave Life in the United States, with a Sketch of the Author's Life*. London: Partridge and Oakey, 1853. At Boston Public Library.

_____. *Places and People Abroad, by William Wells Brown, a Fugitive Slave, with a Memoir of the Author*. Boston: John P. Jewett, 1854. At Schomburg.

_____. *The American Fugitive in Europe; Sketches of Places and People Abroad, with a Memoir of the Author*, 1855. At Schomburg.

Bruce, Henry Clay. *The New Man: Twenty-Nine Years a Slave, Twenty-Nine Years a Free Man*. Recollections of H. C. Bruce. York, Pennsylvania: P. Anstadt and Sons, 1895. At Schomburg.

Bruner, Peter. *A Slave's Advances toward Freedom, Not Fiction, but the True Story of a Struggle*. Oxford, Ohio, n.d. At Schomburg.

Burns, Anthony. *Narrative*. Boston, 1858. At Boston Public Library.

Burton, Annie L. *Memories of Childhood's Slavery Days*. Boston, 1919. At Schomburg.

Campbell, Israel. *Bond and Free; or, Yearnings for Freedom, from My Green Brier House; Being the Story of My Life in Bondage and My Life in Freedom*. Philadelphia, 1861. At Schomburg.

Carver, George Washington. *From Captivity to Fame*. Written by Raleigh H. Merritt. Boston: Meador Publishing Company, ca. 1929.

Chandler, Charles. *The Story of a Slave*. n.p, 1894. At Schomburg.

Clarke, Lewis Garrard. *Narrative of the Sufferings of Lewis Clarke, during a Captivity of More than Twenty-Five Years among the Algerines of Kentucky*. Dictated by himself, written by Joseph C. Lovejoy. Boston: D. H. Eli, 1845. At Schomburg.

Clarke, Lewis Garrard, and Milton Clarke. *Narratives of the Sufferings of Lewis and Milton Clarke, Sons of a Soldier of the Revolution; during a Captivity of More than Twenty Years among the Slaveholders of Kentucky, One of the So-Called Christian States of North America*. Boston: Bela Marsh, 1848. At Schomburg.

Cooper, Thomas. *Narrative of the Life of Thomas Cooper*. New York: Isaac T. Hopper, 1832. At Moorland Foundation.

_____. 4th ed. New York: Isaac T. Hopper, 1837. New York: Arthur Spingarn Library.

Craft, William. *Running a Thousand Miles for Freedom; or, The Escape of William and Ellen Craft from Slavery*. London: W. Tweedie, 1860. At Schomburg.

Davis, Noah. *A Narrative of the Life of Reverend Noah Davis, a Colored Man, Written by Himself.* Baltimore: J. F. Weishampel, Jr., 1859. At Schomburg.

Dinah. *The Story of Dinah, as Related to John Hawkins Simpson, after Her Escape from the Horrors of the Virginia Slave Trade, to London.* London: A. W. Bennett, 1863. At Library of Congress.

Douglass, Frederick. *Narrative of the Life of Frederick Douglass, an American Slave, Written by Himself.* Boston: Published at the Anti-Slavery Office, 1845. At Schomburg.

_____. Dublin: Webb and Chapman, 1845. At Schomburg.

_____. 3d English ed. Wortley, near Leeds: Printed by J. Barker, 1846. At Boston Public Library.

_____. Boston: Bela Marsh, 1850. At Boston Public Library.

_____. *My Bondage and My Freedom.* Part 1: "Life as a Slave," Part II: "Life as a Freeman." New York and Auburn: Miller, Orton, and Mulligan, 1855. At Schomburg.

_____. *Sclaverie und Freiheit Autobiographie.* Aus dem englischen ubertragen von Ottilie Assing. Hamburg: Hoffman und Campe, 1860. At Boston Public Library.

_____. *The Life and Times of Frederick Douglass.* Harford: Connecticut Park Publishing Company, 1881. At Schomburg.

_____. New rev. ed. Boston: De Wolfe, Fiske, and Company, 1892. At Schomberg.

_____. Published for the Frederick Douglass Historical and Cultural League, in preparation for the One Hundredth Anniversary of Douglass's First Public Appearance in the Cause of Emancipation. Substantially a reprint of the last revised and complete work. Introduction by Alaine Locke. New York: Pathway Press, 1941. Also, Centenary Memorial Subscribers' Edition. At New York Public Library.

_____. *Vie de Frederic Douglass, esclave americain, ecrite par lui-meme.* Tr. de l'anglais par S. K. Parkes. Paris: Pagnerre, 1848. At Boston Public Library.

Drumgoold, Kate. *A Slave Girl's Story, The Autobiography of Kate Drumgoold.* Brooklyn, New York, 1898. At Library of Congress.

Eldridge, Elleanor. *Elleanor's Second Book.* Providence, 1839. At Library of Congress.

_____. *Memoirs of Elleanor Eldridge.* Providence, 1843. At Moorland Foundation.

_____. *Memoirs.* Providence, Rhode Island, 1846. At Boston Public Library.

Equiano, Olaudah. *The Interesting Narrative of the Life of Olaudah Equiano, or Gustavus Vassa, the African, Written by Himself.* London: Entered at Stationers' Hall, 1789. At Schomburg.

_____. 2d ed. London, 1789. At Library Company, Ridgeway Brothers, Philadelphia.

_____. 3d ed., enlarged. London, 1790. At Schomburg. *Merkwaardige Lebensgevallen van Olaudah Equiano or Gustavus Vassa, den Afrikaan, eertyds een Negerslaaf.* Rotterdam, 1790. At Boston Public Library.

_____. *The Interesting Narrative of Olaudah Equiano, or Gustavs Vassa, the African: an authoritative text written by himself.* 1st American ed. New York: W. Durell, 1791. At Schomburg.

_____. Dublin, 1791. At Yale University.

_____. London, 1794. At Atlanta University.

_____. Norwich, 1794. At Harvard.

_____. London and Nottingham, 1809.

_____. To which was added poems on various subjects by Phillis Wheatley. Halifax, 1813. At Schomburg.

_____. New ed., corrected. London: J. Nichols, 1815. At Harvard.

_____. Abridged by A. Mott. New York, 1829. At Schomburg.

_____. Boston: Isaac Knapp, 1837. At Harvard.

_____. *Oder Gustav Vassa's des Africaners Mertwurdige lebensgeschichte von ihm geschrieben uns dem Englischen ubersetzt.* Gottingen: Dieterich, 1792. At Schomburg.

Fedric, Francis. *Slave Life in Virginia and Kentucky; or, Fifty Years of Slavery in the Southern States of America. By Francis Fedric, an Escaped Slave.* London: Wertheim, MacIntosh, and Hunt, 1863. At Schomburg.

Frederick, Reverend Francis. *Autobiography of Reverend Francis Frederick, of Virginia.* Baltimore: J. W. Woods, 1869. At New York Public Library.

Grandy, Moses. *Narrative of the Life of Moses Grandy, Late a Slave in the United States of America.* London: C. Gilpin, 1843. At Library of Congress.

_____. 1st American ed. from the last London ed. Boston: O. Johnson, 1844. At Harvard.

_____. 2d American ed. Boston: O. Johnson, 1844. At New York Public Library.

Green, J. D. *Narrative of the Life of J. D. Green, a Runaway Slave from Kentucky, Containing an Account of His Three Escapes, in 1839, 1846, and 1848.* Huddersfield: Printed by Henry Fielding, 1864. At New York Public Library.

Green, William. *Narrative of Events in the Life of William Green, Formerly a Slave, Written by Himself.* Springfield, Massachusetts: L. M. Guernsey, 1853. At Library of Congress.

Grimes, William. *Life of William Grimes, the Runaway Slave, Written by Himself.* New York, 1825. At Boston Public Library.

_____. *Life of William Grimes, the Runaway Slave, Brought Down to the Present Time, Written by Himself.* New Haven, Connecticut: Published by the author, 1855. At New York Historical Society.

Gronniosaw, James Albert Ukawsaw. *A Narrative of the Most Remarkable Particulars in the Life of James Albert Ukawsaw Gronniosaw, An African Prince, as Related by Himself.* 2d ed. n.p., n.d. At Harvard.

_____. Reprint. Newport, Rhode Island: S. Southwick, 1774. At Library of Congress.

_____. *Berr Hanes Pethau Mwaf Hynod ym Mywyd James Albert Ukawsaw Gronniosaw, Troysog o Affrica: fel yr Adroddqyd Ganddo ef ei hun.* Aberhomddu, Argraphwyd dros y Parch. Mr. W. Williams and E. Evans, 1779. At Harvard.

_____.*A Narrative of the Most Remakable Particulars in the Life of James Albert Ukawsaw Gronniosaw, an African Prince, Etc.* Bath: W. Gye and T. Mills, 1780. At New York Public Library.

_____. *A Narrative of the Most Remarkable Particulars in the Life of James Albert Akawsaw [sicl; as Dictated by Himself.* 2d American ed. Catskill, New York: Printed at the Eagle Office, 1810. At the American Antiquarian Society.

_____. *A Narrative of the Most Remarkable Particulars in the Life of James Albert Ukawsaw Gronniosaw, an African Prince as Related by Himself.* Leeds: Printed by Davies and Booth, at the Stanhope Press, Vicar-Lane, 1814. At the New York Historical Society.

Hall, Elder Samuel. *Forty-Seven Years a Slave; a Brief Story of His Life as a Slave and after Freedom.* Washington, Georgia, 1912. At Atlanta University.

Hammon, Briton. *A Narrative of the Uncommon Sufferings, and Surprizing [sic] Deliverance of Briton Hammon, a Negro Man, Servant to General Winslow, of Marshfield, in New-England; Who Returned to Boston, after having been absent almost Thirteen Years. Containing an Account of the many Hardships he underwent from the time he left his master's house, in the year 1747, to the Time of his Return to Boston.——How he was cast away in the Capes of Florida;——the horrid Cruelty and inhuman barbarity of the Indians in murdering the whole Ship's Crew;——the Manner of his being carry'd by them into captivity. Also, An Account of his being Confined Four Years and Seven Months in a close Dungeon.——and the remarkable Manner in which he met with his good old Master in London; who returned to New-England, a Passenger, in the same Ship.* Boston: Printed and sold by Green and Russell, in Queen-Street, 1760. At New York Historical Society.

Hammon, Jupiter. *An Address to the Negroes in the State of New York. By Jupiter Hammon, Servant of John Lloyd, Jun. Esq. of the Manor of Queen's Village, Long Island.* New York: Printed by Carroll and Patterson, 1787. At New York Historical Society.

_____. Philadelphia: Reprinted by David Humphreys, in Spruce Street, 1787. At New York Public Library.

_____. New York: Samuel Wood, 1806. At Arthur Spingarn Library.

Hayden, William. *Narrative of William Hayden, Containing a Faithful Account of His Travels for a Number of Years, Whilst a Slave in the South, Written by Himself.* Cincinnati: Published for the Author, 1846. At Boston Public Library.

Henson, Josiah. *The Life of Josiah Henson, Formerly a Slave, Now an Inhabitant of Canada, as Narrated by Himself to Samuel Eliot.* Boston: A. D. Phelps, 1849. At Schomburg.

_____. With preface by T. Binney. London, 1851. At Schomburg.

_____. London, 1852. At Harvard.

_____. *Truth Stranger than Fiction: Father Henson's Story of His Own Life.* With an introduction by Harriet B. Stowe. Boston: J. P. Jewett and Company; and Cleveland: H. P. B. Jewett, 1858. At New York Public Library.

_____. Dutch trans. Dolgellan, 1877. At Harvard.

_____. French trans. Paris, 1878. At Harvard.

_____. *An Autobiography of the Reverend Josiah Henson, Mrs. H. B. Stowe's "Uncle Tom," from 1789 to 1879.* With a preface by Mrs. H. B. Stowe, introductory notes by

Wendell Phillips and J. G. Whittier, and an appendix on the exodus by Bishop Gilbert Haven. Boston: B. B. Russell and Company, 1879. At Harvard.

_____. Edited by John Lobb. Revised and enlarged, 1789 to 1881, with introduction by George Sturge, S. Morely, Esq., M. P., Wendell Phillips, and J. G. Whittier. London and Ontario: Schuyler, Smith, and Company, 1881. At Harvard.

Horton, George Moses. *The Hope of Liberty, Poems: George Moses Horton, Myself.* Raleigh: Printed by J. Gales and Son, 1829. At Library of Congress.

_____. 2d ed., reprinted under the title, *Poems by a Slave.* Philadelphia, 1837. At Schomburg.

Hughes, Louis. *Thirty Years a Slave, from Bondage to Freedom. The Institution of Slavery as Seen on the Plantation and in the Home of the Planter.* Milwaukee: South Side Printing Company, 1896. At Schomburg.

Jackson, Andrew. *Narrative and Writings of Andrew Jackson, of Kentucky; Containing an Account of His Birth and Twenty-Six Years of His Life While a Slave; His Escape, Five Years of Freedom, Together with Anecdotes Relating to Slavery. Narrated by Himself, Written by a Friend.* Syracuse, New York: *Daily and Weekly Star* Office, 1847. At Library of Congress.

Jacobs, Harriet. *Linda Brent: Incidents in the Life of a Slave Girl, Written by Herself.* Edited by L. Maria Child. Boston, 1861. At Schomburg.

James, Reverend Thomas. *Life of Reverend Thomas James, by Himself.* Rochester, New York, 1886. At Schomburg.

Johnson, Jane. *Narrative.* Related to the Reverend G. W. Offley. Hartford: Published for G. W. Offley. At Schomburg.

Johnstone, Abraham. *The Address of Abraham Johnstone, a Black Man, Who Was Hanged at Woodbury in the County of Gloucester, and State of New Jersey, on Saturday the Eighth Day of July Last.* Philadelphia: Printed for the Purchasers, 1797. At New York Historical Society.

Jones, Thomas H. *The Experience and Personal Narrative of Uncle Tom Jones: Who Was for Forty Years a Slave; also, the Surprising Adventures of Wild Tim, a Fugitive Negro from South Carolina.* New York: G. C. Holbrook, 1854. At Library of Congress.

_____. *The Experience of Thomas H. Jones, Who Was a Slave for Forty-Three Years. Written by a friend as related to him by Brother Jones.* New Bedford, New York, 1871. At New York Public Library.

Joseph and Enoch. *Narrative of the Barbarous Treatment of Two Unfortunate Females, Natives of Concordia, Louisiana, by Joseph and Enoch, Runaway Slaves.* As told by Mrs. Todd and Miss Harrington. New York: Printed for the publishers, 1842. At Massachusetts State Library.

Joyce, John. *Confessions of John Joyce.* Related to Richard Allen. Philadelphia, 1818. At Arthur Spingarn Library.

Keckley, Elizabeth. *Behind the Scenes; or, Thirty Years a Slave and Four Years in the White House, as Mrs. Lincoln's Maid.* New York: G. W. Carleton and Company, 1868. At Schomburg.

Lane, Lunceford. *Narrative of Lunceford Lane, Published by Himself.* Boston: Printed by Hewes and Watson for the Author, 1842. At Schomburg.

Langston, John Mercer. *From Plantation to Congress*. Hartford: American Publishing Company, 1894. At Library of Congress.

Lewis, Joseph Vance. *Out of the Ditch; A True Story of an Ex-Slave, by J. Vance Lewis*. Houston, Texas: Rein and Sons, 1910. At Schomburg.

Loguen, Jermain W. *The Reverend Jermain W. Loguen, as a Slave and as a Freeman. A Narrative of Real Life*. Syracuse, New York: Office of the *Daily Journal*, 1859. At New York Public Library.

Maddison, Reuben. *A True Story*. Birmingham, England, 1832. At Moorland Foundation.

Mallory, William. *Old Plantation Days*. 3d ed. Canada, 1901? In Daniel Murray Collection, Library of Congress.

Mars, James. *Life of James Mars, Written by Himself*. n.p., 1864. At Schomburg.

_____. *Life of James Mars, a Slave Born and Sold in Connecticut, Written by Himself*. Hartford: Case, Lockwood and Company, 1865. At Schomburg.

_____. 6th ed., enlarged. Hartford: Case, Lockwood and Company, 1865. At Boston Public Library.

Mason, Isaac. *Life of Isaac Mason, as a Slave*. Worcester, Massachusetts, 1893. At Schomburg.

Meachum, John B. *An Address to the Colored Citizens of the United States, Prefaced by a Narrative of the Author as a Slave in Virginia*. Philadelphia, 1846. At Library of Congress.

Mountain, Joseph. *Sketches of the Life of Joseph Mountain, a Negro, Who Was Executed at New-Haven, on the 20th Day of October, 1790, for a Rape, Committed on the 26th Day of May Last*. New Haven, Connecticut: Printed and Sold by T. and S. Green, 1790. At Yale University.

Northup, Solomon. *Twelve Years a Slave, Narrative of Solomon Northup, a Citizen of New York, Kidnapped in Washington City in 1841 and Rescued in January, 1853, from a Cotton Plantation near Red River, in Louisiana*. Dedicated to Mrs. Stowe. Auburn, Buffalo, and London: Derby and Miller, 1853. At Schomburg.

Offley, Reverend G. W. *Narrative of the Life and Labors of the Reverend G. W. Offley, a Colored Man and Local Preacher, Written by Himself*. Hartford: Published for the Author, 1860. At Schomburg.

O'Neal, William. *Life and History of William O'Neal; or, The Man Who Sold His Wife*. St. Louis: A. R. Fleming and Company, 1896. At Arthur Spingarn Library.

Paige, C. F. *Twenty-Two Years of Freedom*. n.p., 1876? In Daniel Murray Collection, Library of Congress.

Parker, Janie. *Janie Parker, the Fugitive*. Related to Mrs. Emily Pierson. n.p., 1851. At New York Public Library.

Pennington, James W. C. *The Fugitive Blacksmith; or, Events in the History of James W. C. Pennington, Pastor of a Presbyterian Church, New York, Formerly a Slave in the State of Maryland, United States*. 2d ed. London: C. Gilpin, 1849. At Schomburg.

_____. 3d ed. London: C. Gilpin, 1850. At Harvard.

Peterson, D. H. *The Looking Glass: Being a True Narrative of the Life of the Reverend D. H. Peterson.* n.p., 1854. At Schomburg.

_____. 2d ed., rev. and enlarged. Boston: Published for the Author, 1855. At Library of Congress.

Randolph, Peter. *From Slave Cabin to Pulpit; the Autobiography of Peter Randolph, the Southern Question Illustrated, Sketches of Slave Life.* Preface by Samuel May, Jr. Boston: Published for the Author, 1893. At Schomburg.

Roberts, Ralph. "A Slave's Story. Told by His Owner." *Putnam's Monthly* 9 (June 1857):614–620. At New York Public Library.

Roper, Moses. *A Narrative of Moses Roper's Adventures and Escape from American Slavery; with a Preface by Reverend T. Price.* London: Darton, Harvey, and Darton, 1837. At New York Historical Society.

_____. 2d London ed. London: Harvey and Darton, 1838. At Harvard.

_____. 1st American ed. from the London ed. Philadelphia: Printed by Merrihew and Gunn, 1838. At Library of Congress.

_____. 4th ed. London: Harvey and Darton, 1840. At Schomburg.

_____. Celtic trans. Llanelli: Gan Rees a Thomas, 1841. At Harvard.

_____. Berwick-upon-Tweed: The Author, 1846. At Boston Public Library.

_____. Berwick-upon-Tweed: The Author, 1848. At Boston Public Library.

Sambo. *Sambo: The Slave of Long Ago.* Related by Orrie M. MacDonnell. n.p., 1924. At New York Public Library.

Smith, Harry. *Fifty Years of Slavery in the United States of America.* Grand Rapids, Michigan: Western Michigan Printing Company, 1891. At Library of Congress.

Smith, James L. *Autobiography, Including Also Reminiscences of Slave Life.* Norwich, Connecticut: Bulletin Company, 1881. At Library of Congress.

Smith, Venture. *A Narrative of the Life and Adventures of Venture, a Native of Africa; but Resident about Sixty Years in the United States of America. Related by Himself.* New London, Connecticut: Printed by C. Holt, 1798. At Arthur Spingarn Library.

_____. New London: Reprinted and Published by a Descendant of Venture, 1835. At Schomburg.

_____. Rev. and republished, with traditions by H. M. Selden, of East Haddam. Haddam, Connecticut, 1896. At Library of Congress.

_____. Middletown, Connecticut: J. S. Stewart, printer, 1897. At Library of Congress.

Spear, Chloe. *Narrative of Chloe Spear. By a "Lady of Boston."* Boston: American Anti-Slavery Society, 1832. At New York Historical Society.

Steward, Austin. *Twenty-Two Years a Slave and Fifty Years a Freeman.* New York: W. Alling, 1857. At Harvard.

_____. 3d ed. Rochester, New York: W. Alling, 1861. At Schomburg.

Still, James. *Early Recollections and Life of Dr. James Still.* Philadelphia: Printed for the Author by Lippincott, 1877. At Moorland Foundation.

Still, Peter. *The Kidnapped and the Ransomed: Narrative of Peter Still and His Wife "Vina."* Related to Mrs. Kate E. R. Pickard. Syracuse, New York: W. T. Hamilton Press, 1856. At Schomburg.

Still, William. *The Underground Railroad.* Preface to the revised edition. Philadelphia: Anti-Slavery Society, 1878. At Schomburg.

Stroyer, Jacob. *Sketches of My Life in the South.* Part 1. Salem, 1879. At Schomburg.

_____. New and enlarged ed. Salem: Salem Observer Book and Job Printing, 1885. At Harvard.

_____. 3d ed. Salem: Salem Observer Book and Job Printing, 1890. At Harvard.

Thompson, John. *Life of John Thompson, a Fugitive Slave; Containing His History of Twenty-Five Years,* in *Bondage, and His Providential Escape. Written by Himself.* Worcester, Massachusetts, 1856. At Schomburg.

Tilmon, Levin. A *Brief Miscellaneous Narrative of the More Early Part of the Life of Levin Tilmon, Pastor of a Colored Methodist Church, New York City.* Jersey City: W. and L. Pratt, 1853. At Library of Congress.

_____. 2d ed., enlarged. Jersey City: W. and L. Pratt, 1853. At Harvard.

Tomlinson, Jane. "The First Eugitive Slave Case of Record in Ohio." *Annual Report,* American Historical Society Association, Washington, 1896, pp. 91–100. At Massachusetts State Library.

Truth, Sojourner. *Narrative of Sojourner Truth, a Northern Slave, Emancipated from Bodily Servitude by the State of New York, in 1828.* Narrated to Olive Gilbert, including Sojourner Truth's *Book of Life,* and a dialogue. Boston, 1850. At Library of Congress.

_____. Boston: Published for Sojourner Truth, 1853. At Schomburg.

_____. With introduction by Harriet B. Stowe. Boston, 1855. At Library of Congress. *Narrative of Sojourner Truth, a Bondswoman of Olden Time, Emancipated by the New York Legislature in the Early Part of the Present Century.* Edited by Mrs. Francis W. Titus. Battle Creek, Michigan: *Review and Herald* Office, 1884. At Massachusetts State Library.

Tubman, Harriet. *Scenes in the Life of Harriet Tubman.* As told by Sarah Bradford. New York and Auburn, 1869. At Schomburg.

Turner, Nat. *The Confessions of Nat Turner, the leader of the Late Insurrection in Southampton, Virginia. As fully and voluntarily made to Thomas R. Gray, in the prison where he was confined, and acknowledged by him to be such when read before the court of Southampton, with the certificate under the seal of the court convened at Jerusalem, November 5, 1831, for his trial.* Baltimore: Thomas R. Gray, Lucas and Deaver, printers, 1831. At Schomburg.

Voorhis, Robert. *Life and Adventures of Robert Voorhis, the Hermit of Massachusetts, Who Has Lived Fourteen Years in a Cave, Secluded from Human Society. Comprising an Account of His Birth, Parentage, Sufferings, and Providential Escape from Unjust and Cruel Bondage in*

Early Life—and His Reasons for Becoming a Recluse. Taken from his own mouth by Henry Trumbull, and published for his benefit. Providence, Rhode Island: Printed for Henry Trumbull, 1829. At Schomburg.

Ward, Samuel Ringgold. *Autobiography of a Fugitive Negro: His Anti-Slavery Labours in the United States, Canada, and England.* London: J. Snow, 1855. At Schomburg.

Washington, Booker Taliaferro. "Up from Slavery: An Autobiography." *Outlook,* November 3, 1900 to February 23, 1901.

————. *Up from Slavery: An Autobiography.* New York: A. L. Burt Company, 1900. At New York Public Library.

————. New York: Doubleday, Page and Company, 1901. At Boston Public Library.

————. London: T. Nelson, 1910. At New York Public Library.

————. School ed. New York: Thompson, Brown and Company, 1915.

————. Johannes Knudsen's translation into Danish. Copenhagen: G. E. C. Gao, 1917. At New York Public Library.

————. Garden City: Doubleday, Doran, 1929.

Washington, Madison. *The Heroic Slave, a Thrilling Narrative of the Adventures of Madison Washington, in Pursuit of Liberty.* As told by Frederick Douglass. Boston: Jewett and Company, 1853. At Schomburg.

Watkins, James. *Narrative of the Life of James Watkins, Formerly a Chattel in Maryland, United States.* Bolton, Kenyon, and Abbott, printers, 1852. At Schomburg.

Watson, Henry. *Narrative of Henry Watson, a Fugitive Slave; Written by Himself.* Dedicated to Henry Holt. Boston: Henry Holt, 1848. At Schomburg.

Webb, William. *History of William Webb. Composed by Himself.* Detroit: E. Hoekstra, 1873. At Schomburg.

Wheatley, Phillis. *Letters of Phillis Wheatley, the Negro Slave Poet of Boston.* Boston: Printed by John Wilson and Son, 1864. At Schomburg. Also printed in the *Proceedings of the Colonial Society of Massachusetts* for 1864; and in Woodson, Carter, *Mind of the Negro Prior to 1860,* in the Introduction.

Wheeler, Peter. *Chains and Freedom; or, The Life and Adventures of Peter Wheeler, a Colored Man Yet Living.* Related to C. E Lester. New York: E. S. Arnold and Company, 1839. At Oberlin.

White, George. *Account of Life, Experience, Travels, and Gospel Labours of an African. Written by Himself and Revised by a Friend.* New York: J. C. Tottle, 1810. At Arthur Spingarn Library.

Wilkerson, James. *History of His Travels and Labors in the United States as a Missionary, since Purchase of His Liberty in New Orleans.* Columbus, Ohio, 1861. At Oberlin.

William. *The Negro Servant.* Related by Reverend Richmond Legh. London: Religious Tract Society, printed by J. Tilling, n.d. At Harvard.

————. *The Negro Servant. An Authentic Narrative of a Young Negro, Showing How He Was Made a Slave in Africa; and Carried to Jamaica, Where He Was Sold to a Captain in His*

Majesty's Navy, and Taken to America, Where He Became a Christian; and Afterwards Brought to England, and Baptised. Kilmarnock: H. Crawford, 1815. At Harvard.

_____. Boston: New England Tract Society; Tract no. 53, 1816. At Harvard.

Williams, Isaac. *Sunshine and Shadow of Slave Life. Reminiscences Told to Willam Ferguson Goldie by Isaac Williams.* East Saginaw, Michigan: *Evening News,* 1885. At Library of Congress.

Williams, James. *Narrative of James Williams, An American Slave; Who Was for Several Years a Driver on a Cotton Plantation in Alabama.* As related to John Greenleaf Whittier. New York: n.d.

_____. *Narrative of James Williams, an American Slave.* Abolitionist's Library, No. 3. Boston: Massachusetts Anti-Slavery Society, 1838. Written by John Greenleaf Whittier from Verbal Narrative. In Library of Congress.

_____. 2d edition. Boston: J. F. Trow, printer, 1838. At Harvard.

Williams, James. *Life and Adventures of James Williams, a Fugitive Slave, with a Full Description of the Underground Railroad.* San Francisco: Woman's Union Print, 1873. At Schomburg.

_____. 4th ed. San Francisco: Women's Union Book and Job Printing Office, 1874. At Harvard. Contains additional narrative sketches.

_____. 5th ed. Preface signed "John Thomas Evans, now James Williams." Philadelphia: A. H. Sickler and Company, 1893. At Harvard.

Zamba. *Life and Adventures of Zamba, an African Negro King, and His Experiences of Slavery in South Carolina, Written by Himself, Corrected and Arranged by Peter Neilson.* London: Smith, Elder, and Company, 1847. At Schomburg.

_____. *Der Negerkonig Zamba, Eine Sklavengeschichte Seitenstuck zu "Onkel Tom's Hutte."* Nach dem Englischen bearbeitet von Dr. Chr. G. Barth. Stuttgart, 1853. At Schomburg.

Abernethy, Francis E., Patrick B. Mullen, and Alan B. Govenar, eds. "Musical Traditions of Twentieth Century African-American Cowboys," in *Juneteenth Texas: Essays in African-American Folklore*. Denton: University of North Texas Press, 1996, pp. 195–208.

Anderson, Jervis. *A. Philip Randolph:A Biographical Portrait*. New York: Harcourt Brace Jovanovich, 1972.

Anderson, Robert. *From Slavery to Affluence: Memoirs of Robert Anderson, Ex-Slave*. Steamboat Springs, Colorado: Steamboat Pilot Printer, 1967.

Andrews, Thomas F. "Freedmen in Indian Territory: A Post–Civil War Dilemma," *Journal of the West* 4:3 (July 1965): 367–376.

Apetheker, Herbert. *"One Continual Cry:"DavidWalker's Appeal to the Colored Citizens of the World, 1829–1830*. New York: Humanities Press, 1965.

_____. *American Negro Revolts*. New York: International Publishers, 1987, p. 163.

Arlington, Leonard, and David Bitton. *The Mormon Experience:A History of the Latter Day Saints*. Urbana: University of Illinois Press, 1992.

Athearn, Robert. *The Coloradan*. Albuquerque: University of New Mexico Press, 1976.

_____. *In Search of Canaan: Black Migration to Kansas, 1879–80*. Lawrence: Regents Press of Kansas, 1978.

Bailey, M. Thomas. *Reconstruction in Indian Territory:A Story of Avarice, Discrimination, and Opportunities*. Port Washington, New York: Kennikat Press, 1972.

Ballagh, James Curtis. *A History of Slavery inVirginia*. Baltimore: Johns Hopkins Press, 1902.

Barr, Alwyn. *Black Texans: A History of Negroes in Texas, 1528–1995*. Austin, Texas: Jenkins Publishing Company, 1995.

Barr, Alwyn, and Robert A. Calvert, eds. *Black Leaders: Texans for Their Times*. Austin: Texas State Historical Association, 1981.

Beeth, Howard, and Cary D. Wintz, eds. *Black Dixie: Afro-Texan History and Culture in Houston*. College Station: Texas A&M Press, 1992.

Berlin, Ira, ed. *The Black Military Experience*. New York: Cambridge University Press, 1982.

Berwanger, Eugene. *The Frontier Against Slavery: Western Anti-Negro Prejudice and The Slavery Extension Controversy*. Urbana: University of Illinois Press, 1967.

————. *The West and Reconstruction*. Urbana: University of Illinois Press, 1981.

Betts, Robert B. *In Search of York: The Slave Who Went West to the Pacific with Lewis and Clark*. Boulder: Colorado Associated University Press, 1985.

Billington, Monroe. *New Mexico's Buffalo Soldiers, 1866–1900*. Niwot: University Press of Colorado, 1991.

Blackburn, Robin. *The Overthrow of Colonial Slavery: 1776–1848*. London: Verso, 1988.

Blockson, Charles, L. *The Underground Railroad*. New York: Prentice-Hall, 1987.

Bogle, Donald. *Toms, Coons, Mulattoes, Mammies and Bucks: An Interpretive History of Blacks in American Film*. New York: Viking Press, 1973.

Bonner, Thomas D., ed. *Life and Adventures of James Beckwourth*. Lincoln: University of Nebraska Press, 1972.

Bontemps, Arna. *God Sends Sunday*. New York: Harcourt, Brace and Company, 1931.

————. *Black Thunder: Gabriel's Revolt: Virginia, 1800*. Boston: Beacon Press, 1968.

————, ed. *The Harlem Renaissance Remembered: Essays with a Memoir*. New York: Dodd, Mead, 1972.

Brady, Marilyn Dell. "Kansas Federation of Colored Women's Clubs, 1900–1930." *Kansas History* 9:1 (Spring 1986): 19–30.

Breen, T. H. *Myne Own Ground*. Cambridge, Massachusetts: Oxford University Press, 1980.

Brewer, J. Mason. *Negro Legislators of Texas and Their Descendants*. Dallas: Mathis Publishing Company, 1935.

Bringhurst, Newell G. *Saints, Slaves and Blacks: The Changing Presence of Black People within Mormonism*. Wesport, Connecticut: Greenwood Press, 1981.

Broussard, Albert. *Black San Francisco: The Struggle for Racial Equality in the West, 1900–1954*. Lawrence: University Press of Kansas, 1993.

————. "Slavery in California Revisited: The Fate of a Kentucky Slave in Gold Rush California." *Pacific Historian* 29:1 (Spring 1985): 17–21.

Brown, Elaine. *A Taste of Power: A Black Woman's Story*. New York: Pantheon Books, 1992.

Bruce, Henry Clay. *The New Man: Twenty-Nine Years a Slave, Twenty-Nine Years a Free Man*. New York: Negro University Press, 1969.

Buercker, Thomas R. "One Soldier's Service: Caleb Benson in the Ninth and Tenth Calvary, 1875–1908." *Nebraska History* 74:2 (Summer 1993): 54–62.

Bunch, Lonnie, III. *Black Angelenos: The Afro-American in Los Angeles, 1850–1950*. Los Angeles: California Afro-American Museum, 1988.

Coffin, Levi. *Reminiscences of Levi Coffin, The Reputed President of the Underground Railroad*. New York: Augustus M. Kelley Publishers, 1968.

Cohen, William. *At Freedom's Edge: Black Mobility and the Southern White Quest for Racial Control, 1861–1915*. Baton Rouge: Louisiana State University Press, 1991.

Colburn, David R., and Jane L. Landers, eds. *The African American Heritage of Florida*. Gainsville: University Press of Florida, 1995.

Cole, Thomas R. *NO Color Is MY Kind: The Life of Eldrewey Stearns and the Integration of Houston*. Austin: University of Texas Press, 1997.

Coleman, Ronald. "The Buffalo Soldiers: Guardians of the Uintah Frontier, 1886–1901." *Utah Historical Quarterly* 47:4 (Fall 1979): 421–439.

Coughtry, Jamie, and R. T. King, eds. *Lubertha Johnson: Civil Rights Efforts in Las Vegas 1940s–1960*. Reno: University of Nevada Oral History Program, 1988.

Cowen, Tom, and Jack Maguire. *Timelines of African-American History: 500 Years of Black Achievement*. New York: Roundtable Press, 1994.

Cox, Thomas C. *Blacks in Topeka: A Social History*. Baton Rouge: Louisiana State University Press, 1982.

Crew, Spencer R. *Field to Factory: Afro-American Migration 1915–1940*. Washington, D.C.: Smithsonian Institute, 1987.

Cribbs, Thomas. *Slow Fade to Black: The Negro in American Film, 1900–1942*. New York: Oxford University Press, 1977.

Daniels, Douglass Henry. *Pioneer Urbanites: A Social and Cultural History of Black San Francisco*. Philadelphia: Temple University Press, 1980.

Davis, Charles, and Henry Louis Gates, Jr., eds. *The Slave's Narrative*. Oxford: Oxford University Press, 1985.

De Graaf, Lawrence B. "Negro Migration to Los Angeles, 1930–1950." Ph.D. dissertation, University of California, Los Angeles, 1962.

———. "Race, Sex, and Region: Black Women in the American West, 1850–1920." *Pacific Historical Review* 49:19 (February 1975): 22–51.

Deal, J. Douglas. *Race and Class in Colonial Virginia: Indians, Englishmen and Africans on the Eastern Shore During the Seventeenth Century*. New York: Garland Publishing, Inc., 1993.

Dobak, William A. "Civil War on the Kansas-Missouri Border: The Narrative of Former Slave Andrew Williams." *Kansas History* 6:4 (Winter 1983): 237–242.

Du Bois, W. E. B. *The Philadelphia Negro: A Social Study*. 1899; reprint. New York: Schocken Books, 1967.

Favreau, Marc, and Steven F. Miller, eds. *Remembering Slavery: African Americans Talk about Their Personal Experiences of Slavery and Emancipation*. New York: New Press, 1998.

Fleming, William. *A Narrative of Sufferings and Deliverance*. New York: Garland Publishing, Inc., 1978.

Fogel, Robert William, and Stanley Engerman. *Time on the Cross*. 2 vols. Boston: Little, Brown, 1974.

Fowler, Arlen L. *The Black Infantry in the West, 1869–1891*. Westport, Connecticut: Greenwood Press, 1971.

Franklin, Jimmie Louis. *Journey Toward Hope: A History of Blacks in Oklahoma*. Norman: University of Oklahoma Press, 1982.

Genovese, Eugene. *Roll, Jordan, Roll: The World the Slaves Made*. New York: Vintage Books, 1976.

Govenar, Alan. *The Early Years of Rhythm and Blues: Focus on Houston*. Houston: Rice University Press, 1991.

_____. "African American Ranching in Texas," in *Ranching in South Texas: A Symposium*, Joe S. Graham, ed. Kingsville, Texas: John E. Conner Museum, 1994, pp. 80–85.

_____. *Meeting the Blues: The Rise of the Texas Sound*. New York: Da Capo Press, 1995.

_____. *Portraits of Community: African American Photography in Texas*. Austin: Texas State Historical Association, 1996.

_____, ed. *Osceola: Memories of a Sharecropper's Daughter*. New York: Hyperion Books for Children, 2000.

Govenar, Alan, and Jay F. Brakefield. *Deep Ellum and Central Track: Where the Black and White Worlds of Dallas Converged*. Denton: University of North Texas Press, 1998.

Govenar, Alan, and Les Blank. *Living Texas Blues* (videocassette). Dallas: Dallas Museum of Art (producer), 1985.

Greenbaum, Susan G. *The Afro-American Community in Kansas City, Kansas: A History*. Kansas City, 1982.

Hall, Gwendolyn Midlo. *Africans in Colonial Louisiana: The Development of Afro-Creole Culture in the Eighteenth Century*. Baton Rouge: Louisiana State University Press, 1992.

Halliburton, R., Jr. *Red Over Black: Black Slavery Among the Cherokee Indians*. Westport, Connecticut: Greenwood Press, 1977.

Hanes, Colonel Bailey C. *Bill Pickett, Bulldogger*. Norman: University of Oklahoma Press, 1977.

Harris, N. Dwight. *The History of Negro Servitude in Illinois and the Slavery Agitation in That State, 1719–1864*. New York: Negro Universities Press.

Harris, Theodore, ed. *Negro Frontiersman: The Western Memoirs of Henry O. Flipper, First Negro Graduate of West Point*. El Paso: Texas Western College Press, 1963.

Haviland, Laura. *A Woman's Life-Work: Labors and Experiences of Laura S. Haviland*. Chicago: C. V. Waite and Company, 1887.

Hine, Darlene Clark, Elsa Barkley Brown, and Rosalyn Terborg-Penn, eds. *Black Women in America: An Historical Encyclopedia, 2 vols*. Bloomington: Indiana University Press, 1993.

Hooks, Bell. *Black Looks: Race and Representation*. Boston: South End Press, 1992.

Huggins, Nathan I. *Harlem Renaissance*. New York: Oxford University Press, 1971.

Jones, Le Roi. *Blues People: Negro Music in White America*. New York: William Morrow, 1963.

Katz, William Loren. *Black Indians: A Hidden Heritage*. New York: Antheneum Press, 1986.

_____. *Black People Who Made the Old West*. Trenton, New Jersey: Africa World Press, 1992.

_____. *Black Women of the Old West*. New York: Antheneum Books for Young Readers, 1995.

Kay, Marvin L., Michael Cary, and Lorin Lee Cary. *Slavery in North Carolina: 1748–1775*. Chapel Hill: University of North Carolina Press, 1995.

Kilian, Crawford. *"Go Do Some Great Thing": The Black Pioneers of British Columbia*. Vancouver, British Columbia: Douglas and McIntyre Publishers, 1978.

Lapp, Randolph. *Afro-Americans in California*. San Francisco: Boyd and Fraser Publishing, 1986.

Larsen, Lawrence H. *The Urban West at the End of the Frontier*. Lawrence: Regents Press of Kansas, 1978.

Levine, Lawrence W. *Black Culture and Black Consciousness: Afro-American Folk Thought From Slavery to Freedom*. New York: Oxford University Press, 1977.

Linden, Glenn M. *Desegregating the Schools in Dallas: Four Decades in the Federal Courts*. Dallas: Three Forks Press, 1995.

Litwack, Leon. *Been in the Storm So Long: The Aftermath of Slavery*. New York: Vintage Books, 1979.

Low, Augustus, and Virgil A. Clift, eds. *Encyclopedia of Black America*. New York: Da Capo Press, 1981.

McMillan, James B. *Fighting Back: A Life in the Struggle for Civil Rights*. Reno: University of Nevada Oral Reading Program, 1997.

Miller, Loren. *The Petitioners: The Story of the Supreme Court of the United States and the Negro*. New York: Pantheon Books, 1966.

Natanson, Nicholas. *The Black Image in the New Deal: The Politics of FSA Photography*. Knoxville: University of Tennessee Press, 1992.

Nimmons, Robert Kim. "Arizona's Forgotten Past: The Negro in Arizona, 1539–1965," M.A. thesis, Northern Arizona University, 1971.

Osofsky, Gilbert, ed. *Puttin' on Ole Massa: The Slave Narratives of Henry Bibb, William Wells Brown, and Solomon Northrup*. New York: HarperCollins, 1969.

Overstreet, Everett Louis. *Black on a Background of White: A Chronicle of Afro Americans' Involvement in America's Last Frontier, Alaska*. United States of America: Alaska Black Caucus, 1994.

Painter, Nell Irvin. *Exodusters: Black Migration to Kansas after Reconstruction.* Topeka: University Press of Kansas, 1986.

Phillips, U.B. *American Negro Slavery.* 1918; reprint. Baton Rouge: Louisianna State University Press, 1969.

Pitre, Merline. *Through Many Dangers, Toils, and Snares: Black Leadership in Texas, 1870–1890.* Austin, Texas: Eakin Press, 1997.

Potkay, Adam, and Sandra Burr, eds. *Black Atlantic Writers of the Eighteenth Century, Living the New Exodus in England and the Americas: Selections from the Writings of Ukawsaw Gronniosaw, John Marrant, Quobna Ottobah Cugoano, and Olaudah Equiano.* New York: St. Martin's Press, 1995.

Prather, Patricia Smith, and Jane Clements Monday. *From Slave to Statesman: The Legacy of Joshua Houston, Servant to Sam Houston.* Denton: University of North Texas Press, 1993.

Price, Sammy. *What Do They Want? A Jazz Autobiography.* Chicago: University of Illinois Press, 1990.

Rawick, George P. *The American Slave: An Autobiography.* Westport, Connecticut: Greenwood Press, 1977.

Rice, Lawrence. *The Negro in Texas, 1874–1900.* Baton Rouge: Louisiana State University Press, 1971.

Robinson, Armstead L., and Patricia Sullivan, eds. *New Directions in Civil Rights Studies.* Charlottesville: University Press of Virginia, 1991.

Salzman, Jack, David Lionel Smith, and Cornel West, eds. *Encyclopedia of African American Culture and History, 5 vols.* New York: Simon and Schuster, 1996.

Savage, W. Sherman. *Blacks in the West.* Westport, Connecticut: Greenwood Press, 1976.

Schubert, Frank. "Black Soldiers on the Western Frontier: Some Factors Influencing Race Relations." *Phylon* 32:4 (Winter 1971): 410–415.

Sprague, Stuart Seely, ed. *His Promised Land.* New York: W. W. Norton, 1996.

Stampp, Kenneth. *The Peculiar Institution: Slavery in the Antebellum South.* New York: Knopf, 1956.

Starling, Marion Wilson. *The Slave Narrative: Its Place in American History.* Boston: G. K. Hall, 1981.

Stearns, Marshall W. *The Story of Jazz.* New York: Oxford University Press, 1956.

Still, William. *The Underground Railroad: A Record of Facts, Authentic Narratives, Letters, Etc.* Chicago: Johnson Publishing Company, 1970.

Stuckey, Sterling. *Slave Culture: Nationalist Theory and the Foundations of Black America.* New York: Oxford University Press, 1987.

Tate, Thad W. *The Negro in Eighteenth-Century Williamsburg.* Williamsburg: University Press of Virginia, 1965.

Taylor, Quintard. "The Great Migration: The Afro-American Communities of Seattle and Portland during the 40s." *Arizona and the West* 23 (1981): 109–126.

_____. "Slaves and Free Men: Blacks in the Oregon Country, 1840–1860." *Oregon Historical Quarterly* 83 (1982): 153–170.

_____. *In Search of the Racial Frontier: African Americans in the American West, 1528–1990*. New York: W. W. Norton, 1998.

Turner, Edward Raymond. *The Negro in Pennsylvania: Slavery-Servitude-Freedom, 1639–1861*. Washington, D.C.: American Historical Association, 1911.

Tyler, Lyon Gardiner, ed. *Narratives of Early Virginia: 1606–0625*. New York: Charles Scribner's Sons, 1907.

Walker, Jonathan. *The Trial and Imprisonment of Jonathan Walker at Pensacola, Florida, for Aiding Slaves to Escape from Bondage*. Boston: Dow and Jackson's Power Press, 1845.

Waller, Reuben. "History of a Slave Written by Himself at the Age of Eighty Nine Years." In John M. Carroll, ed., *The Black Military Experience in the West*. New York: Liveright, 1971.

Wax, Darold D. "Robert Ball Anderson, Ex-Slave, a Pioneer in Western Nebraska, 1884–1930." *Nebraska History* 64:2 (Summer 1983): 163–192.

_____. "The Odyssey of an Ex-Slave: Robert Ball Anderson's Pursuit of the American Dream." *Phylon* 45:1 (Spring 1984): 67–79.

White, Richard. *"It's Your Misfortune and None of My Own:" A New History of the American West*. Norman: University of Oklahoma Press, 1991.

Wiggins, Rosilind Cobb. *Captain Paul Cuffe's Logs and Letters, 1808–1817: A Black Quaker's "Voice from within the Veil."* Washington, D.C.: Howard University Press, 1996.

Williams, David A. *Bricks without Straw: A Comprehensive History of African Americans in Texas*. Austin, Texas: Eakin Press, 1997.

Williams, Nudie E. " Black Newspapers and the Exodusters." Ph.D. dissertation, Oklahoma State University, 1973.

_____. "Bass Reeves: Lawman in the Western Ozarks," in *The Handbook of Texas*. Austin: Texas State Historical Association, 1985.

_____. "Black Men Who Wore White Hats: Grant Johnson, United States Deputy Marshall," in *The Handbook of Texas*. Austin: Texas State Historical Association, 1985.

_____. "Black News Journals and the Great Migration of 1879." *Kanhistique: Kansas History and Antiques*, vol. 13, no. 9 (January 1988): 4–5.

_____. "Footnote to Trivia: Moses Fleetwood Walker and the All-American Dream." *Journal of American Culture*, vol. 11, no. 2 (Summer 1988): 65–72.

_____. "The African Lion: George Napier Perkins, Lawyer, Politician, and Editor," *The Chronicles of Oklahoma*, vol. 70, no. 4 (Winter 1992–1993): 450–465.

Williams, William. *Slavery and Freedom in Delaware, 1639–1865*. Wilmington, Delaware: Scholarly Resources, Inc., 1996.

Willis-Braithwaite, Deborah. *VanDerZee Photographer: 1886–1983*. New York: Henry N. Abrams, 1993.

_____, ed. *J. P. Bal: Daguerrean and Studio Photographer*. New York: Garland Publishing, 1993.

Wilson, Elinor. *Jim Beckwourth: Black Mountain Man, War Chief of the Crows, Trader, Trapper, Explorer, Frontiersman, Guide, Scout, Interpreter, Adventurer, and Gaudy Liar.* Norman: University of Oklahoma Press, 1972.

Wilson, Joseph T. *The Black Phalanx: African American Soldiers in the War of Independence, the War of 1812, and the Civil War*. New York: Da Capo Press, 1994.

Winegarten, Ruthe. *Black Women in Texas: 150 Years of Trial and Triumph*. Austin: University of Texas Press, 1995.

Wood, Betty. *Slavery in Colonial Georgia, 1730–1775*. Athens: University of Georgia Press, 1984.

Work Projects Administration, Georgia Writers' Project, Savannah Unit. *Drums and Shadows: Survival Studies Among the Georgia Coastal Negroes*. Athens: University of Georgia Press, 1940.

Index

(Note: page citations in *italic* type refer to illustrations.)